PASS TRAK®

Questions and Answers

D1065983

General
Securities
Representative

*9*th Edition

Dearborn
Financial Publishing, Inc.

The Series 7 Qualification Exam is copyrighted by the New York Stock Exchange. The examination contains the following notice:

> "The contents of this examination are confidential. Neither the whole nor any part of this examination may be reproduced in any form or quoted or used in any way without the written consent of the New York Stock Exchange, Inc."

Dearborn Financial Publishing, Inc. and its employees and agents honor the copyrights of the New York Stock Exchange. We specifically urge each of our students to refrain from any attempts to remove a copy of the exam; or to copy or record any of the questions on the exam.

At press time, this 9th edition of PassTrak Series 7 contains the most complete and accurate information currently available for the NASD Series 7 license examination. Owing to the nature of securities license examinations, however, information may have been added recently to the actual test that does not appear in this edition.

This publication is designed to provide accurate and authoritative information in regard to the subject matter covered. It is sold with the understanding that the publisher is not engaged in rendering legal, accounting, or other professional service. If legal advice or other expert assistance is required, the services of a competent professional person should be sought.

Executive Editor: Kimberly K. Walker-Daniels
Senior Technical Editor: Kenneth R. Walker-Daniels
Managing Editor: Nicola Bell
Product Editor: Brian K. Fauth
Associate Development Editor: Laura Schlachtmeyer

Printed in the United States of America.

97   98   10   9   8   7   6   5   4   3

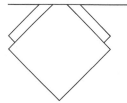

Contents

Trading Securities

Customer Accounts

Brokerage Office Procedures

Margin Accounts

Economics and Analysis

Ethics, Suitability and Recommendations

Acknowledgments

Special thanks to the following persons for their efforts in reviewing this book:

Randy Bauer

Trace Fasano

Phil Keener

Amy Morgan

Richard Smith

Curt Wild

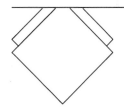

Introduction to PassTrak® Series 7

Welcome to PassTrak® Series 7. Because you probably have a lot of questions about the course and the exam, we have tried to anticipate some of them and provide you with answers to help you on your way.

The Course

How is the course structured?

PassTrak Series 7 consists of three books: a comprehensive textbook, a concise review book and an exam book. The textbook, *Principles & Practices*, contains 20 chapters. Each of the first 19 chapters is devoted to a particular area of general securities sales and regulation that you will need to know in order to pass the General Securities Registered Representative Exam (the Series 7). Chapter 20 helps you answer questions relating to securities quotations as they appear in the financial press. Each chapter is divided into study sections devoted to more specific areas with which you need to become familiar.

The *Review* book also contains 20 chapters. The first 19 chapters cover the same topics as the corresponding chapters in *Principles & Practices,* but present the material in a concise format, omitting much of the explanatory material contained in *Principles & Practices*. Chapter 20 contains mnemonics and study aids designed to help you review some of the important facts you need for the exam.

The exam book, *Questions & Answers,* contains review exams that test the topics covered in *Principles & Practices* and *Review,* and concludes with two final exams composed of questions similar to those you will encounter on the Series 7 exam.

If you have purchased a self-study PassTrak set, you will have received three books: *Principles & Practices*, *Review* and *Questions & Answers*. If you will be attending a Series 7 class, you will have received the special classroom set, which consists of two books: *Review* and *Questions & Answers*.

What topics are covered in this course?

The information needed to pass the Series 7 exam is covered in PassTrak Series 7 through the following chapters:

Chapter 1: Equity Securities
Chapter 2: Debt Securities
Chapter 3: Corporate Debt Securities

How much time should I spend studying?

You should plan to spend about 90 to 120 hours reading the material and working through the questions. Your actual time, of course, may vary depending on your reading rate, comprehension, professional background and study environment.

Spread your study time over the six to eight weeks prior to the date on which you are scheduled to take the Series 7 exam (or, if you will be attending a Series 7 class, over the two to four weeks before the first day of class). Select a time and place for studying that will allow you to concentrate your full attention on the material at hand. You have a lot of information to learn and a lot of ground to cover. Be sure to give yourself enough time to learn the material.

What is the best way to approach the exams?

Approach each review and final exam as if you were preparing to take the actual Series 7 test. Read each question carefully and write down your answer. Then check your answers against the key and read the accompanying rationale. Making yourself go through all of these steps (rather than simply reading each question and skipping directly to the rationale) will greatly increase your comprehension and retention.

At the end of each rationale, you will find a page reference that directs you to the page in *Principles & Practices* where the information is covered. If you are using the classroom set, you will find a special section at the back of the *Review* book that lists the question numbers for each review and final exam, and directs you to the page in *Review* where the information is covered.

Do I need to take the final exams?

The final exams test the same knowledge you will need in order to answer the questions on the Series 7 exam. By completing these exams and checking your answers against the rationale, you should be able to pinpoint any areas with which you are still having difficulty. Review any questions you miss, paying particular attention to the rationale for those questions. If any subjects still seem troublesome, go back and review those topics.

The Exam

Why do I need to pass the Series 7 exam?

Your employer is a member of the New York Stock Exchange (NYSE) or another self-regulatory organization that requires its members and employees of its members to pass a qualification exam in order to become registered. To be registered as a representative qualified to sell all types of securities (except commodities), you must pass the Series 7 exam.

What is the Series 7 exam like?

The Series 7 is a two-part, six-hour, 250-question exam administered by the National Association of Securities Dealers (NASD). The exam is given in two three-hour sessions, each covering different areas of general securities sales and regulation. It is offered as a computer-based test at various testing sites around the country. A paper-and-pencil exam is available to those candidates who apply to and obtain permission from the NASD to take a written exam.

What topics will I see covered on the exam?

This course covers the wide range of topics that the NASD has outlined as being critical functions of the general securities registered representative. The NYSE exam is divided into seven broad function areas:

Critical Function	No. of Questions	Percentage of Exam
Prospecting for and qualifying customers	9	3.6 %
Evaluating customer needs and objectives	4	1.6 %
Providing customers with investment information and making suitable recommendations	123	49.2 %
Handling customer accounts and account records	27	10.8 %
Understanding and explaining the securities markets, their organization and their participants to customers	53	21.2 %
Processing customer orders and transactions	13	5.2 %
Monitoring economic and financial events, performing customer portfolio analysis and making suitable recommendations	21	8.4 %
	250	100.0 %

What score must I achieve in order to pass?

You must answer correctly at least 70% of the questions on the Series 7 exam in order to pass and become eligible for NYSE registration as a general securities representative.

How long does the exam take?

You will be allowed six hours, in two three-hour sessions, in which to finish the exam. If you are taking the computerized version of the exam, you will be given additional time before the test to become familiar with the PROCTOR® terminal.

If English is your second language, you may be entitled to additional time in which to complete the exam. Before scheduling your appointment with the certification center, your firm must send a fax or letter to the NASD in Washington, D.C. stating your name, the exam you are taking and the test location, along with a statement that English is not your first language. The NASD coordinator then authorizes the test location to set the PROCTOR® terminal to reflect additional time. For the Series 7, you will receive an additional 30 minutes per session.

Are there any prerequisites I have to meet before taking the exam?

There are no prerequisite exams you must pass before sitting for the Series 7.

How do I enroll for the exam?

To obtain an admission ticket to the Series 7 exam, your firm must file the proper application form with the NASD along with the appropriate processing fees. The NASD will send you a directory of Certification and Training Service Centers and a PROCTOR® enrollment valid for a stated number of days. To take the exam during this period, make an appointment with a Certification and Training Service Center as far in advance as possible of the date on which you would like to sit for the test.

What should I take to the exam?

Take one form of personal identification that bears your signature and your photograph as issued by a government agency. You are not allowed to take reference materials or anything else into the testing area. Calculators will be available upon request; you will not be allowed to use your personal calculator.

Scratch paper and pencils will be provided by the certification center, although you will not be permitted to take them with you when you leave.

What is PROCTOR®?

The Series 7 exam, like many professional licensing examinations, is administered on the PROCTOR® computerized testing system. PROCTOR® is a nationwide, interactive computer system designed for the administration and delivery of qualifications examinations. Included with your PROCTOR® enrollment, you will receive a brochure describing how the exam is formatted and how to use the computer terminal to answer the questions. When you have completed the exam, the PROCTOR® system promptly scores your answers and within minutes displays your grade for the exam on the terminal screen.

How well can I expect to do on the exam?

The examinations administered by the NASD are not easy. You will be required to display considerable understanding and knowledge of the topics presented in this course in order to pass the Series 7 exam and qualify for registration. If you study and complete all of the sections of this course, and consistently score at least 80% on the review and final exams, you should be well prepared to pass the Series 7 exam.

1 Corporate Ownership and Common Stock Exam

1. At the annual meeting of Consolidated Codfish, five directors are to be elected. Under the cumulative voting system, an investor with 100 shares of COD would have

   A. 100 votes that could be cast for each of five directors
   B. 100 total votes that could be cast in any way the investor chooses among five directors
   C. 500 votes that could be cast for each of five directors
   D. 500 total votes that could be cast in any way the investor chooses among five directors

2. Mountain Brewing would like to distribute treasury stock it currently holds to stockholders of record as a stock dividend. In order to do this, it must

   A. reregister the stock with the NASD
   B. reregister the stock with the NYSE
   C. apply to the SEC for permission to reissue the treasury shares
   D. take no special actions

3. Stockholders must approve

   A. the declaration of a stock dividend
   B. a 3-for-1 stock split
   C. the repurchase of 100,000 shares for the treasury
   D. the declaration of a 15% stock dividend

4. A corporation buys back its stock on the open market in order to

   I. increase earnings per share
   II. reduce interest charges
   III. use it for stock options
   IV. use it for future acquisitions

   A. I and III only
   B. I, III and IV only
   C. II and IV only
   D. I, II, III and IV

5. Cumulative voting rights

   A. benefit the large investor
   B. aid the corporation's best customers
   C. give preferred stockholders an advantage over common stockholders
   D. benefit the small investor

6. Which of the following statements describe treasury stock?

   I. It has voting rights and is entitled to a dividend when declared.
   II. It has no voting rights and no dividend entitlement.
   III. It has been issued and repurchased by the company.
   IV. It is authorized but unissued stock.

   A. I and III
   B. I and IV
   C. II and III
   D. II and IV

7. Limited liability regarding ownership in a large, publicly held U.S. corporation means all of the following EXCEPT

   A. investors might lose the amount of their investment
   B. investors might lose their investment plus the difference between their investment and par value
   C. investors' shares are nonassessable
   D. investors are not liable to the full extent of their personal property

8. Stockholders' preemptive rights include which of the following rights?

   A. Right to serve as an officer on the board of directors
   B. Right to maintain proportionate ownership interest in the corporation
   C. Right to purchase treasury stock
   D. Right to a subscription price on stock

9. Common stockholders' rights include a

   I.   residual claim to assets at dissolution
   II. vote for the amount of stock dividend to be paid
   III. vote in matters of recapitalization
   IV. claim against dividends that are in default

   A. I
   B. I and III
   C. II and III
   D. III and IV

10. When a corporation holds treasury stock, it has the option of

    A. reissuing it as debt securities
    B. not disclosing it to the registrar
    C. retiring it
    D. registering it under any name it chooses

11. The holders of which of the following securities are considered owners of the corporation?

    I.   Mortgage bonds
    II. Convertible debentures
    III. Preferred stock
    IV. Common stock

    A. I, II and III only
    B. III and IV only
    C. IV only
    D. I, II, III and IV

12. A corporation needs shareholder approval for which of the following?

    A. A cash dividend
    B. A 4-for-1 split
    C. A 10% stock dividend
    D. The repurchase of 100,000 of its own shares

◆ Answers & Rationale

1. **D.** With cumulative voting rights, this investor may cast 500 votes for the five directors in any way the investor chooses.   (Page 5)

2. **D.** A company does not have to reregister treasury stock in order to distribute it to the stockholders.   (Page 3)

3. **B.** Stockholder approval is required to change the stated value of stock as would occur with a stock split. Decisions regarding payment of dividends or repurchase of stock are made by the board of directors (management only) because these are considered to be operation decisions.   (Page 5)

4. **B.** These three are reasons why a corporation will buy back its stock. A corporation with cash that is not being totally used may purchase its shares to reduce the number of outstanding shares. If operating earnings remain the same, having fewer shares of outstanding stock will result in an increase in the earnings per share. The repurchased stock may be used for employee stock options or for acquisitions. Stock outstanding may be paid dividends declared by the board of directors, but is not paid interest. The repurchase, therefore, would not reduce interest charges.   (Page 3)

5. **D.** The cumulative method of voting gives an investor one vote per share owned, times the number of directorships to be voted on. For example, if an investor owns 100 stock shares and there are five directorships to be voted on, the investor will have a total of 500 votes. The stockholder may cast all of his votes for one directorship, thereby

giving the small investor more voting power.   (Page 5)

6. **C.** Treasury stock is stock a corporation has issued and subsequently repurchased from the public in the secondary market, It does not carry the rights of other common shares, including voting rights and the right to receive dividends. (Page 3)

7. **B.** Investors can lose no more than the amount of money they invested in the stock.   (Page 8)

8. **B.** A *preemptive right* is the right of a stockholder to purchase enough of any newly issued stock to maintain his proportionate ownership in the corporation.   (Page 8)

9. **B.** As the corporation's owners, common stockholders would have the lowest claim against a company's assets at dissolution or bankruptcy. Holders of common stock are entitled to vote on matters that affect their proportionate ownership. Recapitalization—the alteration of a corporation's capital structure—is an example of a situation that requires a vote of the stockholders.   (Page 5)

10. **C.** Corporations frequently buy back stock (making it Treasury stock) for the purpose of retiring it and thereby increasing earnings per share.   (Page 3)

11. **B.** Common and preferred stock are equity securities, while bondholders are considered creditors of the corporation.   (Page 2)

12. **B.** Shareholders have a right to vote on such items as mergers, reorganizations, recapitalizations and stock splits.   (Page 5)

2 Preferred Stock Exam

1. Which of the following are considered to have an equity position in a corporation?

   I. Common stockholders
   II. Preferred stockholders
   III. Convertible bondholders
   IV. Mortgage bondholders

   A. I and II only
   B. I and III only
   C. II and III only
   D. I, II, III and IV

2. ALFA Enterprises, which has 7% $100 par cumulative preferred stock outstanding, has the following dividend record: last year, 5% was paid to preferred stockholders; the full preferred dividend was paid until last year. Now ALFA wishes to declare a common dividend. Before ALFA can pay dividends to the common stockholders, how much must it first pay on each preferred share outstanding?

   A. $3
   B. $7
   C. $9
   D. $15

3. In a portfolio containing common stock, preferred stock, convertible preferred stock and guaranteed stock, changes in interest rates would be most likely to affect the market price of the

   A. common
   B. preferred
   C. convertible preferred
   D. guaranteed stock

4. A company with cumulative nonparticipating voting preferred stock would

   A. pay the preferred dividend before paying the coupons due on their outstanding bonds
   B. pay past and current preferred dividends before paying dividends on common
   C. pay the current dividends on the preferred but not the past dividends on the preferred before paying a dividend on the common
   D. force conversion of the preferred that is trading at a discount to par and thereby eliminate the necessity of paying past due dividends

◆ Answers & Rationale

1.   **A.**   Owners have equity positions. Common and preferred stockholders are owners. (Page 10)

2.   **C.**   In order to pay this year's common dividend, the corporation must pay the preferred stockholders the 2% not paid last year and this year's 7% dividend; in total, 9%, or $9.   (Page 11)

3.   **B.**   Preferred stock has the closest characteristics to bonds and would be most affected by a change in interest rates.   (Page 10)

4.   **B.**   Current and unpaid past dividends on cumulative preferred stock must be paid before common stockholders can receive a dividend.
(Page 11)

3 Return on Investment Exam

1. Max Leveridge owns 100 shares of Consolidated Codfish and he reads in the paper about a 2-for-1 stock split that has been declared and is payable next week. In order to receive the additional 100 shares, he must

   A. endorse his certificate for 100 shares and send it to the transfer agent, and he will receive a new certificate for 200 shares
   B. endorse his certificate for 100 shares and send it to the registrar, and he will receive a new certificate for 200 shares
   C. see his registered representative, sign a due bill for 100 shares and have his brokerage firm file a request for the additional 100 shares
   D. do nothing; he will receive a second certificate for 100 shares automatically

2. A client has 100 shares of GHI. The stock undergoes a split. After the split, she will have

   A. a proportionately decreased interest in the company
   B. a proportionately increased interest in the company
   C. no effective change in position
   D. a greater exposure

3. A company may pay dividends in which of the following ways?

   I. Stock of another company
   II. Cash
   III. Stock
   IV. Product

   A. I only
   B. II and III only
   C. III only
   D. I, II, III and IV

4. GHI declares a 3-for-2 stock split. How many additional shares will an investor who owns 200 shares be issued?

   A. 100
   B. 300
   C. 400
   D. 500

5. Acme Sweatsocks common stock is currently selling for $75 per share with a quarterly dividend of $.75. The current yield for Acme common stock is

   A. 1.0%
   B. 4.0%
   C. 12.5%
   D. 25.0%

6. GHI stock is $10.00 par value and is selling in the market for $60.00 per share. If the current quarterly dividend is $1.00, what is the current yield of GHI?

    A.   1.0%
    B.   1.6%
    C.   6.6%
    D.   10.0%

7. GHI currently has earnings of $4 and pays a $.50 quarterly dividend. The market price of GHI is $40. What is the current yield?

    A.   1.25%
    B.   5%
    C.   10%
    D.   15%

8. Your customer recently purchased 100 shares of Datawaq at $50 per share. She heard that DWQ has declared a 25% stock dividend, and wants to know how that will affect her holdings after the ex-date. You should tell her she will own

    A.   100 shares at $40
    B.   100 shares at $50
    C.   125 shares at $40
    D.   125 shares at $50

◆ Answers & Rationale

1.   **D.**   Existing stockholders are not required to do anything to receive their additional shares. The investor need not mail in his 100 shares to get 200 back. The investor just sits tight with his original 100 shares, and the issuer will send him an additional 100.   (Page 14)

2.   **C.**   When a stock splits, the number of shares each stockholder has either increases or decreases. The customer experiences no effective change in position or proportionate interest.
                                                         (Page 15)

3.   **D.**   A company may pay a dividend in any of the ways listed.   (Page 14)

4.   **A.**   Multiplying 3/2 by 200 shares gives 300, the total number of shares. To calculate how many additional shares are received, subtract 200 from the total of 300 for 100 additional shares.
                                                         (Page 15)

5.   **B.**

$$\frac{\$3.00 \text{ annual dividend}}{\$75 \text{ market price}} = 4.0\%$$

                                                         (Page 15)

6.   **C.**   The quarterly dividend is $1.00; therefore, the annual dividend is $4.00. $4 divided by $60 (market price) equals 6.6% annual yield (current yield).   (Page 15)

7.   **B.**   The quarterly dividend is $.50; therefore, the annual dividend is $2.00. $2 divided by $40 (market price) equals 5% annual yield (current yield).   (Page 15)

8.   **C.**   The number of shares were increased by 25%, or 25 shares. Total market value remains the same. To calculate the new market price, divide $5,000 (total market value) by 125 to get the after-dividend price of $40 per share.   (Page 14)

4 Transferability of Ownership Exam

1. Which of the following is(are) NOT functions of a registrar?

    I. Recording the names of stockholders on the corporation's books
    II. Accounting for the number of shares outstanding
    III. Canceling old shares
    IV. Transferring shares into the name of the new owner

    A. I
    B. I, III and IV
    C. II and III
    D. III and IV

2. What is the function of the CUSIP number?

    A. It is evidence of ownership in a corporation.
    B. It facilitates tracking and identification of a certificate.
    C. It ensures that the security is fungible.
    D. It is used in place of the registered owner's signature.

3. Which two of the following are necessary to complete a transfer of ownership of common shares?

    I. Owner's signature on the back of the certificate
    II. Owner's signature on a stock power
    III. Broker-dealer's guarantee of the signature
    IV. Officer of a national bank's signature

    A. I and II
    B. I and III
    C. I and IV
    D. II and IV

◆ Answers & Rationale

1.   **B.**   The registrar's function is to be certain that the number of shares outstanding does not exceed the number accounted for on the corporation's books. None of the other functions listed are performed by the registrar.   (Page 17)

2.   **B.**   The Committee on Uniform Securities Identification Procedures assigns a unique number to each certificate of common stock, preferred stock, corporate bond and municipal bond; the number is used to identify and track a particular certificate. The stock certificate itself, not the CUSIP number, is evidence of ownership in the issuing company. The presence of a CUSIP number does not make a security negotiable.   (Page 16)

3.   **B.**   The owner must sign either the back of the certificate or a stock power. Then this signature must be guaranteed by an exchange member, an authorized person of a broker-dealer or an officer of a national bank. An officer of a national bank cannot sign the certificate in place of the owner.
                    (Page 17)

5 Rights and Warrants Exam

1. An investor who wants to subscribe to a rights offering will mail those rights to the

   A. corporation's underwriting department
   B. rights agent
   C. bursar
   D. subscription agent

2. QRS Corporation has a rights offering. Before the rights offering, QRS had 10,000,000 shares of common stock authorized, with 4,000,000 issued and 1,000,000 shares of treasury stock. In a standby rights offering, there are 1,000,000 additional shares offered to the current stockholders. Assume that the existing stockholders subscribe to 600,000 of these shares. After the completion of the rights offering, how many shares of common are outstanding?

   A. 3,000,000
   B. 3,600,000
   C. 4,000,000
   D. 5,000,000

Use the following tombstone to answer questions 3 and 4.

Seven Seas Sailboat Corporation

600,000 Units – $5.00 Per Unit
Each unit represents 4 shares of Preferred plus 1 perpetual Warrant. Warrants may be exercised for 1/2 share of common stock at a value of $50 per share.

The Walrus Capital Group

3. A customer of yours who owns SSS Corp. common saw the tombstone in the local business daily, and has called you with some questions. If SSS's offering is successful, she wants to know, how much money will it be raising?

   A. $2,400,000
   B. $3,000,000
   C. $12,000,000
   D. This cannot be determined from the information given.

4. On completion of the offering of SSS Corp. and if all of the warrants were exercised, how many additional shares would be outstanding?

    I.   2,400,000 preferred shares
   II.   600,000 preferred shares
  III.   600,000 common shares
  IV.   300,000 common shares

    A.   I and III
    B.   I and IV
    C.   II and III
    D.   II and IV

5. What would be the benefits to a corporation of attaching warrants to a new issue of debt securities?

    A.   Dilution of shareholders' equity
    B.   Reduction of the interest rate of debt securities
    C.   Reduction of the number of shares outstanding
    D.   Increase in earnings per share

6. Kelptek is attempting to sell new shares through a rights offering. Hugh Heifer, who chooses to exercise his rights, sends his check to the

    A.   company
    B.   underwriter
    C.   customer's broker
    D.   rights/transfer agent

7. A corporate offering of 200,000 additional shares to existing stockholders is a

    A.   tender offer
    B.   secondary offering
    C.   preemptive offer
    D.   rights offering

8. Which of the following do NOT pay a dividend?

    A.   Warrants
    B.   Mutual funds
    C.   ADRs
    D.   Unit investment trusts

9. Quantum Rapid Search has issued 1 million shares of common stock and is now offering 600,000 units to the public at $5 per unit. Each unit consists of two shares of QRS preferred stock and one perpetual warrant for 1/3 share of common stock, exercisable at $5. When this issue has sold out, QRS has raised

    A. $1,500,000
    B. $1,750,000
    C. $3,000,000
    D. $6,000,000

10. Quantum Rapid Search is offering 600,000 units to the public at $5 per unit. Each unit consists of two shares of QRS preferred stock and one perpetual warrant for 1/3 share of common stock, exercisable at $5. Upon the exercise of all warrants, QRS will be capitalized with

    A.   600,000 preferred shares and 200,000 additional common shares
    B.   600,000 preferred shares and 600,000 additional common shares
    C.   1,200,000 preferred shares and 200,000 additional common shares
    D.   1,200,000 preferred shares and 600,000 additional common shares

11. A corporation issues new stock with a subscription price of $28. The stock is currently selling at $32. Under the terms of the offering, four rights are needed to subscribe to one new share. Using the ex-rights formula, what is the value of a right?

    A. $.80
    B. $1.00
    C. $4.00
    D.   This cannot be determined from the information given.

12. Acme Sweatsocks decides to sell additional shares to its existing stockholders through a rights offering. The current market price of Acme is $32 and the subscription price has been set at $18. Twenty rights will be necessary to purchase one new share. What, approximately, will be the price of the right before the ex-date?

   A. $.67
   B. $.70
   C. $1.00
   D. $1.12

13. A new bond issue will include warrants to

   A. increase the spread to the underwriter
   B. compensate the underwriter for handling the issue
   C. increase the price of the issue to the public
   D. increase the attractiveness of the issue to the public

14. All of the following pay dividends EXCEPT

   A. common stock
   B. preferred stock
   C. convertible preferred stock
   D. warrants

◆ Answers & Rationale

1. **B.** The issuing corporation will appoint a firm to serve as its rights agent. The rights agent will receive the subscription rights sent to it by those individuals who wish to exercise their rights to acquire the corporation's stock.   (Page 20)

2. **C.** Because there were 4,000,000 shares issued, and 1,000,000 shares of treasury stock, this means there were 3,000,000 shares outstanding. The existing stockholders subscribed to 600,000 new shares. However, because a standby (firm) underwriting was used, the additional 400,000 shares were also issued. Hence, a total of 4,000,000 shares will be outstanding.   (Page 20)

3. **B.** 600,000 units are being offered for a price of $5 per unit. If the offering is successful and all of the units are sold, the company will raise $3,000,000.   (Page 20)

4. **B.** 600,000 units each represents four shares of preferred stock for a total of 2,400,000 shares of preferred. Each unit also contains a warrant exchangeable into 1/2 of a share of common stock, for a total of 300,000 shares of common.   (Page 20)

5. **B.** Usually the warrant is issued as a sweetener to make the debt instrument more marketable. This enhancement allows the issuer to pay a slightly lower rate of interest. A warrant may be issued together with bonds or preferred stock, entitling the owner to purchase a given number of common stock shares at a specific price, for a number of years.   (Page 21)

6. **D.** The rights (or transfer) agent receives the checks for a rights offering. The agent can be the company's transfer agent or a special rights agent for the rights offering only.   (Page 18)

7. **D.** The question defines a rights offering.   (Page 18)

8. **A.** Warrants are long-term options to buy stock and do *not* pay dividends.   (Page 21)

9. **C.** 600,000 units are being offered at $5 each; $3,000,000 will be raised.   (Page 21)

10. **C.** Each unit consists of two preferred shares and 1/3 of a common share if the warrant is exercised. 600,000 multiplied by 2 equals 1,200,000 preferred shares and 600,000 multiplied by 1/3 equals 200,000 common shares. (Page 19)

11. **B.** To determine the value of a right, use the ex-rights formula.

$$\frac{\text{Market price} - \text{Subscription price}}{\text{N (number of rights)}}$$

$$= \text{Value of right}$$

$$\frac{\$32 - \$28}{4} = \$1 \text{ per right}$$

(Page 20)

12. **A.** Use the cum rights formula.

$$\frac{\text{Market price (\$32)} - \text{Sub. price (\$18)}}{\text{N(20)} + 1}$$

$$= \frac{14}{21} = .67$$

(Page 20)

13. **D.** Warrants are used as a "sweetener" to increase the attractiveness of a new issue to the public.   (Page 21)

14. **D.** Warrants do not pay dividends under any circumstances. The other instruments listed will pay dividends when declared by the board of directors.   (Page 21)

6 American Depositary Receipts Exam

1. ADRs facilitate which of the following?

   I.   Foreign trading of domestic securities
   II. Foreign trading of U.S. government securities
   III. Domestic trading of U.S. government securities
   IV. Domestic trading of foreign securities

   A. I and II
   B. III
   C. III and IV
   D. IV

2. Which of the following statement(s) is(are) true concerning ADRs?

   I.   They are issued by large commercial U.S. banks.
   II. They encourage foreign trading in U.S. markets.
   III. They facilitate U.S. trading in foreign securities.
   IV. They are registered on the books of the bank that issued the ADR.

   A. I and III
   B. I, III and IV
   C. II
   D. II and IV

3. ADR owners have all of the following rights EXCEPT

   A. voting rights
   B. right to receive dividends
   C. preemptive rights
   D. right to receive the underlying foreign security

4. From which of the following investments is an investor entitled to receive dividends?

   A. ADR
   B. Put option
   C. Call option
   D. Warrant

◆ Answers & Rationale

1. **D.** ADRs (American depositary receipts) are tradeable securities issued by banks, with the receipt's value based on the underlying foreign securities held by the bank. In this way, Americans can trade foreign securities in the United States.

(Page 22)

2. **B.** ADRs are issued by large commercial U.S. banks to facilitate U.S. trading in foreign securities and are registered on the books of the banks that issued them.   (Page 23)

3. **C.** If the foreign company issues additional securities, the ADR owner does not have the right to maintain proportionate ownership of the company.   (Page 23)

4. **A.** An American depositary receipt (ADR) represents ownership in a foreign corporation; thus the owner will receive dividends declared by the corporation. Options and warrants represent the right to buy or sell stock, but do not entitle the owner to receive dividends.   (Page 22)

Characteristics of Bonds Exam

1. Your customer holds a 10M KLP 6s bond callable at 102 in 1995 and maturing in 2001. How much money will the customer receive in total at the debenture's maturity?

   A. $10,000
   B. $10,200
   C. $10,300
   D. $10,600

2. All of the following corporate bonds have a call option, and all have passed their call protection period. Which of these investments is LEAST likely to be called away by the issuer?

   A. 7 1/4% maturing in 2018, callable at 100
   B. 7 1/4% maturing in 2017, callable at 101 1/2
   C. 9 3/4% maturing in 2018, callable at 103
   D. 9 3/4% maturing in 2024, callable at 100

3. The board of Mountain Brewing has come to you for advice. They see a need to increase the company's working capital, but do not want to incur additional fixed charges. Unless there are no other alternatives, they would rather not increase the company's capitalization until the next fiscal year. Which of the following alternatives would you recommend they NOT take over the next six months?

   A. Issue stock dividends in lieu of cash dividends for the next two quarters.
   B. Issue additional shares of common stock to current stockholders through a preemptive rights offering.
   C. Issue two-year notes with no call protection.
   D. Sell a wholly owned foreign subsidiary.

4. Acme Sweatsocks, Inc. has created a sinking fund for the purpose of retiring bonds issued several years ago. The sinking fund is large enough to redeem the outstanding bonds at 102 1/2. If the bonds are trading in the market at 97, Acme's board of directors should

   A. call in part of the issue
   B. purchase bonds at market
   C. wait until the bonds reach parity
   D. convert Acme stock into bonds and arbitrage

5. Consolidated Codfish has decided to prerefund a bond issue that still has several years remaining to maturity. What will be the effect of this action on outstanding bonds?

    A. Outstanding bonds should experience an increase in marketability and rating.
    B. Prerefunding will effectively cancel any call protection the bonds had.
    C. Bondholders can petition the company for immediate tender.
    D. Remaining bondholders will experience an increase in current yield.

6. All of the following are true about bonds registered as to principal only EXCEPT that

    A. coupons are attached
    B. the registered owner may sell the bonds prior to maturity
    C. interest payments are sent directly to the owner twice a year
    D. such bonds can be purchased today in the secondary market

7. A corporation will call in its debt during a period of

    A. rising interest rates
    B. declining interest rates
    C. volatile interest rates
    D. stable interest rates

8. Funded debt is

    A. flower bonds
    B. municipal bonds
    C. U.S. government bonds
    D. corporate bonds

9. Kelptek bonds, which mature in 1993, are callable beginning in 1987 at 103, with the call price to decrease annually by 1/2 a point. The redemption price of the bond in 1990 is

    A. 100 1/2
    B. 101 1/2
    C. 102
    D. 103

10. Max Leveridge purchases $50,000 of 10% corporate bonds at par. At the end of the day, the bonds close down 1/2 a point. Max has a loss of

    A. $25
    B. $250
    C. $2,500
    D. $5,000

11. Your customer has two $5,000 bonds. One has a coupon of 5.1%; the other has a coupon of 5.3%. What is the difference in annual interest payments between the bonds?

    A. $1
    B. $2
    C. $10
    D. $20

12. Which of the following are characteristics of bearer bonds?

    A. They come in registered form.
    B. They have interest coupons attached to the bond.
    C. They have interest coupons detached from the bond.
    D. They pay interest quarterly.

13. Which statement would be true for an investor who purchased $50,000 face value of 5.10 bonds at par due in 2002 and held them to maturity?

    A. The investor would receive $50,000, the final two interest payments and 5.10 market gain at maturity.
    B. The investor would receive $50,000 less 5.10 market discount at maturity.
    C. The investor would receive $50,000 plus 5.10 at maturity.
    D. The investor would receive $50,000 and the final interest payment at maturity.

14. Which bonds are issued all at once and mature over several years?

    A. Serial
    B. Term
    C. Balloon
    D. Series

15. Serial bonds, in comparison to term bonds, have

    A. stable interest payments and stable principal
    B. increasing interest payments and increasing outstanding principal
    C. declining interest payments and declining outstanding principal
    D. declining interest rates and stable principal

16. The difference between par and a lower market price on a bond is called the

    A. reallowance
    B. spread
    C. discount
    D. premium

17. Which of the following factors would be LEAST important in rating a bond?

    A. The bond's coupon
    B. The amount and composition of existing debt
    C. Stability of the issuer's cash flows
    D. Asset protection

18. Texas Powerful Light Company issued Mortgage Senior Lien bonds at 8 7/8, price 96.353. These bonds pay annual interest, per $1,000 bond, of

    A. $85.00
    B. $85.51
    C. $88.75
    D. $96.35

19. New issues of corporate bonds are MOST likely to be offered

    A. in bearer form
    B. registered as to interest only
    C. registered as to principal only
    D. fully registered as to both principal and interest

20. Max Leveridge wants to sell his 20 Datawaq bonds, but tells you that they are registered in book-entry form. What must occur in order for Max to sell his bonds?

    A. Your firm must send the signed Datawaq bond certificate to the transfer agent.
    B. Your firm will send the certificate to the transfer agent who will then destroy the old certificate and issue a new one.
    C. The transfer agent will input the necessary changes in the ownership records on a computer.
    D. The issuer will make the necessary changes in its customer bond record books.

21. Klaus Bruin purchases a bond at a premium. Which of the following call provisions would he prefer?

    A. At par in 7 years
    B. At a premium in 7 years
    C. At par in 14 years
    D. At a premium in 14 years

22. What is the effect of prerefunding a bond issue?

    I. It provides the ultimate in security for the issue.
    II. The quality of the issue improves.
    III. The issue becomes more marketable.
    IV. The price of the bond declines.

    A. I and II only
    B. I, II and III only
    C. III and IV only
    D. I, II, III and IV

23. The issue of bonds in the following listing is an example of what type of maturity?

Amount	Due Feb 1	Rate	Yield or Price
4,165,000	1992	5.20	100
4,165,000	1993	5 1/4	100
4,165,000	1994	5 1/4	5.30
4,165,000	1995	5 1/4	5.35
4,165,000	1996	5 1/4	5.40
4,165,000	1997	5 1/4	5.45
4,165,000	1998	5 1/4	5.50

A. Term
B. Balloon
C. Series
D. Serial

24. An investor owns AA rated Atlanta GO bonds with a coupon rate of 6.5%. The bonds are scheduled to mature in 2015. He receives notice that the bonds will be called at 102 in one month. What should a registered rep advise the investor to do?

I. Hold the bonds until maturity.
II. Trade the bonds in the secondary market.
III. Send the bonds to the issuer for redemption now.

A. I and III only
B. II only
C. III only
D. I, II and III

25. The Mineral Point Opossum Control Authority has issued new bonds and committed the money to paying off the old bonds as soon as they become callable, so the municipality can be said to have

A. retired the issue
B. advance refunded the issue
C. refunded the issue
D. double barreled the issue

26. Randy Bear and Adam Grizzly are conservative investors in their fifties, interested in preservation of principal and high current income from their investments. In which order, from first to last, are the following bonds ranked in terms of their suitability to the customer's needs?

I. A1 Fort Worth Gas 9 1/4s of '25
II. AA+ San Antonio Transit 9 1/4s of '25
III. Aaa Texas Telecom 9 1/4s of '25
IV. AAA– Dallas Electric 9 1/4s of '25

A. III, II, IV, I
B. IV, III, I, II
C. I, II, III, IV
D. III, IV, II, I

◆ Answers & Rationale

1. **C.** 10M bonds denote $10,000 in principal amount to be received by the bondholder at maturity. Each bond pays 6% annual interest of $60; thus, ten bonds pay a total of $600 per year in two semiannual payments of $300. At maturity, the bondholder will receive the $10,000 face amount plus the final semiannual payment ($10,000 + $300 = $10,300).   (Page 28)

2. **B.** The bond with an earlier maturity and a lower coupon is less likely to be called than one with a higher rate. A call price above par is more expensive for the issuer to pay. It is least likely that the 7 1/4% bond callable at 101 1/2 will be called.   (Page 38)

3. **C.** The issuing of short-term debt securities would result in an increase in fixed charges, something the company wants to avoid. The call feature is a "red herring"; it doesn't affect the answer. The other options would increase working capital without increasing fixed charges, although answer B would also increase capitalization.   (Page 28)

4. **B.** If the company is prepared to pay $1,025 for each bond at redemption, it can save $55 per bond by purchasing the bonds back in the market at 97.   (Page 37)

5. **A.** Prerefunding an issue is accomplished by selling new bonds and dedicating the funds raised to retiring an older bond issue at its first call date. The new bonds normally have a lower coupon than the old bonds, effectively lowering the company's fixed interest costs. The funds raised are typically invested in Treasury issues, ensuring their availability to pay off the older issue at the call date.   (Page 39)

6. **C.** A bond that is registered as to principal only will have a certificate registered in some person's name and have bearer coupons attached to the bond certificate. Only the person to whom the bond is registered may sell the securities. Interest will be paid on the bond only if the interest coupons are sent to the paying agent of the bond.   (Page 31)

7. **B.** A corporation will generally call in its debt when interest rates are declining. It can then replace old, high interest rate debt with a new, lower interest rate issue.   (Page 37)

8. **D.** *Funded debt* is the term used to describe long-term corporate debt.   (Page 28)

9. **B.** Using the data given, the call schedule for the bond is:

Year	Price
1987	103
1988	102 1/2
1989	102
1990	101 1/2
1991	101
1992	100 1/2
1993	100

(Page 37)

10. **B.** The customer holds 50 $1,000 bonds. If each bond decreases by 1/2 point, the loss is $5 per bond; multiplied by 50 bonds, this equals $250.   (Page 33)

11. **C.** To determine the dollar difference between the bonds, calculate the two interest payments and find the difference between them ($5,000 × 5.1% = $255; $5,000 × 5.3% = $265; $265 − $255 = $10).   (Page 28)

12. **B.** Bearer bonds, also called *unregistered bonds*, must have the interest coupons attached to the bond.   (Page 31)

13. **D.** Because the 2002 bonds were purchased at par ($1,000 per bond) and will be redeemed at par ($1,000 per bond), the investor will receive $50,000 plus the final six-month interest payment of $1,275 at maturity.   (Page 28)

14. **A.** Serial bonds, by definition, have maturity dates scheduled at regular intervals until the issue is retired. Other bonds may also mature serially, but they don't have to.   (Page 29)

15. **C.** Serial bonds are bonds that mature over a series of years. From the issuer's standpoint, as bonds mature, interest payments and the outstanding principal amount will decline.   (Page 29)

16. **C.** The difference between the par (or face) value of a bond and a market price lower than par is known as the bond's discount from par.   (Page 33)

17. **A.** The coupon rate that a bond pays is not a factor in rating a bond, although the rating that a bond could receive may significantly impact the interest rate the issuers must set.   (Page 35)

18. **C.** A coupon of 8 7/8 represents an annual interest payment of 8 7/8% of $1,000, or $88.75.   (Page 28)

19. **D.** Most corporate bonds are currently being issued in fully registered form.   (Page 31)

20. **C.** Bonds registered in book-entry form are not evidenced by a paper certificate. All records of ownership are retained in computerized form. The transfer agent will make any necessary changes in the computer's records.   (Page 32)

21. **D.** Because the investor purchased the bond at a premium, calling the bond at par or a discount would force the investor to suffer a capital loss. The closer the call period, the quicker the investor would incur this loss. Therefore, the nearest term call at par is most harmful to the investor. It is more desirable to have a call at a premium several years from now to give the investor time to maximize his investment.   (Page 38)

22. **B.** When a bond is prerefunded (advance refunding), the issuer deposits the money to pay off the bond in an escrow account. This account is invested in Treasury securities that mature whenever the issuer can call the bond. Prerefunding provides the ultimate in security for the issue because, technically, the bonds are paid. It improves the quality of the issue, making the bonds more marketable. Often prerefunded bonds are given a Aaa rating. It will not necessarily reduce the price of the bonds.   (Page 39)

23. **D.** An issue of bonds that is redeemed according to a predetermined rate schedule and that retires a similar amount of the issue at set intervals until the entire issue is redeemed is called a *serial maturity*.   (Page 29)

24. **B.** Bonds still trade in the open market after a call notice is issued. The investor's other option, of course, is to deliver the bonds on the call date.   (Page 38)

25. **B.** Municipalities will occasionally pay off an outstanding issue of securities early if they can refinance them by issuing new securities at a substantially lower overall interest cost.   (Page 39)

26. **D.** A plus or minus sign in a Standard & Poor's rating indicates that the bonds fall within, respectively, the top or bottom of that particular category. Moody's uses a "1" after the letter rating to indicate the highest quality bonds within a category. Based on the ratings given, the highest quality bond is the Texas Telecom, rated Aaa, followed in order by the bonds rated AAA–, AA+ and A1.   (Page 34)

8 Bond Yields Exam

1. An inverted yield curve would result from the expectation of

    A. increasing short-term bond prices
    B. increasing long-term bond prices
    C. rising interest rates
    D. falling interest rates

2. If interest rates are changing, which of the following terms would best describe the relationship between prices and yields for corporate bonds?

    A. Reverse
    B. Inverse
    C. Coterminous
    D. Coaxial

3. Of the following bonds in your customer's portfolio, which would be most affected by the risk of changing interest rates?

    A. 8's of '98, yielding 7%
    B. 8.75's of '06, yielding 7.2%
    C. 8's of '13, yielding 7.3%
    D. 8.25's of '04, yielding 7.4%

4. One of your customers owns several 7% and 8% corporate bonds of the same maturity. Because of changes in general interest rates, they are currently trading on a 6.25% basis. If the interest rates decline to 6%

    A. the 7% bond will appreciate the most
    B. the 8% bond will appreciate the most
    C. both bonds will appreciate the same
    D. neither bond will appreciate

5. One of your clients owns two different 9% corporate bonds maturing in 15 years. The first bond is callable in five years, the second has 10 years of call protection, but is callable from then until it matures. If interest rates on bonds of this type begin to fall, which bond is likely to show a greater increase in price?

    A. Bond with the five-year call
    B. Bond with the ten-year call
    C. Both will increase by the same amount.
    D. Both will decrease by the same amount.

6. With fluctuating interest rates, the price of which of the following will fluctuate most?

    A. Common stock
    B. Money-market instruments
    C. Short-term bonds
    D. Long-term bonds

7. How do you calculate the current yield on a bond?

    A. Yield to maturity ÷ Par value
    B. Yield to maturity ÷ Dollar market price
    C. Annual interest payments ÷ Par value
    D. Annual interest payments ÷ Dollar market price

8. The current yield on a bond priced at $950 with a coupon bearing interest at 6% is

    A. the same as the nominal yield
    B. the same as yield to maturity
    C. 6%
    D. 6.3%

9. The current yield on a bond with a coupon rate of 7 1/2% currently selling at 95 is approximately

    A. 7.0%
    B. 7.4%
    C. 7.9%
    D. 8.0%

10. Currently, Kelptek issues 8 1/2% Aaa bonds in the primary market at par. Two years earlier, the corporation had issued 8% Aaa rated debentures at par. Which two statements are true regarding the outstanding 8% issue?

    I.   The dollar price per bond will be higher than par.
    II. The dollar price per bond will be lower than par.
    III. The current yield on the issue will be higher.
    IV. The current yield on the issue will be lower.

    A. I and III
    B. I and IV
    C. II and III
    D. II and IV

11. A bond purchased at $900 with a 5% coupon and a five-year maturity has a current yield of

    A. 5.0%
    B. 5.6%
    C. 7.0%
    D. 7.7%

12. A customer purchased a 5% corporate bond yielding 6%. A year before the bond matures, new corporate bonds are being issued at 4% and the customer sells the 5% bond. The customer

    I.   bought it at a discount
    II. bought it at a premium
    III. sold it at a premium
    IV. sold it at a discount

    A. I and III
    B. I and IV
    C. II and III
    D. II and IV

13. Your firm's fixed-income analyst put out a notice that yield curves are currently flat. If a client calls for information, how would you describe the spread between long- and short-term yields?

    A. Narrow
    B. Wide
    C. Even
    D. Inverse

14. A bond at par has a coupon rate

    A. less than current yield
    B. less than yield to maturity
    C. the same as current yield
    D. higher than current yield

15. What is the calculation for determining the current yield on a bond?

    A. Annual interest ÷ Par value
    B. Annual interest ÷ Current market price
    C. Yield to maturity ÷ Par value
    D. Yield to maturity ÷ Current market price

16. A callable municipal bond maturing in 30 years is purchased at 102. The bond is callable at par in 15 years. If the bond is called at the first call date, the effective yield earned on the bond is

   A. lower than the yield to maturity
   B. the same as the yield to maturity
   C. higher than the yield to maturity
   D. not determinable

17. Which of the following bonds on a broker-dealer inventory sheet would MOST likely be quoted at a price based upon the probability of a call or refunding?

   A. Bond trading at 95, callable at par
   B. Bond trading at 95, callable at premium
   C. Bond trading at 105, callable at par
   D. Bond trading at 105, callable at premium

18. What happens to outstanding fixed-income securities when interest rates drop?

   A. Yields go up.
   B. Coupon rates go up.
   C. Prices go up.
   D. Short-term fixed-income securities are affected most.

19. Two 15-year municipal bonds are issued at par. Both have a 6% coupon rate. One is callable at par in five years and the other is callable at par in ten years. If interest rates decline to 4.8%, which bond will be expected to appreciate the most?

   A. The bond callable in five years will appreciate the most.
   B. The bond callable in ten years will appreciate the most.
   C. Both bonds will appreciate by the same amount.
   D. There is not enough information to determine which will appreciate the most.

◆ Answers & Rationale

1.   D.   An inverted yield curve is the result of short-term bonds yielding more than long-term bonds. When interest rates are high and are expected to fall, the yield to maturity of a long-term bond will also fall as the price increases. Interest rates cause price increases or decreases in the bond market.   (Page 46)

2.   B.   As yields increase, the price of outstanding debt decreases and vice versa. Because the face and coupon on a debt instrument remain unchanged, the market value fluctuates to account for changes in yields.   (Page 45)

3.   C.   Interest rate risk is the danger that interest rates will change while a long-term debt is outstanding. The bond with the most years remaining to maturity and the lowest coupon will be exposed to the greatest risk.   (Page 46)

4.   B.   The rule of thumb for premium bonds is that the farther away from the current market rates a premium bond's yield is, the more volatile its price. Volatility increases as coupon rates decline. Thus the 8% bond will fluctuate more in price than a 7% bond.   (Page 45)

5.   B.   The price of the bond that has the longer call protection will be more volatile, and the basis is therefore likely to increase more as general interest rates fall.   (Page 44)

6.   D.   Long-term debt prices will fluctuate more than short-term debt prices as interest rates rise and fall. When one buys a note or a bond, one is really buying the interest payments and the final principal payment. Money has a time value: the farther out in time money is to be received, the less it is worth today.   (Page 46)

7.   D.   The current yield of a bond equals the annual interest payment divided by the current market price.   (Page 41)

8.   D.   The current yield is:

$$\frac{\$ \text{ Coupon}}{\text{Bond market price}} = \frac{\$60}{\$950} = 6.3\%$$

(Page 41)

9.   C.   Each $1,000 7 1/2% bond pays $75 of interest annually.

$$\text{Current yield} = \frac{\text{Annual interest}}{\text{Bond market price}}$$

$$= \frac{\$75}{\$950} = 7.89\%$$

7.89% is approximately 7.9%.   (Page 41)

10.   C.   Because interest rates in general have risen since the issuance of the 8% bond, the bond's price will now be discounted to give a higher current yield on the bond, making it competitive with the new issues now being sold at 8 1/2%.
(Page 45)

11.   B.   The current yield is the annual interest payment divided by the current market price. Therefore, $50 divided by $900 equals 5.6% current yield.   (Page 41)

12.   A.   If the current yield of a bond is higher than its coupon rate, the bond is selling at a discount from par. If interest rates of newly issued bonds are lower than the rate of a secondary market bond, it is likely that the older bond could be sold at a premium.   (Page 41)

13.   C.   The yield curve illustrates the various yields on a lengthening series of similarly rated debt instruments. With a flat yield curve, short- and long-term securities have the same yields. Therefore, the spread or difference between long- and short-term yields is zero or even.   (Page 47)

14.   C.   When a bond is selling at par, its coupon rate, nominal rate and current yield are the same.
(Page 41)

15.   B.   Dividing the annual interest received by the current market price of the bond will give the current yield.   (Page 41)

16. **A.** If the bond is trading at a premium and is called prior to maturity, the loss of the premium is compressed into a shorter period of time. This reduces the effective yield on the bond. The effective yield if the bond is called is the *yield to call*. Yield to call is calculated as follows:

$$\frac{\text{Annual interest} \pm \dfrac{\text{Gain/loss on call price}}{\text{Number of years to call date}}}{\dfrac{\text{Market price} + \text{Call price}}{2}}$$

(Page 44)

17. **C.** Bonds must be quoted based on the most conservative yield an investor may receive. Any discount bond callable at par or above will have a yield to call that is greater than its yield to maturity. The higher the call price and the sooner the bond is called, the greater the yield to call for a discount bond. A premium bond callable at par or below always has a yield to call that is less than its yield to maturity. The lower the call price and the sooner the bond is called, the lower the yield to call for any premium bond. Recall the rule of thumb method that illustrates these principles:

1. Add the prorated discount to, *or* subtract the prorated premium from, the coupon rate.
2. Divide the result by the average price, which is the price paid for the bond plus the price received upon maturity, divided by 2.

(Page 44)

18. **C.** When the interest rates drop the coupons on new issue bonds will decline to offer lower yields. The price of outstanding bonds will rise to adjust to the lower yields on bonds of comparable quality.   (Page 46)

19. **B.** Call features affect the appreciation of premium bonds. When interest rates decline and the prices of the two bonds increase, the bond with the greater call protection (later call date) will be worth more in the market.   (Page 44)

9 Characteristics of Corporate Bonds Exam

1. In order to read about all of the limitations, promises and agreements about a new corporate bond issue, you would go to the

   A. legal opinion
   B. tombstone
   C. agreement among underwriters
   D. indenture

2. A trust indenture spells out the covenants between

   A. trustee and underwriter
   B. issuer and underwriter
   C. issuer and trustee
   D. issuer and trustee for the benefit of a bondholder

3. In case of bankruptcy, debentures rank on a par with

   A. first-mortgage bonds
   B. equipment trust certificates
   C. unsecured debts of private creditors
   D. collateral trust bonds

4. Bonds that are guaranteed are

   A. insured by AMBAC
   B. required to maintain a self-liquidating sinking fund
   C. guaranteed as to payment of principal and interest by another corporation
   D. guaranteed as to payment of principal and interest by the U.S. government

5. Which of the following statements are true regarding corporate zero-coupon bonds?

   I. Interest is paid semiannually.
   II. Interest is not paid until maturity.
   III. The discount must be prorated and is taxed annually.
   IV. The discount must be prorated annually, with taxation deferred to maturity.

   A. I and III
   B. I and IV
   C. II and III
   D. II and IV

6. An indenture has a closed-end provision. This means that

   A. additional issues will have junior liens
   B. the bonds must be called before maturity
   C. a sinking fund must be established
   D. no additional bonds may be issued

7. In the liquidation of the assets of General Gizmonics, Inc., in what order would the following list of organizations and individuals receive payment?

   I. Internal Revenue Service
   II. Holders of subordinated debentures
   III. General creditors
   IV. Common stockholders

   A. I, II, III, IV
   B. I, III, II, IV
   C. III, I, II, IV
   D. IV, III, II, I

8. Consolidated Codfish has filed for bankruptcy. Interested parties will be paid off in which of the following orders?

    I.   Holders of secured debt
    II. Holders of subordinated debentures
    III. General creditors
    IV. Preferred stockholders

    A. I, II, III, IV
    B. I, III, II, IV
    C. III, I, II, IV
    D. IV, I, II, III

9. When a mortgage bond goes into default, bondholders have a claim against

    A. the principal amount of the loan
    B. the property pledged as collateral
    C. all of the issuer's assets
    D. assets of the parent company

◆ Answers & Rationale

1. **D.** The indenture is the contract between an issuer and the trustee on behalf of its bondholders and contains information regarding all terms, conditions and repayment provisions of a corporate debt issue.   (Page 55)

2. **D.** The trust indenture is a contract between the issuer and trustee for the benefit of a bondholder. It spells out the covenants to be honored by the issuer and gives the trustee the power to monitor compliance with the covenants and the ability to take action on behalf of the bondholder(s) if a default of the covenants is found.   (Page 55)

3. **C.** Debentures represent unsecured loans to an issuer. All of the other bonds are backed by one form or another of collateral.   (Page 55)

4. **C.** A guaranteed bond has additional backing supplied by a corporation other than the issuer (typically a parent corporation guaranteeing the bonds of a subsidiary).   (Page 53)

5. **C.** The investor in a corporate zero-coupon bond receives his return in the form of growth of the principal amount during the bond's life. The bond is purchased at a steep discount and the discount is accrued by the investor and taxed by the government annually.   (Page 54)

6. **A.** A closed-end provision in a bond indenture assures investors in the bonds that no other bonds will be issued with an equal or higher claim against company assets.   (Page 52)

7. **B.** The order in a liquidation is as follows: the IRS (and other government agencies), secured debt holders, unsecured debt holders and general creditors, holders of subordinated debt, preferred stockholders and, finally, common stockholders.
(Page 55)

8. **B.** The order in a liquidation is as follows: the IRS (and other government agencies), secured debt holders, unsecured debt holders and general creditors, holders of subordinated debt, preferred stockholders and, finally, common stockholders.
(Page 55)

9. **B.** Mortgage bonds are secured bonds; in a default situation, the bondholders will lay claim to the property pledged to secure the bond. By liquidating this property, bondholders attempt to retrieve their principal. They do not have a claim on other assets of the issuer or its affiliates.
(Page 52)

1. Lotta Leveridge owns shares of GHI convertible preferred stock. GHI convertible preferred is currently trading at 9 1/2 per share. GHI has just announced that it is offering to redeem shares of GHI convertible preferred at $10 per share. Each share is convertible into one half of a share of the common, currently trading at 18 1/4. What should you advise Mrs. Leveridge to do with her 1,000 shares of GHI convertible preferred?

   A. Sell them in the open market.
   B. Convert them immediately into the common.
   C. Tender the shares to the corporation.
   D. Hold the shares.

2. Lotta Leveridge owns shares of GHI convertible preferred stock. GHI convertible preferred is currently trading at 9 1/2 per share. GHI has just announced that it is offering to redeem shares of GHI convertible preferred at $10 per share. Each share is convertible into one half of a share of the common, currently trading at 18 1/4. Assuming that the market price of the GHI common remains stable, what will happen to the market price of the convertible preferred as the expiration date of the tender offer approaches?

   A. It will slowly decline below the current 9 1/2.
   B. It will slowly rise to just under 10.
   C. It will slowly rise to just under 18 1/4.
   D. It will stabilize at 9 1/8.

3. Acme Sweatsocks has issued both common stock and convertible preferred stock. The convertible preferred has a par value of $100 per share. It is convertible into the common at $25 per share. Acme convertible is trading at 110. What is the parity price of the common?

   A. 25
   B. 27 1/2
   C. 35
   D. 37 1/2

4. Acme Sweatsocks has issued both common stock and convertible preferred stock. The convertible preferred has a par value of $100 per share. It is convertible into the common at $25 per share. Due to a change in interest rates, the market price of the Acme preferred declines to $90 per share. Assume that the common is trading at 20% below parity. What is the market price of the Acme common?

   A. 15 3/4
   B. 18
   C. 22 1/2
   D. 25

5. A corporation has $20,000,000 of 8% convertible debentures outstanding. The bonds have a conversion price of $25 per share. The trust indenture has a provision that prevents dilution of the debenture holder's potential ownership in the corporation. The corporation declares a 10% stock dividend. How will the corporation comply with the dilution covenant of the indenture?

    A. Adjust the conversion price to $16 per share.
    B. Adjust the conversion price to $16.67 per share.
    C. Adjust the conversion price to $22.73 per share.
    D. Offer bondholders the choice of receiving 10 shares of stock or $40 cash.

6. Consolidated Codfish has a $20 million convertible debenture issue outstanding. Each bond converts into 20 shares of COD common stock. The bond indenture contains antidilutive covenants. COD declares a 10% stock dividend. What would be the new conversion price of the bonds?

    A. $32
    B. $33.33
    C. $36.66
    D. $45.45

7. A $1,000 Consolidated Codfish bond can be converted at $50 per share into COD common stock. The bond is currently selling at 110% of parity while the current market value of the stock is $55 per share. What is the bond selling for in the market?

    A. $1,000
    B. $1,100
    C. $1,210
    D. $1,350

8. Which of the following statements are true of convertible and callable bonds?

    I.   If called, the owners have the option of retaining the bonds and they will continue to receive interest.
    II. After the call date, interest will cease.
    III. Upon conversion, there will be dilution.
    IV. The coupon rate would be less than the rate for a nonconvertible bond.

    A. I and III
    B. I, III and IV
    C. II, III and IV
    D. II and IV

9. Which of the following is NOT true concerning convertible bonds?

    A. Coupon rates are usually higher than nonconvertible bond rates of the same issuer.
    B. Convertible bondholders are creditors of the corporation.
    C. Coupon rates are usually lower than nonconvertible bond rates of the same issuer.
    D. If the underlying common stock were to decline to the point where there is no advantage to convert the bonds into common stock, the bonds would sell at a price based on their inherent value as bonds, disregarding the convertible feature.

10. All of the following will remain relatively stable in value in a period of stable interest rates EXCEPT

    A. convertible preferred stock
    B. senior preferred
    C. participating preferred
    D. cumulative preferred

Use the following tombstone to answer questions 11 and 12.

This announcement is neither an offer to sell nor a solicitation of an offer to buy these securities.
The offer is made only by Prospectus.

New Issue   May 5, 1995

$42,000,000
Acme Sweatsocks, Inc.
10 5/8 Convertible Debentures Due 5/31/2025
Price $1,000

Convertible into Acme Sweatsocks Common Stock
at $10.50 per Share through May 31, 2005.

Copies of this Prospectus may be obtained in any State in which this announcement is circulated only
from such of the undersigned as may legally offer these securities
in such State.

Moneyflow and Cash Co.
Millon, Billon, Dillon & Co.   Simpson, Sampson, Sobriquet
Dullard Securities Inc.   Fleecem Runn Skippe

---

11. If an investor wishes to convert, approximately how many whole shares of common stock can she expect per bond?

    A. 90
    B. 95
    C. 100
    D. 105

12. On December 4, 1996, the bonds were trading at 102. Calculation of the parity price of common stock on that date shows it to be approximately

    A. 1 7/8
    B. 9 1/8
    C. 9 3/4
    D. 10 3/4

13. GHI common stock is currently trading at 56 1/2. Your client owns one GHI 6% convertible debenture that closed at 115 1/2 on Friday. Before the open of the market Monday, it was announced that the debenture would be called at 102 1/4. The debenture is convertible into common stock at $59.25 per share. What should he do?

    A. Sell the debenture at 115 1/2.
    B. Convert the debenture and immediately sell the converted shares in the market.
    C. Sell the common stock short against the box.
    D. Allow the debenture to be called.

14. What is the conversion ratio of a convertible bond purchased at face value and convertible at $50?

    A. 2:1
    B. 3:1
    C. 20:1
    D. 30:1

15. Angus Bullwether purchases two newly issued $1,000 par, 5% convertible corporate bonds at par. The bonds are convertible into common stock at $50 per share. During the period in which the investor holds the bonds, the $50 market price of the common stock increases 25%. The parity price of the bond, after the increase in the common stock price, is

    A. $750
    B. $1,000
    C. $1,025
    D. $1,250

16. An investor purchases two newly issued $1,000 par, 5% convertible corporate bonds at parity. The bonds are convertible into common stock at $50 per share. During the period in which the investor holds the bonds, the market price of the common stock increases 25% over her purchase price. Each bond is equivalent to how many converted shares?

    A. 2
    B. 3
    C. 20
    D. 30

17. Acme Sweatsocks convertible bonds are convertible at $50. If the bonds are selling in the market for 90 and the common stock is selling for $45, which two of the following statements are true?

    I.   The bond can be converted into 20 shares of common stock.
    II. There would be a profitable arbitrage situation.
    III. The bonds are trading below parity.
    IV. The bonds are trading at parity.

    A. I and II
    B. I and III
    C. I and IV
    D. II and III

18. Klaus Bruin purchases a 9% convertible bond maturing in 20 years. The bond is convertible into common stock at $50 per share. If the price of the common stock is at parity (57 1/2), how much does Klaus pay for the bond?

    A. $850.00
    B. $942.50
    C. $1,057.50
    D. $1,150.00

19. Belle Charolais owns some $100 par 5 1/2% callable convertible preferred stock that is convertible into common stock at $25. What should she be advised to do should the board of directors call all the preferred at 106 when the common stock is trading at $25.50?

    A. Convert her preferred stock into common stock because the common stock is selling above parity.
    B. Present the preferred stock for the call in order to realize a $6-per-share premium.
    C. Place irrevocable instructions to convert the preferred stock into common stock and sell short the common stock immediately.
    D. Hold the preferred stock in order to continue the 5 1/2% yield.

20. Belle Charolais owns a convertible bond for Consolidated Codfish. She is, therefore,

    A. an owner
    B. a creditor
    C. both owner and creditor
    D. neither owner nor creditor

◆ Answers & Rationale

1. **C.** The customer should do whatever will result in the greatest value. She currently holds 1,000 shares of the preferred with a CMV totaling $9,500 (1,000 × $9.50). She can sell each share in the open market for $9.50. If she converts her preferred, she will get one share of common for two shares of preferred, a conversion value per share of $18.25, and a total market value of $9,125 (500 × 18 1/4). If she tenders the stock, she will receive $10 per share, or $10,000. She can hold the stock, but its retirement by the company means it will no longer earn dividends. She would just be postponing the time at which she receives the $10 per share from the corporation.   (Page 64)

2. **B.** If the corporation is redeeming the entire issue of preferred stock at $10 per share, that fixes the value of those shares as of the call date. As the call date nears, the stock should trade at a slight discount to $10, the call price. This reflects the present value of the funds to be received for tendering the shares to the corporation.   (Page 66)

3. **B.** Acme preferred may be converted into four shares of common (100 ÷ $25 = 4). With the convertible preferred trading at 110, the common stock must be trading at 27 1/2 for four shares of common stock to be of equivalent value with one share of preferred. To calculate the parity price of the common stock, divide the current market price of the preferred stock by the number of shares of common stock that would be received for converting to the preferred ($110 ÷ 4 = 27 1/2).   (Page 64)

4. **B.** The parity price of the common would be 22 1/2 (90 ÷ 4 = 22 1/2). Because the common is trading at 20% below parity, you know that its market price is 80% of 22 1/2 (.80 × 22 1/2 = 18).
(Page 64)

5. **C.** To comply with the dilution covenant, the corporation must adjust the conversion price of the debentures downward to compensate for the 10% stock dividend being received by common stockholders. The new conversion price is calcu-

lated as follows: $1,000 par value divided by $25 conversion price equals 40 shares. Forty shares multiplied by 10% stock dividend equals four shares plus 40 shares equals 44 shares. $1,000 par value divided by 44 shares equals $22.73, the new conversion price.   (Page 64)

6. **D.** Before the dividend, the conversion ratio was 20 and the conversion price was $50 ($1,000 ÷ 20 = $50). Each bondholder received 20 shares of stock per $1,000 face value or par value of bonds owned. After the dividend, the conversion ratio must be increased by 10% to maintain the bondholder's equivalent equity position upon conversion as specified by the antidilutive covenants. The following calculations illustrate the mechanics: 20 (old conversion ratio) multiplied by 110% equals 22 (new conversion ratio), and the new conversion price equals $1,000 divided by 22, or $45.45.
(Page 64)

7. **C.** This is a two-step problem: first, the parity price of the bond must be found. The parity price of a bond equals the market value of common stock times the conversion rate. $55 multiplied by 20 conversion rate (which is $1,000 divided by $50) equals parity price of $1,100 for the bond. If the price of the bond is 110% of parity, then parity times 1.1 equals the market price ($1,100 × 1.1 = $1,210).   (Page 64)

8. **C.** When a bond is called and the owner does not redeem, the interest payments cease. Conversion causes dilution and generally interest rates on convertible bonds are less than straight debt issues.   (Page 61)

9. **A.** Coupon rates are not higher; they are lower because of the value of the conversion feature. The bondholders are creditors, and if the stock price falls, the conversion feature will not influence the bond's price.   (Page 62)

10. **A.** Because interest rate movements drive the prices of preferred stocks, in a period of stable interest rates, preferred stocks will not fluctuate in value. However, convertible preferred stocks will fluctuate with movements in the price of common

stock into which the preferred can be converted.
(Page 62)

11. **B.** Because the debentures are convertible at $10.50, they are convertible into 95.23 shares (95 whole shares).

$$\frac{\$1,000 \text{ per bond}}{\$10.50} = 95.23 \text{ shares}$$

(Page 62)

12. **D.**

$$\frac{\text{Debenture principal } (\$1,000)}{\text{Conversion price } (\$10.50) \text{ common stock}} =$$

$$\frac{\text{Debenture market value } (\$1,020)}{\text{Parity price } (x)}$$

$$\frac{\$1,000}{\$10.50} = \frac{\$1,020}{(x)}$$

$$(x) = \frac{\$10.50 \times \$1,020}{1,000}$$

$$= \$10.71, \text{ rounded to } 10\ 3/4$$

(Page 64)

13. **D.** If the debenture is converted and sold, the sale amount is:

$$\frac{\$1,000}{\$59.25} = 16.877 \text{ shares}$$

$$16.877 \times \$56.50 = \$953.55$$

If the debenture is called, the proceeds would be $102 1/4 or $1,022.50. The call price is the price the investor is guaranteed to receive. There is no guarantee that your client will receive 115 1/2 (the price at market close on Friday).   (Page 64)

14. **C.**

$$\frac{\$1,000 \text{ par value}}{\$50 \text{ conversion}} = 20 \text{ shares per bond}$$

(Page 63)

15. **D.** The bond is convertible into 20 shares ($1,000 ÷ 50 = 20 shares). $50 times 125% equals $62.50. 20 shares multiplied by $62.50 equals $1,250.   (Page 64)

16. **C.** $1,000 divided by 50 equals 20 shares.
(Page 63)

17. **C.** Parity for the bond is $1,000 bond price divided by $50 share price equals 20 shares per bond. If the bond is now selling for 900 and the stock for $45, the conversion rate is $900 divided by 45, which equals 20. The bond and the stock are at parity.   (Page 64)

18. **D.** Because the bond is convertible at $50 per share, each bond can be converted into 20 shares of stock ($1,000 ÷ 50 = 20). The price of the common stock is now 57 1/2. For the bond to be selling at parity, it must sell for 20 multiplied by $57.50 equals $1,150.   (Page 64)

19. **B.** If the preferred is called, each share is worth $106. If the preferred is converted and the equivalent common shares are sold in the market, the dollar value received will be $102 ($100 par at $25 equals 4 shares of common; 4 × $25.50 = $102). Therefore, the stockholder will not retain the stock because dividends cease upon the call.
(Page 66)

20. **B.** A bondholder is a creditor (whether or not the bond is convertible). Only after the bond is converted to stock is she considered to be an owner.
(Page 62)

11 Marketable Government Securities Exam

1. Treasury bills can be described as

    A. issued at par
    B. callable
    C. issued in bearer form
    D. registered

2. The holder of which of the following instruments receives no interest?

    A. Treasury STRIPS
    B. Treasury note
    C. Treasury bond
    D. Treasury stock

3. Which of the following maturities is available to investors in newly issued Treasury bills?

    A. One week
    B. One month
    C. Six months
    D. Nine months

4. Which of the following is true of a Treasury STRIPS but not of a Treasury receipt?

    A. It may be stripped and issued by a securities broker-dealer.
    B. It is backed by the full faith and credit of the federal government.
    C. Its stripped-off interest coupons are sold separately.
    D. Investors may purchase them at a discount.

5. A customer who watches the T bill auctions notices that the average return to investors in the latest T bill auction fell to 4.71%, down from 4.82% at the previous week's sale. When he asks you for your interpretation, you should tell him that

    A. the decline in yields indicates that the supply of short-term funds has decreased relative to demand
    B. investors who purchased bills at this auction paid more for them than purchasers last week
    C. investors who purchased T bills twelve weeks ago paid less than subsequent purchasers
    D. the federal funds rate and other short-term interest rate indicators probably are rising

6. One of your customers would like to invest in a fairly safe security, but is not interested in regular income. Which of the following securities are offered at a discount and would meet his needs?

    A. GNMA certificates
    B. FHLB securities
    C. FNMA certificates
    D. U.S. Treasury STRIPS

7. If interest rates in general are rising, the price of new T bills should

    A. rise
    B. fall
    C. remain steady
    D. fluctuate

8. Which of the following represents a Treasury note quote?

    A. 8:20–8:00
    B. 8.5%
    C. 85:24–85:30
    D. 85 1/2–85 5/8

9. Which of the following represents a Treasury bill quote?

    A. 8.20–8.00
    B. 8.5%
    C. 85.24–85.30
    D. 85 1/2–85 5/8

10. A $25,000 52-week Treasury bill sells at a bid of 4.50%. What is its price?

    A. $26,125
    B. $25,450
    C. $23,875
    D. $11,250

11. All of the following are characteristics of an investment in Treasury notes EXCEPT

    A. interest is paid semiannually
    B. they are issued in a variety of denominations
    C. they are issued with a variety of maturities
    D. they are short-term issues

◆ Answers & Rationale

1. **D.** A registered security is any security for which ownership is recorded in files maintained for this purpose. Even though T bills are book-entry securities (no certificates are issued), ownership records are maintained and, therefore, they are considered registered. (Page 72)

2. **D.** A company that has bought back its own stock and holds it in its treasury does not pay itself dividends on that stock. STRIPS (Separate Trading of Registered Interest and Principal of Securities) are T bonds with the coupons removed. Although STRIPS do not pay interest separately, they are sold at a deep discount and mature at face (par) value, which is considered interest by the IRS. (Page 75)

3. **C.** Investors can acquire Treasury bills at the weekly T bill auction in denominations of $10,000 and up with maturities of three months, six months and twelve months. The U.S. government can issue nine-month certificates, but currently does not. (Page 72)

4. **B.** Treasury receipts are stripped treasuries and, as such, are issued in stripped form by an institution other than the federal government. Only direct issues of the U.S. government are backed by its full faith and credit. (Page 75)

5. **B.** As rates for T bills drop, T bill prices climb (T bill rates and prices have an inverse relationship). T bills are priced at their yield, so an investor who bids 4.71% actually is paying more for a T bill than one who bids 4.82%. (Page 72)

6. **D.** U.S. Treasury STRIPS (Separate Trading of Registered Interest and Principal of Securities) are direct obligations of the U.S. Treasury issued in the form of zero-coupon bonds. Zero-coupon bonds pay no interest. They are issued at a discount and appreciate in value each period until maturity. (Page 75)

7. **B.** Bill prices decrease as interest rates rise. (Page 72)

8. **C.** All Treasury notes and bonds maturing in one year or more are quoted in 1/32nds. Thus, a quote at 85:24 to 85:30 means 85 24/32 to 85 30/32. (Page 73)

9. **A.** Treasury bills are quoted on a yield basis, which is based on a discounted price to par. This results in a yield quote where the bid is greater than the offer. The greater the discount to par (the lower the actual dollar price), the greater the yield. (Page 72)

10. **C.** A Treasury bill is quoted at a discount from par. Its price equals 4.50% less than its face value:

$25,000	Par value of bill
− 1,125	Discount from par
$23,875	Price of bill

(Page 72)

11. **D.** Treasury notes are intermediate-term issues; T bills are short-term issues and T bonds are long-term issues. The other choices are characteristics of T notes. (Page 73)

12 Nonmarketable Government Securities Exam

1. Hugh Heifer received a $1,000 savings bond when he was 13. Now, as an adult, he redeems the bond at maturity. Hugh will pay

   A. federal taxes
   B. state taxes
   C. both federal and state taxes
   D. neither federal nor state taxes

2. All of the following are authorized to sell savings bonds EXCEPT

   A. bank
   B. post office
   C. broker-dealer
   D. Treasury department

3. Your customer would like to purchase a Series HH bond. He can do this by

   A. applying to the Treasury Department
   B. submitting a competitive bid
   C. trading in a T note at maturity
   D. trading in a Series EE bond at maturity

◆ Answers & Rationale

1.   **A.**   In general, earnings from U.S. government securities are exempt from state and local taxes, but subject to federal tax. Savings bonds are debt obligations of the U.S. government.

(Page 76)

2.   **C.**   Savings bonds are not traded on an exchange or over the counter. They must be purchased from the Treasury department or through an issuing agent such as a bank or post office.   (Page 76)

3.   **D.**   Series HH bonds can be purchased only by trading in a Series EE bond at maturity.

(Page 76)

13 ◆ Agency Issues Exam

1. Which of the following statements are true of Freddie Mac?

   I. It issues pass-through securities.
   II. It purchases student loans.
   III. It purchases conventional residential mortgages from financial institutions.
   IV. It issues securities backed directly by the full faith and credit of the U.S. government.

   A. I and III
   B. I and IV
   C. II and III
   D. II and IV

2. Securities offered by the Federal Intermediate Credit Banks are

   A. backed by the full faith and credit of the issuer
   B. issued either in the form of discounted notes or as long-term bonds
   C. neither A nor B
   D. both A and B

3. Which of the following terms would NOT be used to describe the securities that the Federal Intermediate Credit Banks issue?

   A. Stock and equities
   B. Mortgage-backed
   C. Supporting farmers and agricultural producers
   D. Bonds and debentures

4. A client could be assured of federal government backing for an investment issued by which of the following entities?

   A. Federal National Mortgage Association
   B. Federal Home Loan Bank
   C. Government National Mortgage Association
   D. Federal Intermediate Credit Banks

5. In describing GNMAs to a potential investor, you should tell him that

   A. the certificates have the full faith and credit guarantee of the U.S. government
   B. each bond is backed by a pool of insured mortgages
   C. interest payments received by the investor are exempt from both local and federal income taxes
   D. a GNMA can be purchased for as little as $10,000

6. The securities issued by the Federal Farm Credit System could be described as

   A. being issued only in the form of long-term bonds
   B. making federally tax-free interest payments
   C. having the same low risk as direct Treasury issues
   D. being backed by the full faith and credit of the issuer

7. An investor interested in monthly interest income should invest in

    A. GNMAs
    B. Treasury bonds
    C. stock of a utility company
    D. corporate bonds

8. Agency-issued securities have which of the following characteristics?

    I.   Yields quoted in 1/32nds
    II.   Interest-bearing securities quoted as a percentage of par
    III. Redeemable by the purchaser
    IV.   Redeemable by the issuer

    A. I and III
    B. I and IV
    C. II and III
    D. II and IV

9. The Federal Intermediate Credit Banks issue all of the following types of securities EXCEPT

    I.   discount notes
    II.   debentures
    III. pass-through securities
    IV.   preferred stock

    A. I and II
    B. I and IV
    C. II and III
    D. III

10. All of the following issue collateralized mortgage obligations EXCEPT

    A. Fannie Mae
    B. Sallie Mae
    C. Ginnie Mae
    D. Freddie Mac

11. Which of the following collateralized mortgage obligations have a specific maturity date?

    A. TACs
    B. PACs
    C. SAKs
    D. Z tranches

12. Which of the following are characteristics of Ginnie Maes but not of CMOs?

    A. Collateralized by mortgages
    B. Backed by the full faith and credit of the U.S. government
    C. Typically yield more than T bonds
    D. Are pass-through securities

13. Which of the following statements about CMOs is true?

    A. CMO earnings are tax-exempt.
    B. CMOs may not trade at a premium.
    C. CMO returns are affected by interest rate changes.
    D. CMOs are considered junk bonds.

14. CMOs are backed by which of the following?

    A. Mortgages
    B. Real estate
    C. Municipal taxes
    D. Full faith and credit of U.S. government

15. Which of the following securities is characterized by the term "tranche"?

    A. FNMA
    B. T bond
    C. CMO
    D. FHLMC

16. Max receives interest from a CMO investment. At what level is this income taxed?

    I.   At the federal level
    II.   At the state level
    III. At the local level
    IV.   It is not taxable.

    A. I and II
    B. I, II and III
    C. II and III
    D. IV

17. All of the following institutions issue bonds EXCEPT

    A. Federal Farm Credit Bank
    B. Inter-American Development Bank
    C. Federal Reserve Board
    D. Federal Home Loan Bank

18. All of the following statements about government agency securities are true EXCEPT

    A. They may be backed by the federal government.
    B. They are often considered more risky than corporate securities.
    C. Interest paid is always subject to federal income tax.
    D. They are authorized by Congress.

19. If interest rates decline, how is a principal-only CMO investment affected?

    I. Yield decreases
    II. Price increases
    III. Price decreases
    IV. Payments increase

    A. I and II only
    B. I, II and IV only
    C. III and IV only
    D. I, II, III and IV

20. The PSA model is a standard benchmark of

    A. principal amount
    B. prepayment rate
    C. present value
    D. portfolio allocation

21. Most CMOs make interest payments and principal repayments to investors

    A. weekly
    B. monthly
    C. semiannually
    D. annually

◆ Answers & Rationale

1. **A.** "Freddie Mac" stands for Federal Home Loan Mortgage Corporation. Like Ginnie Mae, it issues mortgage-backed pass-through securities. Unlike Ginnie Mae, however, it deals only in conventional residential mortgages.   (Page 79)

2. **D.** Farm Credit System loans are made through Federal Land Banks, Federal Intermediate Credit Banks and Banks for Cooperatives. These banks are federally charted and supervised by the Farm Credit Administration, an independent agency of the federal government. Securities issued by these organizations are not direct obligations of or guaranteed by the U.S. government, but rather by the Farm Credit Agency. The securities are issued in the form of discount notes, six- and nine-month bonds and longer term bonds. Interest is exempt from state and local taxes but is subject to federal income taxes.   (Page 78)

3. **B.** The FICBs make loans to credit companies, agricultural institutions and commercial banks, which in turn lend that money to farmers. Some of these loans take the form of discounted purchases of agricultural "paper" from various financial institutions. FICBs are private corporations and, as such, issue both common and preferred stock in themselves. They raise the funds they lend by issuing short-term debentures, but these bonds are not backed by mortgages on any underlying land, buildings or equipment.   (Page 78)

4. **C.** Only the Government National Mortgage Association issues securities backed by the full faith and credit of the U.S. government. The remainder are considered government agencies and, although their securities are considered second only to U.S. government issues in safety, they do not have direct U.S. government backing.   (Page 80)

5. **A.** The certificates issued by GNMA represent interests in government-insured mortgages pooled by mortgage brokers (who guarantee the monthly cash flow), but it is the U.S. government that actually "backs" GNMA pass-through certificates. GNMA pass-throughs are issued in minimum denominations of $25,000, and all interest earned is subject to federal income tax. (Page 80)

6. **D.** The Federal Farm Credit Consolidation System was set up in 1980 as a means of organizing and reducing the costs of issuing securities for the Federal Land Banks, the Federal Intermediate Credit Banks and the Federal Farm Credit Banks. Issues of the consolidated system are backed in various manners, although—as agencies—none has the full faith and credit backing of the U.S. government. Interest income from all government agency issues is subject to federal income taxes at the ordinary income tax rate.   (Page 78)

7. **A.** The mortgages underlying GNMA pass-through certificates pay interest on a monthly basis. GNMA then passes this monthly income through to investors in GNMA pass-through certificates.   (Page 80)

8. **D.** Agency issue yields typically are quoted on a percentage of par basis. Investors who desire to liquidate their investment must either sell it on the secondary market or wait for the issue to mature.   (Page 77)

9. **D.** The Federal Intermediate Credit Banks make loans to other banks to back agriculture and related financing business. As a private corporation, it can issue stock in itself.   (Page 78)

10. **B.** "Sallie Mae" is the Student Loan Marketing Association, which purchases student loans and packages them for the secondary market. FNMA, GNMA and FHLMC sell mortgage-backed securities.   (Page 81)

11. **B.** Planned amortization classes (PACs) have established (planned) maturity dates. PACs are retired first. Typically, targeted amortization classes (TACs) are the last tranches to mature. SAKs are not CMOs, and Z tranche (accrual bonds) investors receive payment when all other tranches are retired.   (Page 84)

12. **B.** CMOs are not backed by the full faith and credit of the U.S. government. The other statements about Ginnie Maes and CMOs are true.

(Page 81)

13. **C.** Collateralized mortgage obligations are corporate securities issued by loan companies and mortgage bankers. Like all debt securities, they are affected by changes in prevailing interest rates. These bonds are fully taxable at the federal, state and local levels; they may trade at a premium or at a discount. A CMO's rating may be high or low, according to the same scale used to rate other corporate securities. (Page 81)

14. **A.** Collateralized mortgage obligations are collateralized by mortgages on real estate. They do not own the underlying real estate, so they are not considered to be backed by it. (Page 81)

15. **C.** Collateralized mortgage obligations are divided into maturity classes called *tranches*. The tranche determines the maturity schedule and level of risk associated with a particular CMO.

(Page 82)

16. **B.** Interest income from CMOs is fully taxable at the federal, state and local levels.

(Page 84)

17. **C.** The Federal Reserve Board is a regulatory body that oversees the U.S. central bank system; it does not issue securities. All of the other choices issue bonds: the Federal Farm Credit Bank and the Inter-American Development Bank are government agencies, and the Federal Home Loan Bank is operated by a private corporation.

(Page 77)

18. **B.** Corporate securities are generally considered more risky than government agency issues. Agency issues have only a slight risk of default because they are backed by revenues from taxes, fees and interest income. Agency issues include GNMAs, which are backed by the full faith and credit of the government. Some agency issues are exempt from state and local taxation, but they are not exempt from federal taxation. Congress authorizes these agencies to issue debt securities.

(Page 77)

19. **B.** A principal-only (PO) collateralized mortgage bond is affected by changes in interest rates, as is any fixed-income security. When rates go down, current yield decreases. When interest rates decrease, individual mortgage holders may refinance at the lower rates, thereby increasing the amount of principal payments received by the CMO. (Page 83)

20. **B.** The Public Securities Association (PSA) model is a benchmark of prepayment rates for new mortgage loans. The pool of mortgages underlying a CMO issue is compared to the PSA model for the purpose of establishing the projected yield and the projected maturity. (Page 82)

21. **B.** Interest and principal payments on CMOs may vary from issue to issue. However, most CMOs make payments monthly because mortgage holders pay their mortgages monthly, and the payments are passed through to the CMO holders. (Page 84)

14   The Money Market Exam

1. One of the most important functions of a banker's acceptance is its use as a means of

    A. facilitating trades in foreign goods
    B. facilitating trades of foreign securities in the United States
    C. assigning previously declared distributions by foreign corporations
    D. guaranteeing payment of an international bank's promissory note

2. Which of the following types of corporations typically do NOT issue commercial paper?

    A. Commercial banks and holding companies
    B. Investment and finance companies
    C. Industrial and service companies
    D. Brokerage and insurance firms

3. Corporations issue commercial paper with maturities ranging from as little as 1 day to as long as

    A. 7 days
    B. 90 days
    C. 270 days
    D. 365 days

4. The price an investor pays would include market value plus any accrued interest in which of the following securities?

    A. Bankers' acceptances
    B. Negotiable certificates of deposit
    C. Commercial paper
    D. Treasury bills

5. A repurchase agreement is usually initiated by

    I.   the U.S. Treasury
    II. a Federal Home Loan Bank
    III. a commercial bank
    IV. the Federal Reserve Board

    A. I and III
    B. I and IV
    C. II and IV
    D. III and IV

6. What organization or institution would insure a nonnegotiable certificate of deposit issued by a bank?

    A. SIPC
    B. FRB
    C. FDIC
    D. FSLIC

7. Which of the following would be considered a money-market instrument?

    A. Rights with 269 days remaining until expiration
    B. Warrants with seven months remaining to maturity
    C. New issue of T bills
    D. GMAC direct paper

8. Which of the following are characteristics of negotiable CDs?

    I.   Issued in amounts of $100,000 to $1,000,000
    II.   Fully insured by the FDIC
    III. Mature in less than 270 days
    IV.   Trade in the secondary market

    A. I, II and III
    B. I and IV
    C. II, III and IV
    D. III and IV

9. Which of the following are characteristics of commercial paper?

    I.   Backed by money-market deposits
    II.   Negotiated maturities and yields
    III. Issued by commercial banks
    IV.   Not registered as securities

    A. I and II
    B. I, II and III
    C. II and IV
    D. III and IV

10. Your company would like to import raw wool from New Zealand to make into yard goods for shipping next fall. Which of the following instruments could provide your firm with the best means of financing this purchase?

    A. Banker's acceptance
    B. Commercial paper
    C. Eurodollars
    D. Repurchase agreement

11. Because of the cyclical nature of the industry, your firm is experiencing a shortage of cash just at the time it needs to tool up to manufacture new inventory. Which of the following instruments could be used to improve your company's cash flow?

    A. Banker's acceptance
    B. Commercial paper
    C. Repurchase agreement
    D. Reverse repurchase agreement

12. One of your clients is involved in the importation of tropical nuts and oils for a commercial bakery. If the bakery wants to delay payments on purchases of nuts until it is able to sign contracts with a wholesaler, it would use

    A. bankers' acceptances
    B. commercial paper
    C. Eurodollars
    D. foreign currency exchanges

13. Which of the following instruments is commonly used to settle transactions involving imports and exports?

    A. ADRs
    B. Bankers' acceptances
    C. Eurodollars
    D. Foreign currencies

14. One of your corporate clients is interested in learning more about money-market instruments. You would provide him with more information on which of the following?

    I.   Commercial paper
    II.   T bill primary offerings
    III. TANs
    IV.   Repos

    A. I, II and III
    B. I, II and IV
    C. I, III and IV
    D. II, III and IV

15. All of the following are money-market instruments EXCEPT

    A. Treasury bills
    B. municipal notes
    C. commercial paper
    D. newly issued Treasury bonds

16. Which of the following is a money-market instrument?

    A. Short-term debt
    B. Long-term debt
    C. Short-term equity
    D. Long-term equity

17. Which of the following statements are true of negotiable certificates of deposit?

   I.   They are unsecured promissory notes of the issuing bank.
   II. They are callable.
   III. The minimum denominations are $1,000.
   IV. They can be traded in the secondary market.

   A. I, II and III only
   B. I and IV only
   C. II and III only
   D. I, II, III and IV

18. Commercial paper is a

   A. secured note issued by a corporation
   B. guaranteed note issued by a corporation
   C. promissory note issued by a corporation
   D. promissory note issued by a broker-dealer

19. Which of the following money-market instruments finances imports and exports?

   A. Eurodollars
   B. Bankers' acceptances
   C. ADRs
   D. Commercial paper

20. A banker's acceptance is a

   A. promissory note
   B. capital-market instrument
   C. time draft
   D. means to facilitate the trading of foreign securities

21. What is the minimum unit amount on a negotiable CD?

   A. $100,000
   B. $250,000
   C. $500,000
   D. $1,000,000

◆ Answers & Rationale

1. **A.** A banker's acceptance is a time draft typically used to facilitate overseas trading ventures. It is guaranteed by a bank on behalf of a corporation in payment for goods or services.
(Page 92)

2. **A.** Commercial paper is unsecured short-term debt issued by corporations as a means of financing short-term needs. It is issued at a discount from face value and generally matures within 270 days. Commercial banks issue CDs and BAs.
(Page 93)

3. **C.** Commercial paper is issued by corporations with a maximum maturity of 270 days, in part to avoid certain registration requirements under the act of 1933.
(Page 93)

4. **B.** Of the securities listed, only CDs are sold at face value, pay interest and trade with accrued interest. All of the other securities listed are sold at a discount from face value and are redeemed at face value.
(Page 94)

5. **D.** Repurchase agreements (or *repos*) are entered into by a government securities dealer (usually a bank) or by the Federal Reserve Board with an investor (usually a corporation).
(Page 91)

6. **C.** The Federal Deposit Insurance Corporation guarantees money on deposit in banks that are members of the FDIC system. The FDIC insures nonnegotiable CDs up to $100,000 each.
(Page 94)

7. **D.** Only the GMAC direct commercial paper would be considered a money-market instrument. Even though the rights and the warrants have less than 270 days remaining to maturity, they represent rights to equity ownership and do not serve the same purpose as the cash-equivalents normally found in the money market. T bills do not become part of the money market until they begin secondary trading.
(Page 93)

8. **B.** Negotiable CDs are issued for $100,000 to $1,000,000 and, as money-market instruments, are commonly traded in the secondary market. Most are issued with maturities of less than a year, but initial maturities of three to five years can be arranged. The FDIC insures nonnegotiable CDs up to $100,000 each.
(Page 94)

9. **C.** Commercial paper represents the unsecured debt obligations of corporations in need of short-term financing. Both yield and maturity are open to negotiation. Because commercial paper is issued with maturities of less than 270 days, it is exempt from registration under the act of 1933.
(Page 93)

10. **A.** The import and export of goods is often made easier by the use of bankers' acceptances. BAs provide the seller with ready cash, and the buyer with an extended time frame in which to pay.
(Page 92)

11. **B.** The primary purpose of commercial paper is to provide corporations with short-term financing at reasonable rates. Bankers' acceptances are used to finance imports and exports. Repos and reverse repos are used by securities dealers and banks to finance securities inventories. (Page 93)

12. **A.** Bankers' acceptances can be used to delay payment on imports and provide the seller with a bank's guarantee that an account will be paid.
(Page 92)

13. **B.** BAs are used by corporations to settle transactions involving imports and exports of goods.
(Page 92)

14. **C.** T bills do not become part of the money market until they begin secondary trading. All of the others are money-market instruments.
(Page 90)

15. **D.** Newly issued Treasury bonds have a minimum maturity of ten years. Money-market instruments have a maximum maturity of one year.
(Page 90)

16. **A.** A money-market instrument is short-term debt with one year or less to maturity.
(Page 90)

17. **B.** Negotiable certificates of deposit are primarily issued by banks and are backed by the issuing bank. (Page 94)

18. **C.** Commercial paper is a short-term promissory note issued by a corporation. (Page 93)

19. **B.** Bankers' acceptances are used in international trade to finance imports and exports. Eurodollars are not money-market instruments.
(Page 92)

20. **C.** A banker's acceptance is a time draft. It facilitates imports and exports, not the trading of foreign securities. (Page 92)

21. **A.** Although publicized rates are usually on amounts of $1 million or more, a certificate of deposit must have a face value of at least $100,000 to be considered negotiable. (Page 94)

15 Interest Rates Exam

1. You would advise an investor interested in low volatility of interest rates to invest in a security that has a return tied to the

   A. average CD rate
   B. prime rate
   C. federal funds rate
   D. broker call rate

2. An investor interested in the most stable rate of return would NOT want an investment tied to the

   A. prime rate
   B. long-term interest rate
   C. federal funds rate
   D. discount rate

3. Which of the following describes the prime rate?

   A. The base rate on corporate loans at large U.S. money center commercial banks.
   B. Reserves traded among commercial banks for overnight use in amounts of $1 million or more.
   C. The charge on loans to depository institutions by the New York FRB.
   D. The charge on loans to brokers on stock exchange collateral.

4. Which of the following describes the federal funds rate?

   A. The base rate on corporate loans at large U.S. money center commercial banks.
   B. Reserves traded among commercial banks for overnight use in amounts of $1 million or more.
   C. The charge on loans to depository institutions by the New York FRB.
   D. The charge on loans to brokers on stock exchange collateral.

5. Which of the following describes the discount rate?

   A. The base rate on corporate loans at large U.S. money center commercial banks.
   B. Reserves traded among commercial banks for overnight use in amounts of $1 million or more.
   C. The charge on loans to depository institutions by the New York FRB.
   D. The charge on loans to brokers on stock exchange collateral.

6. Which of the following describes the call money rate?

   A. The base rate on corporate loans at large U.S. money center commercial banks.
   B. Reserves traded among commercial banks for overnight use in amounts of $1 million or more.
   C. The charge on loans to depository institutions by the New York FRB.
   D. The charge on loans to brokers on stock exchange collateral.

7. Of the following interest rates, which is considered the MOST volatile?

    A. Discount rate
    B. Federal funds rate
    C. Prime rate
    D. Average CD rate

8. Of the following interest rates, which is considered the LEAST volatile?

    A. Discount rate
    B. Federal funds rate
    C. Prime rate
    D. Average CD rate

◆ Answers & Rationale

1. **A.** Using volatility (the likelihood of changing) as the benchmark, the average CD rate is the least volatile of those listed. All of the other rates fluctuate from occasionally to frequently.
(Page 95)

2. **C.** The federal funds rate is the rate at which banks lend money *overnight* to each other to maintain reserve requirements. It is the most volatile rate and can fluctuate widely even during a business day. The effective federal funds rate is considered to be the average rate each day throughout the country.
(Page 95)

3. **A.** The prime rate is the base rate on corporate loans at large U.S. money center commercial banks. The prime rate is relatively stable and moves only when the major money center banks react to changes in the money supply.
(Page 95)

4. **B.** The federal funds rate represents reserves traded among commercial banks for overnight use in amounts of $1 million or more. The federal funds rate is the most volatile of the interest rates, changing daily in response to the needs of the borrowing banks.
(Page 95)

5. **C.** The discount rate is the charge on loans to depository institutions by the New York FRB.
(Page 95)

6. **D.** The call money rate is the charge on loans to brokers on stock exchange collateral.
(Page 95)

7. **B.** The federal funds rate is the interest rate that banks with excess reserves charge other banks that are associated with the Federal Reserve System and that need overnight loans to meet reserve requirements. Because the federal funds rate is set daily, it is the most sensitive indicator of interest rate direction.
(Page 95)

8. **D.** The average certificate of deposit rate is relatively stable. The prime rate is periodically changed by banks, and the discount rate is periodically changed by the Federal Reserve Board.
(Page 95)

16

Eurodollars and the Foreign Currency Markets Exam

1. The rate at which Japanese yen could be converted into U.S. dollars, or British pounds could be converted into Swiss francs, would be set in the

   A. exchange rate market
   B. interbank market
   C. secondary market
   D. fourth market

2. Which of the following would be considered Eurodollars?

   A. European currencies deposited in U.S. banks
   B. U.S. currency deposited in foreign banks
   C. European currencies deposited in Japanese banks
   D. Japanese currency deposited in European banks

3. Which of the following statements regarding Eurodollar deposits is false?

   A. The interest rate is set by the FRB.
   B. The deposits are dollar-denominated but are held in a foreign bank.
   C. They are more risky than domestic CDs.
   D. They normally pay a higher rate of interest than domestic CDs.

4. Which of the following entities can issue Eurobonds?

   I. Domestic corporations
   II. Foreign corporations
   III. Domestic governments
   IV. Foreign governments

   A. I, II and IV only
   B. I and III only
   C. II and IV only
   D. I, II, III and IV

5. Your firm has entered a number of spot trades for British pounds and Swiss francs in the interbank market. What are the settlement terms it will have to meet?

   A. Same business day
   B. One or two business days
   C. Three business days
   D. One to eighteen months

6. Because of the changes it anticipates in the exchange rates for various foreign currencies, your firm has entered several forward trades for Japanese yen and German deutsche marks. What are the settlement terms it will have to meet?

   A. Same business day
   B. One or two business days
   C. Three business days
   D. One to eighteen months

7. If the U.S. dollar has fallen relative to foreign currencies, which of the following statements are true?

    I.   U.S. imports are likely to rise.
    II. U.S. imports are likely to fall.
    III. Foreign currencies buy fewer U.S. dollars.
    IV. Foreign currencies buy more U.S. dollars.

    A. I and III
    B. I and IV
    C. II and III
    D. II and IV

8. A central bank can cause a strengthening in the value of its own country's currency in the interbank market by

    I.   buying its own country's currency
    II. selling its own country's currency
    III. buying foreign currency
    IV. selling foreign currency

    A. I and III
    B. I and IV
    C. II and III
    D. II and IV

9. A central bank can cause a weakening in the value of its own country's currency in the interbank market by

    I.   buying its own country's currency
    II. selling its own country's currency
    III. buying foreign currency
    IV. selling foreign currency

    A. I and III
    B. I and IV
    C. II and III
    D. II and IV

10. Which of the following statements would constitute a valid reason for investing in Eurobonds?

    A. Eurobonds can provide diversification to a portfolio.
    B. Eurobonds can be purchased more inexpensively than comparable U.S. bonds.
    C. Eurobonds are traded in an unregulated market, free from government intervention.
    D. Eurobonds can provide an exchange rate hedge against a fall in the U.S. dollar.

11. An international, unregulated, decentralized market for trading currencies, as well as debt obligations, where prices are affected by economic policies and conditions, is the

    A. Federal Reserve Board
    B. interbank system
    C. London Stock Exchange
    D. International Monetary Fund

12. Which of the following statements about Eurodollar bonds are true?

    I.   Payment of principal and interest is always in U.S. dollars.
    II. Payment of principal and interest is always in the designated foreign currency of the issuer.
    III. The issuer of Eurodollar bonds may be either a U.S. corporation or a foreign corporation.
    IV. The bonds may be issued either in the U.S. or abroad.

    A. I and III
    B. I and IV
    C. II and III
    D. II and IV

13. Mountain Brewing, a subsidiary of a U.S. corporation, is looking for debt financing by offering a bond denominated in Japanese yen that will be sold in Canada. This bond is a(n)

A. ADR
B. Eurobond
C. Eurodollar bond
D. foreign exchange bond

14. Which of the following entities would NOT be permitted to issue debt securities in the Eurobond market?

A. U.S. domestic corporations
B. Foreign corporations
C. Foreign banks
D. None of the above

15. Interbank transactions in foreign currencies occur in which of the following markets?

I. Spot
II. Forward
III. Pegged
IV. Stabilized

A. I and II only
B. I and III only
C. III and IV only
D. I, II, III and IV

16. The interbank market was formed to trade which of the following?

A. Foreign currencies
B. American depositary receipts
C. Commercial paper
D. Foreign stocks

17. The Japanese yen is losing value in relation to the U.S. dollar. What can the Japanese government do in the open market to stabilize its currency?

A. Sell yen.
B. Buy yen.
C. Sell dollars.
D. Buy dollars.

18. Which of the following may issue U.S. dollar-denominated Eurobonds?

I. Greater Health, Inc., a British company based in London
II. The government of Argentina
III. This Can't Be Sushi, an American company with offices in Japan
IV. The Kenosha, Wisconsin Harbor Authority

A. I and II only
B. I and III only
C. II and IV only
D. I, II, III and IV

◆ Answers & Rationale

1. **B.** The foreign exchange rate for international currencies is determined by buying and selling interest in the interbank market.   (Page 98)

2. **B.** Because the question asks about *Eurodollars*, the only correct answer specifies that U.S. currency (U.S. dollars) is deposited in a foreign country. All of the other answers contain examples of *Eurocurrency*.   (Page 97)

3. **A.** The Federal Reserve Board has no authority over Eurodollar deposits, which are deposits of U.S. dollars held at foreign banks.   (Page 97)

4. **D.** Any entity, public or private, domestic or foreign, can issue bonds in foreign markets that are denominated in U.S. dollars. Many companies and governments do issue Eurobonds to avoid the complexities of U.S. securities registration or to tap a larger market of potential investors.   (Page 97)

5. **B.** Spot trades in foreign currencies are settled in one or two business days. Forward trades settle in more than two business days, and are normally scheduled to settle between one and eighteen months.   (Page 98)

6. **D.** Forward trades settle in more than two business days, and are normally scheduled to settle between one and eighteen months. Spot trades in foreign currencies are settled in one or two business days.   (Page 98)

7. **D.** When the U.S. dollar loses value compared to a foreign currency, the same amount of the foreign currency now buys more dollars. As a result, U.S. goods will be cheaper in terms of that foreign currency, which means that the foreign country will tend to buy more U.S. products and U.S. exports will rise.   (Page 98)

8. **B.** If a central bank wanted to strengthen the value of its own currency, it could decrease the currency's supply (and therefore increase its price) by buying it in the interbank market. It could also increase the supply of foreign currencies (and therefore decrease their price) by selling them in the interbank market.   (Page 98)

9. **C.** If a central bank wanted to weaken the value of its own currency, it could increase the currency's supply (and therefore decrease its price) by selling it in the interbank market. It could also decrease the supply of foreign currencies (and therefore increase their price) by buying them in the interbank market.   (Page 98)

10. **A.** Eurobonds may provide a sophisticated investor with a means of adding diversification to her portfolio. All of the other answers are either untrue statements or represent disadvantages of investing in Eurobonds.   (Page 97)

11. **B.** The interbank system is an international, unregulated, decentralized market involved in trading currencies and debt obligations. As with any market, changes in economic policies and conditions will influence prices.   (Page 98)

12. **A.** Eurodollar bonds are issued outside the United States and are denominated in U.S. dollars by either a domestic or a foreign corporation. Payment of interest and principal on Eurodollar bonds can be made only in U.S. dollars.   (Page 97)

13. **B.** A Eurobond is a debt issue that is denominated and that pays principal and interest in the currency of a country other than that in which the issue is located. A Eurodollar bond is a Eurobond denominated in Eurodollars (U.S. dollars held in banks outside the continental United States).   (Page 97)

14. **D.** U.S. domestic corporations, state and municipal governments, foreign corporations and foreign banks would all be permitted to issue Eurobonds.   (Page 97)

15. **A.** Foreign currency transactions occur in the spot market (same or next day settlement) or the forward market (one to eighteen months' settlement).   (Page 98)

16. **A.** The interbank market is a decentralized, unregulated market formed for the sole purpose of trading foreign currencies.   (Page 98)

17. **B.** The Japanese government can decrease the supply of yen by buying them back for its treasury. A shrinking supply of yen in the market should increase the value of the yen.   (Page 98)

18. **D.** Eurobonds with U.S. dollar denominations are issued and sold outside the U.S. Any foreign corporation, foreign government, domestic corporation or domestic government may issue Eurobonds to reach new sources of revenue and avoid U.S. regulation.   (Page 97)

17 The Regulation of New Issues Exam

1. Which of the following will NOT be found in a final prospectus?

   A. Underwriting agreements and the underwriters' compensation
   B. Stabilization plans
   C. Date and offering price
   D. Statement that the SEC neither approves nor disapproves of the issue

2. Which of the following statements about a red herring is FALSE?

   A. A red herring is used to obtain indications of interest from investors.
   B. The final offering price does not appear in a red herring.
   C. Additional information may be added to a red herring at a later date.
   D. A registered rep may send a copy of the company's research report with it.

3. Datawaq has filed a registration statement for its new issue of common stock with the SEC. As a registered rep you can do which of the following?

   I. Send out your firm's most current research reports to your customers.
   II. Take indications of interest from your customers.
   III. Send a Datawaq preliminary prospectus to each of your customers.
   IV. Take orders for the stock from customers in cash accounts only.

   A. I only
   B. I, II and III only
   C. II and III only
   D. I, II, III and IV

4. As a registered representative, you can use a preliminary prospectus to

   A. obtain indications of interest from investors
   B. solicit orders from investors for the purchase of a new issue
   C. solicit an approval of the offering from the SEC
   D. obtain the NASD's authorization to sell the issue

5. Which of the following statements about new issue underwriting is FALSE?

    A. Underwriting agreements can include a clause that relieves the underwriter of its obligation to sell an issue if certain restrictions are not met.
    B. The preliminary prospectus contains the date and price of the issue in order to assist brokers in obtaining indications of interest.
    C. If the underwriting syndicate discloses that it might engage in stabilization in the preliminary prospectus, it may do so under appropriate circumstances.
    D. If a selling group member sells securities back to the manager of the syndicate during the underwriting period, it may be penalized.

6. Which of the following is NOT required in a preliminary prospectus?

    A. Written statement in red that the prospectus may be subject to change and amendment and that a final prospectus will be issued
    B. Purpose for which the funds that are being raised will be used
    C. Final offering price
    D. Financial status and history of the company

7. Microscam is required to do all of the following if it intends to offer stock EXCEPT

    A. publish a tombstone
    B. issue a prospectus
    C. file a registration statement
    D. register the securities with the SEC

8. Datawaq plans to offer 300,000 shares of its 2,000,000-share new offering of common stock to its own employees. How many shares must it register as being publicly offered?

    A. 300,000
    B. 1,700,000
    C. 2,000,000
    D. 2,300,000

9. If the SEC has cleared an issue, which of the following statements is true?

    A. The SEC has guaranteed the issue.
    B. The underwriter has filed a standard registration statement.
    C. The SEC has endorsed the issue.
    D. The SEC has guaranteed the accuracy of the information in the prospectus.

10. A prospectus must include

    I.   the effective date of the registration
    II. whether the underwriter intends to stabilize the issue if necessary
    III. a statement indicating the SEC has not approved the issue
    IV. disclosure of material information concerning the issuer's financial condition

    A. I, II and IV only
    B. I and IV only
    C. II and III only
    D. I, II, III and IV

11. If his firm is in the process of underwriting a stock issue that is currently in registration, a registered rep is allowed to

    A. accept an order
    B. promise a specific number of shares
    C. perform a private transaction for a customer
    D. accept an indication of interest

12. To which securities market does the Securities Act of 1933 apply?

    A. Primary
    B. Secondary
    C. Third
    D. Fourth

13. In connection with the sale of a new issue and prior to filing a registration statement for that issue, a registered representative is prohibited from

    I.   soliciting indications of interest for the security
    II. soliciting orders
    III. confirming the sale of the security to a customer

    A. I only
    B. II only
    C. II and III only
    D. I, II and III

14. A prospectus for an initial public offering must be sent to customers who purchase the security within how many days after the effective date?

    A. 30
    B. 60
    C. 90
    D. 120

15. In reviewing prospectuses and registration statements, the SEC

    A. guarantees the adequacy of the disclosures made in a prospectus
    B. guarantees the accuracy of the disclosures made in a prospectus
    C. passes on the merits of a particular security covered by the registration statement
    D. does not approve securities registered with it and offered for sale

16. The Securities Act of 1933 covers all of the following EXCEPT

    A. due diligence
    B. prospectus requirements
    C. full and fair disclosure
    D. blue-sky laws

17. Churnum, Burnem, Spurnim is underwriting a third public offering of common stock for This Can't Be Sushi, a company whose stock is listed on the NYSE. Once the offering date has passed, CBS is required to make a prospectus available to purchasers for how many days?

    A. 25
    B. 40
    C. 60
    D. 90

18. Churnum, Burnem, Spurnim is underwriting an additional public offering of common for I Can't Believe This Is Sushi, which has not yet been authorized for listing on either an exchange or on the Nasdaq. Once the offering date has passed, CBS is required to make a prospectus available to purchasers for how many days?

    A. 25
    B. 40
    C. 60
    D. 90

19. Churnum, Burnem, Spurnim is underwriting an initial public offering of common for This Can't Be Sushi. TCB has not yet been authorized for listing on either an exchange or the Nasdaq. Once the offering date has passed, CBS is required to make a prospectus available to purchasers for how many days?

    A. 25
    B. 40
    C. 60
    D. 90

20. Assume that the effective date of an initial public offering is April 10th. Any underwriter that intends to make a market in the security (or any other broker-dealer intending to be a market maker) must provide buying customers with a prospectus

    A. for a 30-day period following the effective date
    B. for a 90-day period following the effective date
    C. for a 120-day period following the effective date
    D. only if shares being sold are public offering shares, meaning that the proceeds are paid to the issuer and/or selling shareholders

21. Which of the following is NOT required to be included in the registration statement for a new issue?

    A. Pending lawsuits on material issues
    B. Statement of owners' equity
    C. Cash flow statement
    D. Balance sheet

22. Kelptek, Inc.'s registration statement for its initial public offering is now effective. Sales of Kelptek shares must be accompanied by a prospectus for up to

    A. 20 days
    B. 25 days
    C. 40 days
    D. 90 days

23. Which of the following are characteristics of the Securities Act of 1933?

    I.   Requires registration of exchanges
    II. Is called the *Truth in Securities Act*
    III. Requires full and fair disclosure
    IV. Requires that debt securities be issued with a trust indenture

    A. I and II
    B. I, II and IV
    C. I and III
    D. II and III

24. Under the Securities Act of 1933, the Securities and Exchange Commission has the authority to

    I.   issue stop orders
    II. approve new issues
    III. review prospectuses

    A. I only
    B. I and III only
    C. II only
    D. I, II and III

25. Full disclosure of all material information about securities offered for the first time to the public is required by the

    A. Securities Act of 1933
    B. Securities Exchange Act of 1934
    C. Trust Indenture Act of 1939
    D. Securities Investor Protection Act of 1970

26. The provisions of the Securities Act of 1933 include the

    I.   regulation of offerings of new securities
    II. prohibition of fraud in the sale of new securities
    III. full and fair disclosure of information
    IV. regulation of insider trading

    A. I only
    B. I, II and III only
    C. II and III only
    D. I, II, III and IV

◆ Answers & Rationale

1. **A.** The underwriting agreements (also known as the *agreement among underwriters*) are separate documents and are not included in a prospectus.   (Page 109)

2. **D.** A registered rep is prohibited from sending a research report with either a preliminary or a final prospectus. During the first 90 days of a new issue, printed information discussing the new issue or the company cannot be circulated.   (Page 108)

3. **C.** Sales of a new issue can be made only by prospectus. Until the issue is through registration, no orders may be accepted, although indications of interest may be taken.   (Page 109)

4. **A.** A preliminary prospectus is used to obtain indications of interest from investors.   (Page 109)

5. **B.** The preliminary prospectus includes much important information relevant to the new issue but does not include the public offering price, the date of the offering or the underwriter's spread.   (Page 108)

6. **C.** A preliminary prospectus is issued before the price is established, and it does not include the eventual offering date or the spread.   (Page 108)

7. **A.** A tombstone advertisement is never required. Tombstones are advertisements that are often placed in the business newspapers to publicize a new issue.   (Page 111)

8. **C.** Even though the shares are being sold to its own employees, those employees are still considered members of the public. The total public offering is for 2,000,000 shares.   (Page 107)

9. **B.** The SEC does not approve, endorse or guarantee the accuracy of a registration statement.   (Page 109)

10. **D.** Choices I and IV should be obvious. If underwriters intend to engage in activities that are designed to stabilize the price of the security, disclosure in the prospectus is required. The SEC disclaimer is required to appear on every prospectus and states that the SEC has neither approved nor disapproved the issue.   (Page 109)

11. **D.** When an issue is in registration (in the cooling-off period) there can be no advertising or sale. The registered representative may, however, distribute preliminary prospectuses and may accept indications of interest from customers. A registered representative may never engage in private securities transactions.   (Page 108)

12. **A.** The Securities Act of 1933 covers the registration and disclosure requirements regarding new issues. The new issue market is the primary market. The trading markets are covered under the Securities Exchange Act of 1934.   (Page 107)

13. **D.** Before the registration statement is filed, there can be no sale of the issue and no soliciting of orders or indications of interest in the issue. Once the registration statement is filed, the issue is in the 20-day cooling-off period. Again, there can be no sale of the issue, nor can orders be solicited. Now, however, it is permissible to accept indications of interest. Once the registration is effective, all three activities are permitted.   (Page 108)

14. **C.** The SEC requires that a prospectus is sent to investors who purchase the security within 90 days after an initial public offering or who purchase the security within 40 days after a primary or registered secondary offering.   (Page 110)

15. **D.** The SEC requires full disclosure regarding a new issue so that the investor can make an informed decision on the security. It does not, however, guarantee the accuracy or adequacy of the disclosure, nor does it approve or disapprove of an issue.   (Page 109)

16. **D.** Blue-sky laws are state laws and are not covered under the federal securities act.   (Page 108)

17. **A.** A prospectus must be made available to purchasers of a new issue listed on a registered exchange for 25 days from the offering date. If the security is not listed on a registered exchange or an electronic interdealer quotation system (such as Nasdaq), the period during which the prospectus must be delivered is 40 days. If the issue is the very first issue of a company, the prospectus delivery period is extended to 90 days.   (Page 110)

18. **B.** A prospectus must be made available to purchasers of a new issue listed on a registered exchange for 25 days from the offering date. If the security is not listed on a registered exchange or an electronic interdealer quotation system (such as Nasdaq), the period during which the prospectus must be delivered is 40 days. If the issue is the very first issue of a company, the prospectus delivery period is extended to 90 days.   (Page 110)

19. **D.** A prospectus must be made available to purchasers of a new issue listed on a registered exchange for 25 days from the offering date. If the security is not listed on a registered exchange or an electronic interdealer quotation system (such as Nasdaq), the period during which the prospectus must be delivered is 40 days. If the issue is the very first issue of a company, the prospectus delivery period is extended to 90 days.   (Page 110)

20. **B.** All purchasers of new issue securities (IPOs) must receive a prospectus for a 90-day period after the effective date, regardless of who the seller is (one of the underwriters, a selling customer or another broker-dealer) or whether the transaction takes place in the public offering market or the secondary market. For public offerings of additional issue securities, the prospectus requirement in the aftermarket is only 40 days.
(Page 110)

21. **C.** The cash flow statement is not a part of the financial information required to be presented in the registration statement. The statement of owner's equity and the balance sheet are required information, since they explain the company's capitalization. Any pending lawsuits against the company are also required to be disclosed.
(Page 108)

22. **D.** For initial public offerings, the prospectus must be provided with every sale for up to 90 days. If the company were issuing additional shares, its registration statement would already be on file with the SEC, and the prospectus sales period would be shortened. Additional issues of unlisted stock are sold with a prospectus for 40 days; additional issues of listed stock, for 25 days.
(Page 110)

23. **D.** The Securities Act of 1933 regulates new issues of corporate securities sold to the public. The act is also referred to as the *Full Disclosure Act*, the *New Issues Act*, the *Truth in Securities Act* and the *Prospectus Act*.   (Page 107)

24. **B.** During the cooling-off period of registration, the SEC reviews the statement. The SEC sometimes issues a stop order, which demands that all underwriting activities cease.   (Page 108)

25. **A.** The Securities Act of 1933 regulates new issues of corporate securities sold to the public.
(Page 108)

26. **B.** The Securities Act of 1933 regulates new issues of corporate securities sold to the public. Although a security might be exempt from the registration requirements, no offering is exempt from the antifraud provisions of the act of 1933. Full and fair disclosure can be found in the prospectus.   (Page 108)

18   The Underwriting Process Exam

1. In the underwriting of a new issue of common stock, all of the following will occur before the public offering price is announced EXCEPT

   A. the formation of the syndicate and selling group
   B. due diligence meetings and investigation
   C. the preparation of the preliminary prospectus
   D. the filing of legal feasibility documents

2. For what period of time can the managing underwriter in a syndicate take action to stabilize an issue?

   A. Only during the offering period
   B. Through one day after the end of the offering period
   C. Through one week after the end of the offering period
   D. Through one month after the end of the offering period

3. All of the following factors are taken into consideration in determining the public offering price of a new issue of corporate stock EXCEPT

   A. past and projected earnings of the company
   B. dividend payment record of the company
   C. how the stock of other corporations in the same industry is priced
   D. selling group's opinion as to a marketable price level

4. Which of the following is probably an example of a stabilizing bid for a new issue by a syndicate?

	Stabilizing Bid	Market Bid	Market Asked
A.	$15	$18	$18 1/4
B.	$21	$21	$21 1/4
C.	$25	$24 1/4	$24 1/2
D.	$35	$34	$34 7/8

5. All of the following will occur during the cooling-off period for a new issue EXCEPT

   I. due diligence meeting
   II. issuance of a preliminary prospectus
   III. stabilization of the issue
   IV. blue-skying the issue

   A. I
   B. I and II
   C. II
   D. III

6. This Can't Be Sushi (TCB) will be offering $7,000,000 of its common stock in its home state and in three other states. For the offering to be cleared for sale by the SEC, TCB must file a(n)

   A. offering circular
   B. registration statement
   C. letter of notification
   D. preliminary prospectus

7. Churnum, Burnem, Spurnim is underwriting a new issue of Consolidated Codfish common. During the distribution period CBS starts buying COD stock in the open market. CBS is engaging in

    A. churning
    B. manipulation
    C. fixing
    D. stabilization

8. Churnum, Burnem, Spurnim is the managing underwriter for a new stock offered at 18 1/2. CBS can stabilize the offering at which of the following prices?

    I.   17 3/4
    II.   18 1/4
    III. 19 1/4
    IV.   19 3/4

    A. I only
    B. I and II only
    C. III and IV only
    D. I, II, III and IV

9. Tallawhosits City Waterworks publishes the following tombstone:

    New Issue

    $20,000,000
    Tallawhosits City Waterworks
    Coupon 7%

    Price 100.65%

    Dewey, Cheatham & Howe

    The bonds are priced above par for what probable reason?

    A. The price reflects the fact that the coupon rate for the bonds at issuance is more than the rate of similar newly issued bonds available in the market.
    B. The amount in excess of par includes accrued interest.
    C. The amount in excess of par represents the underwriter's spread.
    D. The municipality has applied the standard municipal bond servicing charge to the issue price.

10. All of the following are covered under blue-sky laws EXCEPT the

    I.   registration of nonexempt securities
    II.   registration of state-chartered bank issues
    III. registration of government securities
    IV.   licensing of registered representatives

    A. I, II and III
    B. I and III
    C. I and IV
    D. II and III

11. Blue-sky laws require the registration of

    I. small business investment companies
    II. real estate investment trusts
    III. registered representatives
    IV. U.S. government securities

    A. I and II
    B. I, II and III
    C. II and III
    D. III and IV

12. Which of the following is(are) a concern of state securities laws?

    I. Provisions set by the Securities Act of 1933
    II. Adherence to the laws of each state governing the sale of new issues
    III. Revocation of the broker-dealer's registration

    A. I
    B. I and III
    C. II
    D. II and III

13. Which of the following statements about blue-sky laws is NOT true?

    A. They attempt to protect the public from fraudulent sale of securities within a particular state.
    B. A state securities division has the power to revoke the license of a broker-dealer and the license of any securities salesperson for violation of its laws.
    C. An issuer that intends to offer securities for sale in several states must comply with the provisions of the Securities Act of 1933 and all securities laws of the appropriate states.
    D. The Securities Act of 1933 sets forth certain standard provisions that must appear in all blue-sky laws.

14. Subject to the provisions specified in the agreement among underwriters, under what circumstances may a syndicate member sell, without penalty, slow-moving stock or other securities being distributed at a price below the public offering price?

    A. Only on sales made to institutions
    B. Only if released to do so by the managing underwriter
    C. Only to retail customers
    D. One business day after the offering date

15. A due diligence meeting is a meeting between which of the following?

    A. NASD member firm and the NASD's Committee on Corporate Finance, the purpose of which is to discuss the fairness of the underwriting spread on a pending public offering
    B. Underwriter and the SEC prior to the issuance of a final prospectus to insert the public offering price and make any last-minute changes at the SEC's request
    C. Issuing corporation and the underwriters, the purpose of which is to review and reexamine the full details of the pending underwriting and negotiate final terms to be included in the formal underwriting contract
    D. All of the above are forms of due diligence meetings.

16. When the sale of a new-issue stock taken down in a firm commitment underwriting is progressing poorly, a syndicate manager may take which of the following actions to stimulate sales?

    A. Renegotiate the net price to be paid to the issuer
    B. Increase the amount of the selling concession
    C. Lower the public offering price
    D. All of the above

17. Your client wishes to buy securities that are not registered in his state of residence. You can purchase securities for this client's account if the security

    I.   has been traded for at least 12 months
    II. is exempt from registration
    III. is listed on the NYSE
    IV. is listed on the Canadian Stock Exchange

    A. I and II
    B. I, II and IV
    C. II and III
    D. III and IV

18. Which of the following is NOT a basic responsibility of an investment banker?

    A. Distributing large blocks of stock to the public and to institutions
    B. Providing a secondary market for securities that have been issued
    C. Giving advice to corporations on the best way to raise long-term capital
    D. Buying previously unissued securities from an issuer and selling them to the public

19. A secondary distribution is

    A. a distribution that is accomplished without an investment banker
    B. used to achieve a better price than the current market
    C. a method of redistributing a large block of stock without significantly affecting the market price
    D. a new issue of stock or bonds that is being offered by a "second tier" company

20. "Fraud" is defined by the Securities Exchange Act of 1934 as

    A. freeriding and withholding
    B. misleading information in the dealer's offering circular
    C. stabilization above the public offering price
    D. representing an all or none issue as a firm commitment

21. According to the Uniform Securities Act, registration by filing is available to an issuer when the security is

    I.   trading in the secondary market
    II. being registered simultaneously with the SEC
    III. being offered in only one state
    IV. exempt from SEC registration

    A. I
    B. I and II
    C. II and III
    D. III and IV

◆ Answers & Rationale

1. **D.** Each of the activities listed must be performed prior to the publication of the offering price except the filing of legal feasibility documents, because there are no such legal requirements.
(Page 119)

2. **A.** The managing underwriter can place orders to buy the stock being offered at a given price only until the end of the offering period.
(Page 120)

3. **D.** The underwriter determines the selling price and communicates it to the members of the selling group.
(Page 119)

4. **B.** A syndicate is permitted only to stabilize at or below the bid in the market. Any other price could artificially inflate the stock's price in the market.
(Page 120)

5. **D.** The underwriters of a new issue cannot stabilize the offering during the cooling-off period because the issue is not yet in the hands of investors and therefore cannot be traded in the open market.
(Page 120)

6. **B.** Because TCB's $7,000,000 issue is over $5,000,000, it must file a standard registration statement. If the issue were under the $5,000,000 Regulation A filing limit, it would have to file only an offering circular.
(Page 113)

7. **D.** Stabilization of new issues during the offering period is permitted if the fact that an underwriter might stabilize an issue is disclosed in the prospectus. Stabilization is also known as *pegging*, and is not permitted once an offering ends.
(Page 120)

8. **B.** Stabilizing bids may be placed only at or below the public offering price.
(Page 120)

9. **A.** If a bond issue is priced above par, it is usually because the coupon rate at which the bonds

were issued is more than the prevailing rates for other newly issued bonds.
(Page 119)

10. **D.** Blue-sky registration laws apply to the licensing of agents (registered reps) and registration of securities in each state. States require the registration of nonexempt securities. Securities that are exempt, including government issues and state-chartered bank issues, need not be registered in the state.
(Page 118)

11. **C.** Blue-sky laws require state registration of sales representatives and nonexempt securities. Securities that are exempt from registration under the act of 1933 are generally exempt from registration under blue-sky laws. Because U.S. government securities and small business investment companies are exempt under the act of 1933, they are automatically exempt from registration under the blue-sky laws.
(Page 118)

12. **D.** Blue-sky laws cover the registration requirements for broker-dealers and new issues in each state. Only choices II and III are true regarding the blue-sky laws. The Securities Act of 1933 is a federal statute and, as such, does not apply to regulations within a state. The 1933 act applies only to interstate issues and trading. (Page 118)

13. **D.** The Securities Act of 1933 is a federal statute and the federal government does not dictate state law. Blue-sky laws protect the public from securities fraud in each state and must be complied with by issuers and broker-dealers. (Page 118)

14. **B.** A syndicate member is contractually obligated not to sell below the public offering price unless specifically released of contractual obligations and/or authorized to sell at a lower price by the managing underwriter(s). Selling group members are also under contract not to sell securities being distributed below the public offering price.
(Page 120)

15. **C.** A due diligence meeting is held prior to the effective date and is one of the final meetings held prior to the sale of the security to review all aspects of the issue. Attending will be the issuer,

underwriter, their lawyers and accountants.
(Page 119)

16. **B.**   If a public offering is going poorly, one common way to stimulate sales is to increase the selling concession (at the expense of the underwriting fee). Or, if a drastic measure is necessary to move the securities, a managing underwriter may have no choice but to authorize sales at discounts to the offering price.   (Page 120)

17. **C.**   To be sold in a given state, a security must be registered in that state, unless the security is exempt from registration. Most states exempt listed securities from state registration (a *blue chip* exemption). In addition, exempt securities under the act of 1933 are also usually exempt from state registration.   (Page 118)

18. **B.**   The main functions of an investment banker are raising intermediate and long-term capital for corporations through the distribution of securities, buying securities from an issuer and reselling them to the public, distributing large blocks of stock and giving advice to corporations on the best way to raise long-term capital. It is not the responsibility of the investment banker to provide a continuing secondary market for securities once they have been issued.   (Page 113)

19. **C.**   A secondary distribution is the sale of stock that has been previously issued and owned.

A key purpose of a secondary distribution is to redistribute a large block of stock without significantly affecting the market price. Like a primary distribution, an underwriting manager makes distribution arrangements and a syndicate may be formed. In a secondary distribution, the securities are usually offered at a fixed price that is closely related to the current market price so as not to upset the market significantly.   (Page 115)

20. **C.**   Only answer C relates to the Securities Exchange Act of 1934. The other answers are covered under the 1933 act or by NASD regulations.
(Page 120)

21. **B.**   Registration by filing is an option available to an issuer whose registration statement is already on file with the SEC. After the cooling-off period, the federal registration becomes effective, and the state registration will become effective simultaneously. If the federal registration is already effective and the issuer would like to offer shares in a particular state, registration by filing becomes effective after five days. Filing is thus a good choice for both an issuer currently registering with the SEC and an issuer with shares already trading in the secondary market. Registration by qualification is the best choice for a security being offered in only one state. Many securities that are exempt from SEC registration are also exempt from state registration.   (Page 118)

19 The Underwriting Syndicate Exam

1. Why would a syndicate form a selling group?

   A. By forming a selling group, a syndicate cuts its losses if the price of the issue drops.
   B. By forming a selling group, smaller firms may take part in and assist with an underwriting they may not otherwise be able to handle.
   C. The Securities Act of 1933 requires a minimum of one active syndicate manager and three active, participatory selling group members for each new issue in order to provide the public with adequate due diligence.
   D. Permitting other firms into a selling group is a method of repaying those firms for any past favors.

Use the following information to answer questions 2 through 4. Datawaq is raising money by issuing 1,000,000 new shares of common stock at $30 per share. For each share that it sells, the managing underwriter will receive $2.10 plus $.30 for expenses. The selling group will receive $1.80 for each share that it sells.

2. The total spread for the Datawaq offering is

   A. $.30
   B. $1.80
   C. $2.10
   D. $2.40

3. How much money will the managing underwriter receive from the underwriting to cover all of its advertising and other miscellaneous expenses?

   A. $300,000
   B. $1,800,000
   C. $2,100,000
   D. $2,400,000

4. How much money will Datawaq receive from the proceeds of the new issue after all sales and advertising expenses are deducted?

   A. $2,400,000
   B. $27,600,000
   C. $27,900,000
   D. $28,200,000

Use the following tombstone to answer questions 5 and 6.

New Issue

$20,000,000

Tallawhosits City Waterworks

Coupon 7%

Price 100.65%

Dewey, Cheatham & Howe

---

5. Which of the following statements can be made about the underwriting spread charged by Dewey, Cheatham & Howe on the new Tallawhosits City Waterworks bond issue?

    A. The total underwriting spread is larger than the total selling concession.
    B. The total selling concession is larger than the total underwriting spread.
    C. The total reallowance is larger than the total underwriting spread.
    D. The total reallowance is larger than the total selling concession.

6. As a member of the syndicate selling the new issue of Tallawhosits City Waterworks bonds, Dewey, Cheatham & Howe received a 1/2-point takedown on the bonds. You placed 20 of those bonds with a customer. What is DCH's profit per bond?

    A. $.50
    B. $5
    C. $10
    D. $50

7. An underwriting spread is the

    A. amount received by a managing underwriter
    B. amount received by a selling group
    C. amount received by a syndicate
    D. difference between an offering price and the proceeds to an issuer

8. Assume that a corporation is issuing stock to the public at $10 per share. If the syndicate manager's fee is $.10 per share, the underwriting fee is $.25 per share, and the selling concession is $.45 per share, what is the spread?

    A. $.60
    B. $.70
    C. $.80
    D. $.90

9. Which of the following statements about underwriting are correct?

    I.   An underwriting syndicate consists of a group of broker-dealers that have temporarily banded together to distribute new issue securities to the public and whose members have made a financial commitment to the issuer.
    II. A selling group consists of two or more broker-dealers that have agreed to participate in the distribution of new issue securities to the public, and that have made financial commitments to the underwriting syndicate in advance.
    III. An underwriting syndicate consists of a group of broker-dealers that have banded together to buy new issue securities from an issuer, such securities to be held by the syndicate members for investment purposes.
    IV. A selling group consists of two or more broker-dealers that have agreed to participate in the distribution of new issue securities as selling agents only, without principal risk.

    A. I and III
    B. I and IV
    C. II and III
    D. II and IV

10. The largest portion of an underwriting spread normally goes to the

    A. syndicate underwriting members
    B. issuer
    C. selling group
    D. managing underwriter

11. Which of the following elements of an underwriting spread normally accounts for the largest amount?

    A. Reallowance
    B. Managing underwriter's fee
    C. Syndicate members' participation
    D. Selling group concession

◆ Answers & Rationale

1. **B.** Selling groups provide an opportunity for firms that are not large enough to underwrite an entire issue on their own to take part in larger deals. They also help ensure that the syndicate will be able to place the entire issue. (Page 122)

2. **D.** For each share sold, the total spread (the difference between the amount paid to the issuer and the public offering price) is $2.10 plus $.30 expenses, or $2.40. Datawaq will receive $27.60 per share from the deal. (Page 124)

3. **A.** $.30 per share for expenses times 1,000,000 shares is $300,000. (Page 124)

4. **B.** Datawaq will receive $27,600,000 in proceeds from the new issue.

$ 30,000,000	$30 × 1,000,000 shares
− 2,400,000	$2.40 × 1,000,000 shares
$ 27,600,000	Net proceeds

(Page 124)

5. **A.** The underwriting spread is the total difference between the public offering price and the proceeds to the issuer. All expenses incurred and sales concessions paid in an underwriting are deducted from the spread. (Page 124)

6. **B.** Because one bond point equals $10, a 1/2-point takedown per bond represents a profit of $5 per $1,000 bond. (Page 124)

7. **D.** A spread is the difference between a public offering price and the price an underwriter pays an issuer. (Page 124)

8. **C.** The spread for the syndicate is $.80. This is the difference between the $10 public offering price and the $9.20 price to the issuer. (Page 124)

9. **B.** Members of an underwriting (selling) syndicate buy securities from issuers in principal transactions and therefore assume financial risk (in a firm commitment underwriting); members of a selling group act merely as agents and therefore assume no financial risk. (Page 122)

10. **C.** The selling group normally receives the largest portion of a spread. (Page 124)

11. **D.** The largest part of the spread normally is the selling concession, out of which the registered reps selling the issue are paid. (Page 124)

20 Types of Underwriting Commitments Exam

1. What type of agreement would exist if the underwriter of an issue receives a guaranteed amount of money if the minimum amount of the issue is sold, but no more if the maximum is sold?

   A. Mini-max
   B. AON
   C. FOK
   D. Standby

2. Which of the following are terms for different types of underwritings?

   I. Best efforts
   II. All or none
   III. Firm commitment
   IV. Fail-to-receive

   A. I
   B. I, II and III
   C. I and III
   D. II, III and IV

3. Dewey, Cheatham & Howe is the managing underwriter for a new issue of 1,000,000 Microscam common. It has agreed to sell as much of the stock as possible in the market, and Microscam has agreed to take back the rest unsold. What is this type of offering known as?

   A. Standby
   B. Best efforts
   C. All or none
   D. Contingency

4. Dewey, Cheatham & Howe is the managing underwriter for a new issue of 1,000,000 Microscam common. It has agreed to sell all of the stock being offered, and has agreed to buy for its own account any stock that it cannot sell to the public. Microscam will receive the proceeds from the sale of 1,000,000 shares. What is this type of offering known as?

   A. Firm commitment
   B. Best efforts
   C. All or none
   D. Standby

5. Dewey, Cheatham & Howe is the managing underwriter for a new issue of 1,000,000 Microscam common. It has agreed to do its best to sell as much of the stock as possible in the market, but if it cannot sell it all, Microscam will cancel the offering. What is this type of offering known as?

   A. Standby
   B. Best efforts
   C. All or none
   D. Contingency

6. Microscam is engaged in a stock rights offering with the help of Dewey, Cheatham & Howe as managing underwriter. DCH has offered to purchase any of the stock Microscam is unable to sell to current stockholders. This arrangement is known as what type of underwriting?

   A. Special
   B. Best efforts
   C. Standby
   D. All or none

7. Dewey, Cheatham & Howe is the managing underwriter for a new issue of 1,000,000 Microscam common on a firm commitment basis. If part of the Microscam issue remains unsold and results in a loss, the loss will be divided proportionately among the

   I.   underwriting firms
   II. issuing corporation
   III. selling group firms

   A. I only
   B. I and III only
   C. II only
   D. I, II and III

8. Which of the following underwriting arrangements is typically demanded by local statute when general obligation municipal bonds are to be issued?

   A. Best efforts basis
   B. Competitive bid basis
   C. Negotiated basis
   D. All or none basis

9. Underwriters that agree to purchase an entire issue and absorb for their own account any securities not sold are engaging in a(n)

   A. standby underwriting
   B. firm commitment underwriting
   C. best efforts underwriting
   D. all or none underwriting

10. An underwriter that agrees to act as agent for an issuer, but states that any shares not sold will be returned to the issuer engages in a(n)

    A. best efforts underwriting
    B. standby underwriting
    C. firm commitment underwriting
    D. all or none underwriting

11. Assume that an issuing corporation stipulates to an underwriter that it must generate an exact amount of new capital and nothing less; the underwriter responds by saying, "We'll do our best, but we can't guarantee it." What is this type of underwriting called?

    A. Standby underwriting
    B. Best efforts underwriting
    C. Firm commitment underwriting
    D. All or none underwriting

12. Which of the following is(are) true of an underwriter's financial liability if a syndicate is established as an Eastern account?

    I.   Divided liability to purchase securities from the issuer
    II. Undivided liability to purchase securities from the issuer
    III. Divided responsibility for any securities that remain unsold
    IV. Undivided responsibility for any securities that remain unsold

    A. I
    B. I and III
    C. II
    D. II and IV

13. An Eastern account underwriting of $100 million in corporate bonds is established. ALFA Securities agrees to underwrite 10% of the issue and proceeds to sell out the firm's 10% allotment of $10 million. However some of the other firms participating in the deal aren't quite as successful, and $15 million worth of the bonds remain unsold. What is ALFA's financial obligation in this matter?

   A. $0
   B. $150,000
   C. $1.5 million
   D. Pooled responsibility for $15 million

14. A Western account underwriting of $100 million in corporate bonds is established. Dullard Securities agrees to underwrite 10% of the issue and proceeds to sell out the firm's 10% allotment of $10 million. However some of the other firms participating in the deal aren't quite as successful, and $15 million worth of the bonds remain unsold. What is Dullard's financial obligation in this matter?

   A. $0
   B. $150,000
   C. $1.5 million
   D. Pooled responsibility for $15 million

15. When members of a syndicate agree to share financial responsibility for any unsold securities on an undivided basis, this contractual arrangement is called a(n)

   A. Eastern account
   B. best efforts account
   C. selling group account
   D. Western account

16. An underwriter that agrees to purchase any securities an issuing corporation cannot sell to its shareholders in conjunction with a rights offering is engaging in what type of underwriting?

   A. Firm commitment
   B. Best efforts
   C. Standby
   D. All or none

17. In what type(s) of offering(s) does a brokerage firm have no financial obligation for unsold securities?

   I.   All or none
   II.   Best efforts
   III. Standby

   A. I only
   B. I and II only
   C. II and III only
   D. I, II and III

18. What is the name of the clause found in most underwriting agreements that releases a broker-dealer from obligations to proceed with a public offering of an issuer's securities should an adverse material development occur within the issuer's field of business?

   A. Market-out
   B. Back away
   C. Indemnification
   D. Hold harmless

◆ Answers & Rationale

1. **B.** If the underwriter would receive the same amount of money whether the minimum or the maximum amount of an issue is sold, the agreement is probably an all or none (AON). (Page 128)

2. **B.** A fail to receive occurs when a broker-dealer does not receive the securities due it from a buy transaction. The main types of underwritings are:

- Best efforts—when an underwriter will do its best to sell the entire new issue, but will not guarantee success.
- All or none—the underwriter will sell the entire issue or none will be sold.
- Firm commitment—the underwriter will guarantee to sell the entire issue.
- Standby—when a corporation will try and sell the new issue itself through a rights offering, but will have an underwriter standing by to sell the unsold shares.

(Page 127)

3. **B.** A best efforts underwriting is one in which any stock that remains unsold is returned to the issuing corporation. (Page 128)

4. **A.** A firm commitment requires the underwriter to sell the entire issue of stock or to purchase any unsold stock for its own inventory. (Page 127)

5. **C.** An all or none underwriting requires the underwriter to sell the entire issue of stock or to cancel the offering completely. (Page 128)

6. **C.** A standby underwriting arrangement allows a corporation to sell as much of a new issue to current stockholders as possible, backed by the promise of an underwriter to take and sell any unsold shares to the public. (Page 129)

7. **A.** In a firm commitment arrangement, any losses incurred are divided among the underwriters according to their participation. (Page 127)

8. **B.** The majority of municipal underwritings are set up and awarded based on competitive bidding. In most instances, state and local ordinances require competitive bids, especially if general obligation bonds are being issued. (Page 127)

9. **B.** When an underwriter buys an issue from an issuer, the underwriting is a firm commitment underwriting. (Page 127)

10. **A.** The question defines a best efforts underwriting. (Page 128)

11. **D.** The question provides an example of an all or none underwriting. (Page 128)

12. **D.** An Eastern account is undivided as to selling responsibility and liability. (Page 130)

13. **C.** Undivided liability in an Eastern account means that a member is liable for 10% of the unsold bonds (in this case, 10% of $15 million equals $1.5 million). (Page 130)

14. **A.** Divided liability in a Western account means that if a member meets its commitment, it has no liability for other members' unsold shares. (Page 130)

15. **A.** An undivided account, which is an undivided underwriting liability for securities that don't sell, is an Eastern account. (Page 130)

16. **C.** The question defines a standby underwriting. (Page 129)

17. **B.** In a best efforts underwriting, the underwriter serves as an agent with no financial obligation for unsold securities. In an AON offering, the underwriter agrees to devote its best efforts to sell the issue, but the entire offering is canceled if a portion cannot be sold. In a standby underwriting, the underwriter agrees to purchase any unsold shares after a rights offering. (Page 128)

18. **A.** The question defines a market-out clause. (Page 128)

21 Exemptions from the Securities Act of 1933 Exam

1. I Can't Believe This Is Sushi (IBS) wants to offer $4,200,000 of its common stock in six states in the Midwest. For the offering to be cleared for sale, under Regulation A IBS must file a(n)

   A. offering circular
   B. standard registration statement
   C. letter of notification
   D. preliminary prospectus

2. An intrastate offering is exempt from

   A. federal registration
   B. state registration
   C. blue-sky registration
   D. all registration

3. Historically, what is the most common method for an investor to acquire *restricted stock*?

   A. Mergers or acquisitions
   B. Private placements
   C. Standby underwritings
   D. Employee profit-sharing plans

4. Under the Securities Act of 1933, an *accredited investor* is defined as one having a(n)

   I. annual income of at least $1,000,000
   II. annual income of at least $200,000 for the last two years and is expected to have an income of $200,000 this year
   III. net worth of $200,000
   IV. net worth of $1,000,000

   A. I and III
   B. I and IV
   C. II and III
   D. II and IV

5. All of the following are exempt securities EXCEPT

   A. commercial paper
   B. BAs
   C. CDs
   D. ADRs

6. Under the provisions of Rule 144 regarding shares outstanding, what is the percentage of outstanding stock allowed to be sold every 90 days?

   A. 1%
   B. 3%
   C. 4%
   D. 5%

7. All of the following are exempt from registration under the Securities Act of 1933 EXCEPT

    A. small business investment companies
    B. chartered commercial banks
    C. U.S. government issues
    D. utility companies

8. A stock offering to a limited number of non-qualified investors, without SEC registration, is a(n)

    A. private placement
    B. Rule 144 offering
    C. intrastate offering
    D. secondary offering

9. Which of the following governs an individual selling stock under Rule 144?

    A. Investment Company Act of 1940
    B. Maloney Act
    C. Securities Act of 1933
    D. Securities Exchange Act of 1934

10. Which of the following transactions is NOT considered a control stock transaction?

    A. President of Amalgamated Featherbedders buys AMF stock in the open market.
    B. Spouse of Consolidated Codfish's director buys COD stock in the open market.
    C. Joe Kuhl buys 10% of Greater Health, Inc.'s outstanding stock from a broker.
    D. Employee of ALFA Securities buys CowTec stock in a private placement offering.

11. Quantum Rapid Search, Inc. makes a new offering to accredited investors of stock not registered with the SEC. This type of offering is called a(n)

    A. secondary offering
    B. Rule 144 offering
    C. intrastate offering
    D. private placement

12. Which of the following provisions govern the offering of restricted shares to the public without filing a Form 144?

    I. The dollar amount is $1,000,000 or less.
    II. 100,000 shares or less are sold.
    III. 500 shares or less are sold.
    IV. The dollar amount is $10,000 or less.

    A. I and II
    B. I and III
    C. II and IV
    D. III and IV

Use the following information to answer questions 13 and 14. On Tuesday, October 5th, a customer tells you that she wants to sell some Rule 144 stock she holds in ALFAtronics Applied Technology. ALFA has 16,500,000 shares outstanding. Trading volume in ALFA shares for the last few weeks has been as follows:

Week ending:	Shares traded:
Oct. 1	160,000
Sept. 24	170,000
Sept. 17	160,000
Sept. 10	165,000
Sept. 3	170,000
Aug. 27	162,000

13. Assuming all other requirements for Rule 144 are met, what is the maximum number of shares the customer can sell during the next 90 days?

    A. 135,000
    B. 162,000
    C. 165,000
    D. 170,000

14. What would be the maximum permissible sale during the next 90 days if the customer had filed a Form 144 one week ago?

    A. 162,000
    B. 165,000
    C. 166,250
    D. 170,000

15. Filing for a Regulation A exemption covers

   A. an offering of $5,000,000 or less in 12 months
   B. an offering of letter stock
   C. a private offering
   D. an offering of $5,000,000 or more in 12 months

16. An investor and his father own 20% and 10%, respectively, of the outstanding shares of the same corporation. The father wants to sell the holding. According to Rule 144, the father

   I. must file Form 144 to sell the shares
   II. does not have to file a Form 144 to sell the shares
   III. is considered an affiliated person
   IV. is not considered an affiliated person

   A. I and III
   B. I and IV
   C. II and III
   D. II and IV

17. The Securities Act of 1933 exempts all of the following securities EXCEPT

   A. municipal issues
   B. savings and loan issues
   C. real estate investment trusts
   D. U.S. government issues

18. Regulation D covers the minimum standards that must be met by accredited investors in a private placement. These include a(n)

   I. annual income of $200,000 for at least the last two years
   II. annual income of $1,000,000 for at least the last two years
   III. net worth of $1,000,000
   IV. net worth of $200,000

   A. I and III
   B. I and IV
   C. II and III
   D. II and IV

19. Securities exempt under the act of 1933 are not subject to which of the following sections of the Securities Exchange Act of 1934?

   I. Trading restrictions on corporate insiders
   II. Margin requirements imposed under Regulation T
   III. Solicitation of proxies
   IV. Antifraud and market manipulation

   A. I and II only
   B. I, II and III only
   C. III and IV only
   D. I, II, III and IV

20. Which of the following securities is(are) exempt from the SEC registration and disclosure requirements of the Securities Act of 1933?

   I. Securities issued by the United States or any territory
   II. Securities issued by a state or a political subdivision of a state
   III. Securities issued by a common carrier (e.g., a railroad) subject to the Interstate Commerce Act
   IV. Securities issued by banks and savings institutions

   A. I only
   B. I and II only
   C. II and IV only
   D. I, II, III and IV

21. Which of the following securities are subject to the antifraud provisions of the Securities Act of 1933?

   I. U.S. government bonds
   II. Corporate debt instruments maturing in fewer than 270 days
   III. Corporate equity securities issued and sold intrastate
   IV. Municipal bonds

   A. I, II and III only
   B. I and IV only
   C. II and III only
   D. I, II, III and IV

22. Which of the following securities transactions are beyond the regulatory purview of the SEC and the public protection provisions of the 1933 and 1934 acts?

A. Intrastate offerings of corporate securities
B. Interstate offerings of corporate securities
C. Private placements involving unregistered stock
D. Transactions between private parties

23. The maximum amount of securities that can be offered under Regulation A is

A. $500,000 per issue and $500,000 per selling affiliate
B. $500,000 per issue and $100,000 per selling affiliate
C. $1,000,000 per issuer and $500,000 for all selling affiliates
D. $5,000,000 per issuer and $1,500,000 for all selling affiliates

24. Corporate debt securities, such as commercial paper, are exempt from registration under the Securities Act of 1933 if their maturity does not exceed how many days?

A. 30
B. 90
C. 270
D. 365

25. Which of the following securities is(are) exempt from the registration and disclosure provision of the Securities Act of 1933?

I. Securities issued under the jurisdiction of the ICC or another federal government regulatory agency
II. Municipal bonds
III. U.S. government securities
IV. Corporate debt instruments maturing in fewer than 270 days

A. I and II only
B. I and III only
C. II only
D. I, II, III and IV

26. CowTec has its principal office in Illinois and a small branch operation in Michigan. CowTec issues stock in an intrastate offering under Rule 147. Which of the following statements is true?

A. The underwriting broker-dealer is not required to have an office in Illinois.
B. An Illinois resident may purchase CowTec stock.
C. A Michigan resident may purchase CowTec stock.
D. The SEC maintains jurisdiction over the offering.

27. Under the intrastate offering rule (Rule 147), when may a resident purchaser of the securities resell them to a nonresident?

A. Three months after the first sale made in that state
B. Six months after the last sale made in that state
C. Nine months after the first sale made in that state
D. None of the above

◆ Answers & Rationale

1.   **A.**   Because IBS's $4,200,000 issue is under the Regulation A filing limit of $5,000,000, it may file an offering circular.   (Page 132)

2.   **A.**   An intrastate offering is limited to companies that do business in one state and sell their securities only to the residents of that state.
(Page 134)

3.   **B.**   A private placement is an exempt transaction under the Securities Act of 1933, which means that the security issued is not registered with the SEC. The transfer of unregistered securities is restricted and it is known as a *restricted security*. Private placements are the most common way in which restricted securities are acquired. Business merger and acquisition activity occasionally result in the issuance of restricted securities. A standby underwriting is used during a rights offering and is a public distribution of a fully registered security. Profit-sharing plans normally are funded with a share of profits, not stock.   (Page 133)

4.   **D.**   In order to qualify as an accredited investor under Regulation D of the Securities Act of 1933, one must meet one or more of the following: have a net worth of $1,000,000; have an income of $200,000 for each of the past two years with expectations of the same this year; be an institutional investor; or be an insider.   (Page 132)

5.   **D.**   An ADR is an American depositary receipt. It is used to facilitate the trading of foreign securities by U.S. citizens.   (Page 131)

6.   **A.**   Rule 144 (sale of restricted or control stock) allows for the sale of 1% of the outstanding shares or the weekly average of the last four weeks' trading volume, whichever is greater, every 90 days.   (Page 133)

7.   **D.**   Utility companies are not exempted from the Securities Act of 1933. Government issues, small business investment companies and small chartered commercial banks are all exempt under the act.   (Page 131)

8.   **A.**   An offering to a limited number of investors (35 nonaccredited investors or less) is a private placement.   (Page 132)

9.   **C.**   The Securities Act of 1933 encompasses Rule 144, the sale of restricted (unregistered) or control stock.   (Page 133)

10.   **D.**   Stock bought in a private placement is restricted stock, not control stock. Control stock is owned by officers, directors or anyone who owns 10% of that corporation (or their financially dependent relatives). Control stock and restricted stock are subject to many of the same SEC requirements.   (Page 132)

11.   **D.**   A private placement (which is exempt from registration with the SEC) is an offering of a new issue to an unlimited number of accredited investors and a maximum of 35 nonaccredited investors.   (Page 132)

12.   **D.**   Under Rule 144, a Form 144 need not be filed if fewer than 500 shares are sold and the dollar amount is less than $10,000.   (Page 133)

13.   **C.**   Under Rule 144, the maximum sale every 90 days is the greater of 1% of the outstanding shares or the weekly average of the last four weeks' trading volume. 1% of 16,500,000 is 165,000. The average of the last four weeks is: $(160,000 + 170,000 + 160,000 + 165,000) \div 4$, which is 163,750. The greater amount is 165,000 shares.   (Page 133)

14.   **C.**   The average of the four previous weeks' trading volume now becomes: $(170,000 + 160,000 + 165,000 + 170,000) \div 4$, which is 166,250. This is greater than 1% of the outstanding shares, or 165,000.   (Page 133)

15.   **A.**   A Regulation A filing under the Securities Act of 1933 exempts the security from registration and is limited to offerings of $5,000,000 or less within 12 months.   (Page 132)

16. **A.**   Under Rule 144, an *affiliate* is a person who is in a control relationship with the issuer. Because the investors own more than 10% of the stock, they are control persons under Rule 144 and must sell in compliance with the rule. (Page 133)

17. **C.**   REITs are registered nonexempt securities. U.S. government, municipal and savings and loan issues are exempt.   (Page 131)

18. **A.**   The minimum net worth requirement for an investor to be accredited under the private placement exemption is $1,000,000. The minimum income requirement is $200,000.   (Page 132)

19. **B.**   Generally speaking, exempt securities (such as municipal or U.S. government obligations) are exempt from the provisions of the Securities Act of 1933 in terms of disclosure and registration requirements. But all securities issuers, broker-dealers and securities transactions are subject to the antifraud provisions of the act, without exception. In addition, no securities transactions are exempt from the market manipulation prohibitions of the act of 1934.   (Page 135)

20. **D.**   The act of 1933 exempts all of the securities listed from registration and disclosure requirements. But that doesn't mean that banks and common carriers, as examples, can do whatever they want; it simply means that other government regulatory agencies are in charge.   (Page 131)

21. **D.**   All securities and securities transactions are subject to the antifraud provisions of the act of 1933.   (Page 134)

22. **D.**   Transactions between private parties (as in one investor buying stock in a privately held corporation from the president of the company) are not covered under the 1933 or 1934 acts, unless the U.S. mail or interstate commerce are used to accomplish the transaction.   (Page 131)

23. **D.**   Under Regulation A, the dollar limit on sales is $5 million per issuer per year. Persons affiliated with the issuer may sell up to $1,500,000 per year.   (Page 132)

24. **C.**   The time limit placed on maturities of commercial paper exempt from registration is 270 days. Anything longer is considered an investment security subject to registration and disclosure requirements under the act of 1933.   (Page 131)

25. **D.**   All securities listed in choices I through IV are exempt from registration and full disclosure requirements under the act of 1933, but not from the act's antifraud provisions.   (Page 131)

26. **B.**   To qualify as an intrastate offering, all shares must be sold to residents of the state where the company has 80% of its business. The underwriter must have an office in that state, and the state's securities administrator has jurisdiction over the offering.   (Page 132)

27. **D.**   In an intrastate offering, the purchasers of the issue may not sell the securities to a resident of another state for at least nine months after the close of the issue.   (Page 134)

22 Freeriding and Withholding: Hot Issues Exam

1. Underwriters and selling group members are said to engage in freeriding and withholding in the distribution of hot issues when they

   I. retain positions of the new issue by selling to their supported family members
   II. sell blocks of the new issue to accounts of partners or officers
   III. sell to brokers and dealers outside the selling group who position the securities for later resale at higher prices
   IV. withhold issues from sale to the public

   A. I only
   B. II only
   C. III and IV only
   D. I, II, III and IV

2. "Freeriding and withholding" is defined by the

   A. Securities Act of 1933
   B. NASD Rules of Fair Practice
   C. Securities Exchange Act of 1934
   D. SEC Statement of Policy

3. Which of the following individuals may NOT purchase a hot issue under normal circumstances?

   I. Principal of an NASD member firm
   II. Officer, director or employee of an NASD member firm
   III. Senior officer of a savings and loan institution or insurance company
   IV. Employee who is involved in the allocation of the issue

   A. I only
   B. I and II only
   C. II and III only
   D. I, II, III and IV

4. Assume that an NASD member firm is engaged in the distribution of a public offering security that immediately sells at a substantial premium over the offering price in the aftermarket. Under which of the following conditions could the member firm sell the stock at the public offering price to a bank officer?

   I.   Under no circumstances
   II. If the amount sold to the officer is insubstantial
   III. If the securities are purchased in accordance with the officer's normal investment practice
   IV. If the aggregate amount sold to the officer (and other restricted persons) is not disproportionate to the total size of the member's allocation or allotment

   A.   I
   B.   II and III
   C.   II, III and IV
   D.   II and IV

5. NASD freeriding and withholding rules apply to the purchase of public offering stock

   A.   that immediately trades at a discount to the offering price in the secondary market
   B.   that immediately trades at a premium to the offering price in the secondary market
   C.   being distributed to the general public
   D.   The rules apply to none of the above.

6. Under which of the following circumstances may an NASD member sell part of a hot issue to a bank that is buying on behalf of an undisclosed purchaser?

   I.   The order ticket must be initialed by a registered principal of the member firm.
   II. The member firm must make inquiry of the bank, verifying that the true buyer is not subject to the NASD freeriding and withholding restrictions.
   III. A notation must be made on the order ticket or some other document that inquiry has been made to the bank.
   IV. There must be supervisory procedures in place, providing the member firm with a means for close follow-up and review of all transactions, thus providing reasonable assurance that the bank is not being used to hide the identity of persons restricted from buying hot issues.

   A.   I only
   B.   I, III and IV only
   C.   II and IV only
   D.   I, II, III and IV

7. Which of the following statements is(are) true regarding a member firm's obligations to make bona fide public distributions of hot-issue stock?

   I. The member firm may hold part of the issue in inventory for resale to the public at a later time, provided this amount is insubstantial.

   II. The member firm may offer to sell part of the issue to one or more employees, provided these employees regularly purchase new issue securities; also, the total amount offered to employees must be within the NASD's 10% disproportionate allocation guideline.

   III. The member firm may sell part of the issue to the relative of one of its registered representatives if it is the relative's normal investment practice to purchase new issues, the relative receives no financial support from the rep, and the amount sold is insubstantial and not disproportionate in view of the offering's total size.

   IV. The member firm may sell part of the issue to the president or other officer of a bank or trust company if it is consistent with that person's normal investment practice and the amount is insubstantial and not disproportionate.

   A. II and III only
   B. III and IV only
   C. IV only
   D. I, II, III and IV

8. If a registered representative or other associated person wishes to buy a hot issue for his personal account, the NASD Rules of Fair Practice require which of the following?

   I. The order cannot be filled under any circumstances.

   II. The order cannot be filled for the rep's own account, but can be billed to a joint account between the rep and the rep's spouse or supported relative.

   III. The order can be filled for the rep's account, provided he has a history of buying hot issues.

   IV. The order can be filled for the rep's account if the amount of stock sold is insubstantial and not disproportionate to the amount allocated to filling public orders and if the rep has a history of buying hot issues.

   A. I
   B. II and IV
   C. III
   D. IV

9. For the purpose of a hot-issue allocation, which of the following are considered immediate family?

   I. Parents
   II. Parents-in-law
   III. Brothers and sisters
   IV. Aunts and uncles

   A. I and II only
   B. I, II and III only
   C. III and IV only
   D. I, II, III and IV

10. If a registered rep buys a hot issue that her firm is underwriting, but does so on the outside through another broker-dealer that is also participating in the underwriting, which of the following statements is(are) true?

 I. The member firm employing the rep has violated the NASD's freeriding and withholding rules.
 II. The member firm that sold the stock to the rep has violated the NASD's freeriding and withholding rules.
 III. The rep who bought the stock has violated the NASD's freeriding and withholding rules.
 IV. There is no violation if the rep has an investment history of buying new issues.

 A. I and II
 B. I, II and III
 C. II and III
 D. IV

11. "Freeriding and withholding" applies to

 A. new issues that sell at a discount
 B. new issues that sell at a premium
 C. all over-the-counter securities
 D. all of the above

12. If a member firm receives an order from the trust department of a bank for the purchase of a hot issue, the member firm should

 A. require written authorization from the bank, indemnifying the member firm from wrongdoing
 B. fill the order without further inquiry
 C. fill the order only if the name of the customer is disclosed
 D. fill the order after proper inquiry to verify that the customer is not restricted in the purchase of hot issues

13. When selling a hot issue to a bank trust department, a member must

 I. inquire as to whether the buyer is a person subject to the restrictions regarding a hot issue
 II. record and retain a record that proper inquiry was made of the bank involved
 III. not accept the order for an unidentified principal under any circumstances
 IV. send a confirmation to the account's beneficial owner

 A. I and II
 B. I, II and III
 C. II
 D. IV

14. Assume that a registered representative's father wants to purchase a hot issue. Which of the following factors would favor filling his order?

 I. The father is financially independent of the registered representative.
 II. The amount of securities that the father wishes to purchase is insubstantial in relation to the entire issue.
 III. The father has established an investment history of buying new issue securities.
 IV. The father does not reside with the registered representative.

 A. I and II only
 B. I, II and III only
 C. III only
 D. I, II, III and IV

15. When an issuer directs an underwriter to reserve a portion of public offering stock for sale to the issuer's employees, which of the following statements is(are) true?

   A. The amount of stock reserved for employees must be reasonable in relation to the size of the total offering.
   B. Employees for whom securities have been reserved must confirm their commitment to buy not later than ten business days in advance of the effective date.
   C. Employees for whom securities have been reserved are exempt from the NASD's freeriding and withholding provisions.
   D. The underwriter is not required to verify that the employees are not in the restricted account category.

16. The NASD's rules on freeriding and withholding govern purchases of hot issues by supported family members of broker-dealer personnel. Which of the following are considered in determining whether such purchases are a violation?

   I. Number of shares purchased
   II. Suitability of the investment
   III. Buyer's investment history
   IV. Buyer's status as to financial support

   A. I and II only
   B. I, III and IV only
   C. II and III only
   D. I, II, III and IV

17. Which of the following individuals would be permitted to purchase 200 shares of a bioengineering company's $8,000,000 hot issue under certain circumstances?

   I. Employee of a member firm
   II. Investment adviser for an advisory account
   III. Bank president
   IV. Officer of a member firm

   A. I and II
   B. I and IV
   C. II and III
   D. II, III and IV

18. Under the NASD Rules of Fair Practice, freeriding and withholding applies to

   I. debt issued under a prospectus
   II. new equity issues
   III. secondary distributions and Regulation A filings

   A. I only
   B. I and III only
   C. II only
   D. I, II and III

19. The NASD freeriding and withholding policy prohibits which of the following from buying a hot issue at the public offering price?

   I. Officer of the underwriters in the syndicate
   II. Employee of the firms in the syndicate offering the new issue
   III. Bank officer with a long-standing relationship with the underwriter
   IV. Finder of the issue being underwritten

   A. I and II
   B. I and IV
   C. II, III and IV
   D. III and IV

20. A security is trading at a significant premium on the day it is offered. Which of the following would be considered freeriding?

    I. Retaining a block of the securities for the firm's investment account
    II. Selling the securities at the public offering price to good retail customers
    III. Selling the securities to brokerage firms outside the selling group, who later sell the securities at higher prices
    IV. Selling shares to registered representatives of the underwriter at the public offering price

    A. I and III only
    B. I, III and IV only
    C. IV only
    D. I, II, III and IV

21. NASD rules on freeriding and withholding prohibit the purchase of a hot issue except under special circumstances by which of the following persons?

    I. A finder
    II. Bank officer who has a significant relationship with the issuer
    III. Officer of a broker-dealer firm that is an NASD member
    IV. Registered representative

    A. I and II only
    B. I, II and IV only
    C. III and IV only
    D. I, II, III and IV

22. ALFA Securities is a member of the selling group for a new public offering. The securities are expected to sell at an immediate premium in the secondary market. ALFA is permitted to sell shares to which of the following, provided the purchase falls within the person's normal investment practice?

    I. ALFA's vice president
    II. A registered rep with Serendipity Discount Securities, which is not involved in the ALFA underwriting
    III. ALFA's corporate attorney
    IV. Nonsupported relative of ALFA's vice president

    A. I and III
    B. II, III and IV
    C. III and IV
    D. IV

23. Bea Kuhl's brother is a registered representative with Dewey, Cheatham & Howe, one of the member firms underwriting a hot issue of securities. Bea receives material financial support from her brother. Under which of the following conditions may she purchase hot issue shares?

    A. The transaction is consistent with her normal investment practice.
    B. She has never before bought a new issue security.
    C. She does not place the order through Dewey, Cheatham & Howe.
    D. She may not buy hot issues under any circumstances.

24. Angus Bullwether's sister is a registered representative with The Walrus Capital Group, one of the member firms underwriting a hot issue of securities. Angus receives no financial support from his sister. Under which of the following conditions may he purchase hot issue shares?

   I.   The transaction is consistent with his normal investment practice.
   II. He does not place the order through The Walrus Capital Group.
   III. He places the order prior to the effective date of the registration statement.
   IV. He may not buy hot issues in his circumstances.

   A. I
   B. I and II
   C. II and III
   D. IV

◆ Answers & Rationale

1. **D.** The NASD freeriding and withholding policy prohibits the sale of hot issues to other brokers, partners, officers, or employees of firms in the syndicate or selling group offering the issue, or to their supported family members. In other words, the public must get the issue, not insiders who could profit by withholding the issue from sale to the public and then taking a "free ride" on the price escalation of the hot issue.   (Page 136)

2. **B.** Rules regarding freeriding and withholding in conjunction with hot issues are set under the NASD Rules of Fair Practice.   (Page 136)

3. **D.** Under normal circumstances, none of the persons listed may purchase a hot issue. All are considered restricted persons; however, individuals not affiliated with a member firm (such as the senior officer of the savings and loan association mentioned in choice III) may be allowed to purchase a hot issue if they meet certain criteria.   (Page 136)

4. **C.** Although bank officers are considered restricted persons, such persons may be allowed to purchase a hot issue if the requirements set forth in choices II, III and IV are met. The same is true for relatives of member firm employees and for officers and employees of financial institutions, but only if they too meet the requirements set forth in choices II, III and IV.   (Page 137)

5. **B.** Freeriding and withholding applies to hot issues only. A hot issue is one that trades at an immediate premium in the secondary market (also called the *new issue aftermarket*).   (Page 136)

6. **D.** A hot issue can be sold only to a bank for an undisclosed principal if the bank gives adequate information regarding the purchaser. The bank need not disclose the customer's name, but must give assurance that the individual is not subject to freeriding and withholding rules. A written memo of the inquiry must be maintained, all order tickets must be approved by a principal, and bank transac-

tions with the member should be reviewed to ensure compliance with freeriding and withholding rules.   (Page 138)

7. **B.** Hot issues may never be sold to member firms, their officers or their employees. However, employees' nonsupported family members and officers of institutions, while normally not allowed to buy hot issues, may do so if the amount is insubstantial in relation to the total offering and if the purchaser has a history of buying new issue securities routinely.   (Page 137)

8. **A.** A registered representative may never purchase a hot issue.   (Page 136)

9. **B.** For purposes of the freeriding and withholding rule, "immediate family" means parents, brothers, sisters, in-laws and children. (Page 137)

10. **B.** Both member firms and the registered rep have violated the Rules of Fair Practice regarding freeriding and withholding. Member firm employees can never buy hot issues.   (Page 138)

11. **B.** Freeriding and withholding rules apply to hot issues only.   (Page 136)

12. **D.** When a bank wishes to purchase a hot issue for an undisclosed principal, the member must inquire of the bank, in writing, as to whether the owner would be subject to freeriding and withholding regulations.   (Page 138)

13. **A.** When a bank wishes to purchase a hot issue for an undisclosed principal, the member must inquire of the bank, in writing, as to whether the owner would be subject to freeriding and withholding regulations. If the bank responds that the undisclosed principal is not subject to the regulations, the order may be accepted under these circumstances.   (Page 138)

14. **D.** All of the choices listed would tend to favor permitting the father's purchase of the hot issue.   (Page 137)

15. **A.** If too large a portion of a public offering is reserved for sale to employees (or to designated

vendors and professionals doing business with the issuer), the question raised is whether the underwriting is truly an offering of stock to the public. Employees do have to confirm their commitment to buy stock earmarked for them, but answer B is incorrect because confirmation from such persons is due by the close of business on the first business day following the offering's effective date, not ten days in advance of the date. Also if any designated recipients are included on the NASD's list of people restricted from purchasing hot issues, these people are not exempt from the freeriding and withholding rules.   (Page 138)

16. **B.** The Rules of Fair Practice require a member participating in the distribution of a new issue to make a bona fide public offering at the public offering price. Failure to do so is considered freeriding and withholding, which usually occurs when hot issues are being distributed. It is a violation to withhold any securities for the member's account, or sell securities to an employee of a member or to his supported family members. There are exceptions. A member may sell securities to a nonsupported person in the immediate family of an employee of a member if: (1) the securities were sold to such persons in accordance with their normal investment practice with the member; (2) the amount withheld and sold to such accounts is insubstantial and not disproportionate in amount as compared to sales to the public. *Suitability of the investment* has nothing to do with freeriding and withholding.   (Page 137)

17. **C.** The bank president and the investment adviser may purchase shares of a hot issue if they meet certain restrictions. Employees and officers of member firms may never purchase hot issues of securities.   (Page 136)

18. **D.** Freeriding and withholding rules state that a broker cannot withhold a hot issue from sale to the public and ride the price up itself (take a free ride). The policy applies to all new securities (not only equities) that are hot.   (Page 136)

19. **A.** The freeriding and withholding policy categorically prohibits NASD member firms, their officers and their employees from buying a hot issue at the public offering price. However, officers of institutions and finders (persons who introduce a corporation that wants to be underwritten to the underwriter) may be sold shares of a hot issue at the public offering price if they buy an *insubstantial* amount and have demonstrated a history of similar purchases.   (Page 136)

20. **B.** The purpose of the NASD rules against freeriding and withholding is to ensure that a public offering of stock is a bona fide public distribution. Prohibited actions include withholding any of the securities in a member's account, selling any of the securities to an employee or agent of the member and selling any of the securities to any broker or dealer.   (Page 136)

21. **A.** Officers and registered reps of a member cannot buy hot issues *under any circumstances*.   (Page 137)

22. **C.** According to freeriding and withholding rules, employees of NASD members may not purchase shares of a hot issue. A person who acts in a professional capacity in connection with the hot issue and a nonsupported family member of an employee may purchase shares only if it can be shown that they have made similar transactions within the past year.   (Page 137)

23. **D.** Because she is supported by an associated person of a member firm, the customer may not purchase hot issue shares. In the view of the NASD, a supported family member faces exactly the same restrictions as an associated person when seeking to buy hot issues.   (Page 137)

24. **B.** A nonsupported family member of an associated person may purchase hot issue shares if at least one of two requirements is met: the transaction must be consistent with the buyer's normal investment practice or the order must be placed with a firm other than the firm employing the associated person.   (Page 137)

23 The Regulation of Trading Exam

1. Under SEC rules, a registered broker-dealer must report its financial condition to its customers. Which of the following must be reported?

   I.   Inventory positions
   II. Statement of subordinated loans
   III. Statement of net capital
   IV. Unconsolidated balance sheet

   A. I and II
   B. I, II and IV
   C. II, III and IV
   D. III and IV

2. Which of the following is(are) regulated or mandated by the Securities Exchange Act of 1934?

   I.   Full and fair disclosure on new offerings
   II. Creation of the SEC
   III. Manipulation of the market
   IV. Margin requirements on securities

   A. I
   B. I, II and III
   C. II
   D. II, III and IV

3. Corporations are required to issue annual reports by the

   A. Investment Company Act of 1940
   B. Trust Indenture Act of 1939
   C. Securities Exchange Act of 1934
   D. Securities Act of 1933

4. The Securities Exchange Act of 1934 covers which of the following?

   I.   Trading of government securities
   II. Trading of corporate securities
   III. Issuance of financial reports by corporations
   IV. Issuance of government securities

   A. I, II and III
   B. I, II and IV
   C. I and III
   D. II and IV

5. Under the Securities Exchange Act of 1934, the SEC does which of the following?

   I.   Regulates the securities exchanges
   II. Requires the registration of brokers and dealers
   III. Prohibits inequitable and unfair trade practices
   IV. Regulates the over-the-counter markets

   A. I and II only
   B. I and IV only
   C. II, III and IV only
   D. I, II, III and IV

6. The Securities Exchange Act of 1934 contains sections that deal with

   I. the regulation of investment companies
   II. trading activities such as short sales, stabilizing and the registering of over-the-counter brokers and dealers
   III. the form and content of the prospectus that must be given to all prospective purchasers of a security
   IV. the registration of persons engaged in the business of advising others about investment company transactions

   A. I and II only
   B. II only
   C. III and IV only
   D. I, II, III and IV

◆ Answers & Rationale

1.   **C.**   The broker-dealer's report must show the balance sheet, the subordinated loans, a statement of net capital and a statement of aggregate indebtedness. The inventory positions need not be disclosed, and usually are not but are kept secret within the firm.   (Page 145)

2.   **D.**   The Securities Exchange Act of 1934 set up the SEC and regulates the market. The Securities Act of l933 requires full and fair disclosure.
(Page 144)

3.   **C.**   The Securities Exchange Act of 1934 mandates that companies file annual reports with the SEC.   (Page 145)

4.   **A.**   The Securities Exchange Act of 1934 regulates secondary trading or trading markets, while the Securities Act of 1933 regulates the primary, or new issue, market. Trading of corporates and governments would therefore fall under the 1934 act, as does corporate financial reporting. The 1933 act covers the issuance of new securities. Governments are exempt securities under the 1933 act.   (Page 144)

5.   **D.**   The Securities Exchange Act of 1934 (which has greater breadth than the act of 1933) addresses the:

- creation of the SEC;
- regulation of exchanges;
- regulation of credit by the FRB;
- registration of broker-dealers;
- regulation of insider transactions, short sales and proxies;
- regulation of trading activities;
- regulation of client accounts;
- customer protection rule;
- regulation of the OTC market; and
- net capital rule.

(Page 144)

6.   **B.**   The Securities Exchange Act of 1934 (which has greater breadth than the act of 1933) addresses the:

- creation of the SEC;
- regulation of exchanges;
- regulation of credit by the FRB;
- registration of broker-dealers;
- regulation of insider transactions, short sales and proxies;
- regulation of trading activities;
- regulation of client accounts;
- customer protection rule;
- regulation of the OTC market; and
- net capital rule.

(Page 144)

24 Securities Markets and Broker-Dealers Exam

1. An open-ended investment company bought preferred utility stock from a bank through INSTINET. This trade took place in the

    A. primary market
    B. secondary market
    C. third market
    D. fourth market

2. Trading in Microscam stopped on the NYSE because of an influx of orders. What happens to trading in Microscam on the other exchanges?

    A. Trading stops on all other exchanges.
    B. Trading stops on regional exchanges, but not necessarily on the American Stock Exchange.
    C. Trading may continue, but it will not be reported on the Tape until trading resumes on the NYSE.
    D. Trading may or may not continue but it is reported as it occurs.

3. Which of the following securities may be traded over the counter?

    I. Listed registered securities
    II. Unlisted nonexempt securities
    III. Registered unlisted securities
    IV. Unregistered exempt securities

    A. I and II only
    B. I and III only
    C. II and III only
    D. I, II, III and IV

4. If a client tells you that his company regularly trades securities in the fourth market, this means that it trades

    A. listed securities OTC
    B. unlisted securities OTC
    C. unlisted securities on an exchange
    D. securities directly with other institutional owners

5. After the market close yesterday, Datawaq announced that it would be filing for bankruptcy under Chapter 11. The NYSE decides not to open trading in DWQ. In response to the NYSE's announcement, the over-the-counter market

    A. continues to trade DWQ with the NYSE specialist's permission
    B. halts all trading in DWQ until the NYSE reopens it
    C. may either halt or continue trading as it sees fit
    D. applies to the SEC for a decision within 30 minutes of the opening

6. Your firm, Serendipity Discount Securities, has received an order from one of your customers to buy 300 shares of DWQ at the market. Serendipity goes into the market, buys 300 shares of DWQ from another broker-dealer, and delivers them to the account of your customer. Serendipity's role in this transaction was that of a

A. broker acting as an agent for a commission
B. dealer acting as a principal for a profit
C. broker acting as an agent for a profit
D. dealer acting as a principal for a commission

7. Your firm, Serendipity Discount Securities, has received an order from one of your customers to buy 300 shares of DWQ at the market. Serendipity goes into the market and buys 300 shares of DWQ from another broker-dealer for its own inventory. It then takes those shares out of inventory and sells them to the account of the customer. Serendipity's role in this transaction is that of a

A. broker acting as an agent for a commission
B. dealer acting as a principal for a profit
C. broker acting as an agent for a profit
D. dealer acting as a principal for a commission

8. Your firm, Serendipity Discount Securities, has positions in both Datawaq and Microscam. This means that Serendipity

A. holds shares of both stocks in street name for customers
B. is a market maker for both stocks
C. stands ready to buy or sell both stocks on request
D. could be long or short both stocks in inventory

9. Which of the following statements about transactions in the different securities markets is(are) true?

I. Transactions in listed securities occur mainly in the exchange markets.
II. Transactions in unlisted securities occur mainly in the OTC market.
III. Transactions in listed securities that occur in the OTC market are said to take place in the third market.
IV. Transactions in listed securities that occur directly between customers or institutions without using broker-dealers as intermediaries are said to take place in the fourth market.

A. I only
B. I and II only
C. II and III only
D. I, II, III and IV

10. Which of the following trades occur(s) in the secondary market?

I. Specialist on the NYSE buying stocks for his own inventory
II. Municipal bond syndicate selling new issues to the public
III. Registered representative buying unlisted securities for a client
IV. Insurance company buying municipal bonds directly from another insurance company

A. I, II and III
B. I, III and IV
C. II and III
D. IV

11. ALFA Securities, a broker-dealer that is a member of the NYSE, is a position trader. This means that ALFA Securities

A. is trading for its own account
B. is in violation of NYSE regulations
C. is underwriting securities in the primary market
D. acts as a broker for customers

12. Business hours for Nasdaq market makers are

   A.   9:00 am to 5:00 pm Eastern time
   B.   9:30 am to 4:00 pm Eastern time
   C.   10:00 am to 4:00 pm Eastern time
   D.   10:00 am to 4:30 pm Eastern time

13. During a trading halt, an investor could

   A.   cancel an order that was placed prior to the halt
   B.   execute a market order
   C.   execute a limit order
   D.   close an existing position

14. "Position trading" is the term applied to a

   A.   broker arranging a trade for a customer
   B.   dealer buying and selling securities for its own account
   C.   dealer charging a commission for a trade
   D.   broker acting as a market maker

15. A firm executes a customer order, and on the confirmation it discloses both a commission and a markup. Which of the following statements is true?

   A.   The total of the two may not exceed 5%.
   B.   The firm is in violation for making a hidden profit.
   C.   The firm is acting properly in its role as a market maker.
   D.   The firm is engaging in a prohibited practice known as selling away.

◆ Answers & Rationale

1. **D.** The fourth market consists of direct trades between institutions, pension funds, broker-dealers and others. Many of these trades use INSTI-NET. (Page 147)

2. **D.** Each exchange is autonomous in the starting and stopping of trading in securities on that exchange. Generally speaking, other exchanges will stop trading when the NYSE stops trading. Securities listed on the NYSE are not listed on the American Stock Exchange. If trades continue to occur on other exchanges, the Tape will continue to print those trades. (Page 149)

3. **D.** Registered securities that are not listed on an exchange constitute the bulk of the volume of trade of OTC equity securities. Municipal bonds and government securities are exempt from SEC registration requirements. The primary market for these securities is the unlisted OTC market. The third market is the over-the-counter trading market for exchange-listed securities. (Page 147)

4. **D.** The fourth market (INSTINET) is trans-actions between corporations and other large insti-tutions, such as mutual funds and pension plans, that do not involve an intermediary. (Page 147)

5. **C.** The over-the-counter market is not af-fected by actions of the NYSE or other exchanges, and trading may continue in the stock. (Page 149)

6. **A.** Your firm was acting as the customer's agent in acquiring the 300 shares of DWQ. The best way to remember the difference between brokers and dealers is through the letters BAC/DPP. They stand for "Brokers act as Agents for Commissions/ Dealers act as Principals for Profits." *Profit* is another way of saying *markup*. (Page 149)

7. **B.** Your firm was acting as principal in first acquiring the 300 shares of DWQ for its inventory before selling them to the customer. The way to remember the difference between brokers and deal-ers is through the letters BAC/DPP. They stand for

"Brokers act as Agents for Commissions/Dealers act as Principals for Profits." *Profit* is another way of saying *markup*. (Page 150)

8. **D.** To have (or establish) a position means that your firm is either long the stocks (that is, holds them in its own inventory) or is short the stocks (which it will have to replace at some point in the future). (Page 150)

9. **D.** Listed securities traded on exchanges compose the exchange market. Unlisted securities traded over the counter are the OTC market. Listed securities traded OTC compose the third market. Securities bought and sold without the aid of a broker-dealer compose the fourth market. INSTI-NET is a reporting service used by many institu-tions to locate other parties for fourth-market equity transactions. (Page 147)

10. **B.** Underwriters distribute new issues in the primary market. The secondary market is the trad-ing market. In the trading market, a trade can take place on a stock exchange (the first market); in the unlisted or over-the-counter market (the second market); by trading listed securities in the over-the-counter market (the third market); or in a direct institution-to-institution trade without the services of a brokerage firm (the fourth market). (Page 147)

11. **A.** "Position trading" is simply trading as principal, or dealer, for the firm's own account. The opposite role is that of a broker (or agent) trading securities in the secondary market for customers. (Page 150)

12. **B.** Under normal market conditions, Nasdaq trading hours are 9:30 am to 4:00 pm Eastern time, which coincides with trading hours on the NYSE. (Page 148)

13. **A.** If trading is halted in a security, investors cannot buy or sell the security. Of course, an open order can be canceled during a trading halt. (Page 149)

14. **B.** Position trading means that the dealer is buying and selling securities for its own account. A

dealer charges a markup, not a commission, for a trade; a broker acts for clients, not as a market maker. (Page 149)

15. **B.** A firm is prohibited from acting as a broker and a dealer on the same transaction. Charging a markup on an agency transaction or a commission on a principal transaction is known as a "hidden profit." (Page 150)

25   The New York Stock Exchange Exam

1. Which of the following individuals normally trade on the floor of an exchange?

    I. Two-dollar broker
    II. Commission broker
    III. Block trader
    IV. Registered representative

    A. I and II only
    B. I and III only
    C. II, III and IV only
    D. I, II, III and IV

2. The terms "priority," "precedence" and "parity" govern trading at

    A. the New York Stock Exchange
    B. the over-the-counter market
    C. both the exchanges and the OTC
    D. the third market

3. All of the following statements about NYSE-listed securities are true EXCEPT that

    A. securities must qualify for listing on the NYSE
    B. securities can be listed on several exchanges at the same time and may sell at different prices on each exchange
    C. all listed securities are marginable
    D. securities can be delisted any time that the company's board of directors requests it

4. Stock exchanges serve various functions in the trading of securities. Among these functions are

    I. buying and selling securities for public and institutional customers
    II. establishing the price of securities traded on the floor of the exchange
    III. giving traders permission to use the floor of the exchange to transact orders for customers
    IV. providing access to specialists who maintain markets in specific stocks at trading posts on the floor of the exchange

    A. I and II only
    B. II and III only
    C. III and IV only
    D. I, II, III and IV

5. Which of the following can result in the delisting of a stock listed on the NYSE?

    I. The company does not mail out proxies.
    II. Public interest in the stock declines considerably.
    III. The company files for bankruptcy.
    IV. The company issues nonvoting common stock.

    A. I and III only
    B. II and IV only
    C. III and IV only
    D. I, II, III and IV

6. Listing requirements that must be met by a corporation for the NYSE include

   I.   a national interest in trading the stock
   II. voting by stockholders through the solicitation of proxies
   III. 4,000 stockholders of 100 shares or more
   IV. 2,000 stockholders of 100 shares or more

   A. I and II
   B. I, II and III
   C. I, II and IV
   D. III and IV

◆ Answers & Rationale

1. **A.** A registered representative may not trade on the floor of the exchange. Only bona fide traders or specialists (members) may trade on the floor.   (Page 152)

2. **A.** The auction rules of priority, precedence and parity allow for the efficient execution of orders when several bids or offers are made at the same price at a given time on the floor of the NYSE. "Priority" is given to the order first entered. "Precedence" takes place when an entire order can be filled by an opposite order. "Parity" is when two or more orders can fill an opposite order; the brokers match to see who fills the order. The OTC market (including listed securities traded in the third market, over-the-counter) is a negotiated market, not an auction market.   (Page 153)

3. **D.** To be listed on the NYSE, a corporation must satisfy stringent requirements of the Exchange in terms of the total market value of its stock, number of stockholders and earnings. Securities can be listed on several exchanges at once.

Because each exchange is independent of all others, what happens on one exchange will not necessarily affect another exchange. All listed securities are marginable under Federal Reserve Board rules. Once a company is listed on the NYSE, it is difficult to become delisted. A request by the board of directors of a company is insufficient cause for the NYSE to grant a delisting.   (Page 152)

4. **C.** A stock exchange serves as a physical place at which brokers and dealers can conveniently transact business in securities. Specialists add to the efficiency of the system by maintaining a fair and orderly market for certain securities at their trading posts on the floor of the exchange.   (Page 151)

5. **D.** The NYSE considers many factors when determining whether a company should be delisted. Among the factors are all of the choices given.   (Page 152)

6. **C.** To be NYSE listed, a corporation must have at least 2,000 stockholders, allow stockholders to vote, have a national interest in trading the stock and meet minimum earnings and asset tests.   (Page 151)

1. Which of the following kinds of orders may be turned over to the specialist for execution?

   I. Market orders
   II. Stop orders
   III. Limit orders
   IV. Not held orders

   A. I
   B. I and II
   C. I, II and III
   D. III and IV

2. Which of the following activities are NOT part of the function of a specialist on the NYSE?

   A. Setting strike prices for options on the securities he works
   B. Keeping a book of public orders
   C. Guaranteeing an execution price for a trader who requests that the specialist stops stock for him
   D. Buying and selling stock for his own account

3. In order to narrow the spread between the bid and the asked of one of his stocks, a specialist could enter an order to buy for his own account. He would be acting in this transaction as a

   A. broker-dealer
   B. broker (or agent)
   C. dealer (or principal)
   D. market maker

4. The specialist in MCS tells a floor broker who wants to buy 300 shares of MCS for a customer that the stock is stopped at 120. This means that

   A. trading is temporarily frozen in MCS
   B. the highest offering price is 120
   C. exchange approval is required to buy MCS under 120
   D. the specialist has guaranteed to sell the stock at 120 or lower

Use the following information to answer questions 5 and 6. These orders for MCS appear in the specialist's book:

Buy	MCS	Sell
200 BD A	61	
100 BD B	1/8	
100 BD C	1/4	
	3/8	
	1/2	
	5/8	100 BD D
		300 BD E
	3/4	200 BD F
	7/8	100 BD G

5. What is the quote for MCS?

   A. 61–61 7/8
   B. 61 1/4–7/8
   C. 61 1/4–5/8
   D. 61 3/8–1/2

6. What is the size of the market for MCS?

   A. 100 by 100
   B. 100 by 400
   C. 200 by 400
   D. 400 by 700

◆ Answers & Rationale

1.   **C.**   A not held order (NH) is a market order where both price and time discretion have been given to the floor broker by the investor in order to get the best possible execution. This type of order is usually associated with large blocks of stock and is always executed by the floor broker, not the specialist. Limit and stop orders are left with the specialist for execution. Market orders may also be executed by the specialist.   (Page 156)

2.   **A.**   A specialist may engage in any or all of the listed activities in the performance of his duties as a specialist, except setting option strike prices. That is the prerogative of the Options Clearing Corporation (OCC).   (Page 155)

3.   **C.**   A specialist buying for his own account would be operating as a dealer, which means he is acting as a principal in the transaction and hopes to make a profit.   (Page 155)

4.   **D.**   The specialist has made a firm offer to sell MCS at 120 for a short period of time. The floor broker is free to attempt to buy from someone else at a better (lower) price. However, if the floor broker finds no offers, he can go back to the specialist to buy at 120. This is stopping stock. It is a courtesy extended to the floor broker by the specialist for a short period of time. It requires no special approval from the exchange and can be done only for public customer orders, not for member firm trading account orders.   (Page 158)

5.   **C.**   The quote is 61 1/4–5/8.   (Page 155)

6.   **B.**   The size of the market is the number of shares bid and offered just outside the specialist's range of prices. In this case, the size is 100 by 400.   (Page 158)

27 Types of Orders Exam

1. Which of the following statements concerning fill or kill orders and all or none orders are true?

   I.   AON orders must be filled in their entirety.

   II. FOK orders must be filled in their entirety.

   III. AON orders must be canceled if the whole order cannot be executed immediately.

   IV. FOK orders must be canceled if the whole order cannot be executed immediately.

   A. I, II and IV only
   B. I and III only
   C. II and IV only
   D. I, II, III and IV

2. Max Leveridge has placed with his broker an open order to buy 1,600 shares of GHI at $60. GHI declares a 25% stock dividend. On the ex-date this order will be considered a buy limit order for

   A. 1,600 shares at $45
   B. 1,600 shares at $50
   C. 2,000 shares at $48
   D. 2,000 shares at $60

3. Lotta Leveridge has her broker enter an order to buy GHI stock at the opening. Though transmitted promptly, the order does not reach GHI's trading post in time to be filled at the opening. How is the order handled?

   A. The order is canceled.
   B. The order is handled as a market order.
   C. The order is executed in the day, at a price as close to the opening price as possible.
   D. The order automatically becomes an *at-the-open* order the following trading session.

Use the following information to answer questions 4 and 5. Just prior to the close, a customer enters an order to sell short 200 shares of MCS at 21 3/4 stop limit GTC. The order is not elected on that day. The following trades in MCS occur at the opening of the next trading session:

---

21 1/2   21 3/8   21 5/8   21 5/8   21 5/8   21 3/4   21 7/8

---

4. Which transaction elects the order?

    A.   21 3/8
    B.   21 1/2
    C.   21 5/8
    D.   21 3/4

5. At what price is the order executed?

    A.   21 3/8
    B.   21 1/2
    C.   21 3/4
    D.   21 7/8

6. All of the following are reasons for entering a stop order EXCEPT to

    A.   protect established gains in a long position
    B.   limit losses in a long position
    C.   protect profits in a short position
    D.   guarantee execution at a specified price

7. One of your better customers wants you to place an order to sell 200 shares of Microscam with an 18 stop when the stock is trading at 18 7/8. It is the ex-date for a $.55 dividend. What will happen to your customer's stop order?

    A.   Nothing, open sell orders are not adjusted for dividends.
    B.   The stop order will be reduced to 17 3/8.
    C.   The stop order will be increased to 19.
    D.   The stop order will be reduced to 18 1/4.

8. Each of the following types of orders will remain open on the NYSE until certain conditions are met EXCEPT

    A.   stop orders
    B.   good till canceled orders
    C.   all or none orders
    D.   market orders

9. For a client to get immediate execution on an order, the order should be placed as a(n)

    A.   stop order
    B.   good till canceled order
    C.   all or none order
    D.   market order

10. A client bought 100 shares of MCS at 20. The stock rose to 30 and she would like to protect her gain. Which of the following orders should be entered?

    A.   Sell stop order at 29
    B.   Sell limit order at 30
    C.   Sell limit order at 30 1/8
    D.   Sell stop order at 30 1/8

11. KLP common stock has been recently trading between 25 1/4 and 26. Your client would like to buy 500 shares of KLP at 25. While he would like all 500 shares, he is willing to accept fewer shares at that price. Which of the following orders fulfills his intentions?

    A.   Market order to buy 500 shares of KLP at 25
    B.   Limit order to buy 500 shares of KLP at 25 AON
    C.   Limit order to buy 500 shares of KLP at 25 FOK
    D.   Limit order to buy 500 shares of KLP at 25 immediate or cancel

12. A customer sold 100 shares of QRS short when the stock was trading at 19. QRS is now trading at 14 and he would like to protect his gain. What type of order should he place?

    A. Sell stop order at 13 7/8
    B. Sell limit order at 14
    C. Buy limit order at 14
    D. Buy stop order at 14 3/8

13. An investor enters a day order to buy 200 shares of General Gizmonics at 63. Three hours later, with GIZ trading above that price, she calls wanting to change the order to a good till canceled order. The registered representative should

    I. cancel the existing order immediately
    II. leave the existing order on the specialist's books
    III. enter a new limit order to buy 200 shares of GIZ at 63 GTC immediately
    IV. enter a new limit order to buy 200 shares of GIZ at 63 GTC before the opening of the next day

    A. I and III
    B. I and IV
    C. II and III
    D. II and IV

14. Your client, who has sold 100 shares of GIZ short, places a buy stop order at 80. The order is activated when the price of GIZ

    A. falls to 80 or below
    B. falls below 80
    C. rises to 80 or above
    D. rises above 80

15. All of the following statements are true of not held orders EXCEPT that

    A. they are given to a specialist
    B. they give the floor broker discretion over the price and time of execution
    C. the "NH" code is generally used for sizable orders
    D. they may be filled a small portion at a time

16. Rhoda Bear places an order to buy 300 DWQ at 140 stop, but not over 144. This is a

    A. buy stop order
    B. buy limit order
    C. market not held order
    D. stop limit order

17. ALFAtronics has been trading around 70. A customer tells his registered representative that if he can buy 1,000 shares of the stock in one attempt, he will take it. If not, he is not interested. How should this order be entered?

    A. 1,000 ALF at 70
    B. 1,000 ALF FOK
    C. 1,000 ALF GTC
    D. 1,000 ALF IOC

18. Your client feels that General Gizmonics, currently trading around 39, would be a good buy at 38. Therefore, she places an order to buy 200 GIZ at 38 GTC. On the ex-date when the stock splits 2-for-1, her order is still on the specialist's book. How will the order be adjusted on the ex-date?

    A. Buy 100 GIZ at 76 GTC
    B. Buy 200 GIZ at 19 GTC
    C. Buy 400 GIZ at 19 GTC
    D. Buy 400 GIZ at 38 GTC

19. Randy Bear enters an order to buy GIZ at the close. GIZ traded between 70 and 71 all day and then, after a last minute rally, closed up 4 1/4 points at 74 1/4. Randy will receive

    A. the opening price the next morning
    B. the closing price
    C. the same treatment as if he had placed a not held order
    D. a price as near to the close as possible, at the discretion of the floor broker

20. An order ticket is marked: "Buy 20M GIZ
     9% Debentures at 95 AON GTC." All of the
     following statements regarding this order
     are true EXCEPT that

     A. this is a buy limit order
     B. the order will expire at the end of the day
     C. if executed, the customer will pay
         $19,000 or less for the bonds
     D. the trade will be filled in its entirety, or
         not at all

◆ Answers & Rationale

1.   **A.**   Fill or kill (FOK) orders must be executed immediately in their entirety or else canceled. All or none (AON) orders must be executed in their entirety but are not canceled if the whole order cannot be executed right away.   (Page 166)

2.   **C.**   The order is adjusted on the ex-date. The number of shares increases by the percentage of the stock dividend, and the specified price is reduced to compensate. In this case, the number of shares increased to 2,000 (1,600 + 25%), and the specified price is adjusted to $48 per share. To get the adjusted price, divide the total value of the original market order (1,600 × $60 = $96,000) by the new number of shares ($96,000 ÷ 2,000 = $48). The total market value of the order, $96,000, remains the same.   (Page 164)

3.   **A.**   An at-the-opening or at-the-opening-only order is to be filled at the opening price or not at all. At-the-opening orders for multiple round lots are to be filled to the extent possible at the opening price. All or any portion of an order not filled at the opening is canceled. An at-the-opening order arriving later must be canceled. It literally missed the opening and, therefore, could not be filled at the opening. If the at-the-opening order is marked GTC (good till canceled), it is handled differently. If such an order cannot be filled at one day's opening, it will be held and attempts will be made to fill the order at the opening in succeeding trading sessions. Do not assume an order is a GTC order unless it is specifically identified as such.   (Page 165)

4.   **B.**   Someone anticipating a downward turn in MCS might use this strategy. This is an order to sell short at 21 3/4 stop limit GTC (good till canceled). If MCS trades at or below 21 3/4, the customer will be willing to sell short the stock in anticipation of buying it back at a lower price. This downward move will help verify the customer's expectation that he made a correct decision. A stop limit has been used because the customer wishes to receive at least 21 3/4 per share as the proceeds of his short position. On the day the order was placed, it was not elected *(triggered)* because the stock did not trade at or below the stop price and, therefore, MCS was trading above 21 3/4. Before the order may become a limit order, the stop price must be elected. The opening trade of the next session, 21 1/2, triggers the order because it is lower than 21 3/4.   (Page 161)

5.   **C.**   After being triggered, the order has become a limit order at 21 3/4. The customer will accept no less than this price. Because the customer is selling short, the up tick rule also applies. The up tick requirement is met when the stock trades at 21 5/8 (in fact, each subsequent trade after 21 3/8 happens to be a plus tick or zero-plus tick), and the order then fills at 21 3/4.   (Page 161)

6.   **D.**   Stop (loss) orders are entered to protect a profit or to limit a loss. Because a stop order becomes a market order when the stop price is hit, execution at a specific price can never be guaranteed.   (Page 161)

7.   **B.**   Open buy limit orders and open stop orders to sell are reduced on the ex-dividend date. If the dividend cannot be converted exactly into eighths, the amount of reduction will be rounded up to the next eighth ($.55 rounded to the next higher eighth is 5/8).   (Page 164)

8.   **D.**   Market orders are executed immediately at the current market price if the stock is trading. A stop order will not be triggered until a set price is hit or passed through. A good till canceled order will not be filled until its price is hit or passed through. An all or none order will not be filled until the total number of shares specified is bought or sold.   (Page 160)

9.   **D.**   Market orders are executed immediately at the best available market price if the stock is trading. All of the rest of these orders might have a delayed execution if their conditions are not met.   (Page 160)

10.   **A.**   A sell limit order is used to sell out a long position at a higher price (when the market moves up). A sell stop order is used to sell out a long position at a lower price (when the market moves

down). To protect against a loss of the gain, a sell stop order would be placed just below where the stock is currently trading.   (Page 160)

11.   **D.**   Partial execution is permissible on an immediate or cancel order. An AON (all or none) or FOK (fill or kill) order requires execution in full or else the entire order is canceled. Market orders are at the current market price.   (Page 166)

12.   **D.**   A buy limit order is used to buy in a short position at a lower price (when the market moves down). A buy stop order is used to buy in a short position at a higher price (when the market moves up). To protect against the loss of the gain, a buy stop order would be placed just above where the stock is currently trading.   (Page 161)

13.   **D.**   The representative should not cancel the existing order because it would lose priority on the specialist's book. Nor should another GTC order be entered that day because the order could be filled twice. The representative should let the order stay for the day, when it would be canceled automatically if not executed; then, the rep should enter a GTC order the next morning.   (Page 165)

14.   **C.**   A buy stop order is always entered at a price above the current offering price. A buy stop order at 80 means that if the market price rises to 80 or above, the order will become a market order to buy and would be filled immediately.
        (Page 161)

15.   **A.**   In a market not held order, the client agrees not to hold the broker responsible if he cannot fill the complete order within the time limit given. Such orders allow the floor broker to use his judgment on the best execution strategy. Because specialists cannot accept orders that give them discretion over the execution, they cannot accept market not held orders.   (Page 165)

16.   **D.**   The customer has specified a stop limit order. If the stock rises to the stop price of $140, the order is elected and then becomes a buy limit order at 144, meaning an order to buy at $144 or lower.   (Page 163)

17.   **B.**   A fill or kill order designates that the customer wishes that the order be filled in its entirety in one attempt, or be canceled.   (Page 166)

18.   **C.**   In a stock split, the number of shares is increased and the price is reduced proportionately on the ex-date. Any orders on a specialist's book that are below the market will also be adjusted. 200 shares times 2 equals 400 shares; the new price will be 38 times 1/2, which is 19.   (Page 164)

19.   **D.**   When an order is placed *market at the close,* it will be executed as near to the close as possible, at the discretion of the floor broker.
        (Page 165)

20.   **B.**   The customer has placed a limit order to buy 9% debentures issued by General Gizmonics. The limit the customer is willing to pay is 95% of $20,000 worth of bonds, or $19,000 or lower. "AON" means "all or none"—either fill the order in its entirety, or do not execute the order. "GTC" is a good till canceled order, not a day order.
        (Page 165)

1. MCS closed at 32 1/2 on a plus tick on the NYSE on September 22nd. September 23rd is the ex-date for a $.28 dividend. What is the lowest price at which you could execute a short sale at the opening of trading September 23rd?

    A. 32
    B. 32 1/8
    C. 32 1/2
    D. 32 5/8

2. Traders must sell on an up tick when selling short on the

    I. exchanges
    II. over-the-counter market
    III. third market

    A. I only
    B. I and II only
    C. II and III only
    D. I, II and III

3. A customer entered an order to sell short 100 shares of Microscam. The stock closed on an up tick on Friday at 48. The stock will trade ex-dividend $.55 on Monday. What is the lowest price at which the order can be executed at the opening?

    A. 47 3/8
    B. 47 1/2
    C. 48
    D. 48 1/8

4. Randy Bear, an OTC trader, believes that ICBS, a security that trades in the national OTC market, is overpriced at 40 1/2. The current inside bid is lower than the previous bid. Randy can sell ICBS short on the over-the-counter market

    A. only at a price higher than the current inside bid
    B. only if he has an outstanding long position
    C. with no restrictions
    D. under no circumstances

5. Acme Zootech (ZOO) is trading at 50 5/8. Bea Kuhl, who owns 100 shares of the stock, places an order to sell ZOO at 50 1/4 stop limit. The Tape subsequently reports the following trades:

ZOO				
50 5/8	50 3/4	50 1/8	50 1/8	50 1/4

    Bea's order will be executed at

    A. 50 1/8
    B. 50 1/4
    C. 50 5/8
    D. 50 3/4

6. Typically, general obligation bonds are not sold short because

   A. they are backed by the full faith and credit of the issuing authority
   B. MSRB regulations prohibit short selling
   C. it is difficult to cover a short municipal position
   D. they trade over the counter

7. For purposes of the short sale rule, when does a person own a security?

   I. The person or person's agent has title to the security.
   II. The person owns a security convertible into the one that was sold short and has tendered it for conversion.
   III. The person has entered into an unconditional contract to purchase the security, but has not yet received it.
   IV. The person owns an option to purchase the security, but has not yet exercised the option.

   A. I only
   B. I, II and III only
   C. II, III and IV only
   D. I, II, III and IV

8. Sell orders sent to an exchange must be marked

   A. long or short
   B. only if they are long sales
   C. only if they are short sales
   D. Orders need not be marked, only executed in accordance with the appropriate rules.

9. When may a broker-dealer enter an order to sell a stock long?

   I. The broker-dealer has reason to believe that the customer owns the stock and will deliver it promptly.
   II. The security is carried in the customer's account at the broker-dealer.
   III. The customer owns a bond convertible into the stock and will tender the bond for conversion promptly.
   IV. The customer owns a call option on the stock and will execute the call promptly.

   A. I only
   B. I and II only
   C. II and IV only
   D. I, II, III and IV

10. A customer is long 300 shares of COD and simultaneously short 200 shares of COD. To sell the 300 shares in the long account, the customer must sell

    A. all of the shares long
    B. all of the shares short
    C. 100 shares long and 100 shares short
    D. 100 shares long and 200 shares short

11. The Nasdaq short-sale rule applies to all

    A. over-the-counter securities
    B. Nasdaq-listed securities
    C. Nasdaq National Market securities
    D. securities traded by NASD firms

12. A firm is currently long 3,000 shares of DWAQ and, as a qualified market maker, the firm is short 4,000 shares of DWAQ. For purposes of the Nasdaq short-sale rule, the firm is considered

    A. short 1,000 shares of DWAQ
    B. long 3,000 shares of DWAQ
    C. short 4,000 shares of DWAQ
    D. long 7,000 shares of DWAQ

13. An investor places an order to sell short DWAQ at-the-open. DWAQ opens at 15 3/16, the same price DWAQ closed the previous day. The previous day's close was a down bid. At what price may the investor sell short at-the-open?

A. 15 1/8
B. 15 3/16
C. 15 1/4
D. The investor is prohibited from selling short at-the-open.

◆ Answers & Rationale

1. **B.** Ticks carry forward from day to day. Normally, if a stock closed on a plus tick at 32 1/2, the next day an opening trade of 32 1/2 would be considered a zero-plus tick. Changes in price attributable to the dividend when a stock trades "ex" are ignored for tick purposes. The dividend, expressed in 1/8th increments, must always be rounded to the next highest 1/8th amount. In this case, $.28 is between 1/4th and 3/8ths. It is closer to 1/4th ($.25) but is always rounded to the higher amount, or 3/8ths ($.375). If the stock closed at 32 1/2, on a plus tick, the next day's opening trade at 32 1/8 would be considered a zero-plus tick after the dividend adjustment of 3/8ths is taken into account. Any opening trade lower than 32 1/8 would be a minus tick and therefore would not allow the execution of a short trade.   (Page 168)

2. **A.** A dealer that is making a market in an OTC stock must abide by Nasdaq's short sale rule, which is similar to but differs somewhat from the plus tick rule.   (Page 168)

3. **A.** The security price is adjusted for the dividend at its opening price the next morning. The dividend is rounded to the next highest eighth and subtracted from the closing price. The $.55 dividend is rounded to 5/8; 5/8 is subtracted from the closing price of 48. The stock should open at 47 3/8. Because the stock closed on an up tick, an opening at 47 3/8 would be a zero-plus tick and the customer's short sale can be executed.   (Page 168)

4. **A.** The security can be sold short in the OTC market by an OTC trader at a price above the current inside bid. Nasdaq's short sale rule is similar to but differs somewhat from the Exchange's plus tick rule.   (Page 168)

5. **B.** The sell stop limit order is elected (triggered) at 50 1/4 (when the stock trades at or below the stop price of 50 1/4). Now the order becomes a sell limit order at 50 1/4. The order can be executed at that price or higher (the limit placed by the customer). The next trade reported after the trigger is reached is below the limit price. The order will be executed at the next trade of 50 1/4. (Page 168)

6. **C.** Because municipal trading is limited, municipal bonds are not "fungible" (that is, identical to the point of being interchangeable) securities. With fungible securities, such as listed equities, there are many equivalent securities trading at any time. It is easy to short 100 shares of GM (borrow the stock) because an equivalent 100 shares of GM can be purchased on the NYSE at any time. It is not easy to short 5M of 6% NYC GO '05 bonds because it would be very difficult to cover the short position.   (Page 169)

7. **B.** A person is considered long a security if:

- his agent has title to it;
- he has purchased the security or has entered into an unconditional contract to purchase it, but has not yet received it;
- he owns a security convertible into or exchangeable for it and has tendered that security for conversion or exchange; or
- he has an option to purchase and has exercised the option.

     (Page 168)

8. **A.** Every sell order must be marked as either a long sale or a short sale.   (Page 169)

9. **B.** To note that an order is long, a broker-dealer is required either to have the stock in its possession or to have reasonable assurance that the customer actually owns the stock and will deliver promptly.   (Page 169)

10. **D.** In this case the customer is long 300 shares and short 200 shares of the same stock. To sell 300 shares, the customer may sell long only the shares representing the net long position; the balance must be sold short. Thus 100 shares (300 − 200) will be sold long, and the remaining 200 shares will be sold short.   (Page 168)

11. **C.** The Nasdaq short-sale rule applies only to Nasdaq National Market securities. (Page 168)

12. **A.** The firm is considered short 1,000 shares because its positions must be aggregated with its qualified market maker positions. The firm is long 3,000 shares and short 4,000 shares as a market maker, which equals a net position of 1,000 short shares.   (Page 168)

13. **C.** The opening inside bid is a "down bid" if it is lower than the previous day's closing inside bid or if it is the same as the previous day's closing inside bid if that bid was a down bid. Therefore, the opening inside bid in this problem is a down bid, and the investor must sell at least 1/16th higher than the opening bid of 15 3/16, which is 15 1/4.

(Page 168)

1. OTC trading practices in corporate securities are subject to the regulation of which of the following regulatory bodies?

   I.   SIA
   II. SEC
   III. FOMC
   IV. NASD

   A. I and II
   B. I and IV
   C. II, III and IV
   D. II and IV

2. When a broker-dealer is making a market, it is acting as a(n)

   A. agent
   B. principal
   C. broker
   D. underwriter

3. All of the following are true of the over-the-counter market EXCEPT that

   A. it is an auction market
   B. typically, bank and insurance company securities trade OTC
   C. more issues trade OTC than on the exchanges
   D. it handles large block distributions

4. Wholesale corporate bond quotes are found on the

   A. *Pink Sheets*
   B. *Yellow Sheets*
   C. *Blue List*
   D. *Green List*

5. If the broker-dealer for which you work lists a quote in the *Pink Sheets*, you know that the firm will be required to

   A. honor that quote for at least one round lot
   B. give a new quote on request
   C. buy or sell one round lot at that price or pay the difference between its quote and that of the next market maker
   D. do nothing because the *Pink Sheets* quotes are expected to be outdated anyway

6. One of your penny-stock customers wants to sell his 25 shares of This Can't Be Sushi, which he heard has appreciated to 9/16ths per share. There is only one TCBS market maker (the one you called when you sold your customer the stock last week), so where would you have to go to get a quote?

   A. *The Blue List*
   B. The *Yellow Sheets*
   C. The *Pink Sheets*
   D. *The Wall Street Journal*

7. Which of the following securities trade on the over-the-counter market?

    I.   Government and agency securities
    II. Open-ended investment companies
    III. Large block distributions of listed securities
    IV. American depositary receipts

    A. I, II and III
    B. I and III
    C. I, III and IV
    D. II and IV

8. Quotations in the *Pink Sheets*

    A. are reports of last sale prices or closing prices
    B. report bids wanted or offers wanted
    C. are reliable for quoting thinly traded OTC stock prices to customers
    D. are assumed to be firm quotes unless otherwise stated

9. Which of the following reports must be filed by registered market makers in the Nasdaq system?

    I.   Monthly market-making recap report along with the specific data required by the NASD Board of Governors
    II. Quarterly report of profit and loss from market-making activities as required by the Board of Governors
    III. Daily report of trading volume
    IV. Weekly report of trading volume

    A. I and III only
    B. II and IV only
    C. III and IV only
    D. I, II, III and IV

10. For which of the following reasons may a market maker be prohibited from entering quotations in the Nasdaq system?

    I.   The member is undergoing financial or operating difficulties to the point that investors might be jeopardized.
    II. The member has been suspended or expelled from NASD membership.
    III. The member has been suspended or expelled from membership in a national securities exchange.

    A. I only
    B. I and II only
    C. III only
    D. I, II and III

◆ Answers & Rationale

1.   **D.**   The Securities and Exchange Commission (SEC) is responsible for the regulation of nonexempt securities trading throughout the United States. The NASD is the duly authorized SRO for the OTC market. The Securities Industry Association is a trade organization for promoting the interests of the securities business. The Federal Open Market Committee determines the course of open market purchases and sales by the Fed in effecting monetary policy.   (Page 175)

2.   **B.**   Making markets is a principal activity. The broker-dealer stands ready, willing and able to buy or sell securities for its own account. A dealer acts as a principal when it owns the securities it is trading. When the broker-dealer is not acting for its own account, it is acting as a broker or an agent.
(Page 176)

3.   **A.**   The OTC market is a negotiated market; the exchanges are auction markets.   (Page 175)

4.   **B.**   The *Yellow Sheets* provide dealer-to-dealer quotes for corporate bonds traded over the counter. *The Blue List* is for municipal bonds; the *Pink Sheets* are for OTC stocks.   (Page 177)

5.   **B.**   Any market maker that lists a quote for a stock in the *Pink Sheets* will not be held to the quote, but must stand ready to give a new quote for one round lot on request.   (Page 177)

6.   **C.**   Quotes for securities that are inactively traded, have few market makers and are relatively low priced will typically be found in the *Pink Sheets*. The *Pink Sheets* are a publication of the National Quotation Bureau and contain quotes and names of market makers for thousands of thinly traded OTC stocks.   (Page 177)

7.   **C.**   Municipal bonds, government and agency securities and corporate securities all trade in the OTC market. Often, it is easier for institutions to trade large blocks of listed stock off the exchange in a negotiated market, rather than on the exchange, so they also trade OTC. Foreign securities trade in the United States if the companies comply with SEC registration and disclosure requirements. Mutual fund shares (open-end companies) do not trade; they are bought OTC and are redeemed OTC, but there is no trading in the shares. Closed-end investment companies, however, do trade OTC.   (Page 175)

8.   **B.**   Quotes shown in the *Pink Sheets* are never firm quotes; bid and offer prices shown are always subject to prior sale and/or revision. Bids wanted and offers wanted also appear in the *Pink Sheets*.   (Page 177)

9.   **A.**   Reports to be made by all registered market makers are (1) monthly reports of trading data and other information required by NASD rules, and (2) daily reports of trading volume.
(Page 176)

10.   **D.**   Financial difficulties or expulsion from membership in a regulatory body can lead to a member being prohibited from entering quotes.
(Page 176)

Quotations Exam

1. You are a municipal bond trader, and have been given a firm quote with five-minute recall. Forty-five minutes later, the quoting dealer gives you a fill or kill. What does this mean?

   A. The five-minute recall is canceled; you must take the securities immediately or lose the trade.
   B. You have placed the order with the quoting dealer, and it is now going to attempt to fill it.
   C. The quoting dealer wants five minutes' advance notice if you fill the trade.
   D. You have five minutes to fill the order or lose the securities.

2. A market maker gives a firm quote of 20–20 3/8. The purchasing dealer says, "I'll buy 500 shares at the offering price." The market maker must give

   A. 100 shares at 20
   B. 100 shares at 20 3/8
   C. 500 shares at 20
   D. 500 shares at 20 3/8

3. Dullard Securities has made a firm offer for 30 minutes with recall to The Walrus Capital Group. What does this mean?

   I. Dullard cannot change the price for 30 minutes.
   II. Walrus must buy the bonds within the next 30 minutes.
   III. Dullard must call Walrus before selling the bonds to another dealer.

   A. I only
   B. I and III only
   C. II and III only
   D. I, II and III

4. If an OTC market maker provides a firm quote to another broker-dealer, but then refuses to buy or sell at the price quoted, such a market maker is said to be

   A. freeriding
   B. crossing quotes
   C. backing away
   D. interpositioning

5. An OTC quote that must be reconfirmed with the OTC trading room before a broker-dealer takes action on it is called a

   A. representative quote
   B. subject quote
   C. third party quote
   D. firm quote

6. An OTC trader's quote of "60 to 63, work out" in response to a broker holding a customer order to sell a block of stock indicates that the

    A. quote is firm and the customer can sell an unlimited amount of stock at 60 or buy at 63
    B. market maker guarantees that a customer buy order can be filled no higher than 60
    C. quote is firm, but the market maker must be given discretion over when the transaction will take place
    D. quote is tentative (nominal), merely suggesting a range in which the buy order is likely to be filled

7. A market maker entering a two-sided quote on a stock must honor that quote for

    A. the normal trading unit on either side of the market
    B. 300 shares or ten bonds
    C. 500 shares or ten bonds
    D. at least 30 minutes

8. If a market maker is quoting the market 30 to 1/2 and a broker-dealer contacts the market maker offering to buy 300 shares at 30 1/2, the market maker

    A. must sell 300 shares at 30 1/2
    B. must sell 100 shares at 30 1/2
    C. may withdraw the asking price because the other firm is bidding for more than 100 shares
    D. may do none of the above

Use the following information to answer questions 9 and 10. Assume that four market makers are quoting a stock as follows:

Broker-Dealer	Bid	Ask
1	34 1/4	35 1/8
2	34 3/8	35 1/8
3	34 1/2	34 7/8
4	34 3/8	34 3/4

9. Which of these broker-dealers would you trade with if you wanted to buy stock, either for your own account or to fill a customer buy order?

    A. #1
    B. #2
    C. #3
    D. #4

10. Which of these broker-dealers would another dealer trade with if it wanted to sell stock, either for its own account or to fill a customer sell order?

    A. #1
    B. #2
    C. #3
    D. #4

11. How many shares is a Nasdaq market maker obligated to buy or sell on a given market if it receives an order for 1,000 shares?

    A. 100
    B. 1,000
    C. Any part of the order
    D. None of the order

◆ Answers & Rationale

1. **D.** A five-minute recall means that the quoting dealer will hold the securities while you attempt to find a buyer (or seller) at the price the dealer quoted, but it reserves the right to cut the amount of time you have to five minutes if another trader comes in with a firm order.   (Page 179)

2. **B.** The market maker giving the firm quote is only obliged to deliver 100 shares at the asking price of 20 3/8.   (Page 178)

3. **B.** A firm offer for 30 minutes means that the selling firm cannot change the price for this time period. The selling firm further promises to call the buying firm before selling the bonds to another firm. The buying firm is now assured that it can get the bonds from the selling firm. Therefore, the buying firm is free to try to sell them, even without actually purchasing them from the selling firm; the buying firm does not have to buy the bonds unless it so chooses.   (Page 179)

4. **C.** Each quote is good for 100 shares. A dealer who does not honor his quote is said to be "backing away."   (Page 179)

5. **B.** A subject quote must always be reconfirmed with the OTC trader or market maker that provided it before a trade can take place. Subject quotes are typically used in conjunction with thinly traded securities or prior to filling fairly large block orders.   (Page 179)

6. **D.** The term "work out" means that the quote is approximate or nominal. As with a subject quote, the OTC trader who supplied the quote most likely will have to negotiate with a number of market makers in order to get a customer's securities sold or bought.   (Page 180)

7. **A.** Each quote is good for a normal unit of trading, which is customarily, but not necessarily, 100 shares of stock or five bonds.   (Page 179)

8. **B.** Each quote is good for the normal unit of trading, which is customarily 100 shares.
                         (Page 178)

9. **D.** You would want to buy at the least expensive price, which is broker-dealer #4's ask price of 34 3/4.   (Page 180)

10. **C.** If the dealer is selling, of course it wants to get the highest price possible. In this case it would sell to broker-dealer #3 at 34 1/2, the best bid price listed.   (Page 180)

11. **A.** Quotes on Nasdaq are good for only 100 shares. The balance of the order is up for negotiation.   (Page 178)

31 NASD 5% Markup Policy Exam

1. An NASD member firm is selling stock to a customer from inventory. The shares sold have been held by the broker-dealer for several months. What price should the dealer use as a basis for a markup?

   A. Price at which the securities were purchased
   B. Offer price shown in the *Pink Sheets* on the day of the current sale
   C. Broker-dealer's own current offer price
   D. Best offering price quoted in the inter-dealer market

Use the following information to answer questions 2 and 3. Assume that four market makers are quoting a stock as follows:

Broker-Dealer	Bid	Ask
1	34 1/4	35 1/8
2	34 3/8	35 1/8
3	34 1/2	34 7/8
4	34 3/8	34 3/4

2. If broker-dealer #1 sells stock to a customer from inventory at a net price that includes a markup, which base price is used to compute the percentage of markup?

   A. 34 1/4 (broker-dealer #1's bid)
   B. 34 1/2 (broker-dealer #3's bid)
   C. 34 3/4 (broker-dealer #4's ask)
   D. 35 1/8 (broker-dealer #2's ask)

3. If broker-dealer #2 buys stock from a customer for inventory at a net price that includes a markdown, which base price is used to compute the percentage of markdown?

   A. 34 1/4 (broker-dealer #1's bid)
   B. 34 3/8 (broker-dealer #2's bid)
   C. 34 1/2 (broker-dealer #3's bid)
   D. 34 3/4 (broker-dealer #4's ask)

4. The NASD's 5% policy applies to

   I. commissions charged when executing customer agency (broker) transactions
   II. markups and markdowns on principal (dealer) transactions filled for customers from a firm's trading inventory
   III. markups on stock bought for inventory and immediately resold to customers
   IV. markdowns on stocks bought from customers for inventory and then immediately resold to another broker-dealer

   A. I and II only
   B. II only
   C. III and IV only
   D. I, II, III and IV

5. June Polar places an order to sell $10,000 worth of one stock, and the firm adds a commission. With the proceeds, June buys $10,000 worth of another stock, and the firm adds a markup. To comply with fairness guidelines, the member firm

A. should consider the combined commission and markup earned by the firm
B. may handle this type of transaction on an agency basis only
C. may consider each side separately and charge its normal commission or markup on the purchase and the sale
D. should charge either a commission or a markup on only one side of the transaction

6. Which of the following transactions is(are) not subject to the NASD's 5% policy on markups and markdowns?

I. New issue corporate equity securities sold in a public offering
II. Mutual fund shares sold to the public
III. Transactions on the NYSE or other national exchanges
IV. NYSE-listed stock traded in the third market

A. I and II only
B. I, II and III only
C. III only
D. I, II, III and IV

7. Which of the following is true of the NASD's 5% policy?

A. It allows the member to determine fair markups based on the firm's actual acquisition costs.
B. It is a guide to fairness, not a rule.
C. It automatically judges any markup or markdown in excess of 5% to be unfair.
D. It applies only to common stock transactions.

8. The NASD's 5% policy applies especially to a member firm that

I. purchases a security from a market maker to fill a customer buy order, charging the customer a commission
II. purchases a security to fill a customer order
III. purchases a security from a customer for its inventory
IV. sells a customer a mutual fund

A. I, II and III only
B. II and III only
C. IV only
D. I, II, III and IV

9. A dealer disclosing before a transaction the markup amount it will charge and a customer accepting this amount

A. justifies charging markups that otherwise might be considered excessive
B. is one factor in determining the fairness of the broker-dealer's markup or markdown
C. has no bearing on whether a markup or markdown is deemed to be fair or unfair
D. is possible only with new issue securities sold by prospectus

10. Which of the following is(are) relevant in applying the 5% policy?

A. Amount of money involved
B. Type of security
C. Current price of the security
D. All of the above

11. On which of the following would the highest markup be justified?

A. Convertible bond
B. Municipal bond
C. Odd lot of stock selling at a low price
D. Riskless or simultaneous transaction

---

12. The NASD's 5% policy applies to

    I.   agency sales in the OTC market
    II. agency sales on a national exchange
    III. principal transactions in the OTC market
    IV. fourth-market (INSTINET) transactions

    A. I
    B. I and III
    C. I and IV
    D. II and III

13. Assume that a broker-dealer buys stock from a market maker to fill a customer order to buy 100 DWAQ when the market maker is quoting the stock at "20 bid–20 3/4 ask," and this quote represents the inside market. The broker-dealer then fills the customer buy order at 21 1/2 net. What is the percentage markup to the customer?

    A. 3.5%
    B. 3.6%
    C. 3.7%
    D. 7.5%

14. Assume that a broker-dealer is a market maker quoting a particular stock at "16 bid–16 3/4 ask." Another market maker is quoting the same stock at "16 1/4 bid–16 1/2 ask," which is the best two-sided quote at the moment and therefore is the inside market. If the first broker-dealer fills a customer sell order as principal at a net price, which of the following prices must be used as the base figure for determining the percentage markdown to the customer?

    A. 16
    B. 16 1/4
    C. 16 1/2
    D. 16 3/4

15. A broker-dealer purchased 100 shares of stock from a customer at 18 when the broker-dealer's market was 18 3/4–19 1/4. The inside market was 18 7/8–19 1/8. The quote published in the *Pink Sheets* was 18 1/2–19 3/8. What was the markdown percentage to the customer?

    A. 2.7%
    B. 4%
    C. 4.6%
    D. 8%

16. Assume that a customer sells 100 shares of ICBS to a broker-dealer at 25 net. The inside market at the time of this trade was 25 3/4–26 1/4. The customer then buys 100 shares of TCBS at 25 net from the same broker-dealer when the inside market is being quoted 23 1/2–24. What is the total markup (markdown) percentage?

    A. 3.7%
    B. 4.2%
    C. 7.3%
    D. 8.6%

17. Over-the-counter transactions are governed by the NASD 5% markup policy to

    A. limit each customer trade to 5% of the customer's total portfolio value
    B. ensure fair and reasonable customer transactions
    C. set agency commissions at 5% on OTC transactions
    D. set principal markups at 5% on OTC transactions

18. Under the NASD rules for OTC dealers, in an agency transaction commissions are determined by all of the following EXCEPT the

    A. availability of the security
    B. dollar value of the security
    C. costs involved in executing the trade
    D. cost price of the securities held in inventory by the dealer

19. The NASD 5% markup policy applies to dealers trading in

    A. shares of a registered secondary offering requiring a prospectus
    B. open-end investment companies
    C. securities trading in the OTC market by a dealer
    D. all of the above

20. Under the NASD 5% markup policy, an OTC firm that is a market maker in DWAQ common stock will consider which of the following to determine a markup to a customer?

    I.   Cost of services provided by the firm
    II. Price of the security
    III. Amount of the purchase
    IV. Profit or loss to the firm on that specific transaction

    A. I, II and III
    B. I, III and IV
    C. I and IV
    D. II and III

21. The NASD 5% markup policy applies to

    A. principal OTC trades
    B. mutual funds
    C. new issues
    D. all of the above

22. Under NASD rules, a simultaneous trade in the OTC market is

    A. permitted and must conform to the NASD 5% markup policy
    B. permitted and must conform to the 8 1/2% guideline
    C. permitted only when acting as dealer
    D. not permitted

23. A dealer paid 18 for a stock for its inventory. The average price for the stock yesterday was 21 and it closed at 20 7/8. Today, a customer pays 23 net for the stock from the dealer's inventory. At the time of the trade, the interdealer quote for this stock was 20 3/4–21. The percent markup is

    A. 21.7%
    B. 14.2%
    C. 9.5%
    D. 8.7%

24. Riskless or simultaneous transactions

    A. require disclosure of the markup by the firm executing the transactions
    B. are illegal transactions under NASD rules
    C. do not require application of the NASD 5% markup policy
    D. do not require disclosure of the markup by the firm executing the transactions

25. In a proceeds transaction for a customer where the proceeds from the liquidation of one OTC stock are used to purchase another OTC stock, the NASD 5% markup policy applies to

    A. each side of the transaction separately
    B. the combined profit of both the buy side and the sell side
    C. the profit on the buy side only
    D. the profit on the sell side only

◆ Answers & Rationale

1.   **D.**   NASD rules require that a dealer's markup to a customer be based on the current market rather than the dealer's cost. The dealer's potential loss on inventory is considered to be the risk of making a market.   (Page 183)

2.   **C.**   Because the customer is buying, the transaction must be priced off the inside-market ask price, which is broker-dealer #4's asking price of 34 3/4.   (Page 183)

3.   **C.**   This time the customer is selling. Customer sell orders executed as principal must always be priced off the inside-market bid price, which is broker-dealer #3's bid for stock at 34 1/2.   (Page 183)

4.   **D.**   The 5% policy applies both to commission charges on agency transactions and to markups and markdowns on principal transactions with customers.   (Page 182)

5.   **A.**   This question describes a proceeds transaction. The customer is selling one security and using the proceeds to buy another security. The member firm handling this customer must consider both sides of the trade in determining its total profit on the transaction.   (Page 183)

6.   **B.**   The NASD's 5% policy applies to all OTC transactions except public offering stocks (including mutual fund shares) and exempt securities. Because the 5% policy applies to all OTC trading, it includes third-market transactions in listed stocks, but not listed securities traded on an exchange.   (Page 182)

7.   **B.**   The 5% policy is only a guide to fair markups and commissions; it is not a strict rule. Markups or markdowns that amount to more than 5% may very well be justified; and by the same token, a markup of only 1% or 2% could be excessive, depending on the size of the transaction and the dollar amount of the markup or commission charge.   (Page 182)

8.   **A.**   The 5% policy applies to all OTC transactions except for exempt securities and securities sold by prospectus at fixed prices or prices determined by a fixed formula, as is the case with mutual funds.   (Page 182)

9.   **B.**   Advance disclosure of a markup helps justify an unusually large markup, but such action is just one factor to be considered.   (Page 184)

10.   **D.**   Each item listed is part of the relevant circumstances on which the 5% markup is based.   (Page 183)

11.   **C.**   Because of the small size of a trade, a higher markup is justified to defray costs.   (Page 183)

12.   **B.**   The NASD's markup policies do not apply to transactions in listed securities traded on a national securities exchange. Neither do the NASD's regulatory powers extend to the fourth market, which consists of nonmember institutional investors trading among themselves.   (Page 182)

13.   **B.**   A markup or markdown is always based on the inside-market price at the time of the transaction (markups on customer buy transactions are based on the inside-market ask price; markdowns on customer sell transactions are based on the inside-market bid price). In this case the customer is buying at a net price of 21 1/2 ($2,150), which is 3/4ths of a point ($75) higher than the inside-market ask price of 20 3/4 ($2,075). Thus, the markup is 3.6%, computed as follows: $75 ÷ $2,075 = 3.6%.   (Page 182)

14.   **B.**   If a dealer buys from a customer in a principal transaction, the inside-market bid price is always the prevailing market price for markdown calculation purposes. In this case the bid side of the inside market is 16 1/4, the base price all broker-dealers must use in pricing customer sell orders at a net price (which includes a markdown).   (Page 182)

15.   **C.**   The inside market is 18 7/8–19 1/8. The price to the customer is 18. Thus the markdown is 7/8 ($87.50) from the bid price of 18 7/8

($1,887.50), computed as follows: $87.50 ÷ $1,887.50 = 4.6%. (Page 182)

16. **C.** This question describes a combined markup on a proceeds transaction, in which case the profits on both the buy and sell must be taken into consideration. On the customer sell side, the net price to the customer was 25, which is a markdown of 3/4ths of a point ($75) from the inside bid of 25 3/4. On the customer buy side, the net price is again 25, which is one full point ($100) markup on the inside ask price of 24. Thus the broker-dealer's total profit on this transaction is $175. The next step is to compute the percentage markup this $175 represents based on the inside market (24 ask) on the customer buy transaction. The answer is 7.3% ($175 ÷ $2,400). (Page 183)

17. **B.** The NASD 5% markup policy states that the over-the-counter markups and commissions to customers must be fair and reasonable. Five percent is a guideline, not a rule. (Page 182)

18. **D.** Under the NASD 5% markup policy, the factors to be taken into consideration when determining a markup commission include: dollar amount of the trade, size of the trade, difficulty, any special costs incurred, etc. The relevant price from which to mark up the security is the current market price—not the actual cost of the shares in inventory. (Page 183)

19. **C.** The NASD 5% markup policy applies to all over-the-counter trades except exempt securities and those where a prospectus is required. Mutual fund sales require delivery of a prospectus, as do registered offerings. (Page 182)

20. **A.** Any inventory profit or loss is not considered under the NASD 5% markup policy.
(Page 183)

21. **A.** The NASD 5% markup policy applies to agency and principal OTC transactions; it does not apply to prospectus offerings (mutual funds and new issues). (Page 182)

22. **A.** In a normal agency trade, the broker goes to a market maker to buy for a customer and would charge a commission. In a riskless or simultaneous trade, the broker is performing the exact same transaction except that it is accounted for in a different manner. The broker-dealer will buy the security into its inventory account and simultaneously sell the same security out of that account to the customer; this procedure is permissible under NASD rules. The markup or commission that is charged must be fair and reasonable under the 5% policy. (Page 183)

23. **C.** The percent markup is calculated from the prevailing market price of the stock, regardless of the cost to the dealer. The prevailing market price is not simply the closing price; it refers to the inside market price. The amount of the markup is the customer's net price minus the inside ask price, divided by the inside ask price. In this case, 23 minus 21 equals 2; 2 divided by 21 equals 9.5%. (Page 183)

24. **A.** A broker-dealer must disclose the markup in a riskless or simultaneous transaction. (Page 183)

25. **B.** In a proceeds transaction (sell one position; take the proceeds and buy another), the NASD 5% markup policy allows a combined markup or commission representing both sides of the trade. (Page 183)

1. Last sale price information is available for Nasdaq National Market stocks. Which of the following are true concerning the reporting of that information to the system?

   I. The trade must be reported within 90 seconds of execution.
   II. The trade must be reported immediately after the completion of the transaction.
   III. The selling broker-dealer must report the trade.
   IV. The buying broker-dealer must report the trade.

   A. I and III
   B. I and IV
   C. II and III
   D. II and IV

2. The primary purpose for requiring OTC dealers to provide reports of trades in Nasdaq National Market securities is to provide

   A. regulators with a better audit trail
   B. a means of detecting odd lot trading activity
   C. investors with information
   D. a mechanism for preventing short sales in declining markets

3. How many firms must be making markets in a stock before that stock can be entered on Nasdaq Level 1?

   A. One
   B. Two
   C. Five
   D. Ten

4. An over-the-counter dealer has had no activity in the OTC stocks in which it makes a market. When must the market maker report its volume to the Nasdaq?

   A. As soon as the stock begins to trade
   B. Daily
   C. Weekly
   D. Quarterly

5. All of the following statements are true of Nasdaq Level 3 EXCEPT that

   A. it shows volume at the end of the day
   B. actual interdealer quotes are displayed
   C. the quotes are entered by market makers
   D. the system displays trades as they occur

6. Which of the following describes the Nasdaq Level 1 service?

    A. Quotations from all registered market makers currently making a market in the stock
    B. Ability to enter quotations into the system for securities in which a market maker is registered
    C. Best bid and ask quotations on a security in which there are a minimum of two market makers
    D. Representative bid and ask quotations on a security in which there are a minimum of three market makers

7. Which of the following describes the Nasdaq Level 2 service?

    A. Quotations from all registered market makers currently making a market in the stock
    B. Ability to enter quotations into the system for securities in which a market maker is registered
    C. Representative bid and ask quotations on a security in which there are a minimum of two market makers
    D. Representative bid and ask quotations on a security in which there are a minimum of three market makers

8. Which of the following describes the Nasdaq Level 3 service?

    A. Quotations from all registered market makers entering quotes into the system
    B. Ability to enter quotations into the system for securities in which a market maker is registered
    C. Representative bid and ask quotations on a security in which there are a minimum of two market makers
    D. Representative bid and ask quotations on a security in which there are a minimum of three market makers

9. To be accepted as an NNM security, a company must be qualified in which of the following areas?

    I.   Market value of shares
    II.   Number of market makers registered
    III. Annual net income
    IV.   Number of publicly held shares

    A. I and II
    B. I, III and IV
    C. II and IV
    D. I, II, III and IV

◆ Answers & Rationale

1.   **A.**   Reported securities are those that report real time sale information (within 90 seconds). This includes Nasdaq National Market securities. Reporting rules typically require the selling broker-dealer to make a report of the transaction.
(Page 187)

2.   **C.**   Reporting of trades as they occur (price and volume) in certain over-the-counter securities was initiated by the NASD in order to provide the market (investors) with more detailed and current trading information than had previously been available.
(Page 189)

3.   **B.**   A stock must have two active market makers before it can be included on Nasdaq.
(Page 189)

4.   **B.**   Market makers are required to report daily, regardless of the volume of their trading.
(Page 187)

5.   **D.**   Level 3 of the National Association of Securities Dealers Automated Quotation System (Nasdaq) gives current bid/ask quotes. It also shows volume at the end of the day, but trades are never shown. Level 3 is entered by the market makers that have access to the machines to change quotes. Any change in the quote is reflected across the country in five seconds.
(Page 186)

6.   **C.**   Nasdaq Level 1 service shows the best current bid and ask quotation (the inside market) on each security that has at least two market makers.
(Page 185)

7.   **A.**   Nasdaq Level 2 service displays all bids and offers for all market makers in a security.
(Page 185)

8.   **B.**   Nasdaq Level 3 service allows market makers to enter and update quotations on securities in which each market maker is registered with the NASD.
(Page 185)

9.   **D.**   Minimum standards apply in all of these areas in order to qualify the larger issuers for Nasdaq National Market (NNM) listing.
(Page 189)

33 Computerized Order Routing Exam

1. SuperDot is the electronic order system used by which of the following markets for trading common stocks?

   A. New York Stock Exchange
   B. OTC market
   C. Chicago Board Options Exchange
   D. Philadelphia Stock Exchange

2. All of the following actions are prohibited by the NASD when using its Small Order Execution System to trade securities EXCEPT

   A. splitting large customer orders into small ones in order to meet the 1,000-share order-size limit of SOES
   B. entering riskless and simultaneous transactions
   C. the use of SOES by broker-dealers who keep their orders under the maximum size limit
   D. entering odd lot orders for execution at next trade or selling shares short

3. The NASD's Consolidated Quotations Service is primarily designed to

   A. automatically execute trades of between 1,000 and 2,099 shares for public customers
   B. provide both bid and asked quotes from registered market makers in Nasdaq OTC securities to broker-dealers
   C. provide both bid and asked quotes from registered third-market makers in exchange-traded securities only to broker-dealers
   D. automatically execute trades of between 1,000 and 2,099 shares for professional traders

4. The Consolidated Quotation Service provides

   A. bid and ask quotations for all market makers in listed securities
   B. reports of all transactions in OTC securities
   C. reports of all transactions in OTC securities by third-market makers
   D. bid and ask quotations for third-market makers in listed securities

5. The Consolidated Quotation Service is open

   A. from 8:00 am to 7:30 pm Eastern time
   B. from 9:30 am to 6:30 pm Eastern time
   C. from 9:30 am to 5:00 pm Eastern time
   D. from 10:00 am to 5:30 pm Eastern time

6. Unless specified otherwise, for what period of time will a quote entered on Nasdaq's Intermarket Trading System/Computer Assisted Execution System be considered firm?

    A. 30 seconds
    B. 1 minute
    C. 2 minutes
    D. 5 minutes

7. Which of the following statements about the NASD's Consolidated Quotation System are true?

    I.   All NYSE- and AMEX-listed securities are eligible for quotation.
    II. It is designed for third market traders.
    III. Designated securities on regional exchanges are eligible for quotation.
    IV. It facilitates institution-to-institution direct trades.

    A. I and II only
    B. I, II and III only
    C. III and IV only
    D. I, II, III and IV

8. Which of the following statements about SOES are true?

    I.   NNM market makers are not required to participate.
    II. It facilitates trading orders of up to 1,000 shares.
    III. Institutions and broker-dealers may not use it to trade for their own accounts.
    IV. It facilitates fourth market trades.

    A. I, II, and III
    B. I and III
    C. II and III
    D. II and IV

9. All of the following computer systems are used to facilitate order execution EXCEPT

    A. SOES
    B. SuperDot
    C. ORS
    D. CQS

10. The NYSE SuperDot system does all of the following EXCEPT

    A. routes a customer order directly to the specialist
    B. sends an execution report from the commission broker to the brokerage firm
    C. presents an order to the auction market
    D. automatically pairs one order with another through a computer

◆ Answers & Rationale

1.   **A.**   Many markets have introduced computerized automated order routing and execution systems. An automatic execution system automatically executes market orders or limit orders. The system verifies the execution of the trade back to the broker-dealer and to the market maker with which the trade was executed. An order routing system does not automatically execute transactions but electronically directs orders to the appropriate market location of execution. Confirmation of executed trades are then electronically sent to the firm originating the order. The following order routing and execution systems are used:

- The NYSE uses the Super Designated Order Turnaround system. SuperDot can process market orders for up to 2,099 shares, including odd lot orders.
- The OTC market has two automatic execution systems. The Small Order Execution System (SOES) executes trades for 1,000 or fewer shares. The Computer Assisted Execution System (CAES) executes trades mostly in listed securities traded OTC and in some NNM securities.
- The Chicago Board Options Exchange uses the Order Routing System (ORS). The ORS sends trades to the appropriate destinations. Market orders and executable limit orders are sent to the Retail Automatic Execution System (RAES), which is part of ORS.
- The Philadelphia Exchange uses PHLX Automated Communication and Execution system (PACE).

(Page 192)

2.   **B.**   The NASD's Small Order Execution System was designed to help the small investor trade securities. A riskless and simultaneous transaction is one in which a broker-dealer buys stock in the market for its inventory on the order of a customer, and then immediately uses it to fill the customer's order (and the same on the sell side), a permissible use of SOES.   (Page 194)

3.   **C.**   The NASD's Consolidated Quotation System (CQS) is designed primarily to provide bid and asked quotes from registered OTC market makers in exchange-listed securities to broker-dealers. The market makers that use the system must be willing to buy or sell at least one normal trading unit of each security for which they enter a quote.   (Page 195)

4.   **D.**   The Consolidated Quotation Service (CQS) shows trades in exchange-listed stocks executed in the OTC market.   (Page 195)

5.   **B.**   Operating hours for the CQS are 9:30 am to 6:30 pm Eastern time.   (Page 195)

6.   **C.**   Quotes entered by market makers on the ITS/CAES will be considered firm and irrevocable for a period of two minutes unless the market maker specifically states that it is a one-minute quote.

(Page 195)

7.   **B.**   The NASD's CQS provides third-market quotations for listed securities, including certain regionally listed securities. The INSTINET quotation system handles fourth market (institutional) trades.   (Page 195)

8.   **C.**   The Small Order Execution System is designed for public market and executable limit orders of up to 1,000 shares. All Nasdaq National Market market makers must participate. Institutions and broker-dealers may not trade for their own accounts through SOES, since it is not intended for large or frequent trades. The INSTINET quotation system handles fourth market (institutional) trades.   (Page 194)

9.   **D.**   The NASD's Consolidated Quotation System reports quotations and last sales only. It does not actually facilitate the order process. The Small Order Execution System, the NYSE's Super Designated Order Turnaround, and the CBOE's Order Routing System are all electronic systems that facilitate order execution.   (Page 195)

10. **C.** Only the specialist or commission broker can present an order to the auction market. Computerized trading and execution systems handle all types of orders. They speed up the communication of each order and ensure that it reaches the appropriate market maker.   (Page 192)

34 The Consolidated Tape Exam

1. A registered representative observes the following on her quote machine.

IBS.P	B 32 1/2	A 32 3/4	Last 32 5/8

On which exchange and at what price can a customer purchase IBS?

I. PSE
II. PHLX
III. 32 1/2
IV. 32 3/4

A. I and III
B. I and IV
C. II and III
D. II and IV

2. If the following information appeared on your quote machine, how would you respond to a customer inquiry about the current quote on DWAQ stock?

	DWAQ				
L	25 3/8	O	25 3/8	C	24 7/8
B	25	H	25 3/8	NC	+ 1/2
A	25 1/2	L	24 7/8	V	424
				T	9:50

A. "The previous close was at 25 3/8."
B. "The stock last traded at 24 7/8."
C. "DWAQ is quoted 24 7/8 bid–25 3/8 ask."
D. "DWAQ is quoted 25 bid–25 1/2 ask."

3. The Consolidated Tape reported the following transaction:

DWQ Pr	TPL	AMF
5 ^S_S26	26	2s91

This means that

A. 26 shares of DWQ preferred traded short at 5
B. 50 shares of DWQ preferred traded at 26
C. 100 shares of DWQ preferred reverse split 5-to-1 and traded at 26
D. 500 shares of DWQ preferred traded at 26

4. Transactions involving which of the following would NOT appear on the Consolidated Tape?

A. NYSE-listed securities traded on the Chicago and Pacific exchanges
B. options
C. INSTINET
D. NYSE rights and warrants

5. Which of the following securities transactions would have to be reported to the Consolidated Tape?

I. 200 shares of Datawaq bought on the NYSE
II. 1,200 shares of Microscam sold on the Pacific Stock Exchange
III. 25 shares of This Can't Be Sushi bought OTC
IV. 5,000 shares of Consolidated Codfish sold to Microscam by Datawaq's pension account that did not occur through INSTINET

A. I and II
B. II, III and IV
C. III and IV
D. IV

6. An NASD member that is qualified and registered to transact business in listed securities in over-the-counter transactions must report this type of transaction to the Consolidated Tape within how many seconds of execution?

A. 30
B. 60
C. 90
D. 120

7. The Consolidated Tape reads:

TCB	ICB
12.4s11 7/8	29.29 1/8

Which of the following statements is(are) correct?

I. 40 shares of TCB traded at 11 7/8
II. 100 shares of TCB traded at 11 7/8
III. 100 shares of TCB traded at 12
IV. 400 shares of TCB traded at 11 7/8

A. I and III
B. II
C. III
D. III and IV

8. The Consolidated Tape erroneously reported the execution of 100 shares of ALF at 29 1/2. The brokerage firm confirmed the price to the customer. The firm later finds that the actual price was 29 3/4. What price will the customer pay for the shares?

A. 29 1/2
B. 29 5/8, with the difference split between the firm and the customer
C. 29 3/4
D. He has the option of canceling the order.

9. The Consolidated Tape reported the following:

ALF	DWQ
40 1/8.1/4	91.91 1/4

Which of the following statements is(are) correct?

I.   The previous order of 100 shares of ALF at 40 1/8 was in error.
II. 100 shares of ALF sold at 40 1/8.
III. 100 shares of ALF sold at 40 1/4.
IV. ALF closed up 1/4 point.

A. I and III
B. II
C. II and III
D. II and IV

10. The Consolidated Tape reported the following:

ALF.SLD	DWQ
70 1/8	91.91 1/4

The symbol "SLD" means that ALFAtronics stock

A. sold short for 70 1/8
B. sold in a special block sale off the floor
C. has stopped trading at 70 1/8
D. was reported out of sequence

11. Which of the following trades is(are) reported on the Consolidated Tape?

A. NYSE stocks traded on the Pacific Stock Exchange
B. Third-market trades in NYSE-listed stock
C. Secondary distributions of NYSE-listed stock
D. All of the above

12. Which of the following transactions would be reported on the Consolidated Tape?

A. Primary distribution
B. Exercise of warrants
C. Exercise of rights
D. None of the above

◆ Answers & Rationale

1. **B.** The "P" in the quotation is the exchange where the quote originated—the Pacific Stock Exchange. "B" stands for bid; "A" for ask. A customer wanting to buy at the market will pay the ask price. A customer wanting to sell at the market will receive the bid price.   (Page 197)

2. **D.** The "B" represents the bid, the "A" represents the ask price for the security.

	DWAQ					
Last	25 3/8	**Open**	25 3/8	**Close**	24 7/8
Bid	25	**High**	25 3/8	**Net Change**	+ 1/2
Ask	25 1/2	**Low**	24 7/8	**Volume**	424
				Time	9:50

(Page 199)

3. **B.** Certain inactive stocks are traded in round lots of less than 100 shares. The symbol $\frac{s}{s}$ denotes the trading of a 10-share unit on the NYSE. "Pr" is an abbreviation for preferred stock. Thus, 50 shares of DWQ preferred traded at $26 per share.   (Page 198)

4. **B.** Network A of the Consolidated Tape includes trades of NYSE-listed securities traded on the NYSE and other regional exchanges. Although many fourth-market trades (institution-to-institution direct trades) are not reported on the Consolidated Tape, INSTINET trades are included on the B network. Warrants, rights and preferred stock all trade on the exchanges and thus would appear on the Tape on the applicable network. Options do not appear on the Tape.   (Page 197)

5. **A.** The Consolidated Tape reports all transactions involving exchange-listed securities, no matter where they are bought or sold, including fourth market trades done through INSTINET. OTC trades of unlisted securities such as TCBS would not be reported, nor would trades directly between institutions that do not involve broker-dealers and are not done through INSTINET.   (Page 197)

6. **C.** Registered third-market makers are required to report transactions of listed securities traded over the counter to the Consolidated Tape within 90 seconds of execution. Any late reports (trades reported more than 90 seconds after execution) must be designated as late as they are entered into the system.   (Page 197)

7. **D.** The period between "12" and "4s" indicates two trades in TCB. The absence of any volume indication for the first trade means that the 100 shares traded at 12. The "4s" means that 400 shares traded at 11 7/8.   (Page 198)

8. **C.** If the actual price was 29 3/4, the customer must accept the trade at that price even though the trade was erroneously confirmed at a different price.   (Page 199)

9. **C.** The period indicates that two trades in ALF took place. The absence of any volume indication shows that the trades were for 100 shares at 40 1/8 and then 100 shares at 40 1/4.   (Page 198)

10. **D.** "SLD" on the Tape is an indication of a delayed print. This trade was reported out of sequence.   (Page 199)

11. **D.** The Consolidated Tape shows all transactions in NYSE-listed issues.   (Page 197)

12. **D.** None of the transactions listed is reported.   (Page 197)

1. Special procedures must be used whenever a dealer opens a municipal securities account for

   A. a clerical employee of another dealer
   B. the spouse of a trader employed by another dealer
   C. the minor child of an operations supervisor employed by another dealer
   D. all of the above

2. If a municipal dealer maintains an account for the employee of another municipal dealer and the employing dealer has not sent any written instructions, which of the following must be sent to the employing dealer?

   I. Monthly statement of all transactions in the account
   II. Written notice of a security recommended for account purchase
   III. Duplicate confirmations of all securities purchased for the account

   A. I only
   B. I and III only
   C. III only
   D. I, II and III

3. Under MSRB rules a municipal securities broker-dealer opening an account for an employee of another firm must

   A. notify the SEC after each trade
   B. obtain approval of the employer before each trade
   C. refuse all trades unless approved by a municipal principal
   D. send duplicate confirmations to the employer after each trade

4. Joe Kuhl wants to open a cash account with you. In order to open this account, you must do all of the following EXCEPT

   A. get Joe's signature on the new account form
   B. ascertain that Joe is of legal age
   C. get Joe's Social Security number
   D. learn Joe's occupation

5. Joe Kuhl, one of the two general partners in another NYSE brokerage firm, attempts to open an account with your NYSE firm. Which of the following statements is(are) true?

   A. This action is unethical and not allowed.
   B. Mr. Kuhl must provide your firm with written consent from the other partner.
   C. You must receive the other partner's approval and special approval from the exchange on which the trade will take place.
   D. No special approvals are needed.

6. A lawyer with power of attorney over one of your customer's accounts trades for the account because the customer is currently residing in the Near East. The lawyer requests that all statements and trade confirmations be sent to his office. Which of the following statements is true?

A. The lawyer needs approval of the NYSE for such a discretionary account.
B. Statements and trade confirmations must continue to be sent to the customer's official permanent residence.
C. The lawyer's orders must be followed because he has power of attorney.
D. The customer must approve each trade, regardless of where he is currently residing.

7. A nonresident alien wishes to open an account with your firm. The registered rep must obtain which of the following information from the individual?

I. Country of residence
II. Citizenship status
III. Foreign bank reference
IV. Signed proxy statement

A. I and II only
B. I, II and III only
C. III and IV only
D. I, II, III and IV

8. August Polar wants to open an account for his own use but wishes to authorize his son to manage the account. For personal reasons, August does not want the account listed in his own name. The forms required to open this account, in addition to the new account form, are

A. customer agreement and court certificate of his son's appointment
B. customer agreement and two or more accounts form
C. corporate agreement and options disclosure form
D. customer agreement, full trading authorization and numbered account form

9. A customer is going on a trip and wishes to have his brokerage firm stop sending mail. The firm can do all of the following EXCEPT

A. if he is traveling domestically, hold the mail for two months
B. if he is traveling internationally, hold the mail for three months
C. send the mail to a post office box
D. send the mail to the office of the customer's registered rep

10. When a joint options account is opened, the registered rep's responsibilities concerning suitability determination and information disclosure apply

A. to the person with the greatest capital contribution
B. to the person with trading authority for the account
C. to the person with the greatest participation
D. equally to all persons that jointly own the account

11. August Polar wishes to open a cash account with you. You are the registered rep and Mr. Kuhl is the branch manager of your office. Who must sign the new account form in order to open this account?

A. Mr. Polar only
B. You only
C. Mr. Kuhl and you only
D. Mr. Polar, Mr. Kuhl and you

12. Which of the following is true when a customer gives limited power of attorney to his registered rep?

A. The registered rep needs written permission from the customer for each trade.
B. The customer must renew the power of attorney every year.
C. The power of attorney must have the customer's signature.
D. The branch manager must initial each order before it is entered.

13. A registered rep must follow special rules when opening an account for

    A. the six-year-old child of a clerical employee of a competitive brokerage firm
    B. the wife of an operations manager at another brokerage firm
    C. a registered rep at an affiliated brokerage firm that is owned by the same financial holding company
    D. any of the above

14. A customer must sign which of the following documents in order to establish a discretionary account?

    A. Customer's agreement
    B. Trading authorization
    C. Options agreement
    D. New account application

15. According to NYSE rules, duplicate confirmations of transactions must be sent to an account owner's employer when establishing a margin account for whom of the following?

    I. Bank employee
    II. Employee of another broker-dealer
    III. Independent insurance agent
    IV. Officer of another broker-dealer

    A. I and II only
    B. I and III only
    C. II and IV only
    D. III and IV only

16. An account that has been approved only for covered call writing must be reapproved for

    I. ratio writing
    II. spreads
    III. naked option writing
    IV. straddles

    A. I and II only
    B. II and III only
    C. III and IV only
    D. I, II, III and IV

17. A customer wishes to open a new account but declines to provide all of the financial information requested by the member firm. In this case the member firm may

    I. not open an account
    II. open the account if it determines by other means that the customer has the financial resources to carry the account and determines that trading is suitable
    III. not recommend any transactions unless they are suitable for the customer

    A. I
    B. II
    C. II and III
    D. III

18. If a customer wishes to transfer his account from one member firm to another, which of the following statements is(are) true?

    I. A total of seven business days is allowed for completing the transfer.
    II. Transfer requests must be in writing.
    III. The member firm carrying the account must list all of the securities positions in the account.

    A. I only
    B. I and III only
    C. II and III only
    D. I, II and III

19. Customer records must be maintained at which of the following locations?

    I. Branch office
    II. Regional office
    III. Main office

    A. I only
    B. I and III only
    C. II and III only
    D. I, II and III

20. To recommend the sale or purchase of an option to a customer, diligence must be used to obtain certain information. Which of the following information must be obtained?

    I. Present and future financial needs of the customer

    II. Changes in the investment objectives of the customer since the account was approved for options

    III. Changes in the financial situation of the customer since the account was approved for options

    A. I and II only
    B. I and III only
    C. III only
    D. I, II and III

21. Approval to open an options account for a customer must be granted by the

    A. branch manager only
    B. registered representative
    C. branch manager initially, with the subsequent approval of a registered options principal
    D. registered financial adviser

22. A change in which of the following should be indicated in a customer's file?

    I. Name or address
    II. Marital status
    III. Objectives

    A. I only
    B. I and II only
    C. III only
    D. I, II and III

23. Under the act of 1934, the power to set margin requirements for securities transactions was granted to the

    A. SEC, which has established and currently enforces such rules
    B. SEC, which has delegated responsibility to the Federal Reserve Board for enforcing such rules
    C. Federal Reserve Board, which has delegated responsibility to the SEC for enforcing such rules
    D. Department of the Treasury, which has empowered the Federal Reserve Board to establish such rules

24. By definition, "margin" is the

    A. minimum amount of cash that a customer is required to deposit when purchasing securities
    B. maximum amount that a broker is allowed to loan a customer for the purchase of securities
    C. maximum amount of cash that a customer is required to deposit when purchasing securities
    D. minimum amount that a broker is allowed to loan a customer for the purchase of securities

25. If a partner of an NASD member firm wishes to open an account with another member firm, the

    I.   account may not be opened under any circumstances due to the privileged information to which the partner has access

    II.   account may be opened, but the partner may not engage in any transactions in securities recommended by his own firm

    III.   member firm opening the account must send duplicate confirmations or statements to the employing member firm, if requested to do so

    IV.   member firm opening the account is required to give notice to the employing member firm

    A.   I
    B.   II and III
    C.   II and IV
    D.   III and IV

26. Where are penny stocks traded?

    A.   NYSE
    B.   Exchange market
    C.   OTC
    D.   INSTINET

27. Prior to effecting a penny stock transaction the registered rep must

    I.   confirm whether the person is an established customer

    II.   obtain from the customer a signed risk disclosure document

    III.   obtain from the customer a signed penny stock transaction agreement

    IV.   determine suitability based on financial condition, investment experience and investment objectives

    A.   I only
    B.   I and IV only
    C.   II and III only
    D.   I, II, III and IV

28. Under the Penny Stock Rules, what is required for an investor to be considered an established customer?

    A.   Open cash account for one year
    B.   At least three separate penny stock purchases
    C.   Signed risk disclosure statement
    D.   Signed transaction agreement

29. If Bud Charolais wanted to purchase a penny stock, where would the transaction occur?

    A.   INSTINET
    B.   NASD
    C.   Over the counter
    D.   CBOE

30. Which of the following is(are) MOST likely to be covered by the Penny Stock Rules?

    I.   Stock listed only on a regional exchange
    II.   Common stock trading under $5
    III.   Listed options on a stock under $5
    IV.   Stock listed in the *Pink Sheets*

    A.   I only
    B.   I and III only
    C.   II and IV only
    D.   I, II, III and IV

31. Which of the following is(are) MOST likely to be exempt from the Penny Stock Rules?

    I.   Stock listed only on a regional exchange
    II.   Common stock trading under $5
    III.   Listed options on a stock under $5
    IV.   Stock listed in the *Pink Sheets*

    A.   I only
    B.   I and III only
    C.   II and IV only
    D.   I, II, III and IV

32. Which of the following would be included in a penny stock risk disclosure statement?

   I.   Investors' legal rights
   II. Definition of "penny stock"
   III. Risks of investing in penny stock
   IV. Broker-dealer's responsibilities to the investor

   A. I only
   B. I, II and III only
   C. II only
   D. I, II, III and IV

33. The Penny Stock Rules apply to

   I.   non-Nasdaq-listed OTC securities
   II. securities that trade for $5 or less per share
   III. principal transactions

   A. I only
   B. I and II only
   C. II only
   D. I, II and III

34. A registered representative opens an account by soliciting an order from a customer who purchases a speculative stock trading at 7/8–1 1/4. Which of the following statements are true?

   I.   Written permission from the customer must be obtained before executing the order.
   II. The rep must obtain suitability information.
   III. The customer must deposit a minimum of $2,000 to open the account.
   IV. The customer must sign a limited power of attorney.

   A. I and II only
   B. I and III only
   C. II and IV only
   D. I, II, III and IV

35. Joe Kuhl opens an account with Serendipity Discount Securities and signs a loan consent agreement. The firm is permitted to

   A. hypothecate securities in Joe's account
   B. lend out Joe's securities
   C. commingle Joe's securities with securities owned by the firm
   D. lend Joe money and charge interest

◆ Answers & Rationale

1. **D.** Special procedures must be followed whenever an account is opened for the employee of another broker-dealer. The firm opening the account must give the employing broker-dealer written notice that the account is being opened. Duplicate copies of all confirmations must be sent to the employer.   (Page 216)

2. **C.** Unless instructed otherwise, in writing, only duplicate confirmations need be sent.
(Page 216)

3. **D.** Before opening an account for an employee of another municipal firm, the employer must be notified in writing. Duplicate confirmations of each trade must be sent to the employer.
(Page 216)

4. **A.** In opening a cash account, you do not need the signature of the customer. You do need to ascertain whether he is of legal age and to obtain other information, including his Social Security number and his occupation.   (Page 209)

5. **B.** When an employee, partner or spouse of an employee or partner of a brokerage firm wishes to open an account at another NYSE member firm, the employer (or other partner if the account is being opened by a partner) must consent in writing. Duplicate copies of statements and confirms must be sent to a designated partner or officer of that firm.   (Page 216)

6. **B.** Statements and confirms must continue to be sent to the customer's official permanent residence unless the customer instructs the rep in writing to discontinue this service.   (Page 211)

7. **A.** To open an account for a non-U.S. citizen, the registered representative would have to ascertain the person's country of residence and citizenship and obtain a local bank reference. No proxy is required because the person can act or vote as a stockholder on her own behalf.   (Page 209)

8. **D.** The customer has to sign a full trading authorization form giving his son authority to manage the account. If the customer does not want his account identified by name, he must also submit a numbered account form.   (Page 215)

9. **D.** Customer mail may not be sent to the office of the customer's registered rep. This could provide a way for the rep to withhold information from the customer.   (Page 211)

10. **D.** Suitability rules apply to all owners in a joint account.   (Page 209)

11. **C.** The signature of the customer is not required to open a cash account. To open a margin account, the customer's signature must be obtained on the margin agreement. For all accounts, the registered rep must sign the new account form, indicating that the information on the form is true and complete. The branch manager serves as the principal, and must review and accept the new account by signing the form prior to opening the account.   (Page 208)

12. **C.** The registered rep must have prior written authority from the customer and have received approval from a supervisory person before accepting discretionary authority. While a designated principal must frequently review the account, the branch manager need not initial each order before it is entered.   (Page 215)

13. **D.** The NYSE, NASD and MSRB all have rules which require broker-dealers to give special attention to accounts opened by certain individuals. This special attention typically involves permission from, or written notification to, some other broker-dealer regarding establishment of the account. Accounts opened by the following individuals fall within these rules:

- all employees of broker-dealers; and
- all spouses or minor children of employees of broker-dealers.

(Page 216)

14. **B.** In order to establish a discretionary account, written authorization must be received from

the customer(s) in whose name(s) the account has been established. In most cases, this is done by signing either a limited or a full trading authorization: a limited trading authorization allows another individual permission only to buy and sell securities in the account; a full trading authorization allows another individual also to add or remove monies *and* securities from the account.

A signed customer's agreement is required when opening a margin account. A signed options agreement is required within 15 days from the date the options account is approved. A new account application must be signed by the registered representative and the branch manager, but not by the customer.   (Page 215)

15. **C.**   According to NYSE rules, when an employee of a member firm opens an account with another member broker-dealer, duplicate confirmations must be sent to the employer. An officer of a broker-dealer is considered an employee and needs permission from another officer to open the account. The NASD requires duplicate confirmations only upon the request of the employee's firm. Duplicate confirmations are not required to be sent to bank and insurance employers when employees open accounts.   (Page 216)

16. **D.**   An options account that is initially approved only for covered call writing must be reapproved in writing for any other option-related activity.   (Page 213)

17. **C.**   If a customer refuses to provide financial information, the member firm must use whatever information it has available to decide whether to open the account. Any recommendation made to a customer must be suitable, taking into account the customer's investment objectives, financial situation and any other relevant information.   (Page 209)

18. **D.**   If a customer transfers his account to another firm, the transfer request must be in writing and must be completed within seven business days. The carrying broker-dealer must provide a list of the customer's securities positions.   (Page 215)

19. **B.**   Customer records must be kept in the branch office and the firm's main office (supervisory office). There is no requirement to maintain the records also in the firm's regional office.   (Page 216)

20. **D.**   When opening an options account, the firm must obtain the customer's investment objective, financial situation and financial needs. If any of these change, the account form must be updated within 15 days.   (Page 208)

21. **C.**   Approval to open an options account can be given initially by the branch manager. However, if the manager is not a ROP, the ROP must also approve the account.   (Page 213)

22. **D.**   All information that could affect recommendations or the financial situation of a customer must be noted immediately in the file.   (Page 209)

23. **C.**   The extension of credit in the securities industry came under regulation in the Securities Exchange Act of 1934, whereby the Federal Reserve Board was given power to set margin requirements; the FRB delegates the enforcement of these requirements to the SEC.   (Page 211)

24. **A.**   "Margin" is the minimum amount of cash that a customer is required to deposit on the purchase or short sale of securities.   (Page 211)

25. **D.**   The member firm at which the account is being opened must give notice to the employing firm, and the employing firm must receive duplicate copies of all trade confirmations if it requests them.   (Page 216)

26. **C.**   All penny stocks trade over the counter.   (Page 213)

27. **D.**   All of the actions listed must be performed prior to effecting a penny stock transaction.   (Page 214)

28. **B.**   Under the Penny Stock Rules, an established customer is one who has an account open with a broker-dealer and has made a securities

transaction previous to the last year or who has made at least three penny stock purchases from different issuers on different days.   (Page 214)

29. **C.** Penny stocks trade OTC. They are non-Nasdaq-listed equity securities that are traded for prices of less than $5 per share.   (Page 213)

30. **C.** The general definition of penny stock is that it trades at prices under $5 and is not a reported security (that is, it is not listed on an exchange or on Nasdaq). A listed option does not fit the definition, regardless of price. The *Pink Sheets* list primarily penny stocks.   (Page 213)

31. **B.** A stock listed on an exchange is a reported security with current prices and volume and is not considered a penny stock. A listed option is not considered a penny stock regardless of the price. Unlisted stock trading under $5 is considered a penny stock and the *Pink Sheets* quote primarily penny stocks.   (Page 213)

32. **D.** All of the items listed would be explained in a penny stock risk disclosure document.   (Page 214)

33. **D.** The Penny Stock Rules address all of the topics listed, with the intention of protecting investors from fraudulent or deceptive schemes.   (Page 213)

34. **A.** The firm must obtain a signed suitability statement, a signed risk disclosure document, and a signed transaction agreement from the customer prior to the first transaction in penny stocks. No minimum dollar amount or power of attorney is required to open the account.   (Page 214)

35. **B.** The loan consent agreement allows the firm to lend out some of the customer's securities. The other components of a margin agreement, the hypothecation agreement and the credit agreement, are necessary to allow the firm to pledge customer securities and to extend credit to a customer. Securities owned by a customer may not be commingled with firm securities.   (Page 212)

1. The documents that would be required if a customer were to open a cash account and give a sibling trading authorization are

   I. new account card
   II. loan consent agreement
   III. customer agreement
   IV. limited power of attorney

   A. I
   B. I, II and IV
   C. I and IV
   D. II, III and IV

2. A registered representative who learns of a customer's death should

   A. await the proper legal papers
   B. mark the account "deceased"
   C. cancel open orders
   D. do all of the above

3. Upon being informed that one party to a joint tenants in common account has died, a registered representative should

   A. transfer all of the assets to the survivor
   B. freeze the account
   C. maintain the account because one of the parties survives
   D. transfer half of the assets to the survivor

4. Persons wishing to give a broker the right to make investment decisions for them should do so by

   A. providing a letter from an attorney
   B. providing a letter giving discretionary powers
   C. calling the broker each time such an order is to be placed
   D. calling the broker once to advise her to use her own judgment in investment decisions

5. Bud Charolais is opening a new cash account and giving his broker trading authorization. Which of the following documents are needed?

   I. New account card
   II. Customer (margin) agreement
   III. Loan consent agreement
   IV. Limited power of attorney
   V. Partnership resolution

   A. I, II and III
   B. I and IV
   C. I, IV and V
   D. III, IV and V

6. A woman wishes to open a cash account in her name only, and allow her husband to make purchases and receive checks in his name only. She must instruct her broker-dealer to open a

A. margin account
B. cash account with limited power of attorney
C. cash account with full power of attorney
D. cash account

7. All of the following could legally open a margin account EXCEPT

I. the custodian of an UGMA
II. a corporation
III. a trustee
IV. a partnership

A. I
B. I, III and IV
C. II, III and IV
D. III and IV

8. What happens in a partnership account if one partner dies?

A. The surviving partners receive the deceased partner's share.
B. The account must be frozen until an amended partnership agreement is received.
C. The surviving partners are considered joint tenants.
D. The surviving partners are considered joint tenants and receive the deceased partner's share.

9. A registered representative who has an account that is registered as joint tenants with right of survivorship is informed that one of the parties has died. He should

A. maintain the account because one of the parties survives
B. freeze the account
C. transfer half of the assets to the survivor
D. transfer all of the assets to the survivor

10. When a customer wants to open a guardian account, you will need a

A. limited power of attorney
B. full power of attorney
C. signed customer account card, credit agreement and loan consent
D. copy of the court-ordered guardianship papers

11. Which Social Security number is used when opening a custodial account?

A. Parent's or guardian's of the minor
B. Minor's
C. Custodian's
D. Any of the above is acceptable.

12. Which of the following is(are) discretionary order(s) under the Rules of Fair Practice?

I. A customer sends a check for $25,000 to Serendipity Discount Securities and instructs the firm to purchase bank and insurance company stocks when the price appears favorable.
II. A customer instructs a registered representative to buy 1,000 shares of Acme Sweatsocks at a time and price that the representative determines.
III. A customer instructs a registered representative to purchase as many shares of Quantum Rapid Search as the rep deems appropriate.
IV. A customer instructs a registered representative to sell 300 shares of Greater Health, Inc. that are long in the account when the rep thinks the time and price appropriate.

A. I and III only
B. II and IV only
C. III only
D. I, II, III and IV

13. A member firm handling a discretionary account

    A. may not effect transactions that are excessive in size or frequency in view of the customer's resources

    B. must approve each discretionary order in writing on the day the order is entered

    C. must obtain prior written authorization from the customer granting discretionary authority to the registered rep

    D. must comply with all of the above

14. Which of the following statements regarding discretionary accounts is(are) true?

    I. The customer must approve each transaction in writing before the order is executed.

    II. The customer must grant written authorization to the member firm to exercise discretion in the account.

    III. The account may not be accepted unless approved in writing by a partner, officer or designated official of the member firm.

    IV. Each discretionary order must be approved promptly by a partner, officer or designated official of the member firm.

    A. I and III only
    B. II only
    C. II, III and IV only
    D. I, II, III and IV

15. If a customer who has a joint account at your firm dies, which of the following actions should be taken first?

    A. The account should be liquidated and the assets frozen.

    B. Outstanding orders should be canceled.

    C. Assets should be transferred to a surviving spouse.

    D. Nothing should be done in the absence of instructions from an executor.

16. Disclosure of control relationships is required in which of the following types of transactions?

    A. All types of transactions
    B. Principal transactions
    C. Agency transactions
    D. Primary distributions

17. The term "discretionary" refers to an

    A. account in which someone has been given custodial power over another individual's account

    B. account in which the customer has power of attorney over an incompetent individual's account

    C. order that specifies the size of the security, but leaves the choice of time and price up to the registered rep

    D. account where the rep has the power to decide which security and whether to buy or sell without customer authorization for those specific trades

18. A representative wishes to execute an order for the discretionary account of a customer. The municipal dealer has a control relationship with the issuer of the security to be purchased. Under MSRB rules, the representative

    A. may not execute the order

    B. must have specific authorization from the customer

    C. may wait until the firm terminates the control relationship

    D. may refer the customer to a firm that has no control relationship

19. With regard to discretionary accounts, which of the following statements are true?

    I.   The accounts must be accepted in writing by a principal.
    II. All trades in the accounts must be reviewed frequently by a principal.
    III. All account activity must be reviewed frequently by a principal.
    IV. Securities in a discretionary account may never be rehypothecated.

    A. I and II only
    B. I, II and III only
    C. III and IV only
    D. I, II, III and IV

20. Which of the following is(are) required in order to execute orders in a customer's discretionary account?

    I.   The customer must authorize each transaction in writing.
    II. The transactions must be in accordance with the discretionary authorization.
    III. The transaction prices must be fair and equitable.
    IV. The orders must be filled from the best available market.

    A. I
    B. I, II and IV
    C. II and III
    D. II, III and IV

21. Every broker-dealer is required, through a general partner or an officer, to do all of the following EXCEPT to

    A. approve each transaction in a discretionary account before the order is entered
    B. supervise diligently all accounts handled by registered reps of the organization
    C. specifically approve the opening of any account prior to or promptly after the completion of any transaction for the account of a customer
    D. use due diligence to learn the essential facts about every customer

22. Which of the following would be acceptable for a fiduciary acting under the prudent man rule?

    I.   Purchasing AAA rated debentures
    II. Purchasing a growth mutual fund
    III. Purchasing new issues of stock
    IV. Writing covered calls on dividend-paying stock

    A. I only
    B. II only
    C. II and III only
    D. I, II, III and IV

23. Under which of the following circumstances may fiduciaries of trust accounts trade options for those accounts?

    I.   Under no circumstances
    II. If the trust agreement states that trustees have the power to trade options
    III. If the trust's investment objectives are determined to be compatible with options trading

    A. I
    B. II
    C. II and III
    D. III

24. Which of the following statements about discretionary accounts is(are) true?

    I.   The rules regarding churning of accounts do not apply to discretionary accounts.
    II. Discretionary orders must be approved by the branch manager prior to entry.
    III. Discretionary orders must be approved by a principal prior to entry.
    IV. An order in which an investor designates the name of the security, the number of contracts and whether to buy or sell, and that gives the account executive discretion as to time and price only is not considered a discretionary order.

    A. II and III only
    B. II, III and IV only
    C. IV only
    D. I, II, III and IV

25. A customer who had granted power of attorney to her son dies. The power of attorney

    A. remains in effect until canceled by the executor of the estate
    B. remains in effect until canceled by the son
    C. remains in effect only if the son is the sole heir to the estate
    D. is canceled on the death of the principal of the account

26. For which of the following pairs of customers could a registered rep open a joint account?

    I.   Max Leveridge and his 13-year-old son Tiny
    II. Bea Kuhl and June Polar, two adult college roommates
    III. Randy Bear and Adam Grizzly, friends and partners in business for over 20 years
    IV. Belle Charolais and her minor nephew Klaus Bruin, for whom she is guardian

    A. I and III only
    B. II and III only
    C. II and IV only
    D. I, II, III and IV

27. ALFA Enterprises, Inc. wants to open a margin account. Your firm must have on file all of the following documents EXCEPT a

    A. hypothecation agreement
    B. new account form
    C. copy of the corporate charter
    D. copy of the trust agreement

28. A fiduciary wants to establish a trust account that permits margin transactions. Which of the following statements is true?

    A. Margin trading is not permitted.
    B. Margin trading is permitted if the legal documents authorize it.
    C. Margin trading is permitted if the fiduciary observes the prudent man rule.
    D. Margin trading is permitted if the fiduciary shares in the profits or losses.

29. When the customer of a broker-dealer dies, the firm should obtain all of the following documents EXCEPT a(n)

    A. affidavit of domicile
    B. estate tax waiver
    C. certified copy of the death certificate
    D. power of attorney

◆ Answers & Rationale

1. **C.** If one party is giving discretionary privileges to a second party for a cash account, a member firm would require a new account form and a limited power of attorney. A limited power of attorney gives the second party trading authority, but prohibits that party from withdrawing securities from the account.   (Page 218)

2. **D.** When a registered rep learns of a customer's death, she must mark the account "deceased," cancel all open orders and await the appropriate legal documents.   (Page 224)

3. **B.** The assets of a deceased individual eventually go to the surviving party, but a registered representative first cancels all open orders and then awaits the proper papers from the survivor.   (Page 224)

4. **B.** Discretionary accounts always require prior written authorization from the customer in the form of a limited power of attorney.   (Page 220)

5. **B.** New account cards are required for opening new accounts. Margin agreements and loan consent agreements are used only in connection with opening margin accounts. Limited power of attorney is needed to grant the broker trading authorization. A partnership agreement is needed to open a partnership account, but not an individual's account.   (Page 222)

6. **C.** In order for a person other than the person in whose name an account is held to enter trades and withdraw assets, a full power of attorney is required. A limited power of attorney enables someone other than the account owner to enter trades, but not to withdraw assets.   (Page 220)

7. **A.** UGMA specifically prohibits custodians from engaging in speculative trading, including trading on margin. The others will be able to open margin accounts, given the appropriate authority and documentation.   (Page 220)

8. **B.** Upon the death of a partner, a partnership account is automatically frozen until an amended partnership agreement is received.   (Page 219)

9. **B.** No trades may take place and no activity may be initiated until the registered rep has received all necessary documentation.   (Page 223)

10. **D.** Full and limited powers of attorney relate to accounts where the beneficial owner has granted some form of control over the account to another person. Answer C lists the documents needed to open a margin account. A guardian is appointed by the courts to act on behalf of another individual.   (Page 222)

11. **B.** The minor's Social Security number is used because the account will be fully owned by, and taxed to, the minor and not to either the custodian or the parent.   (Page 218)

12. **C.** Discretion is given when the rep chooses the stock, the amount of shares or whether to buy or sell. Discretionary authority must be given to an individual; it may not be given to a firm. Time and price are not considered discretionary decisions.   (Page 224)

13. **D.** Prior to a discretionary trade, the customer's authorization must be obtained in writing. Each trade must have the approval of a principal on the day the order is entered, and cannot be excessive in either size or frequency.   (Page 220)

14. **C.** To establish a discretionary account, a customer must request such an account in writing and grant trading authorization to specific individuals at the broker-dealer. Further, the firm must indicate its willingness to handle the account on a discretionary basis through a signature of a principal of the firm. Once accepted on a discretionary basis, orders can be entered on behalf of the customer without additional prior authorization, either written or verbal. All orders, including those for discretionary accounts, have to be approved promptly (no later than by the end of business on the day the order is entered), but not necessarily prior to execution.   (Page 223)

15. **B.** No trades or other controllable activity may take place in the account of a deceased person pending the arrival of the required documents and instructions from the estate.   (Page 224)

16. **A.** The nature of any control relationship or conflict of interest must be disclosed to the customer. This includes both primary (new issue) and secondary transactions.   (Page 220)

17. **D.** An order is *discretionary* when it is placed by the member firm or its representative for a customer's account without the customer's express authorization for that order. Additionally, for the order to be considered discretionary, the firm must choose more than merely the price and time of execution (for example, the size or the security must be chosen by the firm).   (Page 220)

18. **B.** Even in a discretionary account, a registered rep may not exercise discretion when a control relationship exists between the issuer and the dealer.   (Page 222)

19. **B.** There are no limits placed on the hypothecation or rehypothecation of securities in an account based solely on its discretionary status.   (Page 222)

20. **D.** The customer who has given discretionary authority in writing to another individual does not have to give him written consent for each transaction.   (Page 222)

21. **A.** Although discretionary orders must be approved by an officer or authorized delegate, they do not have to be approved before the order is entered.   (Page 222)

22. **D.** The prudent man rule permits a fiduciary to invest in those securities that a "reasonably prudent man," seeking income and preservation of capital, might buy for his own investments.   (Page 222)

23. **C.** Fiduciary accounts may be opened to trade options if documents prove that the fiduciary has the authority to trade in options and that options are suitable for the account.   (Page 223)

24. **C.** An order is discretionary only if the registered representative selects the size of the trade and/or the security to be purchased. Selecting only price or time of trade does not constitute discretion. Of course, churning rules apply to discretionary accounts, and order tickets must be approved by a principal after the trade, not before.   (Page 222)

25. **D.** When a customer dies, all powers of attorney granted by the customer expire.
(Page 220)

26. **B.** An account owner is the person who can control investments within an account and request distributions of cash or securities from the account. A joint account can be opened only for account owners who are able to legally exercise such control over the account. Minors cannot legally exercise such control, and thus a joint account could not be opened if a minor would be one of the owners.
(Page 218)

27. **D.** All margin accounts must have a new account form and hypothecation agreement on file. A corporation's charter must be provided as proof that margin trading is authorized. Obtaining a copy of the trust agreement is not necessary. (Page 219)

28. **B.** The documents that establish a trust account may include provisions for a margin account. Without specific prior authorization, margin trading by a fiduciary is prohibited.   (Page 220)

29. **D.** All of the documents listed may be required except for the power of attorney. If the decedent had previously executed a power of attorney, it becomes invalid upon death.   (Page 222)

37 Uniform Gifts to Minors Act Accounts Exam

1. A woman wishes to make a gift of securities to her niece's account under the Uniform Gifts to Minors Act. The niece's guardian is opposed to the gift. Under these circumstances, the woman may give the securities

   A. only if the niece approves
   B. as she desires
   C. only with the written approval of the guardian
   D. only after obtaining the permission of the court

2. Under the Uniform Gifts to Minors Act, which of the following is allowable?

   A. A gift from one donor to one child with both parents named as custodian
   B. A gift from two donors to more than one child jointly
   C. A gift from one donor to more than one child jointly
   D. A gift from one donor to one child

3. Under the Uniform Gifts to Minors Act, you can

   I. give an unlimited amount of cash
   II. give securities
   III. give up to $10,000 cash
   IV. revoke a gift

   A. I
   B. I and II
   C. I, II and IV
   D. II and III

4. Under the provisions of an UGMA account, when the minor reaches the age of majority

   A. the account must be turned over to the donee
   B. the account must be turned over to the donor
   C. the account remains as an UGMA account
   D. any securities in the account must be converted to cash

5. Under the Uniform Gifts to Minors Act, the beneficial owner of the securities held in the account is the

   A. custodian
   B. minor
   C. parent of the minor
   D. donor of the securities

6. Under the Uniform Gifts to Minors Act, all of the following are permissible EXCEPT

   A. gifts of cash to a minor
   B. gifts of securities to a minor
   C. the purchase of securities on margin and the securities being held in street name
   D. the donor and the custodian being the same person

7. What information must be included on the application certificate for an UGMA account?

   A. Custodian's name and Social Security number, and minor's name
   B. Minor's and custodian's names
   C. Guardian's name, and minor's name and Social Security number
   D. Custodian's name, minor's name and Social Security number, and state of registration

8. How must stock subscription rights be handled in a custodial account for a minor?

   A. The custodian can exercise or sell rights as she deems prudent.
   B. The custodian cannot exercise or sell rights for a custodial account.
   C. The rights can be exercised or sold only if the stock is held in street name.
   D. The rights can be exercised or sold only if the donor is also the custodian.

9. Max Leveridge is appointed custodian for Klaus Bruin, a minor. Certificates will be registered as

   A. Max Leveridge and Lotta Leveridge as custodians for Klaus Bruin
   B. Max Leveridge as custodian for Klaus Bruin
   C. Klaus Bruin
   D. Klaus Bruin as custodian for Max Leveridge

10. A gift given to a minor may be revoked under UGMA

   A. at any time before the minor reaches majority
   B. if the minor dies before reaching the age of majority
   C. if the custodian dies before the minor reaches majority
   D. under no circumstances

11. The Social Security number of which of the following persons is used when opening a custodial account?

   A. Minor's parent or guardian
   B. Minor
   C. Custodian
   D. Any of the above

12. Which of the following accounts is(are) prohibited from using margin?

   I. Joint account for a husband and wife
   II. Discretionary account
   III. Corporation
   IV. Custodian under the Uniform Gifts to Minors Act

   A. I and II
   B. I, II and III
   C. II and IV
   D. IV

13. How may stock warrants be handled in a custodial account under UGMA?

   A. The custodian may exercise or sell them as he deems prudent.
   B. The custodian may not exercise or sell warrants in a custodial account.
   C. They must be exercised.
   D. They may be exercised or sold only if the custodian is also the donor.

14. Which of the following statements is(are) true of a custodial account in which an individual is custodian for his son under UGMA?

   I.   If the stock is held at a broker-dealer's firm, it may be registered in the name of the custodian or in street name.
   II. The securities will be registered in the parent's name until the son reaches the age of majority.
   III. The custodial relationship is terminated when the son reaches majority.
   IV. The parent's Social Security number is used for purposes of reporting and paying taxes.

   A. II and III only
   B. II and IV only
   C. III only
   D. I, II, III and IV

15. Under the Uniform Gifts to Minors Act, which of the following statements is FALSE?

   A. A gift to a minor is irrevocable.
   B. Only one person may be custodian for one minor in a single account.
   C. The maximum amount of money that may be given to a minor per donor tax free in any one year is $10,000.
   D. Only a parent may give a gift to a minor.

16. Under the Uniform Gifts to Minors Act, a custodian may invest in all of the following EXCEPT

   A. variable annuities
   B. commodity futures
   C. blue chip stocks
   D. corporate bonds

17. A woman has given securities to her ten-year-old niece under the Uniform Gifts to Minors Act and is acting as custodian. The aunt may do which of the following?

   I.   Pay for the niece's support and education out of the niece's funds.
   II. Donate bearer securities to the account.
   III. Buy and sell securities in the custodian account.
   IV. Withhold a reasonable amount of dividends and interest earned in the account as reimbursement for expenses.

   A. I and II
   B. I, II and III
   C. II and III
   D. III and IV

18. Max Leveridge wants to open an UGMA account for his son Tiny. Max may do all of the following EXCEPT

   I.   contribute an unlimited amount of securities and cash
   II. contribute no more than $10,000 worth of securities and cash
   III. keep the account in his name until Tiny reaches the age of majority
   IV. list his son as the beneficial owner of the account

   A. I and III
   B. I and IV
   C. II and III
   D. II and IV

19. Earnings in an UGMA account in excess of the exclusion amount are taxed at the

   I.   minor's rate until the minor reaches 14 years of age

   II. minor's rate after the minor reaches 14 years of age

   III. parent's rate until the minor reaches 14 years of age

   IV. parent's rate after the minor reaches 14 years of age

   A. I and II
   B. I and IV
   C. II and III
   D. III and IV

20. In the event there were legal questions regarding a Uniform Gifts to Minors Act account or its ownership, who would be responsible for answering those questions in a court of law?

   A. Minor
   B. Donor
   C. Guardian
   D. Custodian

21. Grandfather Grizzly is in the 31% tax bracket. He establishes an UGMA account for his 16-year-old grandson, Adam. Adam's parents are in the 28% bracket. How will the earnings in the account be taxed?

   A. At Adam's tax rate
   B. At his parents' tax rate
   C. At his grandfather's tax rate
   D. The earnings are tax exempt.

◆ Answers & Rationale

1. **B.** In a custodian account, any adult, whether related or unrelated, can make gifts. All gifts, however, are irrevocable.   (Page 226)

2. **D.** Under UGMA, an unlimited amount of money or securities may be given by a donor to *one child* with *one* entity named as *custodian.*
(Page 227)

3. **B.** There is no limit to the size of gift that may be transferred under an UGMA account. Gifts under UGMA are irrevocable and may consist of cash and securities.   (Page 226)

4. **A.** Under the terms of the Uniform Gifts to Minors Act, when a minor reaches the age of majority the proceeds must be handed over to the child (donee).   (Page 226)

5. **B.** The minor is the beneficial owner of the securities in an UGMA account, while the securities are held in the name of the custodian.
(Page 226)

6. **C.** UGMA accounts may never be opened as margin accounts; the firm would have no recourse in the event that a stock trade resulted in a deficit in the account.   (Page 227)

7. **D.** Each account set up under UGMA must include the state of registration, the minor's name and Social Security number, as well as the name of the custodian who is the nominal owner of the account.   (Page 227)

8. **A.** The custodian must either buy the securities or sell the rights. The custodian cannot let the rights expire.   (Page 227)

9. **B.** The certificates will be registered as Max Leveridge as custodian for Klaus Bruin. There can only be one custodian for one minor per account.
(Page 227)

10. **D.** The Uniform Gifts to Minors Act states that all gifts to minors are irrevocable. (Page 226)

11. **B.** When a custodial account is opened, the minor's Social Security number is used because it is the minor's account, and it is the minor who pays taxes in the account.   (Page 227)

12. **D.** Although no legal papers are required to open a custodial account, the account must be kept in accordance with state law under the UGMA. This act prohibits securities in a custodial account from being purchased on margin.   (Page 227)

13. **A.** The custodian must either buy the securities or sell the warrants; he cannot let the warrants expire.   (Page 227)

14. **C.** When a minor reaches the age of majority, a custodial account must be reregistered in his name. Securities held in a custodial account cannot be kept at the brokerage firm in street name; the securities are registered, for example, "Max Leveridge as Custodian for Klaus Bruin," not in the name of the parents; and it is the minor's Social Security number that is used.   (Page 227)

15. **D.** Any adult can give a gift to a minor in a custodial account.   (Page 226)

16. **B.** Commodity futures cannot be purchased in a custodial account because commodity futures are purchased on margin. Margin transactions are prohibited in a custodial account.   (Page 227)

17. **B.** A custodian may use custodial property for the support, education and general use and benefit of the minor. A custodian is empowered to collect, hold, manage, sell, exchange or dispose of the property as she deems advisable. However, a donor may not designate herself custodian of bearer securities unless the gift is accompanied by a deed of gift. A custodian may be compensated for reasonable services and reimbursed for necessary expenses if she is not the donor.   (Page 227)

18. **C.** Max may contribute an unlimited amount of cash and securities, and he must put the

account in the custodian's name, listing his son as the beneficial owner.   (Page 226)

19. **C.**   Until the minor reaches age 14, unearned income in an UGMA account is taxed at the parent's top tax rate, after excluding the amount allowed by the IRS. After the minor reaches age 14, unearned income is taxed at the minor's own rate.   (Page 228)

20. **D.**   While the minor is the beneficial owner of an UGMA account, in the event that there were legal questions regarding the account or ownership of the account, the custodian (who has been charged with fiduciary responsibilities in the management of the account) would be responsible for handling such questions and would represent the account in a court of law.   (Page 227)

21. **A.**   The child is a minor over 14, so any earnings in excess of the standard deduction are taxed at his rate.   (Page 228)

38 Brokerage Support Services Exam

1. Under the Uniform Practice Code, regular way transactions settle on the

   A. same day as trade date
   B. second business day following trade date
   C. third business day following trade date
   D. fifth business day following trade date

2. Under the Uniform Practice Code, a seller's option transaction settles

   A. at the discretion of the seller
   B. on or before the expiration date specified in the option
   C. within 35 calendar days of the transaction
   D. within 90 calendar days of the transaction

3. Delivery may be made on a seller's option no sooner than the

   A. trade date
   B. third business day following the transaction
   C. fourth business day following the transaction
   D. fifth business day following the transaction

4. In a seller's option, securities may be delivered prior to the expiration date specified if the seller

   A. gives one day's written notice to the buyer
   B. gives notice to the buyer on the day of delivery
   C. cannot deliver on the specified date
   D. wishes to be paid earlier

5. In a regular way transaction, if a seller delivers prior to the settlement date, the

   A. buyer must accept delivery only if the seller gave advance notice of his intention
   B. seller has violated the Uniform Practice Code
   C. buyer must accept delivery
   D. buyer may accept the stock or may refuse it without prejudice

6. Settlement on when-, as- and if-issued and when-, as- and if-distributed transactions is usually determined by the

   A. buying broker
   B. selling broker
   C. NASD Uniform Practice Committee
   D. Board of Governors

7. The regular way ex-dividend date for stock is the

   A. second business day preceding the record date
   B. second business day following the record date
   C. second business day preceding the settlement date
   D. third business day preceding the record date

8. How many days before the record date must an issuer of securities notify the NASD regarding a dividend or other distribution?

   A. 5
   B. 10
   C. 15
   D. 20

9. Settlement of securities transactions is made

   A. when the selling broker-dealer delivers the securities to the buying broker-dealer's office
   B. at either the office of the buyer or the seller, as specified at the time the parties enter into contract
   C. when the buying broker-dealer delivers a check to the selling broker-dealer's office
   D. when the seller and the buyer come together at the office of the transfer agent

10. Confirmations sent to customers must include

   A. the markup or markdown if the member acted as a principal on a riskless or simultaneous transaction
   B. whether the member acted as agent or principal
   C. the amount of any commissions received
   D. all of the above

11. Under what circumstances does the Uniform Practice Code allow delivery on a seller's option transaction to be made prior to the specified date?

   A. A selling broker-dealer gives written notice one day before delivery.
   B. A buying broker-dealer's client requests early delivery.
   C. A buying broker-dealer requests early delivery.
   D. Under no circumstances may delivery be made early.

12. A due bill would be required when a security is purchased

   A. after the ex-dividend date and delivered after the record date
   B. before the ex-dividend date and delivered after the record date
   C. before the ex-dividend date and delivered before the record date
   D. after the ex-dividend date and delivered before the record date

13. A customer buys $10,000 worth of stock in a cash account and sells the shares for $12,000 without first paying for the buy side in full. The customer then asks that a check for the $2,000 profit be sent to her. Which of the following statements is(are) true?

   I. The $2,000 profit cannot be sent to the customer until she pays for the buy side in full.
   II. The $2,000 can be sent to the customer, but her account will be frozen for 90 days.
   III. If the customer pays for the buy side in full on or before the fifth business day, status as a frozen account is lifted.
   IV. Both trades must be switched to the customer's margin account where buying and selling in this manner are acceptable practices.

   A. I
   B. I and III
   C. II and IV
   D. IV

14. A broker-dealer may request a time extension from

    A. the NASD
    B. the Chicago Stock Exchange
    C. the New York Stock Exchange
    D. its designated examining authority

15. When a client's account is frozen, the client

    A. must deposit the full purchase price no later than the settlement date for a purchase
    B. must deposit the full purchase price before a purchase order may be executed
    C. may make sales but not purchases of securities
    D. may not trade under any circumstances

16. Sell orders sent to an exchange must be

    A. marked as either long or short
    B. marked only if they are long sales
    C. marked only if they are short sales
    D. executed in accordance with the appropriate rules, but not necessarily marked

17. An order memorandum or ticket must be completed

    A. on the trade date
    B. by the business day following the trade date
    C. within three business days
    D. within five business days

18. When an issuing corporation provides a proxy, it is

    A. providing a legal form of absentee voting, effected through a limited power of attorney
    B. providing a document authorizing a third party to buy and sell securities
    C. setting company operating policy
    D. offering the right to present stockholders to purchase more shares below the current market price

19. You received a proxy in the mail from one of your customers. He signed it, but did not specify a vote. Your customer

    A. has given up the right to vote at all
    B. has transferred the power to specify a vote to your firm
    C. must be mailed the proxy for completion
    D. has voted a *none of the above* choice

20. Charges for the collection of dividends, transfer of securities, and safekeeping and custodial services are governed by NASD policy, which

    A. does not allow any service charges beyond normal commissions
    B. permits service charges related to the activity in the account
    C. permits service charges for accounts that have been inactive for more than six months
    D. allows service charges that are reasonable and not unfairly discriminatory between customers

21. The amount of commission must be disclosed on which of the following documents?

    I.   Order ticket
    II. Customer confirmation if an agency transaction
    III. Customer confirmation if a principal transaction

    A. I and II
    B. I and III
    C. II
    D. III

22. Hugh Heifer wants to place an order to sell 200 shares of COD stock. Hugh currently has no COD shares in his account. Which of the following must a rep try to determine before accepting the order?

   A. The name of the broker from whom the stock was purchased
   B. Where the stock is currently held and whether it can be delivered in three business days
   C. The willingness of Hugh to deliver other securities from his account should he fail to deliver the COD stock
   D. Whether Hugh will pledge his other securities as collateral to secure a stock loan to effect timely delivery

23. In a proxy contest, member firms holding securities in street name for their clients who are beneficial owners must

   A. send the proxy material to the beneficial owners at the expense of the member firm
   B. send the proxy material to the beneficial owners at the expense of the issuing company
   C. vote the proxies as they wish
   D. send a list of the names and addresses of the beneficial owners to the issuing company so that they may send proxy materials to those owners

24. A customer purchases securities from a securities dealer. Payment for the purchase is to be made by a bookkeeping entry, transferring money from another account of this customer. The completion of this transaction occurs

   A. when the customer enters the order
   B. when the money is transferred out of the account
   C. on the settlement date of the transaction
   D. on the day the securities are received into the account

25. Customer statements must be sent out at least

   A. daily
   B. weekly
   C. monthly
   D. quarterly

26. A bond that is traded flat may

   I. be an income bond
   II. have interest in arrears
   III. be traded with accrued interest
   IV. have an ex-date and a record date

   A. I and II
   B. I, II and IV
   C. II and IV
   D. III and IV

27. Cash traded bonds settle on the

   A. third day after the payment date
   B. second day after the payment date
   C. trade date
   D. regular way settlement date

28. Karen Kodiak executes a transaction for a customer. Later, she notices that she used the wrong account number. What should she do?

   A. Sell the shares into the correct customer account.
   B. Report the mistake to her manager.
   C. Delay sending the confirmation to the customer until the error is rectified.
   D. Inform the customer in whose account the trade was done that the trade is binding, but that the firm will compensate her for any losses.

29. A customer signs his proxy and sends it to his rep without indicating how he wants his shares voted. Which of the following statements is true?

   A. The rep must return the proxy to the customer.
   B. The customer will not receive any further shareholder communications.
   C. The rep's firm is entitled to vote the shares.
   D. The proxy is irrevocable.

◆ Answers & Rationale

1. **C.** Under the Uniform Practice Code, regular way trades settle three business days after the trade date.   (Page 240)

2. **B.** In a seller's option transaction, the seller may deliver, at his option, between four business days after the trade date until expiration of the option.   (Page 241)

3. **C.** Seller's option trades must settle by the 60th calendar day, but no earlier than four business days after the trade date.   (Page 241)

4. **A.** In a seller's option trade, the seller may deliver, at his option, by giving the buyer written notice one day before the delivery date. (Page 241)

5. **D.** In a regular way trade, the purchaser does not have to accept securities delivered prior to settlement date (three business days after the trade date), but may do so if he wishes.   (Page 240)

6. **C.** Settlement on when issued securities is on a date set by the NASD's Uniform Practice Committee unless such date is determined by an exchange (if the securities are listed) or by the manager of the underwriting syndicate (if new issue securities are involved).   (Page 241)

7. **A.** The regular way ex-dividend date is two business days before the record date. This is the date on which the value of the stock is reduced by the dividend.   (Page 243)

8. **B.** Under SEC Rule 10b-17, issuers must inform the NASD no later than ten days prior to the record date of dividends, stock splits or rights offerings.   (Page 243)

9. **A.** Settlement of securities transactions occurs when the selling broker-dealer delivers to the buying broker-dealer.   (Page 240)

10. **D.** Customer confirmations must disclose the amount of markup for riskless transactions, whether the member acted in an agency or principal capacity, and the amount of commission when acting as an agent.   (Page 237)

11. **A.** Seller's option transactions settle between four business days and 60 calendar days. After the third business day, the seller must give the buyer one day's written notice.   (Page 241)

12. **B.** A due bill is sent when a customer is entitled to receive a dividend, but for some reason did not receive it.   (Page 241)

13. **B.** Any time a customer buys and sells stock in a cash account without paying for the buy side in full, the account is automatically frozen for 90 days, meaning that no orders will be accepted without cash and/or securities on deposit in advance. If the customer pays for the buy side in full within the five-business-day limit imposed by Regulation T, and the customer's check clears the banking system, the sale proceeds can be remitted in full and the frozen account status lifted.   (Page 242)

14. **D.** A time extension must be requested from the broker-dealer's designated examining authority.   (Page 242)

15. **B.** When an account is frozen, the client must deposit the full purchase price prior to any subsequent orders.   (Page 242)

16. **A.** Every sell order must be marked as either a long sale or a short sale.   (Page 236)

17. **A.** When an order is executed, an order ticket must be prepared specifying the details that pertain to the order.   (Page 236)

18. **A.** A proxy is a legal document that can be used by a stockholder to authorize another party to vote her shares at a stockholder's meeting.   (Page 246)

19. **B.** A signed proxy received by the firm indicates that the customer wishes the firm to vote

the customer's shares along with any others the firm has.   (Page 247)

20. **D.** The NASD Rules of Fair Practice allow for the charging of fees for clerical services as long as the charges are fair and reasonable and do not discriminate among customers.   (Page 240)

21. **C.** The amount of the commission is determined after the trade is executed and, therefore, it is not included on the order ticket. It must be disclosed on the confirmation in the case of agency transactions. There is no commission in a principal transaction, only a markup, which does not have to be disclosed on the customer confirmation.
(Page 237)

22. **B.** The rep should ascertain the location of the stock and whether the customer can deliver within three business days, so that the firm can make timely delivery. The broker from whom the securities were purchased, and any other securities held by the customer, are immaterial. (Page 235)

23. **B.** Securities firms that are members of the NASD must forward all proxy material to the beneficial owners for all securities that are held in street name, and the issuer or the corporation in whose name the stocks or bonds are issued must bear the expense of shipping this proxy material. Therefore, in a proxy contest, the members must send the proxy material to the beneficial owners at the expense of the issuing company.   (Page 247)

24. **C.** Completion of any transaction occurs when settlement is made.   (Page 237)

25. **D.** The NASD requires member firms to send out customer account statements at least once per calendar quarter.   (Page 239)

26. **B.** A municipal or corporate bond that is trading "flat" is trading without accrued interest. The bond may be an income bond, which normally pays no interest. If an income bond declares an interest payment, there will be an ex-date and record date. The bond may have defaulted on interest payments, in which case it is also traded flat.
(Page 246)

27. **C.** Cash traded bonds settle on the trade date.   (Page 246)

28. **B.** The rep should report the mistake and not take any action to remedy the mistake without the approval of a principal.   (Page 237)

29. **C.** If the proxy does not address an issue of control of the company, the broker-dealer is permitted to vote shares held in street name. Customers must always receive stockholder communications, and proxies are always revocable.   (Page 247)

1. On February 13th, your customer buys 10M of the 8% Treasury bonds maturing in 1991, for settlement on February 14th. The bonds pay interest on January 1st and July 1st. How many days of accrued interest will be added to the buyer's price?

   A. 14
   B. 43
   C. 44
   D. 45

2. Compute the dollar amount of accrued interest on 10M of an 8% municipal bond bought regular way on Tuesday, March 20, 1998, and maturing on November 1, 1999.

   A. $311.11
   B. $313.33
   C. $315.56
   D. $326.67

3. What does the term "and interest" mean in the sale of a corporate bond?

   A. The buyer must adjust his cost by the amount of interest paid annually.
   B. The seller must adjust his proceeds by the amount of interest paid annually.
   C. The buyer must adjust his cost and the seller must adjust his proceeds, based on the interest accrued to that point.
   D. The transaction was done on a net basis and no adjustment is necessary by either party.

4. The computation for accrued interest on corporate debt obligations is based on

   A. actual-day month and actual-day year
   B. actual-day month and 360-day year
   C. 30-day month and actual-day year
   D. 30-day month and 360-day year

5. KLP 6 1/2% corporate bonds of '99 pay interest on February 15th and August 15th. If a bond is purchased on Friday, March 4th, the seller will receive accrued interest for how many days?

   A. 19
   B. 20
   C. 24
   D. 26

6. Accrued interest for corporate bonds is computed on the basis of

   A. actual days elapsed
   B. 30-day months
   C. 31-day months
   D. SEC accrued interest guidelines

7. Accrued interest for municipal bonds is computed on the basis of

   A. actual days elapsed
   B. 30-day months
   C. 31-day months
   D. SEC accrued interest guidelines

8. Accrued interest for U.S. government bonds is computed on the basis of

   A. actual days elapsed
   B. 30-day months
   C. 31-day months
   D. SEC accrued interest guidelines

9. Which of the following securities trade "and interest"?

   I. Municipal revenue bonds
   II. Certificates of deposit
   III. Treasury bonds
   IV. Zero-coupon bonds

   A. I, II and III only
   B. I and III only
   C. II and IV only
   D. I, II, III and IV

10. The dated date on a municipal bond issue is the

    A. settlement date
    B. trade date
    C. date the bonds are originally issued
    D. date on which the bonds begin accruing interest

11. June Polar buys a municipal bond from you on Monday, December 15th. This bond is a J&J 15. Which of the following statements is true?

    A. The bond settles on December 16th.
    B. Ms. Polar will receive accrued interest on December 15th.
    C. Ms. Polar will receive accrued interest on the settlement date.
    D. Ms. Polar will pay accrued interest when the trade is settled.

12. When August Polar purchases a new municipal bond, the accrued interest is calculated

    I. from the trade date
    II. from the dated date
    III. up to the interest payment date
    IV. up to, but not including, the settlement date

    A. I and III
    B. I and IV
    C. II and III
    D. II and IV

13. If August Polar were to purchase a bond in the secondary market, which of the following would be a factor in calculating the price that he would pay for the bond?

    I. Settlement date
    II. Dated date
    III. Coupon
    IV. Scale

    A. I and III
    B. I and IV
    C. II and III
    D. II and IV

14. June Polar purchases a new issue of a municipal bond on August 1st for cash (same-day settlement). The first interest payment is September 1st. Which of the following statements is(are) true of the interest on this bond?

    I. The bond pays interest on September 1st and March 1st each year.
    II. On September 1st, the buyer will receive all interest due from the dated date to September 1st.
    III. Interest on municipal bonds is computed on a 360-day basis, with each month having an even 30 days.

    A. I only
    B. II only
    C. II and III only
    D. I, II and III

15. An investor purchases five Mt. Vernon Port Authority J&J bonds in a regular way transaction on Wednesday, October 18th. How many days of accrued interest will be added to the price of the bond?

   A. 108
   B. 110
   C. 112
   D. 114

16. One of your customers buys a new issue revenue bond on March 19th. The trade settles on March 24th. The bond pays interest on February 1st and August 1st. The dated date of the bond is March 1st. How many days of accrued interest are due?

   A. 19
   B. 23
   C. 24
   D. 55

17. Which of the following shows the accrued interest formula for U.S. government bonds?

   A. 30 ÷ Actual days to settlement date
   B. Actual days to settlement date ÷ 360
   C. Actual days to settlement date ÷ 30
   D. Actual days to settlement date ÷ Actual days in period

18. All of the following trade with accrued interest EXCEPT

   A. certificates of deposit
   B. zero-coupon bonds
   C. convertible bonds
   D. Treasury bonds

19. An M&N Treasury bond is traded regular way on Wednesday, June 8th. The number of days of accrued interest is

   A. 38
   B. 39
   C. 44
   D. 45

20. A Microscam, Inc. J&J 15 bond is traded for cash on Monday, January 15th. How many days of accrued interest does the buyer owe the seller?

   A. 3
   B. 15
   C. 180
   D. None of the above

◆ Answers & Rationale

Feb. 15 to Feb. 30	=	16 days
Mar. 1 to Mar. 8	=	8 days
Accrued interest:		24 days

(Page 250)

1.   **C.**   Accrued interest for government securities is figured on an actual days elapsed basis. The number of days begins with the previous coupon date and continues up to, but not including, the settlement date. For instance, these bonds pay interest on January 1st; the number of days of accrued interest for January equals 31. The bonds settle February 14th; the number of days of accrued interest for February equals 13. Remember, do not count the settlement date (31 + 13 = 44 days).
(Page 251)

2.   **C.**   Regular way settlement on municipal bonds is three business days.

Settlement date on this transaction is March 23rd. The bonds pay interest on November 1st and May 1st. The number of days of accrued interest is:

Month	Days
November	30 days
December	30 days
January	30 days
February	30 days
March	22 days
Total	142 days (Do not count settlement day.)

The accrued interest formula for municipal bonds is: Principal × Rate × Time; therefore, $10,000 × 8% × (142 ÷ 360) = $315.56.   (Page 250)

3.   **C.**   Accrued interest is added to the price the buyer pays and to the price the seller receives.
(Page 249)

4.   **D.**   Accrued interest on corporate bonds is computed on a 30-day month, 360-day year.
(Page 249)

5.   **C.**   Interest on corporate bonds accrues up to but not including settlement date (March 9th, in this case) and is calculated on a 30-day month and a 360-day year, regardless of the actual days per month.

6.   **B.**   Accrued interest for corporate bonds is calculated on a 360-day year consisting of twelve 30-day months.   (Page 250)

7.   **B.**   Accrued interest for municipal bonds is calculated on a 360-day year consisting of twelve 30-day months.   (Page 250)

8.   **A.**   Accrued interest for U.S. government bonds is calculated on the basis of actual days elapsed, on an actual 365-day year.   (Page 251)

9.   **A.**   Trading "and interest" means trading with accrued interest. Debt instruments that pay interest periodically (for example, municipal bonds or Treasury bonds) trade with accrued interest. CDs are issued at par and trade with accrued interest. Original issue discount obligations, such as T bills, zero-coupon bonds and bankers' acceptances, trade flat. The value of these instruments reaches par at maturity. The difference between the discount price and par is the interest income.   (Page 249)

10.   **D.**   The dated date is the date on which the bonds begin to accrue interest.   (Page 249)

11.   **D.**   When a customer buys a municipal bond, the customer must pay the accrued interest that has built up between the last interest payment date and the settlement date. In this case, the bonds were bought on December 15th, and therefore, they will settle three business days later on December 18th. So, on December 18th the customer must pay the price of the bond, plus the accrued interest that has built up from July 15th to December 18th. Remember, when a municipal bond is purchased, the purchaser pays the accrued interest. The purchaser is not reimbursed for that interest until the next interest payment date which, in this case, is January 15th.   (Page 249)

12.   **D.**   On new issue municipal bonds, purchasers must pay accrued interest to the underwriter for interest earned by the underwriter during the period

the bonds are held before being reoffered to the public. Interest accrues from the bond's dated date until the settlement date of the purchase by the customer.   (Page 249)

13. **A.**   Accrued interest is part of the total dollar amount of a bond transaction. Bond trades occur at a specific price plus accrued interest. In order to calculate accrued interest, you must know the settlement date. The coupon also affects the price—for obvious reasons. The dated date is relevant only with newly issued bonds, and the scale is relevant to the underwriting syndicate when the bonds are first offered to the public. These are not factors in pricing a bond that is trading in the secondary market.   (Page 249)

14. **D.**   Municipal bonds pay interest semiannually. A bond that pays interest on September 1st pays interest six months later, on March 1st. Interest on a new issue bond accrues from the dated date. If she sells this bond in the secondary market, the buyer pays her all interest earned on the bond from the last coupon date. Interest on municipal bonds is computed on a 360-day basis, with each month having an even 30 days.   (Page 250)

15. **C.**   Interest accrues on municipal bonds on the basis of a 360-day year, with all months having 30 days. Therefore, there are 30 days of interest in July, 30 days in August, 30 days in September and 22 days of accrued interest in October, making a total of 112 days.   (Page 250)

16. **B.**   Interest started accruing from the dated date of the bond, March 1st. Interest accrues up to, but not including, settlement. Therefore, 23 days of accrued interest are due. Your customer's first interest payment, the following August, will represent interest that has accrued from the dated date.   (Page 250)

17. **D.**   Accrued interest for U.S. government bonds is calculated by dividing the actual calendar days up to the settlement date by the actual calendar days in the period.   (Page 250)

18. **B.**   Zero-coupon bonds are issued at a deep discount from face value instead of providing semiannual interest payments. The difference between the purchase price and the face value at maturity is the investor's return. T bonds, convertible bonds and CDs all make periodic interest payments, thus the seller receives any accrued interest from the buyer.   (Page 249)

19. **B.**   Accrued interest on government bonds is based on a 365-day year, and settlement occurs on the next business day. This bond pays interest in May and November, with the most recent payment on May 1st. Interest has accrued on this bond for 31 days in May and 8 days in June, for a total of 39 days.   (Page 251)

20. **D.**   When settlement is made on the same day as the interest payment date, no accrued interest is due. The entire interest payment belongs to the seller.   (Page 249)

1. For delivery of mutilated municipal bonds to be considered good delivery, the certificates must be validated. Which of the following entities could validate the mutilated securities?

   I. Issuer
   II. Branch manager
   III. Transfer agent
   IV. Any national bank

   A. I only
   B. I and III only
   C. II and III only
   D. I, II, III and IV

2. Lotta Leveridge wants to place an order to sell 20 TIP bonds. She currently has no TIP in her account. As her registered rep, before accepting the order you must try to determine which of the following?

   A. Name of the broker from which the security was purchased
   B. Where the security is currently held and whether it can be delivered in three business days
   C. Willingness of Ms. Leveridge to deliver other securities from her account should she fail to deliver the TIP
   D. Whether she will pledge her other securities as collateral to secure a loan to effect timely delivery

3. Which of the following persons could sign a stock or bond power to effect good delivery of securities sold from an account set up under the Uniform Gifts to Minors Act?

   A. Minor
   B. Parent
   C. Donor
   D. Custodian

4. A certificate in the name of Joe B. Kuhl, Jr. must be signed

   A. Joe B. Kuhl, Jr.
   B. J. B. Kuhl, Jr.
   C. Joe B. Kuhl
   D. Joe Kuhl, Jr.

5. A power of substitution is used

   A. in discretionary accounts
   B. when the name of the owner has been misspelled on the account
   C. when the uniform transfer instruction form is missing
   D. when the certificate owner has not endorsed the certificate

6. A certificate in the name of Smith & Company may be signed

   A. "Smith & Company" only
   B. "Smith & Company" or "Smith & Co." only
   C. "Smith & Company," "Smith & Co." or "Smith and Company"
   D. "Smith & Company, aka SmitCo"

7. Alterations or corrections on an assignment

   A. invalidate the assignment
   B. must be approved by the transfer agent
   C. may be made if accompanied by a guarantee of signature
   D. have no effect on the assignment

8. A stock power is a(n)

   A. document delegating discretion to purchase or sell securities to another party
   B. authorization delegating voting power to another person
   C. document authorizing transfer of ownership to another party that is usually attached to a stock or bond certificate
   D. legal right of the owner to vote stock as she chooses

9. If a security is sold by the estate of a deceased person, it will be a good delivery if it is signed by a(n)

   A. executor
   B. beneficiary
   C. spouse
   D. branch manager

10. Which of the following is NOT good delivery for 300 shares of stock?

    A. Three certificates for 60 shares each and three certificates for 40 shares each
    B. Three certificates for 100 shares each
    C. Four certificates for 75 shares each
    D. Six certificates for 50 shares each

11. A power of substitution is used under which of the following circumstances?

    A. The registered owner has not endorsed the certificate.
    B. The name of the owner has been misspelled on the certificate.
    C. One of the interest coupons is missing.
    D. The broker requests it from a supervisor.

12. Which of the following certificate registrations or endorsements qualify for good delivery?

    I. Certificates registered in the name of a deceased person, signed by that person before his demise
    II. Certificates registered in the name of a deceased person, signed by the executor of that person's estate
    III. Certificates registered in the name of an executor of a deceased person's estate, signed by the executor so named
    IV. Certificates registered in street name and endorsed by the firm, carried for the account of a deceased person and being sold under the direction of a court-appointed administrator

    A. II only
    B. II, III and IV only
    C. III and IV only
    D. I, II, III and IV

13. Which of the following are good delivery without legal documentation?

    I. Certificates registered in a deceased person's name and signed by an executor
    II. Certificates with an assignment executed by a person who is now deceased
    III. Certificates registered in a guardian's name and signed by the guardian
    IV. Certificates registered in an executor's name and signed by the executor

    A. I and IV only
    B. II and III only
    C. III and IV only
    D. I, II, III and IV

14. Which of the following would NOT be good delivery for 500 shares of stock?

    A. One certificate for 500 shares
    B. Five certificates for 60 shares each and one certificate for 200 shares
    C. Five certificates for 90 shares each and five certificates for 10 shares each
    D. Ten certificates for 50 shares each

15. Which of the following would NOT be good delivery for 470 shares of stock?

   A. Two 100-share certificates and three 90-share certificates
   B. Four 100-share certificates and one 70-share certificate
   C. Eight 50-share certificates, one 40-share certificate and one 30-share certificate
   D. Forty-seven 10-share certificates

16. A broker that has purchased 500 shares from another broker can be required to accept delivery of which of the following?

   I. One certificate for 500 shares
   II. Two certificates for 200 shares each
   III. Three certificates for 100 shares each and eight certificates for 25 shares each
   IV. Ten certificates for 60 shares each

   A. I and II
   B. I, II and III
   C. I and IV
   D. IV

17. The final determination on good delivery is made by the

   A. NASD or MSRB
   B. transfer agent
   C. member firm's cashiering department
   D. SEC

18. Securities sold by a corporation may be signed by

   A. the treasurer or chief financial officer of the corporation only
   B. an individual duly authorized to sign by corporate resolution
   C. the legal counsel of the corporation
   D. any officer of the corporation

19. A stock or bond power is used to

   A. transfer a dividend or interest to a new buyer
   B. assign a certificate to a new owner
   C. permit another party to vote on a specific matter
   D. do all of the above

20. When accepting a client's sell order, a broker-dealer must determine all of the following EXCEPT

   A. if the securities are in deliverable form
   B. the location of the securities
   C. if the client can make delivery promptly
   D. if the securities have been accepted by the transfer agent

21. Mutilated certificates do not constitute good delivery between municipal securities dealers unless they are validated by which of the following?

   I. Delivering dealer
   II. Registered owners
   III. Paying agent
   IV. Trustee

   A. I or II
   B. I and IV
   C. II and III
   D. III or IV

22. A municipal bond in bearer form pays interest each May 1st and November 1st until maturity. Under what circumstances would a seller on a regular way basis be permitted to deliver the bond without the coupon payable on Monday, May 1st?

   I. If the sale is executed before March 15th
   II. If the trade is settled on or after April 1st.
   III. If the issuer announces it will default on the May 1st payment
   IV. If delivery of the certificate is accompanied by a check or draft for the coupon amount

   A. I
   B. I or III
   C. II
   D. II or IV

◆ Answers & Rationale

1. **B.** Mutilated certificates are considered good delivery if validated by the trustee, registrar, transfer agent, paying agent or issuer. (Page 258)

2. **B.** The rep should ascertain the location of the security as well as whether the customer can deliver within three business days, so the firm can make timely delivery. The broker from which the security was purchased and the security holdings of the customer are immaterial. (Page 253)

3. **D.** Custodial securities must be signed by the custodian in order to be good delivery. Securities registered in the name of a custodian for the benefit of a minor, for example, are not good delivery if signed by the minor. (Page 258)

4. **A.** Certificates must be endorsed exactly as registered, unless making the permissible &/and or Company/Co. substitutions. (Page 255)

5. **D.** A power of substitution is a separate form from the stock certificate (although it is normally printed on the back of the stock certificate) and can be used for endorsement if the stock certificate has been left blank. (Page 255)

6. **C.** Corporate signers are the exception to the general rule that endorsement of a certificate must match exactly the name on the front. The words "and Company" can be written in any acceptable way. (Page 255)

7. **C.** Assignments must be properly executed for the securities to be good delivery. An agent of the issuer (that is, the transfer agent) can authenticate mutilated security certificates but cannot verify altered assignments. The certificate must be delivered with a guarantee of the signature (executed by a broker-dealer, federal bank, and so on). (Page 255)

8. **C.** A stock power is an instrument separate from, but usually attached to, the stock certificate by which an owner indicates the intent to transfer ownership of the securities. Answer A describes a type of power of attorney, and answer B describes a proxy. (Page 255)

9. **A.** To effect the sale of a security for the estate of a deceased person, one needs a copy of the death certificate and an appointment of executor. Regulations vary in each state, so check the local laws for the exact forms and procedures. (Page 258)

10. **C.** To be good delivery, certificates must be stackable, or breakable, into 100-share units or multiples of units of 100. Answers B and D clearly meet this requirement; answer A also meets it because 60 plus 40 equals 100. The certificates in answer C, however, cannot be broken into 100-share units. (Page 253)

11. **A.** A power of substitution is used to transfer ownership of securities if the stock certificate has been left blank. (Page 255)

12. **C.** Certificates registered in the name of a deceased person are *never* good delivery, regardless of whether the person signed them. Choices I and II are, therefore, not good for delivery to other broker-dealers; the certificates must first be submitted to the transfer agent. Choice III, in which certificates are registered in an executor's name and endorsed by the same, are good delivery, as are certificates registered in street name (choice IV), provided the broker-dealer has assurance of the administrator's legal authority. (Page 255)

13. **C.** No additional legal documents are required if stock is registered in the name of and signed by either an individual guardian or an individual executor of an estate. The signature of a deceased person is not acceptable. Also, stock registered in the name of a deceased person cannot be assigned by an executor of the estate until the stock is placed in the estate's name. (Page 258)

14. **B.** The unit delivery rule states that certificates must add up to 100 or be in multiples of 100. The shares in answer B do not add up to 100: one certificate of 60 shares equals 60; two certificates

of 60 equals 120; and so on. Therefore, it is not good delivery.   (Page 253)

15. **A.**   Shares must add up to 100 or be in multiples of 100, with the exception of the odd lots.
                                    (Page 254)

16. **B.**   The question does not ask which of these broker-to-broker deliveries is considered good delivery; it asks which of these deliveries the broker must accept. Only choice IV is an unacceptable delivery because certificates of 60 shares each cannot be added to make a 100-share unit. Choice II is acceptable because partial deliveries must be accepted under NASD rules if both firms agree, although partial delivery does not complete the contract.   (Page 254)

17. **B.**   The final determination on good delivery is made by the transfer agent because it ultimately accepts or rejects the certificate.
                                    (Page 253)

18. **B.**   Endorsement of corporate securities must be performed by an individual authorized by corporate resolution.   (Page 258)

19. **B.**   A stock or bond power is used in the event that a certificate is delivered for sale or deposit without being properly endorsed on the back.   (Page 255)

20. **D.**   A broker-dealer must determine answers A through C. Approval of the transfer agent is not a factor when accepting a sell order.   (Page 253)

21. **D.**   A mutilated certificate would not constitute good delivery unless verified by the trustee, registrar, transfer or paying agent or an authorized agent of the issuer.   (Page 258)

22. **D.**   The May 1st coupon would not have to be enclosed if the trade settled on or after April 1st. If a trade settles within 30 days before an interest payment date, the seller may retain the coupon and deliver a bank check for the amount of interest due the buyer.   (Page 254)

41 Extension of Credit in the Securities Industry Exam

1. Regulation T requires a broker-dealer to receive payment in full from a customer for a purchase in a cash account

    A. prior to purchase
    B. within three business days
    C. within five business days
    D. within ten business days

2. Regulation T requires a broker-dealer to receive initial margin deposits from a customer for a purchase in a margin account

    A. prior to purchase
    B. within three business days
    C. within five business days
    D. within ten business days

3. With regard to the requirements of Reg T, if a member firm sells marginable securities as principal to a customer in a margin account, this principal transaction

    A. is exempt from Reg T margin requirements
    B. is not permitted in a margin account and must be rebilled to the customer's cash account
    C. unlike agency trades, must be paid for in full
    D. is treated like an agency transaction under Reg T

4. Regulation T applies to

    A. margin accounts only, for listed securities
    B. margin accounts only, for nonexempt securities
    C. both cash and margin accounts, for listed securities
    D. both cash and margin accounts, for nonexempt securities

5. A customer purchases $10,000 worth of stock on Monday, May 15th. If the stock is bought in a cash account, how much must be deposited and by what date must the deposit be made?

    A. $5,000 no later than Thursday, May 18th
    B. $5,000 no later than Monday, May 22nd
    C. $10,000 no later than Thursday, May 18th
    D. $10,000 no later than Monday, May 22nd

6. A Reg T call must be met

    I. immediately
    II. within five business days in a margin account
    III. within five business days in a cash account
    IV. within ten business days if both a cash and a margin account are maintained

    A. I and IV
    B. II and III
    C. II, III and IV
    D. III and IV

7. Under Regulation T, a funds due notice need NOT be sent if the

    A. amount due does not exceed $100
    B. amount due does not exceed $200
    C. amount due does not exceed $1,000
    D. total amount of the transaction does not exceed $1,000

8. A member firm that sells a customer securities on margin may

    A. permit the customer to meet the margin call by liquidating other securities held in the account on settlement date
    B. permit the customer to meet the margin call by liquidating the securities purchased
    C. permit the customer to defer deposit of the required margin for good cause
    D. obtain the margin or liquidate the transaction

9. In a cash account, a customer has placed a buy order for 300 shares of Flibinite at the market. He calls you and tells you he doesn't have the funds to pay for the stock and asks that you liquidate his position. Because of this set of circumstances, the

    A. customer will be reported to the NASD and cannot trade in future
    B. account must be frozen for 90 days
    C. firm must liquidate all holdings and any credit balance goes to the firm
    D. customer cannot open an account with another broker for 90 days

10. Gwinneth Stout wants to buy shares of Acme Zootech on margin. ZOO is in its initial public offering. How many days must she wait after the public offering date?

    A. 25
    B. 30
    C. 40
    D. 90

11. Regulation T governs the purchase of

    I. American depositary receipts
    II. listed options
    III. corporate convertible bonds
    IV. U.S. government bonds

    A. I, II and III only
    B. I and III only
    C. II and IV only
    D. I, II, III and IV

12. Securities that can be purchased in a margin account include

    I. U.S. government bonds
    II. corporate convertible bonds
    III. state and municipal bonds
    IV. nonconvertible corporate bonds

    A. I and III only
    B. II only
    C. III only
    D. I, II, III and IV

13. Marginable OTC stocks are determined by which of the following?

    A. FRB
    B. SEC
    C. NASD
    D. MSRB

14. Regulation T always allows for purchases on 50% margin of

    A. listed stocks
    B. unlisted stocks
    C. listed options
    D. all of the above

15. Which of the following securities become marginable 30 days after purchase?

    I. UIT unit
   II. Mutual fund share
  III. Insurance contract
  IV. Put option

   A. I and II only
   B. I and IV only
   C. II and III only
   D. I, II, III and IV

16. A broker-dealer is allowed to extend credit for the purchase of all the following securities EXCEPT

   A. U.S. government securities
   B. exchange-traded stock
   C. options
   D. municipal revenue bonds

17. Which regulator sets initial margin requirements for nonexempt securities trading in the OTC market?

   A. SEC
   B. FRB
   C. SIA
   D. NASD

18. To purchase a when issued stock in a cash account, an investor must deposit

   A. the greater of 25% of the purchase price or $2,000 promptly
   B. the greater of 50% of the purchase price or $2,000 promptly
   C. 75% of the purchase price three business days after the trade date
   D. 100% of the purchase price three business days after the trade date

◆ Answers & Rationale

1. **C.** Regulation T requires that a broker-dealer receive payment in full from a customer making a purchase in a cash account no later than five business days after trade date.   (Page 265)

2. **C.** In a margin account, a customer must meet Reg T initial calls not later than the fifth business day after trade date.   (Page 265)

3. **D.** It makes no difference whether margin account transactions are executed as agency or principal trades.   (Page 265)

4. **D.** Regulation T controls credit extended by broker-dealers in all types of accounts and all non-exempt securities.   (Page 265)

5. **D.** Under Regulation T, payment in a special cash account must be made in full within five business days.   (Page 265)

6. **B.** Under Regulation T, the initial margin requirement on purchases in a margin account and full payment in a cash account must be made within five business days.   (Page 265)

7. **C.** Reg T permits a broker-dealer to disregard any amounts due less than $1,000. (Page 267)

8. **D.** Under Regulation T, a customer purchasing on margin must pay promptly, but in no case later than five business days from the trade date; otherwise, the position will be sold out and the account frozen.   (Page 267)

9. **B.** If a customer with a cash account does not pay for a purchase within five business days, then that purchase must be liquidated and the account frozen for 90 days. A frozen account means that all purchases require cash in advance; all sales require delivery of the securities by the customer in advance. In a margin account, the customer may be extended credit by the firm, as long as margin account requirements are met.   (Page 267)

10. **B.** According to Regulation T, new issues may not be purchased on margin for the first 30 calendar days following the public offering date.   (Page 265)

11. **A.** Reg T applies only to nonexempt securities. Because governments and municipals are exempt, there is no federal regulation. However, NASD and NYSE minimum margins still apply.   (Page 265)

12. **D.** Any of the securities listed may be purchased in a margin account as long as the appropriate margin is paid by the customer.   (Page 265)

13. **A.** The Federal Reserve Board determines whether any security is marginable.   (Page 265)

14. **A.** All listed stocks (stocks trading on a national securities exchange) are marginable. Listed options have no loan value and therefore require payment in full. Unlisted stocks are marginable only if they are included on the FRB's OTC margin list.   (Page 265)

15. **A.** UIT units and mutual fund shares are eligible margin securities after 30 calendar days. Insurance contracts and put options are not eligible for purchase on margin.   (Page 265)

16. **C.** Credit is extended on the ownership of stocks and bonds. Options have no loan value and credit cannot be extended on their purchase.   (Page 265)

17. **B.** The Federal Reserve Board is responsible for setting margin requirements for all non-exempt securities regardless of where they are traded. Exempt securities are those that are free from FRB margin requirements.   (Page 265)

18. **B.** In a cash account, 100% of the purchase amount must be deposited. However, for when issued securities, it is not required that payment be made in full until the settlement date, which is set only when the securities are finally issued. Until then, the Reg T minimum margin requirement (the greater of 50% or $2,000) holds.   (Page 267)

42 Margin Accounting Exam

1. Lotta Leveridge purchased 200 shares of Flibinite Health Care from you at $60 per share. She gave you a check for the initial requirement. Flibinite announces that it is selling millions of its new Magic Meditation Machine in Japan, and its stock appreciates on the news to $75. How much cash can Lotta withdraw after this market move?

    A. $0
    B. $1,000
    C. $1,500
    D. $3,000

2. For a couple of months now, Max Leveridge has been watching Microscam and has decided it is time to short the stock. Max sells short 100 shares at $80 per share. He gives you a cashier's check for the initial requirement. The next day, *The Wall Street Journal* carries an announcement that Microscam just signed a big government contract, and its stock appreciates to $90. How much additional cash does Max have to deposit?

    A. $0
    B. $1,000
    C. $2,400
    D. $2,700

3. The formula for computing equity in a margin account is

    A. long market value − short market value + credit balance + debit balance
    B. long market value − short market value + debit balance − credit balance
    C. long market value + credit balance − short market value − debit balance
    D. long market value + short market value − debit balance + credit balance

4. An individual who sells stock short that he owns is selling

    A. short against long
    B. short against the box
    C. short
    D. none of the above

5. An investor's margin account has the following positions:

Long market value	$50,000
Short market value	$27,000
Debit balance	$12,000
Credit balance	$22,000

    What is the total equity in her account?

    A. $10,000
    B. $15,000
    C. $22,000
    D. $33,000

6. In a new account, what is the initial margin requirement for a customer who sells short 100 shares of Acme Sweatsocks at 35?

   A. $1,500
   B. $1,750
   C. $2,000
   D. $3,500

7. An investor will sell stock short to

   A. profit if prices decline
   B. establish a permanent tax loss
   C. defer taxes
   D. liquidate a long stock position

Use the following information to answer questions 8 through 10. Joe Kuhl has a margin account with a debit balance of $37,000. He has the following securities in his account:

Company	No. Shares	Market Price
DWQ	100	$110
MTN	300	$65
TBS	400	$90

8. The equity in Joe's account is

   A. $22,500
   B. $29,500
   C. $33,250
   D. $37,000

9. Joe's account is restricted. How much would he have to deposit to make it a nonrestricted account?

   A. $0
   B. $2,000
   C. $2,500
   D. $3,750

10. The NASD/NYSE margin maintenance requirement for Joe's account is

   A. $8,500
   B. $16,625
   C. $29,500
   D. $33,250

11. An investor purchased $15,000 of stock in a margin account, depositing the Reg T requirement. The account is charged with interest amounting to $100. There has been no other activity in the account. The new debit balance is

   A. $100
   B. $7,400
   C. $7,500
   D. $7,600

12. Which of the following are characteristics of selling short against the box?

   I. Allows a gain on stock to be locked in without selling long
   II. Can be accomplished provided the long position is not liquidated
   III. Turns short-term gains into long-term gains
   IV. Provides general deferral of taxes

   A. I, II and III
   B. I, II and IV
   C. I and III
   D. II and III

13. A customer's debit balance is decreased by all of the following EXCEPT

   A. stock dividends
   B. cash dividends and interest received
   C. deposits of cash
   D. sale of securities

14. An existing margin account that is not in restricted status is credited with a $2,100 dividend from one securities position. The customer would like to withdraw cash immediately. What amount can be sent to the customer?

   A. $0
   B. $900
   C. $1,200
   D. $2,100

15. Hugh Heifer has a margin account containing securities with a market value of $50,000 and no debit balance. If he sold all his stock, he could withdraw

A. $0
B. $7,500
C. $25,000
D. $50,000

16. Hugh Heifer has a margin account containing securities with a market value of $50,000 and no debit balance. How much could he purchase in marginable securities without making a deposit?

A. $7,500
B. $25,000
C. $50,000
D. $100,000

17. Hugh Heifer has a margin account containing securities with a market value of $50,000 and no debit balance. How much would the debit balance be if Hugh purchased the maximum amount of securities without depositing additional cash?

A. $0
B. $12,500
C. $25,000
D. $50,000

18. The NASD/NYSE minimum maintenance requirement on long stock is

A. 25% of the market value
B. 30% of the market value
C. 50% of the market value
D. the same as the initial margin requirement

19. The NASD/NYSE minimum maintenance requirement on short stock selling above $5 is

A. 25% of the market value or $5 per share, whichever is greater
B. 30% of the market value or $5 per share, whichever is greater
C. 50% of the market value or $5 per share, whichever is greater
D. the same as the initial margin requirement

20. What is the Federal Reserve Board minimum margin requirement for municipal securities?

A. 5%
B. 15%
C. 25%
D. There is no requirement.

21. An investor opens a new margin account and sells short 100 shares of ALF at 55 1/2, with Reg T at 50%. What is the investor's required deposit?

A. $1,665
B. $2,000
C. $2,775
D. $5,550

22. An investor opens a new margin account and sells short 100 shares of KLP at 42, with Reg T at 50%. What is the investor's required deposit?

A. $1,050
B. $2,000
C. $2,100
D. $4,200

23. An investor opens a new margin account and sells short 100 shares of COD at 32 1/2, with Reg T at 50%. What is the investor's required deposit?

A. $812.50
B. $1,625
C. $2,000
D. $3,250

24. An investor opens a new margin account and sells short 100 shares of ALF at 10, with Reg T at 50%. What is the investor's required deposit?

A. $250
B. $500
C. $1,000
D. $2,000

25. An investor has an established margin account with a long market value of $24,000 and a debit balance of $19,500, with Reg T at 50%. How much money must the investor deposit to satisfy the NASD/NYSE maintenance requirement?

A. $1,500
B. $4,500
C. $6,000
D. $7,500

26. In a new margin account, June Polar sells short 1,000 shares of Quantum Rapid Search at 15 and makes the required Reg T deposit. The stock drops to 12. What is the equity in her account?

A. $10,500
B. $12,000
C. $15,000
D. $18,000

27. Which of the following sets the minimum maintenance requirement on municipal securities?

A. SEC
B. NASD
C. MSRB
D. Regulation T

28. Max Leveridge wants to buy $1,200 worth of stock on margin. He currently has a margin account with open long positions and equity of $600. What will Max's required deposit be on the purchase of $1,200 of securities?

A. $600
B. $900
C. $1,200
D. $1,400

29. According to Reg T and the NASD/NYSE, initial and maintenance margin requirements for a short account are

A. 50% initial, 25% maintenance
B. 50% initial, 30% maintenance
C. 50% initial, 50% maintenance
D. 70% initial, 50% maintenance

30. An investor opens a new margin account and buys 200 shares of COD at 60, with Reg T at 50%. What is the investor's initial margin requirement?

A. $3,000
B. $3,600
C. $6,000
D. $12,000

31. An investor opens a new margin account and buys 300 shares of DWQ at 47 1/2, with Reg T at 50%. What is the investor's initial margin requirement?

A. $3,562.50
B. $4,275
C. $7,125
D. $14,250

32. An investor opens a new margin account and buys 100 shares of DWQ at 18, with Reg T at 50%. What is the investor's initial margin requirement?

A. $450
B. $900
C. $1,800
D. $2,000

33. An investor opens a new margin account and buys 200 shares of KLP at 18, with Reg T at 50%. What is the investor's initial margin requirement?

    A. $900
    B. $1,800
    C. $2,000
    D. $3,600

34. An investor opens a new margin account and buys 100 shares of DWQ at 50, with Reg T at 50%. If the investor deposits enough cash to meet the initial margin requirement, what is the investor's equity?

    A. $2,500
    B. $3,000
    C. $4,000
    D. $5,000

35. An investor has an established margin account with a current market value of $7,500 and a debit balance of $3,500, with Reg T at 50%. How much equity does the investor have in the account?

    A. $3,500
    B. $3,750
    C. $4,000
    D. $7,500

36. An investor has an established margin account with a current market value of $4,400 and a debit balance of $1,750, with Reg T at 50%. How much buying power does the investor have in the account?

    A. $900
    B. $2,200
    C. $2,650
    D. $4,400

37. An investor has an established margin account with a short market value of $6,500 and a credit balance of $8,250, with Reg T at 50%. How much money must the investor deposit to satisfy the maintenance requirement?

    A. $0
    B. $100
    C. $150
    D. $200

38. A margin account has a long market value of $6,000 and a debit balance of $5,000. This account will receive a call to deposit

    A. $500
    B. $1,000
    C. $2,000
    D. $5,000

39. In a new margin account, a customer buys 100 shares of COD stock at 30 and meets the initial margin requirement. If the stock falls to 25, the equity in the account is

    A. $1,000
    B. $1,500
    C. $2,000
    D. $2,500

40. An investor has an established margin account with a short market value of $12,000 and a credit balance of $15,600, with Reg T at 50%. How much money must the investor deposit to satisfy the maintenance requirement?

    A. $0
    B. $1,800
    C. $3,000
    D. $3,600

41. An investor has an established margin account with a short market value of $17,500 and a credit balance of $23,000, with Reg T at 50%. How much money must the investor deposit to satisfy the maintenance requirement?

   A. $0
   B. $100
   C. $150
   D. $250

42. Although margin requirements are set by the Federal Reserve Board and the NASD and NYSE, member firms may

   A. increase or decrease these requirements through in-house rules
   B. disregard one set of rules if the other is applicable
   C. increase the requirements through in-house rules
   D. follow requirements that are less stringent

43. An investor has an established margin account with a long market value of $10,000 and a debit balance of $7,500, with Reg T at 50%. How much money must the investor deposit to satisfy the NASD/NYSE maintenance requirement?

   A. $0
   B. $500
   C. $1,250
   D. $2,500

44. An investor has an established margin account with a long market value of $6,500 and a debit balance of $3,750, with Reg T at 50%. A maintenance call would be triggered if the long market value decreased below

   A. $2,812.50
   B. $4,875.00
   C. $5,000.00
   D. $8,666.67

45. An investor has an established margin account with a short market value of $4,500 and a credit balance of $6,500, with Reg T at 50%. A maintenance call would be triggered if the short market value increased above

   A. $5,000
   B. $6,750
   C. $9,000
   D. $13,000

◆ Answers & Rationale

1.   C.   Lotta Leveridge could withdraw cash equal to the excess equity. A purchase of 200 shares at $60 per share would require an initial deposit of $6,000 on market value of $12,000. Lotta would have $6,000 in equity and a $6,000 debit. After a rise to $75 a share, the stock's market value would be $15,000. Lotta's debit balance would remain unchanged at $6,000, but her equity would increase to $9,000 ($15,000 CMV – $6,000 DR). Reg T on $15,000 CMV is $7,500. Lotta's $9,000 equity less the $7,500 Reg T leaves her with $1,500 in excess equity.   (Page 273)

2.   A.   At $80 per share, Max had to deposit 50% of the SMV of the shorted stock. At that point, the short account had a $12,000 credit (100 × $80 plus $8,000 × 50%), and Max had equity of $4,000. Maintenance on a short account is 30% of SMV, so initial maintenance was $2,400. If the stock price rises to $90 per share (an increase of $1,000 in SMV), the increase cuts into Max's equity by an equal amount. Max's equity after the price rise is now only $3,000. Maintenance on the stock at a price of $90 would be 30% of $9,000, or $2,700. Max's equity is still greater than the minimum maintenance requirement for the short sale of this stock, but only by $300. Any further price increases will probably result in a maintenance call by your firm.   (Page 281)

3.   C.   The formula for equity in a long account is the long market value minus the debit balance. The formula for equity in a short account is the credit balance minus the short market value. Together, they equal answer C.   (Page 283)

4.   B.   The question defines selling short against the box.   (Page 282)

5.   D.   The equity in a long account is LMV minus debits ($50,000 – $12,000 = $38,000). The equity in the short account is credits minus SMV ($22,000 – $27,000 = –$5,000). The net equity position is $33,000.   (Page 283)

6.   C.   Reg T requires a 50% margin when selling short. $3,500 × .50 = $1,750. However, the NYSE requirement that a client deposit a minimum of $2,000 when opening a short account applies. Therefore, C is the correct answer.   (Page 281)

7.   A.   Short sales are used to profit if prices fall.   (Page 281)

8.   B.   LMV minus debit equals equity.

$ 11,000	DWQ
+ 19,500	MTN
+ 36,000	TBS
$ 66,500	Total LMV
– 37,000	Debit balance
$ 29,500	Equity

(Page 274)

9.   D.   To be nonrestricted, the account must be at 50% margin. 50% of $66,500 equals $33,250 required equity.

$ 33,250	50% of LMV
– 29,500	Actual equity
$ 3,750	Restriction

If the $3,750 is deposited, equity would increase to 50% and the account would not be restricted.
(Page 274)

10.   B.   The NASD/NYSE margin maintenance requirement is 25% of market value in a long account (.25 × $66,500 = $16,625).   (Page 274)

11.   D.   Because the Reg T requirement is 50%, the investor deposits $7,500 and is loaned $7,500 (debit balance) for the $15,000 purchase. If the account is charged with $100 interest expense, the new debit balance is $7,600.   (Page 269)

12.   B.   One cannot use a tax device to convert short-term gains to long-term gains. If an investor sells short against the box on stock that has been held short term, the holding period on the stock is wiped out. Thus, when the short is covered with the delivery of the shares, any gain or loss is always short term. One cannot sell short against the box to lock in a short-term gain and then stretch the gain into a long-term gain.   (Page 282)

13. **A.**   Any cash proceeds can be used to reduce a customer's loan. When shares of stock are increased through a stock dividend, the value of each share will be reduced proportionately. Therefore, stock dividends do not decrease the debit balance.
(Page 271)

14. **D.**   When dividends are received in an unrestricted margin account, the funds can be withdrawn from the account in full. The retention requirement (50%) applies to sales of securities out of a restricted margin account, not to the retention of dividends or interest.   (Page 271)

15. **D.**   Because the stock is paid in full, the customer could take all $50,000 if he sold the stock.
(Page 270)

16. **C.**   Because there is no loan against the $50,000 stock position, the customer can borrow $25,000 in cash (50%). This would allow the purchase of another $50,000 of stock in the account.
(Page 270)

17. **D.**   After the new stock purchase, the account would show:

$ 50,000	Fully paid securities
+ 50,000	New purchase
$100,000	Long market value
− 50,000	Debit balance
$ 50,000	Equity

(Page 270)

18. **A.**   NASD minimum maintenance in a long account is 25% of the market value.   (Page 277)

19. **B.**   NASD minimum maintenance in a short account is 30% of the market value or $5 per share, whichever is greater, for stocks trading above $5. For stocks trading below $5, the minimum maintenance is $2.50 per share or 100% of market value, whichever is greater.   (Page 277)

20. **D.**   The Federal Reserve Board does not set minimum margin requirements for exempt securities, including municipal securities and U.S. government securities. The margin is set by the NASD and NYSE.   (Page 270)

21. **C.**   The required deposit is calculated by multiplying the market value of $5,550 by the Reg T requirement of 50%, which equals $2,775.
(Page 280)

22. **C.**   The required deposit is calculated by multiplying the market value of $4,200 by the Reg T requirement of 50%, which equals $2,100.
(Page 280)

23. **C.**   The Reg T requirement is $1,625 ($3,250 × 50%). When selling stock short in a new account, an investor must meet the NASD/NYSE initial minimum requirement of $2,000.
(Page 281)

24. **D.**   The Reg T requirement is $500 ($1,000 × 50%). When selling stock short in a new account, an investor must meet the NASD/NYSE initial minimum requirement of $2,000.   (Page 281)

25. **A.**   The minimum maintenance requirement for a long margin account is calculated by multiplying the current market value by 25% ($24,000 × 25% = $6,000). The investor has an equity balance of $4,500 in the account and must deposit an additional $1,500 to satisfy the $6,000 minimum requirement.   (Page 278)

26. **A.**   The customer's credit balance after selling short and meeting Reg T is equal to 150% of the proceeds of the short sale, or $22,500. The equity in her account equals the credit balance less the current market value of the shares, which is $12,000. The difference equals $10,500.
(Page 281)

27. **B.**   The NASD sets the minimum maintenance for municipal securities, which is 7% of the principal amount or 15% of the market value, whichever is greater.   (Page 277)

28. **C.** The $2,000 minimum requirement per account of the NASD and NYSE does not require a deposit greater than 100% of the cost of stock being purchased. Normally one has to deposit only the Reg T requirement when buying marginable stock. However, if an existing account has equity of less than $2,000 and the value of stock to be purchased, plus existing equity, is still less than $2,000, the stock must be paid for in full.

(Page 276)

29. **B.** Initial Reg T margin is 50% and the maintenance margin is 30% for short accounts.

(Page 277)

30. **C.** The initial margin requirement is calculated by multiplying the market value of $12,000 by the Reg T requirement of 50%, which equals $6,000. (Page 270)

31. **C.** The initial margin requirement is calculated by multiplying the market value of $14,250 by the Reg T requirement of 50%, which equals $7,125. (Page 270)

32. **C.** The Reg T requirement is $900 ($1,800 × 50%). The investor must meet the lesser of the NASD/NYSE initial minimum requirement of $2,000 or the full price of the stock. Because the full purchase price of the stock is below the $2,000 minimum requirement, the investor need only deposit the price of the stock, which is $1,800.

(Page 270)

33. **C.** The Reg T requirement is $1,800 ($3,600 × 50%). The investor must meet the lesser of the NASD/NYSE initial minimum requirement of $2,000 or the full price of the stock. The investor must deposit $2,000 in his margin account.

(Page 270)

34. **A.** If the investor meets the initial margin requirement by depositing $2,500, the investor has $2,500 in equity in the account. (Page 277)

35. **C.** Equity is calculated by subtracting the debit balance of $3,500 from the current market value of $7,500, which equals $4,000. (Page 277)

36. **A.** The Reg T requirement is 50% of the current market value of $4,400, which equals $2,200. Equity is equal to the current market value of $4,400 minus the debit balance of $1,750, which equals $2,650. Excess equity is calculated by subtracting the Reg T requirement of $2,200 from the current equity of $2,650, which equals $450. Buying power is then calculated by dividing the excess equity of $450 by the Reg T requirement of 50%, which equals $900. (Page 271)

37. **D.** Minimum maintenance requirement for a short margin account is calculated by multiplying the current market value of $6,500 by 30%, which equals $1,950. The investor must have at least $1,950 in equity in the account. The investor has an equity balance of $1,750 in the account and must deposit an additional $200 to satisfy the $1,950 minimum requirement. (Page 281)

38. **A.** The maintenance requirement in a long margin account is 25% of the market value of the stock owned in the account. The equity is $1,000 and the maintenance requirement is $1,500 (25% of the $6,000 long market value). Therefore, the account will receive a margin call for $500.

(Page 277)

39. **B.** The NYSE and the NASD require a minimum of $2,000 to open a margin account when a customer borrows from a broker-dealer. After the customer sends in the required $2,000, the account equity is $2,000. When the market value falls to $2,500 (a decrease of $500), the equity will also decline by the same amount. (Page 277)

40. **A.** The minimum maintenance requirement for a short margin account is calculated by multiplying the current market value by 30% ($12,000 × 30% = $3,600). The investor must have at least $3,600 in equity in the account. Equity is calculated by subtracting the current market value of $12,000 from the credit balance of $15,600, which equals $3,600. The investor's account is exactly at the minimum requirement and would not receive a maintenance call to deposit additional funds.

(Page 281)

41. **A.**   Minimum maintenance requirement for a short margin account is calculated by multiplying the current market value of $17,500 by 30%, which equals $5,250. The investor must have at least $5,250 in equity in the account. The investor has an equity balance of $5,500 in the account and would not be required to deposit any additional money.   (Page 281)

42. **C.**   Firms may set their own margin requirements at more stringent levels than the FRB and NASD/NYSE rules. However, they may never go below the FRB and NASD/NYSE margin requirements.   (Page 279)

43. **A.**   The minimum maintenance requirement for a long margin account is calculated by multi-plying the current market value by 25% ($10,000 × 25% = $2,500). Equity is calculated by subtracting the debit balance of $7,500 from the current market value of $10,000, which equals $2,500. The investor's account is exactly at the minimum requirement and would not receive a maintenance call to deposit additional funds.   (Page 277)

44. **C.**   To determine long market value at maintenance, divide the debit balance of $3,750 by 75%, which equals $5,000.   (Page 278)

45. **A.**   The maximum market value is calculated by dividing the credit balance of $6,500 by 130%, which equals $5,000.   (Page 282)

Use the following information to answer questions 1 and 2. A customer's margin account has a debit balance of $11,000 and contains the following securities (Reg T 50%):

Stock	No. Shares	CMV
ALF	100	$50
COD	500	$20
QRS	200	$80

1. If the market value of the securities increases to $40,000, the customer could withdraw in cash

   A. $3,600
   B. $4,500
   C. $5,000
   D. $9,000

2. If the customer wishes to purchase additional stock after the advance in market value to $40,000, using SMA the customer could purchase a maximum of

   A. $7,000 worth
   B. $9,000 worth
   C. $10,000 worth
   D. $18,000 worth

3. A customer has a margin account with a market value of $20,000, a debit balance of $12,000 and no SMA. Reg T is 50%. If the customer sells $2,000 worth of stock, the amount released to SMA is

   A. $300
   B. $400
   C. $500
   D. $1,000

4. Assume that a customer has an established margin account with no SMA and that the account is restricted. With the Reg T requirement at 50%, the purchase of $1,000 worth of stock would generate a Reg T call of how much?

   A. $250
   B. $500
   C. $2,000
   D. $2,500

Use the following information to answer questions 5 through 8. An account has a $22,000 market value and a debit balance of $6,000, with $5,000 SMA. Reg T is 50%.

5.   The customer could withdraw

A. $0
B. $2,000
C. $5,000
D. $10,000

6.   Without putting up additional margin, the customer could purchase stock worth

A. $2,500
B. $5,000
C. $10,000
D. $15,000

7.   Under NASD rules, the minimum maintenance margin requirement for the account is

A. $5,000
B. $5,500
C. $6,000
D. $6,600

8.   To what level could the market value of the stock decline before a call would have to be sent for additional funds?

A. $6,000
B. $8,000
C. $11,200
D. $16,000

9.   If a customer's account has a market value of $50,000 and a debit balance of $12,000, what is the SMA (Reg T 50%)?

A. $4,800
B. $8,000
C. $13,000
D. $38,000

10.   Which of the following increases SMA?

A.   Receipt of a cash dividend
B.   Decline in market value of long positions
C.   Withdrawal of margin securities
D.   Purchase of margin securities

11.   Max Leveridge's margin account has available SMA of $10,000. How much would he have to deposit to purchase listed options with premiums totaling $18,000?

A. $4,000
B. $6,500
C. $8,000
D. $16,000

12.   Gwinneth Stout is long 200 shares of MTN at 30 and 400 shares of DWQ at 20 in a margin account. The debit balance in the account is $8,000. She sells 200 of the DWQ shares for $4,000. The credit to SMA is

A. $0
B. $1,000
C. $2,000
D. $4,000

13.   By how much would the SMA increase if a customer bought $22,000 of marginable stock in the existing margin account and fully paid for the transaction?

A. $0
B. $5,500
C. $11,000
D. $22,000

14.   Which of the following will cause a change in SMA in a long account?

I.   Purchase of stock
II.   Sale of stock
III.   Increase in market value
IV.   Decrease in market value

A.   I and II only
B.   I, II and III only
C.   III only
D.   I, II, III and IV

15. An investor has an established margin account with a current market value of $4,400 and a debit balance of $1,750, with Reg T at 50%. How much buying power does the investor have in the account?

    A. $900
    B. $2,200
    C. $2,650
    D. $4,400

◆ Answers & Rationale

1.   **D.**   The customer could withdraw $9,000 from the account. The SMA balance, which originally stood at $4,500, increased to $9,000, computed as follows:

$ 5,000	Stock ALF (100 × $50)
10,000	Stock COD (500 × $20)
16,000	Stock QRS (200 × $80)
$ 31,000	
– 15,500	Reg T 50%
– 11,000	Debit balance
$ 4,500	SMA
$ 40,000	CMV
– 20,000	Reg T 50%
– 11,000	Debit balance
$ 9,000	SMA

(Page 286)

2.   **D.**   Buying power is determined by dividing a customer's SMA by the Reg T margin requirement—in this case, $9,000 divided by 50% equals $18,000. At 50% Reg T margin, the math is simple: SMA × 2 = Buying power.   (Page 287)

3.   **D.**   This is an example of a restricted account with equity below the 50% Reg T requirement. In a restricted account, 50% of the sale proceeds is released to SMA (50% × $2,000 = $1,000).   (Page 286)

4.   **B.**   The customer must deposit the full margin requirement of the purchase (50% of $1,000) whether the account is restricted or not; therefore, the call would be for $500. (Also note that the account would be subject to the NASD/NYSE $2,000 minimum equity requirement.) (Page 288)

5.   **C.**   The customer could withdraw the SMA of $5,000. SMA can be withdrawn at any time or can be used towards an additional purchase, provided this action does not cause the equity in the account to fall below 25% equity or the $2,000 minimum maintenance level.   (Page 287)

6.   **C.**   Buying power is determined by dividing the customer's SMA ($5,000) by the margin requirement of 50% ($5,000 ÷ 50% = $10,000). Or, at 50% margin, buying power equals SMA times 2.   (Page 287)

7.   **B.**   Minimum maintenance in a long account is 25% of the market value (25% × $22,000 = $5,500).   (Page 288)

8.   **B.**   If the minimum equity requirement for account maintenance purposes is 25% of the market value, this means the maximum loan value is 75% (reciprocal of 25%). Thus, the debit balance must never be greater than 75% of the market value or else the account would be below the minimum maintenance requirement. To find the minimum market value needed to support a customer's debit balance and keep the account at the minimum equity threshold, use either of the following calculations (both produce the same answer): Debit balance divided by 75% equals market value ($6,000 ÷ 75% = $8,000) or minimum debit balance times 4/3 equals market value ($6,000 × 4/3 = $8,000).   (Page 288)

9.   **C.**   The status of the account is as follows:

$ 50,000	CMV
– 12,000	DR
$ 38,000	EQ
– 25,000	Reg T 50%
$ 13,000	SMA

(Page 286)

10. **A.**   Cash dividends are automatically credited to SMA.   (Page 285)

11. **C.**   The options purchases must be fully paid. The customer has available SMA of $10,000, which means $10,000 may be borrowed from the account. The remaining $8,000 must be deposited by the customer.   (Page 287)

12. **C.**   Because this account is below 50% margin, the account is restricted ($6,000 equity ÷ $14,000 market value = 42.8% equity). When securities are sold in a restricted account, 50% of the proceeds must be retained in the account, with the

other 50% released to the customer. If the funds are not withdrawn, the 50% proceeds are noted in the memorandum account and credited to SMA. This means that the amount of the line of credit can be borrowed from the account or can be applied toward future purchases. Because $4,000 of securities are sold, $2,000 (50%) is credited to SMA.

(Page 286)

13. **C.** Assuming that the customer paid for the securities in full, he would generate $11,000 in SMA. Because the customer need pay only half of the securities' value ($11,000), the additional cash paid ($11,000) would be considered a nonrequired cash deposit and would be credited to the SMA. Another way to look at it is that the customer has fully paid securities with a loan value of 50%, or $11,000.

(Page 285)

14. **B.** Once SMA is created in a long account, it is not reduced by a decline in market value. The SMA may still be taken out as long as it will not bring the account below the maintenance level. An increase in market value as well as a sale of stock increases SMA. The purchase of stock decreases available SMA.

(Page 286)

15. **A.** The Reg T requirement is 50% of the current market value of $4,400, which equals $2,200. Equity is equal to the current market value of $4,400 minus the debit balance of $1,750, which equals $2,650. Excess equity is calculated by subtracting the Reg T requirement of $2,200 from the current equity of $2,650, which equals $450. Buying power is then calculated by dividing the excess equity of $450 by the Reg T requirement of 50%, which equals $900.

(Page 287)

1. Under SEC Rule 15c3-3, customer excess margin securities carried by a broker-dealer are equal to the

   A. difference between the required amount of initial margin and the market value of the margin securities
   B. difference between customer debit balances and the market value of the margin securities
   C. market value of the margin securities in excess of 140% of net customer debit balances
   D. market value of the margin securities in excess of 140% of gross customer debit balances

2. A customer buys 1,000 shares of COW at $50 a share when Regulation T is 50%. The customer's debit balance is $25,000. Assuming that the broker-dealer has hypothecated the maximum amount of stock permissible for the customer, the firm should be holding in segregation how many shares?

   A. 0
   B. 300
   C. 500
   D. 1,000

3. Which of the following statements regarding the handling of a customer's securities by a broker-dealer are true?

   I. The securities may be commingled with those of other customers if all of the customers involved grant consent in writing.
   II. The securities may be commingled with those of the broker-dealer if the customer grants consent in writing.
   III. The broker-dealer may use the customer's securities as collateral to borrow only to the extent of the customer's indebtedness to the broker-dealer.
   IV. The securities may be loaned to another customer if the lending customer grants consent in writing.

   A. I and II only
   B. I, III and IV only
   C. II, III and IV only
   D. I, II, III and IV

4. Under what circumstances may a member firm commingle the securities of two or more customers?

   A. With the customers' written permission
   B. With the SEC's written permission
   C. With the NASD's written permission
   D. Under no circumstances

5. A member firm may commingle the securities of its customers with securities belonging to the firm

    A. with the customers' written permission
    B. with the SEC's written permission
    C. with the NASD's written permission
    D. under no circumstances

6. Fully paid or excess margin securities carried for a customer's account

    A. may be used by a broker-dealer to clear a fail to deliver
    B. may be pledged
    C. may be loaned to another customer of the broker-dealer
    D. must be segregated

7. The SEC prohibits the lending of excess margin securities by a broker-dealer

    A. unless the customer granted permission when he signed the margin agreement
    B. unless the customer has given written consent
    C. unless the customer granted permission when he signed the loan consent agreement
    D. under any circumstances

8. Which of the following phrases commonly refer(s) to SEC Rule 15c3-3?

    I.   Minimum net capital requirements
    II.   Customer protection rule
    III. Reserves and custody of securities
    IV.   Supplemental financial and operational reports

    A. I and IV
    B. II and III
    C. II and IV
    D. IV

9. A customer has a $125,000 debit and a $25,000 credit from short sales. His long account is secured by 2,000 shares of TIP common stock trading at $100 per share. According to SEC Rule 15c3-3, the broker-dealer must segregate what minimum number of shares?

    A. 250
    B. 600
    C. 750
    D. 1,000

◆ Answers & Rationale

1. **C.** Under the rule, excess margin securities are those in excess of 140% of *net* customer debit balances. "Net customer debit balances" means debits net of free credits. Credits arising from short sales are not offset against the customer debits.
(Page 291)

2. **B.** Broker-dealers are allowed to rehypothecate customer margin securities in amounts of up to 140% of an account's debit balance. In this case, the debit balance is $25,000, which means that $35,000 worth of stock ($25,000 × 140%) can be hypothecated. With the stock at 50, a total of 700 shares ($35,000 ÷ $50) can be hypothecated as margin stock, and the balance of 300 shares must be segregated as excess margin stock.
(Page 291)

3. **B.** Under SEC Rule 15c2-1, customer securities may be commingled with those of other customers if all of the customers express their consent in writing. The broker-dealer is permitted to pledge customer securities to a bank to obtain a loan, provided the loan does not exceed the amount the broker-dealer has loaned to the customers. If the customer has signed a separate loan consent, the securities may be loaned by the broker-dealer to another customer. Customer securities may never be commingled with firm positions.   (Page 290)

4. **A.** A member may commingle customer securities with those of other customers only if all of

the customers involved give their written consent.
(Page 290)

5. **D.** A member may never commingle customer securities with firm positions.   (Page 290)

6. **D.** If a broker-dealer holds stock in excess of 140% of a customer's debit balance, or if a customer has no debit balance, the broker-dealer must segregate the stock and may not use it in its business operations for any reason.   (Page 291)

7. **D.** Excess margin securities are fully owned by the customer. SEC rules prohibit broker-dealers from lending these securities or using them as collateral for a loan.   (Page 291)

8. **B.** SEC Rule 15c3-3 is called the "customer protection rule" because of its provisions for safeguarding customer assets. Specifically the rule requires broker-dealers to segregate customers' fully paid and excess margin securities, as well as to establish a special reserve account for certain other customer credits.   (Page 291)

9. **A.** The customer has a $125,000 debit and a $25,000 credit from short sales. This credit is not netted against the debit. Therefore, the amount of the customer's securities that may be rehypothecated equals 140% of $125,000, or $175,000. The customer's debit is collateralized by 2,000 TIP shares valued at $100 each, or $200,000 of stock. Because $175,000 of this stock may be rehypothecated, $25,000 (the excess margin securities) must be segregated (reduced to possession or control). Therefore, $25,000 divided by $100 per share equals 250 shares.   (Page 291)

45 Economics Exam

1. Which of the following is a coincident indicator?

   A. Stock market
   B. Machine tool orders
   C. Industrial production
   D. Agricultural employment

2. Which of the following is a leading indicator?

   A. Stock market
   B. Gross domestic product
   C. Unemployment
   D. Industrial production

3. Which of the following is considered the most accurate method of measuring GDP?

   A. Actual dollars
   B. Constant dollars
   C. Eurodollars
   D. M1 dollars

4. In order to calculate constant dollars, gross domestic product is adjusted

   A. to match foreign GDP
   B. for inflation
   C. to include bank reserves
   D. downward by the balance of payments

5. Which of the following is a lagging indicator?

   A. S&P 500
   B. Housing permits issued
   C. Corporate profits
   D. Hours worked

6. To determine the amount of change in the GDP from one year to another, both years should be converted into

   A. the exchange value of the dollar, as compared with major foreign currencies
   B. international depositary receipts
   C. constant dollars
   D. the current dollar price of gold bullion

7. Arrange the following economic phases in the normal order in which they occur.

   I. Contraction
   II. Expansion
   III. Peak
   IV. Trough

   A. I, II, III, IV
   B. II, III, I, IV
   C. III, II, I, IV
   D. IV, I, III, II

8. Arrange the following economic phases in the normal order in which they occur.

    I.   Recovery
    II. Trough
    III. Recession
    IV. Prosperity

    A. I, IV, III, II
    B. II, I, III, IV
    C. III, IV, I, II
    D. IV, III, I, II

9. During the past two quarters, the GDP declined by 3%, unemployment rose by .7% and the Consumer Price Index fell off by 1.3%. This economic condition is called

    A. inflation
    B. depression
    C. stagflation
    D. recession

10. Which of the following economists is(was) a supporter of demand-side economics?

    A. Adam Smith
    B. John Maynard Keynes
    C. Arthur Laffer
    D. Milton Friedman

11. According to Keynesian economic theory, an economy's health can be ensured if the government

    A. cuts taxes for businesses and the wealthy
    B. increases aggregate demand
    C. increases the money supply
    D. does not interfere

12. If inflation momentum is decreasing, the value of fixed-income securities would be

    A. stable
    B. increasing
    C. decreasing
    D. fluctuating

13. Which kind of economists would encourage a government to spend money to move the economy into an expansionary phase?

    A. Classical
    B. Keynesian
    C. Supply side
    D. Monetarist

14. An increase in inventories is a sign of

    A. increasing consumer demand
    B. deteriorating economic conditions
    C. an expansion of the GDP
    D. increased industrial production

15. Which of the following is considered a lagging economic indicator?

    A. Ratio of consumer credit to consumer income
    B. Building permits and housing starts
    C. Nonagricultural employment
    D. Dow Jones Industrial Average

16. What term do economists use to describe a downturn in the economy that lasts more than two consecutive quarters?

    A. Inflation
    B. Stagflation
    C. Depression
    D. Recession

17. What term do economists use to describe a downturn in the economy that is characterized by both unemployment and rising prices?

    A. Inflation
    B. Stagflation
    C. Depression
    D. Recession

18. Which of the following is considered a lagging economic indicator?

    A. Duration of unemployment
    B. Personal income
    C. Money supply
    D. Orders for durable goods

19. New orders for durable goods is what kind of economic indicator?

   A. Leading
   B. Coincident
   C. Coterminous
   D. Lagging

20. A slowdown in deliveries is what kind of economic indicator?

   A. Leading
   B. Coincident
   C. Coterminous
   D. Lagging

21. Industrial production is what kind of economic indicator?

   A. Leading
   B. Coincident
   C. Coterminous
   D. Lagging

22. Statistics from which of the following industries are considered a leading indicator of economic growth?

   A. Natural gas
   B. New housing
   C. Automotive
   D. High technology

◆ Answers & Rationale

1.   **C.**   Industrial production is a coincident indicator. The stock market anticipates the economy. Agricultural employment is not used by economists as an indicator.   (Page 301)

2.   **A.**   The stock market anticipates the economy and is a leading indicator.   (Page 300)

3.   **B.**   Constant dollars are mathematically adjusted to remove the effects of inflation, so that when comparing the GDP of one period to another economic activity, rather than inflation, is measured.   (Page 299)

4.   **B.**   By adjusting GDP by inflation, one is able to measure economic activity with less distortion. After adjustment, the GDP will be set in constant dollars.   (Page 299)

5.   **C.**   Both the S&P 500 and housing permits are leading indicators. The measure of hours worked is a leading indicator as it reflects changes in the average work week during the current period of time. Corporate profits would be the lagging indicator.   (Page 301)

6.   **C.**   In order to compare GDP from one year to another, and thus compare the amount of real economic activity by comparison, constant dollars must be used to eliminate distortions caused by inflation.   (Page 299)

7.   **B.**   Economists consider expansion (recovery) as the beginning of the business cycle, followed by the peak (prosperity), contraction (recession or deflation) and the trough. (Page 298)

8.   **A.**   Economists consider expansion (recovery) as the beginning of the business cycle, followed by the peak (prosperity), contraction (recession or deflation) and the trough. (Page 298)

9.   **D.**   Two consecutive quarters or more of decline is termed a *recession.*   (Page 298)

10.   **B.**   John Maynard Keynes was the first demand-side economist; he believed that by increasing the income available for spending and saving a government could increase demand and improve the country's economic well-being.   (Page 302)

11.   **B.**   Keynesians theorize that government efforts to increase aggregate demand by increasing its own purchases of goods and services will result in the healthiest economy.   (Page 302)

12.   **B.**   When the rate of inflation is declining, the coupon rate of new issue bonds will be less and yields will decline. The price of outstanding bonds will rise to adjust their yield.   (Page 300)

13.   **B.**   Keynesians advocate government intervention in the workings of the economy through increased government spending, which in turn increases aggregate demand.   (Page 303)

14.   **B.**   Increasing inventories mean that consumer demand is slackening. Thus, disposable income is dropping and economic conditions are deteriorating. Increased consumer demand, a rising GDP and increased industrial production are all positive economic signs.   (Page 300)

15.   **A.**   Consumers tend to borrow more after the economy improves and interest rates go down, and pay back loans after the economy contracts and interest rates go up.   (Page 301)

16.   **D.**   An economic downturn that lasts for more than two consecutive quarters (six months) is known as a *recession.*   (Page 298)

17.   **B.**   *Stagflation* is the term used to describe the unusual combination of inflation and unemployment (stagnation).   (Page 298)

18.   **A.**   The average time it takes an unemployed person to find a new job is a lagging indicator. Employment is usually one of the last things to pick up as the economy enters a period of expansion. Layoffs are one of the last resorts for companies when the economy turns down.   (Page 301)

19. **A.** New orders for durable goods is a leading economic indicator. (Page 300)

20. **A.** Slowdowns in deliveries is a leading economic indicator. (Page 300)

21. **B.** Industrial production is a coincident economic indicator. (Page 301)

22. **B.** A leading indicator is one that predicts future growth trends. The usual indicators involve increases in basic productive processes, which means that more people will be hired and more disposable income will then be available. Such indicators include steel shipments and housing starts. (Page 300)

46 Government Economic Policy Exam

1. The FOMC is purchasing T bills in the open market. Which two of the following scenarios are likely to occur?

   I. Secondary bond prices will rise.
   II. Secondary bond prices will fall.
   III. Interest rates will rise.
   IV. Interest rates will fall.

   A. I and III
   B. I and IV
   C. II and III
   D. II and IV

2. Federal Open Market Committee activities are closely monitored by Wall Street because of the effect of its decisions on all of the following EXCEPT

   A. money supply
   B. interest rates
   C. exchange rates
   D. money velocity

3. If the Federal Reserve Board decided that it was necessary to change the money supply, which of the following instruments would it NOT use?

   A. Bank reserve requirements
   B. Open market operations
   C. Tax rate
   D. Discount rate

4. Which organization or governmental unit sets fiscal policy?

   A. Federal Reserve Board
   B. Government Economic Board
   C. Congress
   D. Secretary of the Treasury

5. In its attempt to increase the money supply, the Federal Open Market Committee is purchasing T bills. This action should cause the yield on T bills to

   A. increase
   B. decrease
   C. fluctuate
   D. stabilize

6. Which of the following situations could cause a fall in the value of the U.S. dollar in relation to the Japanese yen?

   I. Japanese investors buying U.S. Treasury securities
   II. U.S. investors buying Japanese corporations
   III. Increase in Japan's trade surplus over that of the United States
   IV. General decrease in U.S. interest rates

   A. I, II and III
   B. I and IV
   C. II and III
   D. II, III and IV

7. If the Federal Open Market Committee has decided that the rate of inflation is too high, it is MOST likely to

    I.   tighten the money supply
    II. loosen the money supply
    III. lower the discount rate
    IV. raise the discount rate

    A. I and III
    B. I and IV
    C. II and III
    D. II and IV

8. A reduction in the reserve requirement by the FRB will have what sort of effect on total bank deposits?

    I.   Decrease
    II. Increase
    III. Multiplier
    IV. Logarithmic

    A. I and III
    B. I and IV
    C. II and III
    D. II and IV

9. An increase in the reserve requirement by the FRB will have what sort of effect on total bank deposits?

    I.   Decrease
    II. Increase
    III. Multiplier
    IV. Logarithmic

    A. I and III
    B. I and IV
    C. II and III
    D. II and IV

10. The open market operations of the Fed are intended to cause direct changes in

    A. interest rates
    B. exchange rates
    C. money velocity
    D. the money supply

11. Which of the following are responsibilities of the Federal Reserve Board?

    I.   Acting as an agent for the U.S. Treasury
    II. Regulating credit
    III. Serving as the nation's central bank
    IV. Setting the prime rate

    A. I, II and III only
    B. I and III only
    C. II and IV only
    D. I, II, III and IV

12. The open market operations of the FOMC affect all of the following EXCEPT

    A. bank excess reserves
    B. the national debt
    C. the amount of money in circulation
    D. interest rates

13. Which of the following is part of M2 but not of M1?

    A. Currency in circulation
    B. Demand deposits at S&Ls
    C. Money-market mutual funds
    D. Checking accounts at commercial banks

14. The Fed has just increased the discount rate. Which of the following is MOST likely to be adversely affected by this action?

    A. Cyclical industries
    B. Defensive industries
    C. Heavy industries such as steel
    D. Utilities

15. Through its open market operations, the Federal Reserve trades all of the following EXCEPT

    A. Ginnie Maes
    B. Treasury notes
    C. project notes
    D. FICB securities

16. The federal funds rate has fallen to an all-time low. All of the following statements are true EXCEPT that

   A. the Fed is trying to expand credit
   B. the prime rate will rise
   C. banks will have no difficulty borrowing short-term monies
   D. the money supply will increase

17. Disintermediation is MOST likely to occur when

   A. money is tight
   B. interest rates are low
   C. margin requirements are high
   D. the interest ceilings on certificates of deposit have been raised

18. Which of the following conditions might cause the Federal Reserve Board to expand credit?

   I. Decline in the unemployment rate
   II. Falling bond prices
   III. Drop in the GDP
   IV. Increase in the money supply

   A. I, II and IV only
   B. I and III only
   C. II and III only
   D. I, II, III and IV

19. To tighten credit during inflationary periods, the Federal Reserve Board can take any of the following actions EXCEPT

   A. raise reserve requirements
   B. change the amount of U.S. government debt held by institutions
   C. sell securities in the open market
   D. lower taxes

20. The Federal Reserve Board foresees the probability of an overheated economy and the resumption of double-digit inflation. Attempting to avoid the painful results of inflation, the FRB takes actions to slow down the economy, including increasing the discount rate. The likely effects of these moves are a(n)

   I. increase in the prime rate
   II. increase in bond interest and an accompanying decrease in bond prices
   III. slowdown in corporate growth
   IV. decrease in corporate earnings and equity prices

   A. I and II only
   B. I, III and IV only
   C. III and IV only
   D. I, II, III and IV

21. Which of the following is NOT part of M1?

   A. Travelers' checks
   B. Money-market mutual fund
   C. Coins
   D. Consumer checking account

◆ Answers & Rationale

1. **B.** When the Federal Open Market Committee purchases T bills in the open market, it pays for the transaction by increasing the reserve accounts of member banks, the net effect of which will increase the total money supply and signal a period of relatively easier credit conditions. Easier credit means interest rates will decline and the price for existing bonds will rise.   (Page 309)

2. **C.** The FOMC is one of the most influential committees in the Federal Reserve System. Its decisions affect money supplies, interest rates and the speed at which dollars turn over (money velocity). The foreign exchange rate is set in the interbank market.   (Page 309)

3. **C.** The Federal Reserve Board has several tools at its disposal that could be used to change the money supply, including bank reserve requirements, open market operations (trading government securities) and the discount rate.   (Page 306)

4. **C.** Congress sets fiscal policy, while the FRB sets monetary policy.   (Page 304)

5. **B.** The purpose of the FOMC purchase is to increase the attractiveness (market price) of T bills. Because the price will be driven up by an increased market demand and a decreased supply, yields should decrease.   (Page 309)

6. **D.** Increased foreign investment in the United States (choice I) would *raise* the relative value of the U.S. dollar. A decrease in U.S. interest rates (choice IV) would chase money out of the United States and increase the relative value of the foreign currency.   (Page 311)

7. **B.** If the FOMC decides that it is in the economy's interest to lower the inflation rate, it can encourage this to occur by raising the discount rate, which in turn will tighten the money supply.
(Page 309)

8. **C.** If the FRB lowers the reserve requirement, total bank deposits will increase because of the multiplier effect. With a lower requirement, the banks will have more money available to lend.
(Page 307)

9. **A.** If the FRB raises the reserve requirement, total bank deposits will decrease because of the multiplier effect. With a higher requirement, the banks will have less money available to lend.
(Page 307)

10. **D.** The open market transactions of the FOMC have a direct and powerful effect on M1, the largest component of the money supply.
(Page 308)

11. **A.** The Fed is the nation's independent monetary authority and central bank. It acts as the fiscal agent for the Treasury and attempts to maintain monetary stability and regulate credit. The prime rate is set by commercial banks, not by the Federal Reserve.   (Page 306)

12. **B.** When the Fed buys and sells securities on the open market, it is attempting to expand or contract the amount of money in circulation. When the Fed buys, bank excess reserves go up; when the Fed sells, bank excess reserves go down. This, in turn, affects the money supply, credit and, therefore, interest rates. The national debt is affected only when the government issues and redeems T bills, not when it is trading them in the market.
(Page 309)

13. **C.** Money-market funds are part of M2 but not M1. M2 includes everything in M1, plus time deposits and money-market funds.   (Page 305)

14. **D.** If the discount rate increases, all other interest rates are likely to follow. Because utilities are typically the most highly leveraged of all industries, an increase in interest rates could substantially increase their debt service cost and thus reduce earnings.   (Page 308)

15. **C.** The Federal Open Market Committee (FOMC) trades U.S. government and agency securities in the secondary market. The FOMC will buy

securities to inject reserves into the banks and will sell securities to drain reserves from the banks. This includes securities that are fully backed by the U.S. government, such as Treasury notes and GNMA certificates, and agency securities, such as those issued by the Federal Intermediate Credit Banks (FICBs). The Fed does not conduct open market operations with municipal securities.   (Page 308)

16. **B.**   The federal funds market involves short-term loans (sometimes overnight) to one bank from another member bank that has excess reserves. If the funds rate is falling, short-term interest rates are low and banks will have no difficulty borrowing required reserves; therefore, the money supply will expand. These conditions could be the result of deliberate actions on the part of the Fed to expand credit. The prime rate, which is the rate that commercial banks charge their best customers, will undoubtedly fall also.   (Page 308)

17. **A.**   Disintermediation is the flow of deposits out of banks and savings and loans into alternative, higher paying investments. It occurs when money is tight and interest rates are high because these alternative investments may then offer higher yields than S&Ls and banks can offer. However, when interest rates are low, investors may prefer to keep their money in banks and S&Ls. (Page 310)

18. **C.**   If economic conditions are deteriorating, the Fed might loosen the money supply to stimulate credit. A decline in the GDP indicates that the economy is deteriorating. Falling bond prices means that interest rates are rising; therefore, the Fed may have to expand credit. A decline in the unemployment rate, on the other hand, is a positive sign of improving economic conditions. If the money supply is already increased, the Fed may have to tighten, not loosen, credit.   (Page 307)

19. **D.**   To curb inflation, the Fed can sell securities in the open market (thus changing the amount of U.S. government debt held by institutions). It can also raise the reserve requirements, the discount rate or the margin requirements. The Fed has no control over taxes, which are changed by Congress.   (Page 307)

20. **D.**   Attempts of the FRB to slow down the economy will decrease the supply of money with a corresponding increase in interest rates. When interest rates go up, the prime rate increases, bond yields go up and bond prices drop. Higher interest rates have a tendency to slow down corporate growth with a resulting slowdown in earnings. Thus, stock prices tend to fall. All of these occur in approximately the sequence listed in the question.
(Page 308)

21. **B.**   Although money-market funds are highly liquid investments, they are considered time deposits and thus they are part of M2. (Page 305)

47 Technical Analysis Exam

1. According to technical analysis, when the market is consolidating a chart showing the market trendline would appear to be moving

   A. upwards to reach a new peak
   B. downwards to reach a new low
   C. downwards with sporadic upswings
   D. sideways within a narrow range

2. Four of the best known indexes and averages are listed below. How would they rank from the broadest measure of the market to the fewest number of issues in the index?

   I. Dow Jones Industrial Average
   II. NYSE Composite Index
   III. Standard & Poor's 500
   IV. Wilshire 5,000 Index

   A. I, IV, III, II
   B. II, III, I, IV
   C. III, II, IV, I
   D. IV, II, III, I

3. The Dow Jones Industrial Average is a(n)

   A. price-weighted average of 30 primarily industrial stocks
   B. price-weighted average of 300 primarily industrial stocks
   C. unweighted average of 30 primarily transportation stocks
   D. unweighted average of 300 primarily transportation stocks

4. One of your customers noticed that the monthly reports of total short interest of the NYSE have been showing an increase in the number of shares sold short. When he asks you for an interpretation, you should tell him that this signals a

   A. bullish market
   B. bearish market
   C. period of stability in the market
   D. period of volatility in the market

5. In the analysis of a company's stock, a technical analyst would take into consideration all of the following EXCEPT

   A. market price
   B. history
   C. volume
   D. earnings

6. Proponents of which technical theory assume that small investors are usually wrong?

   A. Breadth of market theory
   B. Short interest theory
   C. Volume of trading theory
   D. Odd lot theory

7. According to the Dow theory, reversal of a primary bullish trend must be confirmed by

   A. the duration of the secondary movements
   B. the advance/decline line
   C. the Dow Jones Industrial and Transportation Averages
   D. all of the above

8. A technical analyst would be concerned with all of the following trends EXCEPT

    A. reversals
    B. support levels
    C. PE ratios
    D. changes in the DJIA

9. Which of the following indexes or averages is based on the prices of only 65 stocks (30 industrials, 20 transportation and 15 utilities)?

    A. S&P Composite Index
    B. *Value Line*
    C. Dow Jones Composite Average
    D. Wilshire 5,000 Index

10. Industrial stocks are the largest component of which of the following indexes and averages?

    I.   Dow Jones Composite
    II.   NYSE Composite
    III. Standard & Poor's 500

    A. I only
    B. I and III only
    C. II only
    D. I, II and III

11. Which of the following market analysts is using the efficient market theory?

    A. Before he invests in a company, Max visits its headquarters to see whether management is running the company effectively.
    B. Joe has developed a system for identifying reversals in downward trendlines.
    C. Lotta picks company names out of a hat.
    D. Bea sells stock when she sees small investors buying.

◆ Answers & Rationale

1. **D.** A consolidating market is one that is staying within a narrow price range. When viewed on a graph, the trendline is horizontal and is said to be moving *sideways,* meaning neither up nor down. (Page 314)

2. **D.** Of the indexes and averages listed, the Wilshire 5,000 Index is the broadest measure of the market—it contains 5,000 issues (NYSE, AMEX and OTC securities). The NYSE Composite Index is based on the prices of all the common stocks listed on the exchange. The S&P 500, as the name implies, is based on the prices of 500 stocks—400 industrials, 20 transportation, 40 financial and 40 utility. The index recording the least number of issues is the Dow Jones Industrial Average—only 30 industrial stocks. (Page 313)

3. **A.** The Dow Jones Industrial Average (DJIA), published by Dow Jones & Company, is a price-weighted average of 30 stocks. These stocks represent primarily industrial corporations, but also include AT&T and American Express. (Page 313)

4. **A.** Even though short interest represents the number of people who expect the stock market to take a downward turn, it is considered a bullish indicator by many investors. Each share that has been sold short has to be replaced (covered) at some point. In order to replace the stock shorted, the investor will have to go into the market to buy that stock. When all of those short sellers have to buy back stock they shorted, it puts upward pressure on the price of those stocks. (Page 317)

5. **D.** A market technician (technical analyst) deals primarily with timing of activity and market trends, while a fundamental analyst centers on a particular industry or company within an industry and its relative health and market potential. (Page 312)

6. **D.** Odd lots are usually traded by small investors. Some analysts believe small investors are usually wrong. (Page 317)

7. **C.** Charted price trends can be deceptive, so a trend must be confirmed by the Dow Jones Industrial and Transportation Averages. (Page 316)

8. **C.** Technical analysts are more interested in forecasting market trends and securities prices than in studying individual corporations. Therefore, they are concerned with market prices, trading volumes, changes in the Dow Jones Industrial Average, reversals, support and resistance levels, advance/decline lines, short interest and many other factors that might help them time a buying or selling decision. Fundamental analysts, on the other hand, concentrate on the intrinsic quality of the stock; therefore, fundamental analysts are concerned with PE ratios and earnings per share. (Page 312)

9. **C.** The most widely quoted and oldest measures of changes in stock prices are the Dow Jones averages. They are also the smallest in terms of the number of stocks included in the averages. The Dow Jones Composite Average has only 65 stocks. (Page 313)

10. **D.** The industrial sector is the largest component of all three indexes. Therefore, the values of the indexes are most likely to be affected by a change in industrial stocks. (Page 313)

11. **C.** The efficient market theory holds that any change in the underlying value of a security is immediately reflected in the market price of that security. It then follows that every stock presents an equivalent opportunity to the investor. (Page 318)

48 Fundamental Analysis Exam

1. Which of the following industries would MOST likely be classed as *cyclical*?

   A. Pharmaceutical
   B. Durable goods
   C. Utilities
   D. Food

2. Which of the following industries would MOST likely be classed as *defensive*?

   A. Steel
   B. Automotive
   C. Airline
   D. Clothing

3. Which of the following industries would be MOST adversely affected by increases in interest rates?

   A. Pharmaceutical
   B. Durable goods
   C. Utilities
   D. Automobile

4. A fundamental analyst would MOST likely use the same techniques as a technical analyst to determine

   I. timing
   II. price
   III. industry selection
   IV. company selection

   A. I
   B. I and II
   C. III
   D. III and IV

5. A fundamental analyst would be concerned with all of the following EXCEPT

   A. historical earnings trends
   B. inflation rates
   C. capitalization
   D. trading volumes

6. The common stock of all of the following corporations would be considered defensive stock EXCEPT

   A. Boeing Corporation, an airplane manufacturer
   B. SuperValu, a retail grocery chain
   C. Commonwealth Edison, a utility
   D. Greater Health, Inc., a pharmaceutical company

7. For the past year, disposable personal income has fallen steadily. Which of the following is MOST likely to be affected?

   A. Defense industry
   B. Automotive industry
   C. Tobacco industry
   D. Firm that produces nondurable consumer goods

Use the following information to answer questions 8 and 9.

	ABC	DEF	GHI	JKL
EPS	$1.10	$1.25	$1.50	$1.90
Dividends	0	.25	.75	1.33
Retained earnings ratio	100%	80%	50%	30%

8. Which of the four corporations is MOST likely a growth company?

A. ABC
B. DEF
C. GHI
D. JKL

9. Which of the four corporations is MOST likely a utility company?

A. ABC
B. DEF
C. GHI
D. JKL

10. Growth companies tend to have all of the following characteristics EXCEPT

A. low PE ratios
B. low dividend payout ratios
C. high retained earnings ratios
D. potential investment return from capital gains rather than income

◆ Answers & Rationale

1. **B.** The production of durable goods depends upon whether the economy is in an expansion or a contraction phase. Pharmaceuticals, utilities and food are necessary all of the time.
(Page 319)

2. **D.** Steel, automotive and airline industries are involved in the production of capital goods. Clothing is a necessary item of personal consumption and is not influenced by business cycles (other than luxury items).   (Page 319)

3. **C.** Utilities borrow significantly so that the total capitalization of a utility has a larger amount of long-term debt than would be found in a pharmaceutical, durable goods or automobile concern. As a result, changes in interest rates will significantly affect current income of these highly leveraged companies.   (Page 319)

4. **B.** A fundamental analyst would look over the health and positioning of a company, but might use technical analysis of timing and price to reinforce a decision to buy.   (Page 320)

5. **D.** A fundamental analyst is concerned with the fundamental qualities of an issuer. This would include information such as the economic climate, inflation rate, how the industry is performing, the historical earnings trends for the company, how it is capitalized, and its product lines, management and balance sheet ratios. A technical analyst would be concerned with trading volumes or primary market trends.   (Page 320)

6. **A.** Defensive stocks tend not to be volatile. Firms that produce nondurable consumer goods (tobacco, food, drugs, energy) are more immune to the business cycles than other industries, and are sometimes called *defensive* industries. This term has nothing to do with the defense industry that supplies the Pentagon with goods and services.
(Page 319)

7. **B.** If disposable income is falling, consumers will cut back on purchases. First to be cut are durable goods purchases—automobiles, home appliances, etc. Firms that produce nondurable consumer goods, such as cigarettes, bread and aspirin, are less affected by business cycles and, therefore, are sometimes called *defensive* industries. The defense industries such as aerospace generally are not affected by increases or decreases in personal income levels.   (Page 319)

8. **A.** A growth company will pay out very little in dividends and retain most of its earnings to fund future growth. ABC Corporation has the highest retained earnings ratio and is most likely to be a growth company.   (Page 320)

9. **D.** A utility pays out most of its earnings as dividends and will retain very little savings. Therefore, JKL Corporation, with a low retained earnings ratio, is the most likely to be a utility.   (Page 319)

10. **A.** Growth companies have high PE ratios, low dividend payout ratios and high retained earnings ratios. Growth company market prices are bid up by investors anticipating that fast growth will increase the PE ratio. Such firms retain most earnings (high retained earnings ratios) to fund future growth. Investors select growth companies for growth (capital gain potential), not for investment income.   (Page 320)

49 ◆ Financial Statements Exam

1. Kelptek, Inc. is preparing to report its net income for the past year. An increase in which of the following will cause a decrease in the reported net income?

   I.   Tax rate
   II. Cash dividend
   III. Allowance for bad debts

   A. I
   B. I and II
   C. I and III
   D. II

Select from the following choices to answer questions 2 through 6.

   I.   Current assets
   II. Current liabilities
   III. Working capital
   IV. Total assets
   V.   Total liabilities
   VI. Net worth

2. Which balance sheet items would be affected by a corporation's purchase of a printing press for cash?

   A. I and III
   B. I, III, IV and V
   C. I, V and VI
   D. IV and V

3. Which balance sheet items would be affected when a corporation declares a cash dividend?

   A. I and II
   B. I, II, IV and V
   C. I and VI
   D. II, III, V and VI

4. Which balance sheet items would be affected when a corporation pays a cash dividend?

   A. I and II
   B. I, II, IV and V
   C. I and VI
   D. II, III and VI

5. Which balance sheet items would be affected when the holders of a corporation's convertible bonds convert into common stock?

   A. I and III
   B. I, IV and VI
   C. II, III and V
   D. V and VI

6. Which balance sheet items would be affected when a corporation redeems a bond at par several years before maturity?

   A. I and V
   B. I, III, IV and V
   C. II, III and VI
   D. IV and V

7. The balance sheet equation is

    A. assets + liabilities = net worth
    B. shareholders' equity = assets – liabilities
    C. assets = liabilities – net worth
    D. equity – assets = liabilities

8. The following is the balance sheet for Kelptek:

KELPTEK
Balance Sheet

Assets		Liabilities	
Cash	$ 100,000	Taxes payable	$ 250,000
Accounts receivable	400,000	Accounts payable	100,000
Inventories	500,000	Notes payable	150,000
Machinery/ equipment	1,000,000	Long-term notes	1,500,000
Plant/bldgs/ land	2,000,000	Debentures	1,000,000
Goodwill	100,000		
	$4,100,000		$3,000,000
		Shareholders' equity	$1,100,000

What is the net working capital of Kelptek?

    A. $250,000
    B. $500,000
    C. $600,000
    D. $1,100,000

9. For the past seven months, prices have been rising and analysts are predicting continued upward price movement. Under these conditions, FIFO accounting will cause a corporation to have

    A. higher profits
    B. higher costs of sales
    C. lower costs of inventory on the balance sheet
    D. reduced taxes

10. Additional paid-in capital is

    A. also called *earned surplus*
    B. the total of all residual claims that stockholders have against the assets of a corporation
    C. the difference between the total dollar amount of common stock and par value
    D. the total of all earnings since the corporation was formed, less dividends

11. All of the following are characteristics of extraordinary items on financial statements EXCEPT that

    A. they include nonrecurring expenses
    B. they appear on the balance sheet
    C. the SEC requires them to be listed separately
    D. they include unusual sources of income

12. The balance sheet for ALFA Enterprises shows that its assets increased over the last quarter while its equity remained the same. Which of the following statements is(are) true of ALFA Enterprises?

    I.   Net worth increased.
    II. Total liabilities increased.
    III. Accrued expenses decreased.
    IV. Debt remained the same.

    A. I
    B. I and IV
    C. II
    D. II and III

13. All of the following appear on a corporation's balance sheet as fixed assets EXCEPT

    A. real extate
    B. furniture
    C. computer equipment
    D. inventory

14. Consolidated Codfish declared a stock dividend. Which of the following balance sheet items will be affected?

   I.   Shareholders' equity
   II. Liabilities
   III. Assets
   IV. Retained earnings

   A. I, II and III
   B. I and IV
   C. III and IV
   D. IV

15. A highly leveraged company has the smallest percentage of its total capitalization in

   A. common stock
   B. preferred stock
   C. earned surplus
   D. long-term debts

16. The board of Acme Sweatsocks has voted to pay a $.32 dividend to holders of its common stock. These dividends will be paid from

   A. net income
   B. retained earnings
   C. debt service
   D. new stock issues

17. Total assets of SSS Corporation amount to $780,000; $260,000 represents current assets. Total liabilities are $370,000, of which $200,000 is considered long-term or other liabilities. What is the working capital for SSS Corporation?

   A. $60,000
   B. $90,000
   C. $110,000
   D. $410,000

18. Total assets of SSS Corporation amount to $780,000; $260,000 represents current assets. Total liabilities are $370,000, of which $200,000 is considered long-term or other liabilities. What is the shareholders' equity of SSS Corporation?

   A. $170,000
   B. $410,000
   C. $980,000
   D. $1.15 million

19. Reducing the allowance for bad debts will

   A. increase current assets
   B. decrease current liabilities
   C. increase long-term debt
   D. decrease fixed assets

◆ Answers & Rationale

1. **C.** Dividends are paid out of net income and have no effect on the net income reported by the company.   (Page 328)

2. **A.** Cash (a current asset) decreases, while fixed (noncurrent) assets such as machinery (e.g., a printing press) increase. This leaves total assets unchanged but reduces current assets. Therefore, working capital (current assets minus current liabilities) also decreases.   (Page 323)

3. **D.** When a cash dividend is first *declared,* current liabilities (a part of total liabilities) immediately increase by the amount of dividends payable. Retained earnings, a component of net worth, decreases. Working capital decreases because current liabilities have increased and current assets remain unchanged.   (Page 328)

4. **B.** When the dividend is actually *paid,* current assets (cash) and current liabilities (dividends payable) both decrease equally. Both total assets and total liabilities decrease as well.   (Page 328)

5. **D.** When bondholders convert to common stock, long-term debt (liabilities) decreases because the debt is converted to equity. Shareholders' equity, part of net worth, increases by the amount of debt converted to equity.   (Page 327)

6. **B.** When bonds are redeemed at par, the corporation pays off its obligation to bondholders thus reducing long-term debt liability. This payment is made in cash and therefore reduces current assets and working capital.   (Page 327)

7. **B.** On a balance sheet, assets always equal total liabilities plus shareholders' equity (or net worth). Another way of saying the same thing is: assets − liabilities = shareholders' equity.
                    (Page 321)

8. **B.** Working capital equals current assets minus current liabilities. The total current assets are $1,000,000 (cash + accounts receivable + invento-ries). Total current liabilities are $500,000 (notes payable + taxes payable + accounts payable). Therefore, working capital is $500,000.
                    (Page 324)

9. **A.** In a period of rising costs, FIFO (first-in, first-out) will show greater profits than the alternative LIFO (last-in, first-out) method of inventory valuation. Under FIFO, the cheaper-to-produce "older" inventory is depleted first, resulting in lower cost of sales and hence higher profits. Therefore, taxes are probably higher with FIFO. Because the remaining inventory is valued at the latest price paid, in an inflationary economy FIFO results in increasing the cost of inventory carried on the balance sheet. Under LIFO, the more-expensive-to-produce "newer" inventory is depleted first, resulting in higher costs of sales and hence lower profits.   (Page 326)

10. **C.** Paid-in capital (often called *paid-in surplus*) is shareholders' equity that has not been generated through the retained earnings of the corporation. It is the difference between the dollar amount received from the sale of stock and the par value of the stock. Earned surplus is another name for retained earnings, which are defined by answer D. Answer B is the definition of shareholders' equity.   (Page 324)

11. **B.** Extraordinary items are items of income or expense that will not recur year after year. An example might be the sale of land held for expansion or the sale of a part of the business. These items will not occur in the following year because the transaction has already taken place. The SEC requires registered corporations to list these items separately and not commingle them with operating expenses and revenue. These transactions appear on the income statement after operating income and expenses.   (Page 330)

12. **C.** The formula for the balance sheet is: assets = liabilities + net worth. If assets increase while net worth (equity) remains the same, then total liabilities (debt) must increase. Accrued expenses are liabilities.   (Page 321)

13. **D.** Inventory is not considered a fixed asset because the company expects to convert its inventory into cash within a short period of time. The other choices are fixed assets and cannot be liquidated easily. (Page 323)

14. **D.** Stock dividends are a distribution of additional shares to the shareholders in proportion to their existing holdings. When a stock dividend is declared, retained earnings are reduced because the dividend is paid out of retained earnings. Net worth does not change, nor do current assets or liabilities because no money is paid out. (Page 328)

15. **A.** The total capitalization of a company consists of its long-term capital. This includes long-term debt plus net worth: capital stock (common and preferred), paid-in capital (also called *paid-in surplus*) and earned surplus (or *retained earnings*). By definition, a highly leveraged company has the smallest portion of its capitalization in common stock. Utility companies tend to be highly leveraged. (Page 328)

16. **B.** Cash dividends are typically paid from retained earnings. (Page 328)

17. **B.** Current liabilities equals total liabilities minus long-term and other liabilities:

$ 370,000	Total liabilities
− 200,000	Long-term liabilities
$ 170,000	Current liabilities

Working capital equals current assets minus current liabilities:

$ 260,000	Current assets
− 170,000	Current liabilities
$ 90,000	Working capital

(Page 324)

18. **B.** Total assets equals total liabilities plus shareholders' equity:

$780,000 = $370,000 + Shareholders' equity

Shareholders' equity = $410,000

(Page 324)

19. **A.** Reducing the allowance for bad debts increases accounts receivable (a current asset). Therefore, this action increases current assets. (Page 323)

50 Financial Ratios Exam

1. If your firm wanted to measure the credit risk of Microscam, Inc., it would use the

    A. ratio of total debt to total assets
    B. ratio of total debt to net tangible assets
    C. current ratio
    D. price-earnings ratio

2. Using Table 1, what is the approximate earnings per share for TCB?

    A. $1.00
    B. $1.40
    C. $5.10
    D. $6.36

Table 1

NEW YORK STOCK EXCHANGE COMPOSITE
TRANSACTIONS
Tuesday, September 13, 1998

| 52 Weeks | | | | Yld | P-E | Sales | | | | Net |
High	Low	Stock	Div	%	Ratio	100s	High	Low	Close	Chg.
91 3/8	57 1/2	TCB	1.00	1.4	11	5106	70 5/8	69	69 7/8	−3/8

Use the following information to answer questions 3 through 8.

GHI Financial Statement
as of December 31, 1995

Long-term Debt:	
10% debentures convertible at $25	$10,000,000
Net Worth:	
6% preferred stock	$2,000,000
Common stock ($1 per share par value)	$2,000,000
Paid-in surplus	$18,000,000
Retained earnings	$18,000,000
Depreciation	$2,500,000
Earnings before interest and taxes	$4,000,000

Tax bracket	34%
Market price of common stock	18 5/8
Market price of preferred stock	$90

3. What is GHI's nondiluted earnings per share?

    A. $.93
    B. $.99
    C. $1.26
    D. $2.00

4. What is GHI's return on common shareholders' equity?

    A. 4.89%
    B. 5.21%
    C. 9.30%
    D. 10.52%

5. What is GHI's earnings per share on a fully diluted basis?

    A. $.85
    B. $1.05
    C. $1.10
    D. $1.26

6. What is the current rate of return on GHI's preferred stock?

    A. 3.22%
    B. 6.00%
    C. 6.67%
    D. 7.76%

7. What is the common stock ratio for GHI?

    A. 4%
    B. 40%
    C. 72%
    D. 76%

8. What is GHI's cash flow?

    A. $1,989,000
    B. $3,000,000
    C. $4,000,000
    D. $4,480,000

9. How would you determine a company's margin of profit?

    A. Determine the gross profits per share earned during the fiscal year.
    B. Determine earnings in excess of net income.
    C. Calculate the gross profit retained in business.
    D. Calculate the ratio of gross profit to net sales.

Use the following information to answer questions 10 through 12.

Flibinite Health Care Financial Statement
as of December 31, 1995

Long-term Debt:	
5.5% convertible (at $20) debentures outstanding	$10,000,000
Net Worth:	
8% preferred stock outstanding ($100 par)	$5,000,000
500,000 shares common stock outstanding ($10 par)	$5,000,000
Operating income before taxes and interest	$3,000,000
Tax bracket	34%
Current market value of Flibinite preferred	$40
Current market value of Flibinite common	$20

10. What is the earnings per share of Flibinite?

    A. $2.21
    B. $2.43
    C. $3.23
    D. $4.90

11. What is the approximate interest coverage ratio of Flibinite?

    A. 1.5
    B. 3.5
    C. 5.5
    D. 7.5

12. What is the current return on Flibinite preferred stock?

    A. 5%
    B. 12%
    C. 18%
    D. 20%

13. The following is the balance sheet for General Gizmonics:

GENERAL GIZMONICS
Balance Sheet

Assets		Liabilities	
Cash	$100,000	Taxes payable	$ 250,000
Accounts		Accounts	
receivable	400,000	payable	100,000
Inventories	500,000	Notes payable	150,000
Machinery/		Long-term	
equipment	1,000,000	notes	1,500,000
Plant/bldgs/		Debentures	1,000,000
land	2,000,000		
Goodwill	100,000		
	$4,100,000		$3,000,000
		Shareholders'	
		equity	$1,100,000

What is the current ratio for GIZ?

A. 1:1
B. 1.33:1
C. 1.36:1
D. 2:1

14. What is the return on assets ratio?

A. Net income (after taxes) ÷ Total tangible assets
B. Revenue ÷ Long-term assets
C. Total assets ÷ Shareholders' equity
D. Profit before taxes ÷ Total assets

15. The common stock ratio is

A. long-term debt ÷ total capitalization
B. total liabilities ÷ total assets
C. total liabilities ÷ total shareholders' equity
D. (common at par + capital in excess of par + retained earnings) ÷ total capitalization

16. Using Table 2, if General Gizmonics had earnings of $2.00 per share this year, what was its dividend payout ratio on its common stock?

A. 21.1%
B. 26.7%
C. 37.5%
D. 47.5%

17. A corporation has a net income after taxes of $5.2 million. There are 4 million shares of common stock outstanding. The earnings per share is

A. $.80
B. $1.30
C. $1.78
D. $5.20

Table 2   General Gizmonics — Common $1

Rate – 0.40Q	Pd '99 – 1.60	Pd '98 – 1.45		
Dividend			Record	
Amount	Declared	Ex-date	Date	Payable
0.20	Dec 2	Dec 14	Dec 18	Jan 1
0.20	Mar 2	Mar 9	Mar 13	Apr 1
0.20	Jun 3	Jun 13	Jun 17	Jul 1
0.35	Sep 1	Sep 14	Sep 16	Oct 1

◆ Answers & Rationale

1. **B.**   Credit risk is the danger of default by the issuer. Of the ratios given, the most relevant measure of credit risk is the ratio of total debt to net tangible assets.   (Page 337)

2. **D.**   Price divided by earnings per share equals PE ratio. From the display price, you see that the closing price of TCB was 69 7/8 and the PE ratio was 11. This tells you that the price of 69 7/8 is 11 times the amount of the earnings per share. So, divide 69 7/8 by 11 to get $6.36, which is the approximate earnings per share.   (Page 335)

3. **A.**   Nondiluted earnings per share is calculated without taking into account the potential diluted effects of convertible securities present in a corporation's capital structure; it is calculated by dividing the earnings available to common by the number of common shares outstanding.

$ 4,000,000	Earnings before interest and taxes
− 1,000,000	Interest (10% debentures)
$ 3,000,000	Taxable income
− 1,020,000	Taxes (34%)
$ 1,980,000	Net income (after taxes)
− 120,000	Preferred dividend (6% × $2,000,000)
$ 1,860,000	Earnings available to common

Number of common shares outstanding =

$$\frac{\$2,000,000}{\$1.00 \text{ par value per share}} = 2,000,000 \text{ shares}$$

$$\frac{\$1,860,000}{2,000,000} = \$.93 \text{ earnings per share}$$

(Page 335)

4. **A.**   Return on equity equals earnings available to common divided by common shareholders' equity. In this case, earnings available to common is $1,860,000.

$ 2,000,000	Common stock (at par)
+ 18,000,000	Paid-in surplus
+ 18,000,000	Retained earnings
$ 38,000,000	Common shareholders' equity

$$\frac{\$1,860,000}{\$38,000,000} = 4.89\% \text{ return on equity}$$

(Page 333)

5. **B.**   In order to calculate earnings per share on a fully diluted basis, pretend that all convertible security holders converted to common stock at the beginning of the year. Determine earnings available to common by omitting the interest expense on any convertible debt, and omitting the preferred dividend on any convertible preferred. The preferred stock in this particular question is not convertible.

$ 4,000,000	Earnings before interest and taxes
− 0	Interest
$ 4,000,000	Taxable income
− 1,360,000	Taxes (34%)
$ 2,640,000	Net income (after taxes)
− 120,000	Preferred dividend
$ 2,520,000	Earnings available to common

Now determine the number of common shares that would be outstanding assuming all convertible security holders have converted to common. $10,000,000 debentures convertible at $25 equals 400,000 shares ($10,000,000 ÷ 25).

400,000	Additional shares
+ 2,000,000	Shares outstanding
2,400,000	Total

$$\frac{\$ 2,520,000}{2,400,000} = \$1.05 \text{ fully diluted EPS}$$

Although it is relatively unusual for fully diluted earnings per share to be greater than nondiluted earnings per share, it is not impossible. Do not assume that fully diluted EPS is always lower.

(Page 335)

6.   **C.**   Current rate of return, also known as current yield on common or preferred stock, is calculated as dividends per year divided by current market price. The par value per share of the preferred stock is not given in the question so assume it is $100 per share.

6% dividend rate $\times$ $100 par value $=$ $6 per share

Current market price $=$ $90

$$\frac{\$6}{\$90} = 6.67\%$$

(Page 336)

7.   **D.**   The common stock ratio is defined as common shareholders' equity divided by total capitalization.

Common shareholders' equity was determined to be $38,000,000 (common stock at par plus paid-in surplus plus retained earnings). Total capitalization is:

$ 38,000,000   Common shareholders' equity
+   2,000,000   Preferred stock
+ 10,000,000   Long-term debt
$ 50,000,000   Total capitalization

$$\frac{\$ 38,000,000}{\$ 50,000,000} = 76\% \text{ common stock ratio}$$

(Page 331)

8.   **D.**   Cash flow is defined as net income plus noncash expenses (depreciation).

$ 1,980,000   Net income (after tax)
+ 2,500,000   Depreciation
$ 4,480,000   Cash flow

(Page 332)

9.   **D.**   The margin of profit for a company is a measure of the company's gross profit in comparison with net sales. To calculate margin of profit, subtract cost of goods sold (COGS) from net sales to obtain the ratio known as *gross margin,* or *margin of profit.*   (Page 333)

10.   **B.**   Earnings per share (EPS) is calculated as follows:

$ 3,000,000   Operating income
–   550,000   Interest
$ 2,450,000   Pretax income
–   833,000   Taxes (34%)
$ 1,617,000   Aftertax income
–   400,000   Preferred dividend
$ 1,217,000   Income to common shares
÷   500,000   Common shares
$ 2.43   Earnings per share

(Page 335)

11.   **C.** $3,000,000 operating income divided by $550,000 interest equals 5.45 coverage.

(Page 336)

12.   **D.** $8 preferred dividend divided by $40 preferred market value equals 20% yield (return).

(Page 336)

13.   **D.**   The current ratio equals:

$$\frac{\text{Current assets}}{\text{Current liabilities}} = \frac{\$1,000,000}{\$500,000} = 2 \text{ to } 1$$

(Page 332)

14.   **A.**   The return on assets ratio is net income after taxes divided by total tangible assets.

(Page 333)

15.   **D.**   This is the common stock ratio. Total capitalization is total long-term capital (total long-term liabilities plus shareholders' equity). Answer A is the bond ratio (also known as the *debt ratio*). Answer B is the debt to asset ratio. Answer C is the debt to equity ratio.   (Page 331)

16.   **D.**   The dividend payout ratio is annual dividends paid divided by earnings per share. $.95 ÷ $2.00 $=$ .475 (or 47.5%).   (Page 336)

17.   **B.**   Earnings per share equals net income (less preferred dividends) divided by number of common shares outstanding. Thus:

$$\text{EPS} = \frac{\$5.2 \text{ million}}{4 \text{ million}} = \$1.30$$

(Page 335)

1. The term "churning" refers to

   A. excessive trading in a customer's account for the express purpose of generating commissions
   B. the practice of freeriding in more than one customer's account at a time
   C. manipulation of market prices by a firm
   D. making false or misleading statements to a customer for the purpose of inducing the customer to purchase or sell a security

2. To what does the term "selling dividends" refer?

   A. Encouraging mutual fund customers to sell their holdings just before the fund declares a dividend payment
   B. Enticing customers to buy mutual fund shares just before a dividend payment
   C. Withdrawing dividends rather than reinvesting these amounts in additional shares
   D. Encouraging investors to postpone purchases of mutual fund shares until after the ex-date for a dividend distribution

3. Encouraging a customer to purchase mutual fund shares in an amount just under the next dollar volume bracket, which entitles the customer to a reduction in sales charges, or remaining silent on the matter, is called

   A. breakpoint sales
   B. boiler room selling
   C. double-dip selling
   D. low-ball sales

4. The NASD Rules of Fair Practice govern the actions of its members. All of the following are considered violations of the rules EXCEPT

   A. churning accounts
   B. the blanket recommending of low-price speculative stocks
   C. using discretionary authority
   D. guaranteeing the customer against loss

5. A member firm accepts a limit order from a customer to buy 100 shares of GIZ at 27. Which of the following can the member do before executing the customer's order?

   I. Buy 100 shares of GIZ for its own trading account at 27.
   II. Buy 100 shares of GIZ for its investment account at 27.
   III. Sell 100 shares of GIZ for another customer at 27 1/8.
   IV. Buy 100 shares of GIZ for another customer at 27.

   A. I and II
   B. I and III
   C. II and IV
   D. III and IV

6. According to the Rules of Fair Practice, a member organization must

    A. grant an extension of the settlement date for a purchase made in a special cash account
    B. repurchase from a client any securities offered for sale by the client
    C. quote a quantity discount on lots of more than 100 shares
    D. authorize in writing the sharing of a client's profits or losses by a registered representative

7. As branch manager, you are reviewing your branch's daily trade blotter and note that your biggest producer, Adam Grizzly, purchased 1,000 calls on General Gizmonics for his own account a few minutes before he entered an order to buy 10,000 shares of GIZ for his biggest client. Mr. Grizzly is guilty of

    A. capping
    B. support
    C. front-running
    D. hedging

8. Your customer Adam Grizzly is short 1,000 calls on Microscam. Mr. Grizzly starts to sell large quantities of MCS long to put pressure on the price. This practice is called

    A. front-running
    B. capping
    C. pegging
    D. hedging

9. A member firm may assume a customer's loss under which of the following circumstances?

    I.   The firm has an agreement in writing from the customer allowing the sharing of profits in a managed account.
    II. The registered rep or the member firm has a proportionate capital investment.
    III. The approval of the exchange was obtained to assume the loss.
    IV. The loss resulted from an error.

    A. I
    B. I and II
    C. III and IV
    D. IV

10. An investor sells calls and, just prior to their expiration, sells the underlying stock. Her intent is to keep the price from rising above the exercise price. Such an action is called

    A. pegging
    B. supporting
    C. capping
    D. front-running

11. A member firm receives an order from an institutional account to purchase 20,000 shares of stock. Before the order is transmitted for execution, the member firm buys calls on the same security for its own account. This would constitute

    A. pegging
    B. supporting
    C. capping
    D. front-running

12. Which of the following would constitute manipulative or prohibited activities?

   I.   An investor sells GIZ Jul 50 calls at one firm and purchases the same calls at another firm at the same time.

   II.   A registered representative quotes an option at 3 1/8–3 3/8 to a customer when he knows the option is trading at 2 5/8– 2 3/4.

   III.   A customer who has written calls makes substantial short sales in underlying stock.

   A.   I only
   B.   II and III only
   C.   III only
   D.   I, II and III

13. A rep signs an agreement to borrow money from a customer. This is permitted

   A.   with written permission from your firm
   B.   with written permission from the NASD
   C.   if the customer is a bank
   D.   under no circumstances

14. An associated person of Dullard Securities owns a vacation home. She is permitted to rent it

   A.   with prior written approval of Dullard Securities
   B.   after notifying Dullard Securities
   C.   without restriction
   D.   under no circumstances

15. Randy Bear, a registered rep, is also an amateur filmmaker. He and his film colleagues decide to form a limited partnership and sell a few units in order to finance a short film. Before acting as a general partner in this enterprise, Randy must

   I.   provide written notice to his employer

   II.   provide his employer with a list of the names of the limited partners

   III.   comply with blue-sky laws regarding the sale of limited partnership interests

   IV.   comply with SEC regulations regarding the sale of exempt securities

   A.   I
   B.   I and IV
   C.   I, III and IV
   D.   II, III and IV

16. When determining whether a registered representative is churning an account, which of the following are taken into consideration?

   I.   Frequency of trades
   II.   Motive of rep
   III.   Rating of securities traded
   IV.   Size of positions traded

   A.   I
   B.   I, II and IV
   C.   I and III
   D.   III and IV

17. A registered representative is hired to be a guest speaker and will be paid a fee. The representative must

   A.   register as an investment adviser
   B.   be a certified financial planner
   C.   receive permission from the NASD
   D.   notify her firm in writing

◆ Answers & Rationale

1. **A.** "Churning" describes trading that is excessive in light of a particular customer's circumstances or trading more excessive than what would normally be considered suitable. This is equally true for both discretionary and nondiscretionary accounts.   (Page 346)

2. **B.** "Selling dividends" is an unethical sales practice in which a seller intentionally or unintentionally misleads customers into believing they will be getting the equivalent of a rebate on their investments because the fund will soon be paying a distribution. The customers suffer out-of-pocket losses because the cash immediately coming back is dividend income, subject to tax.   (Page 346)

3. **A.** "Breakpoint sales" are those in which a customer unknowingly buys investment company shares in an amount just under a dollar bracket amount that would qualify the customer's investment for a reduction in sales charges. As a result the customer pays a higher dollar amount in sales charges, which reduces the number of shares purchased and results in a higher cost basis per share.   (Page 347)

4. **C.** Use of discretionary authority is not a violation of the Rules of Fair Practice, but abuse of that authority by excessive trading and the misuse of a customer's funds or securities is. Answers A, B and D are clear violations. Recommendations should be based on the customer's financial status and objectives. Low-priced stocks may result in a higher percentage of commission.   (Page 345)

5. **D.** A member firm may only execute for the firm's own account at prices above a customer's outstanding buy limit. Trades for other customers, however, can be executed at the same price (the trader should use time priority for customer limit orders).   (Page 350)

6. **D.** According to the NASD Rules of Fair Practice, members and persons associated with them are forbidden to:

- guarantee that a customer will not sustain a loss; or
- share in the profits or losses of a customer's account unless the firm's prior written approval has been obtained and the associated person shares only to the extent of his proportionate contribution to the account. (Note that accounts of the immediate family of the associated person are exempt from the proportionate share limitation.)
                              (Page 348)

7. **C.** "Front-running" is the term used to describe the actions of registered representatives who place orders for their personal accounts for the purpose of benefiting from subsequent orders they place for their clients. This procedure is forbidden.   (Page 350)

8. **B.** "Capping," an illegal procedure, involves placing selling pressure on the stock to keep the price lower than an exercise price. (Page 350)

9. **C.** If the firm makes an error in executing an order that results in a loss to the customer, the firm may assume the loss; also, if the exchange approves, the firm may assume a loss not the result of a firm error. Otherwise, the firm may not take on a loss from a customer's account. Note, however, that the firm may share in (not assume) the gains and losses of an account if a joint account is opened with the customer and the sharing is in direct proportion to the capital contributed to the account.
                              (Page 348)

10. **C.** The investor is attempting to cap the price of the stock in the market: selling the underlying stock to keep her short call positions from going in-the-money.   (Page 350)

11. **D.** Front-running is the use of trade information in the securities market before the customer trade is executed; this is prohibited.   (Page 350)

12. **D.** All choices listed are manipulative practices. Choice I is a wash sale—there is no change of ownership in the security, yet the appearance of trading activity is given. Choice II is a fictitious

quote, which is misleading. Choice III is capping, which is a prohibited practice.   (Page 345)

13. **C.** The prohibition against borrowing money from customers does not include customers who are in the business of lending money. Otherwise, borrowing money or securities from customers is strictly prohibited.   (Page 347)

14. **C.** Receiving payment for rent of a vacation home does not constitute a private securities transaction, so no approval or notification is required.   (Page 344)

15. **C.** Forming a limited partnership requires compliance with state and federal laws regarding registration or exemption of securities. This activity is also considered an outside business activity by the NASD, thus the rep must provide prior

written notice to his employing firm. The NASD does not require the rep to provide the names of the investors to the employing firm.   (Page 344)

16. **B.** Excessive trading, whether in terms of size or frequency, in a customer's account is a prohibited practice known as *churning*. When regulators investigate allegations of churning in an account, the possible motivation of the registered rep is taken into consideration.   (Page 346)

17. **D.** If a registered representative will receive income from a source other than the employing firm, she is required to notify the employing firm. Registration as an investment adviser is not necessary if the rep is giving advice within the scope of her employment with the broker-dealer.
        (Page 344)

1. To open a new account, the registered representative must obtain information about the client's

    I.   financial needs
    II. investment objectives
    III. financial condition

    A. I and II only
    B. I and III only
    C. II and III only
    D. I, II and III

2. Which of the following characteristics best define(s) the term "growth"?

    A. Value of the investment increasing over time
    B. Increasing principal and accumulating interest and dividends over time
    C. Investments that appreciate tax deferred
    D. All of the above

3. Which of the following investments is least appropriate for a client who is primarily concerned with liquidity?

    A. Preferred stock
    B. Municipal bond mutual funds
    C. Bank savings accounts
    D. Direct participation programs

4. A registered representative has a new client who has just received a $25,000 inheritance. The client wishes to use the money to purchase 8 1/4% Tallawhosits City general obligation bonds selling at an 8.45% yield. The $1 million bond issue is due in 15 years and is rated Ba. All of the following factors would result in your recommending *against* such a purchase EXCEPT that

    A. the client is in the 18% tax bracket
    B. this would be the client's only investment
    C. the client is willing to accept a moderate amount of risk
    D. the client's job is not secure

5. All of the following are used to determine the suitability of recommendations made to a municipal bond customer EXCEPT the

    A. tax bracket of the customer
    B. reciprocal exemptions
    C. state of residence of the customer
    D. structure of the customer's existing portfolio

6. To determine whether a particular type of options trading is suitable for a customer, the member firm should consider the customer's

   I. understanding of the strategies being employed
   II. ability to calculate maximum profit or loss
   III. ability to assume risk
   IV. ability to meet the margin call

   A. II and IV only
   B. III only
   C. III and IV only
   D. I, II, III and IV

7. An oral recommendation by a registered representative must be

   A. followed by a statement of risks
   B. followed by an example of the strategy recommended
   C. followed by a prospectus
   D. approved by a registered options principal

8. A person's investment decisions should be based primarily on her

   I. risk tolerance
   II. rep's recommendations
   III. investment needs

   A. I only
   B. I and III only
   C. II and III only
   D. I, II and III

◆ Answers & Rationale

1.   **D.**   Under Rule 405 (the NYSE "Know Your Customer" Rule), all of this information is considered essential before opening an account.
(Page 351)

2.   **A.**   "Growth" refers to an increase in the value of an investment over time.   (Page 353)

3.   **D.**   An investment is liquid if an investor can sell it quickly at face value or at a fair market price without losing significant principal. Direct participation programs (DPPs) are considered very illiquid because there does not exist a ready secondary market for them.   (Page 354)

4.   **C.**   A "Ba" rating is consistent with the client's willingness to accept moderate risk. The client's tax bracket might be too low to take full advantage of the bond's tax-exempt feature. The bonds would also not be very liquid because only 1,000 bonds were issued. If the client lost her job and needed cash, the bonds might be difficult to sell.   (Page 352)

5.   **B.**   To determine suitability when recommending municipals, the tax bracket of the customer, the state of residence (because intrastate issues are triple exempt) and the structure of the customer's existing portfolio would all be considered.   (Page 353)

6.   **D.**   All factors would be considered when determining suitability: understanding of strategies; ability to calculate maximum profit or loss; ability to assume risk; and ability to meet a margin call.   (Page 352)

7.   **A.**   Any recommendation that implies that a gain can be made must be followed by a statement of the attendant risks of the transaction.
(Page 351)

8.   **B.**   Understanding and acceptance of risk, along with the reasons for investing, will shape a client's portfolio. A rep's recommendations should suit the client's needs—they should not be used to drive investment decisions.   (Page 352)

53 Analyzing Financial Risks and Rewards Exam

1. Gwinneth Stout wishes to buy Datawaq bonds. You, as her representative, have advised her that the trade is unsuitable. If she decides to go ahead with the purchase, you must

   A. execute the trade specifically as she has directed you to do
   B. execute the trade if the NASD approves
   C. execute the trade only if Mrs. Stout has previous trading experience in similar securities
   D. not execute the trade

2. If a customer is concerned about interest rate risk, which of the following securities would a rep NOT recommend?

   A. Treasury bills
   B. Project notes
   C. 10-year corporate bonds
   D. 18-year municipal bonds

3. You have a convertible corporate bond available that has an 8% coupon, is yielding 7.1%, but may be called some time this year. Which feature of this bond would probably be LEAST attractive to your client?

   A. Convertibility
   B. Coupon yield
   C. Current yield
   D. Near-term call

4. Credit risk involves

   A. safety of principal
   B. fluctuations in overall interest rates
   C. the danger of not being able to sell the investment at a fair market price
   D. inflationary risks

5. Bondholders face the risk that the value of their bonds may fall as interest rates rise. This is known as

   A. credit risk
   B. reinvestment risk
   C. marketability risk
   D. market risk

6. Randy Bear is 27 years old, in a low tax bracket and wants an aggressive long-term investment. His rep recommends a high-rated municipal general obligation bond. The rep has

   A. violated the suitability requirements of NASD and MSRB rules
   B. recommended a suitable investment because GOs are good long-term investments
   C. committed a violation because municipal bonds weather the ups and downs of the markets well
   D. not committed a violation if the customer agrees to the transaction

7. Which of these statements regarding suitability of recommendations and transactions for customers is FALSE?

 A. No MSRB member may effect transactions in a discretionary account that are excessive in size or frequency.
 B. Municipal securities transactions initiated by MSRB members in discretionary accounts must first be determined to be suitable for the customer.
 C. If a municipal securities transaction is determined to be unsuitable, it may still be executed at the customer's direction.
 D. In the absence of complete background information, an MSRB member may not recommend municipal securities transactions to a customer, even if they appear to be suitable.

8. Any recommendations made to customers by a broker-dealer must be suitable for the customer based on an investigation of the customer's

 I. investment objectives
 II. financial background
 III. tax status

 A. I only
 B. I and II only
 C. II and III only
 D. I, II and III

9. If a customer wishes to place an order for 30 GNMAs that the broker-dealer feels is unsuitable for her, the broker-dealer must advise the customer of its opinion and

 A. not execute the order
 B. execute the order only with the prior approval of a senior partner of the firm
 C. execute the order only with prior MSRB approval
 D. execute the order at the customer's direction

10. A municipal securities dealer shall not recommend transactions in municipal securities to a customer

 A. unless the customer has requested, in writing, such recommendations
 B. unless the dealer is long the securities that are the subjects of the recommendation
 C. that are excessive in size or frequency for that customer
 D. that include securities which contain a call feature exercisable by the issuer

11. The risk of not being able to convert an investment into cash at a time when cash is needed is known as

 A. legislative risk
 B. liquidity risk
 C. market risk
 D. reinvestment risk

12. Which of the following activities are responsibilities of a registered representative?

 I. Determining a customer's suitability for investing
 II. Describing the characteristics and benefits of various securities products
 III. Offering tax advice and assisting customers in completing tax returns
 IV. Personally holding a customer's securities for a future transaction

 A. I and II
 B. I and III
 C. II and IV
 D. III and IV

◆ Answers & Rationale

1.   **A.**   If a customer wishes to purchase a security that the registered representative feels is unsuitable, the trade may be executed if the customer specifically directs it. The ticket should be marked "Unsolicited." (Most firms require that the customer sign a nonsolicitation letter for this type of trade, meaning that the customer was not solicited to do this trade by the firm.)   (Page 355)

2.   **D.**   Interest rate risk is the danger that interest rates will change over the life of the debt instrument and adversely affect the price of a bond. This risk is greatest for long-term bonds.   (Page 356)

3.   **D.**   The near-term call would mean that no matter how attractive the bond's other features, the client may not have very long to enjoy them.
(Page 358)

4.   **A.**   Credit risk is the risk of losing all or part of one's invested principal through failure of the issuer.   (Page 357)

5.   **D.**   Market risk is the risk of losing some or all of one's principal due to price volatility in the marketplace. Prices of existing bonds can fluctuate with changing interest rates.   (Page 356)

6.   **A.**   In recommending a conservative, tax-exempt investment to this customer, the rep has failed to make a suitable recommendation.
(Page 355)

7.   **C.**   The MSRB states that a broker must obtain all necessary information regarding a customer's financial background, tax status and investment objectives before it may recommend municipal securities to a customer. If a broker feels that a municipal securities transaction is unsuitable for a customer, it may not execute that transaction, even at the demand of the customer.   (Page 355)

8.   **D.**   A customer's financial status, tax bracket and investment objectives should be taken into consideration when recommending a security.
(Page 355)

9.   **D.**   Under NASD/NYSE rules, even though the security appears unsuitable to the registered rep, the trade may be executed at the demand of the customer.   (Page 355)

10.   **C.**   The dealer may not recommend to the customer any securities transactions that would be considered excessive in size or would be considered "churning."   (Page 355)

11.   **B.**   Liquidity risk is the measure of marketability—or how quickly and easily a security can be converted to cash.   (Page 357)

12.   **A.**   A registered rep is primarily responsible for determining customer suitability and for explaining different investments to prospective investors. A registered rep is not responsible for helping prepare tax returns, and he is not permitted to hold customer funds or securities.   (Page 355)

54   Portfolio Analysis Exam

1. Your client is following a constant dollar investment plan. The market value of his equity portfolio has increased from $100,000 to $120,000. To maintain his investment plan, he should

   A. transfer $20,000 from his equity portfolio to his bond portfolio
   B. increase his bond portfolio so it will also have a market value of $120,000
   C. continue to invest a fixed dollar amount each month in specific equity securities
   D. continue to invest a fixed dollar amount in both equity and debt securities

2. Changing any of the following characteristics of the stocks and bonds in an investor's portfolio would probably add diversification to the investor's holdings EXCEPT changes made strictly according to the

   A. geographic location of the issuer
   B. relative prices of the securities
   C. industries in which investment is being made
   D. types of securities

3. Lotta and Tiny Leveridge are in a high tax bracket and are interested in maximizing their aftertax income while diversifying their portfolio. You should recommend that they buy

   A. TANs
   B. GNMAs
   C. tax-exempt convertible bonds
   D. tax-exempt unit trusts

4. When trying to diversify a bond portfolio, which of the following is NOT considered?

   A. Price
   B. Quality
   C. Geographical location or industry
   D. Maturity

5. Max Leveridge owns three municipal bonds:

   Aa rated City of New York,
     8% GOs, due 2001

   AA rated Ohio Turnpike Authority,
     7.9% revenue bonds, due 2000

   Aaa rated University of California,
     7.8% revenue bonds, due 2003

   What type of diversification does this represent?

   I. Geographical
   II. Quality
   III. Maturity
   IV. Price

   A. I
   B. I and IV
   C. II and III
   D. II and IV

6. A portfolio manager analyzing the beta co-efficient of his portfolio relative to a stock index is concerned about

    A. capitalization of his portfolio versus the index
    B. yield on his portfolio relative to the index
    C. volatility of his portfolio relative to the index
    D. past performance on his portfolio

7. A portfolio manager adjusting a hedge in index options by the portfolio beta factor is trying to reduce which of the following risks?

    A. Financial
    B. Systematic
    C. Purchasing power
    D. Selection

8. Which of the following investment strategies is(are) defensive?

    I.   Constant dollar plan
    II.   Margin purchasing
    III. Dollar cost averaging

    A. I
    B. I and II
    C. I and III
    D. II and III

9. Diversification will help protect against which of the following?

    A. Systematic risk
    B. Market risk
    C. Nonsystematic risk
    D. Inflation risk

◆ Answers & Rationale

1.   **A.**   In a constant dollar plan, an investor keeps a constant dollar amount of his portfolio in equity securities. If the market value of the equities rises, then the excess is transferred to fixed income securities. If the market value of the equities falls, then the debt is liquidated and the equity position restored to its constant value. This procedure serves to balance an investor's portfolio.   (Page 361)

2.   **B.**   Diversification of a portfolio is rarely done by price alone.   (Page 361)

3.   **D.**   Each of the other answers is a debt instrument that finances a single project or item. Unit trusts are typically composed of several underlying securities.   (Page 360)

4.   **A.**   One of the reasons for diversifying a bond portfolio is to spread the risk among the portfolio's issues. This can be accomplished by buying bonds of differing maturities and geographical locations (for a municipal portfolio) or industries (for a corporate portfolio), as well as quality. *Quality* relates to a bond's credit rating (i.e., lower quality bonds have greater risk than higher quality bonds). The price of bonds when purchased is not taken into account for diversifying a portfolio.   (Page 360)

5.   **A.**   The bonds are from different issuers from around the country; hence, they offer geographical diversification. The quality, measured by Moody's and Standard & Poor's ratings, is nearly identical; in fact, a Aa Moody rating equals a AA S&P rating. The coupon rates and maturities (and hence price) of the issues are all similar.   (Page 360)

6.   **C.**   Beta is used to compute the number of index contracts needed in putting on a hedge.   (Page 362)

7.   **B.**   *Systematic risk* refers to the impact of the overall market on an equity portfolio's value.   (Page 362)

8.   **C.**   Purchasing securities on margin is an aggressive investment strategy. A constant dollar plan and dollar cost averaging are defensive investment strategies.   (Page 361)

9.   **C.**   By owning a diversified portfolio, nonsystematic risk (which is associated with the decline in value of an individual security) is reduced. Systematic risk and market risk (the risk that the prices of securities trend together) and inflation risk affect all securities and therefore are not eliminated by diversification.   (Page 360)

1. Which of the following taxes are known as *progressive taxes*?

   I. Sales
   II. Gasoline
   III. Income
   IV. Gift
   V. Estate

   A. I and II only
   B. II and IV only
   C. III, IV and V only
   D. I, II, III, IV and V

2. An investor has effected the following transactions in her account:

   Bought 100 TCB at 40 on June 15, 1995

   Bought 100 TCB at 33 on November 30, 1995

   Sold 100 TCB at 32 on December 20, 1995

   Bought 100 MTN at 22 on January 18, 1995

   Sold 100 MTN at 27 on October 31, 1995

   Bought 100 MTN at 28 on November 15, 1995

   What is the tax consequence of these transactions?

   A. Net loss of $400
   B. Net loss of $300
   C. Net gain of $400
   D. Net gain of $500

3. A corporation in a 35% tax bracket reports operating income of $4,000,000 for the year. The firm also received $200,000 in preferred dividends. Assuming no other items of income or expense, what is the company's tax liability?

   A. $1,360,000
   B. $1,370,200
   C. $1,421,000
   D. $1,756,000

4. An investor in a 28% tax bracket has a $5,000 loss after netting all capital gains and losses realized. How much may the investor deduct from income that year?

   A. $0
   B. $2,500
   C. $3,000
   D. $5,000

5. An investor in a 28% tax bracket has a $5,000 loss after netting all capital gains and losses realized. The following year this investor has a $1,000 capital gain. After netting his gains and losses, what will be his tax situation that second year?

   A. He will have a $1,000 gain.
   B. He will have a $1,000 loss to carry over to the next year.
   C. He will offset $1,000 ordinary income this year.
   D. There will be no tax consequences.

6. Max Leveridge bought a $100,000 7 3/8% GHI bond at 94 and paid 60 days' accrued interest on the purchase. What was his cost basis?

    A. $708
    B. $5,000
    C. $94,000
    D. $94,000 plus interest

7. By which government is the income from Eurodollar bonds taxed?

    A. Government of the country in which the investor pays taxes
    B. Government of the country that issued the bonds
    C. Government of the country in whose currency the bonds are denominated
    D. No tax is levied.

8. By which government is the income from Inter-American Development Bank bonds taxed?

    A. Government of the country in which the investor pays taxes
    B. Government of the country that issued the bonds
    C. Government of the country in whose currency the bonds are denominated
    D. No tax is levied.

9. Which of the following groups of taxpayers would be MOST affected by a regressive tax?

    A. Low income
    B. Middle income
    C. High income
    D. Passive income

10. Which of the following taxes would be considered *regressive*?

    A. Income
    B. Sales
    C. Inheritance
    D. Estate

11. Max Leveridge is calculating his income taxes and goes through the alternative minimum tax calculations as well. He has both numbers, but doesn't know what they mean. You should tell him that

    A. the alternative minimum tax is added to the regular tax
    B. he pays the regular tax or the alternative tax, depending on his bracket
    C. the excess of the alternative tax over the regular tax is added to his regular tax
    D. he pays the lesser of the regular tax or the alternative tax

12. Mini Leveridge has not followed your investment advice and now has net capital losses of $10,000 for the year. How much of these losses can she offset against her non-passive income for the year?

    A. $1,500
    B. $3,000
    C. $6,000
    D. $10,000

13. Gwinneth Stout, retired and in the 15% tax bracket, has a long-term capital gain of $3,000. What percentage of this gain will be paid as tax?

    A. 15%
    B. 20%
    C. 28%
    D. 40%

14. Klaus Bruin, in the 28% tax bracket, bought 100 shares of DWQ common at 50 and 19 months later sold the shares at 70. What is his maximum tax liability on this investment?

    A. $224
    B. $400
    C. $560
    D. $2,000

15. A husband and wife who file jointly received $300 in corporate dividends, $500 in interest income from corporate bonds and $1,000 in interest income from general obligation bonds. How much of their total investment income is subject to federal taxes?

    A. $600
    B. $800
    C. $1,500
    D. $1,800

16. Your customer bought an original issue discount bond issued by the Mt. Vernon Port Authority. How is the discount on this bond taxed?

    A. As capital gains upon maturity or the sale of debenture
    B. As income upon maturity or the sale of debenture
    C. It is accreted during the life of the bond and used to adjust the bond's cost basis
    D. It is tax-exempt

17. A customer owns 10M of 7% U.S. Treasury bonds. She is in the 28% federal tax bracket and the 10% state tax bracket. What is her annual tax liability on these bonds?

    A. $70
    B. $98
    C. $196
    D. $266

18. TCB, Inc., a successful chain of sushi bars, is in the maximum corporate tax bracket. It will be allowed to exclude from taxation 70% of income earned on investments in

    A. government and agency securities
    B. municipal bonds from the same state the corporation is located in
    C. corporate common and preferred stock
    D. industrial development bonds

19. A client in the highest tax bracket wants to minimize her tax burden. The interest on which of the following securities is exempt from federal, state and local taxes?

    A. City of New York general obligation bonds
    B. GNMA pass-through certificates
    C. Treasury bills
    D. Bonds issued by the Commonwealth of Puerto Rico

20. A married couple who file jointly have a $5,000 long-term capital loss with no offsetting capital gains. Which of the following statements is NOT true of the tax treatment of this loss?

    A. The maximum they can deduct this year is $3,000.
    B. They can carry forward $2,000 to future years.
    C. Capital losses can only be used to offset capital gains.
    D. Capital losses can be deducted dollar-for-dollar.

21. June Polar owns TCB stock and wants to continue holding the security. The stock has fallen from 26 when she bought it on February 2nd to a 52-week low of 20 7/8. She sells the stock on December 1st at the low and repurchases it at the same price on December 15th. What are the tax consequences of this investment?

    A. June has a capital loss.
    B. By repurchasing the investment at the same price, she keeps the same cost basis.
    C. The holding period for the stock was wiped out.
    D. The tax loss is not allowed.

22. A customer who earns more than $200,000 a year owns 200 shares of Datawaq. He bought it at 60 ten years ago and it is now trading at 90. If he donates the stock to a not-for-profit corporation, how much can he claim as a tax deduction for this donation?

   A. $0
   B. $6,000
   C. $12,000
   D. $18,000

23. On Monday, August 22, 1998, an investor purchased 5M MTN 11.5% debentures due October 1, 2013, at 89 1/4. He sells them on March 17, 1999. How much interest income from the October 1st payment on these bonds would be taxable to the investor in 1998?

   A. $11.50
   B. $57.50
   C. $201.25
   D. $287.50

24. On Monday, July 5, 1991, an investor buys 5M of 9 3/8% Treasury bonds at 88 1/4. The bonds mature on September 1, 1996. If he sells the bonds on February 7, 1992, at 90 7/8, what is the amount of interest he would recognize for federal tax purposes in 1991?

   A. $72.60
   B. $156.25
   C. $220.05
   D. $234.50

25. How does the net yield of a municipal bond that would subject its owner to AMT compare to the yield of one that would not?

   A. Higher yield
   B. Lower yield
   C. Same
   D. Does not affect yield

26. An investor owns 2,000 shares of stock in Czarnina, Inc., a Slovenian corporation. The stock has a cash dividend of $2. Slovenia withholds 15% of the cash dividend as a tax. How does the U.S. investor report the Slovenian withholding on his tax return?

   A. Declares all $4,000 as income
   B. Declares $3,400 as dividend income and claims a 15% foreign tax credit
   C. Claims a 15% foreign tax credit
   D. Declares $3,400 only as income

27. A married couple sets up a JTWROS account with a balance of $1,000,000. If the wife dies, what is the husband's estate tax liability?

   A. He pays federal and state taxes on the entire balance.
   B. He pays federal and state taxes on $500,000.
   C. He pays federal taxes only on $500,000.
   D. He does not pay estate tax on any amount.

28. Your high-income customer is subject to AMT. Which of the following preference items must be added to adjusted gross income to calculate his tax liability?

   A. Interest on private purpose municipal bond issued in September 1987
   B. Interest on municipal bond issued to finance highway construction
   C. Income from municipal security issued to finance parking garages
   D. Distributions from corporate bond mutual fund

29. Which of the following are federally tax exempt for a corporation?

   I. Municipal bond interest
   II. U.S. preferred stock dividends
   III. Foreign corporate stock dividends
   IV. Capital gains

   A. I
   B. I and II
   C. II and III
   D. II and IV

30. Which investment should a rep recommend to a corporation whose objective is current income?

   A. Preferred stock
   B. Aggressive growth fund
   C. Money-market fund
   D. High-yield bonds

31. Eve Grizzly receives stock from the estate of her mother. Eve's cost basis in this stock is the

   A. original cost of the stock to her mother
   B. original cost of the stock to her mother adjusted for any estate taxes paid
   C. market value on the date of death
   D. market value on the date of distribution to the customer

32. A mother makes a gift of securities to her ten-year-old son. The son's cost basis in the stock is the

   A. original cost of the securities to the mother
   B. market value of the securities on the date of the gift
   C. market value of the securities on April 15th of the year the gift is made
   D. market value of the securities on December 31st of the year the gift is made

◆ Answers & Rationale

1.   **C.**   With a progressive tax, the amount of tax (percentage) increases with an increase in the taxable amount such as income, estates and gifts (taxes are paid by the donor). Gasoline and sales taxes are considered to be regressive taxes because all persons pay the same percentage tax regardless of their wealth.   (Page 363)

2.   **D.**   The 30-day wash sale rule of the IRS states that the purchase of substantially identical securities within 30 days of a securities transaction at a loss will result in the loss being disallowed for tax purposes. The 30-day time period is considered to be either before or after the sale date. The purchase of 100 shares of TCB on November 30, 1995, is within 30 days of the sale on December 20, 1995, therefore no loss on these transactions is allowed.   (Page 368)

3.   **C.**   The corporation's $4,000,000 operating income will be taxed at a rate of 35%. For tax purposes, corporations can exclude 70% of all dividends received from domestic common and preferred stocks. Thus, 30% of the $200,000 received from preferred dividends will be taxed at the 35% tax rate. $200,000 × 30% = $60,000. The $4,000,000 in income plus $60,000 received in taxable dividends equals $4,060,000. $4,060,000 multiplied by a 35% tax rate equals taxes of $1,421,000.   (Page 370)

4.   **C.**   The maximum deduction of capital losses in any one year is $3,000. Any remaining losses can be carried forward into the next year.   (Page 367)

5.   **C.**   The losses carried forward from the previous year are $2,000. These losses are netted against the gain of $1,000 for a net loss of $1,000. That $1,000 loss can be used to offset $1,000 of ordinary income. In other words, the net $1,000 loss is deducted from the investor's income. No further loss remains to carry forward.   (Page 367)

6.   **C.**   Accrued interest is not counted in establishing the cost basis of a bond for tax purposes.   (Page 365)

7.   **A.**   The income from a foreign investment is taxable to the investor under the rules of the country in which he retains citizenship.   (Page 366)

8.   **A.**   The Inter-American Development Bank was created in 1959 in partnership with the governments of 20 Latin American countries, and is treated as an agency of the U.S. government. A U.S. investor would pay U.S. taxes on income from its securities.   (Page 365)

9.   **A.**   A regressive tax (for example, a sales tax) is one that takes a larger percentage from a person with a low income than it does from a person with a high income.   (Page 363)

10.   **B.**   All of the other taxes listed are progressive. Income taxes, inheritance taxes and estate taxes all take a larger bite from a person with a high income than from a person with a low income. Sales tax takes a proportionally higher part of the income from a low-income family.   (Page 363)

11.   **C.**   The excess is added to the regular tax.   (Page 369)

12.   **B.**   Net capital losses are deductible against earned (nonpassive) income to a maximum of $3,000 per year. The balance of such losses can be carried forward to the next year.   (Page 367)

13.   **A.**   Capital gains are currently taxed at ordinary income rates up to a maximum rate of 28%. Because the customer is in the 15% tax bracket, this percentage is the maximum she will pay on the gain.   (Page 364)

14.   **C.**   The sale of securities held over 12 months results in a long-term capital gain or loss. Under current tax law, both long-term and short-term gains are taxed at ordinary tax rates up to a maximum rate of 28%. In this case, the investor bought 100 shares at $50 ($5,000) and sold at $70 ($7,000), resulting in a $2,000 capital gain. 28% × $2,000 = $560 tax liability.   (Page 364)

15. **B.** The dividend exclusion has been repealed. The couple's corporate dividend income of $300 and their interest income of $500 from the corporate bonds are subject to federal income taxes. Interest income from general obligation bonds is exempt from federal income taxes.

(Page 364)

16. **C.** Under IRS rules, owners of original issue discount bonds are required to adjust the cost basis of the bond by accreting the discount over the life of the bond. (Page 368)

17. **C.** $1,000 times 7% equals $70 annual interest per bond; $70 times 10 equals $700 annual interest, which is taxable only by the federal government. $700 × 28% = $196 tax liability.

(Page 365)

18. **C.** Corporate ownership of another company's stock allows the owner to exclude 70% of the dividends from taxation. (Page 370)

19. **D.** Bond issues by protectorates of the United States (Guam, Puerto Rico and the U.S. Virgin Islands) are triple tax-exempt: federal, state and local. Interest income from municipal bonds is federal tax exempt, but is not state tax exempt unless the bondholder is a resident of the state where the bonds are issued. Interest from Treasury bills and most other government and agency securities is state tax exempt, but is subject to federal taxes. Exceptions are GNMA and FNMA securities, which are taxed on all levels. (Page 365)

20. **C.** Capital losses are deducted from ordinary income and so reduce tax liability. The maximum individuals or married couples can deduct is $3,000 annually. If the long-term capital loss exceeds the maximum, the excess losses are carried forward to future years (up to the $3,000 limit) until the loss is exhausted. Under current IRS regulations, $1 of losses results in $1 of deductions.

(Page 367)

21. **D.** The IRS will not allow the loss. The customer is in the same position (holding the same security) and, therefore, has not made a true transaction; thus, the IRS will disallow the paper loss.

It would have been allowed had the customer bought it back after 30 days; this is the wash sale rule. Note that the loss will be allowed when the new shares are ultimately sold. (Page 368)

22. **D.** Securities that have been owned for more than one year can be gifted to a charity and deducted at their fair market value. Securities owned for less than one year can be deducted at their acquisition cost only. (Page 363)

23. **B.** Only interest income received during the year is taxable. Because the bond matures on October 1st, interest is paid on April 1st and October 1st. August 25, 1998, (trade settlement date) to October 1, 1998, includes 36 days during which interest will accrue. The investor will receive a $287.50 interest payment on October 1st. However, the investor must pay back accrued interest he is not entitled to from April 1st up to, but not including, the settlement date of August 25th. The number of days in this period is 144. The amount of interest for this period is $5,000 times .115 (which is 11 1/2%) times .4 (144 ÷ 360), which equals $230. The amount of interest income reported for tax purposes is $57.50, the difference between what was received ($287.50) and $230, the accrued interest the investor had to pay back.

(Page 366)

24. **A.** Interest computation is always the same: principal × rate × time. In this example, we know that the bond will pay interest on March 1st and September 1st. March 1st to August 31st equals 184 days. The investor owned the bonds from July 6th to August 31st, or a total of 57 of those 184 days. The rate of interest is divided by two because only half is paid each six months. $5,000 × (9 3/8% ÷ 2) × (57 ÷ 184) = $72.60. (Page 365)

25. **B.** Any bond that is subject to additional taxes, such as might apply if the owner is subject to the alternative minimum tax (AMT), would have a lower net yield than one that is not subject to additional taxes. (Page 369)

26. **C.** The Foreign Tax Credit (FTC) is 15% on dividends distributed by foreign corporations.

(Page 366)

27. **D.** Estate taxes are paid on assets transferred to others according to the provisions of a will. Establishing a joint tenants with right of survivorship account eliminates the need to will the account balance to the other joint tenant. Therefore, no taxes are paid.   (Page 363)

28. **A.** If more than 10% of a bond's proceeds go to private entities, the interest on the bond is a tax preference item for the alternative minimum tax. Earnings from public purpose bonds are tax deductible. Earnings from nonessential public bonds (such as the one financing parking garages) and corporate bonds are taxable and thus would not have been deducted from the customer's taxable income.   (Page 370)

29. **A.** Like individual taxpayers, U.S. corporations do not pay tax on earnings from municipal bonds. U.S. stock dividends are only partially tax-exempt. Corporations pay taxes on foreign stocks and on capital gains, though at a reduced rate.   (Page 370)

30. **A.** Preferred stock will generate a steady flow of current income; it is paid in the form of dividends, thus the income has the additional benefit of being 70% tax-exempt to the corporation. The money-market fund will provide a comparatively low level of current income, and the high-yield bonds are accompanied by a high level of risk. As a rule, aggressive growth funds strive for capital appreciation rather than current income.   (Page 370)

31. **C.** The cost basis of inherited stock is adjusted to reflect the fair market value on the date of the decedent's death. The date of distribution to the beneficiary is not considered.   (Page 369)

32. **A.** The cost basis of stock received as a gift is not adjusted for the new owner. After ownership of the securities is transferred, the new owner's cost basis is the original purchase price paid by the donor.   (Page 369)

56 ◆ Insider Trading Act of 1988 Exam

1. Under the Securities Exchange Act of 1934, insiders include

    I.   the attorney who wrote the offering circular for the company
    II. a bookkeeper in the accounting department of the company
    III. the wife of the president of the company
    IV. a brother of the president of the company

    A. I only
    B. II only
    C. II, III and IV only
    D. I, II, III and IV

2. The Chinese Wall prohibitions refer to which of the following situations?

    A. Difficulties a U.S. client would encounter in attempting to trade foreign stocks directly instead of using ADRs
    B. Registered rep calling the corporate finance department of his firm to get information about a company it is helping underwrite a new issue of stock
    C. Affirmative action program originally created on Wall Street to expand the brokerage network in California
    D. Refusal of traders on the Tokyo Stock Exchange to recognize Taiwanese securities

3. When assessing whether an individual has acted properly in the purchase and sale of option contracts based on inside information, which of the following factors will be considered?

    I.   Whether the individual with inside information made a profit on the transaction
    II. Whether the other party was privy to the same information
    III. Method by which the information was released to the public
    IV. Time of the transaction in relation to the time when the information was released to the public

    A. I and II only
    B. II and IV only
    C. III and IV only
    D. I, II, III and IV

4. Tex Longhorn is in possession of material inside information about General Gizmonics, Inc. He may communicate this information to a customer

    A. if the customer knows it's inside information
    B. the day before the information is made public
    C. if the customer enters an unsolicited order
    D. under no circumstances

◆ Answers & Rationale

1.   **D.**   While the act of 1934 defines an insider as an officer, director or 10% stockholder of the company, the courts have broadened the definition to include anyone who has inside information.

(Page 376)

2.   **B.**   The Chinese Wall rules were designed to prevent the sharing of insider information between the corporate finance section of a broker-dealer and the retail sales department. Much of the information obtained when the corporate finance department helps an issuer underwrite a new issue of securities could, if it wasn't public knowledge, be used to affect the stock price unfairly.   (Page 378)

3.   **C.**   Under the act of 1934, insiders cannot profit from inside information (i.e., information not available to the general public). To determine whether information is still "inside" (i.e., not in the public domain), the SEC considers the method by which the information is released to the public (i.e., it must be broadly disseminated) and the timing of trades relative to when other people also have the information. The SEC does not consider the profit made or the loss avoided when determining whether a violation occurred; the SEC's concern is whether the information was nonpublic at the time of the trade.   (Page 376)

4.   **D.**   Inside information may never be discussed until it is made public, at which point it is no longer inside information. Violations may be punished with civil penalties as well as prison sentences.   (Page 376)

57 Securities Investor Protection Corporation Exam

1. A husband and wife have both a joint cash account and a joint margin account. In addition, each has an individual retirement account. SIPC would cover

   A. the joint accounts separately and the retirement accounts as one
   B. the retirement accounts separately and the joint accounts as one
   C. all accounts combined as one
   D. all accounts individually and separately

2. The trustee for a bankrupt broker-dealer must

   I. notify customers of the bankruptcy
   II. handle the liquidation of the broker-dealer
   III. distribute all property specifically identified as belonging to customers
   IV. make sure books and records are accurate

   A. I, II and IV only
   B. I and III only
   C. III and IV only
   D. I, II, III and IV

3. Securities distributed by a trustee operating under SIPC authorization will be valued for coverage based on the

   A. market value of the securities on the day on which the trustee is appointed
   B. average value of the securities between the date of the bankruptcy and the distribution date
   C. value of the securities as of the distribution date
   D. purchase price

4. A client not covered by SIPC in a broker-dealer bankruptcy would

   A. become a secured creditor
   B. become a general creditor
   C. become a preferred creditor
   D. lose his investment

5. In the event of the bankruptcy of a broker-dealer, the Securities Investor Protection Corporation covers

   A. $100,000 per separate customer
   B. $100,000 per account
   C. $500,000 per separate customer
   D. $500,000 per account

6. The determination of a broker-dealer's financial failure is made under the provisions of the

A. Securities Act of 1933
B. Securities Exchange Act of 1934
C. Securities Investor Protection Act of 1970
D. specific determination of the SEC

7. Client coverage under SIPC is $500,000 for

A. securities losses only
B. cash and securities losses
C. securities losses, and $500,000 for cash losses
D. cash and securities losses, of which no more than $100,000 may be for cash losses

8. Which of the following customer accounts is(are) NOT SIPC-insured?

I. Customer margin account
II. JTWROS account with spouse
III. JTIC commodities account with son
IV. JTIC account with business partner

A. I
B. II and III
C. II, III and IV
D. III

9. A client has a special cash account with stock valued at $460,000 and $40,000 in cash. The same client also has a joint account with a spouse that has a market value of $320,000 and $180,000 in cash. SIPC coverage would then be

A. $460,000 for the special cash account and $320,000 for the joint account
B. $500,000 for the special cash account and $420,000 for the joint account
C. $500,000 for the special cash account and $500,000 for the joint account
D. a total of $1,000,000 for both accounts

10. A corporation opens a trading account with ALFA Financial Services. At the same time, a director of the corporation opens an individual trading account with ALFA. According to SIPC rules, how will the accounts be treated?

A. Both accounts will be combined as one separate customer account.
B. The corporation's account will be covered under SIPC, but the director's account will not.
C. The director's account will be covered under SIPC, but the corporation's account will not.
D. Each account will be treated as a separate customer.

11. Which of the following market values is used by SIPC for valuing customer claims when a broker-dealer becomes insolvent?

A. Market value on the date the broker-dealer becomes insolvent
B. Market value on the date that a federal court is petitioned to appoint a trustee
C. Market value on the date that the trustee pays the balances to the customers
D. Average market value from the time the trustee is appointed to the payment date

12. Under SIPC, when a trustee is appointed customer claims are filed with the

A. court-appointed trustee
B. failed broker-dealer's SRO
C. Securities and Exchange Commission
D. Securities Investor Protection Corporation

13. If a brokerage firm goes bankrupt, the dollar amount of insurance coverage applicable to a customer's special cash account with a balance of $100,000 is

A. $0
B. $100,000
C. $200,000
D. $500,000

14. A fidelity bond is a(n)

    A. bond that protects customer accounts against loss of value

    B. truth-in-lending statement that must be furnished to customers prior to opening an account

    C. insurance bond that protects broker-dealers from losses due to theft or embezzlement by employees

    D. corporate debt issue backed by the faith and credit of the issuer

15. SIPC provides coverage for which of the following securities held in a customer account?

    I. Common stock
    II. Preferred stock
    III. Rights and warrants
    IV. Corporate bonds

    A. I and II only
    B. II, III and IV only
    C. III and IV only
    D. I, II, III and IV

◆ Answers & Rationale

1.   **B.**   SIPC provides up to $500,000 of protection to each separate customer account. Multiple accounts held by the same person would be considered as only one customer for SIPC purposes (remember that the definition of "person" can include individuals, groups, companies, and so on). However, there are different elements of beneficial ownership. If a woman has an account in her name, a man has an account in his name and they are joint owners of a third account, SIPC will treat them as three separate customer accounts.   (Page 381)

2.   **D.**   Upon being appointed by the court, a trustee must inform all customers of the broker-dealer's condition, conduct a rapid and orderly liquidation of the broker-dealer's business, and distribute all identifiable assets. As part of this process, the trustee will review the broker-dealer's books and records to ensure their accuracy.
(Page 379)

3.   **A.**   The value of a customer account under SIPC is set as of the date that SIPC applies to the courts to appoint a bankruptcy trustee. (Page 380)

4.   **B.**   Any customer claims not covered by SIPC will result in the customer's becoming a general (unsecured) creditor of the company.
(Page 380)

5.   **C.**   Coverage under SIPC amounts to $500,000 per separate customer account, with no more than $100,000 of that amount going to cover cash and cash equivalents.   (Page 382)

6.   **C.**   The determination of financial failure is made under the Securities Investor Protection Act of 1970.   (Page 379)

7.   **D.**   SIPC coverage for each separate customer account is $500,000, with cash coverage not to exceed $100,000.   (Page 380)

8.   **D.**   SIPC coverage applies to accounts holding *securities* only. Commodities accounts, therefore, are not covered.   (Page 382)

9.   **B.**   SIPC coverage is $500,000 per separate customer account, with cash not to exceed $100,000. Thus, in the single-name account, SIPC provides full coverage, while in the joint account SIPC covers the full value of the securities but only $100,000 of the $180,000 in cash. The remaining $80,000 becomes a general debt of the bankrupt broker-dealer.   (Page 381)

10.   **D.**   The corporate account (in corporate name) will be treated as a separate customer account from the individual account. (Note that if the director of the corporation were a director of the broker-dealer, the account would not be covered.)
(Page 381)

11.   **B.**   Under SIPC rules, customer claims are valued on the day customer protection proceedings commence; this would be the day that a federal court is petitioned to appoint a trustee. (Page 380)

12.   **A.**   Customer claim forms are filed with the trustee.   (Page 380)

13.   **B.**   Coverage is $500,000 maximum with cash not to exceed $100,000. An individual with $100,000 of securities in a special cash account is covered for $100,000.   (Page 380)

14.   **C.**   Broker-dealers are required to maintain fidelity bond coverage to protect the firm's assets from loss due to theft or embezzlement by officers or employees.   (Page 382)

15.   **D.**   SIPC provides coverage for up to $500,000 worth of securities held in a customer account. All types of securities are covered up to the maximum.   (Page 380)

58 Other Federal and State Legislation Exam

1. The Trust Indenture Act of 1939 covers all of the following securities transactions EXCEPT a(n)

   A. public issue of debentures worth $5,500,000 sold by a single member firm throughout the United States
   B. sale of an issue of $50,000,000 worth of Treasury bonds maturing in 2011
   C. corporate bond issue sold interstate worth $10,000,000
   D. equipment trust bond worth $5,000,000

2. Serendipity Discount Securities has its principal office in New Jersey and recently registered a branch office in Minnesota. Which of the following statements is true?

   A. Registered reps working in the principal office may take unsolicited orders from Minnesota residents.
   B. Registered reps working in the branch office may take unsolicited orders from New Jersey residents.
   C. Each rep is automatically registered in both states.
   D. Each rep must be registered in the appropriate state before soliciting or taking orders.

◆ Answers & Rationale

1. **B.** The Trust Indenture Act of 1939 requires all corporate debt issues that are sold publicly to contain a trust indenture. U.S. governments are exempt. (Page 383)

2. **D.** According to the provisions of the Uniform Securities Act, reps must be registered in every state in which they conduct business. (Page 384)

59 Registration and Regulation of Broker-Dealers Exam

1. Which of the following brokerage house staff are NOT subject to the mandatory fingerprinting rule?

   A. Associated persons employed as sales representatives
   B. Auditors and accountants in charge of the firm's money and securities accounting records
   C. Officers or partners who supervise the cashiering and accounting departments of the firm in sales production
   D. Associated persons engaged exclusively in securities research

2. If a registered representative is suspended by a member firm, the member firm must report the suspension to

   A. its designated examining authority
   B. the state securities commissioner
   C. the SEC
   D. the news media

◆ Answers & Rationale

1. **D.** SEC Rule 17f-2 requires that all officers and employees of a broker-dealer organization be fingerprinted if they (1) engage in the sale of securities, (2) have access to physical securities, cash or accounting records, or (3) directly supervise employees who handle securities, cash or accounting records.   (Page 390)

2. **A.** If a registered representative is suspended by a member firm, the firm must report the suspension to its designated examining authority (DEA)—typically the NASD or exchanges where the firm is a member. Each DEA is a self-regulatory organization.   (Page 390)

60 NASD Bylaws Exam

1. A statutory disqualification applies to an employee or official of a broker-dealer who, within the past ten years, has

   A. been charged with assaulting a police officer
   B. been convicted of a misdemeanor in the securities industry
   C. been convicted of breaking a car window at a dealership that sold him a lemon
   D. not paid income taxes

2. It is ethical for a broker-dealer to pay commissions under a continuing commission contract to which of the following?

   I. Retired employee or his widow, for continuing business
   II. Broker-dealership purchased by you for that broker-dealer's continuing business
   III. Retired employee who refers an old neighbor to the broker-dealer
   IV. Retired employee who, in the course of his travels, acquires new business for the broker-dealer

   A. I and II only
   B. II and III only
   C. III and IV only
   D. I, II, III and IV

3. Which of the following individuals are required to register as principals with the NASD?

   I. Any person soliciting orders from the public who is also a partner of a member firm
   II. Manager of an office of supervisory jurisdiction
   III. Directors who are actively engaged in a member firm's securities business
   IV. Assistant vice president involved in training registered reps for a member firm

   A. I and II only
   B. II and IV only
   C. III and IV only
   D. I, II, III and IV

4. You would be exempt from registration as an investment adviser under the Uniform Securities Act if you had no place of business in the state and if, in any consecutive twelve-month period, you directed business communications to no more than how many customers?

   A. Five
   B. Ten
   C. Fifteen
   D. Unlimited

5. According to the NASD Bylaws, which of the following must be recorded for a person who seeks a job that involves handling funds or securities?

    I.   Arrest or indictment for any crime involving the purchase, sale or delivery of securities
    II. Denial of membership in any national securities exchange
    III. Disclosure of the person's business connections over the past ten years
    IV. Educational institutions attended within the past ten years

    A. I and II only
    B. I, III and IV only
    C. II and III only
    D. I, II, III and IV

6. In order to be qualified to solicit orders for unit investment trusts and mutual funds that invest exclusively in municipal securities, a person must be registered as a(n)

    I.   general securities representative
    II. insurance agent
    III. municipal securities representative
    IV. certified financial planner

    A. I
    B. I and III
    C. I, III and IV
    D. II and IV

7. An individual duly registered with the MSRB who wishes to sell shares of a unit investment trust may do so

    A. if she is registered to sell investment company shares with the MSRB
    B. if she is registered to sell investment company shares with the NASD
    C. with written permission of the MSRB
    D. with no written permission

8. The NASD Uniform Practice Code was established to

    A. require that practices in the investment banking and securities industry be just, reasonable, and nondiscriminatory between investors
    B. eliminate advertising and sales literature that the SEC considers to be in violation of standards
    C. provide a procedure for handling trade complaints from investors
    D. maintain similarity of business practices among member organizations in the securities industry

9. Which of the following persons are qualified to solicit orders for unit investment trusts and mutual funds that invest exclusively in municipal securities?

    I.   Registered life insurance broker
    II. Registered municipal securities representative
    III. Bank manager
    IV. Registered general securities representative

    A. I , II and III
    B. I, II and IV
    C. III
    D. IV

10. A sales assistant who takes options orders from the customers of a registered representative

    A. does not need to be registered if properly supervised by a registered person
    B. needs only to be registered with the NASD as a Series 6
    C. must be registered and certified to do options trading
    D. must have a Series 11 license

11. A sales assistant takes messages from customers regarding the purchase and sale of securities during the rep's absence. The sales assistant is not licensed. This activity is

   A. a violation of exchange rules and will subject both the sales assistant and the registered representative to disciplinary proceedings
   B. a violation of exchange rules and will subject the registered representative to disciplinary proceedings
   C. permitted
   D. permitted only if the registered representative reviews the activities of the sales assistant on a daily basis

12. Consolidated Codfish would like to offer its new issue of 1,000,000 shares of common through Churnum, Burnem, Spernim to investors in the three states in which it has customers. What registration and sales restrictions will apply?

   I. The offering needs to be registered only in Consolidated Codfish's home state.
   II. COD shares can only be sold by registered reps licensed to sell securities in those states.
   III. CBS must arrange to have tombstones published in each of those states.
   IV. The offering must be blue-skyed in each of the three states in which the issue will be sold.

   A. I and III
   B. II, III and IV
   C. II and IV
   D. III and IV

13. Blue-sky laws pertain to all of the following EXCEPT

   A. registration of securities within a state
   B. regulation of securities trading in other countries
   C. regulation of securities trading in a state
   D. registration of securities salespersons in a state

14. Most blue-sky laws have provisions for all of the following EXCEPT

   A. revoking a registration or license when a state securities division determines that a broker-dealer or salesperson has violated any part of the blue-sky laws
   B. registering all broker-dealers and their salespeople in each state in which they do business
   C. selling securities issued in other states
   D. comparably compensating salespeople registered in more than one state

15. A registered representative left her firm a year ago to write a screenplay. She is ready to return to the industry. Which of the following statements is FALSE?

   A. Her registration was terminated.
   B. She must requalify by examination.
   C. Her old firm filed a U-5 Form.
   D. Her new firm must file a U-4 Form.

16. A registered representative is convicted of a felony involving the sale of a security. For how many years will she be disqualified from associating with an NASD member firm?

   A. One
   B. Three
   C. Seven
   D. Ten

17. Randy Bear, a Series 11-licensed assistant representative, is paid an hourly wage. Which of the following is another permitted form of compensation?

   A. Bonus based on new accounts opened
   B. Commission based on customer orders entered
   C. Profit-sharing program based on company's success
   D. Bonus based on number of unsolicited orders transacted

18. A Series 11-licensed representative may

  A. qualify new customers
  B. make investment recommendations
  C. accept unsolicited orders
  D. provide advice to customers

19. According to the rules that established SROs, these organizations are

  I. accountable to the SEC for supervising securities practices within their assigned jurisdictions
  II. government agencies
  III. permitted to issue securities
  IV. responsible for either over-the-counter or exchange trading

  A. I and II
  B. I and III
  C. II and IV
  D. I and IV

20. Which of the following must be included in an advertisement that identifies a nonbranch office of an NASD member?

  A. Statement that the advertisement was filed with the NASD prior to use
  B. NASD approval of the nonbranch's registration
  C. Address and telephone number of the nonbranch's office of supervisory jurisdiction
  D. Name of the registered principal with supervisory responsibility for the nonbranch office

◆ Answers & Rationale

1. **B.** Anyone who has been convicted within the past ten years of a misdemeanor involving securities or any felony is subject to the NASD's statutory disqualification rules. A member firm may hire someone who has a record of convictions for misdemeanors outside the industry, although that person's application for registration will be reviewed by the Association before approval.
(Page 401)

2. **A.** A member firm may continue to pay commissions either to a retired employee (or to a retired employee's spouse) or to a broker-dealer purchased by the firm for continuing business, provided that a prior written contract exists.
(Page 395)

3. **D.** Any person who is actively engaged in the management of a member's business (including supervising, soliciting or training other persons for any of these functions) must be registered with the NASD as a principal.
(Page 399)

4. **A.** This investment adviser would be exempt from the USA's registration requirements if he contacted no more than five customers.
(Page 396)

5. **D.** Under the NASD Bylaws, a broker must have a record of all of the items listed. (Page 394)

6. **A.** Persons licensed to sell only municipal securities must limit their activities to securities issued by municipal issuers, the federal government and government agencies. Municipal bond mutual funds or unit investment trusts are investment company securities; the sale of these securities requires either a general securities or an investment company/variable contracts representative license. A general securities license would be required to sell both investment company products and municipal securities.
(Page 397)

7. **B.** UIT shares are investment company shares and may be sold only if the broker is registered with the NASD to do so.
(Page 397)

8. **D.** The Uniform Practice Code is designed to standardize the customs, practices and trading techniques employed in the investment banking and securities business.
(Page 393)

9. **D.** Persons licensed to sell only municipal securities must limit their activities to securities issued by municipal issuers, the federal government and government agencies. Municipal bond mutual funds and unit investment trusts are investment company securities; the sale of these securities requires a general securities or investment company/variable contract representative license.
(Page 397)

10. **D.** A sales assistant who accepts options orders must be Series 11-licensed as an AROP.
(Page 397)

11. **C.** As long as the sales assistant does not solicit or take orders, she need not be licensed. However, her activities should be supervised by the registered representative.
(Page 396)

12. **C.** In order to sell an issue in any state, the broker-dealer, the registered reps and the security itself must each be registered in that state. Registering an issue in a state is known as *blue-skying* the issue.
(Page 398)

13. **B.** Blue-sky laws are developed within a state for control of securities trading within that state.
(Page 398)

14. **D.** The typical blue-sky laws have provisions for revoking the license of a broker-dealer or salesperson. The provisions require the registration of all broker-dealers, salespeople and provisions for the sale of securities issued in other states (they need to be registered in that state). By process of elimination, you can conclude that there are provisions for everything except comparable compensation for salespeople registered in more than one state. The blue-sky laws do not tell a brokerage firm how to compensate people.
(Page 398)

15. **B.** Only after a leave of absence of two years or more must registered reps requalify. When the rep left the old firm, her registration was terminated and a U-5 Form was filed by the firm. When she is employed by a new firm, she must reapply for registration on a U-4 Form. (Page 395)

16. **D.** A felony conviction within the ten years preceding application for registration is considered a statutory disqualification. The same restriction applies to convictions for misdemeanors if they involve securities or money-related offenses.
(Page 401)

17. **C.** A Series 11-licensed assistant representative may participate in company-sponsored profit-sharing bonuses. He may not receive bonuses or commissions based on transactions or account activity. (Page 398)

18. **C.** A Series 11 Assistant Representative–Order Processing may accept unsolicited orders, but may not determine suitability or otherwise provide recommendations or advice. (Page 397)

19. **D.** Self-regulatory organizations were established to ensure compliance with SEC regulation in a particular jurisdiction. Some SROs, such as the NYSE and the CBOE, are responsible for exchange trading; others, such as the NASD, supervise OTC trading. Since all SROs are independent membership corporations, they may not issue capital stock. (Page 391)

20. **C.** A nonbranch office of a broker-dealer must identify the name, address and telephone number of its OSJ on letterheads, business cards, telephone directory listings and advertisements.
(Page 394)

61 Codes of Procedure and of Arbitration Procedure Exam

1. The Board of Governors of the NASD has the authority to

   I. suspend a person, prohibiting him from associating with any exchange
   II. censure a partner of a member firm
   III. suspend or expel a member firm from membership in the NASD
   IV. either suspend or bar a person from further association with a member firm

   A. I and III only
   B. II, III and IV only
   C. II and IV only
   D. I, II, III and IV

2. The Code of Procedure was designed for all of the following purposes EXCEPT settling

   A. when-, as- and if-issued securities transactions between member firms
   B. complaints between or among members
   C. complaints between registered reps and members
   D. complaints made by customers against members

3. The NASD may take which of the following actions against members who violate the Rules of Fair Practice?

   I. Expulsion
   II. Censure
   III. Fine
   IV. Suspension

   A. I, II and IV only
   B. I and IV only
   C. II and III only
   D. I, II, III and IV

4. Findings under the NASD Code of Arbitration Procedure

   A. are binding on members, but not on customers
   B. are binding on all parties involved in the dispute
   C. may be appealed to the NASD's Board of Governors
   D. may be appealed to the SEC

5. A registered representative may be disciplined for an infraction of the Rules of Fair Practice

    I.   at the request of a customer
    II. at the request of the Board of Governors
    III. by the District Business Conduct Committee

    A. I and III only
    B. II only
    C. II and III only
    D. I, II and III

6. Arbitration under the NASD Code of Arbitration Procedure may be used to resolve which of the following disputes?

    I.   Member against a person associated with a member
    II. Member against another member
    III. Member against a public customer
    IV. Public customer against a member

    A. I only
    B. I, II and IV only
    C. II only
    D. I, II, III and IV

7. The Code of Arbitration is mandatory when there are disputes between a broker-dealer and

    A. the Securities and Exchange Commission
    B. another broker-dealer
    C. the general public
    D. the National Association of Securities Dealers

8. Which of the following statements apply to the Code of Procedure?

    I.   The Board of Governors may review the findings of the District Business Conduct Committee within 45 days.
    II. All answers by respondents must be in writing and must be submitted to the District Business Conduct Committee within 20 calendar days.
    III. All complaints must be in writing.
    IV. The SEC will approve or disapprove the penalty assessed within 60 days.

    A. I and II only
    B. I, II and III only
    C. III and IV only
    D. I, II, III and IV

9. The dollar limit for simplified arbitration procedures between members is

    A. $1,000
    B. $2,500
    C. $5,000
    D. $10,000

10. If not appealed to the Board of Governors, findings by a District Business Conduct Committee become effective

    A. immediately
    B. only after review by the SEC
    C. no sooner than 10 days from the date of the decision
    D. no sooner than 45 days from the date of the decision

11. Who can lodge a complaint against a registered rep?

    A. NASD Board of Governors
    B. Client
    C. Member broker-dealer
    D. Anyone

12. How long does a client have in which to submit a claim against a registered representative or a member firm under the Code of Arbitration?

    A. Six months
    B. One year
    C. Six years
    D. Ten years

13. The maximum fine in a summary complaint proceeding is

    A. $1,000
    B. $2,500
    C. $5,000
    D. $10,000

14. How are disputes between NASD members regarding delivery and payment for securities transactions settled?

    A. By the SEC
    B. Under the provisions of the Code of Arbitration
    C. By the Board of Governors
    D. By the District Business Conduct Committee

15. Who may assess the penalties on, suspend, or expel a firm or registered representative from NASD membership?

    I.   District Business Conduct Committee
    II. NASD Board of Governors
    III. Uniform Practice Committee

    A. I and II
    B. II
    C. II and III
    D. III

16. Binding arbitration is required in all the following disputes EXCEPT

    A. broker-dealer against broker-dealer
    B. associated person against broker-dealer
    C. broker-dealer against customer
    D. broker-dealer against associated person

17. Which of the following means of settling disputes is attractive to broker-dealers because of its relatively low cost?

    A. Litigation
    B. Coterminous defeasance
    C. Repatriation
    D. Arbitration

18. In settling disputes between member firms, arbitration is preferable to litigation because arbitration

    A. is not binding on both parties
    B. is less costly
    C. does not allow for arguments from parties outside the industry
    D. gives more time to prepare arguments

19. A customer might choose to go through arbitration with a dispute rather than take it to court because

    A. the arbitrators tend to favor the customer
    B. a customer has no choice and must arbitrate
    C. arbitration is generally less expensive than court procedures
    D. a public customer is not permitted to use arbitration

20. The time limitation for submitting a dispute to the National Arbitration Committee is how many years from the time the act occurred?

    A. One
    B. Two
    C. Three
    D. Six

21. Brought to arbitration is a matter involving a $50,000 discrepancy. The panel hearing this dispute will consist of

    A. not fewer than three or more than five arbitrators
    B. five arbitrators
    C. seven arbitrators
    D. a number of arbitrators determined by the arbitration committee

22. Unless the law directs otherwise, all awards rendered under or proceeding before the arbitration panel shall be

    A. subject to review by the MSRB
    B. subject to review by the SEC
    C. subject to appeal to the federal courts
    D. deemed final and not subject to review or appeal

23. When initiating an arbitration proceeding, the document filed by the initial party that states the relevant facts of the cases and the remedies sought is called the

    A. submission agreement
    B. statement of claim
    C. official statement
    D. director's brief

24. What is(are) the responsibilities of a respondent when the party learns that it is involved in a simplified customer arbitration dispute?

    I.   The respondent must file the appropriate forms with the Director of Arbitration within 20 calendar days of the receipt of service.
    II. In its answer, the respondent must put forth all defenses to the statement of claim.
    III. The respondent may set forth a counterclaim, if any, against the initiating party or a third party.

    A. I only
    B. I and II only
    C. III only
    D. I, II and III

25. A customer involved in a dispute with a broker-dealer signs the required submission agreement. The customer

    A. must abide by any decision in the customer's favor
    B. must abide by any decision in the firm's favor
    C. must abide by any decision
    D. is not required to abide by any decision

◆ Answers & Rationale

1. B. The Board of Governors of the NASD may censure, suspend or expel a member or a person associated with a member. It has no jurisdiction over the exchanges and cannot prohibit any person from associating with them.   (Page 404)

2. A. The Code of Procedure is a mechanism for settling complaints between or among members or between members and nonmembers. The Uniform Practice Code establishes standard operating procedures for the settlement of transactions.
(Page 403)

3. D. Members or employees of members found to violate the Rules of Fair Practice can be subjected to any penalty in the NASD's arsenal.
(Page 404)

4. B. Members and associated persons must submit disputes to arbitration. Customers are subject to arbitration only if they agree to submit to arbitration. Findings under the Code of Arbitration are considered binding on all parties involved.
(Page 406)

5. C. Members or associated persons may be disciplined only after it is determined that they have violated the rules. This finding could come from the District Business Conduct Committee or the NASD's Board of Governors.   (Page 404)

6. D. The Code of Arbitration is mandatory in member against member disputes. In a dispute between a member and a public customer, the public customer cannot be forced to arbitrate by the member, but arbitration may be used at the customer's request.   (Page 405)

7. B. The Code of Arbitration covers inter-dealer disputes.   (Page 405)

8. B. The Board of Governors may review any findings by the DBCC within 45 days if it sees fit. In every instance, charges by complainants and replies by respondents must be in writing. Respon-dents have 20 calendar days in which to answer a complaint.   (Page 404)

9. D. Simplified arbitration procedures are allowed and encouraged between member broker-dealers for disputes estimated to have a value of less than $10,000.   (Page 406)

10. D. If not appealed, District Business Conduct Committee decisions become final 45 days after the decision date.   (Page 404)

11. D. Anyone can lodge a complaint against a registered rep for infractions of the Rules of Fair Practice.   (Page 403)

12. C. Under the Code of Arbitration, no dispute or claim is eligible for submission to arbitration six years after the date of occurrence of the dispute. The statute for arbitration does not extend applicable state statutes of limitations (typically two years).   (Page 405)

13. B. The maximum fine in a summary complaint is $2,500, according to the NASD Code of Procedure.   (Page 405)

14. B. Disputes regarding the provisions of the Uniform Practice Code (UPC) are handled through the NASD Code of Arbitration. The UPC specifies the mechanics of member-to-member dealings.
(Page 405)

15. A. Under the NASD Code of Procedure, both the DBCC and the Board of Governors are empowered to penalize, suspend or expel a member firm or an associated person.   (Page 403)

16. C. In disputes involving only associated persons and broker-dealers, all must submit to binding arbitration. In the case of either a broker-dealer against a customer, or a customer against a broker-dealer, the customer is not compelled to submit to arbitration. The customer may *elect* to arbitrate, and in signing documentation to that effect he is bound by the decision of the arbitrators.
(Page 405)

17. **D.** Arbitration is a system for resolving disputes between parties by submitting the disagreement to an impartial panel, consisting of one, three or five people. Arbitration expedites binding decisions involving disputes and avoids costly litigation. (Page 405)

18. **B.** Arbitration is the preferred method for settling disputes between member firms because it is less costly than litigation. (Page 405)

19. **C.** Answers A, B and D are false statements. (Page 405)

20. **D.** The limitation for submitting a dispute to the National Arbitration Committee is six years from the time the act occurred. (Page 405)

21. **A.** In disputes involving more than $30,000, the code dictates that there be no fewer than three arbitrators but no more than five arbitrators. (Page 406)

22. **D.** All decisions made by the arbitration committee are deemed final and binding. (Page 404)

23. **B.** The filing of the claim in a dispute is called the *statement of claim*. (Page 405)

24. **D.** The respondent in a simplified customer arbitration must respond to the notice within 20 calendar days, at which time he may set forth his defense and/or file a counter or additional claim. (Page 403)

25. **C.** The submission agreement is filed along with the statement of claim when a dispute is submitted for arbitration. Under the NASD's Code of Arbitration Procedure, a customer cannot be forced to submit to arbitration; however, if the customer gives written consent, he must abide by the final decision of the panel. (Page 405)

62 NYSE Constitution and Rules Exam

1. Under NYSE rules, prior to a registered representative taking a second job written permission must be granted by the

    A. registered rep's employer
    B. NYSE
    C. SEC
    D. NASD

2. The employing NYSE firm of a registered rep who wishes to work outside the firm after hours would notify the

    A. compliance department of the member firm
    B. NASD
    C. NYSE
    D. SEC

3. If a registered representative violates Exchange rules, the Exchange may

    A. impose a fine only
    B. expel the representative only
    C. recommend that disciplinary action be taken, but only the SEC can take such action
    D. fine, censure, suspend or expel the representative

4. An NYSE disciplinary hearing panel may impose all of the following penalties EXCEPT

    A. imprisonment
    B. monetary fine
    C. temporary suspension of registration
    D. permanent barring from the Association

◆ Answers & Rationale

1.   **A.**   In order to take a second job, a registered representative must get prior written permission from his employer.   (Page 409)

2.   **C.**   The registered rep must get permission from his firm, which in turn will notify the NYSE.   (Page 409)

3.   **D.**   If Exchange rules are broken by a registered representative, the Exchange has the power to fine, censure, suspend or expel the rep.   (Page 410)

4.   **A.**   The NYSE does not have authority to impose a jail sentence on a member or associated person. The NYSE may censure, impose fines and suspend registrations; it may also expel and bar members or associated persons from the securities business.   (Page 410)

1. All advertisements recommending securities must include the

   I. fact that the member firm intends to buy or sell the security
   II. price at the time the original recommendation was made
   III. fact that the member firm makes a market in the security if such is the case
   IV. name of the member firm providing the recommendation

   A. I and III only
   B. II and IV only
   C. III only
   D. I, II, III and IV

2. When a member firm refers to its previous recommendations, it must also

   I. indicate that the market was generally rising if such is the case
   II. show all of its recommendations of the same type of securities made within the previous twelve months
   III. indicate the date and price of the security at the time of recommendation
   IV. give the amount of profit or loss that would have been realized had an individual acted on all of the recommendations

   A. I, II and III only
   B. II and III only
   C. I, II, III and IV
   D. None of the above

3. A testimonial used by a member firm must state

   A. the qualifications of the person giving the testimonial if a specialized or experienced opinion is implied
   B. that past performance is not indicative of future performance and that other investors may not obtain comparable results
   C. the fact that compensation was paid to the person giving the testimonial if such compensation was paid
   D. all of the above

4. Which of the following is NOT considered either advertising or sales literature?

   A. Radio advertisement that describes the range of services offered by a firm
   B. Advertisement for the firm published in the telephone directory
   C. Press release sent to national newspapers stating an analyst's view of the economy
   D. Market letters sent to a firm's customers

5. For how many years must advertisements, sales literature and market letters be maintained in an easily accessible place?

   A. One
   B. Two
   C. Three
   D. Five

6. Which of the following is(are) subject to NASD rules on advertising and sales literature?

I. Newspaper advertisements offering an opportunity for employment as a registered representative
II. Material used in a newspaper or on television
III. Letters sent to an individual discussing investments relating to his securities portfolio
IV. Form letters sent to customers

A. I
B. I and II
C. I, II and IV
D. III and IV

7. Which of the following must be included in a testimonial made on behalf of a member firm and distributed to potential clients?

I. Qualifications of the person giving the testimonial if a specialized or expert opinion is implied
II. Length of time the testimonial covers
III. That the returns and investment performance cited in the testimonial may not be easily duplicated
IV. Whether compensation was paid to the person giving the testimonial

A. I, III and IV only
B. I and IV only
C. II and III only
D. I, II, III and IV

8. With respect to recruiting advertising by NASD member firms, which of the following statements is(are) correct?

I. Recruiting advertising is not subject to NASD filing rules.
II. Recruiting advertising may not contain exaggerated claims about opportunities in the securities business.
III. Recruiting advertising is not permitted.
IV. Recruiting advertising for the firm's first year of business must be filed with the NASD.

A. I
B. II and III
C. II and IV
D. III

9. Advertising and sales literature concerning which of the following investment product lines must be filed with the NASD's advertising department within ten days of first use?

A. New issue equity securities
B. Corporate straight debt securities
C. Open-end investment company securities
D. Closed-end investment company securities

10. Which of the following forms of written communication must be approved prior to its use by a branch officer or manager?

A. Letter to a customer confirming an annual account review appointment
B. Letter sent to 30 customers offering advice about a stock
C. Interoffice memorandum
D. Preliminary prospectus

11. Recommendations by a registered rep to a customer

    A. must be approved in advance by a principal and must be suitable based on the facts disclosed by the customer regarding other holdings and financial situations
    B. must be suitable based on the facts disclosed by the customer regarding other holdings and financial situations
    C. must be approved in advance by a principal
    D. are not covered by NASD rules

12. In recommending securities to customers, a member firm must

    I. not make guarantees as to future performance
    II. have a suitable basis for the recommendations
    III. disclose or offer to disclose supporting documentation

    A. I only
    B. I and II only
    C. II only
    D. I, II and III

13. The recommendation to purchase ALFA Enterprises' stock should NOT contain

    A. the stock's price at the time of the recommendation
    B. the disclosure of market-making activity or ownership of warrants to purchase the stock by the member firm
    C. a statement forecasting a continued decline in the security's price
    D. an offer to provide supporting information on request

14. Which of the following activities is(are) likely to lead to a charge of rule violation by the NASD and/or the SEC?

    I. A featured columnist for a nationally distributed financial newspaper writes a favorable report on a certain company and is invited on an all-expenses-paid vacation sponsored by a market maker in the company's securities.
    II. A paid advertisement is placed in a local newspaper by a broker-dealer publicizing the range of investment banking services the firm has provided for locally based corporations.
    III. A broker-dealer agrees to fund a major portion of the circulation expenses incurred by the sponsor or publisher of a monthly investment newsletter in exchange for priority placements of news items and research opinions at the direction of the broker-dealer.
    IV. A broker-dealer offers sales incentives in the form of higher selling concessions to registered representatives, but only on buy orders for a select list of equity securities in which the firm makes markets.

    A. I
    B. I and III
    C. I, III and IV
    D. II, III and IV

15. Which of the following are included under the terms "advertising" and "sales literature" with respect to mutual funds?

   I.   Commercial messages broadcast on radio and television

   II.   "Sales ideas" and marketing literature sent by issuers to broker-dealers to be used as internal sales development materials

   III. Sales aids and product literature distributed to broker-dealers by a fund's principal underwriter, such materials to be sent to prospective buyers or displayed for their viewing

   IV. Written communications such as direct mail pieces sent to the general public

   A.   I and II only
   B.   I, III and IV only
   C.   III and IV only
   D.   I, II, III and IV

16. If ArGood Mutual Funds uses performance charts and return on investment statistics in its sales literature, which of the following NASD policy statements apply?

   I.   Performance charts and similar financial information displays should cover a minimum of ten years (or the life of the fund, if shorter); periods in excess of ten years can be reported in five-year increments.

   II.   All earnings and total return figures should provide a separate accounting of dividends and capital gains.

   III. In computing and reporting historical yields and return on investment, the shares' maximum offering price should be used.

   IV. Current yield figures must be based on the fund's income distributions only.

   A.   I and III only
   B.   II and IV only
   C.   III and IV only
   D.   I, II, III and IV

17. Which of the following must be approved by a supervisory analyst?

   A.   Research reports
   B.   Market letters
   C.   Personal appearances
   D.   Television advertising

18. Under NYSE rules, which of the following communications with the public requires approval of a supervisory analyst?

   A.   Market letter
   B.   Television interview
   C.   Research report
   D.   Seminar

19. Which one of the following is classified as "sales literature," not as "advertising"?

   A.   Reprint of newspaper advertisement
   B.   Billboard
   C.   Telephone directory listing
   D.   Prerecorded telemarketing message

20. A research report distributed by a member firm must disclose that the member firm

   I.   is a market maker in the issue
   II.   holds call options on the issue
   III. was a selling group member in an underwriting of the company's stock within the past two years
   IV. was a managing underwriter of the company's stock within the past three years

   A.   I and II
   B.   I, II and III
   C.   I, II and IV
   D.   III and IV

21. Under NYSE rules, prior approval of sales literature and research reports must be given by a(n)

    I.   chartered financial analyst
   II.   supervisory analyst
  III. allied member
  IV. individual member

  A. I
  B. I, III and IV
  C. II and III
  D. II, III or IV

22. All of the following are considered advertising or sales literature EXCEPT

  A. market letters
  B. research reports
  C. prospectuses
  D. telephone directory listings

23. Which one of the following is classified as "advertising," not as "sales literature"?

  A. Form letter
  B. Script for a television program
  C. Research report
  D. Tape of a radio commercial

24. Written recommendations prepared by a registered representative need the prior approval of

  A. the appropriate SRO
  B. a principal of the firm
  C. the SEC
  D. the FCC

25. All of the following statements are true EXCEPT that

  A. a market letter distributed in electronic form only is considered sales literature
  B. all sales literature must be approved by a supervisory analyst
  C. candidates for registration must agree to appear before any committee of the exchange and give evidence on any subject under investigation
  D. allied members of the NYSE are not authorized to transact business on the floor of the exchange

26. Which of the following parties are covered under the Telephone Consumer Protection Act of 1991?

  A. University survey group
  B. Nonprofit organization
  C. Church group
  D. Registered representative

27. Joe receives a cold call from a registered representative, and he tells the rep he is not interested in this investment or in making any future investments. Which of the following actions is required by the Telephone Consumer Protection Act of 1991?

  A. The rep may send a letter notifying Joe of her intentions before calling again.
  B. A principal of the firm may call Joe the next time.
  C. The rep may never make cold calls again.
  D. No calls may be made to Joe by anyone at the firm.

28. A new customer comes to you with questions about a growth mutual fund. As a registered rep, you may NOT tell the customer

A. "Because this is a growth fund, your shares will increase in value."
B. "Your shares may be redeemed at any time, but you should consider this a long-term investment."
C. "This fund has performed in the top 25% of funds with similar objectives over the past ten years, according to the information compiled by ZBest Mutual Fund Rating Service."
D. "You may choose to have all distributions automatically reinvested in the fund."

29. A newspaper advertisement describes an initial public offering of common stock. The advertisement mentions the stock's par value and the name and phone number of the firm to contact for a prospectus. The advertisement must also include which of the following statements?

A. "This stock is issued by Acme Sweatsocks, Inc."
B. "Acme Sweatsocks, Inc. is a clothing manufacturer."
C. "The SEC has approved Acme Sweatsocks, Inc.'s stock offering."
D. "This notice does not constitute an offer to sell Acme Sweatsocks, Inc. securities."

30. Educational material prepared by an options broker-dealer must be approved by the CROP and the

A. ROP
B. NASD
C. general securities principal
D. SEC

31. Which of the following must a rep do when making cold calls?

I. Immediately record the names and phone numbers of customers who ask to not be called again.
II. Inform the customer of the name and phone number or address of the firm.
III. Limit calls to between the hours of 8:00 am and 9:00 pm of the time zone in which the customer is located.
IV. Not call customers who make a do-not-call request.

A. I and II only
B. I and IV only
C. II and III only
D. I, II, III and IV

32. Which of the following is exempt from the Telephone Consumer Protection Act?

A. Nonprofit charitable organization calling to sell raffle tickets
B. Small business calling in the immediate neighborhood
C. Telemarketing service calling between 8:00 am and 9:00 pm
D. Radio station calling to survey listeners for an advertiser

33. Max Leveridge receives a telephone solicitation from a registered rep at Stern, Sterner, Sternest. Under which of the following conditions is this solicitation exempt from the Telephone Consumer Protection Act of 1991?

I. Max asked the rep to call him with any investment recommendations.
II. Max is an active trader with an account at Stern, Sterner, Sternest.
III. Max is an active trader with an account at another firm.
IV. The rep received permission from a principal of the firm.

A. I and II
B. I, II and III
C. II
D. IV

34. Which of the following telephone solicitations are exempt from the Telephone Consumer Protection Act?

   I. Calls made by tax-exempt nonprofit organizations
  II. Calls made on behalf of tax-exempt nonprofit organizations
 III. Calls made for debt collection
 IV. Calls made to established business customers

  A. I, III and IV only
  B. I and IV only
  C. II and III only
  D. I, II, III and IV

◆ Answers & Rationale

1.   **D.**   All items listed here must be disclosed in advertisements recommending securities: the source of the recommendation, the security's price, any member firm interest in the security or the fact that the member firm is a market maker in the security.   (Page 415)

2.   **A.**   When referring to past recommendations, a member must show the whole universe of recommendations in the past year, not only the winners. A member must indicate whether the overall market was generally rising and the date and price of the security at the time of recommendation.   (Page 415)

3.   **D.**   Testimonials must state whether the testimonial giver was paid, that the giver's experience may not be indicative of other investors' experience, and the qualifications of the giver if a specialized or experienced opinion is implied. (Page 418)

4.   **C.**   Publications of a general nature (that is, not recommending securities or promoting a firm) are not considered advertising.   (Page 411)

5.   **B.**   All advertisements must be maintained on file for three years after use, the first two years in an easily accessible place.   (Page 413)

6.   **C.**   Individual letters to customers of a specific nature are not considered advertisements.   (Page 411)

7.   **A.**   When a member firm uses a testimonial, the testimonial must be accompanied by the following disclosures: (1) a statement that this person's experience does not necessarily represent that of other customers; (2) any compensation paid, if material; and (3) the qualifications of the testimonial giver if an expert opinion is implied.   (Page 418)

8.   **C.**   All advertising during a firm's first year of business must be filed with the NASD ten days prior to use. Recruiting advertising may not contain exaggerated claims about brokerage business opportunities.   (Page 420)

9.   **C.**   Although NASD rules require that all advertising and sales literature be closely monitored and approved by an officer or a designee of the member firm prior to first use or publication, only certain investment products are subject to the ten-day filing requirement. Chief among these products are registered investment company securities, including mutual funds, variable annuity contracts and unit investment trusts. Closed-end investment company securities are treated as corporate equity securities and are not subject to filing under this rule.   (Page 414)

10.   **B.**   Form letters fall into the category of sales literature and must be approved by the principal or manager prior to use.   (Page 411)

11.   **B.**   Recommendations made to a customer must be suitable for that customer.   (Page 415)

12.   **D.**   Choices I through III are applicable to customer recommendations.   (Page 415)

13.   **C.**   Because this is a purchase, it would be inappropriate for a firm to recommend a stock if it projects a continued decline in the security's price.   (Page 415)

14.   **C.**   Rule 9a-5 of the act of 1934 and the NASD's Rules of Fair Practice both prohibit the activities and inducements described in all of the choices except choice II. The rules on what is permissible cover promotional materials that are clearly distinguishable as paid advertising.   (Page 412)

15.   **B.**   The terms "advertising" and "sales literature" refer only to materials prepared for publication or broadcast to a mass audience or investors in general. Materials intended for internal use within a broker-dealer's organization are not considered advertising or sales literature—assuming, of course, that the firm keeps them away from customers.   (Page 411)

16. **D.** Performance charts should cover a sufficient number of years to allow prospective buyers to evaluate a mutual fund's performance during good times as well as bad, which is why the NASD approves of ten-year performance histories. The NASD also believes that prospective buyers should be alerted as to whether a fund's performance is based on reinvestment of capital gains only or on reinvestment of capital gains and dividends. Further, for purposes of both reporting fairness and statistical consistency, yield and total return figures should be based on the maximum offering price during the period covered.   (Page 416)

17. **A.** Research reports must be prepared or approved by a supervisory analyst acceptable to the NYSE. Advertisements and market letters must be approved by a member, allied member or authorized delegate prior to their release. Member organizations must also establish specific written supervisory procedures applicable to members, allied members and employees who engage in presenting speeches, writing newspaper or magazine articles or making radio or television appearances.   (Page 413)

18. **C.** The firm would be liable for the accuracy and content of the research report because it would be prepared by the firm and would supposedly have the firm's name and reputation behind it. All the other pieces are prepared on a more individualized, local basis and would not fall under the jurisdiction of the supervisory analyst. (Page 413)

19. **A.** A reprint of an advertisement that is distributed to customers is classified as sales literature. All of the other answers make use of the public media and are, therefore, classified as advertising.   (Page 411)

20. **C.** In its research report on a company, the member firm must disclose if it has any financial interest in the company (e.g., owning the company's stock, owning call options, or having acted as an underwriter in an offering of the company's stock). However, the member firm need not disclose that it was a selling group member in an underwriting of the company's stock.   (Page 415)

21. **D.** The NYSE rules require that all sales literature and research reports be approved by a member, allied member or supervisory analyst prior to use. A chartered financial analyst is not qualified to approve reports.   (Page 413)

22. **C.** Advertising is any communication to the general public. The first three answers fit this definition. Prospectuses are not considered advertising.   (Page 411)

23. **D.** Of the answers listed, the radio commercial makes use of the public media and thus is considered advertising. The other answers describe communications that may be made available to the public or to customers and, therefore, they are classified as sales literature.   (Page 411)

24. **B.** A written recommendation sent to a customer is classified as sales literature. Therefore, a principal must review and approve the communication prior to use.   (Page 413)

25. **B.** Any communication distributed or made available by a member organization for general distribution to customers or the general public must be approved by a member, allied member, supervisory analyst or authorized delegate prior to its release. Research reports, but not other sales literature, must be approved by a supervisory analyst. The definition of sales literature includes material distributed electronically.   (Page 413)

26. **D.** The Telephone Consumer Protection Act of 1991 covers all registered reps. Each firm must have a "do-not-call list" that every registered rep is required to check before soliciting any person. The act applies to commercial solicitation and does not include a university survey group or nonprofit organization.   (Page 421)

27. **D.** Joe's name must be placed on the firm's "do-not-call list," and no one at the firm may call him.   (Page 421)

28. **A.** Share price and investment return will vary, and no mutual fund company can guarantee that an investment will produce positive returns. Reps must comply with rules intended to protect

the public; they must not imply that funds are suitable for short-term trading or discuss performance information without revealing the source of the material. Discussing services offered by the fund, such as dividend reinvestment, is permissible. (Page 416)

29. **D.** A tombstone advertisement does not constitute an offer to sell the security; that can be done only through a prospectus. The tombstone is an announcement of an offering. If it chooses, the issuer may include its name and principal area of business, but it is not required to do so. Implying SEC approval of an issue is not permitted. (Page 412)

30. **B.** Educational material must be approved by the NASD (or by an SRO having the same standards as the NASD), as well as by the broker-dealer's compliance registered options principal. General securities principals approve communications material *unless* it is specific to options. (Page 414)

31. **D.** All of the choices are requirements of the Telephone Consumer Protection Act of 1991. (Page 421)

32. **A.** Exemptions from the Telephone Consumer Protection Act (TCPA) include calls made by nonprofit charitable organizations, calls made to current established business customers, calls without a commercial purpose and calls made with express permission or invitation by the customer. (Page 421)

33. **A.** The Telephone Consumer Protection Act of 1991 exempts calls made to established customers and calls made at the invitation of prospective customers. A registered principal does not have the authority to exempt certain calls from the provisions of the act. (Page 421)

34. **D.** All of the choices listed describe calls exempted from the TCPA. (Page 422)

1. Which of the following is considered a double-barreled bond?

   A. New Housing Authority bond
   B. Bridge authority revenue bond guaranteed by the full faith and credit of a city
   C. Moral obligation bond
   D. Dome stadium bond with provisions for emergency ceiling support

2. Which of the following are considered sources of debt service for general obligation bonds?

   I. Personal property taxes
   II. Real estate taxes
   III. Fees from delinquent property taxes
   IV. Liquor license fees

   A. I and IV only
   B. II and III only
   C. II, III and IV only
   D. I, II, III and IV

3. Which of the following taxes are considered sources of debt service for special tax bonds?

   I. Business license
   II. Alcohol
   III. Gasoline
   IV. Ad valorem

   A. I, II and III only
   B. I and III only
   C. II and IV only
   D. I, II, III and IV

4. The provision in a revenue bond indenture specifying that any bonds issued at a later date with an equal claim on project revenues can only be issued if debt service coverage is adequate is known as the

   A. additional bonds test
   B. rate covenant
   C. nondiscrimination covenant
   D. MSRB covenant

5. User-charge revenue bonds typically contain a rate covenant requiring the issuer to set rates sufficiently high to meet the requirements for all of the following EXCEPT

   A. optional call provisions
   B. expenses incurred for operation and maintenance of the facility
   C. debt service requirements
   D. renewal and replacement fund payments

6. Who has the final responsibility for debt service on an industrial revenue bond?

   A. A municipal authority established by the issuer
   B. The MSRB
   C. The corporation leasing the facility
   D. The municipal issuer of the bonds

7. The primary obligor defaults on a moral obligation bond. If funds are to be appropriated to make debt service payments, which of the following parties would take action?

A. Governor
B. Municipal Securities Regulatory Board
C. State supreme court
D. Legislative branch of the state government

8. The City of Waterloo is issuing BANs for capital formation. All of the following are true EXCEPT that

A. the municipality wishes to raise short-term funds
B. long-term financing will be secured at a later date
C. eventually, the project will be funded through general tax receipts
D. these are general obligation securities

9. Which of the following is true of a moral obligation bond?

A. It generally is used in conjunction with a sale leaseback arrangement.
B. The legislature has the authority, but not the obligation, to pay back the bond.
C. Mandatory sinking funds must be established to pay the bond in case revenues are insufficient.
D. It commonly is associated with projects with socially desirable purposes, such as low-income housing.

10. Which of the following is true of a lease-rental bond?

A. It is a double-barreled bond.
B. It often is used to finance state office buildings.
C. Under this arrangement, once the facility is built, the issuing agency sells it to a private corporation.
D. It is a type of GO.

11. Which of the following sources of funds back revenue bonds?

I. Federal revenue sharing
II. Special taxes on tobacco and alcohol
III. Rental payments under leaseback arrangements
IV. Tolls and fees

A. I and II only
B. II, III and IV only
C. III and IV only
D. I, II, III and IV

12. All of the following provisions might be included in the trust indenture of a revenue bond EXCEPT

A. allocation of funds
B. interest rates
C. yield to maturity
D. protective covenants

13. A promise that income from a proposed facility will be sufficient to pay for operation and maintenance of the facility as well as interest and principal on the debt is called a

A. bond trust indenture
B. rate covenant
C. reserve fund requirement
D. net revenue pledge

14. August Polar is interested in investing $50,000 in a revenue bond being issued by the Kenosha Harbor Authority. Before he commits this money, August would like to make certain that the issuer will maintain the property, keep its books properly, maintain rates on the facility at a high enough level to cover all costs, and report revenues. What document will reveal such information to August?

A. Bond resolution
B. Bond certificate
C. Legal opinion of the bond counsel
D. Bond Basis Book

15. Which of the following statements is(are) true of industrial development bonds?

    I.   They are a primary obligation of the corporation.
    II. They are issued by municipalities to provide funds for local industries.
    III. The credit rating of the bonds is the same as the credit rating for the municipality.

    A. I and II
    B. II
    C. II and III
    D. III

16. Which of the following municipal issues is backed by the full faith and credit of the United States government?

    A. Industrial revenue
    B. New Housing Authority
    C. Tax assessment
    D. General obligation

17. Which of the following might lead to an industrial development bond being called?

    I.   The facility is destroyed by a storm.
    II. Interest rates are falling.
    III. Funds are available in the surplus account to call the bond.
    IV. The municipality is approaching a statutory debt limit.

    A. I, II and III only
    B. I and III only
    C. II only
    D. I, II, III and IV

18. Which of the following statements are NOT true concerning revenue bonds?

    I.   They are secured by a specific pledge of property.
    II. They are a type of general obligation bond.
    III. Generally, they are not subject to the statutory debt limitations of the issuing jurisdiction.
    IV. They are analyzed primarily on the project's ability to generate earnings.

    A. I and II
    B. I, II and IV
    C. II and III
    D. III and IV

19. The doctrine of tax-free reciprocity for municipal bonds originated in

    A. U.S. Supreme Court decisions
    B. state laws
    C. federal laws
    D. IRS interpretations

20. Investors buy municipal bonds for which of the following reasons?

    I.   The interest is federally exempt for qualifying issues.
    II. The interest is locally and state exempt.
    III. Issues and maturities may be diversified.

    A. I
    B. I and II
    C. I and III
    D. II

21. Which of the following are characteristics of a variable-rate municipal demand note?

    I.   It is a long-term investment.
    II. Its price should remain relatively stable.
    III. It is payable on demand.
    IV. The interest is federally tax-exempt.

    A. I and IV only
    B. II and III only
    C. II, III and IV only
    D. I, II, III and IV

22. Which of the following special revenue bonds is backed by the full faith and credit of the U.S. government?

    A. New Housing Authority bonds
    B. Special tax bonds
    C. Industrial revenue bonds
    D. Lease rental bonds

23. A municipality issues a variable-rate demand note. One of the reasons for this may be that the

    A. municipality is building a new office complex that it will rent to state agencies
    B. municipality has exceeded its statutory limits on debt
    C. length of time before the municipality receives permanent funding is uncertain
    D. taxpayers approved the new issue in a referendum

24. All of the following entities may issue municipal bonds EXCEPT

    A. New York/New Jersey Port Authority
    B. Holy Name Cathedral, Chicago
    C. Territory of Puerto Rico
    D. City of Little Rock

◆ Answers & Rationale

1. B. Double-barreled bonds are backed not only by a specified source of revenues, but also by the full faith and credit of a municipal issuer with authority to levy taxes. Double-barreled bonds are sometimes classified in the broader category of general obligation bonds. The additional backing of NHAs is the full faith and credit of the U.S. government. The additional backing of moral obligation bonds are legislative appropriations that are not mandatory. (Page 434)

2. D. All of the fees and taxes listed are payments received by the municipality that are not the result of a revenue-producing facility. General revenues of the municipality may be used to pay the debt service on a general obligation bond. (Page 431)

3. A. Special tax bonds are sometimes included in the larger and more general category of revenue bonds. Ad valorem taxes, on the other hand, support general obligation bonds. Bonds payable only from the proceeds of specified income generators, such as gasoline, cigarettes, liquor and business licenses, are special tax bonds. (Page 433)

4. A. The *additional bonds test* is an earnings test that must be met under the provisions of a revenue bond indenture before additional bonds having an equal lien on project revenues (parity bonds) can be issued. (Page 432)

5. A. Protective covenants of a municipal revenue bond indenture (the agreement between the issuing municipality and the trustee for the benefit of the bondholders) usually contain a rate covenant specifying a minimum margin of safety of revenue coverage. This means that the issuer promises to charge rates that are sufficient to generate revenues from the facility that exceed the amounts required for operation and maintenance, debt service, debt service reserve and repairs (renewal and replacement fund). Any excess revenue coverage provides additional protection to the bondholder. (Page 432)

6. C. The issuer of industrial revenue bonds is a municipality or an authority established by a municipality. However, no municipal assets or general revenues are pledged to secure the issue. The net lease payments by the corporate user of the facility are the source of revenue for debt service. Therefore, the ultimate responsibility for the payment of principal and interest on an industrial revenue bond rests with the corporate lessee. (Page 433)

7. D. Legislation authorizing the issuance of moral obligation securities usually grants the state legislature the authority to apportion money to support debt service payments on such securities, but does not legally require the legislature to do so. (Page 434)

8. C. Bond anticipation notes (BANs) are issued by municipalities to raise funds immediately. The community is planning a future bond sale to raise funds to pay off the notes. Therefore, eventually, the project will be funded through the sale of bonds, not general tax receipts. Capital formation means that the bonds are being issued for general purposes, not for a specific project. Usually, BANs (like TANs and RANs) are general obligation securities. TANs (tax anticipation notes) are funded eventually by general tax receipts, and RANs (revenue anticipation notes) by revenues other than tax receipts. (Page 434)

9. B. Moral obligation bonds are issued with a covenant that states that if revenue collections are not sufficient to meet debt service requirements, the state legislature has the authority, but not the obligation, to appropriate funds necessary to meet payments. This is the moral obligation; the state is morally obligated to pay, but not legally required to do so. (Page 434)

10. B. Certain revenue bonds are secured by a leaseback arrangement. For example, the state may set up an agency to construct a new office complex to house all state agencies. This authority issued the bonds. Once the facility is built, the state leases the complex from that authority. The bonds are backed by the lease payments of that authority. (Page 433)

11. **B.** Typical sources of funds for revenue bonds include user charges, special taxes, payments under leaseback arrangements, lease revenues, and tolls and other fees from the operation of the facility. Federal revenue sharing is not a funding source for revenue bonds.   (Page 432)

12. **C.** The trust indenture (sometimes referred to as the *bond indenture* or *bond resolution*) is a legal statement of the terms of the agreement between the issuing municipality and the bondholder. It will spell out such things as how the issuer is going to pay back the principal and interest (allocation of funds), interest rates and any protective covenants (such as minimum reserve requirements, insurance protection, antidiscrimination clauses, rate covenants, etc.). Yield to maturity will not be found in the indenture because it is determined primarily by the sales price of the bond in the marketplace.   (Page 430)

13. **B.** The rate covenant is a promise to keep raising rates that a facility charges so that enough funds will be available to pay off the bondholders. It is found in the bond trust indenture. (Page 432)

14. **A.** The bond resolution is essentially the same as the trust indenture. In the resolution, the issuer makes protective covenants to the bondholders. These might include the promise to keep the books properly, report revenues collected, maintain the facility properly and maintain rates on the facility at a level high enough to cover all costs. One difference between a resolution and a trust indenture is that the trustee is appointed to monitor the issuer's compliance with these covenants. With a simple resolution, however, there is no policeman monitoring compliance.   (Page 429)

15. **A.** Although IDBs are issued by municipalities to provide funds for local industries, they are a primary obligation of the corporation, not the municipality. The municipality merely acts as a conduit in issuing the bonds. Thus, the bonds' credit rating depends on the corporation's credit rating, not the municipality's.   (Page 433)

16. **B.** The New Housing Authority is a federal agency that backs public housing municipals by making annual contributions to subsidize rental revenues.   (Page 434)

17. **A.** All of the events listed might lead to an industrial revenue bond being called except for choice IV. Unlike general obligation bonds, revenue bonds generally are not subject to statutory debt limits.   (Page 433)

18. **A.** Revenue bonds are not secured by a specific pledge of property and are not a type of general obligation bond.   (Page 432)

19. **A.** The doctrine of reciprocal immunity, or mutual exclusion, was determined in the Supreme Court Case of *McCulloch v. Maryland.* (Page 428)

20. **C.** Because municipal bonds typically are serial bonds, it is easy to diversify maturities. The interest on municipal bonds is exempt from federal income tax, but subject to state and local tax.
                    (Page 428)

21. **C.** Variable-rate notes have short maturities. Because the rate of interest will change with the prevailing interest rate environment, their market value should remain relatively stable. Principal is repaid to the holder when the issuer demands, and, like other municipal bonds, they provide tax-exempt income.   (Page 434)

22. **A.** NHAs are backed by the federal government; they are issued by municipal housing authorities to develop and improve low-income housing. Special tax bonds are backed by taxes collected from the users of the facility being constructed. Industrial revenue bonds and lease-rental bonds are backed by rental payments received from the corporation or public entity occupying the facility.   (Page 434)

23. **C.** Variable-rate demand notes are issued in anticipation of receiving long-term funding; the municipality will repay principal when funding is available. Financing a new office building is normally done through a lease rental bond. If the municipality has exceeded statutory limits on debt,

it may not issue additional notes. Taxpayer approval is required only for new issues of GO bonds. (Page 434)

24. **B.** Only U.S. territorial possessions, legally constituted taxing authorities and public authorities are permitted to issue municipal debt securities. Churches may issue bonds, but they do not offer the tax benefits of municipal bonds. (Page 429)

1. Your firm is the managing underwriter for a syndicate underwriting a new issue of general obligation municipal bonds. The director of your municipal bond department decides to allocate the bonds in a somewhat different priority than that specified in the agreement among underwriters. Which of the following statements is true?

   A. As long as the bonds affected total less than 25% of the entire underwriting, this is within the discretionary authority of the manager and no further action is required.
   B. She must justify her action to show that it was in the best interest of the syndicate as a whole.
   C. She must file the appropriate papers with the MSRB and amend the agreement among underwriters.
   D. This is not permitted under any circumstance.

2. A municipal issuer has accepted a bid from an underwriting syndicate to purchase a bond offering at a premium. The premium

   A. is an addition when calculating net interest cost
   B. is a subtraction when calculating net interest cost
   C. reflects the issuer's high credit rating
   D. reflects the issuer's low credit rating

3. The placement ratio listed in *The Bond Buyer* is arrived at by dividing

   A. bonds placed by visible supply
   B. bonds placed by new issues offered
   C. new issues offered by visible supply
   D. bonds traded over by issues offered

4. One of your clients has heard that Mount Vernon municipal bonds are currently being offered by your firm and would like to know when the new issue will be delivered. You can find the answer for him by looking in

   A. *The Blue List*
   B. the official statement
   C. *Munifacts*
   D. *The Wall Street Journal*

5. A customer of yours is interested in up-to-the-minute information on municipal bonds. To get the most accurate, current information available, you would go to

   A. *The Blue List*
   B. *The Bond Buyer*
   C. *The Yellow List*
   D. *Munifacts*

6. A member of an undivided $5,000,000 municipal syndicate has a $500,000 commitment. At the close of the offering, there are $1,000,000 of bonds left. The member sold $300,000 of its commitment. How many dollars worth of bonds will it have to buy?

A. $100,000
B. $200,000
C. $300,000
D. $500,000

7. Place in the proper sequence from highest to lowest priority the following methods of allocating bond orders in a new municipal underwriting.

I. Presale
II. Group net
III. Designated
IV. Member

A. I, II, III, IV
B. I, III, IV, II
C. I, IV, III, II
D. IV, I, III, II

8. A municipality reviewing bids to determine the lowest net interest cost would use which of the following calculations?

I. Add any premium received to total interest cost.
II. Subtract any premium received from total interest cost.
III. Add any discount to total interest cost.
IV. Subtract any discount from total interest cost.

A. I and III
B. I and IV
C. II and III
D. II and IV

9. Which of the following statements would be included in an unqualified legal opinion?

A. The issue may be marketed in various states.
B. The issuer has authority to incur debt for the project.
C. The attorney has qualified the official statement.
D. The attorney has qualified the interest payments.

10. All of the following are municipal securities underwriting terms EXCEPT

A. firm
B. when issued
C. standby
D. AON

11. Which of the following terms is usually used in connection with a new issue of GO bonds?

A. Private placement
B. Best efforts
C. Negotiated
D. Competitive

12. In connection with the issuance of a municipal general obligation bond, the bond counsel will register an opinion on all of the following EXCEPT the

A. statutory authority of the issuer
B. Internal Revenue Code aspect of the annual interest
C. fairness of the underwriting spread
D. circumstances under which the issue can be called

13. An underwriting bid for a municipal GO issue would include which two of the following?

    I.   Dollar amount bid
    II. Coupon rate
    III. Yield to maturity
    IV. Underwriting spread

    A. I and II
    B. I and III
    C. II and III
    D. II and IV

14. The manager of a municipal bond syndicate must confirm syndicate members' orders at least

    A. 20 days after the sale
    B. 20 days prior to the settlement
    C. 6 days after the sale
    D. 6 days prior to the settlement

15. Which of the following references would an underwriter use to find the amount of anticipated competitive bid and negotiated sales in municipal bonds for the coming month?

    A. *Munifacts*
    B. *The Blue List*
    C. Visible supply
    D. *Moody's Manual*

16. All of the following statements are true of competitive bidding for a new municipal bond issue EXCEPT that

    A. the underwriter will be selected on the basis of the lowest interest rate
    B. prior consultation between investment bankers and the municipality issuing the bonds is prohibited
    C. most states require that municipalities use competitive bidding for GO bonds
    D. the municipality selects an investment banker

17. The Walrus Capital Group is the manager of a municipal syndicate. Which of the following activities is(are) the underwriting manager responsible for?

    I.   Taking the largest position in the new issue
    II. Closing the underwriting arrangements with the issuing municipality
    III. Writing the legal opinion for the issue
    IV. Acting as underwriter's counsel

    A. I only
    B. II only
    C. III only
    D. I, II, III and IV

18. Who is responsible for unsold securities in an Eastern underwriting arrangement?

    A. Syndicate members that have not sold their allotted commitment
    B. Managing underwriter
    C. Selling group
    D. Each underwriter for its proportional share

19. All of the following are found on the official notice of sale of a municipal bond offering EXCEPT

    A. instructions on the bidding procedure
    B. names of the underwriters
    C. good faith deposit requirement
    D. interest rate limitations

20. The legal opinion of the bond counsel on a new issue might state all of the following EXCEPT

    A. that capital gains are exempt from federal taxes
    B. that the interest is exempt from federal taxes
    C. that the interest is exempt from state and local taxes
    D. whether the bonds have been authorized in accordance with the law

21. What would be included on the confirmation of a municipal bond that is offered "when-, as- and if-issued"?

    I.   Number of bonds
    II. Settlement date
    III. Yield to maturity
    IV. Total dollar amount

    A. I and III
    B. I and IV
    C. II and III
    D. II and IV

22. An initial customer confirmation on a purchase of a when issued municipal security will include the

    A. settlement date
    B. total principal value
    C. underwriters' names
    D. dated date

23. Under MSRB rules, a dealer selling a new issue to a customer must provide all of the following EXCEPT

    A. final confirmation of the transaction, showing the amount due
    B. a copy of the official statement
    C. written notice if the issuer does not intend to prepare a final official statement
    D. a copy of the agreement among underwriters

24. In the municipal bond business, the function of a broker's broker is to

    I.   help sell municipal bonds that a syndicate has been unable to sell
    II. protect the identity of the firm on whose behalf the broker's broker is acting
    III. help prepare bids for an underwriting syndicate
    IV. serve as a wholesaler, offering bonds at a discount from the current bid and offer

    A. I
    B. I and II
    C. III
    D. III and IV

25. As a registered representative, you are soliciting orders for a new municipal issue. Which of the following investors must receive a preliminary official statement?

    A. Only those who request the document
    B. All prospects, before you discuss the issue with them
    C. All prospects, including those who have already received the official statement
    D. All clients who buy the issue, on or before the date the final confirm is received

26. A broker-dealer is acting as a financial adviser in a municipal underwriting. When must the financial adviser deliver the final official statement to the syndicate manager?

    A. Three business days after bonds are delivered to syndicate members
    B. Two days before bonds are delivered to syndicate members
    C. Two days before the award is made
    D. Before it is used as an advertisement in public media

27. Which of the following is NOT a type of municipal securities underwriting?

    A. Competitive bid
    B. Firm commitment
    C. Standby
    D. Negotiated

28. An analyst is studying the official statement in a municipal offering. Which equation does he use to determine the net total debt?

    A. Net direct debt divided by total population
    B. Net direct debt plus self-supporting debt
    C. Overlapping debt plus net direct debt
    D. Self-supporting debt plus overlapping debt

29. Which organization owns and operates *Munifacts?*

A. MSRB
B. *The Bond Buyer*
C. Standard & Poor's
D. NYSE

◆ Answers & Rationale

1. **B.** MSRB rules require a manager to establish a priority for the acceptance of orders placed for a new issue. However, the manager is allowed to deviate from the established priority if such action benefits the syndicate as a whole. The manager must be prepared to justify that any deviation satisfies this condition. (Page 445)

2. **B.** In a competitive underwriting for municipal bonds, competing syndicates submit bids to the issuer. The municipal industry commonly uses the net interest cost (NIC) formula to determine the lowest interest cost. NIC considers the premium or discount of the issue and provides a method of calculating the payments by the issuer beyond the amounts borrowed over the life of the bond. Unlike the true interest cost method (TIC), NIC ignores the time value of money.

$$NIC = \frac{\substack{\text{Total interest} \\ \text{payments}} \pm \substack{\text{Discount/} \\ \text{premium}}}{\text{Bond years}}$$

(Page 443)

3. **B.** The placement ratio serves to show the relationship between the number of bonds actually placed (sold) out of the total number available in the market that week. (Page 437)

4. **A.** *The Blue List* will contain information regarding the delivery date of a new issue as well as other important information about municipal offerings including par value, maturity dates, prices and yields. (Page 438)

5. **D.** *Munifacts* supplies up-to-the-minute information via computer terminal to the subscribers to its service. *Munifacts* is a service offered by *The Bond Buyer*. (Page 437)

6. **A.** In an undivided (or Eastern) syndicate, each member is responsible for its proportion of the offering, regardless of how many bonds it has already placed. If the member was committed to sell 10% of the original dollar value of the issue, it will be committed to sell 10% of any bonds remaining unsold. (Page 442)

7. **A.** Presale orders get filled first because they were placed even before the syndicate manager had purchased the securities from the issuer. Group net orders are filled next; although the buyer didn't indicate a desire to purchase the bonds until after the beginning of the sale period, the buyer has agreed to pay the public offering price and the entire group splits the takedown according to the percentage of their individual participation in the syndicate. Designated orders are the next filled because the buyer is still willing to pay the full public offering price, but would like to designate which syndicate members will receive the credit for the sale. The last orders filled are those of the members themselves, who will be allocated bonds less whatever takedown or concession for which they are eligible. (Page 446)

8. **C.** The lowest net interest cost is calculated by adding any discounts given to and subtracting any premiums received from the total interest cost. (Page 443)

9. **B.** The purpose of a legal opinion is twofold: first, the counsel attests to the fact that, to the best of its knowledge, the issuer has the legal right to issue the securities in question, and second, that the interest that will be paid on the bonds by the issuer will be exempt from federal taxation. An unqualified legal opinion expresses no reservations about the legality of the issue or about the tax-exempt status of the interest payments. (Page 436)

10. **C.** The term "standby" is usually used to indicate a brokerage firm that has agreed to purchase any part of an issue that has not been subscribed to through a rights offering. (Page 443)

11. **D.** GO bonds are issued on a competitive basis. Revenue bond issues are typically negotiated. (Page 435)

12. **C.** The bond counsel is not concerned with the amount of the underwriting spread. (Page 436)

13. **A.** Because "How much money can we raise?" and "How much is it going to cost us?" are the only two things the issuer wants to know, those are the two things that a firm bidding on the issue would include in its bid. The investor would want to know the yield to maturity in order to determine whether the investment makes sense. The members of the syndicate would want to know the underwriting spread so that they could decide whether it would be profitable for them to take part.

(Page 435)

14. **D.** The syndicate manager must send confirms to the members of the syndicate or account at least six business days before the settlement date.

(Page 448)

15. **C.** The 30-day visible supply is used by issuers and dealers to determine the amount of new issues expected in the market in the next 30 days. Updated weekly, the visible supply is the par value of all competitive bids and negotiated sales that are scheduled to be reoffered by syndicates within the coming 30 days.

(Page 437)

16. **D.** The first three statements describe the competitive bidding process. Because general obligation bonds are backed by the taxing power of the municipality, most states require the municipality to obtain a loan at the lowest possible interest rate. This means competitive bidding. In a negotiated underwriting, the municipality selects the investment banker, and the price is negotiated.

(Page 435)

17. **B.** The managing underwriter will act as the representative for the underwriting group. The other three choices are wrong.

(Page 444)

18. **D.** In an Eastern (undivided) account, every underwriter is responsible for the entire underwriting. Thus, an underwriter that has sold its 2% allocation remains liable for 2% of any bonds that remain unsold by any other underwriters. The selling group does not underwrite the securities; they make no commitments to the issuer and are never liable for unsold securities.

(Page 442)

19. **B.** The official notice of sale is the advertisement placed by a municipality soliciting bids from underwriters for an issue it wishes to sell. It does not include two key pieces of information—the rating of the bond and the names of the underwriters. Neither item has been determined yet.

(Page 435)

20. **A.** The legal opinion will state whether the bonds are issued in accordance with the law. It will also state that, in the opinion of the counsel, the interest is exempt from federal tax as well as state and local tax if purchased by a state resident. Capital gains on municipals, however, are taxable.

(Page 436)

21. **A.** On a new municipal bond offering, where the customer receives a when-, as- and if-issued confirmation, the final settlement date is not known; therefore, the amount of accrued interest is unknown (because it is payable until settlement). Thus, the dollar amount is unknown (because it includes accrued interest). Also, MSRB rules state that the extended principal amount (meaning total dollar amount for the bonds excluding accrued interest and any other charges) need not be included. Note that all of these items would be included on the final confirmation sent to the customer once the settlement date is announced.

(Page 448)

22. **B.** The customer's preliminary confirmation will indicate the total face amount he has committed to purchase. The rest of the information will not be provided until the issue and settlement dates are known.

(Page 448)

23. **D.** The agreement among underwriters is a private, nonpublic contractual agreement that the underwriters are not required to disclose.

(Page 441)

24. **B.** A broker's broker helps sell any bonds the syndicate has left and, as a rule, does not disclose the identity of the firm on whose behalf it is acting. Brokers' brokers do not charge fees for quoting a security. They will sometimes attempt to sell for clients, but may not effect the sale if a buyer cannot be found at an acceptable price. (Page 447)

25. **D.** Until the official statement is ready, a preliminary official statement is delivered to municipal bond purchasers. The preliminary statement must be delivered at the time of confirmation of the purchase if the final statement is not available from the issuer. Note that official statements are not mandatory for all municipal new issues, but are required by many states. (Page 450)

26. **B.** The statement must be delivered as promptly as possible after the award is made, and no later than two days before the securities are delivered. (Page 453)

27. **C.** Standby underwritings are only available to publicly held corporations issuing additional stock. An underwriting of municipal bonds may be conducted through a competitive bid or negotiated process; a competitive bid involves a firm commitment on the part of the underwriter to which the issue is awarded. (Page 435)

28. **C.** The net total debt is equal to the debt owed by the municipality on GOs and short-term notes (net direct debt) plus its share of the debt owed by other districts whose boundaries overlap the municipality (overlapping debt). (Page 451)

29. **B.** *Munifacts* is a subscription wire service of *The Bond Buyer*. (Page 437)

1. Which of the following is(are) required by the MSRB on customer confirmations?

   I. Source of any commission received on an agency transaction
   II. Amount of any commission received on an agency transaction
   III. Amount of markdown or markup on a principal transaction
   IV. Notification if the bonds are in other than bearer form

   A. I, II and IV
   B. I and III
   C. II
   D. II, III and IV

2. A client must be given all of the following information regarding a negotiated municipal underwriting EXCEPT the

   A. amount of the underwriting spread
   B. amount of any fee received by the firm as agent for the issuer
   C. initial offering price of each maturity in the issue
   D. members of the underwriting syndicate

3. Under MSRB rules, which of the following calls must be considered in determining the dollar price a customer must pay for a municipal bond trading at a premium?

   A. In-whole
   B. Sinking fund
   C. Partial
   D. Catastrophe

4. Under MSRB rules, subject or nominal quotes can be given for

   A. information purposes
   B. general obligation bonds only
   C. revenue bonds only
   D. none of the above

5. The price-to-call date must be recorded on the confirmation of which of the following municipal issues?

   A. 6% nominal yield quoted on a 9.5% basis, callable '98
   B. 6% nominal yield quoted on a 10% basis, callable '98
   C. 9% nominal yield quoted on a 6.5% basis, callable '98
   D. 9% nominal yield quoted on a 9% basis, callable '98

6. According to MSRB rules, dealers must do all of the following regarding quotations EXCEPT give

   A. bona fide quotes
   B. quotes that represent the best bid prices and asked prices in the market
   C. firm quotes
   D. subject quotes

7. Bud Charolais buys a City of New York municipal bond at a premium and, two years later, sells it at a discount. The capital loss from this investment can be used to offset

   A. all other taxable gains and losses
   B. only gains from other tax-exempt investments
   C. only passive income
   D. no other income—capital losses on municipal bonds are not deductible

8. Belle Charolais, of Oklahoma City, is considering buying a 7.125 Oklahoma Municipal Power Authority bond at a yield to maturity of 7.18. The bond will mature in 2015. Which of the following statements is(are) true of the tax-equivalent yield on this investment?

   I.   It cannot be calculated with the information given.
   II. It is based on a yield of 7.125.
   III. It will be higher than the coupon yield and the yield to maturity.
   IV. It will change with the price movements of the bond.

   A. I
   B. I, III and IV
   C. II and III
   D. II and IV

9. Your client owns $100,000 of a 6% municipal bond that he bought at 105. In December, the bonds are trading at 99 and his financial adviser suggests a municipal bond swap. In making this swap, he should be concerned about all of the following EXCEPT

   A. nominal yield
   B. bond rating
   C. issuer
   D. accrued interest

10. Belle Charolais buys $10,000 worth of new issue municipal bonds at a price of 104. The bonds have ten years to maturity. Four years after purchasing the bonds, she sells them at 99. What is her tax loss on these bonds?

    A. $160
    B. $340
    C. $400
    D. $500

11. Bud Charolais buys $5,000 worth of new issue municipal bonds at 97 and holds the bonds until maturity, in five years. What are the tax consequences at maturity?

    A. $0
    B. $150 long-term gain
    C. $150 ordinary income
    D. $300 long-term gain

12. Lotta Leveridge, retired and living in Florida, owns $100,000 worth of A rated City of Philadelphia GOs. Her stockbroker suggests a municipal bond swap. All of the following may be reasons for performing this swap EXCEPT to

    A. improve the yield to maturity
    B. generate commissions
    C. incur a tax loss
    D. increase her interest income

13. Rhoda Bear of Los Angeles buys $10,000 worth of State of California municipal bonds in the secondary market at 96. The bonds have 20 years to maturity. She sells in five years at 99. What is her long-term capital gain on this investment?

    A. $0
    B. $80
    C. $200
    D. $300

14. A client buys a $5,000 municipal revenue bond with a 20-year maturity for 104. Ten years later, she sells it for 103. What is the tax consequence of this investment?

   A. $50 capital loss
   B. $50 capital gain
   C. $100 capital loss
   D. $100 capital gain

15. Randy Bear purchases $5,000 worth of new issue municipal bonds at 101 and holds the bonds ten years until maturity. What is the tax consequence of this investment upon maturity?

   A. $50 capital gain
   B. $50 capital loss
   C. $100 capital loss
   D. No taxes are due upon maturity.

16. Your customer owns $10,000 worth of an A rated 6% Kenosha Harbor Authority municipal revenue bond that is due to mature on January 1, 2015. He bought the bonds on the secondary market three years ago at 102, and they are trading now at 98. In December, he decides to swap his municipal bonds and incur a tax loss. He can reasonably expect to pay a higher price if he substitutes bonds with any of the following characteristics EXCEPT

   A. longer maturities
   B. AA ratings
   C. coupon rate over 6%
   D. better quality

17. Your client buys an original issue municipal discount bond and sells it two years later, before it matures. Which of the following items does his tax adviser need to know in order to calculate the accretion amount on this investment?

   I. Purchase date
   II. Sale date
   III. Purchase price
   IV. Sale price

   A. I and II
   B. I, II and III
   C. I and III
   D. II, III and IV

18. Which of the following ultimately determines the annual accretion of the discount on municipal original issue discount bonds?

   A. Issuer
   B. Underwriter
   C. Internal Revenue Service
   D. Federal Reserve

19. One of your clients purchased a municipal bond at 110 that matures in eight years. Six years later, he sells the bond for 106. What is his cost basis at the time of sale?

   A. 100
   B. 101 1/2
   C. 102 1/2
   D. 106

20. Under MSRB rules, which of the following call provisions could affect the yield required to be shown on a customer's municipal bond confirmation?

   A. Sinking fund
   B. Catastrophe
   C. In-whole
   D. Extraordinary

21. Randy Bear, who is in the 28% tax bracket, is considering buying a 7.3% Tallawhosits City Waterworks revenue bond with a yield to maturity of 6.9%. What is the tax-equivalent yield on this bond?

   A. 8.83%
   B. 9.34%
   C. 9.58%
   D. 10.14%

22. All of the following are common characteristics of municipal dollar bonds EXCEPT

   A. optional call provisions
   B. term maturities
   C. call provisions
   D. serial maturities

23. An investor in the 28% income tax bracket is considering purchasing either an 8% municipal bond or a 10.5% corporate bond. Which of the following is true about the aftertax yields of the two bonds?

   A. The yields on the two bonds are equivalent.
   B. The corporate yield is higher than the municipal yield.
   C. The municipal yield is higher than the corporate yield.
   D. The yield difference cannot be determined.

24. Which of the following BEST describes an *out firm* quote in municipal bond trading?

   A. Indication that another interested buyer has been given a quote that is firm for a specified length of time
   B. Quote that *permits* a dealer to buy the bonds at a fixed price for a fixed period of time (such as one hour)
   C. Quote that *requires* a dealer to buy the bonds at a fixed price for a fixed period of time (such as one hour)
   D. Price that is currently subject, but will be firm at a certain point in time (such as the opening of trading on the next business day)

25. Your municipal securities firm has an out firm quote from another dealer on a block of municipal bonds. This means that

   A. your firm must confirm the final price before finalizing the transaction
   B. your firm can sell these bonds before buying them
   C. a firm quote on the same bonds was given to another broker-dealer
   D. the bonds have not yet been priced

26. According to MSRB Rule G-15, what must the customer confirmation disclose?

   I. Settlement date
   II. Highest potential yield
   III. Lowest potential yield
   IV. Semiannual interest payment dates

   A. I and II
   B. I, III and IV
   C. II and IV
   D. III and IV

27. Chip Bullock sells a municipal bond at a profit. Which of the following statements is true?

   A. Gains will be taxed at the capital gains rate.
   B. Gains will be taxed at the alternative minimum tax rate.
   C. Gains are exempt from federal tax.
   D. Gains are exempt from state and local tax.

28. Which of the following BEST describes a municipal firm quote?

   A. It is not bona fide.
   B. The dealer gives a price and a time period during which orders at that price will be accepted.
   C. The dealer indicates the approximate market value for informational purposes only.
   D. It is always delivered in writing.

◆ Answers & Rationale

1. **A.** The amount of markup or markdown must be fair and reasonable, but need not be disclosed.   (Page 457)

2. **D.** All of the information except the membership of the syndicate is considered material to the client's decision.   (Page 456)

3. **A.** When determining the dollar price of serial bonds quoted on a yield to maturity (YTM) basis, any call provision on the series as a whole must be considered and the bond price adjusted to the lower dollar value of YTM or yield to call. Only calls with a reasonable certainty of occurrence are considered for this calculation. With an in-whole call, all of a particular maturity is callable at a certain date—this reasonable certainty exists. Partial calls, sinking fund calls (which are random order) and catastrophe calls do not have a reasonable certainty of occurrence and are not considered.   (Page 457)

4. **A.** According to MSRB rules, subject to market or nominal quotes are allowed for informational purposes.   (Page 454)

5. **C.** When a municipal is quoted at a premium, if the bond is called prior to maturity, the premium is lost faster, reducing the yield to the customer. These issues must be priced to the near call date, which assumes that the customer will get the promised yield, even if the issue is called. Only answer C is a premium bond. The others are bonds priced either at par or at a discount. These are priced to maturity. If these bonds were called early, the yield would be the same or improved (because the discount is earned faster).   (Page 457)

6. **B.** The MSRB allows dealers to give firm and subject quotes. A quote that represents the best bid and asked price is found only on the Nasdaq system and is not relevant.   (Page 454)

7. **A.** Because municipal bond capital gains are taxable and municipal bond losses are deduct-ible, these gains and losses can be used to offset all other taxable gains and losses.   (Page 458)

8. **B.** You cannot calculate the tax-equivalent yield on this investment because you do not know the customer's tax bracket. Because municipal securities are tax exempt, the tax-equivalent yield on this investment will be higher than the nominal yield or the yield to maturity, regardless of whether she is in the 15% or 28% tax bracket. Calculating the aftertax yield enables you to compare this investment with the yields offered by taxable bonds.   (Page 459)

9. **D.** In a municipal bond swap, at the end of the year a client will sell a municipal holding to incur a tax loss and replace it with another municipal holding having a different rating or interest rate. To avoid a wash sale, the new bonds cannot be too similar to the old bonds or the IRS will disallow the tax deduction. Therefore, your client should be concerned with the issuer. The amount of accrued interest due is irrelevant to the tax swap decision.   (Page 460)

10. **B.** The premium on a new issue municipal bond must be amortized. To amortize the premium annually, divide the amount of the premium ($400) by the number of years until maturity (ten). Thus, in this case, the customer will write down the cost of the bond by $40 per year. After four years, the bond that was purchased at $10,400 will be written down to $10,240 (4 years × $40 per year = $160). If the bonds are sold for $9,900, the tax loss is $340 ($10,240 − $9,900 = $340).   (Page 458)

11. **A.** Original issue discount bonds must be accreted. Therefore, at maturity the entire discount would have been accreted and the bond would be valued at par. There would be no gain or loss at maturity.   (Page 458)

12. **B.** A bond swap is done to incur a loss for tax purposes. At the same time, it may be possible to improve the bond's yield (increasing the customer's interest income and improving cash flow) or to improve the bond's quality. A registered representative may never make transactions for a customer solely to generate commissions. (Page 460)

13. **D.** Because the municipal bonds were bought at a discount in the secondary market, there is no requirement to accrete the discount. The bonds are valued at cost ($9,600) for tax purposes. If the bonds are sold for $9,900, the taxable gain is $300. Note that, although the interest is tax exempt, capital gains on municipal bonds are taxable.
(Page 459)

14. **B.** The premium on municipal bonds must be amortized on a straight-line basis. The $5,000 bond bought at 104 has a $200 premium to be amortized over a 20-year period. This amounts to writing down the cost of the bond by $10 a year. After ten years, $100 has been amortized and the bond has an adjusted cost basis of $5,100. If the bond is sold for 103 ($5,150), there is a $50 taxable gain.
(Page 458)

15. **D.** If a new issue municipal bond is bought at a premium, the premium must be amortized over the life of the bond. Thus, at maturity there would be no capital gain or loss because the premium would have been amortized.
(Page 458)

16. **A.** Your customer could expect to pay more for the bonds with shorter maturities, higher coupon rates and/or better quality (as indicated by their rating). Why shorter maturities? In a normal yield curve, the bond with the shorter maturity has the lower yield. With a lower yield, the bond price is higher.
(Page 460)

17. **B.** The discount on original issue discount bonds must be accreted so that at maturity the bond is valued at par. If the bond is sold prior to maturity, the appropriate accretion amount is determined from the purchase date to the sale date. The dollar amount is based on the portion of the discount earned over this period; therefore, the purchase price of the bond is required. The sale price is needed only to compute the gain or loss on the sale. It is not needed to compute the accretion amount.
(Page 458)

18. **C.** The IRS ultimately would decide the discount on an OID bond because the discount must be accreted annually and is treated as interest income. As the discount is accreted, the adjusted cost basis of the bond is increased. This changes the capital gain or loss that would be realized each year if the bond were sold.
(Page 458)

19. **C.** The premium deducted yearly for the period held is deducted from the original cost to establish the new basis. $100 ÷ 8 = $12.50; $12.50 × 6 = $75; $1,100 − $75 = 102 1/2.
(Page 458)

20. **C.** MSRB rules require customer confirmations to disclose the lowest of yield to maturity, yield to premium call or yield to par option. (Par option is a call provision at par.) The rules distinguish between *in-whole* and *in-part* call provisions. Sinking fund calls are *in-part* calls. Only *in-whole* calls are used to calculate a yield to call. Extraordinary optional redemptions (call of the bonds when the property is prepaid) or extraordinary mandatory redemptions (*catastrophe call* when the facility is destroyed by fire) are not used when calculating yield to call.
(Page 457)

21. **C.** The municipal bond is priced at a premium to yield 6.9%. The 7.3% nominal yield is not relevant because the customer will get a 6.9% yield. The equivalent corporate yield is:

$$\frac{\text{Tax-exempt yield}}{100\% - \text{Tax bracket}} = \frac{6.9\%}{100\% - 28\%}$$

$$= 6.9\% \div 72\% = 9.58\%$$
(Page 459)

22. **D.** A municipal dollar bond is a term issue, which is quoted as a percentage of par. Most term bonds are callable prior to maturity. Serial bonds are quoted on a yield basis and can also be callable.
(Page 457)

23. **C.** Investors are primarily interested in their return after taxes—in other words, what they really get to keep. To compare the two bonds in a meaningful fashion, you can use the tax-equivalent yield formula:

$$\text{Tax-equivalent yield} = \frac{\text{Tax-exempt yield}}{100\% - \text{Tax bracket}}$$

$$= \frac{8\%}{100\% - 28\%} = 11.11\%$$
(Page 459)

24. **A.** When a municipal securities dealer gives another dealer a firm quote that is good for a specified period of time (for example, one hour), the next dealer to inquire about the bonds is given a quote that is described as *out firm*.   (Page 455)

25. **C.** With an out firm quote, one firm has been offered the bonds at a firm price for a limited period of time (for example, one hour). If the selling dealer receives another inquiry about the same security during that time period, he may respond with an out firm quote, indicating that an interested buyer has already received the right to purchase that security at the quoted price.

(Page 455)

26. **B.** Confirms must indicate the lowest possible yield the customer might receive; this may or may not be the same as the yield to maturity. They must also include the details of the transaction, including the settlement date. In addition, they must accurately describe the security, which includes disclosing the interest payments the bondholder will receive.   (Page 457)

27. **A.** The customer realizes a capital gain on the sale of the bond if his selling price exceeds the price paid. The sale of a capital asset such as a bond is taxed as a capital gain; capital gains are not exempt from federal, state or local taxes.

(Page 459)

28. **B.** A firm quote allows a municipal dealer to guarantee that it will fill a market order at the stated price for a given period of time. This is a bona fide quote, because the dealer is obliged to trade that security according to the terms of the quote. A nominal or subject quote is given for informational purposes only; any means of communication is permissible.   (Page 455)

1. In addition to regularly collected property taxes, which of the following are sources of money that a municipality can tap into in order to service bonds backed by that municipality's full faith and credit?

   I. Delinquent ad valorem tax collections
   II. Fines and penalties for late tax payments
   III. Tax increases

   A. I only
   B. I and II only
   C. III only
   D. I, II and III

2. How do municipal bond analysts view an increase in tax rates and assessed values of property?

   A. Both are negative events.
   B. Both are positive events.
   C. An increase in tax rates is a positive event.
   D. An increase in assessed values is considered a positive event.

3. The City of Cedar Rapids, Iowa, recently issued municipal revenue bonds to finance a new regional business center. During the subsequent operation, revenues from the project are inadvertently commingled with other city revenues and attributed to other revenue sources. What is the impact of this on the business center bonds?

   A. Lower debt service coverage ratio, lower price, and higher yield
   B. Higher debt service coverage ratio, higher price, and lower yield
   C. Lower debt service coverage ratio, lower price, and lower yield
   D. Higher debt service coverage ratio, higher price, and higher yield

4. Which of the following would insure payment of principal and interest on the outstanding debt of a municipal bond issue if the issuer experiences financial difficulty?

   I. MBIA
   II. FDIC
   III. FRB
   IV. AMBAC

   A. I and II only
   B. I and IV only
   C. II, III and IV only
   D. I, II, III and IV

5. All of the following should be evaluated when considering the purchase of a municipal revenue bond EXCEPT

   A. the existence of competitive facilities
   B. a project feasibility study
   C. a legal opinion signed by a qualified bond counsel
   D. the municipality's operating budget

6. The gross revenue on a bond issue is $12 million, operating expenses are $6 million, interest is $2 million and principal is $1 million. If the trust indenture specifies a net revenue pledge, what is the debt service coverage?

   A. 1.33 to 1
   B. 2 to 1
   C. 4 to 1
   D. 6 to 1

7. Which of the following is LEAST important to a municipal bond analyst?

   A. Legality of the issue
   B. Debt service to annual revenues
   C. Revenue collection record
   D. Net tangible assets per bond

8. The ratio of net debt to assessed valuation is important for which of the following types of bonds?

   A. Municipal revenue bonds
   B. Equipment trust certificates
   C. Collateral trust bonds
   D. General obligation bonds

9. Which of the following ratios normally is considered adequate coverage of interest charges for a municipal revenue bond?

   A. 1:1
   B. 2:1
   C. 5:1
   D. 7.5:1

10. Max Leveridge, who owns a municipal revenue bond, asks his registered representative for a bond appraisal. Max will receive

    A. the tax-equivalent yield of his bond
    B. the S&P rating of the bond
    C. background information from *Moody's Manual*
    D. the market price of a similar security

11. An issuer would go to which of the following parties to purchase insurance on its new issue?

    A. FDIC
    B. SIPC
    C. FNMA
    D. Investor-owned insurance companies

12. An analyst for a rating service reviewing the financial health of a general obligation bond would be most likely to look over the

    A. feasibility study
    B. municipal budget
    C. competitive facilities
    D. bond counsel's opinion

13. A customer of yours is concerned that the municipal bonds you are describing might have overlapping debt. In which of the following situations would that become a concern?

    A. You are selling bonds of coterminous taxing authorities.
    B. You are selling bonds of a recreation authority located in a public park.
    C. You are selling bonds of a harbor authority located in a school district.
    D. You are selling bonds of a mosquito control authority within municipal city limits.

14. The University of Michigan is issuing revenue bonds to construct a college dormitory. Which of the following factors will MOST likely be considered when analyzing the quality of this issue?

   A. Per capita debt in the area
   B. Competing facilities
   C. Fluctuations in interest rates
   D. Willingness of the university to pay

15. Which of the following represents an advantage of a general obligation bond over a revenue bond?

   A. GO bonds do not dilute the borrowing limits of the municipality.
   B. GO bonds involve less risk.
   C. The only requirement for issuing GO bonds is a feasibility study.
   D. Only the users of a facility pay for it.

16. To evaluate the creditworthiness of a bond issue, analysts studied property tax valuations, ad valorem taxes and per capita income. What type of bond issue are they evaluating?

   A. General obligation bond
   B. Revenue bond
   C. Original issue discount bond
   D. Project notes

17. Which of the following items would be analyzed by the consulting engineer for a municipal school bond issue?

   I. Cost estimates
   II. Estimate of additional taxes or revenues required
   III. Flow of funds
   IV. Dilution of borrowing limits

   A. I only
   B. I and II only
   C. III and IV only
   D. I, II, III and IV

18. An investor is debating between two municipal revenue bonds. Both are issued to construct bridges on the turnpike. One is being offered at a yield to maturity of 6.8%; the other is trading at 6.3%. Which of the following is NOT a possible explanation for the price difference between the two bonds?

   A. They have different S&P ratings.
   B. They have different maturities.
   C. One has a competing toll-free bridge nearby; the other does not.
   D. One of the issuing authorities has a higher debt limit than the other.

19. Which of the following are used to analyze a general obligation bond issue of the City of San Francisco?

   I. Statutory debt limitations
   II. Amount of overlapping debt
   III. Assessed property valuation
   IV. Net revenues

   A. I, II and III only
   B. I and III only
   C. II and IV only
   D. I, II, III and IV

20. Which of the following are MOST likely considered when evaluating the credit risk of a revenue bond for a new section of the turnpike?

   I. Accessibility of alternative routes
   II. Area traffic patterns
   III. Municipality's ability to pay
   IV. Coverage ratios

   A. I and II only
   B. I, II and IV only
   C. III and IV only
   D. I, II, III and IV

21. An analyst is assessing the relative weakness of a GO bond. Which of the following is a cautionary sign?

    A. The maturity of the bond extends beyond the life span of the facility.

    B. The bond is insured by the MBIA.

    C. The tax collection ratio is very low.

    D. The issuer has only limited taxing power.

◆ Answers & Rationale

1. **D.** Bonds backed by the full faith and credit of a municipal issuer are serviced from the general revenues of the municipality. Property taxes (ad valorem taxes) are the principal component of general revenues for municipal issuers below the state level. Fines provide additional revenues.
(Page 462)

2. **D.** An increase in the tax rates is potentially a problem because higher taxes can discourage new business investment and result in a flight of existing businesses or citizens that find the taxes excessive. An increase in assessed valuation of property will increase the real estate tax receipts to the issuer without raising tax rates. The increase of the assessed value is not as burdensome as an increase in tax rates. The higher assessed value recognizes the increased economic value of the property.
(Page 462)

3. **A.** If revenues from the project were attributed to other sources, the project's revenues would be understated. This would cause the debt service coverage ratio to be lower. The lower coverage ratio would create the appearance of increased risk of default, which would lead to a lower price in the open market. Lower prices equal higher yields.
(Page 464)

4. **B.** The Municipal Bond Investors Assurance Corp. (MBIA) and AMBAC Indemnity Corporation (AMBAC) insure municipal bonds' principal and interest. Currently insured issues are AAA rated. The Federal Reserve Board (FRB) sets reserve requirements, establishes the discount rate and controls credit extended in the margining of securities. The Federal Deposit Insurance Corporation (FDIC) protects customer accounts against bank financial failure.
(Page 465)

5. **D.** Answers A, B and C are all important factors in evaluating a municipal revenue bond. The main characteristic of revenue bonds is that they are payable only from the specific earnings of a revenue-producing enterprise, such as a toll bridge, airport or college dormitory. Such bonds are not payable from general taxes and the full faith and credit of the issuer is not pledged. Therefore, the municipality's operating budget does not apply.
(Page 463)

6. **B.** Debt service coverage (the coverage ratio) is net revenue divided by debt service. Net revenue is gross revenue less operating expenses ($12 million − $6 million = $6 million). Debt service includes both principal and interest ($2 million + $1 million = $3 million). Therefore, the coverage ratio is 2 to 1 ($6 million to $3 million). This is the minimum standard for municipal revenue bonds (except utility bonds, which, because of their stable and reliable flow of income, can have coverage ratios as low as 1.25 to 1).   (Page 464)

7. **D.** The net tangible assets per bond is a ratio used to analyze corporate bonds.   (Page 464)

8. **D.** When analyzing a GO bond, analysts evaluate the ratio of net debt to assessed valuation to determine how much debt that property base is already supporting.   (Page 464)

9. **B.** A coverage of two times is considered adequate for a municipal revenue bond because the flow of revenues normally is quite consistent.
(Page 464)

10. **D.** Max wants to know the approximate value of his bond.   (Page 465)

11. **D.** AMBAC and MBIA are investor-owned corporations.   (Page 465)

12. **B.** A general obligation bond is backed by the strength of the municipality, its financial health and its budget, not by any specific revenues or revenue-generating facility.   (Page 461)

13. **A.** Municipalities that share the same boundaries and that can issue debt independently of each other are known as *coterminous taxing authorities*.   (Page 462)

14. **B.** Revenue bonds are not backed by the full faith and credit of the issuing authority. Rather, the

debt is paid by the people who use the facilities. Therefore, competing facilities would be important. The other factors have little bearing in determining the inherent quality of a municipal revenue bond issue.   (Page 463)

15. **B.** GO bonds are less risky than revenue bonds and, therefore, tend to have lower interest rates. The other three statements refer to the advantages revenue bonds offer over GO bonds. There is no limit on revenue bonds. No public referendum need be held to sell revenue bonds—only a feasibility study must be performed. Such bonds are paid off by revenue generated from the use of the facilities, not by public taxes.   (Page 461)

16. **A.** General obligation bonds are paid off by property taxes. Therefore, an analysis of the bonds would encompass property valuation, tax rates (ad valorem taxes) and per capita income. (Page 463)

17. **A.** The engineer for the project would be responsible for estimating construction and related costs and would work on portions of the feasibility study. Once the issuer has these cost projections, marketing consultants would be hired to anticipate taxes needed and the effect on the statutory borrowing limits of the municipality. A flow of funds statement is important in a revenue bond, not a GO bond issue (such as a school bond issue).
(Page 461)

18. **D.** Debt limits apply only to GO bonds, not revenue bonds. Remember that revenue bonds are paid from the revenues generated by the facility. Therefore, if there is a competing bridge nearby, that authority might have problems generating the necessary revenues to pay off the issue. It would then have to offer a higher yield to attract investors. Similarly, bonds with lower S&P or Moody's ratings and long-term bonds generally trade at higher yields because investors expect to be compensated for the greater risks associated with such investments.   (Page 463)

19. **A.** All three are important when evaluating GO bond issues. Debt limits of an individual municipality can be misleading; overlapping debts must also be considered. Overlapping debt refers to debt incurred by multiple taxing authorities or tax districts. Net revenues are important for revenue bonds, not GO bonds.   (Page 462)

20. **B.** Revenue bonds are paid off by revenues from the facility. Therefore, an analysis should consider the bond's economic justification (for example, area traffic patterns), competitive facilities (for example, alternative routes) and coverage ratios (a ratio of the amount of money available to pay the interest compared to the interest itself). Because revenue bonds are not backed by the taxing power of the municipality, this factor is not important in analyzing revenue bonds. (Page 463)

21. **C.** If the amount of taxes collected is small in relation to the amount of taxes assessed, the issuer's financial condition may be deteriorating. Concerns about revenue from a specific project or facility apply to revenue bonds, not general obligation bonds. Risk of default is decreased if a bond issuer purchases insurance. Limited taxing power also decreases risk by ensuring that the municipality does not borrow excessively.   (Page 464)

68 Municipal Securities Rules and Regulations Exam

1. MSRB rules prohibit which of the following during the apprenticeship period of a new registered representative?

   I. Being compensated on a per transaction basis
   II. Conducting municipal securities business with the public
   III. Conducting municipal securities business with other dealers
   IV. Performing any of the duties of a municipal securities representative

   A. I and II
   B. II and III
   C. II and IV
   D. III and IV

2. In connection with a registered representative's apprenticeship period, MSRB rules require that the new registered rep pass the appropriate exam

   I. before effecting transactions for public customers
   II. within 180 days after becoming associated with a dealer in order to continue performing any municipal securities representative activities
   III. within 90 days of being hired
   IV. before effecting transactions with municipal dealers

   A. I and II
   B. I and III
   C. II and III
   D. III and IV

3. MSRB rules requiring certain books and records to be kept for specific lengths of time apply to which of the following?

   I. Records of all principal and agency transactions
   II. Written customer complaints
   III. Official statements
   IV. Client account records

   A. I, II and IV only
   B. I and IV only
   C. II and III only
   D. I, II, III and IV

4. Under MSRB rules, which of the following is necessary for a bond to be considered good delivery?

    A. Three-day delivery
    B. Hand-delivered in three days
    C. Notice sent in three days
    D. Endorsed with legal opinion attached

5. Under MSRB rules, arbitration could be used in which of the following situations?

    I. Dealer-to-customer disputes
    II. Customer-to-dealer disputes
    III. Broker-to-dealer disputes

    A. I only
    B. I and III only
    C. II only
    D. I, II and III

6. Serendipity Discount Securities, a municipal securities dealer, hires a new trainee who has no industry experience. The trainee has not passed the SRO-required exam. Which of the following statements are true?

    I. The trainee can execute customer trades immediately.
    II. The trainee can execute trades with broker-dealers immediately.
    III. The trainee can execute customer trades after 90 days' probation.
    IV. The trainee must pass the SRO-required exam within 180 days or he is terminated.

    A. I and II
    B. II and III
    C. II and IV
    D. III and IV

7. Under MSRB rules, required customer account information includes

    I. whether the customer is of legal age
    II. the name and address of the customer's employer
    III. the signature of the representative introducing the account
    IV. the customer's tax identification number

    A. I and IV only
    B. II and III only
    C. III and IV only
    D. I, II, III and IV

8. Under MSRB rules, unless otherwise agreed, good delivery of a municipal bond trade between dealers would include all of the following EXCEPT

    A. properly endorsed bond certificates
    B. the legal opinion of the issuer's bond counsel
    C. the delivery ticket
    D. the trust indenture

9. Under MSRB rules, a municipal registered representative can engage in all of the following municipal activities EXCEPT

    A. act as a financial adviser to an issuer
    B. participate in an underwriting
    C. supervise or train other representatives
    D. act as a trader for institutional accounts

10. Broker-dealer B has received a mutilated bond from Broker-dealer A. The bond was accompanied by a bond power and a legal opinion. To be considered good delivery under MSRB rules, authentication is required from the

    A. delivering dealer
    B. principal of the delivering dealer
    C. transfer agent
    D. delivering registered representative

11. Which of the following employees of a firm subject to the rules of the MSRB must be registered as a municipal securities representative?

   I. Municipal securities trader who only does business with other securities professionals
   II. Salaried clerk who receives telephone orders and is closely supervised by municipal principals
   III. Bank employee who refers depositors to registered representatives and who is compensated for the resulting trades

   A. I only
   B. I and III only
   C. II and III only
   D. I, II and III

12. Which of the following individuals are in violation of the MSRB rules regarding trainees?

   I. Previously qualified general securities representative who sells municipal bonds to a public customer one week after employment
   II. Salaried trainee who sells government bonds to an institutional account one month after employment
   III. Commissioned trainee who sells municipal bonds to another securities professional two months after employment
   IV. Investment counselor who sells municipal bonds to the public

   A. I and II
   B. I and III
   C. II and IV
   D. III and IV

13. An MSRB dealer, in compliance with MSRB rules, must do which of the following?

   I. Maintain records and books
   II. Verify delivery procedures
   III. Receive and verify comparison confirmations
   IV. Designate a principal to supervise books and records

   A. I, II and III only
   B. I and IV only
   C. II, III and IV only
   D. I, II, III and IV

14. A customer of an MSRB firm may gain access to an MSRB rule book

   A. only by writing the MSRB directly with a specific question involving an MSRB rule
   B. only with the written permission of a principal
   C. only with the verbal permission of a registered branch manager (sales supervisor)
   D. upon request to the broker-dealer—no restrictions exist

15. Every municipal securities firm must adopt written supervisory procedures that the

   A. MSRB specifies
   B. NASD specifies
   C. SEC specifies
   D. firm itself must develop

16. Which of the following are regulated directly by the MSRB?

   I. Issuers of municipal bonds
   II. Banks that conduct municipal securities business
   III. Broker-dealers that conduct municipal securities business

   A. I only
   B. II only
   C. II and III only
   D. I, II and III

17. Which of the following do NOT have authority to enforce MSRB rules?

   I.   MSRB
   II. Treasury Department
   III. Comptroller of the Currency
   IV. Federal Reserve Board

   A. I and II only
   B. I, II and IV only
   C. III and IV only
   D. I, II, III and IV

18. A municipal securities principal must approve all of the following EXCEPT

   I.   legal opinions
   II. the opening of new customer accounts
   III. each transaction in municipal securities
   IV. the handling of written customer complaints

   A. I
   B. I and IV
   C. II, III and IV
   D. III

19. Which of the following is the maximum amount of business-related gratuities and gifts that may be received by a registered representative from one person per year, according to MSRB rules?

   A. $0
   B. $25
   C. $50
   D. $100

20. Under MSRB rules, municipal securities firms may engage in all of the following EXCEPT the

   A. dissemination of an out firm quote in response to a request from an investment company
   B. solicitation of municipal transactions from the investment company as compensation for shares sold of the investment company
   C. acceptance of a presale order on behalf of an investment company for a new municipal issue
   D. All transactions in municipal securities by investment companies are prohibited.

21. A registered representative is about to close a large municipal bond sale to a new customer. The customer voices some concern about near-term price risks due to a potential increase in interest rates. Which of the following actions by the registered representative are prohibited by MSRB rules?

   I.   Including a municipal bond put or repurchase agreement in the transaction for an additional charge
   II. Guaranteeing the customer against any loss
   III. Sharing in profits resulting from the transaction
   IV. Personally offering to repurchase the bonds at a specified price and date

   A. I and III only
   B. II, III and IV only
   C. II and IV only
   D. I, II, III and IV

22. A municipal securities dealer has made no investment in an account. Are there any circumstances under which the dealer is allowed to share in the profits or losses of the account?

   I. Yes—when a written instrument is created and included with the confirmation of all transactions

   II. Yes—when the customer requests it in writing

   III. No

   A. I
   B. I and II
   C. II
   D. III

23. MSRB rules define which of the following as "advertising" ?

   I. Official statements

   II. Reports, circulars, and market letter excerpts

   III. Preliminary official statements

   IV. Abstracts or summaries of official statements

   A. I, II and III only
   B. I and III only
   C. II and IV only
   D. I, II, III and IV

24. A customer is in the 15% tax bracket and wishes to buy municipal bonds. You feel this is unsuitable for the customer. MSRB rules require that you advise the customer of your opinion and

   A. refuse to execute the order
   B. execute the order only after approval of a principal
   C. execute the order only after MSRB approval
   D. execute the order as directed by the customer

25. Representative Max Leveridge's customer wants to place an order for municipal securities that Max feels is completely suitable for the customer, despite the fact that the customer has refused to disclose his financial background or tax status. Max

   A. may choose not to execute the order
   B. may execute the order
   C. must get the permission of a municipal securities principal before executing the order
   D. must refuse to execute the order

26. Representative Max Leveridge's customer wants to place an order for a specific municipal bond. The customer provides the bond's issuer, coupon, maturity date and CUSIP number. The customer has not disclosed his financial background or tax status. Max

   A. must determine whether the transaction is suitable
   B. may execute the order and mark it "unsolicited"
   C. may recommend a different bond of the same issuer with a higher rating
   D. must refuse the order

◆ Answers & Rationale

1. **A.** MSRB Rule G-3 states that during the 90-day apprentice period, a municipal securities representative may function in a representative capacity provided he does not conduct business with any member of the public. Also, he may not be compensated for transactions during this time. Securities dealers are not considered to be members of the public.   (Page 468)

2. **A.** MSRB rules require an apprenticeship period for persons not previously engaged in the securities business who become associated with a municipal securities broker-dealer. During the 90-day apprenticeship period, these persons are not allowed to transact business with any member of the public or be compensated for any transactions involving municipal securities. They are allowed to perform any other functions of a municipal securities representative such as: underwriting, trading and sales of municipal securities; providing financial advice to issuers; or providing research or investment advice about municipal securities, as long as they are not dealing with members of the public.

Municipal securities broker-dealers and professionals are not considered to be members of the public. The rules go on to require a person to pass the qualifying examination within 180 days of becoming associated with a municipal securities broker-dealer in order to continue performing any municipal securities representative activities. MSRB rules do not require the examination to be passed within the 90-day apprenticeship period, but do require that it be passed prior to transacting business with public customers.   (Page 468)

3. **A.** The MSRB, NASD and NYSE each requires retention of broker-dealer records for specific periods. Offering documents, such as official statements and prospectuses, are issuer documents and not considered broker-dealer records.
(Page 468)

4. **D.** MSRB rules generally do not cover *procedural* items. The time allowed for delivery would be considered procedural, while the condition of the certificate would not.   (Page 469)

5. **D.** The MSRB rules on arbitration permit its use in all of the circumstances listed.
(Page 474)

6. **C.** The trainee may have no contact with public customers, but may deal with other member broker-dealers. The minimum apprenticeship period required by the MSRB is 90 days, and the trainee has a maximum of 180 days to qualify by exam (Series 52 or Series 7) or be terminated.
(Page 468)

7. **D.** All of the information listed is required under MSRB rules.   (Page 468)

8. **D.** Although municipal revenue bonds may be issued with a trust indenture, this is not a requirement for good delivery.   (Page 469)

9. **C.** Supervisory and training functions are never placed under the control of individuals who are only registered as representatives. These functions are handled by duly authorized and appropriately registered principals.   (Page 468)

10. **C.** For MSRB purposes, good delivery means an attached and signed bond power, an attached legal opinion and authentication by the transfer agent.   (Page 469)

11. **B.** Any individual compensated either directly or indirectly, on either a commission or per-trade basis, must be registered. An individual compensated by a flat salary need not be registered.
(Page 468)

12. **D.** The individual in choice I already qualified, so no training period is necessary. The individual in choice II is not compensated on a commission or per-trade basis. The individuals in choices III and IV would both need to satisfy training requirements.   (Page 468)

13. **D.** MSRB Rules 9, 12, 14 and 27 state that firms must maintain records and books, verify de-

livery procedures, receive and verify comparison confirmations and designate a principal to be responsible for maintaining and preserving books and records. (Page 468)

14. **D.** MSRB Rule 29 requires that each municipal securities broker-dealer maintain a copy of the rules of the MSRB and also that it make these rules available to customers on request. (Page 473)

15. **D.** MSRB Rule 27 requires that each firm establish its own written supervisory procedures. (Page 473)

16. **C.** Issuers are specifically excluded from MSRB jurisdiction. (Page 467)

17. **A.** Neither the MSRB nor the Treasury Department have the authority to enforce the Municipal Securities Rulemaking Board's rules. Inspection and enforcement of the rules among their own members is left to the Securities and Exchange Commission, the National Association of Securities Dealers, the Federal Deposit Insurance Corporation, the Federal Reserve Board and the Comptroller of the Currency. (Page 467)

18. **A.** Legal opinions are written by independent legal experts hired by the issuer. The issuer is not under the authority of the MSRB. (Page 473)

19. **D.** MSRB Rule G-20 prohibits gifts that exceed $100. (Page 472)

20. **B.** The basic idea behind the municipal anti-reciprocal rule is that the investment companies should not attempt to induce municipal broker-dealers to sell shares of the fund. This could be done if the investment company ran its portfolio trades only through those broker-dealers that sold the most fund shares. This practice is prohibited under MSRB rules. Of course, presale orders for new municipal issues may be accepted and transactions between investment companies and municipal bro-ker-dealers are allowed (otherwise, how could the fund's portfolio be traded?). (Page 474)

21. **B.** MSRB rules specifically prohibit associated persons of a municipal securities dealer from guaranteeing a customer against loss or promising to repurchase customer securities at a set price for their own accounts. MSRB rules specifically permit the sale of bona fide put options or repurchase agreements to customers by municipal securities dealers. Sharing in profits or losses is also prohibited. (Page 473)

22. **D.** MSRB rules specifically prohibit associated persons of a municipal securities dealer from sharing in a customer's account unless the sharing is solely in direct proportion to the associated person's investment in that account. (Page 473)

23. **C.** MSRB rules consider all forms of mass public communication to be advertising except the listing of dealer inventories, official statements, and preliminary official statements. (Page 472)

24. **A.** If a broker-dealer has reason to believe that a transaction in municipal securities is unsuitable for a customer MSRB Rule G-19 prohibits the broker-dealer from entering the transaction, even if the customer directs the broker-dealer to do so. (Page 472)

25. **D.** MSRB Rule G-19 specifically prohibits a broker-dealer from entering a municipal securities transaction for a customer without first obtaining the customer's financial background, tax status and investment goals. (Page 472)

26. **B.** When a customer wants to buy a specific municipal bond and possesses all of the material information about the bond, MSRB Rule G-19 allows the rep to execute the order and mark it "unsolicited." This happens only rarely in the municipal bond market. The rep may not recommend any municipal bond without knowing the customer's financial objectives and tax status. (Page 472)

1. An investor will be in a position to acquire stock under which of the following circumstances?

   I.   She is a buyer of a call.
   II.   She is a buyer of a put.
   III.   She is a seller of a call.
   IV.   She is a seller of a put.

   A.   I and III
   B.   I and IV
   C.   II and III
   D.   II and IV

2. An investor will be in a position to sell stock under which of the following circumstances?

   I.   He is a buyer of a call.
   II.   He is a buyer of a put.
   III.   He is a seller of a call.
   IV.   He is a seller of a put.

   A.   I and III
   B.   I and IV
   C.   II and III
   D.   II and IV

3. Karen Kodiak owns 50 CowTec calls. She may do all of the following EXCEPT

   A.   sell the CowTec calls
   B.   exercise the calls and purchase shares of CowTec
   C.   let the CowTec calls expire
   D.   trade the calls for 50 shares of CowTec

4. Options normally expire within how many months?

   A.   6
   B.   9
   C.   12
   D.   24

◆ Answers & Rationale

1. **B.** The holder of a call has the right to buy stock at the strike price; the seller of a put is obligated to buy stock at the strike price if exercised. (Page 480)

2. **C.** The holder of a put has the right to sell stock at the strike price; the seller of a call is obligated to sell stock at the strike price if exercised. (Page 480)

3. **D.** The investor has three alternatives: exercise the option, allow it to expire or trade it to another investor. (Page 480)

4. **B.** Options are short-term instruments that expire within nine months of being issued. (Page 480)

70 Equity Options Exam

1. Trading in expiring options series concludes on the business day before expiration date at

   A. 12:00 pm EST
   B. 3:10 pm EST
   C. 4:10 pm EST
   D. 5:00 pm EST

2. Listed options expire at

   A. 3:00 pm EST on the third Friday of the expiration month
   B. 4:30 pm EST on the third Friday of the expiration month
   C. 4:30 pm EST on the Saturday immediately following the third Friday of the expiration month
   D. 11:59 pm EST on the Saturday immediately following the third Friday of the expiration month

3. A firm may assign option exercises by which of the following methods?

   I. FIFO
   II. Random assignation
   III. LIFO

   A. I only
   B. I and II only
   C. II only
   D. I, II and III

4. When an investor exercises a call or a put, how does the OCC assign the exercise to a clearing member firm?

   A. Randomly
   B. On a first-in, first-out basis
   C. By finding out who wrote the option
   D. By any of the above methods

5. The OCC will automatically exercise an option contract in the absence of instructions from the owner of the account if the contract is in-the-money by

   I. 3/4ths of a point or more for a public customer
   II. 3/4ths of a point or more for a member firm
   III. 1/4th of a point or more for a public customer
   IV. 1/4th of a point or more for a member firm

   A. I and II
   B. I and IV
   C. II and III
   D. III and IV

6. If a 50% stock dividend is declared, the owner of 1 XYZ Jul 30 call will now own

A. two contracts for 100 shares with an exercise price of 20
B. two contracts for 150 shares with an exercise price of 20
C. one contract for 150 shares with an exercise price of 20
D. one contract for 100 shares with an exercise price of 20

7. Which of the following statements regarding the adjustment of the strike price of a listed option are true?

I. Adjustments are made for all distributions except cash dividends.
II. Cash distributions that are considered to be a return of capital do not cause an adjustment in the terms of the contract.
III. Stock splits that are an uneven multiple (such as 3-for-2) result in an increase in the number of shares and a decrease in the exercise price.
IV. Adjustments are always made to the next lowest 1/8th of a point.

A. I and III only
B. I, III and IV only
C. II and IV only
D. I, II, III and IV

8. When opening a new options account, in which order must the following actions take place?

I. Obtain approval from the branch manager.
II. Obtain essential facts from the customer.
III. Obtain a signed options agreement.
IV. Enter the initial order.

A. I, II, III, IV
B. I, II, IV, III
C. II, I, III, IV
D. II, I, IV, III

9. When must a new options customer, who has not yet traded options, receive the current disclosure document of the Options Clearing Corporation?

A. At or before the time the registered representative signs the customer approval form
B. Within 15 days after the CROP has approved the customer's account for options trading
C. At or before the time the account has received final approval for options trading from the ROP
D. No later than 15 days after the ROP signs the options customer approval form

10. Which of the following statements about discussing options with customers is true?

A. An OCC Options Disclosure Document must be in the hands of the customer before options can be discussed.
B. In every discussion about the benefits of options, a statement must be made regarding the corresponding risks.
C. Covered call writing has such a limited risk that it is unnecessary to point out risk factors.
D. All of the above statements are true.

11. Options cease trading at

A. 11:00 am EST on the business day prior to the expiration date
B. 4:10 pm EST on the business day prior to the expiration date
C. 1:00 am EST on the expiration date
D. 4:10 pm EST on the expiration date

12. Which of the following methods is(are) used by the Options Clearing Corporation in assigning exercise notices?

    I.   Random selection
    II. First in, first out
    III. To the member firm holding a long position that first requests an exercise
    IV. On the basis of the largest position

    A. I
    B. I, II and III
    C. I and III
    D. II and IV

13. An investor purchases 100 shares of stock trading at 50 and writes a 50 call on the stock for a premium of 3/4. The stock declares a $.75 dividend. If the investor wants to be assured of receiving the dividend, he should

    A. sell the stock prior to the ex-date
    B. sell the stock on the ex-date
    C. close the call position prior to the ex-date
    D. lose the call position after the ex-date

14. Which term describes options of the same exercise price and expiration date for the same underlying security?

    A. Class
    B. Series
    C. Issue
    D. Type

15. What is the effect on an existing series of options if a new series of similar options is established by the Exchange?

    A. They are restricted to closing transactions only.
    B. They are suspended.
    C. No more than five contracts per day for any single customer may be traded.
    D. There is no effect.

16. When determining the position limit, the member firm will aggregate which of the following positions?

    I.   Long calls and long puts
    II. Long calls and short puts
    III. Short calls and short puts
    IV. Short calls and long puts

    A. I and III only
    B. II and IV only
    C. I, II, III and IV
    D. None of the above

17. On the day after the ex-dividend date for a cash dividend, a holder of a call tenders an exercise notice. The holder will be

    A. entitled to the dividend
    B. entitled to the dividend only if he sells the underlying stock
    C. not entitled to the dividend
    D. required to pay the dividend to the writer

18. If an investor maintaining a short contract is assigned an exercise notice, the investor

    A. may refuse exercise under certain circumstances
    B. must accept the exercise notice
    C. may offset her obligation with a closing transaction up to the end of trading on the same day
    D. may offset her obligation with a closing transaction within three days

19. If a listed stock underlying an option contract has been trading below $5 for the past six months, the exchange will

    A. immediately delist existing options
    B. cease trading in the option until the price rises above $5
    C. not add any new options series
    D. allow only closing transactions

20. If a 12% stock dividend is declared, 1 GIZ Jul 30 call will

   A. not be adjusted
   B. be adjusted to 100 shares at an exercise price of 26 3/4
   C. be adjusted to 112 shares at an exercise price of 26 3/4
   D. be adjusted to 112 shares at an exercise price of 33 5/8

21. The holder of a listed put who is long the underlying stock would be required to pay any dividend she receives on the stock to the writer

   A. whenever the dividend is declared
   B. if the holder exercises the contract prior to the ex-dividend date
   C. if the holder exercises the contract after the ex-dividend date
   D. if the holder exercises the contract after the record date

22. An investor has exercised the following number of contracts in COD, a security that qualifies for the highest position limit:

Monday, July 15th	9,000 contracts
Tuesday, July 16th	1,000 contracts
Wednesday, July 17th	200 contracts

   On Friday, July 19th, the investor would, at a maximum, be allowed to exercise how many additional COD contracts?

   A. 300
   B. 3,000
   C. 3,000, as long as he limited exercises to puts
   D. None, he already exceeds the limit for that class of security

23. What is the maximum LEAPS option contract expiration?

   A. 6 months
   B. 9 months
   C. 15 months
   D. 39 months

24. What is the maximum LEAPS option contract expiration?

   A. Six years
   B. Five years
   C. Four years
   D. Two years

25. For purposes of determining position limits on ALF stock options trading, short-term options contracts and LEAPS contracts on the same side of the market

   A. are considered separately
   B. must be aggregated
   C. are added to increase the position limit
   D. do not have position limits

26. Joe Kuhl owns 6,000 ALF 90 put options. His wife Bea wants to sell ALF LEAPS call options. Without violating position limits, Bea can sell

   A. 4,500 because positions in short-term options are aggregated with LEAPS when determining position limits
   B. 6,000 because a position in LEAPS is limited to the number of short-term options held
   C. 9,000 because LEAPS are long term and therefore only 50% are considered in determining position limits
   D. 10,500 because positions in short-term options are not aggregated with LEAPS when determining position limits

27. Which of the following are characteristics of long-term equity options?

   I. Premiums are generally lower than ordinary options.
   II. There is a reduced chance of the option expiring worthless.
   III. Conventional options strategies apply to them.
   IV. They are available on all listed equities.

   A. I, II and III
   B. I and III
   C. II and III
   D. II and IV

28. What is the size of one LEAPS contract?

    A. 100 shares
    B. 1,000 shares
    C. More than 1,000 shares
    D. There is no standard LEAPS contract size.

29. Which of the following statements is(are) true of LEAPS options positions maintained for more than twelve months?

    I. The LEAPS writer's gains are taxed as short-term gains.
    II. The LEAPS writer's gains are taxed as long-term gains.
    III. The LEAPS buyer's gains are taxed as short-term gains.
    IV. The LEAPS buyer's gains are taxed as long-term gains.

    A. I
    B. I and IV
    C. II and III
    D. IV

◆ Answers & Rationale

1.   **C.**   The official close is 4:10 pm EST on the business day before the expiration date. However, trading that is in process at the closing bell may be completed even if this runs a few minutes beyond 4:10 pm. Expiring options may be exercised until 5:30 pm EST on the business day before the expiration date.   (Page 492)

2.   **D.**   Options expire on the Saturday immediately following the third Friday of the expiration month at 11:59 pm EST. Options trading stops on Friday, so this expiration time gives member firms all day Saturday to balance their books and correct errors.   (Page 492)

3.   **B.**   A firm may assign an exercise by either the random or the FIFO method. LIFO is not acceptable.   (Page 492)

4.   **A.**   Puts and calls are assigned at random by the OCC. The member firm may assign the exercise to its client on a FIFO basis or at random.   (Page 492)

5.   **B.**   On the day prior to expiration, the OCC will automatically exercise options in-the-money by 3/4ths of a point or more for customer accounts and by 1/4th of a point or more for member firm accounts.   (Page 492)

6.   **C.**   When a company pays a stock dividend or effects a fractional stock split, the underlying option is adjusted by increasing the number of shares covered by the contract and reducing the strike price proportionately.   (Page 490)

7.   **A.**   Options are adjusted for stock dividends and splits but not for cash dividends. Cash dividends that are a return of capital are not a true dividend and would cause the option to be adjusted. Adjustments are made to the *nearest* 1/8th, not the next highest or lowest 1/8th.   (Page 490)

8.   **D.**   The steps in opening an options account are:

1.   Obtain essential facts about the customer.
2.   Give the customer an options disclosure document.
3.   Have the account approved by the manager.
4.   Enter the initial order and then obtain written approval.
5.   Have the options agreement verified by the customer within 15 days.
                    (Page 489)

9.   **C.**   Customers must be furnished with an options disclosure document before or at the time their accounts receive approval by the ROP.
                    (Page 489)

10. **B.**   Any description of options must include a description of the risks. This ruling applies to advertisements as well as to personal conversations. Covered call writing is not suitable for all customers. The customer must receive a current disclosure document either before or at the time that the account receives final approval for options transactions.   (Page 489)

11. **B.**   Options cease trading at 4:10 pm EST (3:10 pm CST) on the business day prior to expiration.   (Page 492)

12. **A.**   The OCC assigns exercise notices to member firms on a random order basis. The members may choose the customer to be exercised on either a random order or FIFO basis.   (Page 492)

13. **C.**   Because the investor owns the stock, he will be on record to receive the dividend as long as the stock is not called away. To make sure this does not happen, the investor must close out the short call before the ex-date. Then the stock cannot be taken away from him before the record date.
                    (Page 490)

14. **B.**   Options of the same class, exercise price and expiration month for the same underlying security are considered a single series of options.
                    (Page 483)

15. **D.**   If new options series are created, this has no effect on existing options.   (Page 482)

16. **B.** Contracts on each side of the market are used for determining position limits. Long calls and short puts are on the same side (bullish); long puts and short calls are on the same side (bearish).   (Page 491)

17. **C.** If the holder of a call exercises before the ex-date, then the trade settles on or before the record date. The holder would then be on record for the dividend. If the holder exercises after the ex-date, then the trade settles after the record date. The holder will not be on record for the dividend and is not entitled to the dividend.   (Page 490)

18. **B.** Once exercised, a contract can no longer be traded to another individual. The exercised party must either deliver the stock in three business days (call) or buy the stock in three business days (put).   (Page 492)

19. **C.** If the underlying stock's price stays below $5 for six months, no new options contracts can be issued. Existing contracts still trade until expiration, however.   (Page 486)

20. **C.** The new contract will cover 112 shares at a new reduced strike price. 30 ÷ 1.12 = 26.78, which is 26 3/4. Note that the aggregate value of the contract is unchanged: 112 shares at 26 3/4 equals $3,000.   (Page 490)

21. **B.** If the holder exercises the put before the ex-date, she is selling the stock and will settle before the record date. The buyer of the stock will be on record to receive the dividend (the writer of the contract). If the trade, for some reason, settles after record date, then the holder of the stock would erroneously receive the dividend. Because she is not entitled to the dividend, it must be paid to the buyer of the stock—the writer of the put.   (Page 490)

22. **A.** The investor has exercised 10,200 contracts in three successive days. Because the maximum number of contracts that may be exercised is 10,500 in five consecutive days, another 300 contracts may still be exercised.   (Page 491)

23. **D.** Rules authorize LEAPS with expirations of up to 39 months; however, all of the LEAPS currently being offered extend approximately two years.   (Page 492)

24. **D.** Rules authorize LEAPS with expirations of up to 39 months; however, all of the LEAPS currently being offered extend approximately two years.   (Page 492)

25. **B.** LEAPS and short-term options on the same side of the market on the same underlying security must be aggregated and remain within position limits.   (Page 491)

26. **A.** LEAPS and short-term options on the same side of the market and on the same underlying security must be aggregated when determining position limits. The 10,500 contract position limit less Joe's 6,000 contracts leaves a total of 4,500 that Bea may sell.   (Page 491)

27. **C.** Because these options have expirations of up to three years, there is a better chance that they will be in-the-money at some point before expiration. Long-term equity options are available as calls or puts and lend themselves to conventional options strategies. Investors pay higher premiums for long-term options because of their greater time value. Long-term options are currently available on a limited number of blue-chip stocks.   (Page 493)

28. **A.** The standard LEAPS contract covers 100 shares of the underlying stock.   (Page 493)

29. **B.** The LEAPS writer's premium is taxed as a short-term gain. The LEAPS buyer has taken a position for longer than twelve months, so any profits are considered long-term capital gains.   (Page 492)

71 Option Trading and Strategies Exam

1. Your client Eve Grizzly has sold her business to Microscam, Inc. for $100,000 cash and a large block of Microscam's stock. This stock is not restricted. Mrs. Grizzly has told you that she wishes to generate additional income but does not want to take additional capital gains this year. Which of the following strategies should you recommend to Mrs. Grizzly?

   A. Sell some of her stock.
   B. Deposit her stock with your firm and write out-of-the-money calls that do not expire until next year.
   C. Deposit her stock in her margin account and borrow against it.
   D. Do none of the above.

2. Which of the following positions subject an investor to unlimited risk?

   I. Short naked call
   II. Short naked put
   III. Long put
   IV. Short sale of stock

   A. I and II
   B. I, II and IV
   C. I and IV
   D. II, III and IV

3. A call is in-the-money when the

   A. strike price is above the market price of the underlying stock
   B. strike price is equal to the market price of the underlying stock
   C. strike price is below the market price of the underlying stock
   D. intrinsic value plus the premium is above the market price of the underlying stock

4. Adam Grizzly is short 100 shares of IBS at 35. The market price is 35 1/4. He believes there will be a near-term rally. Which of the following strategies would best hedge his position?

   A. Buy an IBS call with an exercise price of 35.
   B. Buy an IBS call with an exercise price of 40.
   C. Write an IBS put with an exercise price of 40.
   D. Write an IBS call with an exercise price of 40.

5. In which of the following circumstances would an investor risk an unlimited loss?

    I.   Short 1 IBS Jul 50 put
    II.   Short 100 shares of IBS stock
    III. Short 1 IBS Jul 50 uncovered call
    IV.   Short 1 IBS Jul 50 covered call

    A. II only
    B. II and III only
    C. III and IV only
    D. I, II, III and IV

6. An investor is interested in purchasing 1 IBS Jul 50 call representing 115 shares of stock selling at a premium of 14 1/2. His cost will be

    A. $1,450
    B. $1,667.50
    C. $1,750
    D. $3,550

7. An investor writes 1 TCB 320 put for 21 3/8. TCB stock closes at 304 1/2 and he makes a closing transaction at the intrinsic value. The resulting profit or loss is

    A. $155 profit
    B. $155 loss
    C. $587.50 profit
    D. $587.50 loss

8. An investor wants to purchase TCB stock, currently trading at 38. He expects that the price of TCB stock is going to rise slowly in the near future. If he would like to purchase the stock below its current market value, he should

    A. write a call at 35
    B. buy a put and exercise the option
    C. write a put at 35 and buy the stock
    D. buy a call and exercise the option

9. Before writing a naked option, an investor should consider

    A. the risk/reward ratio
    B. the loss potential
    C. the possibility of exercise
    D. all of the above

10. By buying a put option, an investor can

    I.   avoid selling a security on which she has large capital gains and yet participate in additional gains if the security continues to increase in price
    II.   avoid selling a security on which she has large capital gains and be assured that she can sell the security at its strike price during the term of the option
    III. protect a profit on her current stock position

    A. I and II only
    B. I and III only
    C. II and III only
    D. I, II and III

11. Which of the following has an unlimited dollar risk if it is the only position in the account?

    A. Long put
    B. Long call
    C. Short put
    D. Short call

12. In April, a customer purchases 1 TCB Jul 85 call for 5 and purchases 1 TCB Jul 90 put for 8. TCB stock is trading at 87. If TCB stays at 87 and both options are sold for the intrinsic value, the customer would realize a(n)

    A. $800 loss
    B. $500 profit
    C. $1,000 profit
    D. $1,100 profit

13. An investor bought 1 IBS Apr 40 call for 6 and 1 IBS Apr 50 put for 8 when IBS was 45. If the stock goes to 44 and both the call and the put are sold close to expiration (no time value), the result would be a

    A. $400 loss
    B. $100 loss
    C. $100 profit
    D. $400 profit

14. A registered representative wishes to enter an order to buy one contract on an exchange at 2 1/2 and immediately sell the contract on another exchange at 2 5/8. You would

   A. allow him to enter the order
   B. ask for additional information regarding the customer's investment objectives
   C. advise him that arbitrage is not permitted in listed options
   D. not allow the order to be entered as it is uneconomical

15. An investor is long stock at 50. If he does not expect the price to change in the immediate future and wishes to generate income, his best strategy would be to

   A. sell a call
   B. sell a put
   C. sell a straddle
   D. buy a straddle

16. An investor sells short at 50 and sells a 50 put at 5. If the put is exercised when the stock is trading at 45, the investor will realize

   A. neither gain nor loss
   B. a gain of $500
   C. a gain of $1,000
   D. a gain of $1,500

17. An investor writes 1 IBS 280 put for 16 5/8. The stock declines to 265 1/4 and the put is bought for its intrinsic value. The investor would realize a

   A. loss of $237.50
   B. loss of $187.50
   C. profit of $147.50
   D. profit of $187.50

18. An investor owns stock with a current price of $62. He feels the stock will temporarily decline in price but that the long-term trend is favorable. In order to take advantage of the temporary decline, he would probably

   A. sell a call
   B. sell a put
   C. buy a straddle
   D. set up a spread

19. An investor is interested in buying a stock that is currently trading at 47. She does not think the price will change in the near future and would like to reduce the effective cost of purchasing the stock. She should

   A. write a put at an exercise price of 45
   B. buy a put at an exercise price of 45
   C. write a put at an exercise price of 49
   D. buy a put at an exercise price of 49

20. Upon exercise of the option, the holder of a long call will realize a profit if the price of the underlying stock

   A. falls below the exercise price
   B. falls below the exercise price minus the premium paid
   C. exceeds the exercise price
   D. exceeds the exercise price plus the premium paid

21. Which of the following strategies would be considered MOST risky in a strong bull market?

   A. Buying calls
   B. Writing naked calls
   C. Writing naked puts
   D. Either writing naked calls or writing naked puts

22. The holder of a long put will realize a profit upon exercise of the option if the price of the underlying stock

   A. exceeds the exercise price
   B. exceeds the exercise price plus the premium paid
   C. falls below the exercise price
   D. falls below the exercise price minus the premium paid

23. In buying listed call options as compared to buying the underlying stock, which of the following is NOT an advantage?

   A. Buying a call would require a smaller capital commitment.
   B. Buying a call has a lower dollar loss potential than buying the stock.
   C. The call has a time value beyond an intrinsic value that gradually dissipates.
   D. Buying a call allows greater leverage than buying the underlying stock.

24. If TCB is trading at 43 and the TCB Apr 40 call is trading at 4 1/2, what is the intrinsic value and the time value of the call premium?

   A. Intrinsic value 4 1/2; time value 0
   B. Intrinsic value 3; time value 4 1/2
   C. Intrinsic value 3; time value 1 1/2
   D. Intrinsic value 1 1/2; time value 3

25. All of the following usually result in a profit to a naked call writer EXCEPT the

   A. option contract expires without being exercised
   B. price of the underlying security falls below and remains below the exercise price of the option
   C. call is exercised and the price of the underlying security is greater than the exercise price plus the premium received
   D. price of the option contract declines

26. Bea Kuhl and June Polar buy 100 shares of Acme Zootech (ZOO) at 55 and write a ZOO 50 call at 7 1/2. Acme Zootech goes to 60, and the call is exercised. Disregarding commissions, they have a

   A. $250 gain
   B. $500 gain
   C. $500 loss
   D. $750 loss

27. An investor buys 1 DWQ Sep 50 call at 2 1/2. What is the investor's breakeven point?

   A. 47 1/2
   B. 50
   C. 52 1/2
   D. 55

28. An investor buys 1 DWQ Sep 50 call at 2 1/2. What is the investor's maximum potential gain?

   A. $4,750
   B. $5,000
   C. $5,250
   D. Unlimited

29. An investor buys 1 DWQ Sep 50 call at 2 1/2. What is the investor's maximum potential loss?

   A. $250
   B. $500
   C. $5,250
   D. Unlimited

30. An investor sells 1 COD Jun 50 call at 3 1/2. What is the investor's breakeven point?

   A. 46 1/2
   B. 50
   C. 53 1/2
   D. 57

31. An investor sells 1 COD Jun 50 call at 3 1/2. What is the investor's maximum potential gain?

   A. $350
   B. $4,650
   C. $5,350
   D. Unlimited

32. An investor sells 1 COD Jun 50 call at 3 1/2. What is the investor's maximum potential loss?

   A. $350
   B. $4,650
   C. $5,350
   D. Unlimited

33. An investor buys 1 ALF Jan 50 put at 2. What is the investor's breakeven point?

    A. 48
    B. 49
    C. 50
    D. 52

34. An investor buys 1 ALF Jan 50 put at 2. What is the investor's maximum potential gain?

    A. $200
    B. $4,800
    C. $5,200
    D. Unlimited

35. An investor buys 1 ALF Jan 50 put at 2. What is the investor's maximum potential loss?

    A. $100
    B. $200
    C. $4,800
    D. $5,200

36. An investor sells 1 DWQ Feb 30 put at 4 1/2. What is the investor's breakeven point?

    A. 25 1/2
    B. 27 1/2
    C. 30 1/2
    D. 34 1/2

37. An investor sells 1 DWQ Feb 30 put at 4 1/2. What is the investor's maximum potential gain?

    A. $450
    B. $2,550
    C. $3,450
    D. Unlimited

38. An investor sells 1 DWQ Feb 30 put at 4 1/2. What is the investor's maximum potential loss?

    A. $450
    B. $2,550
    C. $3,450
    D. Unlimited

◆ Answers & Rationale

1.   **B.**   The customer will receive premiums for the calls she sells. If the calls she will write are out-of-the-money, the stock will probably not be called away and, therefore, will not produce capital gains until next year.   (Page 498)

2.   **C.**   Short stock and short naked calls subject an investor to unlimited risk because no one knows how high the price of a stock might rise. Risk can be defined for the other positions.   (Page 501)

3.   **C.**   An option is in-the-money when it has intrinsic value. A call option is in-the-money when the price of the underlying security is higher than the exercise price of the option.   (Page 494)

4.   **A.**   The best hedge for a short stock position is to buy a call, not to sell a put. If the stock goes up, the investor has the right to exercise the call and use the stock to close out the short position. To obtain the most protection, the call's strike price should equal the short sale price.   (Page 496)

5.   **B.**   A short stock position gives an investor unlimited risk potential if the stock should rise because the investor eventually must buy back the stock at the higher price. Because stock can rise an unlimited amount, there is unlimited risk. The sale of a naked call requires that, if exercised, the writer must buy the stock in the market and deliver it at the strike price. Because the stock can rise an unlimited amount, the writer assumes unlimited risk. The sale of a covered call does not pose this risk because the writer already owns the stock at an established price. When selling a naked put, if exercised, the writer is required to buy stock at a fixed price. Because the price of the stock can only drop to zero, the writer's maximum loss is fixed; the worst that can happen is that he is forced to buy worthless stock.   (Page 501)

6.   **B.**   This option has been adjusted for a stock dividend. Because the contract now covers 115 shares, at a premium of 14 1/2 per share, the cost is $1,667.50 (115 × 14 1/2).   (Page 496)

7.   **C.**   The investor opened the position and received 21 3/8 for selling the option. He closed the position by buying the option at its intrinsic value, which is equal to the difference between the stock's market price and the option's strike price. In this example, 320 minus 304 1/2 equals an intrinsic value of 15 1/2. The investor's gain is the difference between the sale price of 21 3/8 and the purchase price of 15 1/2, which equals 5 7/8, or $5.875. His profit is $5.875 times the multiplier of 100, which equals $587.50.   (Page 499)

8.   **C.**   If the investor writes any put, he collects premiums. If the stock price rises, the put will go out-of-the-money and will expire. The investor keeps the premiums, which help offset his purchase cost of $38 per share. He will not write a call at 35 because, as the stock price slowly rises, the call will go in-the-money. It would then either be exercised (and the stock taken away) or be bought back at a higher premium for a loss.   (Page 500)

9.   **D.**   A naked writer would consider all choices—the risk/reward ratio, the loss potential and the possibility of exercise.   (Page 498)

10.   **D.**   The purchase of a put allows the holder of stock to lock in a sale price and thus protect any gain already made on the stock. If the price were to continue to rise, the investor would not exercise the put. She would let it expire and sell the stock at the higher market price.   (Page 499)

11.   **D.**   Short calls that are uncovered give unlimited dollar risk.   (Page 498)

12.   **A.**   The opening purchase of the TCB Jul 85 call was made at 5 and the closing sale of that call was made at 2. The difference of 3 represents a $300 loss. The opening purchase of the TCB Jul 90 put was made at 8 and the closing sale of that put was made at 3. The difference of 5 represents a $500 loss. The total loss for the account was $800.   (Page 495)

13.   **A.**   The opening purchase of the IBS Apr 40 call was made at 6 and the closing sale of that call was made at 4. The difference of 2 represents a $200 loss. The opening purchase of the IBS Apr 50

put was made at 8 and the closing sale of that put was made at 6. The difference of 2 represents a $200 loss. The total loss for the account was $400. (Page 495)

14. **D.** Because the potential profit on the two trades is only 1/8th of a point, any commissions would result in a net loss to the customer. This trade is uneconomic. (Page 494)

15. **A.** The most conservative strategy for generating income is to sell a covered call. An investor who writes a put must be able to afford the entire purchase price of the stock if the put is exercised. (Page 498)

16. **B.** When the short put is exercised, the investor buys stock at $50, which then can be used to cover the $50 short sale. There is no gain or loss on the stock. However, the writer of the put collected $500 in premiums, so the writer has a gain of $500. (Page 500)

17. **D.**

Opening sale:
   1 IBS 280 put   16 5/8
Closing purchase:
   1 IBS 280 put   14 3/4
                     1 7/8 ($187.50 gain)

(Page 500)

18. **A.** The sale of a call will allow the investor to collect premiums. Because he owns the stock, the option is covered and no margin is required. Alternatively, the investor could buy a put, which would move more in-the-money as the stock price falls temporarily. He could then liquidate the put at a profit. (Page 498)

19. **A.** Because the market price is 47, by writing a put at 45 (2 points out-of-the-money), the investor will collect some premiums. Because she does not think the price will change, the put will expire and she will keep the premiums. This will reduce her cost on the purchased stock. (Page 500)

20. **D.** To profit on a long call, the market price must exceed the strike price plus the premiums paid. (Page 497)

21. **B.** Writing naked calls gives unlimited upside risk. Writing naked puts results in the put expiring if the market rises. (Page 501)

22. **D.** Breakeven for the buyer and for the seller of a put is the strike price of the option minus the premium paid for the option. (Page 501)

23. **C.** Call options allow greater leverage than buying the underlying stock, and the capital requirements are smaller, allowing for a smaller loss potential. The fact that options expire (that is, have a time value that erodes as the option nears expiration) is a disadvantage of options. Because stock purchases have no time value component, there is no expiration and, therefore, no value erosion due to this factor. (Page 497)

24. **C.** The option is in-the-money by 3 points because the strike price on the call is 40 and the market price is 43. This sets a minimum premium of $3 per share. Because the actual premium is 4 1/2, the balance of 1 1/2 represents time value. (Page 495)

25. **C.** If the option expires out-of-the-money, the naked call writer keeps the premiums. This occurs when the market price stays below the strike price. Breakeven is the strike price plus the premiums. If the price rises above this, the naked call writer, when exercised, will lose. (Page 501)

26. **A.** Bea and June received $750 when they sold the ZOO 50 call at 7 1/2. Their cost for the stock was $5,500 ($55 × 100). When the ZOO call was exercised at 50, they delivered the stock that they had purchased at 55 for a $500 loss ($5,500 – $5,000). Their $750 proceeds from writing the call less their $500 loss on the sale of the stock left them with a net gain of $250 before commissions. (Page 498)

27. **C.** The breakeven point on a long call is calculated by adding the premium to the strike price. Add the premium of 2 1/2 to the strike price

of 50 to determine the breakeven point of 52 1/2. (Page 500)

28. **D.** The maximum gain on a long call is unlimited because theoretically there is no limit on a rise in stock price. (Page 500)

29. **A.** The maximum loss on a long call is equal to the premium paid for the option. One contract represents 100 shares and the buyer paid a 2 1/2 dollar per share premium, which equals $250. (Page 500)

30. **C.** The breakeven point on a short call is calculated by adding the premium to the strike price. Add the premium of 3 1/2 to the strike price of 50 to determine the breakeven point of 53 1/2. (Page 501)

31. **A.** The maximum gain on a short call is equal to the premium received by the seller. One contract represents 100 shares and the seller received a 3 1/2 dollar per share premium, which equals $350. (Page 501)

32. **D.** The maximum loss on a short call is unlimited because theoretically there is no limit on a rise in stock price. (Page 501)

33. **A.** The breakeven point on a long put is calculated by subtracting the premium from the strike price. Subtract the premium of 2 from the strike price of 50 to determine the breakeven point of 48. Remember, the investor is bearish on the stock and wants the price to go down. (Page 498)

34. **B.** The maximum gain on a long put is calculated by subtracting the premium from the strike price. Subtract the premium paid of 2 from the strike price of 50 to determine the maximum potential gain of 48 per share. One contract represents 100 shares, so the buyer's maximum gain is $4,800. (Page 501)

35. **B.** The maximum loss on a long put is equal to the premium paid for the option. One contract represents 100 shares and the buyer paid a 2 dollar per share premium, which equals $200. (Page 501)

36. **A.** The breakeven point on a short put is calculated by subtracting the premium from the strike price. Subtract the premium of 4 1/2 from the strike price of 30 to determine the breakeven point of 25 1/2. (Page 502)

37. **A.** The maximum gain on a short put is equal to the premium received by the seller. One contract represents 100 shares and the seller received a 4 1/2 dollar per share premium, which equals $450. (Page 502)

38. **B.** The maximum loss on a short put occurs when the stock drops to $0 and is calculated by subtracting the premium from the strike price. Subtract the premium received by the seller of 4 1/2 from the strike price of 30 to determine the maximum loss of 25 1/2 per share. One contract represents 100 shares, so the seller's maximum loss is $2,550. (Page 501)

1. Which two of the following are spreads?

   I. Long 1 FLB May 40 call; short 1 FLB May 50 call
   II. Long 1 FLB May 40 call; long 1 FLB May 50 call
   III. Long 1 FLB Aug 40 call; short 1 FLB May 40 call
   IV. Long 1 FLB Aug 40 call; short 1 FLB Aug 50 put

   A. I and II
   B. I and III
   C. II and III
   D. II and IV

2. Hugh Heifer sells an FLB Mar 35 call. To establish a straddle he would

   A. sell an FLB Mar 40 call
   B. buy an FLB Mar 35 put
   C. sell an FLB Mar 35 put
   D. buy an FLB Mar 40 call

3. A registered representative executes the following trades for an options account: buy 1 FLB Apr 40 call at 9 and sell 1 FLB Apr 45 call at 4. Are these suitable trades?

   A. It depends on the customer's investment objectives.
   B. It is impossible to tell.
   C. No, because the customer has no chance of making a profit on these trades.
   D. Yes, because the trades will result in a small profit.

4. An active options trader establishes the following position: long 10 ALF Apr 40 calls at 6, short 10 ALF Apr 50 calls at 2. What is the breakeven point?

   A. 4
   B. 40
   C. 44
   D. 46

5. An options trader establishes the following position: long 10 ALF Apr 40 calls at 6, short 10 ALF Apr 50 calls at 2. What will be the client's maximum gain and loss?

   A. Gain 2, loss 6
   B. Gain 4, loss 2
   C. Gain 6, loss 4
   D. Gain unlimited, loss 6

6. An options trader establishes the following position: long 10 ALF Apr 40 calls at 6, short 10 ALF Apr 50 calls at 2. What is the risk to reward ratio?

   A. 4:6
   B. 6:4
   C. 40:44
   D. 40:50

7. Your client writes a combination that consists of a DWQ 45 call and a DWQ 50 put. The premiums total $650. Your client will break even when the price of the underlying stock is

   I. $43.50
   II. $50.50
   III. $51.50
   IV. $56.50

   A. I and III
   B. I and IV
   C. II and IV
   D. IV

8. Hugh Heifer bought 5 ALF Sep 50 calls at 5 and also bought 5 ALF Sep 50 puts at 3. This position is called a

   A. spread
   B. ratio write
   C. straddle
   D. combination

9. A customer is long 100 shares of stock and has written 5 calls against that stock. This option strategy is called a

   A. triple-covered write
   B. reverse spread
   C. ratio (variable) write
   D. combination

10. Chip Bullock bought a Jan 30 CowTec call for 4 1/2 and sold a Jan 35 call for 2 1/2. If he is to profit from this position, the spread between the prices of the two options will have to

    A. widen
    B. narrow
    C. remain the same
    D. fluctuate

11. If a customer buys 1 COW Nov 70 put and sells 1 COW Nov 60 put when COW is selling for 65, this position is a

    A. bull spread
    B. bear spread
    C. combination
    D. straddle

12. Tippecanoe Ferry Co. issues a news release that your customer believes will greatly affect the market price of its stock, but he is not sure whether the effect will be positive or negative. In this situation, which of the following strategies would be best?

    A. Buy a call.
    B. Write a call.
    C. Write a straddle.
    D. Buy a straddle.

13. All of the following are credit spreads EXCEPT

    A. write 1 COW Nov 35 put; buy 1 COW Nov 30 put
    B. buy 1 COW Apr 40 call; write 1 COW Apr 30 call
    C. buy 1 COW Jul 50 call; write 1 COW Jul 60 call
    D. buy 1 COW Jan 50 put; write 1 COW Jan 60 put

14. In which of the following strategies would the investor want the spread to widen?

    I.   Buy 1 ALF May 30 put; write 1 ALF May 25 put.
    II. Write 1 ALF Apr 45 put; buy 1 ALF Apr 55 put.
    III. Buy 1 ALF Nov 65 put; write 1 ALF Nov 75 put.
    IV. Buy 1 ALF Jan 40 call; write 1 ALF Jan 30 call.

    A. I and II
    B. I and IV
    C. II and III
    D. III and IV

15. Which of the following statements regarding straddles is(are) true?

    I.   An investor who wishes to generate income and who does not anticipate that the price of a stock will change will sell a straddle.
    II. An investor who anticipates a substantial advance in the price of a stock will buy a straddle.
    III. An investor who anticipates a substantial decline in the price of a stock will sell a straddle.
    IV. An investor who anticipates substantial fluctuations in the price of a stock will buy a straddle.

    A. I only
    B. I and IV only
    C. II and III only
    D. I, II, III and IV

16. GHI is currently trading at 62. An investor anticipates a substantial decline in the price of the stock and wishes to obtain maximum leverage. He would be MOST likely to

    A. buy the GHI Jul 60 put
    B. buy the GHI Jul 70 put
    C. buy a GHI straddle
    D. sell a GHI straddle

17. An investor buys QRS stock at 60. He subsequently writes 1 QRS 60 call at 4 and 1 QRS 60 put at 5. If QRS stock is trading at $74 on the expiration date, the investor will realize a profit of

    A. $100
    B. $400
    C. $500
    D. $900

18. A customer would incur an unlimited financial risk if he were

    A. long 1 TCB Jan 50 put
    B. short 1 TCB Jan 50 put
    C. short 1 TCB Jan 50 put and short 100 shares of TCB stock
    D. short 1 TCB Jan 50 put and long 100 shares of TCB stock

19. In April, a customer sold short 100 shares of QRS stock at $50 and simultaneously wrote 1 QRS Jan 50 put for a premium of $7. At what price will he break even?

    A. $43
    B. $50
    C. $57
    D. $64

20. In April, a customer sold short 100 shares of QRS stock at $50 and simultaneously wrote 1 QRS Jan 50 put for a premium of $7. If the January put is exercised when the market value of QRS is 43 and the stock acquired is used to cover the short stock position, what would be the customer's profit or loss per share?

    A. $0
    B. $7 loss
    C. $7 gain
    D. $14 loss

21. An investor purchases 1,000 shares of DWQ stock and sells 1 DWQ put and 1 DWQ call with the same terms. He subsequently sells the stock. His position now would be which of the following?

    A. Spread
    B. Straddle
    C. Covered writer
    D. Combination

22. In a margin account, an investor is long a call on DWQ stock and is short DWQ stock. The short stock should be marked to market

    A. whenever the price of the stock becomes higher than the strike price of the option
    B. daily
    C. weekly
    D. if the price of DWQ stock declines

23. If an investor primarily interested in speculation does not expect the price of DWQ stock to change, he would

    A.   write an uncovered straddle
    B.   write a straddle and buy stock
    C.   write a straddle and short the stock
    D.   buy a straddle

24. An investor purchased DWQ stock at 50. The stock is now 60 and he fears that the price will decline to 55. He should

    A.   sell a straddle at 60
    B.   buy a straddle at 60
    C.   buy a 60 put and write a 60 call
    D.   write a 60 put and buy a 60 call

◆ Answers & Rationale

1. **B.** Choices I and III fit the definition of a call spread because each includes one long and one short option of the same type with different strike prices (I, a price spread) or different expiration dates (III, a time spread). Choice II involves options of the same type, but both are long. Choice IV involves options of different types. (Page 503)

2. **C.** Straddles involve options of different types, but both options must be long or both must be short. They must have the same expiration date and strike price. (Page 504)

3. **C.** These trades are not suitable because a customer would have no chance of making a profit on them. (Page 506)

4. **C.** Add the difference in premiums (6 – 2 = 4) to the lower strike price. (Page 507)

5. **C.** The area of gain is between 44 and 50 for a gain of 6. Should the stock decline, both options will expire for a loss of 4 (6 – 2). (Page 506)

6. **A.** The client's risk is $400 and the potential reward is $600. Expressed as a ratio, the risk/reward is 4:6. (Page 504)

7. **A.** Your client will break even when one of the options is worth $650 and the other is worthless. When the price of the stock is $43.50, the put is $650 in-the-money. When the price of the stock is $51.50, the call is $650 in-the-money. (Page 511)

8. **C.** An investor establishes a straddle by buying or writing a call and a put, both of which have the same strike price and expiration date. (Page 504)

9. **C.** A stockholder establishes a ratio write by writing a call that covers more shares than he owns. This strategy is also called a *variable hedge*. (Page 514)

10. **A.** The customer bought the more expensive option. This option created a debit. A debit spread is profitable when the difference between the premiums widens. (Page 509)

11. **B.** This put spread is established at a debit because the customer pays more for the 70 put than he receives for the 60 put. Bears buy puts and write put spreads having debit balances. (Page 507)

12. **D.** If the stock goes either up or down sharply, the customer will profit from owning a straddle. (Page 509)

13. **C.** The lower the strike price, the more expensive the call option. The investor has purchased the more expensive option with the lower strike price; therefore, this is a debit spread. (Page 505)

14. **A.** Choices I and II are debit spreads. An investor wants a debit spread to widen. As the distance between premiums increases, the investor's potential profit also increases. This is because the investor intends to sell the option with the higher premium and buy back the option with the lower premium. (Page 509)

15. **B.** A long straddle is the purchase of a put and a call on the same stock with both options having the same terms. The long call is profitable if the market moves upward, while the long put is profitable if the market moves downward. In this manner, both sides of the market are *straddled*. (Page 509)

16. **A.** To profit from a decline in the market price and obtain the greatest leverage (use the least cash), the purchase of a put is best. The lowest premium would be on a put that is currently at- or out-of-the-money. Because the market price of the stock is 62, a Jul 60 put is 2 points out-of-the-money, while a Jul 70 put is 8 points in-the-money. The Jul 60 put, therefore, would require a lower premium. (Page 507)

17. **D.** With QRS trading at 74 on the expiration date, the QRS 60 call will be exercised while the QRS 60 put will expire. The investor originally bought the stock in the market at 60, and will

deliver the stock at 60 to satisfy the exercised call. (Page 510)

18. **C.** A short stock position gives unlimited loss potential as the stock rises in price. A short put, on the other hand, is profitable if the stock price rises. With a short put, the writer's loss is limited to the purchase of worthless stock at the strike price of the option (if exercised). (Page 514)

19. **C.** If the stock price falls, the loss on the short put is exactly offset by the gain on the short stock position. The customer then keeps the premiums of $700. On the other hand, if the price rises above 50, the short put will expire. The short stock position is then losing money. Because $700 was collected in premiums, the short stock position can lose 7 points and still break even (50 + 7 = 57 breakeven point). (Page 514)

20. **C.** Because the stock is purchased upon exercise of the short put for $50 and is then used to cover the $50 short sale, there is no gain or loss on the stock. The writer of the put still keeps the $700 collected in premiums, for a profit of $7 per share. (Page 514)

21. **B.** The investor's position after the sale of the stock is short 1 DWQ call and short 1 DWQ put, both at the same terms. This is a short straddle. (Page 504)

22. **B.** All stock positions in margin accounts, whether long or short, are marked to the market daily. (Page 513)

23. **A.** An investor who expects prices to remain stable would write an uncovered straddle (short straddle). In selling the put and call at the same terms, the writer collects double premiums. Both expire if the price remains stable; however, if the price moves, then one side or the other will lose money. (Page 510)

24. **C.** The investor bought the stock at $50 and the stock has risen to $60. To protect against a decline in the price of the stock, he could buy a 60 put, which locks in a $60 sale price. By writing the $60 call, he collects premiums that offset the premium paid to buy the $60 put. If the price falls, he is protected; but if the price rises, the short call will be exercised and he will lose the stock. (Page 509)

1. The S&P 100 and AMEX Major Market indexes are examples of which of the following?

   A. Broad-based indexes
   B. Narrow-based indexes
   C. Equity options
   D. Debt options

2. When an index option is exercised, cash settlement must take place how many business days after exercise?

   A. One
   B. Two
   C. Three
   D. Five

3. On November 4th, Chip Bullock writes an S&P 100 Jan 185 put at 6. His maximum potential gain on this position is

   _____

4. On November 4th, Chip Bullock writes an S&P 100 Jan 185 put at 6. Chip will achieve the maximum gain on his position if, on the expiration date, the S&P 100 closes at what price?

   _____

   _____

5. Rhoda Bear writes an AMEX Major Market 250 call at 13. The market closes that day at 262.34. Rhoda will break even on her short call if, on the expiration date, the index closes at which of the following prices?

   A. 237
   B. 250
   C. 262.34
   D. 263

6. Randy Bear establishes a spread by purchasing an S&P 100 Nov 185 call and writing a Nov 180 call. Is his position a credit spread or a debit spread?

   _____

7. Randy Bear establishes a spread by purchasing an S&P 100 Nov 185 call and writing a Nov 180 call. Does he want his spread to widen or narrow?

   _____

8. Randy Bear establishes a spread by purchasing an S&P 100 Nov 185 call and writing a Nov 180 call. The index closes at 180 on the expiration date. Does Randy realize his maximum gain or maximum loss?

   _____

Table 1

Value Line Index Options
October 21, 1997

Strike Price	Calls			Puts		
	Nov	Dec	Jan	Nov	Dec	Jan
180	...	...	...	3/16	7/16	...
185	8 3/8	...	...	1/2	1	...
190	4 3/8	5 7/8	...	1 1/16	2	...
195	1 5/8	3	...	...	3 3/4	...
200	7/16	1 5/8	...	...	7 7/16	...
205	...	3/8	1 1/8	...	...	...

Use Table 1 to answer questions 9 through 13.

9.   If the multiplier for *Value Line* Index options is 100, what is the dollar amount of the premium for Nov 185 calls?

_____

Trades involving index options must be settled in cash. In questions 10 through 13, write in the blanks the amount of cash that will be required in each settlement.

10.   Chip Bullock is short a Nov 190 call on the *Value Line* Index. If he is assigned an exercise on October 21st, when the index closes at 193.72, how much will he owe?

_____

11.   If Chip buys back the Nov 190 call on October 21st before being assigned an exercise, how much will that closing purchase cost?

_____

12.   Chip buys back a Nov 190 call on October 21st before being assigned an exercise. How much of the amount paid in Chip's closing transaction is due to the premium's intrinsic value?

_____

13.   Chip buys back a Nov 190 call on October 21st before being assigned an exercise. How much of the premium is due to time value?

_____

14.   Your client Adam Grizzly purchases 1 Dec 90 T bill call option at a premium of .40. How much does he pay for the option in dollars?

A. $100
B. $400
C. $1,000
D. $4,000

15.   The exercise price of a yield-based option is 62.50. This represents a yield of

A.   .0625%
B.   .625%
C.   6.25%
D.   62.5%

16.   In November, Clara Bullock writes a Mar 102 call at 1.20 on a 9 5/8% five-year T note when the note is trading at 101 22/32. How much does she receive for writing the option?

A. $1,031
B. $1,200
C. $1,625
D. $2,000

17. In November, Clara Bullock writes a Mar 102 call at 1.20 on a 9 5/8% five-year T note when the note is trading at 101 22/32. Clara is bearish on the price of T notes. She will break even on her investment when the price of the underlying note is which of the following?

    A. 98 12/32
    B. 101 11/32
    C. 102
    D. 103 20/32

18. What security underlies a yield-based option?

    A. Treasury bond
    B. Income stock
    C. Debenture
    D. Revenue bond

19. Chip Bullock purchases a Nov 106 put on five-year 10 3/4% T notes and sells a Nov 108 put on the same notes. Which of the following statements are true?

    I. Chip believes interest rates are going to decline.
    II. Chip is bearish on the price of Treasury securities.
    III. Chip has created a debit spread.
    IV. If Chip closes his position with notes selling at 108, he will realize his maximum gain.

    A. I and II
    B. I and IV
    C. II, III and IV
    D. II and IV

20. Using yield-based options, what hedging strategy would offer a bond portfolio manager the greatest protection against rising long-term interest rates?

    A. Sell 30-year T bond yield-based calls
    B. Buy 30-year T bond yield-based calls
    C. Sell 30-year T bond yield-based puts
    D. Buy 30-year T bond yield-based puts

21. Adam Grizzly, an investment manager, believes that interest rates will go up soon. Which of the following strategies will be most profitable if he is correct?

    A. Buy T bills at the next auction.
    B. Buy puts on T bills.
    C. Buy calls on T bills.
    D. Write calls on long-term bonds.

22. In reading the foreign currency option quotes in *The Wall Street Journal,* you find that the exchange rate for British pounds is listed at 148.47. What does this mean?

    A. One dollar is equivalent to 1.4847 pounds.
    B. One dollar is equivalent to 14.847 pounds.
    C. One pound is equivalent to 1.4847 dollars.
    D. One pound is equivalent to 14.847 cents.

23. How many yen must an investor have on deposit in a Tokyo bank to cover 1 short call on yen?

    A. 62,500
    B. 125,000
    C. 6,250,000
    D. 12,500,000

24. An investor writes a Dec 45 call on Swiss francs at a premium of 2.76. How many cents does the investor receive per franc in the contract?

    A. 0.0276
    B. 0.276
    C. 2.76
    D. 27.60

25. An investor exercises a Dec 150 put on British pounds with the spot price at 148.47. As a consequence, the investor

    A. receives £31,250 for $45,937.50
    B. receives £31,250 for $46,875
    C. sells £31,250 for $45,937.50
    D. sells £31,250 for $46,875

26. What does an investor receive when he exercises a capped SPX option?

    A. Common stock
    B. Cash equal to the cap interval
    C. Cash equal to the market value at the open of trading
    D. Capped index options cannot be exercised.

27. Which of the following are considered features of a capped index option?

    I. Automatic exercise as soon as the option is out-of-the-money by the amount of the cap interval
    II. Automatic exercise as soon as the option is in-the-money by the amount of the cap interval
    III. The cap price is set by the Exchange at the time of listing.
    IV. Automatic exercise when the underlying index hits or goes through the cap price

    A. I, III and IV
    B. I and IV
    C. II and III
    D. II, III and IV

28. A capped index call option has an exercise price of 370 and a cap interval of 25. The index reaches 380. Which of the following statements is FALSE?

    A. The option may be traded on the CBOE.
    B. The owner may exercise the option only if it expires the following day.
    C. The option will automatically be exercised when the index reaches or exceeds 395.
    D. The option will automatically be exercised when it is in-the-money.

29. Joe Kuhl buys a capped index call option for a premium of $1,400. The strike price is 360. The option is automatically exercised at the cap price of 390. What is Joe's gain or loss?

    A. $1,400 loss
    B. $1,600 gain
    C. $3,000 gain
    D. $4,400 loss

◆ Answers & Rationale

1. **A.** Broad-based indexes attempt to reflect the status of the market as a whole, not the status of particular market segments.   (Page 516)

2. **A.** Exercised stock index options settle on the next business day.   (Page 518)

3. $600. Potential gain on a short option is the premium received on the transaction.   (Page 518)

4. At or above 185. At this price and above, the put expires worthless and the customer keeps the premium he received for writing the option.   (Page 518)

5. **D.** To break even, the customer would have to lose an amount equal to her initial gain—13 points. That will happen if her short call is in-the-money by 13 points and she is assigned an exercise.   (Page 518)

6. Credit spread. The customer sold the call with the lower strike price. The lower the strike price of a call, the higher the premium. Therefore, he received more for his short call than he paid for his long one. He has a credit spread.   (Page 518)

7. Narrow. The investor who opens a credit spread wants the spread between premiums to narrow. Ideally, both premiums will become zero, and there will be no spread between them. (Page 518)

8. Gain. As the writer of a bear credit spread, the investor wants the price of the index to drop until the calls expire worthless so he can keep the initial credit.   (Page 518)

9. $837.50. 8 3/8 × 100.   (Page 516)

10. $372. $193.72 − 190 = 3.72; 3.72 × 100 = $372.   (Page 516)

11. $437.50. Premium of 4 3/8 times the multiplier of 100.   (Page 516)

12. $372. With the index at 193.72, the 190 call is in-the-money by 3.72.   (Page 516)

13. $65.50. $437.50 − 372 = $65.50. Premium equals intrinsic value plus time value. (Page 516)

14. **C.** T bill premiums are quoted in 1/100ths of 1% of the underlying. The short-cut calculation is 40 times $25.   (Page 520)

15. **C.** Divide the strike price by ten to calculate the percentage yield of the underlying Treasury security. In this example, 62.50 divided by 10 equals a yield of 6.25%.   (Page 520)

16. **C.** In premium quotes for options on Treasury notes and bonds, 1.0 equals $1,000. The .20 indicates 20/32, which multiplied by the par value of $1,000 equals $625. Another way to calculate this is to remember that each 1/32nd of a point equals $31.25, and 20 times $31.25 equals $625. The total premium is $1,000 plus $625, which equals $1,625.   (Page 520)

17. **D.** The customer receives the premium of 1 20/32. When the bond price moves against her by that amount, to the strike price plus 1 20/32, she stands to lose as much as she gained on the opening sale.   (Page 520)

18. **A.** Yield-based interest rate options are based on the yields of Treasury bills, notes and bonds.   (Page 521)

19. **B.** The customer has written the spread at a credit. Because bulls write puts and put spreads, you know he is bullish on the price of the notes. If the price of the T notes goes up, interest rates will go down. The customer hopes to keep the credit received when the puts expire worthless, which will happen at 108 or any higher price. (Page 519)

20. **B.** If the portfolio manager bought the 30-year T bond yield-based calls, the options would increase in value as the actual yield on the 30-year Treasury bonds rose above the yield value represented by the strike price of the option. Note that the opposite strategy of buying puts would be used if the bond portfolio manager were using par-based

interest rate options, because the par-based puts would increase in value as bond prices fall as a result of rising interest rates.   (Page 522)

21. **B.**   Answers A and C would work only if rates fell. Answers B and D are effective ways to profit from rising rates and falling debt security prices, but short-term T bills are more affected by near-term rate changes.   (Page 521)

22. **C.**   The exchange rate refers to U.S. cents per British pound; 148.47¢ = $1.4847. (Page 524)

23. **C.**   The PHLX option is on 6,250,000 yen.   (Page 523)

24. **C.**   Premiums for options on the Swiss franc are quoted in cents per franc.   (Page 523)

25. **D.**   By exercising a put, the investor sells £31,250 at the strike price of 150; therefore, $1.50 × 31,250 = $46,875.   (Page 523)

26. **B.**   When exercising an index option, the investor receives cash in an amount equal to the difference between the strike price and the index's market value. For a capped index option, this amount is equal to the cap interval set by the Exchange.   (Page 517)

27. **D.**   Cap prices are set at a certain in-the-money interval by the Exchange. These options are exercised only when the underlying index hits or goes through the cap price.   (Page 518)

28. **D.**   When a capped index option is in-the-money *by the amount of the cap interval*, it is automatically exercised. If it does not reach the cap price by its expiration date, the owner may exercise the option.   (Page 518)

29. **B.**   When the index call option is exercised, the customer receives, in cash, the difference between the option's strike price and its market value—in this case, $3,000. To calculate his gain, the customer subtracts the $1,400 premium he paid for the option.   (Page 516)

74 Tax Rules for Options Exam

1. An investor who is long TCB stock for six months buys 1 call on TCB. If the call expires in eight months and the investor sells the stock three months after the call expires, he would realize on the stock a

   A. short-term gain or loss
   B. long-term gain or loss
   C. short-term gain or a long-term loss
   D. long-term gain or a short-term loss

2. An investor sells 1 TCB Jul 40 put and buys 1 TCB Jul 50 put. If she subsequently sells the Jul 50 put, she will realize

   A. a capital gain or loss
   B. a long-term capital gain if she sells at a profit or a short-term capital loss if she sells at a loss
   C. a short-term capital gain if she sells at a profit or a long-term capital loss if she sells at a loss
   D. ordinary income or ordinary loss

3. After having held 100 shares of GHI stock for 15 months, a customer purchases 1 GHI Sep 50 put in December. Which two of the following statements would be true if the put were exercised prior to the expiration date and the long stock were delivered?

   I. The premium would be added to the proceeds of the sale.
   II. The premium would be deducted from the proceeds of the sale.
   III. Any gain would be long term.
   IV. Any gain would be short term.

   A. I and III
   B. I and IV
   C. II and III
   D. II and IV

4. In February, a customer sells 1 GHI Oct 60 put for 3 and buys 1 GHI Oct 70 put for 11. If the customer closed the Oct 70 put prior to expiration, the resulting profit or loss

   A. is treated as ordinary income or loss
   B. depends on the disposition of the short Oct 60 put
   C. is treated as a capital gain or loss
   D. cannot be determined from the information given

5. An investor who is short IBS stock and subsequently buys a call option

   A. terminates the holding period on the short position
   B. does not affect the holding period on the short position
   C. will cause any gain on the short position to be short term and any loss to be long term
   D. will cause suspension of the holding period on the short position until the call is closed out or expires

6. An investor's account reflects the following activity:

   May 1995
       BOT 100 shares of TCB at 40

   June 1995
       BOT 200 shares of TCB at 42

   January 1996
       BOT 1 TCB Jul 45 call at 5

   July 1996
       SLD 1 TCB Jul 45 call at 7

   August 1996
       SLD 300 shares of TCB at 51

   The investor would have realized

   A. a short-term capital gain on 300 shares of TCB stock
   B. a long-term capital gain on 300 shares of TCB stock
   C. ordinary income on 300 shares of TCB stock
   D. none of the above

7. Which of the following would affect the holding period on a long position in IBS stock?

   I. Purchase of 1 IBS call
   II. Purchase of 1 IBS put
   III. Sale of 1 IBS out-of-the-money call
   IV. Sale of 1 IBS out-of-the-money put

   A. I only
   B. II only
   C. III and IV only
   D. I, II, III and IV

8. On July 15, 1993, an investor sells 1 TCB Jan 50 put at 7. The put expires unexercised. The investor will realize

   A. a $700 short-term capital gain reportable for tax year 1993
   B. a $700 short-term capital gain reportable for tax year 1994
   C. $700 ordinary income reportable for tax year 1993
   D. $700 ordinary income reportable for tax year 1994

9. For federal income tax purposes, which of the following transactions could affect the holding period of the long position in the underlying stock if it has been held for twelve months or less?

   I. Opening put spread
   II. Closing put purchase
   III. Opening put sales
   IV. Opening put purchase

   A. I, II and IV
   B. I and III
   C. I and IV
   D. II and IV

10. Bea Kuhl has a short position in Microscam that she has held for almost 11 months. If she bought a call on Microscam, what effect would this purchase have on the holding period of the stock for tax purposes?

    A. It would eliminate the holding period.
    B. It would freeze the holding period for the interval that she owned the call.
    C. It would automatically reduce the holding period by the number of months remaining until the expiration of the call.
    D. It would have no effect.

11. In September, an investor writes 2 DWQ Jan 60 puts at 3. If the investor buys back the 2 puts at 4 1/2, the result for tax purposes is a

    A. $150 capital gain
    B. $150 capital loss
    C. $300 capital gain
    D. $300 capital loss

12. In September, an investor writes 2 DWQ Jan 60 puts at 3. If the puts expire in January, what is the tax consequence for the writer?

    A. $600 gain realized in September
    B. $600 loss realized in September
    C. $600 gain realized in January
    D. $600 loss realized in January

13. On January 1st, an investor buys 1 DWQ Apr 50 call at 4 and 1 DWQ Apr 50 put at 2 1/2. Both options expire unexercised. What is the result of the call transaction for tax purposes?

14. On January 1st, an investor buys 1 FLB Apr 50 call at 4 and 1 FLB Apr 50 put at 2 1/2. Both options expire unexercised. What is the result of the put transaction for tax purposes?

15. An investor buys 300 shares of Flibinite and one month later buys 1 FLB Jul 50 put. How does this affect the holding period on his stock?

    A. It does not interrupt the holding period on his long stock.
    B. It ends the holding period on 100 shares.
    C. It ends the holding period on 300 shares.
    D. It ends the holding period on the put.

16. An investor has owned stock for five months on which he has an unrealized loss. If he wishes to retain the stock and keep his loss from becoming a long-term loss, he

    A. must dispose of the stock before six months have elapsed or his loss will become a long-term loss
    B. should sell a call
    C. should buy a call
    D. should buy a put

17. An investor who has owned Flibinite stock for two years buys 1 FLB Oct put. This will

    A. have no effect on his holding period
    B. end his holding period and cause any gain or loss to be short term
    C. end his holding period and cause any gain or loss to be long term
    D. end his holding period and cause any loss to be long term and any gain to be short term

◆ Answers & Rationale

1. **B.** The purchase of a call has no effect on a long stock position's holding period because the call only allows more stock to be purchased—it does not allow the stock to be sold. The stock was held for 17 months, which is longer than the holding period required for long-term capital gains treatment.   (Page 528)

2. **A.** The investor opens with a vertical (price) spread. If she closes out one of the legs of the spread, on that position (buy Jul 50 put/sell Jul 50 put) she will have a capital gain or loss for tax purposes as of the closing trade date.   (Page 527)

3. **C.** Because the customer already held the stock long term when purchasing the put, he was not trying to stretch a short-term gain into a long-term gain. There is no effect on his established holding period of 15 months. Whenever a put is exercised, the sale price of the stock (exercise price) is reduced by the premium paid for buying the put. Because it cost the amount of the premium to sell, this accurately computes the net sales proceeds that the customer receives.   (Page 528)

4. **C.** All listed options trades, with resulting gains or losses, are treated as capital gains or losses.   (Page 527)

5. **B.** The purchase of a call has no effect on a short stock position's holding period. By the way, there is no holding period for a short stock because the stock is never owned. All gains and losses from shorting stock are always short term.   (Page 527)

6. **B.** Because the 300 shares of TCB were purchased in May and June 1995, the sale of the stock in August 1996 means that position was held long term. The sale of the call has no effect on the holding period for the stock.   (Page 528)

7. **B.** Only the purchase of a put affects a stock's holding period when the stock has been held short term at the time of the purchase of the put. The put purchase wipes out the stock's holding

period. With regard to transactions in calls, only the sale of an in-the-money call can affect a stock's holding period.   (Page 528)

8. **B.** For tax purposes, the gain to the writer of premiums earned is recognized at the expiration date. Because the maximum life on a listed option is nine months, the gain is short term. (Page 527)

9. **C.** The IRS does not allow individuals who own stock short term to lock in a sale price using the purchase of a put and then "stretch" the holding period to long term before exercising the put and selling the stock. Upon purchasing the put, whatever holding period the owner of the stock has accrued is wiped out. The holding period does not start again until the put expires or is sold. This rule applies to all opening put purchases whether the put is purchased alone or in combination with other options transactions.   (Page 528)

10. **D.** A profit or loss resulting from a short position is always taxed as a short-term capital gain or loss, so a short position has no holding period.   (Page 527)

11. **D.** $900 closing cost minus $600 opening proceeds equals a $300 loss.   (Page 527)

12. **C.** Expiration of a short option generates a gain at the time the option expires.   (Page 527)

13. $400 capital loss.   In a straddle, the options are treated separately for tax purposes. (Page 527)

14. $250.   A $250 capital loss.   (Page 527)

15. **B.** The purchase of the put wipes out the holding period on the number of shares owned that the put allows the holder to sell. Because the holder owns 1 put, this wipes out the holding period on 100 shares owned. The other 200 shares are unaffected.   (Page 528)

16. **D.** The purchase of the put, while the stock is held short term, will wipe out any accumulated holding period. A new holding period starts when the put expires or is sold.   (Page 528)

17. **A.**   Because the investor held the stock long term when the put was acquired, there is no effect on the holding period.   (Page 528)

1. Any of the following could be considered a redeemable security under the Investment Company Act of 1940 EXCEPT a(n)

    A. security that pays out each investor's proportionate share of the company's assets
    B. security that can be sold on an exchange at the fair market price the buyers and sellers have established
    C. investment company security issued as common stock
    D. security issued by an open-end investment company

2. Under the definition of a management company, all of the following would qualify EXCEPT

    I.   face-amount certificate companies
    II. unit investment trusts
    III. closed-end investment companies
    IV. open-end investment companies

    A. I
    B. I and II
    C. I, II and III
    D. III and IV

3. A unit investment trust is an

    A. investment contract that represents an obligation on the part of the issuer to pay a determinable sum at a fixed date more than 24 months after the date of issue
    B. investment company that issues redeemable securities, each of which represents an undivided interest in a portfolio's securities, which are professionally selected
    C. issuer who acquires investment securities exceeding 40% of the value of the issuer's total assets
    D. account established and managed by an insurance company under which income, gains and losses (whether or not realized) are credited to or charged against such account

4. GEM Precious Metals Fund, a diversified open-end investment company, invested 5% of its total assets in Monaghan Minerals and Mining, Inc. The market soared and, because of Monaghan's phenomenal appreciation, Monaghan securities now make up 8% of the GEM Fund's total assets. GEM Fund

    A. must sell enough of Monaghan securities to reduce its holdings in Monaghan to 5% of its total assets
    B. must sell out its holdings in Monaghan completely
    C. must sell Monaghan shares only if the 8% investment represents more than 10% of Monaghan's outstanding voting securities
    D. does not have to sell Monaghan shares, but cannot buy more Monaghan shares and still advertise itself as a diversified company

5. Face-amount certificate companies can include any or all of the following conditions in their contracts EXCEPT

    A. require the payment of a stated sum of money on a fixed date by the issuer
    B. require the payment of stated sums by the purchaser at fixed intervals
    C. provide a return that varies daily based on market fluctuation
    D. provide a fixed rate of return during periods of prolonged market decline

6. A typical unit investment trust has

    A. no investment adviser
    B. listed securities
    C. securities representing a divided interest in a unit of specified securities
    D. a board of directors

7. An investment company that is not classified as either a unit investment trust or a face-amount certificate company would be classified as a(n)

    A. mutual fund
    B. management investment company
    C. open-end company
    D. closed-end company

8. A diversified investment company must invest at least ____ of its assets such that no more than ____ of its assets are in any one company and each investment may represent no more than ____ of the voting securities of the target company.

    A. 50%—10%—5%
    B. 75%—5%—10%
    C. 75%—10%—5%
    D. 100%—5%—15%

9. Which of the following statements is(are) FALSE regarding a unit investment trust?

    A. It invests according to stated objectives.
    B. It charges no management fee.
    C. Overall responsibility for the fund rests with the board of directors.
    D. The transfer agent may limit sales to current unit holders.

10. All of the following statements are true of a closed-end investment company EXCEPT that it

    A. can redeem its own shares
    B. is a type of management company
    C. sells at the market price plus a commission
    D. may not be referred to as a mutual fund

11. Which of the following statements are true of open-end investment companies?

   I. They may constantly issue new shares.
   II. They redeem shares at any time.
   III. They may leverage common shares by issuing bonds.

   A. I and II only
   B. I and III only
   C. II and III only
   D. I, II and III

12. According to the Investment Company Act of 1940, what is the maximum percentage of a corporation's voting securities that a diversified mutual fund may hold?

   A. 5%
   B. 10%
   C. 50%
   D. 75%

13. The ArGood Fund, a diversified investment company, has a net asset value of $225 million. ArGood wishes to invest in General Gizmonics, Inc. GIZ stock is selling at $30 a share, and there are 100,000 shares outstanding. The maximum number of GIZ shares that ArGood Fund could buy and still be diversified is

   A. 5,000
   B. 10,000
   C. $11,250,000 worth
   D. $12,500,000 worth

14. A regulated, diversified investment company cannot own more than what percentage of the outstanding shares of any one company?

   A. 2%
   B. 5%
   C. 8%
   D. 10%

15. To be considered a diversified investment company by the SEC, the company must meet which of the following requirements?

   A. At least 25% of the fund's assets must be invested in one industry.
   B. The fund must be invested in at least 20 different industries.
   C. 75% of the fund's assets must be invested, with no more than 5% invested in any one company and with no investment representing more than 10% of a single company's stock.
   D. The fund must be invested in both stocks and bonds.

16. Which of the following would be classified as an investment company?

   I. Closed-end company
   II. Open-end company
   III. Qualified plan company
   IV. Nonqualified plan company
   V. Fixed annuity company

   A. I and II
   B. I, II and V
   C. II
   D. III, IV and V

17. Where can closed-end investment company shares be purchased and sold?

   A. In the secondary marketplace
   B. From the closed-end company
   C. In the primary market
   D. All of the above

18. Which of the following statements describe(s) an open-end investment company?

   I. It can sell new shares in any quantity at any time.
   II. It must redeem shares in any quantity within seven days of request.
   III. It provides for mutual ownership of portfolio assets by shareholders.

   A. I and II only
   B. II only
   C. III only
   D. I, II and III

19. All of the following statements concerning investment companies are true EXCEPT

    A. a nondiversified company is any management company not classified as a diversified company
    B. to be considered a diversified investment company, the company must invest at least 75% of its total assets in cash and/or securities
    C. an investment company that invests the majority of its assets in one company or industry is considered a nondiversified company
    D. a diversified company can be only an open-end investment company

20. Any of the following could be considered a redeemable security under the Investment Company Act of 1940 EXCEPT a(n)

    A. security that pays out each investor's proportionate share of the company's assets
    B. security that can be sold on an exchange at the fair market price the buyers and sellers have established
    C. investment company security issued as common stock
    D. security issued by an open-end investment company

21. Which of the following statements describe an open-end investment company?

    I. The company may sell new shares in any quantity at any time.
    II. The company must sell new shares in any quantity at any time.
    III. The company may redeem shares in any quantity at any time but may restrict the redemption of shares at the discretion of the board of directors.
    IV. The company must redeem shares in any quantity at any time except that it may suspend the redemption of shares with SEC approval.

    A. I and III
    B. I and IV
    C. II and III
    D. II and IV

◆ Answers & Rationale

1.   **B.**   A redeemable security is one that is purchased from and redeemed with the issuer of the security. If the security can be traded on a secondary market, it is not considered a redeemable security. Open-end shares are redeemable securities; closed-end shares are not.   (Page 537)

2.   **B.**   As defined in the act of 1940, closed-end and open-end funds are subclassifications of management companies (actively managed portfolios). Face-amount certificate companies and unit trusts are separate investment company classifications under the act.   (Page 537)

3.   **B.**   A unit investment trust issues redeemable securities representing an undivided interest in a portfolio of securities that have been professionally selected. A UIT does not actively manage its portfolio. Answer A refers to face-amount certificate companies (FACs). Answer C defines investment companies in general. Answer D describes a separate account but, because the portfolio is managed, the account is set up as a management investment company, not as a UIT.   (Page 536)

4.   **D.**   A fund will not lose its diversified status because of market movement. While this fund may not purchase more Monaghan shares, it is not required to sell off any part of its Monaghan holdings.   (Page 538)

5.   **C.**   Face-amount certificate companies pay a fixed return.   (Page 536)

6.   **A.**   Unit investment trusts issue redeemable securities that are traded by the issuer only (the issuer must maintain a second market); the securities are not listed on an exchange. The shares (units) of a UIT evidence an undivided interest in a portfolio of securities that is not actively managed. A UIT has neither an investment adviser nor a board of directors.   (Page 536)

7.   **B.**   Management investment companies are the third classification of investment companies under the Investment Company Act of 1940. Open-end funds (mutual funds) and closed-end funds are subclassifications of management investment companies.   (Page 537)

8.   **B.**   A management company must be at least 75% invested, its investments must be diversified so that no more than 5% of its assets are in any one company and no single investment can represent more than 10% of the voting securities of another company.   (Page 538)

9.   **C.**   A unit investment trust has no board of directors. Answers A and B are true: a UIT must follow a stated investment objective (as must any investment company); and it does not charge a management fee because it is not a managed portfolio.   (Page 536)

10.   **A.**   A closed-end investment company does not redeem its own shares. The term "mutual fund" refers to an open-end investment company.   (Page 537)

11.   **A.**   An open-end company must stand ready to redeem shares within seven days of receiving a customer's request and may continuously offer its shares for sale. Although an open-end company may invest in just about any security, it may issue only one class of voting stock. The company cannot issue any type of debt.   (Page 537)

12.   **B.**   To be considered a diversified investment company, a mutual fund can own no more than 10% of the voting securities of a target company. Additionally, no diversified investment company may have more than 5% of its portfolio invested in the securities of a single company.   (Page 538)

13.   **B.**   A diversified investment company has at least 75% of its assets invested so that no more than 5% of its assets own more than 10% of a company's stock. In this question, 5% of ArGood Fund's assets could purchase the entire General Gizmonics company. Therefore, the ArGood Fund is limited to

only 10% of GIZ stock, or 10,000 shares.

(Page 538)

14. **D.**   To be considered a diversified investment company, the fund's portfolio must be invested to at least 75% so that no more than 5% of the *assets* own no more than 10% of a company's outstanding *stock*. Remember: 75% invested, 5% assets, 10% stock.   (Page 538)

15. **C.**   By definition, a diversified investment company must invest at least 75% of its assets, have no more than 5% of its assets concentrated in any one company and own no more than 10% of any single company's voting securities.   (Page 538)

16. **A.**   Open-and closed-end funds are classified as investment companies. Plan companies offer plans in which an investment company may be selected as an investment vehicle, but are not investment companies themselves. Fixed annuities are offered by insurance companies only.

(Page 537)

17. **A.**   A closed-end company share is bought *and sold* in the secondary marketplace. (Page 537)

18. **D.**   An open-end investment company can sell any quantity of new shares, redeem shares within seven days and provide for mutual ownership of portfolio assets by shareholders.

(Page 537)

19. **D.**   A diversified company could be either a closed-end company or an open-end company.

(Page 537)

20. **B.**   A redeemable security is one that is purchased from and redeemed with the issuer of the security. If the security can be traded on a secondary market, it is not considered a redeemable security. Open-end shares are redeemable securities; closed-end shares are not.   (Page 537)

21. **B.**   Under the Investment Company Act of 1940, an investment company selling mutual funds is not required to continuously offer new shares for sale; in fact, a fund will often suspend sales to new investors when it grows too large to adequately meet its investment objective. The act of 1940 does require the fund to continuously offer to redeem shares, and this redemption privilege may be suspended only during nonbusiness days or with the approval of the SEC.   (Page 537)

76 Characteristics of Mutual Funds Exam

1. The ZBest Invest Fund is a mutual fund that has as its primary objective the payment of dividends, regardless of the current state of the market; preservation of capital and capital growth are secondary objectives. Which of the following industry groups would be appropriate for the ZBest Invest Fund's portfolio?

   A. Aerospace
   B. Public utilities
   C. Computer technology
   D. Consumer appliances

2. All of the following characteristics are typical of a money-market fund EXCEPT that

   A. the underlying portfolio normally is made up of short-term debt instruments
   B. it is offered as a no-load investment
   C. it has a high beta and is safest in periods of low market volatility
   D. its net asset value normally remains unchanged

3. All of the following statements are true of money-market funds EXCEPT that

   A. investors pay a management fee
   B. interest is computed daily and credited to the investor's account monthly
   C. investors can buy and sell shares quickly and easily
   D. high interest rates are guaranteed

4. Mutual fund shares represent an undivided interest in the fund, which means that

   A. investors can purchase only full shares
   B. the fund can hold securities of only certain companies
   C. the number of shares outstanding is limited to a predetermined maximum
   D. each investor owns a proportional part of every security in the portfolio

5. Lotta Leveridge owns 150 shares of American Conservative Equity Fund. Which of the following statements are true?

   I. When a dividend is declared by the fund, she will receive a cash dividend for each share owned.
   II. She will have difficulty liquidating her shares.
   III. The amount of her dividend will reflect her proportional interest in the value of the fund portfolio on the record date.
   IV. She will receive dividends from only 150 shares of stock held in the fund portfolio.

   A. I, II and IV
   B. I and III
   C. II and III
   D. II, III and IV

6. Max Leveridge believes that the electronics industry will be very successful in the next ten years. If he wants to invest in the industry but does not want to limit his investments to only a few companies, he should invest in a

    A. bond fund
    B. money-market fund
    C. hedge fund
    D. specialized fund

7. Last year the bond market was very profitable, and ZBest Invest Fund had 70% of its assets in bonds. Next year the fund's managers expect the stock market to do well, and they adjust the fund's portfolio so that 60% will be invested in stock. ZBest Invest is probably what type of fund?

    A. Balanced
    B. Hedge
    C. Specialized
    D. Aggressive growth

8. ZBest Invest Fund pays regular dividends, offers a high degree of safety of principal and especially appeals to investors seeking tax advantages. ZBest Invest is a(n)

    A. corporate bond fund
    B. money-market fund
    C. aggressive growth fund
    D. municipal bond fund

9. Your client asks whether he should invest in a particular investment company. You should tell him to check the investment company's

    I.   investment policy
    II.   track record
    III. portfolio
    IV.   sales load

    A. I, II and III only
    B. I and IV only
    C. III only
    D. I, II, III and IV

10. Which of the following probably would be found in the portfolio of a money-market fund?

    I.   T bills
    II.   T bonds with a short time to maturity
    III. Bank certificates of deposit
    IV.   Common stock

    A. I and II only
    B. I, II and III only
    C. III and IV only
    D. I, II, III and IV

11. An investor who owns shares of a mutual fund in fact owns

    A. an undivided interest in the fund's debt capitalization
    B. specific shares of stock in the fund's portfolio
    C. an undivided interest in the fund's portfolio
    D. certain unspecified securities among those owned by the fund

12. The portfolio of a diversified common stock fund would MOST likely consist of

    A. all growth stocks within one particular industry
    B. stocks of many companies in many different industries
    C. convertible bonds and other debt instruments
    D. bargain stocks

13. A balanced fund is one that at all times invests

    A. a portion of its portfolio in both debt and equity instruments
    B. equal amounts of its portfolio in common stock and corporate bonds
    C. equal amounts of its portfolio in common and preferred stock
    D. a portion of its portfolio in both common stock and government securities

14. All the following are advantages of mutual fund investment EXCEPT

   A. the investor retains personal control of her investment in the mutual fund portfolio
   B. exchange privileges within a family of funds managed by the same management company
   C. the ability to invest almost any amount at any time
   D. the ability to qualify for reduced sales loads based on accumulation of investment within the fund

15. Which of the following investments would provide high appreciation potential together with high risk?

   A. Balanced fund
   B. Bond fund
   C. Income fund
   D. Sector fund

16. Which of the following is(are) characteristics of money-market funds?

   I. Portfolio of short-term debt instruments
   II. High beta
   III. Offered without a sales load
   IV. Fixed NAV

   A. I
   B. I, II and IV
   C. I, III and IV
   D. II, III and IV

17. A mutual fund's expense ratio is its expenses divided by

   A. average net assets
   B. public offering price
   C. income
   D. dividends

18. Although alternatives are available to a mutual fund issuer regarding the details of redemption procedures, by law the issuer must

   A. make payment for shares within seven days of tender
   B. inform the investor of his loss or profit
   C. redeem shares at the public offering price
   D. redeem shares at the net asset value minus the sales charge

19. A tax-exempt bond fund may invest in

   A. corporate bonds
   B. short-term money-market instruments
   C. common stock
   D. municipal bonds

20. An elderly widower explains to his rep that he requires his investments to provide high current income. The rep should recommend

   A. a growth fund
   B. a zero-coupon bond
   C. a mutual fund that matches the investor's stated objective
   D. the ZBest Widow Fund, a fund structured specifically for this type of investor

◆ Answers & Rationale

1. **B.** Utilities belong to the group known as *defensive industries*, as compared to the other types mentioned. They more consistently produce dividends, although their relative growth potential is limited. (Page 542)

2. **C.** A money-market fund has no price volatility; the rate of interest fluctuates in line with that of the instruments underlying the original money-market certificates. (Page 544)

3. **D.** Money-market instruments earn high interest rates but the rates are not guaranteed. Money-market funds are typically no-load funds with no redemption fee, but investors do pay a management fee. The interest earned on an investor's shares is computed every day and credited to the account at month end. An advantage of money-market funds is the ease with which shares can be purchased and sold. (Page 544)

4. **D.** A mutual fund shareholder owns an undivided interest in the portfolio of the investment company. Because each share represents one class of voting stock, the investor's interest in the fund reflects the number of shares owned. (Page 540)

5. **B.** A mutual fund share represents an undivided interest in the fund's portfolio. If a dividend is declared, the shareholder receives a dividend for each mutual fund share held. Dividends are paid in cash unless the investor elects to reinvest the cash distribution for the purchase of more fund shares. (Page 540)

6. **D.** A specialized or sector fund invests all of its assets in a particular type of security or a particular industry. (Page 543)

7. **A.** This fund is invested in both stock and bonds; it is likely to be a balanced fund. The percentage invested in the two types of securities will be adjusted to maximize the yield that can be obtained. The percentages are seldom fixed. (Page 543)

8. **D.** Municipal bonds are considered second only to U.S. government securities in terms of safety. Also, interest received from the bonds is exempt from federal income tax. (Page 544)

9. **D.** All of these elements should be checked when assessing a fund. (Page 545)

10. **B.** Money-market instruments are considered short-term, very liquid debt instruments. Because common stock is equity, it would not be in a money-market fund. (Page 544)

11. **C.** Each shareholder owns an undivided (mutual) interest in the fund portfolio. (Page 540)

12. **B.** A diversified common stock fund will have stocks from many companies and many industries. (Page 542)

13. **A.** Balanced funds carry both equity and debt issues but not necessarily in equal amounts. (Page 543)

14. **A.** Control of the investment is given over to the investment manager. All of the other items mentioned are considered advantages. (Page 540)

15. **D.** A specialized or sector fund offers a higher appreciation potential (coupled with higher risk) than an income-oriented fund. (Page 543)

16. **C.** Money-market mutual funds invest in a portfolio of short-term debt instruments such as T bills, commercial paper and repos. They are offered without a sales load or charge. The principal objective of the fund is to generate current interest income, and generally the NAV does not appreciate. (Page 544)

17. **A.** By dividing a mutual fund's expenses by its average net assets, you can calculate the fund's expense ratio. (Page 546)

18. **A.** The Investment Company Act of 1940 requires an open-end investment company to redeem shares upon request within seven days from receipt of the request. (Page 540)

19. **D.** The fund will distribute taxable income or dividends unless it invests in municipal bonds. Because the fund's stated investment objective is to provide tax-exempt income, it must invest in instruments that enable it to achieve this objective.
(Page 544)

20. **C.** Investors should be careful not to be misled by a mutual fund's name. Although the name of a fund should bear a resemblance to its objective, the investor and the rep should read the fund's prospectus carefully to be sure that the fund's objective matches the investor's. Growth funds and zero-coupon bonds are not designed to meet the requirement of providing maximum current income.
(Page 545)

77 Investment Company Registration Exam

1. The shareholders of an investment company must vote to approve a change

   I. from a diversified company to a nondiversified company
   II. from an open-end company to a closed-end company
   III. in operations that would cause the firm to cease business as an investment company
   IV. in the objectives of the fund

   A. I and IV only
   B. II and III only
   C. II, III and IV only
   D. I, II, III and IV

2. In order to make a public offering, a registered investment company must have a minimum net worth of

   A. $100,000
   B. $1,000,000
   C. $10,000,000
   D. $100,000,000

3. Each of the following is considered an investment company EXCEPT a

   A. face-amount certificate company
   B. company that has invested 65% of its assets in securities
   C. bank investment advisory account
   D. company that issues redeemable securities

4. Which of the following actions is permissible if the investment company receives the approval of a majority of its voting shares?

   A. Participating in a joint trading account
   B. Lending money to other corporations for use as venture capital
   C. Selling portfolio securities short
   D. Purchasing government bonds on margin

5. An investment company must register with the SEC, and in doing so must provide all of the following information EXCEPT its

   A. intention to borrow money
   B. intended trading practices
   C. present or future plans to issue senior securities
   D. intention to concentrate its investments in a single industry

6. SEC rules and regulations regarding securities issued by investment companies prohibit

    I.   closed-end funds from issuing preferred stock
    II. open-end funds from issuing preferred stock
    III. closed-end funds from issuing bonds
    IV. open-end funds from issuing bonds

    A. I and II
    B. I and IV
    C. II and III
    D. II and IV

7. A senior security is one issued under the

    A. Investment Company Act of 1940
    B. Investment Advisers Act of 1940
    C. Maloney Act
    D. Trust Indenture Act of 1939

8. According to the Investment Company Act of 1940, what is the minimum amount of net assets a fund must have before it can sell shares to the public?

    A. $10,000
    B. $100,000
    C. $500,000
    D. $1,000,000

9. An open-end investment company may do all of the following EXCEPT

    A. continuously offer shares
    B. borrow money
    C. lend money
    D. issue bonds

10. The Investment Company Act of 1940 allows closed-end investment companies which of the following privileges that are not allowed open-end investment companies?

    A. To issue preferred stock
    B. To issue voting stock
    C. To borrow money from a bank
    D. To borrow more than one-third of its NAV

11. An open-end investment company wishes to change its investment objective. It may do so only with a

    A. majority vote of the outstanding shares
    B. majority vote of the outstanding shareholders
    C. two-thirds vote of the outstanding shareholders
    D. unanimous vote of the board of directors

12. An open-end investment company must maintain what percentage of net assets to debt?

    A. 33 1/3%
    B. 50%
    C. 100%
    D. 300%

13. The Investment Company Act of 1940 requires that a mutual fund

    I.   issue a statement of investment policy
    II. have $100,000 minimum capitalization
    III. ensure that 40% of the directors are neither officers nor investment advisers of the company

    A. I only
    B. II only
    C. II and III only
    D. I, II and III

14. Which of the following statement(s) is(are) true regarding money-market funds?

    I.   The rate of return is generally two points over the prime rate.
    II. The owners are shareholders.
    III. A prospectus must precede or accompany the original purchase.
    IV. The client is subject to a substantial penalty for early withdrawal.

    A. I
    B. I and II
    C. II and III
    D. II and IV

15. Which of the following are required of investment companies under the Securities Act of 1933?

I. Filing a registration statement with the SEC
II. Providing a prospectus to potential purchasers
III. Publishing a tombstone advertisment giving the name of the issuer and a brief description of the issuer's type of business
IV. Obtaining the SEC's approval of the truthfulness of the information in the prospectus

A. I and II only
B. I and III only
C. II and IV only
D. I, II, III and IV

16. Financial information cannot be used in a prospectus if the information is aged more than

A. 60 days
B. 9 months
C. 12 months
D. 16 months

17. An investment company offering securities registered under the act of 1933 may make which of the following statements?

I. "The SEC has passed on the merits of these securities as an investment."
II. "The SEC has passed on the adequacy of the information in our prospectus."
III. "The SEC has passed on the accuracy of the information in our prospectus."
IV. "These securities have been approved for retirement accounts and institutional clients by the SEC."

A. I
B. I and II
C. II, III and IV
D. None of the above

18. A member firm can be sued for damages if an investor purchases an open-end fund and

I. receives no prospectus
II. is told an untrue statement by the member or by a person associated with the member
III. is given a prospectus that omits a material fact
IV. loses 20% or more in the investment within the first 30 days after the initial purchase

A. I
B. I, II and III
C. II and III
D. II, III and IV

19. A prospectus must be delivered to the purchaser of a unit investment trust

A. prior to the purchase
B. with the first confirmation
C. with each confirmation
D. between 45 days and 18 months following the initial deposit

20. All of the following would be violations of NASD rules EXCEPT

A. sending a prospect a prospectus and sales literature at the same time
B. selling a mutual fund without first distributing a prospectus
C. selling a mutual fund with sales literature that is not a prospectus describing the fund's performance over a ten-year period
D. sending a customer sales literature that represents performance history for five years for a fund that has been in existence for ten years

21. An investor must be provided with a "Statement of Additional Information" about a mutual fund

A. annually
B. in addition to the prospectus
C. upon request
D. included in the prospectus

22. In a mutual fund portfolio, it is permissible to buy all of the following securities EXCEPT

A. index options
B. junk bonds
C. shares of other mutual funds
D. stock on margin

◆ Answers & Rationale

1. **D.** Any substantive change in the form, structure, investment objectives or business operations of an investment company must be approved by a majority vote of the outstanding shares.
(Page 551)

2. **A.** No investment company may register an offering with the SEC unless it has a minimum net worth of $100,000 (or will have within 90 days).
(Page 548)

3. **C.** A bank advisory account is specifically exempted from the definition of an investment company.
(Page 549)

4. **B.** Mutual funds may not participate in joint accounts, sell short or buy securities on margin, regardless of approval by a majority vote. An investment company may lend money as long as the practice conforms to the company's investment policy.
(Page 551)

5. **B.** Investment companies do not need to outline their trading practices. However, the registration statement is required to describe any intent to borrow money or issue senior securities. A company's concentration of investments would be part of its required investment policy description.
(Page 548)

6. **D.** Closed-end funds are permitted to issue more than one class of securities, including debt issues and preferred stock. Open-end funds are allowed to issue only one class of voting stock; they are prohibited from issuing any senior security. Open-end funds may borrow from a bank, but they are limited to the same asset coverage requirements as closed-end funds that issue debt (300%).
(Page 550)

7. **D.** The term "senior security" generally indicates a corporate security that has certain rights and preferences over other securities in the event of a liquidation or dissolution of a corporation (corporate debt would be considered senior to common stock). All nonexempt corporate debt security issues of $1,000,000 or more must be issued under the Trust Indenture Act of 1939. Investment company securities are required to be registered under the act of 1940. Persons who give investment advice for a fee must register under the Investment Advisers Act of 1940. The Maloney Act allows for the registration of self-regulatory organizations (such as the NASD and the NYSE).   (Page 550)

8. **B.** Before operations can begin, an investment company must have a net capital of at least $100,000. Thereafter the net capital can fluctuate.
(Page 548)

9. **D.** A mutual fund is prohibited from issuing any senior securities, although it may purchase just about any type of security as an investment. All shares of a mutual fund must be of the same class.
(Page 550)

10. **A.** A closed-end company may issue different classes of securities: common stock, preferred stock and bonds. An open-end company may issue only one class of stock.   (Page 550)

11. **A.** The Investment Company Act of 1940 requires the fund to have a clearly defined investment objective. The only action that can be taken to change the investment objective is a majority vote of the outstanding shares (shares vote, not shareholders).   (Page 551)

12. **D.** The Investment Company Act of 1940 prohibits a mutual fund from borrowing more than one-third of its net asset value. In other words, the fund must maintain at least 300% assets to debt.
(Page 548)

13. **D.** The Investment Company Act of 1940 requires a mutual fund to have an initial capitalization of $100,000, at least 100 shareholders and a clearly defined investment objective. Additionally, the interlocking directorate rules state that at least 40% of the fund's directors must be independent from the operations of the fund.   (Page 548)

14. **C.** All mutual funds, as new issues, require delivery of a prospectus; there is no penalty for

early withdrawal. Investors are shareholders in the fund and have voting rights. The interest rate depends on the performance of the fund's portfolio, and is not pegged to the prime rate.   (Page 549)

15. **A.** The Securities Act of 1933 sets forth the registration and prospectus requirements for all companies contemplating the issuance of securities. There is no requirement to publish a tombstone; and the SEC does not approve, pass on the adequacy of, or pass on the completeness of an offering.   (Page 550)

16. **D.** An investment company may distribute a prospectus to prospective investors if the information it contains is no more than 16 months old. The fund is also required to send an audited financial report to current shareholders at least annually and an unaudited one every six months.

(Page 549)

17. **D.** The SEC neither approves nor disapproves of an issue, nor does it pass on the adequacy, accuracy or completeness of the information presented in a prospectus.   (Page 550)

18. **B.** Federal securities laws require that purchasers of newly issued securities be given a full disclosure of material information concerning the issuer and the security. Choice I states that the purchaser received no disclosures. Choices II and III imply a measure of fraud or improper disclosure, and in each of these cases the purchaser could

sue to recover damages and costs. A drop in an investment's value (choice IV) is not grounds for suit—unless the loss was directly related to improper disclosure by the company.   (Page 550)

19. **B.** Purchasers of newly issued securities must receive a prospectus no later than with receipt of the confirmation of their purchase.   (Page 549)

20. **A.** Any solicitation for sale must be preceded or accompanied by a prospectus that meets the guidelines put forth by the Securities Act of 1933.   (Page 549)

21. **C.** The "Statement of Additional Information" may be obtained by the investor upon request from the fund. The prospectus contains information on the fund's objective, investment policies, sales charges and management expenses, services offered and a 10-year history of per share capital changes. The "Statement of Additional Information" typically contains the fund's consolidated financial statements including the balance sheet, statement of operations, income statement and portfolio list at the time the statement was compiled.   (Page 550)

22. **D.** Mutual funds may not purchase securities on margin because, in the event of a margin call, they have no recourse to investors' funds. A fund is not prohibited from buying options, low-quality bonds and other mutual funds. (Page 551)

78 Management of Investment Companies Exam

1. If its policy permits such loans, an investment company may loan money to one of its officers

    A. if it notifies both the SEC and the NASD in writing
    B. if a majority of the voting shareholders approve the loan prior to its taking effect
    C. if the board of directors issues a statement of approval and gives the shareholders notice through a quarterly statement
    D. under no circumstances

2. What is the minimum percentage of a fund's outstanding stock that Belle Charolais would have to own in order for her to be considered an affiliated person of that investment company?

    A. 5%
    B. 10%
    C. 25%
    D. 75%

3. The Securities and Exchange Commission would consider which of the following to be affiliated persons of an investment company?

    I. Customer who owns 5% of the investment company's shares
    II. Corporation in which the investment company has a 22% ownership
    III. Treasurer of the Amusement Technology Fund
    IV. Amusement Technology Fund's independent investment adviser

    A. I, II and III only
    B. I and III only
    C. II and IV only
    D. I, II, III and IV

4. The maximum length of a contract that an investment company may enter into with its investment adviser is

    A. one year
    B. two years
    C. three years
    D. five years

5. When selecting a board of directors, a registered investment company must take care not to include more than what percentage of interested persons?

   A. 10%
   B. 40%
   C. 50%
   D. 60%

6. Each registered investment company must provide and maintain a fidelity bond covering each officer and employee of the company. The minimum amount of the bond is determined by the

   A. number of people the bond covers
   B. capital reserves of the company if it is currently under 27(d) for surrender rights
   C. total gross assets of the company
   D. board of directors at its annual bond advisory meeting

7. Under the Investment Company Act of 1940, investment companies must

   I. limit the membership of their boards of directors to a maximum of 60% interested persons
   II. state and adhere to their investment objectives
   III. maintain adequate debt/equity diversification
   IV. have a minimum of $100,000 in capital before embarking on a public offering

   A. I
   B. I and II
   C. I, II and IV
   D. III and IV

8. The board of directors of a mutual fund cannot be elected for a term exceeding

   A. one year
   B. two years
   C. three years
   D. five years

9. Which of the following are functions of an investment company's custodian bank?

   I. Safekeeping of portfolio securities and cash
   II. Providing portfolio advice regarding transactions
   III. Maintaining books and records for accumulation plans
   IV. Safekeeping of customer securities

   A. I and III only
   B. I, III and IV only
   C. II and IV only
   D. I, II, III and IV

10. All of the following are interested persons under the Investment Company Act of 1940 EXCEPT

   I. a broker-dealer registered under the Securities Act of 1933
   II. an employee of the fund's investment adviser
   III. the SEC
   IV. members of the board of directors

   A. I, II and IV only
   B. III only
   C. III and IV only
   D. I, II, III and IV

11. A management investment company must do all of the following EXCEPT

   A. hold all portfolio securities in a custodian bank
   B. hold all cash in a custodian bank
   C. maintain a bond for persons who have access to monies or securities
   D. investigate the employment record of the officers of the custodian bank

12. A noninterested member of a board of directors would include a director

    A. whose spouse is the principal underwriter
    B. whose only involvement with the company is her role as a member of the board
    C. who is the attorney for the investment adviser
    D. who is also president of the custodian bank

13. Under the Investment Company Act of 1940, shareholders must receive financial reports

    A. monthly
    B. quarterly
    C. semiannually
    D. annually

14. The contract between an investment company and its investment adviser must

    A. be approved annually by the shareholders
    B. show the compensation paid by the investment company to the adviser
    C. be approved annually by the directors
    D. meet all of the above requirements

15. CBS Investment Services charges a fee for its services in managing several mutual funds. Which of the following would be included in the services CBS supplies?

    I. Ensuring that the fund portfolio meets diversification requirements
    II. Attempting to meet the investment objectives of the fund
    III. Analyzing the market and deciding when securities in the portfolio should be bought or sold
    IV. Changing investment objectives in order to maximize potential gain for the shareholders

    A. I, II and III only
    B. I and IV only
    C. II and III only
    D. I, II, III and IV

16. Usually the fee received by the management company from an investment company depends on the

    A. net assets of the fund
    B. profit of the fund
    C. volume of new shares sold
    D. type of securities in the fund portfolio

17. The money holder of a mutual fund's account would generally be a

    A. commercial bank
    B. investment banker
    C. savings and loan association
    D. stock exchange member

18. The investment adviser's contract must be approved by the

    A. board of governors of the NASD
    B. SEC
    C. NASD district committee
    D. board of directors of the fund and the shareholders

19. The investment adviser in a regulated, diversified open-end investment company performs which of the following functions?

    I. Makes sure the fund invests in such a manner as to retain its diversified status
    II. Attempts to fulfill the fund's investment objective by means of careful investing
    III. Changes investment objectives as he believes is in the best interest of the investors
    IV. Investigates the tax status of potential investments

    A. I, II and III
    B. I, II and IV
    C. II and IV
    D. III and IV

20. An investment adviser of a mutual fund can liquidate shares held in the fund's portfolio

   A. only with the consent of a majority vote of the shareholders
   B. only with the consent of the board of directors
   C. as long as the liquidation is within the guidelines set forth by the fund's objective
   D. only with the consent of the board of directors and a majority vote of the shareholders

21. Mutual funds are like other types of corporations in that

   I. they may issue equity and debt
   II. the board of directors makes policy decisions
   III. shareholders have ownership rights

   A. I and III only
   B. II only
   C. II and III only
   D. I, II and III

22. According to the Investment Company Act of 1940

   I. a fund must have $1,000,000 in assets before it may begin operations
   II. at least 40% of the board of directors must be noninterested persons
   III. a fund must have at least 100 shareholders before it may begin operations
   IV. a fund may not borrow more than 33 1/3% of its asset value

   A. I and III only
   B. II, III and IV only
   C. II and IV only
   D. I, II, III and IV

23. June Polar wants to buy $1,000 worth of an open-end investment company. She may buy shares through

   I. the sponsor of the fund
   II. a brokerage firm
   III. the custodian of the fund
   IV. a bank acting as dealer

   A. I and II
   B. I, II and IV
   C. II
   D. III and IV

24. The principal underwriter of an open-end investment company is also known as the

   A. sponsor
   B. dealer
   C. trustee
   D. registrar

25. Which of the following has the authority to approve an investment adviser's contract with the investment company?

   A. NASD District Business Conduct Committee
   B. Board of directors of the fund
   C. Board of governors of the NASD
   D. SEC

◆ Answers & Rationale

1. **D.** An investment company is not permitted to make loans to affiliated or interested persons under any circumstances. An officer is an affiliated person of an investment company.   (Page 556)

2. **A.** An affiliated person is any person owning 5% of a company's stock. Also, an investment adviser, or depositor of assets (in the case of a unit trust), is an affiliated person.   (Page 555)

3. **D.** By definition, an affiliated person includes: a person who owns a 5% or greater share in the company; a corporation in which the investment company has a 5% or greater holding; all officers and directors; all investment advisers; and all depositors of assets (in unit trusts). (Page 555)

4. **B.** Investment advisory contracts must be approved annually by the investment company's board of directors, its shareholders or both. Such contracts have a maximum length of up to two years, but are subject to annual reapproval.
(Page 554)

5. **D.** The Investment Company Act of 1940 requires that at least 40% of the board be independent (that is, noninterested) directors. Consequently, no more than 60% of the directors can be interested persons as defined by the act.
(Page 553)

6. **C.** The SEC sets minimum bonding requirements based on an investment company's gross assets at the end of the most recent fiscal quarter.   (Page 558)

7. **C.** According to the Investment Company Act of 1940, 40% of a company's directors must be independent, a company must state and follow a clearly defined investment objective (which may be changed only with a majority vote of the outstanding shares), and a company must have a minimum of $100,000 in assets before it may begin to operate.   (Page 553)

8. **D.** The board of directors may be appointed for a minimum of one year and a maximum of five years.   (Page 553)

9. **A.** The custodian bank performs bookkeeping and clerical functions and, principally, retains the fund's cash and securities for safekeeping. The adviser offers portfolio advice and management services. The custodian does not provide for safekeeping of investors' securities.   (Page 556)

10. **C.** Interested persons are those who may influence, or are associated with, a person in control. The SEC, although interested in the workings of an investment company, is a regulator and is not defined as an interested person. A director of an investment company is an affiliated person but is not considered an interested person if he acts only in the capacity of a director.   (Page 555)

11. **D.** The investment company is not required (and would probably find it difficult) to investigate the employment records of the officers of its custodian bank. The Investment Company Act of 1940 requires only that investment companies keep all cash and securities with a custodian bank and maintain a bond.   (Page 556)

12. **B.** A director who holds no other position in the fund is exempt from the interested person definition. However, a director associated with or employed in another capacity with the fund is considered interested. The act of 1940 requires that at least 40% of the directors are independent (that is, noninterested persons).   (Page 555)

13. **C.** Investment company shareholders must receive financial reports at least semiannually (that is, every six months).   (Page 559)

14. **D.** The advisory contract can be approved by the board, the shareholders or both. The contract must be in writing and must indicate the compensation paid to the adviser.   (Page 554)

15. **A.** The objective of the fund may be changed only by a majority vote of the outstanding shares. The fund manager is assigned the day-to-day management responsibilities of the fund. Du-

ties would include attempting to meet the objective as set out by the fund and buying and selling securities to be held in the portfolio.   (Page 554)

16. **A.** The management company usually receives a fee based on the average annual net assets of the fund managed.   (Page 554)

17. **A.** The money holder of a mutual fund is its custodian. In most instances, the custodian will be a commercial bank.   (Page 556)

18. **D.** The investment adviser's contract is approved annually by the board of directors and/or a majority vote of the outstanding shares (shareholders).   (Page 554)

19. **B.** The investment adviser is responsible for making investments according to the objective stipulated by the fund. The fund's objective may be changed only with a majority vote of the outstanding shares.   (Page 554)

20. **C.** A mutual fund investment adviser is given authority to select and make investments in the fund portfolio. The fund must follow the adviser's advice.   (Page 554)

21. **C.** Mutual funds may issue only one class of voting stock. Like corporate stockholders, mutual fund shareholders do have various rights, one of which is the right to elect the board of directors, which sets policies for the fund.   (Page 553)

22. **B.** A company must have commitments for at least $100,000 in assets before it begins operations. All of the other items listed are true.
(Page 553)

23. **A.** The custodian does not sell the shares, but holds them for safekeeping. A bank cannot be a member of the NASD and therefore cannot act as a dealer (although subsidiaries independent of the bank may be set up as broker-dealers). (Page 557)

24. **A.** The term "sponsor" is synonymous with the term "underwriter."   (Page 557)

25. **B.** The investment adviser's contract is approved by the board of directors of the fund and often a majority vote of the outstanding fund shares. An investment adviser must be registered with, not approved by, the SEC.   (Page 554)

Mutual Fund Marketing, Pricing and Valuation Exam

1. A registered representative is seeking to sell shares in an investment company to a client. Which of the following statements would be accurate and permissible for him to say regarding his recommendation?

   I. "When you redeem your shares, you will not know immediately the dollar value of your redeemed shares."
   II. "If you purchase the shares of two or more funds in the same family of funds, you may be entitled to a reduced sales charge."
   III. "If you invest just before the dividend distribution, you can benefit by receiving the added value of that dividend."

   A. I and II only
   B. I and III only
   C. II and III only
   D. I, II and III

2. What services must a mutual fund sponsor offer in order to be permitted to charge the maximum allowable sales charge for the fund shares?

   I. Rights of accumulation
   II. The privilege to reinvest dividend distributions at no sales charge
   III. Price breakpoints offering reduced commissions for larger purchases

   A. I and II only
   B. I and III only
   C. II and III only
   D. I, II and III

3. Lotta Leveridge signed a letter of intent stating that she would purchase $25,000 worth of ACE Fund over the next 9 months. After 13 months, she had invested only $12,000. What will be the effect of her actions?

   A. Her entire investment will be charged an 8 1/2% sales charge.
   B. She qualifies for the second breakpoint only, and will be charged 8%.
   C. The entire amount is still due because she signed a binding contract when she signed the letter of intent.
   D. Nothing; she will be charged whatever sales charge she is entitled to for the actual amount she invested.

4. Minnie Leveridge is explaining mutual funds to a prospective investor. Which of the following statements could she use?

   I. "Mutual fund shares are liquid, so you can use them as either short-term or long-term investments."
   II. "The fund will always redeem shares at NAV, so there is very little chance of a financial loss."
   III. "The redemption value of the shares fluctuates according to the value of the fund's portfolio."
   IV. "Because mutual funds are required to make payment within seven days of redemption, you will always be able to receive a return of your original investment."

   A. I, II and IV
   B. I and III
   C. III
   D. III and IV

5. An investment company share that is purchased at its net asset value and can be redeemed later at the then current net asset value is a share issued by a(n)

   A. open-end investment company
   B. closed-end investment company
   C. front-end load company
   D. no-load open-end investment company

6. In order to get cash for an emergency that arose, Max Leveridge redeemed his shares in a mutual fund that offered reinstatement privileges. Within how many days of redemption could he reinvest in the same fund without having to pay additional sales charges?

   A. 7
   B. 30
   C. 45
   D. 60

7. The NASD allows sales charges up to a maximum of

   A. 9% on mutual funds and variable annuities
   B. 9% on mutual funds and contractual plans
   C. 8 1/2% on mutual funds and contractual plans
   D. 8 1/2% on mutual funds and variable annuities

8. In general, the NASD Rules of Fair Practice permit selling concessions and discounts

   A. as consideration for services rendered by nonmember broker-dealers in obtaining business
   B. to member broker-dealers engaged in the investment banking or securities business
   C. to anyone that deals in securities transactions
   D. within certain percentage limits

9. The maximum sales load may be charged on the purchase of shares from an open-end investment company that offers

   I. dividend reinvestment
   II. rights of accumulation
   III. quantity discounts
   IV. exchange privileges

   A. I and II only
   B. I, II and III only
   C. III and IV only
   D. I, II, III and IV

10. A purchase or redemption order for investment company shares must be executed at a price based on the

   A. net asset value next computed after the fund receives the order
   B. net asset value last computed before the fund receives the order
   C. net asset value computed at the close of trading on the NYSE on the day before the fund receives the order
   D. best net asset value computed the same day the fund receives the order

11. Which of the following describes a qualified investor eligible for a quantity discount?

   I. Pension plan trustee
   II. Investor in an individual retirement account
   III. Investment club
   IV. Woman and her husband in a joint account

   A. I and II only
   B. I, II and IV only
   C. III and IV only
   D. I, II, III and IV

12. The quantity of securities an investor owns for purposes of rights of accumulation could be based on the

   I. current net asset value of the securities
   II. current public offering price of the securities
   III. total purchases of shares at the actual offering prices
   IV. current value of all redeemable securities owned by the investor within the same family of funds

   A. I and III only
   B. II only
   C. III only
   D. I, II, III and IV

13. Letters of intent can be backdated up to how many days?

   A. 30
   B. 60
   C. 90
   D. 120

14. A member can allow reduced sales charges for purchases by nonmembers under certain circumstances. Among these are

   I. the signing of a letter of intent by the customer
   II. a lump-sum purchase that qualifies for a breakpoint
   III. additional purchases that qualify for breakpoints under rights of accumulation
   IV. special level access charges

   A. I
   B. I, II and III
   C. I and IV
   D. II and III

15. A "sales load" is defined as the

   A. difference between the public offering price and the net asset value
   B. commissions paid on the purchase or sale of securities
   C. fee paid to the investment adviser
   D. concessions allowed on the purchase or sale of securities

16. The practice of selling mutual fund shares at a dollar amount immediately below the price stated in the prospectus that would qualify an investor to receive a reduced sales charge is called

   A. breakpoint selling
   B. conditional orders
   C. selling dividends
   D. freeriding and withholding

17. An investor is redeeming 200 shares in the ACE Fund. The current POP is $12.50, and the NAV is $11.50. The investor will receive

   A. $2,200
   B. $2,300
   C. $2,400
   D. $2,500

18. If the value of securities held in a fund's portfolio increases and the amount of liabilities stays the same, the net assets of the fund will

A. increase
B. decrease
C. stay the same
D. be more liquid

19. The ArGood Mutual Fund experienced an unrealized loss last month. This loss will result in

I. a lower NAV per share
II. lower dividend payments to the shareholders
III. a reduction in the proceeds payable to shareholders who liquidate their shares

A. I and II only
B. I and III only
C. II and III only
D. I, II and III

20. A customer wishes to redeem 1,000 shares of a mutual fund. The bid and ask quote is 11–11.58. A 1/2% redemption fee will be charged. How much will the customer receive?

A. $10,945
B. $11,000
C. $11,522
D. $11,580

21. A client deposits $2,200 in an open-end investment company. After 60 days, he signs a letter of intent for the $10,000 breakpoint. Six months later, he deposits $11,000. He will

A. receive a reduced load on $1,000 worth of the shares
B. receive a reduced load on $8,800 worth of the shares
C. receive the beneficial effect of a reduced load on $13,200 worth of the shares
D. not receive any break in the sales load

22. The exchange privilege offered by open-end investment companies allows investors to

A. exchange personally owned securities for shares of the investment company
B. exchange shares of one open-end fund for those of another fund in the same company on a net asset value basis
C. purchase new fund shares from dividends
D. delay payment of taxes

23. To qualify for the quantity discount, which of the following could NOT be joined together under the definition of "any person"?

I. A father and his 35-year-old son investing in separate accounts
II. A husband and wife investing in a joint account
III. A husband and wife investing in a separate account
IV. A trust officer working on behalf of a single trust account

A. I
B. II, III and IV
C. II and IV
D. III and IV

24. A letter of intent for a mutual fund does NOT contain which of the following provisions?

A. The time limit is 13 months.
B. The letter can be backdated 90 days to include a previous deposit.
C. The fund can halt redemption during the period of time the letter of intent is in effect.
D. The fund might keep some of the initially issued shares in an escrow account to ensure full payment of the full spread.

25. Class A shares of a mutual fund have a

A. back-end load
B. level load
C. front-end load
D. asset-based fee

26. The price of a no-load mutual fund can be described by all of the following EXCEPT

   A. POP
   B. NAV
   C. bid
   D. book value

27. A mutual fund collects 12b-1 fees. Which of the following statements are true?

   I. The fund may use the money to pay for mailing sales literature.
   II. Advertising materials may state that the fund is no-load.
   III. The fund may use the money to pay for commissions on securities transactions.
   IV. The fund's prospectus is required to disclose the fee.

   A. I and II only
   B. I and IV only
   C. II and III only
   D. I, II, III and IV

28. When is the sales charge deducted from purchases of mutual fund shares made under a letter of intent?

   A. Monthly
   B. Annually
   C. When each purchase is made
   D. When each letter of intent is completed

◆ Answers & Rationale

1. **A.** Purchase of two funds in the same family of funds may qualify an investor for combination privileges. At redemption, he will receive the next price calculated (forward pricing), which is not yet known. Purchase of a mutual fund just prior to a dividend distribution is a detriment: the distribution about to be paid is included in the purchase price and, when received by the investor, will be treated as ordinary income—even though he is essentially being returned a portion of his investment.   (Page 569)

2. **D.** NASD rules prohibit sales charges in excess of 8 1/2% on mutual fund purchases by public customers. Unless a mutual fund grants its shareholders certain privileges, the amount charged must be lower than 8 1/2%. To qualify for the maximum sales charge (8 1/2%), *all* of the following privileges must be extended to the fund's shareholders:

- rights of accumulation
- dividend reinvestment at net asset value
- quantity discounts (breakpoints)

(Page 567)

3. **D.** An LOI is not a binding contract, so the customer is not required to deposit the rest of the money. She will be entitled to whatever breakpoint her $12,000 investment qualifies for.   (Page 568)

4. **C.** Mutual funds are very marketable but, because of the sales charge, they are recommended for long-term investments. Shares are redeemed at NAV. However, the NAV will fluctuate, and upon redemption the investor may have more or less money than originally invested.   (Page 562)

5. **D.** A share purchased at its NAV and sold at its NAV is a no-load fund. NAV plus the sales charge equals the POP; if there is no sales charge, the NAV equals the POP.   (Page 561)

6. **B.** Funds offering the reinstatement privilege allow the investor to redeem and reinvest shares within 30 days without an additional sales charge. The privilege can be used only once, and only the amount withdrawn can be reinstated.   (Page 570)

7. **D.** The NASD's maximum allowable sales charges are: contractual plans (periodic pay unit trusts), 9%; mutual funds, 8 1/2%; variable annuities, 8 1/2%.   (Page 563)

8. **B.** NASD Rules of Fair Practice permit member broker-dealers to allow concessions and discounts only to other members. There are some exceptions, such as dealings in exempt securities or with foreign nonmembers.   (Page 561)

9. **B.** Investment companies may charge the maximum sales load if they offer all of the following benefits: dividend reinvestment, rights of accumulation and quantity discounts (also known as *breakpoints*). If none of these services is offered, a member cannot assess a sales charge of more than 6.25%.   (Page 567)

10. **A.** Purchase or redemption of mutual fund shares may occur at the net asset value next calculated after the order is received; this is known as *forward pricing*.   (Page 570)

11. **B.** The NASD defines a "person" as: any individual; a joint account held by any combination of an individual, spouse or children; or a trustee purchasing for a single account. It allows quantity discounts to any of these. Investment clubs do not qualify under the definition, nor do groups of individuals who form a business or organization for the sole purpose of investment.   (Page 568)

12. **D.** All of the methods listed are permitted. The choice is up to the investment company; however, it must disclose the method it chooses. (Generally the greater of choices I or III is the option offered.)   (Page 569)

13. **C.** The time limit for a letter of intent (LOI) is 13 months, but the letter can be backdated by up to 90 days from the date it was filed.   (Page 569)

14. **B.** Reduced sales charges are allowed for purchases made under a letter of intent, large purchases that have reached breakpoints and purchases made under a customer's rights of accumulation.
(Page 567)

15. **A.** A sales load is the difference between the public offering price and the amount actually added to the investment company's portfolio (at the current NAV). Commissions, concessions and allowances are part of the sales load.   (Page 564)

16. **A.** The term "breakpoint sale" refers to a sale made just below a breakpoint (that point at which an investor would qualify for a quantity discount) for the sole purpose of earning a higher commission.   (Page 570)

17. **B.** Shares are redeemed at NAV. If the investor is redeeming 200 shares at an NAV of $11.50, he will receive $2,300 (200 × $11.50).
(Page 571)

18. **A.** An appreciation in value of fund assets without an attendant increase in liabilities would lead to an increase in the fund's net asset value (assets − liabilities = NAV).   (Page 562)

19. **B.** An unrealized loss is the same as a depreciation in asset value, which results in a lower NAV per share. An investor would receive less at redemption than he would have received if the redemption had taken place prior to the depreciation of the asset.   (Page 562)

20. **A.** Always redeem at NAV (bid): 1,000 shares × 11 = $11,000. Next, determine the redemption fee: $11,000 × .005 (a 1/2% redemption fee) = $55. Finally, subtract the fee from the gross redemption proceeds: $11,000 − $55 = $10,945. A shortcut alternative to the last two steps is to multiply the gross redemption proceeds by the complement of the redemption fee: $11,000 × .995 = $10,945.   (Page 571)

21. **C.** An investor signing a letter of intent has 13 months to contribute funds to reach the reduced load. The investor may also backdate a letter within 90 days to include an amount previously deposited.
(Page 568)

22. **B.** Exchange privileges allow investors to move from fund to fund within a family of funds without paying an additional sales charge.
(Page 570)

23. **A.** For the purpose of qualifying for breakpoints, the definition of "any person" includes family units, but only minor children—not someone 35 years old.   (Page 568)

24. **C.** A letter of intent is not binding on the client in any way. Should the client decide to liquidate the account prior to completion of the letter, the company may reduce the redemption only by the amount of shares held in escrow.   (Page 568)

25. **C.** Class A shares have a front-end load; Class B shares have a back-end load; and Class C shares have a level load that is an asset-based fee.
(Page 564)

26. **A.** No-load open-end investment company shares are sold to investors and redeemed through the issuer at their book value, which is the same as their net asset value or "bid" price.   (Page 562)

27. **B.** 12b-1 fees may be used only to cover promotional expenses for funds that act as distributors of their own shares. The amount of the fee must be disclosed in the prospectus, and the fund may not use the term "no-load" in any communications with the public.   (Page 565)

28. **C.** When the customer makes her first investment under a letter of intent, the reduced sales charge applies immediately. At the time each additional investment is made, the same reduced charge is deducted. If the investor does not invest the amount stated in the letter, then the full sales load applies retroactively to the total investment.
(Page 568)

80 Mutual Fund Purchase and Withdrawal Plans Exam

1. An advantage of dollar cost averaging during a bull market is that it will result in an average cost per share that is *less* than the cost of the stock on any given day, assuming that

   I. the price of the underlying shares fluctuates
   II. a set number of shares is purchased regularly
   III. a set dollar amount is invested regularly
   IV. a set dollar amount of investments is maintained

   A. I and II
   B. I and III
   C. II and III
   D. III and IV

2. After opening an account in a mutual fund, an investor can generally make additional periodic investments in minimum amounts

   A. of $50
   B. of $100
   C. of $500
   D. as set forth in the prospectus

3. Under the spread-load plan provision of the 1970 amendments to the Investment Company Act of 1940, an investor may have no more than what percentage deducted from any one payment?

   A. 8 1/2%
   B. 9%
   C. 16%
   D. 20%

4. A customer canceling a contractual plan will have all of his sales charge refunded if he cancels the plan within

   A. 15 days of receiving the notice by the custodian bank
   B. 30 days of the mailing of the notice by the custodian bank
   C. 45 days of the mailing of the notice by the custodian bank
   D. 18 months of receiving the notice from the custodian bank

5. The average sales charge on a spread-load contractual plan over the plan's first four years can be no more than

   A. 9%
   B. 16%
   C. 20%
   D. 50%

6. A customer purchased a front-end load periodic payment plan last year. The investment company stopped receiving payments from her after six months. Because she hasn't been heard from for the last four months, the investment company

   A. must recalculate the deposits, retain its 50% sales charge and return the balance from the escrow account
   B. must send a notice to the customer informing her of both the value of the account and the refund to which she is entitled if she decides to cancel the plan
   C. must refund all sales charges in excess of 15% of the deposits and return the net asset value of her investment
   D. may sue the customer for the past due payment(s)

7. A subscriber to a front-end load contractual plan that has a ten-year life is expected to make payments totaling $12,000 over that period of time. Instead, he has decided to cancel after the tenth month and spend the remaining amount on health club dues. How much of the sales charge already paid will be refunded to him?

   A. $0
   B. $350
   C. $425
   D. $500

8. Periodic payment plan certificates represent what type of interest in the underlying securities?

   A. Divided
   B. Undivided
   C. Personal
   D. Fractional

9. The maximum sales charge on a unit investment trust using mutual funds for its underlying investment is

   A. 7%
   B. 8%
   C. 8 1/2%
   D. 9%

10. One risk of a withdrawal plan is that the

    A. sales charge for the service will be high
    B. cost basis of the shares will be high
    C. plan is illegal in many states
    D. principal value will fluctuate

11. June Polar has signed up for a mutual fund contractual plan with a 50% front-end load and $300 monthly payments. She has decided to cancel the plan after her second payment but within 45 days. If her current NAV is $340, how much will she get back from the plan?

    A. $340
    B. $550
    C. $600
    D. $640

12. An investor in a spread-load plan wants to withdraw after investing $150 a month for eight months. The plan has taken $240 in sales charges. If the NAV has not changed, how much refund will the investor receive?

    A. $600
    B. $960
    C. $1,020
    D. $1,200

13. June Polar has just invested a lump sum in the ACE Fund. If she wishes to purchase additional shares by reinvesting all dividends and capital gains, she can set up a(n)

    A. accumulation plan
    B. regular plan
    C. dollar cost averaging plan
    D. lump-sum plan

14. June Polar and Joe Kuhl each have open accounts in the ArGood Mutual Fund. June has decided to receive all distributions in cash, while Joe is automatically reinvesting all distributions. How do their decisions affect their investments?

   I. Receiving cash distributions may reduce June's proportional interest in the fund.
   II. June may use the cash distributions to purchase shares later at NAV.
   III. Joe's reinvestments purchase additional shares at NAV rather than at the offering price.

   A. I and II only
   B. I and III only
   C. II and III only
   D. I, II and III

15. Which of the following characteristics describe a contractual planholder?

   I. Receives a plan certificate
   II. Owns a specific portion of the underlying mutual fund shares
   III. Owns specific shares in the underlying portfolio
   IV. Must complete the contractual plan

   A. I and II
   B. I and III
   C. II and IV
   D. III and IV

16. Klaus Bruin has decided to terminate his contractual plan one month after opening it. At the time he opened the account, the NAV was $11.50, and it is now $11.80. He has acquired 212 shares and has paid sales charges of $930. What will Klaus's refund be?

   A. The total NAV for his shares at the time of their purchase plus 50% of the sales charges
   B. The current NAV of his shares plus all sales charges
   C. Only the current NAV of his shares
   D. The current NAV of his shares plus sales charges that exceed 15% of gross payments

17. Which of the following statements describe contractual plans?

   I. They cannot be sold in certain states.
   II. They do not obligate the planholder to complete the contracted number of payments.
   III. They have a predetermined fixed schedule of sales charges.

   A. I and II only
   B. I and III only
   C. II and III only
   D. I, II and III

18. An investor has requested a withdrawal plan from his mutual fund and is currently receiving $600 per month. This is an example of a

   A. contractual plan
   B. fixed-share periodic withdrawal plan
   C. fixed-dollar periodic withdrawal plan
   D. fixed-percentage withdrawal plan

19. June Polar owns $24,000 of ZBest Invest Fund shares. She chooses to have the money forwarded to her, using a ten-year fixed-time withdrawal. She will receive a

   A. fixed number of dollars for a variable amount of time
   B. variable number of dollars for a fixed amount of time
   C. fixed number of dollars for a fixed amount of time
   D. variable number of dollars for a variable amount of time

20. A customer has a contractual plan. The customer's daughter is in college and needs money for expenses. The customer has been investing $150 per month into the contractual plan. What would you recommend she do to provide her daughter with expense money?

A. Give the daughter $100 per month, and invest $50 per month instead of $150 per month into the contractual plan.
B. Liquidate the plan.
C. Continue to invest, and make periodic withdrawals from the plan.
D. Set up a systematic withdrawal plan, and continue to make investments.

21. A customer canceling a front-end load contractual plan will have all or part of his sales charge refunded if he cancels the plan within

A. 8 months
B. 18 months
C. 28 months
D. 38 months

◆ Answers & Rationale

1. **B.** Dollar cost averaging will result in a lower average cost per share as long as the price of the shares fluctuates, the general trend of the stock price is up, and the same number of dollars is invested during each interval.   (Page 577)

2. **D.** Periodic investments differ from fund to fund, and the rep must refer to the prospectus.
(Page 572)

3. **D.** Under the Investment Company Act Amendments of 1970, a spread-load plan cannot take more than 20% of any plan payment in the first year as a sales charge. Therefore, total sales charges cannot exceed 20% in the first year and cannot average more than 16% over the first four years of the plan. A maximum sales charge of 9% is permitted over the life of the plan; 8 1/2% is the maximum sales charge permitted by the NASD for single pay unit trusts and investment company open accounts.
(Page 574)

4. **C.** Under the Investment Company Act of 1940, contractual planholders must be allowed a full refund if they return their shares within 45 days of the mailing of the notice by the custodian bank.
(Page 575)

5. **B.** The Investment Company Act Amendments of 1970 states that a spread-load plan cannot take more than 20% of any plan payment as a sales charge and the sales charge cannot exceed an average of more than 16% over the first four years of the plan investment.   (Page 574)

6. **B.** Purchasers of front-end load plans have surrender rights for 18 months after their initial investment. The purchaser must be officially notified of these rights if she misses any three payments within the first 15 months or misses one or more payments between the 15th and the 18th month. Under these rights, the purchaser will be refunded some (but not all) of the sales charges as well as the current value of the account.   (Page 575)

7. **B.** Under the act of 1940, the subscriber would receive the sales charge of $500 (one half of the $1,000 in premiums already paid) less 15% of $1,000 ($150); $500 − $150 = $350.   (Page 576)

8. **B.** Periodic payment plan certificates represent an undivided interest in a pool of underlying securities. Typically the pool is composed of open-end investment company shares.   (Page 573)

9. **D.** A UIT investing in mutual fund shares is most likely a contractual plan operating under the Investment Company Act of 1940 or the 1970 act amendments. The maximum sales load permissible under either type of plan (front-end load or spread-load) is 9% over the life of the plan.   (Page 574)

10. **D.** Withdrawal plans have no guarantee of payment. The investor's account value is at the mercy of market fluctuations.   (Page 578)

11. **D.** Under the Investment Company Act of 1940, an investor terminating a plan within 45 days is entitled to a refund of all sales charges plus the current value of the account. Because the customer has made two payments of $300 each, a total of $600 was invested. From that $600, 50% ($300) was deducted as a sales charge. The current value of the account is $340, so the customer will receive $640 as a refund.   (Page 575)

12. **B.** Refunds from a spread-load plan that has been in effect for more than 45 days are limited to a return of net asset value only. The investor would receive the difference between the amount invested (NAV remains the same) and the sales charges deducted. In this case, a total investment of $1,200 minus the sales charge of $240 equals a refund of $960.   (Page 575)

13. **A.** The customer can elect to reinvest fund distributions through an accumulation plan.
(Page 572)

14. **B.** By electing to receive distributions in cash while others are purchasing shares through reinvestment, the customer's proportional interest in the fund will decline. Most funds allow reinvestment of dividends at net asset value. Cash invested

is considered a new purchase, and the shares will be purchased at the public offering price, not NAV. (Page 572)

15. **A.** A contractual planholder receives a certificate evidencing ownership of shares held in trust by the plan company. Remember, plan companies are unit investment trusts that invest in shares of mutual funds. The plan participant holds units in the trust, not specific shares of the mutual fund. (Page 572)

16. **B.** Termination of a contractual plan within 45 days results in a refund of all sales charges plus the current value of the account. (Page 575)

17. **D.** Contractual plans are not legal in several states; the contract is unilateral (only the company is bound); and the prospectus will detail the specific charges to be deducted from each payment over the life of the plan. (Page 573)

18. **C.** If the investor is receiving $600 a month, the dollar amount of the withdrawal is fixed; this must be a fixed-dollar plan. (Page 578)

19. **B.** Under a fixed-time withdrawal plan, only the time period of the distribution is fixed. The amount of money received each month or the number of shares liquidated will vary. (Page 578)

20. **A.** The best choice is to reduce the contractual plan payments to $50 per month and give the daughter $100 per month (allowed by most plans). By doing so, the contractual plan remains intact (although the time necessary to accumulate the plan's stated investment is extended). By liquidating, or withdrawing from the plan, the customer is using money that has been subject to heavy sales charges (50% or 20% loads). Clearly, using money reduced by heavy sales charges is not in the best interest of the customer. (Page 572)

21. **B.** Purchasers of front-end load plans have surrender rights for 18 months after their initial investment. Under the Investment Company Act of 1940, an investor terminating a plan within 18 months is entitled to a refund of all sales charges in excess of 15% of the total (gross) payments made to date, plus the current value of the investment, which is liquidated at current NAV (and may result in a profit or loss). (Page 575)

81 Mutual Fund Distributions and Taxation Exam

1. Investment companies are prohibited from distributing capital gains to their shareholders more frequently than

   A. monthly
   B. quarterly
   C. semiannually
   D. annually

2. When calculating net investment income, an investment company would include

   A. only dividends
   B. only interest
   C. both dividends and interest
   D. both dividends and interest, minus operating expenses

3. Three months after you have purchased 100 shares of an open-end investment company, the company pays a $.32 per share capital gain distribution. On your tax return you will

   A. report the distribution as ordinary income
   B. report the distribution as a capital gain
   C. claim the distribution under your $200 dividend exclusion if you itemize
   D. report your registered rep for selling dividends

4. An investment company must inform all shareholders of their right to reinvest dividends at net asset value at least

   A. annually
   B. quarterly
   C. at the time of each distribution
   D. at the time of the original purchase

5. Which of the following statements is permitted under the Rules of Fair Practice?

   I. "This fund distributed a $.30 dividend from investment income and $.70 from realized security profits, for a total yield of 7% on its current price of $13.58."
   II. "This fund distributed a $.30 dividend from investment income and $.70 from realized security profits, for a 5.1% yield on its current price of $13.58."
   III. "This fund distributed a $.30 dividend from investment income and $.70 from realized security profits, for a 2.2% return on its current price of $13.58."
   IV. "You would be advised to purchase this fund at this time in order to benefit from the already announced and pending capital gain distribution."

   A. I and II
   B. I and III
   C. III
   D. IV

6. The document that must accompany each distribution an investment company pays out to its mutual fund shareholders is a

A. Form 1099B IC/VC
B. prospectus
C. W-2 statement
D. statement as to the source of the distribution

7. A customer transfers his proceeds from one fund to another within the same family of funds. The tax consequence is

A. no gain or loss is recognized until redemption
B. gains are taxed and losses are deferred
C. losses are deducted and gains are deferred
D. on the date of the transaction, any gain or loss is recognized for tax purposes

8. What is the source of dividend distributions to mutual fund shareholders?

A. Capital gains from portfolio transactions
B. Gross income of the fund
C. Net income of the fund
D. Net income of the fund less sales charges

9. Unrealized gain in a mutual fund portfolio

I. affects the value of fund shares
II. represents the growth in market value of securities held in the portfolio
III. is realized by shareholders only when they redeem their shares

A. I and II only
B. I and III only
C. II and III only
D. I, II and III

10. An investor purchased 200 shares of the ACE Fund when the POP was $11.60 and the NAV was $10.60. The current POP of the ACE Fund is $12.50, and the current NAV is $11.50. If the investor liquidates her 200 shares now, she will have a

A. loss of $200
B. loss of $20
C. gain of $20
D. gain of $200

11. An investor in the 36% tax bracket has received dividends and capital gains distributions on shares she has held for four months. The investor will pay

A. long-term tax rates on the capital gains distributions and ordinary income tax rates on the dividends
B. ordinary income tax rates on both the capital gains distributions and the dividends
C. long-term or short-term capital gains rates, depending on the length of time the fund has held the securities
D. no tax until she liquidates the shares

12. The conduit theory of taxation means that

I. the fund is not taxed on earnings it distributes
II. retained earnings are taxed as regular corporate income
III. the earnings distributed by a regulated mutual fund are taxed three times

A. I and II only
B. I and III only
C. II and III only
D. I, II and III

13. Belle Charolais's Form 1099B from a mutual fund investment listed her earnings for last year as follows:

Reinvested capital gains	$5,000
Undistributed capital gains	3,000
Reinvested dividends	7,000

If she filed a separate return and had no other dividend income, what would be Belle's taxable income from this investment?

A. $10,100
B. $10,200
C. $14,900
D. $15,000

14. The ACE Fund in which Max and Lotta Leveridge have invested paid $62 in taxes on their share of retained capital gains. How would they report this?

A. They would claim the $62 paid by ACE as a credit against taxes they owe.
B. They would exclude an additional $62 from dividend income.
C. They would pay an additional $62 in taxes and have to refund the $62 paid by the fund.
D. Their tax liability is not affected by the $62 paid by ACE.

15. Three years ago, Bea Kuhl purchased 300 shares of ACE Fund. She sold the shares on August 15th, for a loss of $400. On September 4th of the same year, she repurchased the shares. How would she record the loss for tax purposes?

A. Forty percent of the loss is deductible.
B. Fifty percent of the loss is deductible.
C. Sixty percent of the loss is deductible.
D. The loss is not deductible.

16. The ACE Tax Free Money Market Fund advertises itself as a triple tax-free investment for purchasers residing in New York City. This means ACE's portfolio

I. most likely holds City of New York short-term notes or similar city income tax-exempt securities
II. is invested so that more than 10% of its assets hold a single issue of City of New York short-term notes
III. has an average maturity of 90 days or less
IV. has at least 95% of the securities held rated in the top investment grade for money-market instruments

A. I and IV only
B. II and III only
C. III only
D. I, II, III and IV

17. If you invest in a regulated investment company, any dividend you receive from that investment will be taxed

A. as long-term capital gains
B. as long-term or short-term capital gains, depending on how long you have been an investor
C. to you as ordinary income but will not be taxed at the fund's level
D. to you as capital gains but will not be taxed at the corporate level

18. For the year 1994, the ACE Mutual Fund showed the following information:

Average net value	$28,000,000
Dividend income received	2,100,000
Interest income received	800,000
Long-term capital gains	2,000,000
Operating expenses	300,000

If ACE wishes to retain its designation as a regulated investment company under the Internal Revenue Code Subchapter M, it must distribute to its shareholders an amount closest to which of the following?

A. $1,890,000
B. $2,340,000
C. $5,940,000
D. $8,550,000

19. Which of the following costs cannot be deducted as an expense from the investment income of an open-end investment company?

A. Custodial fees
B. Auditing fees
C. Advertising fees
D. Accounting fees

20. As the owner of mutual fund shares, you will pay no tax on

A. dividends that are reinvested in the fund
B. unrealized capital gains
C. capital gains that are issued as additional shares
D. dividends that do not qualify for the $100 dividend exclusion

21. Randy Bear buys the ACE Growth Fund and enjoys a substantial paper capital gain. When Randy believes the market has reached its peak, he switches into the ACE Income Fund within the ACE Family of Funds. He incurs a small service fee, but he is not charged an additional sales charge. What is the tax effect?

A. Any gain or loss is deferred until he liquidates the ACE Income Fund.
B. The tax basis of the ACE Income Fund is adjusted to reflect the gain in the ACE Growth Fund.
C. It is a tax-free exchange.
D. Any gain in the ACE Growth Fund is taxable because the switch is treated as a sale and a purchase.

22. During an inflationary cycle, a mutual fund with the objective of providing high current income by investing in bonds and other fixed rate investments distributes a 5% dividend to shareholders. Excluding transaction costs, this distribution will result in

I. a decline of the fund's net asset value if the shareholders do not reinvest the distribution
II. a decline of the fund's net asset value per share if the shareholders reinvest the distribution
III. no change in the fund's net asset value if the shareholders reinvest the distribution
IV. no change in the net asset value per share if the shareholders reinvest the distribution

A. I and II
B. I, II and III
C. II and III
D. III and IV

23. Your client has asked about automatic dividend reinvestment offered by the ACE Fund. In describing the differences between dividend reinvestment and receiving distributions in cash, you can say

   I. one benefit of dividend reinvestment is that distributions reinvested are tax deferred, whereas dividends received in cash are taxable in the year received

   II. the taxation of the dividend distribution is not affected by your choice to reinvest or receive the dividend in cash

   III. the shareholder's proportionate ownership in the ACE Fund will decline if she elects to receive dividend distributions in cash

   IV. the shareholder's proportionate ownership in the ACE Fund is guaranteed to increase if dividend reinvestment is elected

   A. I and III
   B. I and IV
   C. II and III
   D. II and IV

◆ Answers & Rationale

1. **D.** Under the act of 1940, investment companies are prohibited from distributing capital gains more frequently than once per year. This does not require gains to be distributed, as the fund may retain gains for reinvestment.   (Page 580)

2. **D.** Net investment income is equal to gross investment income minus operating expenses. Gross investment income is interest and dividends received from securities in the investment company's portfolio. Capital gains are not included in investment income.   (Page 579)

3. **B.** If a fund makes a capital gains distribution, shareholders are required to report it as capital gain on their individual tax returns (the investment company will provide both the shareholder and the IRS with a 1099B form reflecting the distribution). The distribution is a capital gain taxed at ordinary rates. The dividend exclusion has been repealed by the Tax Reform Act of 1986.   (Page 582)

4. **A.** Notification of the right to reinvest dividends at net asset value (if offered) must occur at least annually.   (Page 580)

5. **C.** While a fund can advertise both capital gains and dividend distributions, the two amounts cannot be calculated as one figure and represented as the yield received from the fund. The dividend distribution of $.30 divided by $13.58 equals the yield. Choice IV is selling dividends, which also violates the Rules of Fair Practice.   (Page 579)

6. **D.** A statement as to the source of the distribution must accompany the distribution of dividends if the source of the dividend is from other than retained or current net income. The 1099B form is sent after the close of the year and details tax information related to distributions for the year.   (Page 581)

7. **D.** An exchange is a taxable event. The NAV of the investment must be compared to the cost basis of those shares. Any gain is taxable (or loss is deductible) in the year of the exchange. The exchange privilege allows the investor to avoid paying an additional sales charge; it does not allow the investor to avoid taxes.   (Page 584)

8. **C.** Dividend distributions are made from the fund's net investment income. Net investment income is gross income (dividends, interest and, if identified, short-term gains) minus fund expenses.   (Page 579)

9. **D.** Unrealized gains in portfolio securities are the result of the asset's appreciation in value. This appreciation in value will be reflected in an appreciation of the mutual fund shares themselves. An investor wanting to cash in on this appreciation can do so only by selling the shares (realizing the gain).   (Page 581)

10. **B.** The investor's cost base in the shares is $11.60. If she liquidates, she will receive the net asset value of $11.50, resulting in a loss of $.10 per share. Liquidating 200 shares, therefore, results in a total loss of $20 (200 × $.10).   (Page 582)

11. **A.** Income distributions from a mutual fund are considered ordinary income for tax purposes. Under current tax rules, capital gains are taxed at the investor's ordinary income rate up to a maximum of 28%. Thus, for an investor in a tax bracket higher than 28%, the two types of distributions will be taxed at different rates.   (Page 584)

12. **A.** Under the conduit (or pipeline) theory of taxation, which is applied to qualified regulated investment companies, the fund is liable for taxes only on the income retained. The investor benefits because the income is taxed only twice (at the corporate level and at the individual level) and not three times by adding taxation at the fund level.   (Page 582)

13. **D.** Under the Tax Reform Act of 1986, income and gains distributions are taxable at ordinary income tax rates. The capital gains exclusion has been repealed, as has the dividend exclusion. Undistributed gains are still taxable to the shareholder. The taxes paid by the fund on the retained gain are credited to the shareholder.   (Page 581)

14. **A.** If a fund realizes a gain but declines to distribute it to shareholders, the gain is still taxable to the investor. The fund will pay taxes on the gain on behalf of the shareholders (similar to a withholding tax) and will issue as part of the 1099B a statement showing their share of taxes paid. In this question, that share equalled $62. The Leveridges can elect to use that share as a credit against their tax liability or can elect to have it refunded. The basis of the shares is increased by the amount of the undistributed gain included in income, less the taxes paid by the fund.   (Page 582)

15. **D.** The customer repurchased the shares within 30 days of the loss transaction, and the loss is disallowed (a wash sale).   (Page 583)

16. **A.** Nontaxable money-market funds come under the same restrictions (Rule 2a-7 of the Investment Company Act of 1940) as taxable money-market funds. However, tax-exempt money-market funds are excluded from the 90-day-or-less average maturity restriction. Finally, a triple tax-exempt fund would most likely have City of New York issues in its portfolio as well as State of New York issues.   (Page 581)

17. **C.** A mutual fund qualifying as a regulated investment company distributes at least 90% of its net investment income as a dividend to shareholders. Because the company has qualified, the fund pays no tax on the income distributed. However, the shareholders are taxed at their ordinary income tax rate on the distribution.   (Page 582)

18. **B.** To qualify as a regulated investment company, the fund must distribute at least 90% of its net investment income. Net investment income for the purposes of IRC Subchapter M is income, without regard to gains, minus expenses. For ACE, dividend income ($2,100,000) plus interest income

($800,000) minus expenses ($300,000) equals a net investment income of $2,600,000. Ninety percent of $2,600,000 is $2,340,000.   (Page 582)

19. **C.** Advertising costs are an expense of the underwriter and are paid from the sales charge collected on the sale of investment company shares.   (Page 579)

20. **B.** A gain is not taxable until it is realized or sold.   (Page 581)

21. **D.** The exchange is treated as a sale, regardless of the holding period and the fact that it does not involve a new sales charge. The gain (or loss) on the ACE Growth Fund is determined by comparing the cost basis with the net asset value of the shares at the time of the exchange. Any difference is a capital gain or loss.   (Page 584)

22. **B.** By making a dividend distribution, the net asset value of the fund will decline if the dividend is not reinvested. If the dividend is reinvested by the shareholders, the NAV of the fund will remain the same as it was prior to the distribution. However, even though the dividend reinvestment may not change the fund's NAV on a per share basis, the NAV declines as the reinvestment will purchase additional shares, and so the same amount of money is divided over more shares. (Page 583)

23. **C.** Dividend reinvestment does not defer taxation of the distribution. Whether the dividend is received in cash or reinvested, the distribution is still taxable in the year paid. An investor electing to receive distributions in cash will see his interest in the fund decline if others are reinvesting. However, reinvestment of distributions does not guarantee an investor will increase his proportionate interest in the fund.   (Page 580)

1. All of the following require written customer verification of his financial condition EXCEPT the

    A. purchase of real estate investment trust shares
    B. establishment of an options account
    C. purchase of a new construction real estate limited partnership interest
    D. purchase of a new computer-leasing limited partnership interest

2. Which of the following is(are) characteristics of REITs?

    I.   They offer limited liability.
    II. They offer the opportunity for capital gains.
    III. They offer a pass-through of losses.

    A. I
    B. I and II
    C. I and III
    D. II and III

3. Which of the following statements is(are) true about REITs?

    I.   Operating losses flow through directly to REIT owners.
    II. Profits from operations usually flow through directly to REIT owners.
    III. They are a type of direct participation program.
    IV. They provide long-term financing to real estate projects.

    A. I, II and III only
    B. II and IV only
    C. IV only
    D. I, II, III and IV

4. In order to avoid taxation at the corporate level, a REIT must derive at least 75% of its income from real property and must distribute what percentage of its net income to shareholders?

    A. 75%
    B. 90%
    C. 95%
    D. 98%

5. REITs provide which of the following features to investors?

    A. Flow-through of income and deductions
    B. Diversification with limited capital investment
    C. Switching privileges between REITs in a family
    D. Management fees that are lower overall than those of mutual funds

◆ Answers & Rationale

1.   **A.**   A customer's financial condition does not have to be certified in writing before he may purchase shares of a real estate investment trust (REIT). Written certification is required to establish an options account and for any purchases of limited partnerships.   (Page 585)

2.   **B.**   Operating losses do not flow through REITs, which offer limited liability. The investor cannot lose more than he has invested. Also, the REIT can appreciate in value, thus offering capital gains opportunities to the investor.   (Page 585)

3.   **B.**   Real estate investment trusts (REITs) are companies, usually traded publicly, that manage equity and debt investments in real estate in order to earn profits for shareholders. Although REITs must by law pass through 95% or more of their earnings to retain their status as REITs, they do not pass losses through directly to investors and, therefore, are not direct participation programs.
(Page 585)

4.   **C.**   REITs must distribute at least 95% of their net income to the shareholders in order to avoid corporate taxation.   (Page 585)

5.   **B.**   REITs consist of diversified portfolios of real estate and real estate mortgages. Because REITs are bought and sold on exchanges and over the counter as shares of beneficial interest, investors can purchase as few or as many shares as they choose, and can vary their investment size accordingly.   (Page 585)

83 Individual Retirement Accounts Exam

1. A registered representative who is recommending investments for a qualified IRA would give primary consideration to

   A. maximum current income
   B. tax status of the beneficiary
   C. liquidity
   D. risk

2. Which of the following investment activities are suitable for an individual retirement account?

   I. Writing uncovered calls
   II. Writing covered calls
   III. Buying puts on stock held long
   IV. Writing naked puts

   A. I and II only
   B. I and IV only
   C. II and III only
   D. I, II, III and IV

3. Which of the following would be the MOST suitable investment for the IRAs of a young couple with a combined annual income of $42,000?

   A. Stock in a growth fund
   B. Initial public offerings of small companies
   C. Options on blue chip common stock
   D. Partnership interests in an oil and gas drilling program

4. Lotta Leveridge makes $65,000 a year as an advertising executive, and her husband, Tiny, makes $40,000 a year as Lotta's assistant. How much can the Leveridges contribute to IRAs?

   A. They cannot make a contribution because their combined income is too high.
   B. They can contribute up to $2,250 split over both accounts, with no more than $2,000 in either account.
   C. They can each contribute $2,000 to an IRA.
   D. They can each contribute $2,500 to an IRA.

5. Lotta and Tiny Leveridge are both in their twenties and have been married only a few years. They have asked for your recommendation as to an investment for their IRAs. You should suggest

   A. growth-oriented mutual funds
   B. penny precious metals stocks
   C. oil and gas exploration limited partnerships
   D. index options

6. Max Leveridge has been reading the financial news and thinks that interest rates will decline soon. He wants to protect the principal he has accumulated in his IRA, and plans to begin making withdrawals in seven years. Under the circumstances, you would recommend

A. purchasing seven-year zero-coupon Treasury STRIPS
B. leaving all of his cash in money-market funds
C. withdrawing now and investing in corporate debentures
D. a unit investment trust that begins to mature in seven years

7. Your client, who is 50 years of age, wants to withdraw funds from her IRA. She asks you about the tax implications of early withdrawal. You should tell her that the withdrawal will be taxed as

A. ordinary income
B. ordinary income plus a 10% penalty
C. capital gains
D. capital gains plus a 10% penalty

8. A customer has just started an IRA. She will be vested

A. immediately
B. in two years
C. in five years
D. at age 70 1/2

9. Which of the following statements regarding individual retirement accounts is NOT true?

A. IRA rollovers must be complete within 60 days of receiving the distribution.
B. Cash-value life insurance is a permissible IRA investment but term insurance is not.
C. The investor must be under 70 1/2 years of age to open an IRA.
D. Distributions may begin at age 59 1/2 and must begin by age 70 1/2.

10. One of your customers and his wife are going to make their annual contribution to their IRA. He earned $40,000 this year and his wife earned $45,000. How much may they contribute?

A. $2,000
B. $2,250
C. $4,000
D. $5,000

11. Which of the following individuals will NOT be penalized on an IRA withdrawal?

A. Man who has just become disabled
B. Woman who turned 59 one month before the withdrawal
C. Person, age 50, who decides on early retirement
D. Man in his early 40s who uses the money to buy a house

12. Under IRS rules, IRA distributions upon retirement can go to the

I. employee only
II. employee jointly with the employee's spouse
III. employee, and at the employee's death, to a designated beneficiary
IV. employee's designated beneficiary

A. I only
B. I, II and III only
C. IV only
D. I, II, III and IV

13. Distribution from an IRA can begin at age 59 1/2 and must begin no later than

A. 65
B. 68
C. 70 1/2
D. 15 years from the individual's date of retirement

14. Premature withdrawals from an IRA are subject to a penalty of

    A. 5%
    B. 10%
    C. 15%
    D. 25%

15. A married couple are both employed and are not covered under either a Keogh plan or a pension plan. Their combined income is $28,000, and both wish to open IRAs. For them to make the maximum tax-deductible contribution, they should deposit

    A. $1,000 in separate individual IRAs
    B. $2,000 in separate individual IRAs
    C. $2,250 in a joint IRA
    D. $4,000 in a joint IRA

16. Two of your clients, a husband and wife, wish to open IRAs. Both are employed at separate firms: she works as an engineer and earns $25,000 a year; he is employed as an editorial assistant earning $10,000 a year. Their maximum contribution to IRA accounts is

    A. a joint contribution of $4,000 into a single IRA
    B. $2,000 in her IRA, $1,500 in his IRA
    C. a joint contribution of $4,250 into a spousal IRA
    D. $2,000 in her IRA, $2,000 in his IRA

17. Which of the following statements is(are) true of spousal IRAs?

    I.   Contributions must be distributed equally between the accounts.
    II. Contributions can be greater than in a regular IRA.
    III. Rollover to a new plan is 18 months rather than the one-year rollover allowed in a regular IRA.

    A. I and II
    B. I and III
    C. II
    D. II and III

18. An IRA with a spousal option differs from one without such an option in that it has a

    I.   higher aggregate contribution limit
    II. higher minimum contribution requirement
    III. requirement of joint filing of the couple's tax return

    A. I
    B. I and III
    C. II
    D. II and III

19. Excess IRA contributions are subject to a penalty of what percentage annually until they are used up or withdrawn?

    A. 6%
    B. 10%
    C. 12%
    D. 15%

20. An employee not covered under his company's pension plan has been contributing to an IRA for five years. He now leaves his old job, starts a new job and is covered under the new corporation's pension plan. Which of the following statements is true?

    A. His IRA must be closed.
    B. Nondeductible contributions to his IRA may continue.
    C. The money in his IRA must be combined with any money he will receive from the pension plan.
    D. Contributions to his IRA must stop; the money in the account will be frozen, but interest and dividends can accrue tax-free until he retires.

21. Which of the following can be rolled over into an IRA?

   I.   Another IRA
   II. Corporate pension plan
   III. Corporate profit-sharing plan
   IV. Keogh plan

   A. I and IV only
   B. II and III only
   C. II, III and IV only
   D. I, II, III and IV

22. The maximum allowable contribution to an IRA is

   A. $250 per individual account
   B. $2,000 per individual account
   C. $2,250 per individual account
   D. There is no limit because contributions to IRAs are no longer allowed.

23. A premature distribution from an IRA is subject to a

   A. 5% penalty plus tax
   B. 6% penalty plus tax
   C. 10% penalty plus tax
   D. 50% penalty plus tax

24. A woman opening an IRA and including her unemployed husband may deposit

   A. $2,000 in a single joint account
   B. $2,250 in a single joint account
   C. $2,250 in an account for the wife and $250 in a separate account for the husband
   D. up to $2,250 divided between two accounts so that no more than $2,000 is placed in either account

25. The maximum contribution allowed under an IRA is 100% of annual earnings

   A. before taxes or $2,000, whichever is the greater
   B. before taxes or $2,000, whichever is the lesser
   C. after taxes or $2,000, whichever is the greater
   D. after taxes or $2,000, whichever is the lesser

26. An employee makes a withdrawal from her IRA at age 52. She pays no penalty tax if she

   A. has retired
   B. is disabled
   C. had no earned income that year
   D. transferred her account to another custodian

27. You work for the Tippecanoe Ferry Co. and are a participant in its 401K plan. How much can you invest in an IRA?

   A. $0
   B. $2,000
   C. $2,250
   D. Up to 25% of annual compensation

28. Which of the following securities would a registered rep recommend to a customer who wants to set up an IRA?

   A. Municipal bond fund shares
   B. Term insurance contract
   C. Growth stock
   D. Put options

29. Sandy and Klaus Bruin are married and file a joint tax return. Their AGI is $62,000 this year and both are active participants in qualified retirement plans. The couple may

   A. contribute to IRAs and deduct the full amount of their contributions
   B. contribute to IRAs, but may only deduct a portion of their contributions
   C. contribute to IRAs, but may not deduct their contributions
   D. not contribute to IRAs

30. Chip Bullock received a lump-sum distribution from a 401K plan when he left his job. He may now

    I.   roll over his account within 60 days

    II. transfer his account without taking possession of the money

    III. keep the funds and pay ordinary income tax

    IV. invest in a tax-exempt municipal bond fund to avoid paying tax

    A. I and II
    B. I and III
    C. II and IV
    D. III and IV

31. Which of the following statements about SEP-IRAs is true?

    A. They are used primarily by large corporations.
    B. They are used primarily by small businesses.
    C. They are set up by employees.
    D. They cannot be set up by self-employed persons.

32. The money contributed to a SEP vests

    A. according to a preset schedule
    B. immediately
    C. beginning at the fifth anniversary of establishment
    D. after the employee retires

33. Which of the following is required to establish a SEP?

    A. 50% of the eligible employees must have an IRA.
    B. 75% of the eligible employees must have an IRA.
    C. 100% of the eligible employees must have an IRA.
    D. The employer must establish a separate IRA for each eligible employee.

34. June Polar works for a small business and would like to participate in a SEP. Which of the following statements is true?

    A. June may not participate in a SEP because she has been employed by this company for only five years.
    B. The maximum SEP contribution is higher than the maximum IRA contribution.
    C. June's employer must match her contributions.
    D. Contributions over $2,000 are not tax deductible.

◆ Answers & Rationale

1.   **D.**   Risk is the key consideration in an IRA. Such an account seeks to preserve capital and achieve a reasonable rate of return. This is a *prudent man* type of investment guideline. Seeking high-income investments (such as junk bonds) without regard to their riskiness is imprudent.

The tax status is not relevant because investments that are fully taxable (such as corporate bonds) are treated as tax-free investments as long as they are in an IRA. Liquidity is less important in retirement accounts because they are presumed to be long-term investments.   (Page 592)

2.   **C.**   In a retirement account, investment activities generally strive to seek reasonable income, preserve capital and avoid speculative investments. In regard to options strategies, writing covered calls and buying puts on stock held in the portfolio are considered conservative positions. Writing uncovered calls and puts subject the investor to a high degree of risk and are considered unsuitable.   (Page 592)

3.   **A.**   The IRA for this couple should be established with an eye towards long-term appreciation. Answers B and C are riskier and are generally considered inappropriate for IRAs. The DPP is inappropriate because tax losses in an IRA cannot be used to offset gains.   (Page 592)

4.   **C.**   No matter how much an individual or a couple make, IRA contributions can still be made. Each spouse is entitled to contribute 100% of earned income up to $2,000 (insofar as both spouses are working).   (Page 590)

5.   **A.**   A growth mutual fund is appropriate for a young couple's IRA. All other answers bear a high risk that is not appropriate for a retirement account.   (Page 592)

6.   **A.**   Max will be able to lock in an interest rate and be assured of safety of principal with zero-coupon Treasury STRIPS. By purchasing bonds that mature in seven years, he will be able to match his withdrawal plans with their maturity.   (Page 592)

7.   **B.**   An early withdrawal from an IRA is taxed as ordinary income plus a 10% penalty.   (Page 594)

8.   **A.**   Investors are always vested immediately in their IRAs.   (Page 591)

9.   **B.**   Cash-value life insurance is not a permissible IRA investment, nor are term insurance or collectibles. Answers A, C and D are true.   (Page 592)

10.   **C.**   Individuals may contribute 100% of earned income up to $2,000. Because both the husband and his wife work, together they may contribute a maximum of $4,000. If the wife did not work, the husband could contribute a maximum of $2,250. However, their combined income is over the cut-off for deductibility of contributions.   (Page 590)

11.   **A.**   Disability allows an IRA owner to make a withdrawal without penalty before age 59 1/2. The other individuals described will pay a 10% penalty on the withdrawal because they are under 59 1/2 years of age.   (Page 593)

12.   **D.**   Under IRS rules, when an employee retires IRA payments can be made to the employee or jointly to the employee and spouse. In the event that the account owner dies, payments may continue to be made to a designated beneficiary; a person's rights to accumulated IRA benefits do not stop at the death of that person.   (Page 593)

13.   **C.**   As a result of the Tax Reform Act of 1986, the owner of an IRA or a Keogh retirement plan has until April 1st of the year after the year in which he turns 70 1/2 to begin withdrawing from the account.   (Page 593)

14.   **B.**   Except in the case of death or disability, withdrawals that begin before the account owner reaches 59 1/2 are subject to a one-time penalty of 10% of the gross amount withdrawn, in addition to any taxes due the government.   (Page 593)

15. **B.** Because both spouses are employed, both are eligible for individual retirement accounts with a maximum contribution limit of $2,000. (Page 591)

16. **D.** Because they are both employed, each is eligible to make a contribution of $2,000 to an IRA. (Page 591)

17. **C.** If only one spouse of a married couple works and they file a joint tax return, the couple can open an IRA with a spousal option. The couple can contribute a maximum of $2,250 to the two accounts and can divide it between the accounts in any manner they choose as long as they put no more than $2,000 in either account. (Page 591)

18. **B.** There is no minimum contribution requirement for IRAs. (Page 591)

19. **A.** Excess IRA contributions are subject to a yearly penalty of 6% until they are withdrawn or are applied to the following year's contribution limit. (Page 591)

20. **B.** An employee covered under a qualified retirement plan may continue to own and contribute to an IRA. The contributions may not be fully tax deductible, depending on the amount of compensation earned, but the employee benefits from the tax deferral of IRA earnings. (Page 591)

21. **D.** Assets from any qualified corporate plan or from another IRA may be rolled over into an IRA. (Page 592)

22. **B.** The maximum allowable contribution to an IRA (independent of whether the contribution is deductible) is currently $2,000. (Page 590)

23. **C.** A person who takes a premature distribution from an IRA will be liable for taxes on the amount at the current rate plus a penalty of 10%. (Page 593)

24. **D.** The maximum annual contribution that can be made is $2,250 divided between two separate accounts with no more than $2,000 in any one account. (Page 591)

25. **B.** The maximum annual contribution to an IRA plan is 100% of earnings before taxes or $2,000, whichever is less. (Page 591)

26. **B.** An IRA account holder may withdraw money before the age of 59 1/2 without incurring a penalty tax only in the case of death or disability. A transfer between custodians does not constitute a withdrawal from the account. (Page 591)

27. **B.** The maximum annual contribution to an IRA is $2,000, whether or not the account owner participates in a qualified retirement plan. The full amount of the contribution may not be tax deductible, but all earnings in the account are still tax deferred. (Page 590)

28. **C.** Although a municipal bond fund is permissible, earnings on IRA accounts are always tax deferred, so the tax advantage of municipal investments is not a benefit. Insurance contracts are ineligible IRA investments, and options investments are generally inappropriate for retirement accounts owing to their high risk. (Page 591)

29. **C.** Their IRA contributions are not tax deductible because they participate in qualified retirement plans and their adjusted gross income is more than $50,000. Regardless of participation in an employer-sponsored qualified retirement plan, an investor may contribute to an IRA. (Page 592)

30. **B.** If the investor does not roll over the money into an IRA account, it will be taxed as ordinary income. Because he has already received the lump sum, he cannot transfer the account to a new custodian. Any amount he does not roll over will be taxed as income even if he invests it in tax-exempt bonds. (Page 592)

31. **B.** SEP-IRAs are used primarily by small businesses because they are much easier and less expensive to set up than other plans; they are also used by self-employed persons. The employer sets up and administers the SEP-IRA. (Page 592)

32. **B.** SEP contributions, like IRA contributions, are fully vested immediately. (Page 595)

33. **C.** In order for a small business to establish a SEP, each eligible employee must have an IRA. If an employee refuses to establish an IRA, the employer *must* open an IRA in that employee's name. (Page 595)

34. **B.** The contribution limit is 15% of earned income up to $30,000 for a SEP retirement plan, compared to just $2,000 for a regular IRA, and the entire amount is tax deductible. Full-time employees who have been employed for at least three of the immediately preceding five years are automatically eligible to participate. The entire amount of the employer's contribution up to the maximum contribution is tax deductible. (Page 595)

84 Keogh (HR-10) Plans Exam

1. Your client, who is 40 years of age, wants to withdraw funds from her Keogh. She asks you about the tax implications of early withdrawal. You should tell her the withdrawal will be taxed as

   A. ordinary income
   B. ordinary income plus a 10% penalty
   C. capital gains
   D. capital gains plus a 10% penalty

2. Hugh Heifer has a salaried, full-time position but his employer does not offer a company retirement plan. Hugh also has his own clock repair business, which earns less than his salaried position. He wants to invest for his retirement. Which of the following investments are options for him?

   A. An IRA if he does not have a Keogh plan
   B. A Keogh plan if he does not have an IRA
   C. Both an IRA and a Keogh plan
   D. An IRA, but not a Keogh plan because his self-employment is not his main source of income

3. Which of the following are characteristics of a Keogh plan?

   I. Dividends, interest and capital gains are tax-deferred.
   II. Distributions after age 70 1/2 are tax-free.
   III. Contributions are allowed for a non-working spouse.
   IV. Lump-sum distributions are allowed.

   A. I and II
   B. I and III
   C. I and IV
   D. II and III

4. All of the following factors influence the amount of money that can be contributed to a Keogh plan in one year EXCEPT

   A. the rules regarding maximum contributions
   B. whether the plan is qualified or non-qualified
   C. the amount of self-employment income
   D. whether the participant is an employee or a business owner

5. Which of the following would disqualify a person from participation in a Keogh plan?

   A. She turned 70 eight months ago.
   B. She has a salaried position in addition to her self-employment.
   C. Her spouse has company-sponsored retirement benefits.
   D. She has an IRA.

6. Under Keogh plan provisions, a full-time employee would be defined as one working at least how many hours per year?

    A. 100
    B. 500
    C. 800
    D. 1,000

7. An employer makes $75,000 and contributes the maximum to her own Keogh account. She must contribute how much to the Keogh of a full-time employee earning $12,000?

    A. $1,200
    B. $2,400
    C. $3,000
    D. $7,500

8. What are the two consequences when a participant in a Keogh plan makes a voluntary contribution?

    I. The contributions are tax-deductible.
    II. The contributions are not tax-deductible.
    III. Interest and dividends accumulate tax-deferred.
    IV. Interest and dividends do not accumulate tax-deferred.

    A. I and III
    B. I and IV
    C. II and III
    D. II and IV

9. Which of the following statements about contributions to a Keogh in excess of 25% or the $30,000 annual limit is(are) true?

    I. Excess contributions are not permitted.
    II. Excess contributions are permitted, but are not tax deductible.
    III. Excess contributions are allowed for both employee and employer.
    IV. Excess contributions may be subject to a 10% penalty tax.

    A. I
    B. II, III and IV
    C. II and IV
    D. IV

10. Under a Keogh plan, which of the following would be an acceptable investment?

    A. Unit investment trust
    B. Variable annuity
    C. U.S. government bond
    D. All of the above

11. An employee who is covered under a Keogh plan will become fully vested

    A. depending on the vesting schedule chosen by the employer
    B. after one year
    C. after two years
    D. after three years

12. Which of the following people would not be eligible to start her own Keogh, but would be eligible to open an IRA?

    A. College professor who makes $10,000 on the sale of a book and several articles
    B. Corporate officer who earns $40,000 plus an additional $10,000 as a part-time speaker
    C. Doctor who receives $10,000 from a restaurant she owns
    D. Corporate officer who receives a $5,000 bonus

13. Which of the following individuals are entitled to participate in a Keogh plan?

    I.   Doctor
    II. Security analyst who makes $2,000 giving lectures
    III. Engineer of a corporation who earns $5,000 making public speeches
    IV. Executive of a corporation who receives $5,000 in stock options from his company

    A. I
    B. I and II
    C. I, II and III
    D. IV

14. Chip Bullock is registered in a corporate profit-sharing plan as an employee. He also runs a small business on the side. Chip may participate in which of the following?

    I.   IRA
    II. Keogh plan
    III. Corporation's pension plan
    IV. Personal mutual fund account

    A. I only
    B. I, II and III only
    C. II only
    D. I, II, III and IV

15. Early withdrawals may be made without penalty from a Keogh plan in all of the following circumstances EXCEPT

    A. the account owner's death
    B. the account owner's disability
    C. from the voluntary, nondeductible contributions
    D. from the tax-deductible contributions

16. The maximum contribution a self-employed person is allowed under a Keogh plan is

    A. 25% of precontribution income or $30,000, whichever is greater
    B. 25% of precontribution income or $30,000, whichever is less
    C. 25% of after-contribution income or $30,000, whichever is greater
    D. 25% of after-contribution income or $30,000, whichever is less

17. An individual earned $75,000 in royalties from his writings; $5,000 from interest and dividends; $2,000 from long-term capital gains in the stock market; and $3,000 from rents on two cottages. He could contribute to his Keogh plan

    A. $12,570
    B. $12,750
    C. $15,000
    D. $18,750

18. Clara Bullock earns $18,000 a year as a free-lance writer and is paid an additional $4,000 for her part-time work at a private corporation that has no pension plan. She could deposit in a Keogh

    A. $1,500
    B. $3,600
    C. $4,500
    D. $7,500

19. A nurse had been participating in her employer's Keogh plan. Upon leaving the clinic, she may roll over the distributed Keogh assets into an IRA and defer taxes on these assets if the transaction is completed within

    A. 30 days
    B. 60 days
    C. 90 days
    D. 6 months

20. A nurse had been participating in her employer's Keogh plan. Upon leaving the clinic, she wishes to roll over the distributed Keogh assets into an IRA. She may deposit into the IRA

    A. $15,000 for each year the Keogh was in force
    B. $2,000 for each year the Keogh was in force
    C. the entire lump sum from the Keogh
    D. $15,000 per year

21. A person works for an accounting firm that has a retirement plan. He is paid $28,000 a year. He also works part time as a self-employed Lionel electric train wholesaler, from which he earned $12,000 last year. The maximum he can contribute for his personal retirement on a tax-deductible basis is

    A. $0
    B. $2,400
    C. $3,500
    D. $4,000

22. Which of the following persons may participate in a Keogh plan?

    I. Self-employed doctor
    II. Analyst who makes money giving speeches outside his regular working hours
    III. Individual with a full-time job who has income from freelancing
    IV. Corporate executive who receives $5,000 in stock options from his corporation

    A. I
    B. I and II
    C. I, II and III
    D. II, III and IV

23. Chip Bullock earns $2,000 as a self-employed, part-time set designer. What is the maximum dollar amount of part-time earnings he can contribute to a Keogh plan?

    A. $300
    B. $400
    C. $1,000
    D. $2,000

24. A Keogh plan would not be available to a(n)

    A. artist whose annual income comes from sales of paintings
    B. doctor whose income is derived from her practice
    C. person whose income is exclusively capital gains and interest
    D. advertising agency executive whose income is derived from a salary plus $5,000 in outside consulting fees

25. Which of the following employees need not be included in a Keogh plan if the business owner has a Keogh account?

    I. Waitress who works 30 hours a week for twelve months
    II. Bookkeeper who works full time for eight months of the year
    III. Janitor who works full time for three months of the year
    IV. Clerical assistant who works 20 hours a week for 20 weeks

    A. II and III only
    B. III and IV only
    C. IV only
    D. I, II, III and IV

26. Gwinneth Stout is 45 years old, self-employed and in the 31% tax bracket. She withdraws $40,000 from her Keogh account. What is the total amount she must pay to the IRS on the withdrawal?

    A. 0%
    B. 10%
    C. 31%
    D. 41%

27. Max Leveridge earned $100,000 this year and would like to make a large contribution toward his retirement. Because he is self-employed, you should recommend that he contribute to a(n)

A. IRA
B. Keogh account
C. 401K plan
D. TSA

◆ Answers & Rationale

1. **B.** An early withdrawal from a Keogh is taxed in the same way as an early withdrawal from an IRA—as ordinary income plus a 10% penalty. (Page 598)

2. **C.** The investor can start an IRA, assuming that he is under age 70 1/2. How much of his IRA contributions are deductible depends on his income level. He is also eligible to invest in a Keogh plan because he is self-employed, regardless of how much or how little he earns from his self-employment or how those earnings compare to his salary. Investment in an IRA does not affect his eligibility for a Keogh plan. (Page 596)

3. **C.** Keogh plan earnings from dividends, interest and capital gains are tax-deferred. Lump-sum distributions are allowed, as well as regular payment distributions. Distributions are taxable, regardless of age. Contributions for a nonworking spouse are not allowed in a Keogh plan. (Page 598)

4. **B.** By definition, Keogh plans are qualified plans. (Page 596)

5. **A.** A person can participate in a Keogh plan if she is self-employed. The fact that she is a salaried employee and also has an IRA does not affect her eligibility. However, because withdrawals from a Keogh must begin by age 70 1/2, she is no longer eligible to contribute because of her age. (Page 596)

6. **D.** "Full-time" is defined as 1,000 hours or more per year, regardless of the number of days, weeks or months worked. In other words, to be considered full time, a person must work more than 50% of the 2,000 hours a normal employee works in a year. (Page 597)

7. **C.** Because she is self-employed, the employer must calculate her Keogh contribution based on post-contribution income. If she makes her maximum contribution of 25% of her post-con-

tribution gross income (which is equivalent to 20% of her precontribution gross income), she will contribute $15,000. Her employee, by definition, is not self-employed; thus the Keogh plan, like other qualified plans, sets a maximum of 25% of total earnings or $30,000, whichever is less. The employer then must contribute 25% of her employee's income of $12,000, which is $3,000. (Page 597)

8. **C.** Individuals with Keogh retirement plans are permitted to make nondeductible contributions. The interest and dividends on these contributions will accumulate tax-deferred until the owner withdraws them. (Page 597)

9. **B.** Excess contributions may be subject to a 10% penalty tax. (Page 597)

10. **D.** The only investments that are not permitted in Keoghs are commodities, term life insurance, collectibles and antiques, precious metals (other than U.S.-issued gold and silver coins) and uncovered options. (Page 598)

11. **A.** Benefits vest to an employee according to the schedule chosen by the employer, usually over five or seven years. (Page 597)

12. **D.** Anyone can open an IRA; the tax deductibility of a person's contributions will depend on the availability of an employer-sponsored qualified retirement plan and on the person's income. Each of the listed individuals had income earned from self-employment except for the corporate officer receiving a bonus. (Page 596)

13. **C.** Stock options, dividends, capital gains and interest are not considered income earned from self-employment. (Page 596)

14. **D.** The investor may make deposits into any one or more of the investment and retirement vehicles listed. The deductibility of his contributions to the IRA will be determined by his income, because his company offers a qualified retirement plan and because he has his own Keogh. (Page 596)

15. **D.** A Keogh account owner can always withdraw her own voluntary contributions, and

tax-deductible contributions can be withdrawn without penalty in the event of the account owner's death or disability. (Page 598)

16. **D.** IRS guidelines state that a self-employed person's contribution to a Keogh plan is limited to 25% of after-contribution income, or $30,000, whichever is less. (Page 596)

17. **C.** Only the royalties count as self-employment income; therefore 20% of $75,000 equals $15,000. (Page 596)

18. **B.** The investor's $18,000 of self-employment income would allow a $3,600 tax-deductible Keogh contribution ($18,000 × 20%). (Page 596)

19. **B.** Rollovers may take place once a year and must occur within a 60-day period. There are no limits on direct transfers of retirement assets. (Page 598)

20. **C.** All money received as a rollover distribution is eligible for the IRA. (Page 598)

21. **B.** This person can establish a Keogh for himself and make a tax-deductible contribution to it of $2,400 ($12,000 × 20%). His combined income of $40,000 puts him past the IRA phaseout for single filers, so he is not eligible to make deductible IRA contributions. He is still eligible to make voluntary Keogh contributions, as well as nondeductible IRA contributions of up to $2,000. (Page 596)

22. **C.** The corporate executive would not be considered self-employed and, therefore, would not be eligible to contribute to a Keogh. (Page 596)

23. **B.** A self-employed person's Keogh contribution is limited to 20% of precontribution income. (Page 596)

24. **C.** Keogh plans are limited to individuals who are self-employed. Persons with passive income cannot make tax-deductible contributions to a Keogh. (Page 596)

25. **B.** An employee who works at least 1,000 hours a year must be included in an employer's Keogh plan. The janitor and the clerical assistant described here do not meet this requirement. (Page 597)

26. **D.** The withdrawal becomes part of Gwinneth's gross income for that year; she pays 31% in tax on the full amount. She has not reached age 59 1/2; therefore, she is assessed an additional 10% penalty tax. (Page 598)

27. **B.** Keogh plans allow contributions of 25% of earned income up to $30,000 in a single tax year, while contributions to IRAs are limited to $2,000. Both TSAs and 401K plans are administered by employing companies, so this investor could not participate. (Page 596)

85 Corporate Retirement Plans Exam

1. In a defined benefit plan

   A. all employees receive the same benefits at retirement
   B. all participating employees are immediately vested
   C. high-income employees who are near retirement will benefit the most
   D. the same amount must be contributed for each eligible employee

2. Which of the following statements is(are) true about a qualified, noncontributory defined benefit plan?

   I. Contributions are taxable.
   II. Distributions are taxable.
   III. Contributions may vary.

   A. I and II
   B. II
   C. II and III
   D. III

3. Which of the following plans require the services of an actuary?

   A. Profit-sharing
   B. Defined benefit
   C. Defined contribution
   D. 401K

4. A qualified profit-sharing plan has all of the following features EXCEPT

   A. the contribution is tax deductible to the employee
   B. the contribution is reported by the employee
   C. the contribution is taxable upon payment at retirement
   D. upon retirement the beneficiary may average out the income

5. The amount paid into a defined contribution plan is set by the

   A. ERISA-defined contribution requirements
   B. trust agreement
   C. employer's age
   D. employer's profits

6. When an employee's voluntary contribution to an employer-sponsored qualified pension plan is distributed to the employee, it is

   A. returned tax free
   B. taxed at a reduced rate
   C. taxed at the beneficiary's ordinary tax rate
   D. taxed at the current capital gains rate

7. Corporate pension plans have all of the following features EXCEPT that payments

   A. cannot exceed Social Security benefits
   B. can be tied to Social Security benefits
   C. will depend on length of service and salary
   D. will depend on an employee's value to the company

8. Corporate profit-sharing plans must be in the form of a(n)

   A. trust
   B. conservatorship
   C. administrator
   D. beneficial ownership

9. When Angus Bullwether retires, he will receive a retirement income that equals a percentage of the average of his last three years of compensation. In which kind of plan is Angus MOST likely participating?

   A. Keogh
   B. Defined contribution
   C. Defined benefit
   D. TSA

◆ Answers & Rationale

1. **C.** The rules regarding the maximum amount of contributions are different for defined contribution plans and defined benefit plans. Defined benefit plans set the amount of retirement benefits that a retiree will receive as a percentage of the previous several years' salaries. For the highly paid individual who is nearing retirement, the defined benefit plan allows a larger contribution in a shorter period of time. Answer D describes a defined contribution plan rather than a defined benefit plan.   (Page 599)

2. **C.** Contributions to a qualified, noncontributory plan are made by the employer, not the employee. Contributions are not taxed until they are received as distributions by the participant. Because the benefits provided by this type of qualified plan may vary (depending upon the participant's age, sex, income, etc.), the contributions made on his behalf will vary. All distributions from the plan are taxed upon receipt by the participant.   (Page 600)

3. **B.** Because the payout is set and the contributions must adequately cover the benefits, calculations for a defined benefit plan are performed by an actuary based on employees' life expectancies.   (Page 599)

4. **A.** Qualified retirement plans are tax-deductible to the employer, not to the employee.   (Page 601)

5. **B.** The retirement plan's trust agreement will contain a section explaining the formula(s) used to determine the contributions to a defined contribution plan.   (Page 599)

6. **A.** All voluntary employee contributions to a qualified retirement plan are made with aftertax dollars. Therefore, because the employee already paid taxes on the money, it will be returned tax-free. All earnings attributable to employee contributions as well as all employer-contributed money will be taxed at the employee's ordinary income rate at the time of distribution.   (Page 601)

7. **A.** Payments made to an employee at retirement can be of any amount and are not limited by Social Security payments. All the other statements are true.   (Page 600)

8. **A.** All corporate pension and profit-sharing plans must be set up under a trust agreement. The plan's trustee will have fiduciary responsibility for the plan.   (Page 599)

9. **C.** A defined benefit plan specifies the amount of money to be paid to employees upon retirement. The maximum benefit is 100% of the employee's average compensation for the final three years of employment. Keogh plans, defined contribution plans and tax-sheltered annuity plans all specify the amount of money to be contributed to the plan.   (Page 600)

86 Nonqualified Corporate Retirement Plans Exam

1. Each of the following is an example of a qualified retirement plan EXCEPT a(n)

   A. deferred compensation plan
   B. individual retirement account
   C. pension and profit-sharing plan
   D. defined benefit plan

2. Which of the following statements is(are) true of deferred compensation plans?

   I. They are available to a limited number of select employees.
   II. They must be nondiscriminatory.
   III. They cannot include corporate officers.
   IV. They cannot include members of the board of directors.

   A. I
   B. I and IV
   C. II
   D. III and IV

3. Deferred compensation plans need the prior approval of the

   A. employer
   B. plan trustee
   C. IRS
   D. Keogh Committee

4. Acme Zootech begins a nonqualified retirement plan. Which of the following statements is true?

   A. Employee contributions are tax deductible.
   B. Employer contributions are tax deductible.
   C. Employee contributions grow tax deferred if they are invested in an annuity.
   D. The employer must abide by all ERISA requirements.

◆ Answers & Rationale

1.   **A.**   A deferred compensation plan is considered a nonqualified plan because no IRS approval is required to initiate a deferred compensation plan for employees. Only qualified retirement plans need IRS approval.   (Page 602)

2.   **B.**   Deferred compensation plans can be offered to select employees; however, directors are not considered employees.   (Page 603)

3.   **A.**   Deferred compensation plans do not require IRS approval (only qualified plans need that); there is no plan funding (which eliminates a plan trustee); and there is no such thing as a Keogh Committee. Deferred compensation plans are an arrangement between an employer and an employee.   (Page 603)

4.   **C.**   Earnings accumulate tax deferred if the plan is funded by an investment vehicle that offers tax deferral, such as an annuity contract. Tax is paid on all amounts contributed to the plan by the employees and by the employer. Nonqualified plans do not have to comply with all of the ERISA requirements.   (Page 602)

87 Annuity Plans Exam

1. Which of the following represent rights of investors who have purchased variable annuities?

   I. Right to vote on proposed changes in investment policy
   II. Right to approve changes in the plan portfolio
   III. Right to vote for the investment adviser
   IV. Right to make additional purchases at no sales charge

   A. I and III
   B. I and IV
   C. II and III
   D. II and IV

2. Ms. Charolais invests in a variable annuity. At age 65, she chooses to annuitize. Which of the following statements are true?

   I. She will receive the entire value of the annuity in a lump-sum payment.
   II. She may choose to receive monthly payments for the rest of her life.
   III. The value of the accumulation unit is used to calculate the total number of annuity units.
   IV. The accumulation unit value is used to calculate the annuity unit value.

   A. I and III
   B. I and IV
   C. II and III
   D. II and IV

3. For a retiring investor, which of the following is the MOST important factor in determining the suitability of a variable annuity investment?

   A. The fact that the annuity payment may go up or down
   B. Whether the investor is married
   C. Whether the investor has concerns about taxes
   D. The fact that the periodic payments into the contract may go up or down

4. Ms. Charolais purchases a nonqualified annuity at age 60. Before the contract is annuitized, she withdraws some of her funds. What are the consequences?

   A. 10% penalty plus payment of ordinary income on all funds withdrawn
   B. 10% penalty plus payment of ordinary income on all funds withdrawn in excess of basis
   C. Payment of capital gains tax on earnings in excess of basis
   D. Payment of ordinary income tax on earnings in excess of basis

5. Once a variable annuity has been annuitized, which of the following statements is true?

A. The value of each annuity unit varies but the number of annuity units is fixed.
B. The value of each annuity unit is fixed but the number of annuity units varies.
C. The number of accumulation units is fixed but the value per unit varies.
D. The value of each annuity unit and the number of annuity units vary.

6. Which of the following statements are true regarding both variable annuities and mutual funds?

I. They contain managed portfolios.
II. The property of the owner must pass to his estate at the time of his death.
III. They are regulated by the Investment Company Act of 1940.
IV. All income realized by the portfolio through investment income and capital gains is taxable to the owner in the year in which it is generated.

A. I and III
B. I and IV
C. II and III
D. II and IV

7. Your 65-year-old client owns a nonqualified variable annuity. $29,000 was originally invested four years ago; it now has a value of $39,000. The client makes a lump-sum withdrawal of $15,000. He is in the 28% tax bracket. What tax liability results from the withdrawal?

A. $0
B. $2,800
C. $3,800
D. $4,200

8. Under the Tax Reform Act of 1986, all of the following investments offer either full or partially tax-deductible contributions to individuals who meet eligibility requirements EXCEPT

A. IRAs
B. Keogh plans
C. variable annuities
D. defined contribution plans

9. In a variable annuity, total accumulation units are equal to

A. the investor's bookkeeping value
B. the investor's percentage of ownership of the separate account
C. reinvested dividends
D. the offering price

10. Holders of variable annuities receive the largest monthly payments under which of the following payout options?

A. Life annuity
B. Life annuity with period certain
C. Joint and last survivor annuity
D. All options offer the same payout.

11. Changes in payments on a variable annuity will correspond MOST closely to fluctuations in the

A. cost of living
B. Dow Jones Industrial Average
C. value of underlying securities held in the separate account
D. prime rate

12. The owner of a nontax-qualified variable annuity withdraws funds before the contract is annuitized. He would incur which of the following tax consequences?

A. Taxable income or nondeductible losses
B. Capital gains or losses
C. Tax-deferred income
D. Ordinary income in excess of basis

13. All of the following are true statements concerning the assumed interest rate EXCEPT that the

   A. AIR is used in projecting earnings for variable annuities
   B. higher the AIR, the lower the assumed payment
   C. higher the AIR, the higher the initial payment
   D. more conservative the AIR, the more likely the target payment will be achieved

14. Clara Bullock is 43 years old and decides to withdraw the total value of her nonqualified annuity. According to tax code rules, the

   I. entire amount is taxed as ordinary income
   II. earnings are taxed as ordinary income
   III. earnings are taxed as capital gains
   IV. earnings are subject to a 10% penalty

   A. I
   B. II
   C. II and IV
   D. III and IV

15. If a variable annuity has an assumed investment rate of 5% and the annualized return of the separate account is 4%, what would be the consequence?

   I. The value of the accumulation unit will rise.
   II. The value of the annuity unit will rise.
   III. The value of the accumulation unit will fall.
   IV. The value of the annuity unit will fall.

   A. I and II
   B. I and IV
   C. II and III
   D. III and IV

16. An investor is in the annuity stage of a variable annuity purchased 15 years ago. During the present month, the annuitant receives a check for an amount that is less than the previous month's payment. Which of the following events would have caused the annuitant to receive the smaller check?

   A. The performance of the account was less than the previous month's performance.
   B. The performance of the account was greater than the previous month's performance.
   C. The performance of the account was less than the assumed interest rate.
   D. The performance of the account was greater than the assumed interest rate.

17. The separate investment account funding a variable annuity that is managed by the insurance company offering the variable contract is considered

   A. a unit investment trust
   B. a face-amount certificate company
   C. a management investment company
   D. none of the above

18. The separate account funding a variable annuity that purchases shares in a mutual fund offered by the life insurance company is considered

   A. a unit investment trust
   B. a face-amount certificate company
   C. a management investment company
   D. none of the above

19. Adam Grizzly is about to buy a variable annuity contract. He wants to select an annuity that will give him the largest possible monthly payment. Which of the following payout options would do so?

   A. Life annuity with period certain
   B. Unit refund life option
   C. Life annuity with ten-year period certain
   D. Life only annuity

20. Adam Grizzly owns a variable annuity contract with an AIR of 5%. In January the realized rate of return in the separate account was 7%, and Adam received a check based on this return for $200. In February the rate of return was 10%, and Adam received a check for $210. To maintain the same payment Adam received in February, what rate of return would the separate account have to earn in March?

A. 3%
B. 5%
C. 7%
D. 10%

21. Your client tells you he wants a source of retirement income that is stable, but that also could offer some protection against purchasing power risk in times of inflation. You should recommend

A. a variable annuity
B. a fixed annuity
C. a combination annuity
D. common stocks and municipal bonds

22. Which of the following statements about a straight-life variable annuity is(are) true?

I. The number of annuity units a client redeems never changes.
II. The number of accumulation units a client owns never changes.
III. If the client dies during the annuity period, the remaining funds will be distributed to the beneficiary.
IV. The monthly payout is fixed to the Consumer Price Index.

A. I only
B. I and II only
C. II and III only
D. I, II, III and IV

23. According to the NASD, the maximum sales charge on a variable annuity contract is

A. 8.5% of the total amount invested
B. 8.5% of the net amount invested
C. 9% of the total amount invested
D. unlimited

24. At age 65, Adam Grizzly purchased an immediate variable annuity contract. Adam made a lump-sum $100,000 initial payment and selected a life income with ten-year period certain payment option. Adam lived until age 88. The insurance company made payments to Adam

A. until his initial payment of $100,000 was exhausted
B. for ten years
C. for 23 years
D. at a fixed rate for ten years and at a variable rate up until his death

25. The difference between a fixed annuity and a variable annuity is that the variable annuity

I. offers a guaranteed return
II. offers a payment that may vary in amount
III. will always pay out more money than a fixed annuity
IV. attempts to offer protection to the annuitant from inflation

A. I and III
B. I and IV
C. II and III
D. II and IV

26. Belle Charolais purchased a nonqualified annuity when she was 42 and chose to defer payment of benefits. Now she is 55 and withdraws half of the assets in the annuity. What is her tax liability?

A. She owes tax on the entire amount withdrawn.
B. She owes tax on the earnings portion of her withdrawal.
C. She owes tax on the contributions portion of her withdrawal.
D. She incurs no tax liability.

27. An investor begins to receive the payout on a variable annuity. Which of the following statements is true?

   A. Accumulation units are converted to annuity units.
   B. Annuity units are converted to accumulation units.
   C. The value of the annuity unit is fixed.
   D. The amount of each payment is fixed.

28. A joint life with last survivor annuity

   I. covers more than one person
   II. continues payments as long as one annuitant is alive
   III. continues payments as long as all annuitants are alive
   IV. guarantees payments will be made for a certain period of time

   A. I and II
   B. I and III
   C. I and IV
   D. II and IV

29. Which of the following statements about variable annuities is FALSE?

   A. The rate of return is determined by the value of the underlying portfolio.
   B. These annuities are designed to combat inflation risk.
   C. The AIR guarantees a minimum rate of return.
   D. The number of annuity units becomes fixed when the contract is annuitized.

30. Distributions from both an IRA and a variable annuity are subject to which of the following forms of taxation?

   A. Short-term capital gains tax
   B. Long-term capital gains tax
   C. No income tax
   D. Ordinary income tax

31. Eve Grizzly is 65. She made monthly contributions into a tax-deferred annuity. Her contributions totaled $10,000 and the current value of her account is $16,000. For tax purposes, what is Eve's cost basis?

   A. $0
   B. $6,000
   C. $10,000
   D. $16,000

◆ Answers & Rationale

1. **A.** Owners of variable annuities, like owners of mutual fund shares, have the right to vote on changes in investment policy and the right to vote for the investment adviser every two years. They also have the benefit of enjoying reduced sales charges for large dollar purchases.   (Page 604)

2. **C.** When a variable contract is annuitized, the number of accumulation units is multiplied by the unit value to arrive at the total current value. An annuity factor is taken from the annuity table, which considers the investor's sex, age, etc. This factor is used to establish the dollar amount of the first annuity payment. Future annuity payments will vary according to the value of the separate account.   (Page 610)

3. **A.** The most important consideration in purchasing a variable annuity is that benefit payments will fluctuate with the investment performance of the separate account. Answer D is not a consideration because normally the payments into an annuity are level or in a lump sum. (Page 605)

4. **D.** Contributions to a nonqualified variable annuity are made with aftertax dollars. This is in contrast to tax-qualified retirement vehicles (such as an IRA or a Keogh), in which contributions are made with pretax dollars. Distributions from a tax-qualified plan are considered to be 100% taxable ordinary income because the original contributions were never subject to tax. Distributions from a nonqualified plan represent both a return of the original investment made in the plan with aftertax dollars (a nontaxable return of capital) and the income from that investment. Because the income was deferred from tax over the plan's life, it is taxable as ordinary income once it is distributed.   (Page 611)

5. **A.** The annuity period of a variable annuity is the payout period that occurs after the contract has been annuitized. Payments are based on a fixed number of annuity units established when the contract was annuitized. This number of annuity units is multiplied by the value of an annuity unit (which can vary) to arrive at the payment for the period. Accumulation units relate to the accumulation phase of a variable annuity when payments by owners are made to the contract.   (Page 610)

6. **A.** Both mutual funds and variable annuities are regulated by the act of 1940. Mutual funds owned in a single name pass to the estate of the owner at death. Variable annuity proceeds, however, typically pass directly to the owner's designated beneficiary at death, like a typical insurance policy. Investment income and capital gains realized generate current income to the owner of mutual funds, but in variable annuities income is deferred until withdrawal begins.   (Page 605)

7. **B.** This annuity is nonqualified, which means the client has paid for it with aftertax dollars and, therefore, has a basis equal to the original $29,000 investment. Consequently, the client will pay taxes only on the growth portion of the withdrawal ($10,000). The tax on this is $2,800 ($10,000 × 28%). Because the client is over age 59 1/2, there will be no 10% premature distribution penalty tax. However, had the client been *under* age 59 1/2, a $1,000 penalty tax ($10,000 × 10%) would be payable in addition to the $2,800 income tax.   (Page 611)

8. **C.** Contributions to a variable annuity are not tax-deductible. Contributions to an IRA or a Keogh may be tax-deductible, depending on the individual's earnings and his access to company-sponsored retirement plans.   (Page 611)

9. **B.** Accumulation units are an accounting measure that represent an investor's share of ownership in the account.   (Page 609)

10. **A.** A life-simple annuity will provide the investor with the largest payments when the contract is annuitized.   (Page 609)

11. **C.** Payments from a variable annuity depend on the value of the securities in the underlying investment portfolio of the separate account.   (Page 605)

12. **D.** If funds are withdrawn from a nontax-qualified variable annuity before it is annuitized, the owner would be liable for ordinary income tax on all withdrawals that exceed his cost basis. (Page 611)

13. **B.** The level of the AIR alone does not determine the payment. (Page 610)

14. **C.** When receiving a distribution from a nonqualified annuity, the customer pays taxes on the earnings portion only (the amount that exceeds the cost basis). Because the customer is making a withdrawal before age 59 1/2, she must pay a 10% penalty on the taxable amount of the withdrawal. (Page 611)

15. **B.** The accumulation unit will increase in value as the portfolio earned 4%; however, the annuity unit value will decrease because actual return of the portfolio (4%) was less than the assumed interest rate of 5% necessary to maintain payments. (Page 611)

16. **C.** In the annuity stage of a variable annuity, the amount received will depend on the performance of the account compared to the assumed interest rate. If actual performance is less than the AIR, the value of the check will decline. (Page 611)

17. **C.** A separate account that is managed by an insurance company and is used to fund variable contracts is defined by the Investment Company Act of 1940 as a management investment company. (Page 605)

18. **A.** A separate account purchasing shares of mutual funds to fund variable contracts does not actively manage the securities held; instead, the account holds the shares in trust for the contract holders. This account is classified as a unit investment trust under the act of 1940. (Page 605)

19. **D.** Generally a life only contract will pay the most per month because payments cease at the death of the annuitant. (Page 609)

20. **B.** If the actual rate of return equals the assumed interest rate, the check will stay the same.

Recall that the payout is based on an accumulated value to be distributed over the life of the annuitant (like compounding). Therefore, for the investor to receive the $210 in March the account must earn 5%. (Page 610)

21. **C.** Because the investor wants the objectives provided by both a fixed and variable annuity, a combination annuity would be suitable. (Page 606)

22. **A.** Annuity units are fixed; their current value when cashed in determines the payout amount. A life only annuity ceases payments at the death of the annuitant. The company keeps any undistributed payments. Accumulation units will fluctuate in value and number during the accumulation period. (Page 610)

23. **A.** NASD rules allow a maximum sales charge on a variable annuity contract of 8 1/2%. (Page 607)

24. **C.** An annuity with life and ten-year certain will pay for the greater of ten years or the life of the annuitant. The investor lived for 23 more years, which is more than the ten certain. (Page 609)

25. **D.** Variable annuities are different from fixed because the payments vary and they were designed to offer the annuitant protection against inflation. (Page 605)

26. **B.** Because this is a nonqualified annuity, all the investor's contributions are made with after-tax dollars; she does not owe tax on the contributions portion of her withdrawal. However, investment earnings in annuity contracts are tax-deferred. Therefore, she must pay tax on the portion of the withdrawal that is attributable to investment growth. (Page 611)

27. **A.** To determine the amount of the payment, accumulation units are converted to annuity units. In a variable annuity, neither the value of the annuity unit nor the amount of the monthly payment can be fixed. (Page 609)

28. **A.** A joint life with last survivor contract covers multiple annuitants and ceases payments at the death of the last surviving annuitant. A period certain contract guarantees payments for a certain amount of time. (Page 609)

29. **C.** The assumed interest rate provides an earnings target for the annuity contract, not a guarantee. Variable annuities provide a rate of return based on the performance of the separate account, which is generally invested in growth instruments with the intention of keeping pace with inflation. At the time the investor begins receiving payments, accumulation units are converted to annuity units. (Page 609)

30. **D.** All distributions from retirement accounts in excess of cost basis are subject to taxation at the owner's then-current ordinary tax rate. The advantage of most retirement accounts is that withdrawals usually begin after the account owner has dropped into a lower tax bracket (i.e., upon retirement). (Page 611)

31. **C.** Contributions to a nonqualified annuity are made aftertax. The growth of the annuity is deferred representing ordinary income when withdrawn. Cost base is $10,000. (Page 611)

Qualified Annuity Plans Exam

1. Adam Grizzly invests in a tax-qualified variable annuity. What is the tax treatment of the distributions he receives?

   A. Partially tax-free; partially ordinary income
   B. Partially tax-free; partially capital gains
   C. All ordinary income
   D. All capital gains

2. Whom of the following would be ineligible for a tax-sheltered 403B annuity?

   A. Professor at a land grant college
   B. Custodian at a municipal public school
   C. Student at a private college
   D. Employee of a county high school

3. Your customer works as a nurse in a public school. He wants to know more about participating in his school's TSA plan. You should tell him

   I. contributions are made with before-tax dollars
   II. he is not eligible to participate
   III. distributions before age 59 1/2 are normally subject to penalty tax
   IV. mutual funds and CDs are available investment vehicles

   A. I, II and III
   B. I and III
   C. I, III and IV
   D. II

4. Of the following statements describing IRAs, which one is NOT true of TSA qualified plans?

   A. A self-employed person may participate.
   B. Contributions are tax deferred.
   C. Distributions must begin by age 70 1/2.
   D. Distributions after age 59 1/2 will be taxed as ordinary income.

◆ Answers & Rationale

1.   **C.**   In a tax-qualified annuity, the annuitant has no basis unless voluntary aftertax contributions were made. Such aftertax contributions are the exception and are not mentioned in this question. Because the annuitant has no basis, all payments are considered ordinary income. In a nonqualified annuity, contributions are made with aftertax dollars, which establish the annuitant's basis. Annuity payments from nonqualified annuities are treated as ordinary income to the extent that they exceed the basis.   (Page 616)

2.   **C.**   All of the individuals listed meet the requirement of being an employee of a school system except for the student.   (Page 613)

3.   **C.**   Because he is employed by a public school system, your customer is eligible to participate in the tax-sheltered annuity plan. Employee contributions to a TSA plan are excluded from gross income in the year in which they are made. Like other retirement plans, a penalty tax is assessed on distributions received before age 59 1/2. A TSA plan may invest in various instruments, including mutual funds, stocks, bonds and CDs, in addition to annuity contracts.   (Page 613)

4.   **A.**   Only employees of schools, church organizations and nonprofit organizations are eligible to participate in 403B TSA plans. The provisions for contributions and distributions are the same for IRAs and TSA qualified plans.   (Page 613)

89 ERISA Exam

1. What was the primary purpose for establishing ERISA?

   A. To establish a retirement fund for government employees
   B. To establish a means for self-employed persons to provide for their own retirement
   C. To protect employees from the mishandling of retirement funds by corporations and unions
   D. To provide all employees, both government and nongovernment, with an additional source of retirement income in the event that the Social Security system defaults

2. The requirements of the Employee Retirement Income Security Act apply to pension plans established by which of the following?

   A. Self-employed individuals with no employees
   B. Only public entities, such as the City of New York
   C. Only private organizations, such as Exxon
   D. Both public and private organizations

3. Regulations regarding how contributions are made to tax-qualified plans relate to which of the following ERISA requirements?

   A. Vesting
   B. Funding
   C. Nondiscrimination
   D. Reporting and disclosure

4. A qualified payroll deduction plan

   I. requires advance approval from the Department of Labor and the IRS
   II. must comply with nondiscrimination rules
   III. must cover all its employees within three years
   IV. provides tax-deferred growth potential

   A. I only
   B. I, II and III only
   C. II, III and IV only
   D. I, II, III and IV

◆ Answers & Rationale

1. **C.** ERISA was created originally to protect the retirement funds of members of unions and employees of large corporations. ERISA has set guidelines stating that all qualified retirement plans must: be in writing; not be discriminatory; segregate funds from corporate or union assets; invest in prudent investments; and report to the participants annually. All of these activities are audited under ERISA. (Page 617)

2. **C.** ERISA was established to protect the retirement funds of employees working in the private sector only. It does not apply to self-employed persons or public organizations. (Page 617)

3. **B.** *Vesting* describes how quickly rights to a retirement account turn over to an employee. *Nondiscrimination* refers to employee coverage by the plan. All retirement plans must meet ERISA's fiduciary reporting and disclosure requirements. Only *funding* covers how an employer makes contributions to (or funds) a plan. (Page 617)

4. **D.** Every qualified retirement plan must meet the ERISA requirements listed. (Page 618)

1. All of the following statements are true with respect to a limited partnership subscription agreement EXCEPT the

    A. investor's registered representative must verify that the investor has provided accurate information
    B. general partner endorses the subscription agreement, signifying that a limited partner is suitable
    C. investor's signature indicates that he has read the prospectus
    D. general partner's signature grants the limited partners power of attorney to conduct the partnership's affairs

2. Which of the following handles registration of the securities and packages the program for a limited partnership?

    A. Syndicator
    B. Property manager
    C. General partner
    D. Underwriter

3. A general partner may be allowed to do all of the following EXCEPT

    A. make general management decisions regarding the partnership
    B. sell property to the limited partnership
    C. act as an agent for the partnership in managing partnership assets
    D. borrow money from the partnership

4. Limited partners have all of the following rights EXCEPT the right to

    A. monitor the partnership
    B. sue the general partner for violations of the partnership agreement
    C. justified returns
    D. decide which properties will be purchased by the partnership

5. The managing partner of a limited partnership has responsibility for all of the following EXCEPT

    A. organizing the business
    B. managing the operations
    C. providing unlimited capital for the partnership business
    D. paying the debts of the partnership

6. Your client's real estate limited partnership goes bankrupt. Who will be paid before your client?

    I.   Fellow limited partners
    II.   Bank that holds the mortgage on the property
    III. Bank that holds the unsecured note
    IV.   General partner

    A. I and II
    B. II and III
    C. II, III and IV
    D. III and IV

7. What might be the effect of a limited partner's making business decisions for the partnership?

A. He might be removed from the partnership.
B. His limited liability status would be maintained.
C. His limited liability status might be jeopardized.
D. There would be no effect, because of partnership democracy.

8. Programs that allow for the direct pass-through of losses and income to investors include all of the following EXCEPT

A. REITs
B. Subchapter S corporations
C. oil and gas drilling direct participation programs
D. new construction real estate direct participation programs

9. If your objective is capital appreciation, in which type of DPP should you invest?

A. Raw land
B. Oil and gas exploratory drilling
C. Existing property
D. Equipment leasing

10. Which of the following statements are true regarding the risk and return potential of oil and gas direct participation programs?

I. Exploratory drilling programs are less risky than developmental programs.
II. Income programs provide the lowest return potential.
III. Developmental programs are speculative investments.
IV. A successful exploratory program provides a higher rate of return than a successful developmental program.

A. I and II
B. II and IV
C. II, III and IV
D. IV

11. An investor expects to have a large amount of passive income over the next two years. Which type of partnership is likely to provide the largest amount of shelter?

A. Equipment-leasing program
B. Undeveloped land purchasing program
C. Oil and gas drilling program
D. Real estate income program

12. Which of the following BEST describes an intangible drilling cost?

A. Labor, fuel, or drilling rig rental
B. Proven reserves of oil or gas
C. Tax liability
D. Exploratory well drilling

13. In considering a direct participation program, rank the following in order of priority.

I. Tax write-offs
II. Liquidity and marketability
III. Potential for economic gain

A. I, II, III
B. II, III, I
C. III, I, II
D. III, II, I

14. A method of analyzing limited partnerships by identifying the sources of revenues and expenses is known as

A. capital analysis
B. cash flow analysis
C. technical analysis
D. liquidity analysis

15. Which two of the following could be used by an analyst to establish the rate of return on a direct participation program?

I. Present value
II. Internal rate of return
III. Yield to maturity
IV. First in, first out

A. I and II
B. I and III
C. II and III
D. II and IV

◆ Answers & Rationale

1. **D.**   The limited partner's signature on the subscription agreement grants the general partner power of attorney to conduct the partnership's affairs. The subscription agreement for a limited partnership is deemed accepted when the general partner signs the subscription agreement.
(Page 625)

2. **A.**   In putting the deal together by organizing the administrative apparatus and handling registration of the securities, the person is acting as a syndicator. The general partner is responsible for buying the partnership assets. The property manager handles the day-to-day activities. The underwriter is responsible for distributing the partnership's interest.   (Page 625)

3. **D.**   In all these situations, there is the potential for conflicts of interest; however, the general partner is not forbidden by law to engage in any of these acts, except for borrowing money—the general partner may never borrow money from the partnership.   (Page 627)

4. **D.**   The limited partners have the right to inspect partnership records and to sue a general partner who acts outside the partnership agreement. The compensation of the general partner is normally set by the general partner in the original agreement. The general partner makes all management decisions relative to the partnership's interests.   (Page 627)

5. **C.**   The general partner organizes and manages the partnership. He assumes unlimited liability, including paying all partnership debts. However, it is the limited partner who usually provides the bulk of the capital.   (Page 627)

6. **B.**   Creditors, both secured and unsecured, have priority over partners. Your client's fellow limited partners will be paid at the same time as your client. The general partner will receive his money last.   (Page 626)

7. **C.**   If a limited partner has control over the partnership operation (i.e., he makes partnership decisions), he could be judged a general partner and thus have unlimited liability. This should not jeopardize the status of other limited partners. Partnership democracy refers to what the limited partners can do as a group without putting their status in jeopardy (e.g., sell assets, remove the general partner and so on).   (Page 628)

8. **A.**   REITs allow for the direct pass-through of income but not of losses. The other programs are all forms of business that allow for pass-through of income and losses.   (Page 629)

9. **A.**   Raw land is purchased solely for its appreciation potential. Exploratory drilling, existing property and equipment leasing programs all offer income rather than capital appreciation.
(Page 629)

10. **C.**   Income programs generate income from proven oil or gas reserves, making them the safest and lowest yielding type of oil and gas DPP. Both exploratory and developmental drilling programs are speculative. An exploratory program offers the highest level of risk and the highest potential return on investment.   (Page 629)

11. **C.**   Oil and gas drilling programs allocate the majority of investment dollars to drilling. These costs are intangible drilling costs (IDCs), which are 100% deductible when drilling occurs. In equipment-leasing programs, the investment dollars are recovered through depreciation over the life of the leased assets.   (Page 629)

12. **A.**   Intangible drilling costs are a part of oil and gas exploratory drilling programs. These costs are generally written off in the first year of operations. None of the other choices listed are costs of operating an exploratory drilling program.
(Page 630)

13. **C.**   Economic viability of the program is the first commandment of DPPs. Programs that are designed solely to generate tax benefits but that are not really economically viable are the ones the IRS considers abusive.   (Page 631)

14. **B.** Cash flow analysis compares income (revenues) to expenses. (Page 631)

15. **A.** The present value (of the dollars the investor will receive as principal at the maturity of the partnership) and the internal rate of return (the present values of the future cash flow) are both used by analysts to establish a rate of return for a DPP. (Page 631)

1. All of the following lend money EXCEPT the

   A. GNMA
   B. FRB
   C. FHLB
   D. FICB

2. The Federal Farm Credit Bank system consists of all of the following EXCEPT the

   A. FICBs
   B. banks for cooperatives
   C. Federal Land Bank
   D. Federal Home Loan Bank

3. Income from which of the following qualifies for the 70% corporate dividend exclusion?

   I. Common stock
   II. Preferred stock
   III. Convertible bonds
   IV. Municipal bonds

   A. I and II
   B. II, III and IV
   C. II and IV
   D. III and IV

4. Bond trust indentures are required for which of the following?

   A. Corporate debt securities
   B. Municipal general obligation bonds
   C. Municipal revenue bonds
   D. Treasury securities

5. What is the advantage of a Treasury receipt over a Treasury bill?

   A. The investor does not have to pay taxes on accrued interest.
   B. All interest is paid at maturity.
   C. The capital requirement is less.
   D. Interest is taxed as it accrues yearly, regardless of whether it has been received.

6. Using Table 1, what was Consolidated Codfish's close on September 12th?

   A. 68
   B. 71 1/2
   C. 74 1/2
   D. 78

7. Using Table 1, what was Consolidated Codfish's approximate earnings per share?

   A. $.75
   B. $3.00
   C. $6.00
   D. $33.29

Table 1

NEW YORK STOCK EXCHANGE COMPOSITE TRANSACTIONS
Tuesday, September 13, 1998

52 Weeks High	Low	Stock	Div	Yld %	P-E Ratio	Sales 100s	High	Low	Close	Net Chg.
80	40	COD	.75	.1	12	3329	78	68	73	–1 1/2

8. Which of the following investments would produce the LEAST market risk?

   A. Stocks
   B. Fixed-income debentures
   C. Treasury bills
   D. Zero-coupon bonds

9. Which is the earliest date a customer can sell a stock and still receive a previously declared dividend?

   A. Ex-date
   B. Payable date
   C. Record date
   D. Next day

10. In order to be paid a dividend, an owner's name should be recorded on the stock record book of the issuer's transfer agent by the

   A. ex-date
   B. payable date
   C. record date
   D. next day

11. An investor purchasing 1,000 shares of a mutual fund that has a maximum sales charge of 8 1/2% and an NAV of $10.30 at the time of purchase will pay a total sales charge (rounded to the nearest dollar) of

   A. $88
   B. $96
   C. $875
   D. $957

12. Government securities settle on the

   A. ex-date
   B. payable date
   C. record date
   D. next business day

13. Using Table 2, how much would an investor have received and reported as taxable income per share in 1998?

   A. $1.00
   B. $1.40
   C. $1.50
   D. $1.60

14. A customer owns 100 shares of DWQ at a cost basis of $25 per share. DWQ distributes a 5% stock dividend. Under the Internal Revenue Code, what is the customer's basis in this stock?

   A. 100 shares at a cost of $25 and 5 shares at a cost of $0
   B. 105 shares at an average cost of $23.81 per share
   C. 105 shares at an average cost of $25 per share
   D. 100 shares at a cost of $25 and 5 shares at a cost of $21 3/4

15. If a broker-dealer executes a registered bond trade between two customers, which of the following must be notified?

   A. National Clearing Corporation
   B. National Association of Securities Dealers, Inc.
   C. Issuer's transfer agent
   D. Issuer's registrar

16. Which of the following are actively traded?

   I. Rights
   II. Nondetachable warrants
   III. Common stocks
   IV. Options on stock

   A. I, III and IV only
   B. II only
   C. II and IV only
   D. I, II, III and IV

Table 2

Rate 0.40Q   Pd'97—$1.40
ALFAtronics, Inc.   Com p—$1.00

Divd $	Declared	Ex-date	Record Date	Payable
0.50	Nov 16	Dec 4	Dec 6	Jan 15
0.40	Feb 15	Mar 2	Mar 6	Apr 15
0.40	May 16	Jun 7	Jun 9	Jul 15
0.20	Sep 16	Oct 19	Oct 23	Nov 15
0.40	Nov 22	Dec 7	Dec 9	Jan 15 '99

17. Which of the following statements is(are) true regarding rights and warrants?

   I. Warrants are issued with an exercise price higher than the underlying stock.
   II. Rights are issued with an exercise price lower than the underlying stock.
   III. Warrants are long-lived, may even be perpetual, and may be issued to anyone.
   IV. Rights are short-lived and are issued only to present stockholders.

   A. I only
   B. I and II only
   C. II and III only
   D. I, II, III and IV

18. Which of the following is issued with a maturity of 12 months or less?

   A. Treasury bill
   B. Treasury note
   C. Treasury bond
   D. Treasury stock

19. Which of the following is considered to have intermediate maturity?

   A. Treasury bill
   B. Treasury note
   C. Treasury bond
   D. Treasury stock

20. Which of the following is considered to have long-term maturity?

   A. Treasury bill
   B. Treasury note
   C. Treasury bond
   D. Treasury stock

21. Using Table 3, the bid price of the 8 1/2 of Nov 1997 is

   A. $1,000
   B. $1,001.25
   C. $1,001.875
   D. $1,005

22. Which of the following is the issuer of government securities?

   A. Federal Reserve Banks
   B. Federal Reserve Board
   C. Treasury Department
   D. Commerce Department

23. All of the following are true of a negotiable CD EXCEPT that

   A. yields are quoted for no shorter than a 14-day time period
   B. interest is paid at maturity
   C. it is guaranteed by the issuing bank
   D. it is registered

24. Which of the following do NOT trade in the secondary market?

   A. Bankers' acceptances
   B. Commercial paper
   C. Repurchase agreements
   D. Treasury bills

25. If enough stop orders are entered in the market, which two of the following statements would be true?

   I. Buy stops will accelerate a bull market.
   II. Sell stops will accelerate a bull market.
   III. Buy stops will accelerate a bear market.
   IV. Sell stops will accelerate a bear market.

   A. I and II
   B. I and IV
   C. II and III
   D. III and IV

Table 3

TREASURY BONDS AND NOTES					
Rate	Mat. Date	Bid	Asked	Chg.	Yld.
7 5/8	1997 Nov n	99.30	100.1	−.1	3.65
8 1/2	1997 Nov	100.4	100.6	+.1	4.51

26. Which of the following best describe the information displayed on Level 3 of the Nasdaq system?

I. Highest bid
II. Highest ask
III. Lowest bid
IV. Lowest ask

A. I and II only
B. I and IV only
C. II and III only
D. I, II, III and IV

27. The *broker* part of the term "broker-dealer" indicates which of the following?

A. Acting for others in both purchase and sale
B. Acting for others in both purchase and sale, and selling from inventory
C. Acting for the firm and for others in both purchase and sale
D. None of the above

28. Which of the following is true of a GTC order on the specialist's book?

A. It is automatically canceled after six months.
B. If properly renewed, it doesn't lose its priority.
C. It must be reentered after one year.
D. It never has to be reviewed or renewed.

29. If a customer designates an order as "not held," which of the following statements is true?

A. The floor broker has been given discretion as to time and price.
B. The registered representative has been given discretion as to time and price.
C. The order will not be held up; it will be executed immediately.
D. The order will be given to the specialist for execution.

30. A customer is long 2,000 shares of SSS and sells 2,000 shares of SSS short against the box for $30,000. Under NYSE rules, how much money may he withdraw from his margin account on completion of this transaction? (Reg T is 50%.)

A. $15,000
B. $26,000
C. $28,500
D. $30,000

31. A customer opens a new cash account. The signature(s) of which of the following is(are) required before orders can be executed?

I. Customer
II. Registered representative
III. Registered principal

A. I only
B. I and II only
C. II and III only
D. I, II and III

32. A new customer deposits $32,000 cash in his margin account. How much can he buy in marginable securities? (Reg T is 50%.)

A. $16,000
B. $32,000
C. $48,000
D. $64,000

33. A change in which of the following should be indicated in a customer's file?

I. Name or address
II. Marital status
III. Objectives

A. I only
B. I and II only
C. III only
D. I, II and III

34. Adam Grizzly has $300,000 worth of securities with Churnum, Burnem, Spurnim, his spouse has $300,000 in securities, and they have a joint account with $400,000 in securities. CBS files for bankruptcy. What is the couple's SIPC coverage?

   A. $300,000
   B. $600,000
   C. $700,000
   D. $1,000,000

35. All of the following are characteristics of an investment in a REIT EXCEPT

   A. ownership of real property without management responsibilities
   B. diversification of real estate investment capital
   C. pass-through tax treatment of income
   D. pass-through tax treatment of operating losses

36. An investor is in a low tax bracket and wishes to invest a moderate sum in an investment that will provide him with some protection from inflation. Which of the following would you recommend?

   A. Municipal unit investment trust
   B. Growth stock mutual fund
   C. Money-market mutual fund
   D. Ginnie Mae fund

37. Which of the following mutual funds would provide high appreciation potential together with high risk?

   A. Balanced
   B. Bond
   C. Income
   D. Specialized

38. Two customers who combine their capital would NOT qualify for which of the following?

   A. Avoiding the odd-lot differential
   B. Opening a joint tenants in common account
   C. Breakpoints on a mutual fund purchase
   D. Joint registration on stock certificates

39. Which of the following statements about the NASD 5% markup policy are true?

   I. The type of security is a consideration.
   II. A transaction in common stock customarily has a higher percentage markup than a bond transaction of the same size.
   III. A riskless transaction is not generally covered by the 5% markup policy.
   IV. The markup policy does not apply to securities sold at a specific price and with a prospectus.

   A. I, II and IV only
   B. I, III and IV only
   C. II and III only
   D. I, II, III and IV

40. A doctor has compensation of $160,000. What is the maximum he may contribute to his Keogh plan?

   A. $5,000
   B. $22,000
   C. $28,000
   D. $30,000

41. An investment in a REIT unit differs from an investment in a real estate limited partnership interest in that the REIT investment

   A. does not pass through losses
   B. has limited liability
   C. cannot be traded on an exchange
   D. passes through income

42. If the Federal Reserve Board changes the reserve requirement, the effect of the change to the economy will MOST likely be

   A. regressive
   B. nonregressive
   C. multiplied
   D. deflationary

43. An economic downturn that lasts for six months is called

   A. a recession
   B. a depression
   C. progressive
   D. regressive

44. Orders for durable goods are considered what type of indicator?

A. Leading
B. Lagging
C. Coincident
D. Coterminous

45. Which of the following is a coincident indicator?

A. Duration of unemployment
B. Durable goods
C. S&P 500
D. Personal income

46. A company with cumulative nonparticipating voting preferred stock would

A. pay preferred dividends prior to paying the coupons due on their outstanding bonds
B. pay past due and current preferred dividends before paying dividends to their common stockholders
C. pay the current dividends on the preferred but not the past dividends on the preferred before paying a dividend on the common
D. force conversion of the preferred that is trading at a discount to par and thereby eliminate the necessity of paying past due dividends

47. Which of the following situations might fall into the category of hot issues?

A. A new issue is offered at $30 and immediately appreciates to $35.
B. A new issue is offered at $30 and immediately decreases to $25.
C. A market maker buys at $17 and immediately sells with a spread of $2.
D. A broker-dealer sells inventory at $60 three weeks after buying at $30.

48. At 1:30 pm Eastern time, the Dow Jones Industrial Average is down 250 points from the prior day's close. The NYSE will halt all trading for a period of

A. 15 minutes
B. 30 minutes
C. 1 hour
D. 2 hours

49. Which of the following debt instruments does not generate current income?

A. Treasury STRIPS
B. Treasury note
C. Treasury bond
D. Treasury stock

50. Which of the following statements is(are) true of a Treasury STRIPS?

I. The rate of return is locked in.
II. There is no reinvestment risk.
III. The interest is taxed as a capital gain.
IV. The interest is realized at maturity.

A. I
B. I, II and III
C. I, II and IV
D. II and IV

51. Which of the following is NOT an advantage offered by a REIT investment?

A. Liquidity
B. Tax deferral
C. Diversification
D. Professional management

52. Securities issued by which of the following are backed by the federal government?

A. Federal National Mortgage Association
B. Federal Home Loan Mortgage Corporation
C. Government National Mortgage Association
D. Federal Intermediate Credit Bank

53. Which of the following statements is true of GNMA mortgage-backed securities?

   A. They are backed by the Federal National Mortgage Association, which may borrow from the Treasury to pay principal and interest.
   B. They are backed by a pool of mortgages.
   C. Interest payments are exempt from federal income taxes.
   D. The minimum purchase is $25,000.

54. Federal Farm Credit System Consolidated Systemwide Issues are characterized by which of the following statements?

   A. They are issued only in the form of discount notes.
   B. The interest on them is not subject to federal income tax.
   C. They have the same degree of safety as Treasury issues.
   D. They are backed only by the full faith and credit of the issuer.

55. All of the following pay semiannual interest EXCEPT

   A. GNMAs
   B. Treasury bonds
   C. Treasury notes
   D. public utility bonds

56. T bills are issued with all of the following maturities EXCEPT

   A. one month
   B. three months
   C. six months
   D. twelve months

57. Which of the following have authority to enforce MSRB rules?

   I. SEC
   II. NASD
   III. Comptroller of the Currency
   IV. Federal Reserve Board

   A. I and II only
   B. I, II and IV only
   C. III and IV only
   D. I, II, III and IV

58. All of the following statements are true of a Treasury receipt EXCEPT that

   A. it may be issued by a securities broker-dealer
   B. it is backed by the full faith and credit of the federal government
   C. the interest coupons are sold separately
   D. it may be purchased at a discount

59. Which of the following best describes the federal funds rate?

   A. Average rate for short-term bank loans of the previous week
   B. Rate charged by major New York City banks
   C. Rate that changes daily and that banks charge each other
   D. Rate that major New York City banks charge broker-dealers

60. Which of the following are characteristics of the interbank system?

   I. Unregulated
   II. Regulated by the Federal Reserve Board
   III. Centralized
   IV. Decentralized

   A. I and III
   B. I and IV
   C. II and III
   D. II and IV

61. Which of the following do NOT issue commercial paper?

    A. Commercial banks
    B. Finance companies
    C. Service companies
    D. Broker-dealers

62. Which of the following is(are) characteristics of a money-market fund?

    I. Portfolio of short-term debt instruments
    II. High beta
    III. Offered without a sales load
    IV. The NAV does not appreciate

    A. I
    B. I, II and IV
    C. I, III and IV
    D. II, III and IV

63. A newly issued bond has call protection for the first five years after it is issued. This feature would be most valuable if, during this five-year period, interest rates are generally

    A. fluctuating
    B. stable
    C. falling
    D. rising

64. The capitalization of a corporation includes $1,000,000 of 7% preferred stock and $1,000,000 of 7% convertible debentures. If all the convertible debentures were converted into common stock, what would happen to the company's earnings?

    A. They would increase.
    B. They would decrease.
    C. There would be no change.
    D. The change in earnings cannot be forecast.

65. NASD rules on freeriding and withholding restrict the purchase of a hot issue by which of the following people?

    I. Nonregistered employee of a member of the NASD
    II. Bank officer who has a significant relationship with the issuer
    III. Officer of a broker-dealer firm that is a member of the NASD
    IV. Registered representative

    A. I and II only
    B. I, III and IV only
    C. III and IV only
    D. I, II, III and IV

66. The newspaper indicates that T bill yields have gone down. This means that T bill prices

    A. are up
    B. are mixed
    C. are down
    D. cannot be determined

67. A customer requests information on a security offering that is not yet effective. She asks her registered rep to circle the important information in the preliminary prospectus and jot down the company's most recent performance numbers. This is permitted

    A. if it is an additional issue of listed stock
    B. if it is an initial public offering
    C. without restriction
    D. under no circumstances

68. Which of the following securities are exempt from the 1933 act?

    I. Federal and state issues
    II. Small business investment companies
    III. Nonprofit organizations
    IV. State-chartered commercial banks

    A. I only
    B. I and II only
    C. II, III and IV only
    D. I, II, III and IV

69. An insider can sell securities under Rule 144 without being required to file notice with the SEC if the

I.   number of shares is 500 or less
II. value of the shares is $10,000 or less
III. value of the shares is greater than $1 million
IV. number of shares is greater than 100,000

A. I and II
B. I and III
C. II and IV
D. III and IV

70. A 5% bond is purchased with an 8% yield to maturity. If the bond is held to maturity, the aftertax yield will be

A. less than 5%
B. 5%
C. between 5% and 8%
D. 8%

71. Which of the following clients is exempt from the Penny Stock Rules?

A. Bea Kuhl signed and dated a copy of the *Important Information on Penny Stocks* statement.
B. Joe Kuhl returned a signed copy of his suitability determination statement to his broker.
C. Randy Bear has purchased three different penny stocks over the past year.
D. Rhoda Bear signed and dated a transaction agreement naming the penny stock and number of shares bought.

72. The doctrine of tax-free reciprocity for municipal bonds originated in

A. U.S. Supreme Court decisions
B. state laws
C. federal laws
D. IRS interpretations

73. All of the following trade flat or without accrued interest EXCEPT a

A. bond in default of interest
B. zero-coupon bond
C. bond for which the settlement date and the interest payment dates are the same
D. registered industrial revenue bond

74. The settlement for a government bond trade in a cash account is

A. the same day
B. the next business day
C. three business days after the trade date
D. five business days after the trade date

75. Which two of the following statements are true regarding an NASD Form DK?

I.   It is sent to the contra broker.
II. It is sent to the customer.
III. It is sent to the NASD or NYSE.
IV. It is used to report unmatched trades.

A. I and III
B. I and IV
C. II and III
D. II and IV

76. What is typically NOT a reason for a fail to deliver of a certificate?

A. Rapidly changing market
B. Incorrect delivery instructions
C. Mutilated certificate
D. Partially called issue

77. ALFA Enterprises intends to acquire Microscam. The terms are one share of ALF for three shares of MCS. ALF is trading at 30 and MCS at 10 1/2. The acquisition is being reviewed for possible problems with antitrust laws. A trader has sold short 4,000 shares of ALF at 30 and has bought 12,000 shares of MCS at 10 1/2. This trader's transaction would be considered a

A. bona fide arbitrage
B. risk arbitrage
C. straddle
D. reverse hedge

78. A client is interested in penny stock investments. Where would the registered representative locate current quote information?

   A. *The Blue List*
   B. *Yellow Sheets*
   C. *Pink Sheets*
   D. Consolidated Quotation System

79. A customer is buying 800 shares of DWQ stock. The trader responds to the firm's request for an 800-share quote with bid–15, ask–15 1/2. The trader must sell

   A. 100 shares at 15
   B. 100 shares at 15 1/2
   C. 800 shares at 15
   D. 800 shares at 15 1/2

80. A customer enters a day order to sell 400 shares of QRS at 34 1/2. During the day QRS trades between 33 and 33 3/4. If prior to the close the customer wishes to change the order to a good till canceled order, you should suggest that the customer

   A. cancels the day order promptly and immediately reenters it as a GTC order
   B. cancels the day order, and enters a new GTC order the next day at the opening
   C. enters a new GTC order promptly and allows the day order to remain on the books until expiration
   D. allows the day order to remain on the books and, if it is not executed, reenters it the next day as a GTC order

81. Which of the following limited partnership programs would be LEAST appropriate for an investor seeking to shelter current passive income?

   A. Oil and gas income program
   B. Oil and gas exploratory program
   C. Sale-leaseback arrangement
   D. Program investing in existing apartment buildings

82. In general, a registered representative could have power of attorney for accounts of each of the following EXCEPT a(n)

   A. corporation
   B. individual
   C. partnership
   D. custodian

83. A registered representative of an NYSE member firm who wishes to work outside the firm after hours would require permission from the

   A. member firm
   B. NASD
   C. NYSE
   D. SEC

84. Which of the following orders would have to be marked "short"?

   A. You have exercised warrants and sold the underlying stock.
   B. You have sold part of a long position when you are short against the box.
   C. You have sold stock owned long.
   D. You have exercised a call and then sold the underlying stock.

85. Which of the following statements is true of a limited power of attorney that a customer gives his rep?

   A. The rep needs written permission from the customer for each trade.
   B. The customer must renew the power of attorney every year.
   C. The customer can still enter independent orders.
   D. The branch manager must initial each order before it is entered.

86. A mutual fund has an NAV of $13.37. An investor was charged a 4% sales charge on a lump-sum purchase of $50,000. How many shares were purchased?

   A. 3,422
   B. 3,564
   C. 3,589
   D. 3,595

87. All of the following are true of taxable zero-coupon bonds EXCEPT that

    A. the discount is accreted
    B. tax is paid annually
    C. interest is paid semiannually
    D. they are purchased at a discount

88. In a margin account, marking to the market may result in a request for an additional deposit equal to the difference between

    A. Reg T and the maintenance margin
    B. Reg T and the current market value
    C. the settlement and the contract price
    D. the maintenance margin and the current equity

89. Which of the following statements about a bond quoted as "GMA Zr 12" would be true?

    A. The bond pays $12 interest annually.
    B. The bond pays $120 interest annually.
    C. The bond pays no interest until maturity.
    D. None of the above statements is true.

90. After short selling a stock at 60, an investor holds the position as the stock declines to 42. The investor could use which of the following strategies to lock in the gain?

    A. Buy stop limit at 44
    B. Write calls
    C. Write puts
    D. Buy calls

91. Where does a customer get the information needed to determine the amount of accretion on an original issue discount bond?

    A. Investor
    B. Underwriter
    C. IRS
    D. Issuer

92. The federal funds rate has been increasing for a long time. Which of the following is likely to occur?

    A. The FRB will increase bank reserve requirements.
    B. Member banks' deposits at Federal Reserve Banks will decrease.
    C. Money-market interest rates will decrease.
    D. The prime rate will decrease.

93. All of the following information may be included in an advertisement for a CMO issue EXCEPT a

    A. statement that the CMO is guaranteed by the U.S. government
    B. disclosure of the CMO's coupon rate and final maturity date
    C. generic description of the CMO tranche
    D. disclosure that payment assumptions may or may not be met

94. A bond issuer establishes a sinking fund. The bond is most likely to be retired

    A. if the facility providing revenue is severely damaged
    B. on the initial call date
    C. on or before the maturity date
    D. during the year following the maturity date

95. An investor in COD stock has a margin account that is restricted by $800. COD pays a dividend of $1,000. The investor can withdraw

    A. $0
    B. $200
    C. $500
    D. $1,000

96. A customer bought a T bill on margin. What is the required margin? (Reg T is 50%.)

    A. $0
    B. 30%
    C. 50%
    D. NASD/NYSE minimum margin

97. An improvement in the business cycle is indicated by an increase in all of the following EXCEPT

A. industrial production
B. inventory levels
C. S&P Index
D. consumer orders

Use the following information to answer questions 98 and 99. ALFA Enterprises has the following capitalization:

$100,000 of 5% debentures convertible at $20
$100,000 of 5% preferred stock cumulative
$100,000 of common stock, par $20

98. With operating income of $50,000 and a 34% tax bracket, EPS is

A. $3.50
B. $4.94
C. $5.60
D. $5.94

99. With operating income of $50,000, the corporation has fully diluted EPS of

A. $2.00
B. $2.47
C. $2.80
D. $5.60

100. An investor's portfolio includes ten bonds and 200 shares of common stock. If both positions increase by 1/2 of a point, what is the gain?

A. $50
B. $105
C. $110
D. $150

101. A U.S. company that sells stereo equipment places a 600,000,000 yen order in August for Japanese stereo components for its Christmas inventory. Payment must be made in Japanese yen in three months. At the time the order is placed, the yen is worth 50 hundredths of a cent. However, the U.S. company thinks that the dollar may weaken against the yen. Which of the following foreign currency option transactions would best protect the U.S. company from a possible weakening of the dollar against the yen?

A. Buy calls on Japanese yen.
B. Buy puts on Japanese yen.
C. Sell calls on Japanese yen.
D. Sell puts on Japanese yen.

102. Karen Kodiak buys 100 shares of AMF stock at 49 and sells an AMF 50 call at 3. The stock's price rises to 57 and the option is exercised. For tax purposes, Karen must report

A. sale proceeds of $5,300 and cost basis of $4,900
B. sale proceeds of $5,000 and cost basis of $4,600
C. sale proceeds of $5,700 and cost basis of $4,900
D. sale proceeds of $5,700 and cost basis of $5,500

Use the following information from Moody's bond page to answer questions 103 and 104.

GMAC ZR '12 54 1/4
DWQ 5's '93 78 7/8

103. The annual interest received on the GMAC bond is

A. nothing until the bond matures
B. $ 12.00
C. $ 24.00
D. $ 54.25

104. The annual interest on 50 DWQ bonds is

    A. $93
    B. $500
    C. $930
    D. $2,500

105. Adam Grizzly needs to determine if a certain company's bonds are investment grade. This information is provided by all of the following EXCEPT

    A. Fitch's
    B. Standard & Poor's
    C. Moody's
    D. *Value Line*

106. Which of the following statements is NOT true of a prerefunded bond issue?

    A. It is no longer considered part of the company's debt.
    B. It will be called at the first call date.
    C. It is a high-risk investment.
    D. The new issue is sold at a lower coupon than the original issue.

107. Which of the following issues would be referred to as a "junk" bond?

    A. Low-yielding corporate bond
    B. Bond that has missed one interest payment
    C. New Housing Authority bond
    D. Corporate bond rated Baa by Moody's

108. What is the normal priority for filling orders in a municipal underwriting?

    A. Group orders, presale orders, designated orders, member takedown orders
    B. Designated orders, presale orders, member takedown orders, group orders
    C. Presale orders, group orders, designated orders, member takedown orders
    D. Presale orders, designated orders, group orders, member takedown orders

109. Your firm is a member of the underwriting syndicate of a municipal bond issue. Why would your firm be willing to enter a net designated order on behalf of a customer to purchase $50,000 of the bonds held by the syndicate?

    A. To earn a larger takedown credit on those bonds
    B. To comply with MSRB syndicate sharing regulations
    C. To give the order priority ahead of the member takedown orders
    D. For all of the above reasons

110. Your firm is the managing underwriter for a syndicate underwriting a new issue of general obligation municipal bonds. The director of your municipal bond department decides to allocate the bonds in a different priority than that specified in the agreement among underwriters. Which of the following statements is true?

    A. As long as the bonds affected total less than 25% of the entire underwriting, this is within the discretionary authority of the manager and no further action is required.
    B. He must justify his action to show that it was in the best interests of the syndicate as a whole.
    C. He must file the appropriate papers with the MSRB and amend the agreement among underwriters.
    D. This is not permitted under any circumstances.

111. Before executing a penny stock transaction, a registered rep must disclose to a customer all of the following EXCEPT the

    A. amount of commission he will earn
    B. financial history of the broker-dealer
    C. amount of shares to be purchased
    D. amount of commission the broker-dealer will earn

112. An issuer would go to which of the following parties to purchase insurance on its new issue?

    A. FDIC
    B. SIPC
    C. FNMA
    D. Investor-owned insurance companies

113. When explaining aftertax yields on a security to a customer, you might use which alternative term?

    A. Current yield
    B. Gross yield
    C. Yield to maturity
    D. Tax-equivalent yield

114. The placement ratio listed in *The Bond Buyer* is arrived at by dividing

    A. bonds placed by visible supply
    B. bonds placed by new issues offered
    C. new issues offered by visible supply
    D. bonds traded by issues offered

115. One of your clients has heard that Mt. Vernon Port Authority bonds are currently being offered by your firm, and would like to know when the new issue will be delivered. You can find the answer by looking in

    A. *The Blue List*
    B. the official statement
    C. *Munifacts*
    D. *The Wall Street Journal*

116. An analyst for a rating service reviewing the financial health of a general obligation bond would be MOST likely to look over the

    A. feasibility study
    B. municipal budget
    C. competitive facilities
    D. bond counsel's opinion

117. Your customer is interested in up-to-the-minute information on municipal bonds. To obtain the most accurate, current information available, you would go to

    A. *The Blue List*
    B. *The Bond Buyer*
    C. The *Yellow List*
    D. *Munifacts*

118. An order designated FOK means the order must be executed

    A. immediately and in its entirety
    B. in its entirety, but not immediately
    C. immediately, but a partial execution is acceptable
    D. at the opening of trading

119. The Mineral Point Opossum Control Authority has issued new bonds and committed the money to paying off the old bonds as soon as they become callable. The municipality can be said to have

    A. retired the issue
    B. advance refunded the issue
    C. refunded the issue
    D. double-barreled the issue

120. In order for a municipality considering a new offering of bonds to meet the additional bonds test, it must know that

    A. additional bonds can be issued only as junior lien bonds if these are backed by the same collateral and revenues
    B. applicable revenues must cover the debt service on the outstanding bonds plus the amortization of principal and interest on the new bonds, times a preset multiplier
    C. additional general obligation bonds cannot be issued
    D. an analysis of the existing bonds outstanding must be performed by a qualified analyst before the sale of additional bonds

121. The Tallawhosits City Waterworks would probably choose to issue a general obligation bond rather than a revenue bond if

   I. the overall interest costs of a general obligation issue would be appreciably less

   II. the costs for the planned expansion are assessed only to current and future users

   III. the facility is used by the municipality

   IV. it wishes to avoid the formalities of obtaining voter approval

   A. I, II and III only

   B. I and III only

   C. II and IV only

   D. I, II, III and IV

122. The Mt. Vernon Port Authority wants to issue bonds to pay for a new yacht club, and wants to make the offering as attractive as possible. Which of the following would be of LEAST concern to potential investors?

   A. Size of the offering

   B. Dated date

   C. Insurance on the bond

   D. Maturity and call dates

123. Mountain Brewing wants to refinance by calling in $1 million of 6% preferred stock and issuing $1 million of 6% debentures. The company is in the 34% tax bracket. How will this refinancing affect the EPS of Mountain Brewing?

   A. It will have no effect on the EPS.

   B. The EPS will increase.

   C. The EPS will decrease.

   D. The EPS will remain unchanged but the stock price should increase.

124. Which of the following would have an inflationary effect?

   A. The discount rate increases from 4.4% to 6%.

   B. Government spending has increased and there is a tax rebate.

   C. Last year there was a high level of defense spending and wages and taxes rose.

   D. The rate for federal funds moves up, taxes are decreased and government spending is reduced.

125. Which of the following would probably lead to an increase in the money supply?

   I. Increase in time and savings deposits at commercial banks

   II. Sale of securities in the open market by the Federal Reserve

   III. Increase in bank loans and investments

   IV. Lowering the reserve requirements

   A. I and II only

   B. I, III and IV only

   C. II, III and IV only

   D. I, II, III and IV

◆ Answers & Rationale

1.   **A.**   GNMAs sell pass-through certificates, which represent ownership interests in a pool of mortgages.   (Page 80)

2.   **D.**   The Federal Farm Credit Bank system consists of: the Federal Land Banks, which make low-interest mortgages to farmers; the Federal Intermediate Credit Banks, which make short-term loans to financial institutions serving farmers; and the Banks for Cooperatives, which make agricultural loans to cooperatives owned by farmers. The Federal Home Loan Bank works with the savings and loan industry.   (Page 78)

3.   **A.**   Dividends paid from one corporation to another are 70% exempt from taxation, unless the holder has 20% or more of the company's stock. If the holder qualifies by owning 20% or more, the exclusion is 80%. Because it is a dividend exclusion, only securities that issue dividends (common and preferred stocks) would be included.
(Page 370)

4.   **A.**   Nonexempt issuers of debt securities (such as corporations) are required by the Trust Indenture Act of 1939 to include a bond contract. Exempt issuers (such as municipalities and the U.S. government) are not required to enter into a trust indenture, although most municipalities do anyway.   (Page 383)

5.   **C.**   The Treasury receipt is a creation of a broker-dealer. The broker-dealer buys Treasury bonds and "strips" them of their coupons. They sell the coupons separately and create a pool with the bonds. The investor will purchase a piece of the pool and receive a receipt for his purchase (called a *Treasury receipt*). Because the investor can purchase a unit of the pool, instead of an actual stripped bond, the capital requirement could be less.
(Page 75)

6.   **C.**   The September 13th close was at 73, down (or net change of) 1 1/2 from the previous day's close of 74 1/2.   (Page 637)

7.   **C.**   Earnings per share is not given in the display. It can be calculated by using the PE (or price-earnings) ratio. The PE is the market price per share divided by earnings per share (EPS). To find the EPS, divide the market price by the PE. $73 \div 12 = 6.083$.   (Page 637)

8.   **C.**   Market risk is a measure of how much the price of a given security will change when general interest rates change. The longer the security's maturity, the greater the change in its price for a given change in interest rates. Of the securities listed, Treasury bills have the shortest maturity. (Stocks, although they do not have an actual maturity date, are highly responsive to interest rate fluctuations.)   (Page 356)

9.   **A.**   If the customer is holding the stock and wishes to sell the stock yet still receive the dividend, he must wait until the ex-date to sell. Remember that the ex-date is two business days prior to the record date. The regular way settlement is three business days. If he sells on the ex-date, the transaction will settle the day after the record date. The record date is set by the corporation and is used to determine who qualifies for the dividend (usually the holder of record on that day).   (Page 243)

10.   **C.**   To receive a dividend, the buyer must be the bona fide owner (in other words, he must be on the books of the issuer as the owner) on or by the record date.   (Page 243)

11.   **D.**   The 1,000 shares have a net asset value of $10,300. Divide that amount by the complement of 8 1/2% (91 1/2%). The result is $11,257, which is the amount of the current offering price. The difference is $957.   (Page 566)

12.   **D.**   Regular way settlement of government securities occurs on the next business day.
(Page 242)

13.   **C.**   Investors pay tax on what they have actually received in that calendar year; therefore, you must look at the payable date instead of the record date. The total dividends received, based on the payable dates, are $1.50.   (Page 364)

14. **B.** The customer has 100 shares of stock that he purchased for a total of $2,500. After the 5% dividend he has 105 shares of stock with the same total cost basis of $2,500. Each share is now worth $2,500 divided by 105, for a basis of $23.81 per share. The Internal Revenue Code (IRC) requires that with stock splits or dividends, the basis (or cost) of the stock must be adjusted to reflect the new value of the shares.   (Page 367)

15. **C.** The transfer agent must be notified so that it can change the registration of the bonds from the seller to the buyer. The issuer must be notified as to the change because the ownership of principal and interest is listed on the books of the corporation.   (Page 31)

16. **A.** Rights, common stock and options all have an active secondary market.   (Page 21)

17. **D.** Warrants are usually issued as a sweetener to a deal. For example, if a company wants to issue bonds at an interest rate lower than general market rates, the company could add warrants to make the bonds more attractive. Warrants are usually issued with a very long life, and give the holder the right to purchase stock above the current market price. When a corporation has common stock outstanding and wishes to issue more common stock, it must offer the shares to the current stockholders first (preemptive rights).   (Page 20)

18. **A.** T bills have maturities of three, six and twelve months.   (Page 72)

19. **B.** T notes are intermediate-term securities issued with one- to ten-year maturities.   (Page 73)

20. **C.** Treasury bonds are long-term securities, having maturities of 10 to 30 years.   (Page 73)

21. **B.** U.S. government securities are quoted in 1/32nds of a point. (Remember that a point is $10.) Therefore, the bid price for the November is 100 4/32. 4/32nds of a point ($10) is .3125 times 4, or $1.25; so the bid price of the bond is $1,001.25.   (Page 642)

22. **C.** The Treasury Department is the issuer of government securities.   (Page 72)

23. **D.** Because certificates of deposit are issued by banks, they are exempt from registration under the act of 1933.   (Page 94)

24. **C.** Repurchase agreements are not as much a security as they are a contract between two parties. Although one party may transfer its obligations or rights to a third party, there really is no active secondary market for repos.   (Page 91)

25. **B.** Buy stops are placed above the current market and, when activated, become market buy orders. This will bring more buy orders into a rising (or bull) market. Sell stops are placed below the current market and are used to protect profits. They become market sell orders as the market reaches the stop price. These can accelerate bear markets.   (Page 163)

26. **D.** Level 3 is used by market makers to enter bids and askeds. The market maker needs to see all of the quotes of the various market makers, including the lowest ask, highest ask, lowest bid, highest bid and everything in between. Level 2 also shows all of these quotes, but a subscriber with Level 2 service is not able to enter and change quotations through it.   (Page 185)

27. **A.** When the term "broker" is used, it means that the firm is acting as an agent and is bringing a buyer and a seller together. Answers B and C describe a dealer.   (Page 149)

28. **B.** Good till canceled (open) orders must be reconfirmed the last day of April and October in order to remain on the specialist's book. If the order is not verified, it will be canceled and lose its position.   (Page 165)

29. **A.** When a customer wants to buy or sell certain shares of stock but does not know at what price or when, the customer can say, "Sell my 200 shares of COD at the time you think best and the price you think best, and you will not be held responsible."   (Page 165)

30. **C.** The customer has sold his securities short against the box to defer a tax liability while freeing up some cash. Because the customer holds long shares of the same security he sold short, the NYSE requires him to maintain only 5% of the CMV of the underlying security in his account. Because the customer sold the securities short for $30,000 (the CMV), he can withdraw everything in excess of 5% of that amount, or $30,000 less $1,500, which equals $28,500.   (Page 282)

31. **C.** When a customer opens a new account, the card is signed by the registered rep introducing the client to the firm and the principal who is accepting the client for the firm. The customer is not required to sign the new account card. The customer's signature is required only on a margin account.   (Page 209)

32. **D.** If the customer deposits $32,000 in cash, he has $32,000 in SMA. With $32,000 of cash, the customer can purchase twice the amount in securities at 50% margin.   (Page 271)

33. **D.** All of the information that affects your recommendations or the financial situation of a customer must be noted immediately in the file.   (Page 209)

34. **D.** SIPC insurance is figured by account ownership. Adam is covered for his $300,000 in securities. His wife is covered for her $300,000 in securities. The joint account will be treated separately, and would be covered for the $400,000 in securities. The total securities coverage for the two of them and their three accounts is $1,000,000. Insurance coverage per account is $500,000, no more than $100,000 of which can be in cash.   (Page 381)

35. **D.** REITs serve as *conduits* for the income received from their underlying investments in real estate, and pass through that income to their investors. The Internal Revenue Code requires 95% of all income received by a REIT to be distributed to investors in order for that REIT to be exempt from taxation on that income. But a REIT is not a direct participation program: REIT operating losses do not flow through to investors.   (Page 585)

36. **B.** A growth fund will give the investor some protection from inflation. Historically, common stock is a better inflation hedge than fixed-income instruments. The other three answers are income-oriented funds.   (Page 542)

37. **D.** A specialized fund has a higher appreciation potential (coupled with higher risk) than an income-oriented fund.   (Page 543)

38. **C.** In order to qualify for a breakpoint, the investor must be a *separate legal individual*. Two customers pooling their money solely to qualify for the benefits of breakpoints do not constitute a *separate* individual.   (Page 568)

39. **A.** Riskless transactions are covered by the 5% markup policy.   (Page 183)

40. **D.** Keogh contributions are limited to 25% of aftercontribution income (the equivalent of 20% of precontribution income) to a maximum of $30,000. The doctor's $160,000 income times 20% equals $32,000, $2,000 more than the maximum contribution.   (Page 596)

41. **A.** Although REITs pass through 95% or more of their income directly to their investors, they do not pass through any of the losses they incur.   (Page 585)

42. **C.** Whenever the Federal Reserve changes a national policy or requirement (such as reserve requirements, margin requirements or the discount rate), the effect tends to be multiplied throughout the economy. If the reserve requirement is raised, money will be tightened because banks have to hold more in reserve, thus causing interest rates to rise; in turn, those companies that borrow will have to raise prices, and so on.   (Page 307)

43. **A.** When the economy is bad for six months (or two consecutive quarters), it is in a recession; if this situation continues, it is in a depression.   (Page 298)

44. **A.** The production of durable goods, housing starts and the stock market are all considered leading indicators: the movement up or down of

these indicators predicts the economy of the future. The production of nonessential items (nondurable goods) such as clothing, small appliances, etc., are called lagging indicators because they lag behind the economy. (Page 300)

45. **D.** Duration of unemployment is a lagging indicator. Orders for durable goods and the S&P 500 are leading indicators. (Page 301)

46. **B.** Current and unpaid past dividends on cumulative preferred stock must be paid before common stockholders can receive a dividend. (Page 11)

47. **A.** When a stock rises in price dramatically upon issue, it is said to be *hot*. Although there is no mathematical formula, a rise in price of 1/8th to 1/4th point or more upon issue is generally considered an indicator of a hot issue. (Page 136)

48. **C.** The NYSE will impose a one-hour trading halt in response to extraordinary market volatility. This provision is part of an NYSE rule that attempts to control extreme movements in stock prices. (Page 153)

49. **A.** STRIPS are sold at a discount and generate no current income for investors. The rate of return is locked in and the *interest* is realized at maturity. There is no reinvestment risk because you are not receiving anything over the life of the bond to reinvest. The interest is taxed as ordinary income and must be accreted annually. Treasury stock is not a debt instrument and pays neither interest nor dividends. (Page 75)

50. **C.** A STRIPS has no reinvestment risk because the investor receives no interest payments that have to be reinvested. Because there is no reinvestment risk, the total rate of return is locked in, or set at issuance. The interest on the bond is paid at maturity but it is taxed as interest income over the life of the bond. (Page 74)

51. **B.** REITs offer professional management of a diversified portfolio of real estate holdings. REITs are considered liquid because many are actively traded on exchanges and over-the-counter.

However, the IRS does not allow tax deferral for REIT investors. (Page 585)

52. **C.** GNMAs are guaranteed by the government. These are the only agency issues that are backed directly by the government. The other answers are indirect federal debt. (Page 80)

53. **D.** GNMAs are issued in minimum denominations of $25,000. (Page 80)

54. **D.** Federal Farm Credit System Consolidated Systemwide Banks issue short-term discount notes, as well as short- and long-term bonds that are agency-backed. (Page 78)

55. **A.** GNMA issues monthly checks that include both principal and interest payments. (Page 80)

56. **A.** T bills are issued with three-, six- and twelve-month maturities. (Page 72)

57. **D.** The Comptroller of the Currency, the FRB and the FDIC regulate banks. The NASD enforces MSRB rules with NASD members that trade municipals. (Page 467)

58. **B.** Although the Treasury securities underlying Treasury receipts are backed by the full faith and credit of the federal government, the stripped securities are not. (Page 74)

59. **C.** The federal funds rate is what banks charge each other for overnight loans. It can fluctuate hourly. (Page 95)

60. **B.** The interbank system is a market that trades in foreign currencies and government debt obligations. It is international, decentralized and unregulated. (Page 98)

61. **A.** Commercial paper is not issued by commercial banks. The CP market was developed to circumvent banks so that corporations could lend to and borrow from each other more economically. CPs are unsecured corporate IOUs. (Page 93)

62. **C.** Money-market mutual funds invest in a portfolio of short-term debt instruments such as T bills, commercial paper and repos. They are offered without a sales load or charge. The principal objective of the fund is to generate current interest income, and generally the NAV does not appreciate. (Page 544)

63. **C.** In this case, call protection means that the bonds cannot be called by the issuer for at least five years. If interest rates are falling, the issuer would have reason to want to call the bonds in and, perhaps, issue new bonds at a lower interest rate. Therefore, the call feature protects the investor for a specific period of time. (Page 38)

64. **A.** Bond interest is an expense of the firm and, when it is paid, it reduces the earnings of the firm. If the bonds were to convert, there would be no more interest payments; therefore, the company would have higher earnings. There will be more shares of common stock outstanding and this will normally translate to a lower earnings per share for the common. Interest costs would be reduced, earnings would increase and the number of shares would increase. (Page 61)

65. **D.** Officers and directors of a broker-dealer can never buy a hot issue, nor can the firm for its own inventory. Neither a registered rep nor an associated person can buy a hot issue. The bank officer's ability to purchase a hot issue is restricted; the purchase must meet the three tests of insubstantial amount, not disproportionate allocation and normal investment practice. (Page 137)

66. **A.** If the yields have gone down, it means that the discount has been reduced; therefore, the dollar cost of the bills has gone up. (Page 72)

67. **D.** The rep may not disseminate additional information on the issuer nor on the securities until after the registration statement is effective. It is misleading to imply that some of the information contained in the red herring is less important; in addition, the prospectus is a legal document and may not be altered for any reason. (Page 108)

68. **D.** Each of the securities listed is exempt from registration under the act of 1933. Others would include commercial paper, Rule 147, Regulation A and Regulation D issues. (Page 131)

69. **A.** Because Rule 144 was designed to allow the SEC to monitor insider trading, the intent is to monitor insiders selling large positions that might affect the price of the stock. This rule also might indicate the trading on insider or nonpublic information. The SEC does not require that the trade be reported if the number of shares sold is 500 or less and the total sale price is $10,000 or less. (Page 133)

70. **C.** Because the yield is above the coupon, this bond is trading at a discount. Therefore, if it is held to maturity the customer will realize a return on the bond of 8% and incur a capital gains tax. Because the tax paid will reduce the return on his investment, the effective yield will be less than 8%. (Page 368)

71. **C.** Randy fits the description of an "established customer," so he is exempt from the requirements of the Penny Stock Rules. The other three investors have fulfilled some of the requirements for making penny stock transactions, but the Penny Stock Rules still apply. (Page 214)

72. **A.** The doctrine of reciprocal immunity or mutual exclusion was determined in the Supreme Court Case of *McCulloch vs. Maryland.* (Page 428)

73. **D.** Like most bonds, industrial revenue bonds trade with accrued interest. If a bond is in default it means the bond is not paying interest payments; therefore, interest would not accrue. If the settlement day is the first day of the new interest period, then the seller would be entitled to receive the entire six months' payment and the bond will trade without accrued interest. Zeros are stripped bonds; therefore, there is no interest. (Page 249)

74. **B.** Be careful to distinguish between a cash account and a cash transaction. Regular way settlement for a government bond is next business day.

Most other securities settle regular way on the third business day.   (Page 242)

75. **B.** A DK (Don't Know) notice is sent broker-to-broker if the comparisons do not match up. When a trade occurs, a confirmation is sent to the customer and a comparison is sent to the contra broker no later than the next business day. If the two brokers do not agree on what is to happen on the settlement day, a DK must be sent and received no later than the fourth business day.   (Page 248)

76. **A.** A fail does not occur when the value of the securities has changed. A fail occurs when one broker-dealer fails to comply with the terms of a trade.   (Page 259)

77. **B.** Because the outcome of the merger is still in question and the trader has already established positions, he is in a risk situation. He is attempting to make money on the disparity of prices; therefore, this is an arbitrage situation. If the merger goes through, the speculator will deliver the MCS shares to cover the short position.
(Page 154)

78. **C.** The *Pink Sheets* quote primarily penny stocks.   (Page 213)

79. **D.** The trader has responded to a quote for a specific size.   (Page 179)

80. **D.** Orders are filled in the order in which they are received. The customer will lose his position by canceling the order.   (Page 165)

81. **A.** An oil and gas income program provides few tax benefits.   (Page 630)

82. **D.** A custodian for an UGMA account cannot grant trading authority to a third party.
(Page 227)

83. **A.** A rep always needs to get permission from her own firm before working for another firm.
(Page 344)

84. **B.** The SEC considers a short against the box as a net position of zero. All later sales must be marked "short" because the investor does not have a net long position.   (Page 169)

85. **C.** The registered rep must have prior written authority from the customer and must have received approval from a supervisory person before accepting discretionary authority. While a designated principal must frequently review the account, the branch manager need not initial each order before it is entered.   (Page 222)

86. **C.** The first step is to determine the complement of the sales charge percentage (100 − 4% = 96%); then divide the NAV by the complement ($13.37 ÷ 96% = $13.93). The final step is to divide the invested amount by the purchase price ($50,000 ÷ $13.93 = 3,589), and this is the number of shares purchased.   (Page 566)

87. **C.** A portion of the original issue discount on taxable zero-coupon bonds must be declared as income and taxed annually until the bonds mature. This is known as *accreting the discount*.
(Page 368)

88. **D.** As the market price of a security changes, the broker-dealer may mark to the market and require a deposit of additional funds from an investor.   (Page 277)

89. **C.** The GMA is a zero-coupon bond maturing in the year 2012. Zero-coupon bonds are bought at a discount and mature at face value. If the bonds are held to maturity, the difference between the purchase price and the maturity price is considered interest.   (Page 640)

90. **D.** Only the purchase of a call could guarantee the investor a purchase price for the stock. A buy stop limit may never be executed if the limit is missed (answer A). Writing a call would obligate the investor to sell more stock (answer B). Writing a put would not protect him if the market went up, except by the amount of the premium. (Page 513)

91. **D.**   The issuer determines the amount of accretion and will be entitled to an interest deduction for that year.   (Page 368)

92. **B.**   If the cost of borrowing funds is increasing, members will need to keep more of their own funds available.   (Page 306)

93. **A.**   The U.S. government does not issue or back CMOs (although several government agencies do). It is also misleading to state or imply that a CMO's anticipated yield or average life is guaranteed. According to the NASD, CMO advertisements must include the coupon rate, the final maturity date, a description of the tranche and a disclosure that returns may fluctuate.   (Page 81)

94. **C.**   A sinking fund is usually established to facilitate the retirement of a bond issue before the maturity date. This bond may be redeemed any time between the initial call date and the maturity date. A *catastrophe call* provides for redemption of bonds if the facility that provides revenue for interest and principal payments is damaged.   (Page 37)

95. **D.**   A customer may withdraw 100% of the interest and dividends even if the account is restricted.   (Page 275)

96. **D.**   U.S. government obligations and political subdivisions are exempt from Reg T, though not from the NYSE margin requirements.   (Page 266)

97. **B.**   If inventories are going up, it is generally taken as an indication that sales are going down.   (Page 301)

98. **B.**

$ 50,000	Operating income
– 5,000	Interest ($100,000 × 5%)
$ 45,000	Income before taxes
– 15,300	Taxes
$ 29,700	Aftertax income
– 5,000	Preferred dividends ($100,000 × 5%)
$ 24,700	Earnings available to common
÷ 5,000	Shares of common ($100,000 × $20 par)
$ 4.94	

(Page 335)

99. **C.**

$ 50,000	Operating income
– 17,000	Taxes
$ 33,000	Aftertax income
– 5,000	Preferred dividends
$ 28,000	Earnings available
÷ 10,000	Shares outstanding
$ 2.80	

$100,000 convertible debentures divided by $20 conversion price results in 5,000 shares more after conversion.   (Page 335)

100. **D.**   The gain would be $50 for the ten bonds (1/2 of a point for one bond is $5) and $100 for the common stock (1/2 point = $.50; $.50 × 200 shares = $100).   (Page 640)

101. **A.**   If the dollar weakens against the yen, the purchase of 600,000,000 yen will cost more in dollars. To guard against this possibility, the U.S. company could purchase calls on Japanese yen, which would guarantee that the firm could purchase yen at no more than the strike price.   (Page 523)

102. **A.**   When a call option is exercised, the writer's sale proceeds are equal to the sum of the strike price plus the call premium ($5,000 + $300 = $5,300). The cost basis of the stock is the original

purchase price, which equals $4,900. The investor's total gain is $400.   (Page 527)

103. **A.**   The GMAC bond is a zero-coupon bond (ZR), meaning that no interest payments are made. These bonds sell at a deep discount and the tax law requires annual accretion of the discount.
(Page 54)

104. **D.**   "DWQ 5's" means 5% bonds. 5% of $1,000 par equals $50 interest per bond annually. For 50 bonds, the annual interest is $2,500.
(Page 640)

105. **D.**   The *Value Line Investment Survey* ranks individual stocks. The remaining three rate bonds.
(Page 34)

106. **C.**   Prerefunded bonds are virtually riskless; the proceeds from the new issue are held in an escrow account, then the old bonds are called at the first call date and the escrowed funds are used to redeem them. Prerefunding terminates the issuer's debt obligation; the new issue replaces the old issue at a lower coupon rate.   (Page 39)

107. **B.**   Any bond that has missed one or more interest or principal payments is considered non-investment grade, or "junk."   (Page 35)

108. **C.**   The typical priority for filling municipal orders is: presale orders, group orders, designated orders, member takedown orders.   (Page 446)

109. **C.**   Even though on designated orders syndicate members share the takedown credit with other designated members (and thus earn less money on those particular bonds), they are willing to accept them because designated orders have a higher priority than an individual member's order. In an oversubscribed issue, this difference in priority can make the difference between the order being filled and not being filled. Remember the order priority for a municipal bond underwriting: presale orders, group orders, designated orders and, finally, member takedown orders.   (Page 446)

110. **B.**   MSRB rules require a manager to establish a priority for the acceptance of orders placed for a new issue. However, the manager is allowed to deviate from the established priority if such action benefits the syndicate as a whole. The manager must be prepared to justify that any deviation satisfies this condition.   (Page 445)

111. **B.**   Of the items listed, only the financial history of the firm is not required as part of the transaction agreement.   (Page 214)

112. **D.**   AMBAC, FGIC and MBIA are all investor-owned corporations.   (Page 465)

113. **D.**   The aftertax yield of a corporate or U.S. government bond (that is, the amount of income left for the investor after all federal income taxes have been paid) is also known as that bond's *tax-equivalent yield*. Tax-equivalent yield is the yield an investor would have to receive from a municipal bond in order to have the same amount of cash in pocket after taxes.   (Page 459)

114. **B.**   The placement ratio serves to show the relationship between the number of bonds actually placed (sold) out of the total number available in the market that week.   (Page 437)

115. **A.**   *The Blue List* contains information regarding the delivery date of a new issue, as well as other important information about municipal offerings, including par value, maturity dates, prices and yields.   (Page 438)

116. **B.**   A general obligation bond is backed by the strength of the municipality, its financial health and its budget, but not by any specific revenues or revenue-generating facility.   (Page 461)

117. **D.**   *Munifacts* supplies its subscribers with up-to-the-minute information via computer terminals. *Munifacts* is a service offered by *The Bond Buyer*.   (Page 437)

118. **A.**   The initials FOK on an order mean "fill or kill." This phrase signifies that an order is to be executed immediately and in its entirety, or else the entire order must be canceled. An immediate or cancel order (IOC) can be partially filled.
(Page 166)

119. **B.** Municipalities occasionally pay off an outstanding issue of securities early if they can refinance those securities by issuing new securities at a substantially lower overall interest cost.

(Page 39)

120. **B.** Before a municipality can issue additional revenue bonds backed by the same facility as the previously issued bonds, it must first be able to show that the debt service of both issues will be adequately covered by the projected revenues of the facility (including a multiplier that serves as a safety factor). (Page 432)

121. **B.** If the cost of raising money is lower for a GO bond, a municipality will generally issue a GO bond rather than a revenue bond, especially if the facility serves the entire municipal community.

(Page 431)

122. **B.** The actual dated date (the date from which interest will begin to accrue, regardless of the actual delivery date) is rarely a factor in a bond's marketability. (Page 249)

123. **B.** Interest is paid with before-tax dollars and is tax deductible. Preferred dividends, on the other hand, are paid with aftertax dollars and are not deductible. On an aftertax basis, the net interest cost is 3.96% (34% of the 6% interest is tax deductible). The preferred dividend rate is 6% on an aftertax basis. Because the debt financing is "cheaper" than the preferred stock financing, reported earnings per share will increase. (Page 335)

124. **B.** During inflationary periods, people buy more goods than can be produced. Increased government spending tends to aggravate inflation by increasing demand. Decreasing taxes also contributes to inflation by making more funds available for spending. A decrease in government spending accompanied by an increase in taxes tends to have a deflationary effect. (Page 309)

125. **B.** An increase in time and savings deposits at commercial banks results in an increase in the money supply; then such deposits are by definition part of M2. An increase in bank loans and investments results in an increase in funds available to businesses and consumers, thereby increasing the money supply. Lowering reserve requirements creates excess reserves that banks can use for loans; this also increases the money supply. The sale of securities in the open market by the Federal Reserve decreases the money supply because banks use their reserves to purchase these securities.

(Page 309)

1. A Mar 60 put will be expiring in two days. The current market value is 45. What is the MOST likely premium?

   A. 3/4
   B. 1 1/2
   C. 15 1/4
   D. 18

2. Riskless and simultaneous transactions by a broker-dealer are

   A. not possible under any circumstances
   B. permissible as long as they comply with a 5% markup policy
   C. permissible only if there is profit for a customer
   D. permissible only in new issue underwritings

3. All of the following statements are true of revenue bonds EXCEPT that

   A. they are not backed by ad valorem taxes
   B. they generally have sinking funds
   C. they are usually double-barreled
   D. users pay expenses

4. Who insures municipal issues?

   I. FRB
   II. MBIA
   III. AMBAC
   IV. FDIC

   A. I
   B. I, II and III
   C. II and III
   D. III and IV

5. The excess revenues received by the issuers of a revenue bond are

   A. placed in the general reserve
   B. deposited in a sinking fund
   C. invested by the issuer's treasurer
   D. used to call the bonds

6. The formula used to compare corporate return with municipal return is

   A. $\dfrac{\text{Yield to maturity}}{100\% - \text{Investor's tax bracket}}$

   B. $\dfrac{\text{Current yield}}{100\% - \text{Investor's tax bracket}}$

   C. $\dfrac{\text{Nominal yield}}{100\% - \text{Investor's tax bracket}}$

   D. $\dfrac{\text{Coterminous yield}}{100\% - \text{Investor's tax bracket}}$

7. All of the following are characteristics of an order book official on the CBOE EXCEPT that he

   A. is an employee of the exchange
   B. cannot trade for himself above the public price
   C. cannot accept a limit order
   D. is responsible for the inside price on his book

8. The premium of an option is the

   A. cost of the option
   B. profit on the option
   C. cost to exercise the option
   D. exercise price

9. Which of the following guarantees a listed option?

   A. OCC
   B. NASD
   C. NYSE
   D. SEC

10. A manufacturing company sold goods to a London firm and agreed to accept payment of 1 million British pounds in two months. In which of the following ways could the company protect the payment?

    A. Buy pound puts or sell pound calls.
    B. Buy pound calls or sell pound puts.
    C. Buy U.S. dollar puts or sell U.S. dollar calls.
    D. Buy U.S. dollar calls or sell U.S. dollar puts.

11. If interest rates are rising, which interest rate option strategies would be profitable?

    I.   Buy T bond calls.
    II. Buy T bond puts.
    III. Sell T bond calls.
    IV. Sell T bond puts.

    A. I and II
    B. I and IV
    C. II and III
    D. II and IV

12. Which of the following types of options would be used to protect against systematic risk?

    A. Stock
    B. Index
    C. Currency
    D. Interest rate

13. The CBOE uses which of the following criteria to determine which stocks are optionable?

    I.   Number of shares outstanding
    II. Number of shareholders
    III. Trading volume
    IV. Market price

    A. I only
    B. I and II only
    C. II and III only
    D. I, II, III and IV

14. Foreign currency option premiums are quoted in which of the following?

    A. U.S. cents
    B. Units of foreign currency
    C. Percentage of the value of the foreign currency
    D. Both B and C

15. In order for an individual to trade in a corporate cash account, the brokerage firm will need a

    A. corporate agreement
    B. hypothecation agreement
    C. corporate charter
    D. legal opinion

Use the following information to answer questions 16 through 18.

Company	Sales	High	Low	Close	Change
Best 7 3/4's '95	5	92 1/2	91 1/4	92	− 1/2
Bre 7's '96	10	84 1/4	83 3/8	83 7/8	− 3/8
Bzdt 7 1/2's '99	30	95 3/8	95	95 7/8	+ 5/8

16. How many Bzdt bonds were sold on this day?

    A. 3
    B. 30
    C. 300
    D. 30,000

17. Best's bonds closed the day before at

   A. 91 1/2
   B. 92
   C. 92 1/2
   D. This cannot be determined from the information given.

18. The current yield for Bre's 7% bonds is

   A. 8.25%
   B. 8.31%
   C. 8.35%
   D. 8.54%

19. Which of the following statements about the advertising of municipal securities is(are) true?

   I. A principal must approve an advertisement before its first appearance.
   II. The MSRB must approve an advertisement before its first appearance.
   III. The firm must maintain a file containing the firm's current and past advertisements.

   A. I and II only
   B. I and III only
   C. III only
   D. I, II and III

20. A customer owns $565,000 worth of securities and also has $150,000 in a cash account. If the firm were to go bankrupt, the customer could recover up to

   A. a maximum value of $500,000
   B. either $500,000 in securities or $100,000 in cash
   C. the total amount
   D. $500,000 in securities and $100,000 in cash

21. According to MSRB rules, which of the following items is(are) considered advertising?

   I. Summaries of official statements
   II. Official statements
   III. Offering statements
   IV. Market letters

   A. I and II only
   B. I, III and IV only
   C. III only
   D. I, II, III and IV

22. Which of the following activities would be the MOST appropriate in a pension fund portfolio?

   A. Buying government securities and writing uncovered calls
   B. Buying government securities and writing uncovered puts
   C. Buying government securities and writing covered calls
   D. Shorting government securities and writing covered calls

23. All of the following may be called at par. Which confirmation must show yield to call?

   A. 6% municipal, basis 10%, due 2018
   B. 9% municipal, par, due 2018
   C. 6% municipal, basis 9.5%, due 1998
   D. 9% municipal, basis 6.5%, due 1998

24. Which of the following is the LEAST important source of income to support a state's general obligation bonds?

   A. Income taxes
   B. Ad valorem taxes
   C. License fees
   D. Sales taxes

25. A corporation buys a public purpose municipal bond at a premium with a maturity of ten years at 110. Five years later the bond is called at 105. What are the tax consequences if the bond is delivered at the call?

   A. No gain, no loss
   B. $50 capital loss
   C. $50 capital gain
   D. $50 ordinary income

26. Geographic diversification of municipal securities investments protects against all of the following EXCEPT

   A. adverse legislation in a particular area
   B. economic decline in a particular area
   C. a change in interest rates
   D. default by a particular issuer

27. A municipal syndicate is structured with a 3/4-point concession and an additional takedown of 1 point. A syndicate member selling 100 bonds will receive

   A. $250
   B. $750
   C. $1,000
   D. $1,750

28. The syndicate manager takes which of the following actions in a divided municipal syndicate that does not sell out?

   A. Prorates the bonds according to syndicate participation
   B. Confirms the bonds to the member that did not sell its share
   C. Holds an auction
   D. Returns the bonds to the issuer

29. What secures an industrial revenue bond?

   A. State tax
   B. Municipal tax
   C. Trustee
   D. Net lease payments from the corporation

30. A municipal bond counsel uses which of the following in forming a legal opinion for a new issue of revenue bonds?

   I. State constitution
   II. Municipal bylaws charter
   III. Court cases and legal proceedings
   IV. Voter referendum

   A. I, II and III only
   B. I and III only
   C. II and IV only
   D. I, II, III and IV

31. A municipal bond rating service would consider which of the following when evaluating a general obligation issue?

   A. Public's attitude toward debt
   B. Consultant's report
   C. Debt service coverage ratio of the issuer
   D. Operating revenues of the issuer versus its long-term liabilities

32. A *flow of funds* clause would be found in the indenture of which of the following issues?

   A. General obligation bonds
   B. Project notes
   C. Bond anticipation notes
   D. Revenue bonds

33. If an insured municipal bond defaults, the insurance company is obligated to pay

   A. interest only
   B. principal only
   C. both principal and interest
   D. neither principal nor interest

34. Which of the following is limited in the case of a limited tax municipal bond?

   A. Rate of tax that can be levied
   B. Number of taxpayers
   C. Number of buyers
   D. Amount of bonds issued

35. An unqualified legal opinion in a municipal bond underwriting would indicate that the

    A. bond attorney is not qualified to express the opinion
    B. opinion is without restriction or condition
    C. municipality has exceeded its debt limits on revenue bond issues
    D. legal opinion may not be printed on the bond

36. Which of the following types of covenants on a municipal revenue bond will insure adequate coverage for maintenance, debt service and debt service reserve?

    A. Maintenance
    B. Insurance
    C. Additional bond
    D. Rate

37. In a municipal securities underwriting, the term "takedown" refers to the discount at which members of the syndicate can buy municipal securities from the

    A. syndicate
    B. issuer
    C. selling group
    D. market maker

38. Which of the following would insure that the principal and interest are paid when a municipal issuer is in financial difficulty?

    I.   MBIA
    II. AMBAC
    III. SIPC
    IV. FDIC

    A. I and II only
    B. III only
    C. III and IV only
    D. I, II, III and IV

39. In a gross revenue pledge, the first claim on revenues is

    A. operations and maintenance
    B. debt service
    C. debt service reserve
    D. repair and replacement

40. A customer has a restricted account and wants to sell $1,000 worth of securities. How much can be withdrawn by the customer?

    A. $500
    B. $1,000
    C. $1,500
    D. $2,000

41. A customer buys 100 TCB at 50 and 1 TCB 50 put for 5. The breakeven point for the customer is

    A. 30
    B. 45
    C. 50
    D. 55

Use the following tombstone to answer questions 42 and 43.

Tallawhosits City Waterworks

Mortgage Bonds
Senior Lien bonds
7 7/8%

Price: 95.75

42. The bonds pay annual interest per $1,000 of

    A. $77.50
    B. $78.75
    C. $85.00
    D. $95.75

43. What is used to secure the debt?

    A. Power plant built with the proceeds of the issue
    B. Full faith and credit of the company
    C. Property owned by the company
    D. Principal mortgages of property owned by the residents of Tallawhosits

44. A new customer is interested in trading options. When opening an options account, the rep must

    I.   determine her financial status
    II. ascertain her investment history and objectives
    III. provide her with a copy of the OCC Options Disclosure Document
    IV. obtain a signed copy of a customer options agreement within 15 days of approval

    A. I and II only
    B. I and IV only
    C. III and IV only
    D. I, II, III and IV

45. If a municipal firm purchases a block of municipal bonds in anticipation of a price increase, the firm is engaged in

    A. arbitraging
    B. hedging
    C. position trading
    D. in-house trading

46. An investor acquires limited partner status in a direct participation program at the time

    A. he submits a signed copy of the subscription agreement
    B. he and the general partner have both signed the subscription agreement
    C. the certificate of limited partnership is filed in its home state
    D. his money is received by the general partner

47. The newspaper reports a Tippecanoe Ferry Co. bond is priced at $1,012.50. This price is written as

    A. 100 1/8
    B. 101 1/4
    C. 101 1/2
    D. 101.25

48. Why would a trader normally NOT sell short a municipal bond?

    A. Short sales are illegal under the 1934 act.
    B. The market is limited due to interest rate fluctuation.
    C. There is an increased likelihood of default.
    D. A municipal bond shorted may not be available later in the secondary market.

49. Which of the following represents a corporate bond quote?

    A. 8.20–8.00
    B. 8.5%
    C. 85.24–85.30
    D. 85 1/2–85 5/8

50. A broker-dealer that is a financial adviser to a municipal issuer cannot also act as a negotiated underwriter unless the

    I.   financial adviser relationship is terminated
    II. broker-dealer discloses to the issuer the potential conflict of interest
    III. broker-dealer discloses to the issuer the amount of profit it will make on the underwriting

    A. I and II only
    B. II only
    C. III only
    D. I, II and III

51. Your customer buys a put. Prior to expiration, the put is exercised. What is your customer required to deposit?

    I.   Cash equal to the aggregate exercise price
    II. The margin that is required for a short position
    III. 100 shares of the underlying stock

    A. I
    B. I or II
    C. II
    D. II or III

52. The NYSE Composite Index consists primarily of

    A. industrial securities
    B. financial securities
    C. utility securities
    D. transportation securities

53. Where would you find the bid worksheet on a new municipal bond issue?

    A. *The Bond Buyer* Worksheet
    B. *The Blue List*
    C. *Munifacts*
    D. *Moody's*

54. Which of the following appears on the confirmation statement for a when issued trade of municipal bonds?

    A. Settlement date
    B. Total contract price
    C. Accrued interest
    D. Principal or agency trade

55. A corporation purchases a $100,000 par value public purpose municipal bond in the secondary markets at 90, ten years prior to maturity. For accounting purposes, the corporation uses straight-line accretion to determine the book value of this investment. After three years, the corporation sells the bond at 93. What is the reported gain or loss on this investment for tax purposes?

    A. $1,500 loss
    B. $1,500 gain
    C. $3,000 loss
    D. $3,000 gain

56. What is the spread on a U.S. government security with a bid price of 97.12 and an offering price of 97.16?

    A. $0.04
    B. $1.00
    C. $1.25
    D. $12.50

57. All of the following would affect option premiums EXCEPT the

    A. volatility of the stock
    B. stock price
    C. time to expiration
    D. account position

58. An investor has purchased a municipal bond at a premium and sold the same bond before maturity. Each of the following would be needed to determine capital gain or loss EXCEPT the

    A. issue date
    B. purchase date
    C. sale date
    D. maturity date

59. All of the following debt securities are issued with a fixed maturity date EXCEPT a

    A. CMO
    B. GO bond
    C. Treasury STRIPS
    D. nonnegotiable CD

60. Your spouse wants to open a trading account with Dullard Securities. Because you are a registered rep with Worthmore, Moola, you must comply with NYSE requirements by obtaining prior written approval from

    A. Worthmore, Moola
    B. Dullard Securities
    C. the NYSE
    D. the NASD

61. Which of the following characteristics are associated with real estate mortgage investment conduits?

   I. REMICs may be issued either as shares of beneficial interest or as debt securities.
   II. The flow-through treatment of income from a REMIC may provide investors with tax and accounting benefits.
   III. Some investors in a REMIC might receive income payments faster than other investors in the same REMIC.
   IV. A REMIC can issue both junior and senior classes of securities with differing payment allocations.

   A. I, II and III only
   B. I and IV only
   C. II, III and IV only
   D. I, II, III and IV

62. The advantages of a REMIC investment include all of the following EXCEPT that

   A. the conduit treatment of its income provides for significant tax savings at the corporate level
   B. it is formed as a subchapter M corporation, passing both interest and capital gains through to investors
   C. it is generally like a limited partnership, passing deductions through to owners of units, and is just as difficult to liquidate
   D. interests in it are sold either as shares of stock or as bonds, depending on the individual REMIC

63. Which of the following information is distributed via *Munifacts*?

   I. New issue information
   II. Issues still available from dealers
   III. Quantities of new issues still available
   IV. Economic indicators

   A. I and II only
   B. I and III only
   C. II and III only
   D. I, II, III and IV

64. The Municipal Securities Rulemaking Board does not permit a municipal securities firm to engage in certain business activities with an investment company. The activities NOT permitted include

   A. accepting presale orders
   B. hiring officers from the investment company
   C. soliciting transactions in municipal securities as compensation for selling investment company shares
   D. refusing to transact business with the investment company

65. An open-end mutual fund has a bid price of $16.00 and an offering price of $17.39. The sales charge for buying an investment of $50,000 to $99,000 is 5%. How many shares can an investor purchase if he invests $60,000?

   A. 3,125
   B. 3,450
   C. 3,562
   D. 3,700

66. A member of an undivided $5,000,000 municipal syndicate has a $500,000 participation. At the close of the offering, there are $1,000,000 of bonds remaining. The member sold $300,000 of its commitment. How many dollars' worth of bonds will it have to buy?

   A. $100,000
   B. $200,000
   C. $300,000
   D. $500,000

67. Place in the proper sequence from highest to lowest priority the following methods of allocating bond orders in a new municipal underwriting.

I.   Presale
II. Group net
III. Designated
IV. Member

A. I, II, III, IV
B. I, III, IV, II
C. I, IV, III, II
D. IV, I, III, II

68. A registered rep receives a call from a custodian wishing to buy shares of a specific new issue security. The rep should

A. refuse to accept the order
B. accept the order only if it is placed in a margin account
C. discuss and review suitability
D. talk the investor into buying another stock

69. Which of the following statements would be included in an unqualified legal opinion?

A. The issue may be marketed in various states.
B. The issuer has authority to incur debt for the project.
C. The attorney has qualified the official statement.
D. The attorney has qualified the interest payments.

70. All of the following are municipal securities underwriting terms EXCEPT

A. firm
B. when issued
C. standby
D. AON

71. Each of the following four bonds has a 6.1% coupon rate. A 5-basis-point change in each bond would have the greatest effect on the dollar price of which bond?

A. 1 year to maturity, 6.10 basis
B. 2 years to maturity, 6.50 basis
C. 2 1/2 years to maturity, 7.25 basis
D. 2 3/4 years to maturity, 7.35 basis

72. Which of the following terms is commonly used in connection with a new issue of GO bonds?

A. Private placement
B. Best efforts
C. Negotiated
D. Competitive

73. Which of the following documents would include information about the financial condition of the issuer?

A. Notice of sale
B. Trust indenture
C. Official statement
D. Bond resolution

74. In connection with the issuance of a municipal general obligation bond, the bond counsel will register an opinion on all of the following EXCEPT the

A. statutory authority of the issuer
B. Internal Revenue Code aspect of the annual interest
C. fairness of the underwriting spread
D. circumstances under which the issue can be called

75. An underwriting bid for a municipal GO issue would include which two of the following?

    I.   Dollar amount bid
    II. Coupon rate
    III. Yield to maturity
    IV. Underwriting spread

    A. I and II
    B. I and III
    C. II and III
    D. II and IV

76. A municipal bond dealer that submits an order to a syndicate must disclose that the securities are being purchased for all of the following EXCEPT

    A. its dealer account
    B. a bank president
    C. the account of a related portfolio
    D. an accumulation account

77. What does the Trust Indenture Act of 1939 require trust indentures to include?

    A. Trustee's name
    B. Protective covenants
    C. Schedule of interest payments
    D. Investors' names

78. A registered representative has a new client who has just received a $25,000 inheritance and who wishes to use the money to purchase 8 1/4% Steel City industrial development bonds selling at an 8.45% yield. The $1,000,000 bond issue is due in 15 years and is rated Ba. Which of the following factors would support a recommendation of a purchase of these bonds?

    A. The client is in the 18% tax bracket.
    B. This would be the client's only investment.
    C. The client is willing to accept a moderate amount of risk.
    D. The client's job is not very secure.

79. How would the net yield of a municipal bond that would subject its owner to AMT compare to one that would not?

    A. The yield would be higher.
    B. The yield would be lower.
    C. The two yields would be the same.
    D. The yield is not affected by AMT.

80. One of your clients purchased a municipal bond at 110 that was eight years from maturity. Six years later, she sells the bond for 106. What is her cost basis at the time of sale?

    A. 100
    B. 101 1/2
    C. 102 1/2
    D. 106

81. Municipal securities regulations are enforced by which of the following?

    I.   SEC
    II. IRS
    III. NASD
    IV. NYSE

    A. I and III only
    B. I and IV only
    C. II and III only
    D. I, II, III and IV

82. Which of the following represents a municipal term dollar bond quote?

    A. 8.20–8.00
    B. 8.5%
    C. 85.24–85.30
    D. 85 1/2–85 5/8

83. Which of the following represents a municipal serial bond quote?

    A. 8.20–8.00
    B. 8.5%
    C. 85.24–85.30
    D. 85 1/2–85 5/8

84. General obligation bonds are usually NOT sold short because

    A. they are backed by the full faith and credit of the issuing authority
    B. MSRB regulations prohibit short selling
    C. it is difficult to cover a short municipal position
    D. they trade over the counter

85. How long must a customer who sold a bond at a loss wait before he can buy back a substantially identical bond and not have the sale classified as a wash sale?

    A. 5 days
    B. 20 days
    C. 30 days
    D. There is no waiting period.

86. Which of the following includes the amount of anticipated competitive bid and negotiated sales in municipal bonds for the coming month?

    A. *Munifacts*
    B. *The Blue List*
    C. The visible supply
    D. *Moody's Manual*

87. Bea Kuhl agrees to buy $10,000 of a new issue of municipal bonds that are being traded when-, as- and if-issued. Which of the following items would appear on her confirmation of this transaction?

    I. Amount of accrued interest
    II. Settlement date
    III. Description of the securities
    IV. Total cost of the transaction

    A. I, II and III only
    B. II only
    C. III only
    D. I, II, III and IV

88. A head and shoulders bottom formation is an indication of

    A. a bearish market
    B. a bullish market
    C. the reversal of an upward trend
    D. the reversal of a downtrend

89. The *dated date* on a municipal bond issue refers to the

    A. settlement date
    B. trade date
    C. date on which the bonds were originally issued
    D. date on which the bonds begin accruing interest

90. All of the following actions would increase a deficit in the U.S. balance of payments EXCEPT

    A. investments by U.S. firms abroad
    B. purchases by foreigners of U.S. securities
    C. U.S. foreign aid
    D. U.S. citizens buying Japanese cars

91. Flibinite, Inc. has a PE ratio of 8.0 and earnings per share of $1.30, and paid $.64 per share of common. What is the dividend payout ratio of Flibinite?

    A. 10%
    B. 12.50%
    C. 16.25%
    D. 49%

92. This Can't Be Sushi declares bankruptcy and is to be liquidated. In what order of preference, starting with the first claims on the assets of TCB, will the following creditors be paid?

I.   Preferred stockholders
II. Internal Revenue Service
III. Holders of unsecured debentures
IV. Common stockholders

A. I, IV, III, II
B. II, III, I, IV
C. III, II, I, IV
D. IV, I, III, II

93. General Gizmonics, with an EPS of $2.20, paid dividends of $.15 per quarter for the first three quarters of the year. Due to an excellent fourth quarter, the directors declared a $.30 dividend for the final quarter. What is the dividend payout ratio for GIZ?

A. 20%
B. 29%
C. 34%
D. 49%

94. To tighten credit, the Fed begins selling securities in the open market. What is the first interest rate to feel this change in Fed policy?

A. Money-market rates
B. Prime rate
C. Interest rates on long-term debentures
D. Federal funds rate

95. Payment on Eurodollar bonds is made in which of the following ways?

A. Interest and principal in a foreign currency
B. Interest and principal in U.S. dollars
C. Interest in a foreign currency, principal in U.S. dollars
D. Interest in U.S. dollars, principal in a foreign currency

96. The U.S. dollar has been appreciating against foreign currencies. All of the following statements are true EXCEPT that

A. the U.S. dollar buys more of foreign currencies
B. U.S. exports become more competitive
C. U.S. goods become more expensive in foreign countries
D. foreign goods become cheaper in the United States

97. Kelptek has 300,000 shares of common stock outstanding, no preferred stock and $500,000 in net earnings after taxes. Kelptek declares a 1-for-3 reverse split. The new EPS will be

A. $.55
B. $1.66
C. $5.00
D. the same as the previous EPS

98. Which of the following statements concerning highly leveraged companies are true?

I.   Historically, utilities are highly leveraged.
II. They are most likely to trade on equity.
III. Their debt ratios are high.
IV. If sales increase, EPS will increase dramatically.

A. I and II only
B. I and III only
C. III and IV only
D. I, II, III and IV

99. The economy has entered an uncertain period, with interest rates fluctuating. Which of the following statements are true?

I. Short-term interest rates will fluctuate more sharply than long-term interest rates.
II. Short-term bond prices will fluctuate more sharply than long-term bond prices.
III. Prices of long-term bonds are most affected by changes in the yield.
IV. The most volatile fluctuations are found in the federal funds rate.

A. I, II and III only
B. I, III and IV only
C. II and IV only
D. I, II, III and IV

100. When the Federal Reserve Board buys securities in the open market, which of the following will occur?

I. The federal funds rate will tend to decrease.
II. Treasury notes will tend to increase in price.
III. Banks will have more money to lend.
IV. The call loan rate will increase.

A. I only
B. I, II and III only
C. III and IV only
D. I, II, III and IV

101. Which of the following statements regarding the declaration of cash dividends is FALSE?

A. Total liabilities increase.
B. Total assets decrease.
C. The market price of the stock may change.
D. Growth companies are more likely to declare stock dividends than cash dividends.

Use the following information to answer questions 102 through 104. Greater Health, Inc. is a start-up company formed by a group of investors to manufacture and market biomedical technology. GHI is in the 34% tax bracket. At the time of its formation it had:

$ 1,000,000	7% $1,000 par debentures (convertible at $20)
1,000,000	10,000 shares of 5% preferred ($100 par)
2,000,000	200,000 shares of common ($10 par)
$ 4,000,000	Total capitalization

In its first year of operation, it had $1,000,000 of operating income.

102. What is the earnings per share of GHI during its first year of operation?

A. $1.89
B. $2.65
C. $2.82
D. $3.05

103. What is the return on common equity during GHI's first year of operation?

A. 19%
B. 25%
C. 29%
D. 50%

104. GHI stock is trading at $25 per share. If all the GHI debenture holders converted, what would happen?

A. EPS would decrease.
B. EPS would increase.
C. Neither the EPS nor the PE ratio would be affected.
D. The PE ratio would be affected, but not the EPS.

105. Tex Longhorn's portfolio has a beta coefficient of 1.1. If the overall market goes up 10%, the portfolio's value is likely to

   A. increase by 10%
   B. increase by 11%
   C. decrease by 10%
   D. decrease by 11%

106. Texas Powerful Light Company has issued convertible bonds with a fixed rate of interest. Last year, TPL increased its operating profit by 25%. The earnings per share for the company

   A. will increase
   B. will decrease
   C. will remain the same
   D. cannot be determined from the information given

107. After three consecutive quarters of decline, the Fed takes action to expand credit. Which of the following actions would have LEAST impact on the economy?

   A. Buying securities in the open market
   B. Lowering margin requirements
   C. Lowering reserve requirements
   D. Lowering the discount rate

108. Interest rates have been declining for the past three months. Which of the following statements are true?

   I. Long-term discount bonds benefit the most.
   II. Bond prices gain in proportion to the loss in yield.
   III. Bond prices of newly issued bonds remain the same.

   A. I and II only
   B. I and III only
   C. II and III only
   D. I, II and III

Use the following information to answer questions 109 through 111.

> Buy 2 MCS Jun 40 calls at 2
> Sell 2 MCS Jun 30 calls at 4 1/4

109. What is this position called?

   A. Bearish spread
   B. Bullish spread
   C. Combination
   D. Variable hedge

110. What will be the investor's overall net profit or loss if both calls expire unexercised?

   A. $450 loss
   B. $450 profit
   C. $1,250 loss
   D. $1,250 profit

111. At what price in the stock will the investor break even?

   A. 30
   B. 32 1/4
   C. 40
   D. 44 1/4

112. A partnership comprised of seven individual partners wants to open a trading account. One partner has received authorization to trade in the account. For the purposes of suitability requirements, the registered rep should obtain the financial condition and investment objectives of

   I. the partner authorized to trade in the account
   II. all seven individual partners
   III. the partnership itself
   IV. the general partner

   A. I only
   B. II, III and IV only
   C. III only
   D. I, II, III and IV

113. Assume that TCB declares a 6% stock dividend. What will be the exercise price of the TCB Jan 50 call option after the ex-dividend date?

   A.   47
   B.   47 1/8
   C.   47 1/4
   D.   50

114. Fleecem Runn Skippe advertised its bond underwriting department in *The Wall Street Journal* as "unequaled in service and impeccably professional." However, its underwriting department is less than one year old and is staffed by inexperienced people. This advertisement

   A.   was false and misleading
   B.   was acceptable
   C.   would have been acceptable if more than one securities principal of the firm had approved it
   D.   would have been acceptable if the MSRB had approved it before publication

115. Using Table 1, what price would DWQ need to reach in order for the investor who bought 10 May 60 DWQ calls to break even? (Disregard commissions.)

   A.   57 3/4
   B.   60
   C.   61 3/4
   D.   62 1/4

116. Using Table 1, when will the 10 May 60 DWQ calls expire?

   A.   11:59 pm EST Saturday, May 19th
   B.   Noon EST Saturday, May 19th
   C.   4:10 pm EST Friday, May 18th
   D.   3:10 pm EST Friday, May 18th

117. Using Table 1, if the 10 May 60 DWQ calls expire unexercised, how much money will the investor lose?

   A. $2,250
   B. $5,950
   C. $6,000
   D. $8,250

118. A customer tells his registered rep to purchase $10,000 worth of shares in whatever pharmaceutical company the rep thinks looks good. In what type of account could the rep accept this type of order?

   A.   Custodial
   B.   Discretionary
   C.   Margin
   D.   Special cash

Table 1

Option & NY Close	Strike Price	Calls—Last			Puts—Last		
		May	Jun	Jul	May	Jun	Jul
DWQ	60	2 1/4	r	r	1/16	7/8	1 3/8
58 1/4	65	1/4	r	r	7 1/2	8	8 5/8

Use the following information to answer questions 119 and 120. On November 24, 1998, an investor buys 1 OEX Dec 575 call at 7 when the index was at 581.96. On December 1, 1998, the index closes at 584.50 and the investor would now like to take some gain.

Wednesday, December 1, 1998

OPTIONS
CHICAGO BOARD
S&P 100 INDEX – $100 times index

Strike	Calls – Last			Puts – Last		
Price	Nov	Dec	Jan	Nov	Dec	Jan
565	10 3/8	14	...	1 1/4	4 1/8	6 3/4
570	7 1/4	11 7/8	13	2 5/8	7 5/8	9 1/2
575	4 1/8	9 7/8	10 1/8	7 1/8	11 1/2	12 5/8
580	2 3/8	6 1/4	8 5/8	10 1/2	13	15 1/2
585	1 1/4	4 1/2	6 1/4	15	...	...
590	1/4	3 1/8	5	20	...	...
595	1/8	2 1/8	4 1/8	...	...	...

Total call volume 174,908   Total call open int. 1,282,742
Total put volume 164,129   Total put open int. 1,113,492
The index: High 585.78 Low 582.12 Close 584.50 +2.42

---

119. Which of the following courses of action would result in the largest gain?

    A. Sell the option at the close.
    B. Lock in a 2.50-point gain by exercising the option when the index is at 584.50.
    C. Exercise the option any time on December 1, 1998.
    D. Continue to hold the option and allow it to expire.

120. Which of the following OEX options were in-the-money at the close on December 1, 1998?

    I. Jan 565 call
    II. Jan 570 put
    III. Dec 585 put
    IV. Jan 595 call

    A. I and III
    B. II, III and IV
    C. II and IV
    D. III

121. Investors who have diversified stock holdings usually write covered calls so as to

    A. increase their rate of return on the stocks held in their portfolios
    B. increase the number of shares they own
    C. further diversify their portfolios
    D. lock in profits

122. An investor buys 1 IBS Apr 40 call and sells 1 IBS Jul 50 call. What is this position?

    A. Variable hedge
    B. Straddle
    C. Diagonal spread
    D. Vertical spread

123. Using Table 2, an investor purchased a deutsche mark Mar 64 call on the last sale of the day. How much did the investor pay for the option?

    A. $126.00
    B. $478.80
    C. $787.50
    D. $1,260.00

124. Using Table 2, the investor exercises the call with the deutsche mark at 65.50. What was the investor's net cost?

    A. 64.00 cents per mark
    B. 65.26 cents per mark
    C. 65.50 cents per mark
    D. 66.76 cents per mark

Table 2

Option & Underlying	Strike Price	Calls—Last			Puts—Last		
		Nov	Dec	Mar	Nov	Dec	Mar
62,500 German marks-cents per unit							
DMark	...63	0.21	0.42	r	0.23	0.89	s
67.60	...64	0.66	0.88	1.26	r	1.14	r
67.60	...65	r	r	0.74	r	r	r

125. An investor would like to profit from a market advance that she believes will occur in the near future, but she is uncertain which specific stocks will be affected. She also wishes to limit her risk to a specific amount. Which of the following actions would be MOST appropriate to take in attempting to meet this objective?

   A.   Buy calls on a broad-based stock index.
   B.   Sell puts on a narrow-based stock index.
   C.   Buy calls on a narrow-based stock index.
   D.   Purchase several blue chip stocks on margin.

◆ Answers & Rationale

1. **C.**   This is a judgment question. The put is in-the-money by 15 points (the holder of the put could buy the stock at 45 and sell it at 60). Because the premium includes intrinsic value (amount in-the-money) and time value (intangible value), the premium must be greater than 15. Because there are only two days remaining before expiration, the time value will be very little; therefore, 15 1/4 is the best answer.   (Page 495)

2. **B.**   The 5% markup policy applies to all types of secondary market transactions, including riskless and simultaneous transactions. (Page 183)

3. **C.**   A revenue bond is backed only by the revenue generated by the facility, whereas a GO bond is backed by the full faith, credit and taxing power of the issuer (and is therefore considered safer). A double-barreled bond is a revenue bond that is additionally backed by the full faith, credit and taxing power of the municipality.   (Page 434)

4. **C.**   Financial Guaranty Insurance Company (FGIC), Bond Investors Guaranty Insurance Co. (BIGI), AMBAC Indemnity Corp. (AMBAC), MGIC and MBIA all insure municipal bonds.
(Page 465)

5. **A.**   Extra funds received normally are placed in the general reserve. If at a later date the municipality decides to call the bonds, the funds will be transferred from the general reserve to the sinking fund (if there is one) and the bonds will be called.   (Page 464)

6. **A.**   Municipal securities are quoted in yield to maturity, so that is the yield you must use. This is the formula for tax-equivalent yield. (Page 459)

7. **C.**   One of the functions of the order book official (sometimes called the *board broker*) is to maintain a record of all limit orders. The OBO displays the inside market. The CBOE employs the OBO.   (Page 486)

8. **A.**   The premium is the cost (or price) of the option. The profit on an option represents gain. The cost to exercise an option is the exercise or strike price. Premiums equal intrinsic value plus time value.   (Page 483)

9. **A.**   The Options Clearing Corporation issues, guarantees and exercises options for the industry. The firm handles all of the clerical functions. The Options Clearing Corporation guarantees the performance of the option contract.
(Page 489)

10. **A.**   The manufacturing company wants to protect the value of the British pound payment. Just as in any hedge used to protect against a decrease in value, the hedger buys puts or sell calls.
(Page 523)

11. **C.**   If rates are rising, bond prices are falling. Buying puts or selling calls would be profitable.
(Page 519)

12. **B.**   Systematic risk is also called *market risk*. Index options allow the investor to protect against any decrease in the value of stocks due to market factors. This is different from nonsystematic or company-specific risk, which can be hedged with equity options. All stocks have both types of risks: the risk of what the market does and the risk of what happens to the individual company.
(Page 516)

13. **D.**   To determine which stocks are optionable, the CBOE considers the number of shares outstanding (minimum of 7,000,000), number of shareholders (minimum of 2,000), trading volume (minimum of 2,400,000 in the past 12 months on all exchanges) and market price (minimum of $7.50 for the majority of days in the past 3 months prior to listing).   (Page 486)

14. **A.**   Foreign currency options traded in the United States are always quoted in U.S. cents.
(Page 523)

15. **A.**   The corporate agreement (also known as the *corporate resolution*), which must be signed by the secretary of the corporation, identifies the offi-

cers authorized to make transactions. In a margin account, a copy of the corporate charter and a hypothecation agreement would also be required. (Page 219)

16. **B.** Sales on bonds are quoted in $1,000 par value unit. 30 = 30 $1,000 bonds = $30,000 face amount. (Page 640)

17. **C.** Today, Best closed at 92, down 1/2. Therefore, Best closed the day before at 92.50, or 92 1/2. (Page 640)

18. **C.**

$$\frac{\text{Annual interest}}{\text{Bond price}} = \frac{\$70}{\$838.75}$$

$$= .0835 = 8.35\%$$

(Page 640)

19. **B.** The MSRB does not need to approve advertisements before they appear. Each firm must have either a municipal securities principal or a general securities principal who is responsible for the content of the advertisements and who must approve each advertisement before its appearance. Firms are expected to keep records of all advertisements on file. (Page 472)

20. **A.** SIPC insures the customer to maximum of $500,000. The maximum amount of cash included in the $500,000 total is $100,000. (Page 380)

21. **B.** The MSRB rule states that advertising is any material designed for use in the public media or any promotional literature designed for dissemination to the public. An official statement provides information on a new issue of securities and must be prepared under separate and explicit guidelines, so it is not considered advertising. Summaries of official statements, offering statements and market letters are typical publications considered to be advertisements. (Page 451)

22. **C.** Pension funds normally must follow very conservative investment strategies. Of the strategies listed, only answer C represents transac-

tions that would be appropriate for this type of account. An investor who writes uncovered options or shorts securities is taking on very great risks for the returns that are possible. (Page 498)

23. **D.** The requirement is that if a bond is callable, it must be quoted in yield to maturity or yield to call, whichever yield is lower. In relation to the coupon, the yield to call is farthest away, so if the bond is trading at a discount the yield to call will be the highest yield; if the bond is trading at a premium, the yield to call will be the lowest yield. (Page 457)

24. **B.** Most states levy both income tax and general state sales taxes. They also charge licensing fees to private schools, hospitals, etc. Real estate taxes are normally charged by a county or city and are used for general expenses. (Page 431)

25. **A.** Because this is a premium bond, the premium must be amortized over the life of the bond (this is true whether it was purchased in the primary or secondary market). The bond was purchased for a $100 premium and will mature in 10 years, so the bond will be amortized at $10 per year. After 5 years, the $50 ($10 × 5) amortized would have dropped the cost basis to $1,050 (or 105). Therefore, at the time of sale there is no loss or gain. (Page 458)

26. **C.** If the interest rates change, geographic diversification will not help. A change in interest rates will affect all of the yields. (Page 360)

27. **D.** Normally the concession is part of the takedown. However, in this example it has been separated. Because the total takedown includes the concession, it is 1 3/4% of $100,000, or $1,750. In this question, the total takedown is 1 3/4 points (takedown of 3/4 plus additional takedown of 1 point). A syndicate member that sells the bond will receive the whole takedown. (Page 445)

28. **B.** Because this issue is a divided, or Western, syndicate, each member is responsible for a specified number of securities to be sold. If a member does not sell its share, it receives the bonds for

its inventory. Answer A would be correct for an undivided, or Eastern, syndicate.   (Page 441)

29. **D.** IDRs are issued by municipalities to construct a facility that will be used by, or is being constructed for, the benefit of a corporation. When this is done, the corporation is required to sign a long-term lease. Although classified as a municipal security, IDRs are backed by the revenues of the corporation participating in the project. (Page 433)

30. **A.** The bond counsel (bond attorney) is paid to do whatever research is necessary to render an opinion on the legality and the tax-exempt status of the issue, and may use any or all of the items listed when rendering a legal opinion. If the issue is a revenue bond, the issue is not subject to the approval of a voter referendum.   (Page 430)

31. **A.** Answers B, C and D are revenue bond considerations.   (Page 462)

32. **D.** Because revenue bonds are backed solely by the user fees paid to the facility, it is important to know how these funds will flow (what is paid first, second, etc.). Because GO bonds have full faith and credit backing, flow of funds is not an issue.   (Page 463)

33. **C.** Municipal bond insurance is purchased to insure the payments of principal and interest in the event the issuer defaults.   (Page 465)

34. **A.** A general obligation bond may be backed by a specific tax, and that tax may be limited by a ceiling on either its rate or amount.
(Page 431)

35. **B.** An unqualified legal opinion is one that is issued by the bond counsel with no restrictions. It confirms that there is no problem or potential problem with either the tax-exempt status or the legality of the issue.   (Page 436)

36. **D.** The rate covenant will have within it the promise to charge enough for the use of the facility to cover expenses. It will also include a gross or net revenue pledge stating in what order the revenue received will be used.   (Page 432)

37. **A.** The manager of the syndicate buys the securities from the issuer and in turn sells them to the other members of the syndicate at a discount, known as the *takedown*.   (Page 445)

38. **A.** Municipal Bond Investors Assurance Corp. (MBIA) and AMBAC Indemnity Corporation (AMBAC) both insure municipal bonds. Securities Investor Protection Corporation (SIPC) insures securities account holders from broker-dealer default; Federal Deposit Insurance Corporation (FDIC) insures bank account holders from bank default.   (Page 465)

39. **B.** In a gross revenue pledge, debt service comes first; in a net revenue pledge, operations and maintenance have first claim.   (Page 463)

40. **A.** When a customer makes a sale in a restricted account, 50% of the proceeds are released to SMA and can, therefore, be withdrawn by the customer. The customer sold $1,000 worth of securities, so $500 can be released.   (Page 286)

41. **D.** The customer owns stock that he purchased for $50 a share. To protect that price, he purchased (or paid for) a put that allows him to sell the stock for $50 a share. The cost of the put was $500, or $5 a share. Therefore, he has invested a total of $55 for this position, which will be his breakeven. If the stock trades at 55 or above, he will be able to sell his stock for enough to cover the cost of the put he purchased, as protection against downside risk.   (Page 501)

42. **B.** The annual interest can be determined by looking at the coupon. The annual interest is 7 7/8% of $1,000 face value, or $78.75.   (Page 640)

43. **C.** Senior lien bonds are backed by property owned by the company. They are backed by a first mortgage.   (Page 52)

44. **D.** Before opening an options account, the rep must determine the suitability of options trading for this customer; information about financial status, investment history and objectives must be recorded on the options account forms. In addition, the customer must be sent the Options Disclosure

Document and sign a customer options agreement within 15 days of approval acknowledging that she read it.   (Page 213)

45. **C.** The dealer is buying for its inventory. This is called *position trading*.   (Page 149)

46. **B.** The investor must sign a copy of the subscription agreement, but he is not considered a limited partner until the agreement is also signed by the general partner indicating acceptance of the limited partner.   (Page 625)

47. **B.** Corporate bond prices are expressed as percentages of the principal amount of a bond, or $1,000. Each bond point is equal to $10, with the minimum variation for bond quotes at 1/8 of a point. Therefore, a quote of 101 1/4 is equal to $1,012.50 (101.25 × $10). A quote expressed as 101.25 is used for government securities quotations and is equal to 101 25/32.   (Page 640)

48. **D.** The trader may not be able to borrow the bonds to cover the short because many municipal issues have a thin float.   (Page 169)

49. **D.** Corporate bond quotes, like dollar bond quotes, are based upon a percentage of face amount. Corporate bonds have a par value of $1,000. Therefore, a quote of 85 1/2–85 5/8 is 85 1/2% to 85 5/8% of $1,000, or $855.00 to $856.25.   (Page 640)

50. **D.** The MSRB has specified that all of the listed requirements be met by the broker-dealer.   (Page 452)

51. **D.** To exercise a put, an investor can either deliver the shares of the underlying stock or deposit the required amount of cash to sell short the stock.   (Page 484)

52. **A.** The largest portion of all broad-based indexes are industrial securities.   (Page 313)

53. **A.** Before a bid is placed, a preliminary price meeting of syndicate members is held. Each member enters onto *The Bond Buyer* Worksheets proposed prices or yields for each maturity of the issue.   (Page 435)

54. **D.** A when issued trade establishes the contract price but not the settlement date. Because the settlement date will not be established until the securities become available, the amount of accrued interest and the total amount due cannot be calculated at the time of the trade.   (Page 457)

55. **D.** The corporation receives interest free of federal tax while holding the bond. Appreciation or depreciation of the bond's value is treated as a capital gain or loss upon sale. The gain or loss is calculated using the purchase and sale prices, not the adjusted bond value.   (Page 459)

56. **C.** Always assume a $1,000 bond face value unless otherwise stated. U.S. government notes and bonds are quoted as a percentage of par in 1/32nds. 97 16/32 (97.5% of par) is $975.00. 97 12/32 (97.375% of par) is $973.75. The spread is $1.25.   (Page 642)

57. **D.** The number of contracts that a client owned (long) or owed (short) would not affect the option premiums.   (Page 494)

58. **A.** The amount of the premium that would be amortized (and, therefore, affect the cost basis for determining capital gains or losses) is based on the price at which the bond is purchased, the date it was purchased, the length of time remaining until maturity, the sale date and the proceeds.   (Page 458)

59. **A.** A CMO is issued with a projected maturity date, based on assumptions that may or may not be met about the rate of mortgage prepayments. Because of the uncertainty about prepayments, a CMO does not have a fixed date on which it will mature.   (Page 81)

60. **A.** The employing firm must provide prior written approval before an employee, or a spouse or minor child of an employee, opens an account with another firm.   (Page 216)

61. **D.**   Each of the choices describes an essential characteristic of the real estate mortgage investment conduit (REMIC). REMICs can be issued as shares of beneficial interest (stock) or as debt (bonds). They offer some tax and accounting advantages to investors. REMICs can issue both junior and senior securities, and each of these levels can receive different amounts of payments at different times.   (Page 85)

62. **C.**   REMICs are more like REITs than they are like limited partnerships. REMICs do not pass through any tax advantages to investors in the form of deductions against passive income. Additionally, they are easier to liquidate because there is no established secondary market for limited partnerships.   (Page 85)

63. **D.**   *Munifacts* is a private wire system similar to the Dow Jones wire system. It continually prints general news affecting the municipal bond market, new information about issues and pricing information.   (Page 437)

64. **C.**   The MSRB has rules against manipulative practices such as this.   (Page 474)

65. **C.**   Because the client is investing $60,000, the breakpoint at $50,000 applies. Therefore, it is necessary to calculate the offering price at this breakpoint as follows: Take the net asset value and divide it by 100% less the sales charge percentage. $16.00 ÷ 95% = $16.84. $60,000 will purchase 3,562 shares at $16.84 per share.   (Page 566)

66. **A.**   In an undivided (or *Eastern*) syndicate, each member is responsible for its proportion of the offering, regardless of how many bonds it has already placed. If the member was committed to sell 10% of the original dollar value of the issue, it will be committed to sell 10% of any bonds remaining unsold.   (Page 442)

67. **A.**   Presale orders get filled first because they were placed even before the syndicate manager had purchased the securities from the issuer. Group net orders are filled next; although the buyer didn't indicate a desire to purchase the bonds until after the beginning of the sale period, the buyer has

agreed to pay the public offering price and the entire group splits the takedown according to the percentage of their individual participation in the syndicate. Designated orders are the next orders filled; the buyer is still willing to pay the full public offering price, but would like to designate which syndicate members will receive the credit for the sale. The last orders filled are those of the members themselves, who will be allocated bonds minus whatever takedown or concession for which they are eligible.   (Page 446)

68. **C.**   There are no restrictions that apply specifically to the purchase of new issues in a custodial account, as long as the registered rep has discussed and reviewed the suitability of the investment.   (Page 220)

69. **B.**   The primary purposes of a legal opinion are twofold: the counsel attests to the fact that, to the best of its knowledge, the issuer has the legal right to issue the securities in question, and the interest that will be paid on the bonds by the issuer will be exempt from federal taxation.   (Page 436)

70. **C.**   The term "standby" usually is used to indicate that a brokerage firm has agreed to purchase any part of an issue that has not been subscribed to through a rights offering.   (Page 443)

71. **D.**   The change in yields must be made up over a longer period, so that the yield change results in a greater change in price for a longer term bond.   (Page 45)

72. **D.**   GO bonds are issued on a competitive basis. Revenue bond issues are typically negotiated.   (Page 435)

73. **C.**   The official statement is used to disclose all material information that an investor would need to know about an issuer to make an intelligent and informed decision regarding the purchase of the issue.   (Page 430)

74. **C.**   The bond counsel is not concerned with the amount of the underwriting spread. (Page 436)

75. **A.** Because "How much money can we raise?" and "How much is it going to cost us?" are the only two things the issuer wants to know, they are the two things that a firm bidding on the issue would include in its bid. The investor would want to know the yield to maturity in order to determine whether the investment made sense for her. The members of the syndicate would want to know the underwriting spread so they could decide whether it would be profitable for them to take part.
(Page 442)

76. **B.** The municipal dealer does not have to disclose purchases of securities by individuals.
(Page 448)

77. **B.** The Trust Indenture Act of 1939 requires trust indentures to include clauses protecting the bondholders.
(Page 55)

78. **C.** A "Ba" rating is consistent with the client's willingness to accept moderate risk. The client's tax bracket might be too low to take full advantage of the bond's tax-exempt feature. The bonds would also not be very liquid because only 1,000 bonds were issued. If the client lost his job and needed cash, the bonds might be difficult to sell.
(Page 35)

79. **B.** Any bond subject to additional taxes, such as might occur with an investor subject to alternative minimum tax (AMT), would have a lower net yield than one that was not subject to additional taxes.
(Page 369)

80. **C.** The premium deducted yearly for the period held is deducted from the original cost to establish the new basis: $100 \div 8 = \$12.50$; $\$12.50 \times 6 = \$75$; $\$1,100 - \$75 = 102\ 1/2$.
(Page 458)

81. **A.** The SEC regulates all securities, and was empowered to do so by the Securities Act of 1933. The IRS was not empowered to act directly in securities matters. The NASD was empowered under the Securities Exchange Act of 1934 to regulate broker-dealers.
(Page 467)

82. **D.** Term dollar bond quotes are based upon a percentage of face amount. Bonds have a par value of $1,000. Therefore, a quote of 85 1/2–85 5/8 is 85 1/2% to 85 5/8% of $1,000, or $855.00 to $856.25.
(Page 457)

83. **B.** Municipal serial bonds are issued at one time with differing maturity dates. They are quoted on a yield basis such as 8.5%. Term bonds, in contrast, compose a large part or all of a particular issue and come due at the same time. These bonds (dollar bonds) are quoted in terms of dollar prices rather than yields.
(Page 457)

84. **C.** Because municipal trading is limited, municipal bonds are not *fungible* (that is, identical to the point of being interchangeable) securities. With fungible securities, such as listed equities, there are many equivalent securities trading at any time. It is easy to short 100 shares of GM (borrow the stock) because an equivalent 100 shares of GM can be purchased on the NYSE at any time. It is not easy to short 5M of 6% NYC GO bonds M '05 because it would be very difficult to cover the short position with the same bonds.
(Page 169)

85. **C.** When a customer sells a security at a loss, he cannot buy back a substantially identical security between 30 days prior to and 30 days after the sale that established the loss.
(Page 368)

86. **C.** The 30-day visible supply is used by issuers and dealers to determine the amount of new issues expected in the market in the next 30 days. Published monthly, the visible supply is the par value of all competitive bids and negotiated sales that are scheduled to be reoffered by syndicates within the coming 30 days.
(Page 435)

87. **C.** When an order is taken for a bond *when-, as- and if-issued*, the bond is a new issue without a final settlement date. Because the settlement date is not set, the amount of accrued interest payable to the seller (the underwriter in this case) is not known. If the amount of accrued interest is not known, the total cost of the transaction cannot be determined.
(Page 448)

88. **D.** A head and shoulders bottom formation is also known as an *inverted* head and shoulders formation. It is that part of a graph where a down-

trend has reversed to become an uptrend. It is not, however, an indicator of the bullishness or bearishness of the market as a whole. It is an indication only of the direction of a trend, which may be either short or long in duration.   (Page 315)

89. **D.**   The dated date is the date on which the bonds begin to accrue interest.   (Page 249)

90. **B.**   There is a deficit in the balance of payments in the United States when the country has been paying out more money abroad than it has been taking in. This happens when the United States imports more than it exports, invests money abroad, or sends money to foreign countries in the form of foreign aid. However, when foreigners purchase U.S. securities, foreign currency flows into the country, not out. Answer B, therefore, will decrease the deficit in the balance of payments.   (Page 311)

91. **D.**   The dividend payout ratio is 49%.

$$\frac{\text{Annual dividends per share of common}}{\text{Earnings per share}} =$$

$$\frac{\$.64}{\$1.30} = 49.23\%$$

In other words, Flibinite is paying out about half of its earnings in dividends.   (Page 336)

92. **B.**   In the event of a liquidation, the order of preference is:

1. unpaid wages
2. taxes
3. secured claims (e.g., mortgages)
4. secured liabilities (bonds)
5. unsecured liabilities (debentures) and general creditors
6. subordinated debt
7. preferred stockholders
8. common stockholders

(Page 55)

93. **C.**   Total dividends paid each quarter during the year are $.15 + $.15 + $.15 + $.30 = $.75. The dividend payout ratio is:

$$\frac{\text{Annual dividends per share of common}}{\text{Earnings per share}} =$$

$$\frac{\$.75}{\$2.20} = 34.09\%$$

(Page 336)

94. **D.**   The Federal Reserve's actions to influence the money supply are first felt on the discount rate and the federal funds rates. These are the rates for loans of reserves.   (Page 309)

95. **B.**   Eurodollar bonds are issued by either domestic or foreign corporations in a currency other than that of the country of issue. They are denominated in U.S. dollars and payment of interest and principal is made in U.S. dollars. (Page 97)

96. **B.**   When the U.S. dollar strengthens, foreign goods become cheaper in the United States because the dollar buys more. At the same time, U.S. goods become more expensive in foreign countries because their currency would buy less of U.S. goods. Therefore, when the dollar appreciates relative to foreign currency, U.S. exports become less competitive and foreign imports become more competitive.   (Page 99)

97. **C.**   Earnings per share are earnings available for common divided by the outstanding shares. Because Kelptek has no preferred stock, all the earnings after taxes are earnings for common. The reverse split means that three outstanding shares will be traded in for one new share. Thus, after the split, the company will have 100,000 shares outstanding. The new EPS will be $5.00 per share ($500,000 ÷ 100,000 shares).   (Page 335)

98. **D.**   Historically, utility stocks have a high percentage of debt in their capitalization. Thus, like all highly leveraged companies, their debt ratios are high. Because of this, they are most likely to trade on equity. Because they pay fixed debt interest fees, if sales increase there is no increase in debt cost. The earnings increase flows to the relatively small equity base and can increase earnings per share

greatly. Because leverage magnifies earnings swings, it also magnifies EPS changes. EPS changes are direct influences on the stock's price.
(Page 331)

99. **B.** Short-term interest rates fluctuate more than long-term interest rates. Long-term bond prices fluctuate more than the price of short-term debt instruments (so choice II is false). Because long-term bonds must make up the difference in yield over the years, as yields change the prices on long-term bonds are affected the most. The federal funds rate is the rate at which banks loan money overnight to each other to maintain reserve requirements; due to its very short-term nature, it is the most volatile money-market rate.   (Page 95)

100. **B.** When the Fed buys securities in the open market, it is putting money into the banking system. This tends to ease the money supply and lower interest rates.   (Page 308)

101. **B.** Upon the declaration of a cash dividend, retained earnings are reduced because dividends are paid out of retained earnings. Until the dividends are paid, liabilities increase. Assets are not affected until the cash dividend is paid. A decision to pay a dividend impacts the market price of the stock. A corporation is not required to pay cash dividends to common stockholders; the decision is made at the discretion of the board of directors. Indeed, growth companies are less likely to pay cash dividends than stock dividends (which require no outlay of cash) because they want to retain most of their earnings for future growth.   (Page 328)

102. **C.** Calculate earnings per share as follows:

$ 1,000,000	Operating income
– 70,000	Interest on convertible debentures
$ 930,000	Income before taxes
– 316,200	Taxes at 34%
$ 613,800	Income after taxes
– 50,000	Preferred dividends
$ 563,800	Earnings for common

$$\frac{\text{Net income available for common}}{\text{No. shares of common outstanding}} = \frac{\$563,800}{200,000}$$

$$= \$2.82 \text{ EPS}$$

(Page 335)

103. **C.** The rate of return per share of common equals:

$$\frac{\$563,800 \text{ earnings for common}}{\$2,000,000 \text{ common equity}} = 28.19\%$$

(Page 333)

104. **A.** If all bondholders converted, no bond interest would be paid. Note the effect on the income statement:

$1,000,000	Operating income
– 0	Interest on convertible debentures
$1,000,000	Income before taxes
– 340,000	Taxes at 34%
$ 660,000	Income after taxes
– 50,000	Preferred dividends
$ 610,000	Earnings for common

These earnings are spread over 200,000 original common shares plus 50,000 converted shares. Because of this, earnings per share decreases:

$$\frac{\text{Net income available for common}}{\text{No. shares of common outstanding}} = \frac{\$610,000}{250,000}$$

$$= 2.44 \text{ EPS}$$

(Page 335)

105. **B.** A beta of 1.1 means the portfolio is considered to be 1.1 times more volatile than the overall market. Therefore, if the market is up 10%, the portfolio with a beta of 1.1 is likely to be up 11%.   (Page 362)

106. **A.** Because a company's interest expense is fixed, if the sales and operating margin (operating profit) increases, the EPS (profit on equity) will increase. For example:

	Typical Year	Good Year
Sales	$ 1,000,000	$ 1,400,000
Expenses	– 500,000	– 775,000
Operating margin	$ 500,000	$ 625,000
Bond interest	– 100,000	– 100,000
Income before taxes	$ 400,000	$ 525,000
Income after taxes (35% rate)	$ 260,000	$ 341,250
EPS (200,000 common shares)	$1.32	$1.73

(Page 335)

107. B.   Changing the margin requirement affects the credit extended only on securities transactions. The other actions listed will affect credit throughout the entire economy.   (Page 306)

108. B.   When interest rates decline, long-term bonds benefit the most due to the compounding effect of the interest rate decline over the life of the bond. Because the bonds are still issued at or near par value, bond prices on newly issued bonds remain the same. However, as interest rates decline, the loss in yield will be accompanied by a gain in the price of bonds in the secondary market. This relationship between yield and price is not proportionate because of the different times to maturity. The price of a bond that will mature in one year will not move as much as the price of a bond that will mature in 30 years.   (Page 46)

109. A.   The investor has a net credit, so he *sold* the call spread. When an investor sells a call spread by buying the call with the higher exercise price, the spread is considered *bearish.*   (Page 508)

110. B.   If both calls expire, the investor will lose $400 on the call that he bought and make a profit of $850 on the call that he wrote, for a net profit of $450.   (Page 508)

111. B.   The investor will break even if the MCS Jun 30 call is trading at 4 1/2. This price means that the stock was trading at 32 1/4.   (Page 508)

112. C.   The beneficial owner of the account is the partnership itself, although only one partner is authorized to trade in the account. To determine suitability, the rep must consider the financial condition and objectives of the beneficial owner.   (Page 209)

113. B.   In the event of a stock dividend, the call contract would become a call on 106 shares. Divide 106 shares into the total contract price of $5,000 to determine the adjusted exercise price. After rounding off to the nearest 1/8th, the result is 47 1/8.   (Page 490)

114. A.   This representation is obviously misleading; therefore, it is unacceptable under all circumstances.   (Page 451)

115. D.   Calculate the breakeven point of a purchased call by adding the cost of the call to the exercise price. 2 1/4 + 60 = 62 1/4.   (Page 496)

116. A.   Listed stock options expire at 11:59 pm EST on the Saturday immediately following the third Friday of the expiration month.   (Page 492)

117. A.   The investor will lose 100% of his investment if the calls expire unexercised, which means he will lose $2,250.   (Page 496)

118. B.   In a discretionary account, the registered rep can make decisions with respect to the specific security and the quantity to purchase, as well as to time and price.   (Page 222)

119. A.   If the investor sold the option at the close, the gain would have been 2 7/8 points, or $287.50 (9 7/8 closing sale price minus 7 opening purchase price). If the option had been exercised, the gain or loss would have been calculated based on the closing index value for that day. The gain would have been the difference between the closing index value (584.50) and the strike price (575) less the premium paid (7) for a net gain of 2.50, or $250. If the option expires, the investor has a loss equal to the premium.   (Page 516)

120. A.   A call is in-the-money if the index value is greater than the strike price, whereas a put is in-the-money if the index value is lower than the strike price.   (Page 516)

121. **A.**   Individuals with diversified stock holdings may write calls against their positions, thus deriving the premiums for these calls. Writing calls, therefore, increases the rate of return on the stocks that they hold.   (Page 498)

122. **C.**   Both the exercise price and the expiration date are different. This is a diagonal spread.   (Page 503)

123. **C.**   The premium of 1.26 represents 1.26 cents per unit times 62,500 units per contract, for a total premium of $787.50.   (Page 524)

124. **B.**   When the investor exercises the call, he must pay the strike price of 64 cents per mark, to which the premium of 1.26 cents per mark must be added, for a net cost of 65.26 cents per mark.   (Page 524)

125. **A.**   A broad-based stock index is designed to track the market as a whole rather than any particular market segment. If the market rises, both index call buyers and index put sellers will profit.   (Page 516)

Notes

Notes

Notes